THE WAR OF THE WORLDS

Also Available from Bloomsbury

The Reception of H. G. Wells in Europe, edited by
Patrick Parrinder and John S. Partington
The Invisible Man: The Life and Liberties of H. G. Wells, Michael Coren

Also by Peter J. Beck

Presenting History: Past and Present (2012)
*Using History, Making British Policy: The Treasury
and the Foreign Office, 1950–76* (2006)
*Scoring for Britain: International Football and
International Politics, 1900–1939* (1999)
*British Documents on Foreign Affairs. Reports and Papers from the Foreign
Office Confidential Prints: The League of Nations 1918–1941, 1–10* (1992–5)
The Falkland Islands as an International Problem (1988; 2014)
The International Politics of Antarctica (1986; 2014)

THE WAR OF THE WORLDS

From H. G. Wells to Orson Welles, Jeff Wayne, Steven Spielberg and Beyond

Peter J. Beck

Bloomsbury Academic
An imprint of Bloomsbury Publishing Plc

B L O O M S B U R Y
LONDON · OXFORD · NEW YORK · NEW DELHI · SYDNEY

Bloomsbury Academic

An imprint of Bloomsbury Publishing Plc

50 Bedford Square	1385 Broadway
London	New York
WC1B 3DP	NY 10018
UK	USA

www.bloomsbury.com

BLOOMSBURY and the Diana logo are trademarks of Bloomsbury Publishing Plc

First published 2016

© Peter J. Beck, 2016

Peter J. Beck has asserted his right under the Copyright, Designs and Patents Act, 1988, to be identified as Author of this work.

British Library Cataloguing-in-Publication Data

A catalogue record for this book is available from the British Library.

ISBN:	HB:	978-1-4742-2988-3
	PB:	978-1-4742-2987-6
	ePDF:	978-1-4742-2990-6
	ePub:	978-1-4742-2989-0

Library of Congress Cataloging-in-Publication Data

A catalog record for this book is available from the Library of Congress.

Cover design: Hugh Cowling
Cover image © Hugh Cowling

Typeset by Fakenham Prepress Solutions, Fakenham, Norfolk NR21 8NN
Printed and bound in India

For Ethan

CONTENTS

Part I
INTRODUCTION

Part II
WRITING AND PUBLISHING *THE WAR OF THE WORLDS*

Part V
CONCLUSION

LIST OF TABLES

LIST OF ILLUSTRATIONS

ACKNOWLEDGEMENTS

Extracts from correspondence and publications by H. G. Wells are quoted by permission of United Agents LLP on behalf of the Literary Executors of the Estate of H. G. Wells. Wells's correspondence was consulted at and is quoted with the permission of the Beinecke Rare Book and Manuscript Library, Yale University, New Haven; the Harry Ransom Center, The University of Texas at Austin; and the Rare Book and Manuscript Library, University of Illinois at Urbana-Champaign; and through the invaluable anthology edited by Bernard Loing. Material from David C. Smith's *The Correspondence of H. G. Wells* is quoted by permission of Taylor & Francis. Extracts from the William Heinemann archive, held at the Random House Archive, Rushden, are quoted by permission of The Random House Group Ltd. Extracts from Woking Borough Council archive, held at the Surrey History Centre, are quoted by permission of the Surrey History Centre. Material from the H. G. Wells collection held at the Local Studies Library, Bromley, is quoted by permission of Bromley Local Studies and Archives. Photographic, online and other sources, especially those from http://www.thewaroftheworlds. com/, relating to Jeff Wayne are quoted by permission of Jeff Wayne, with many thanks also to Damian Collier. Figure 15.1 is a photograph taken by Roy Smiljanic. Extracts from the Mass Observation archives are reproduced by permission of Curtis Brown Group Ltd, on behalf of the Trustees of the Mass Observation Archive. The covers of Dell's 1938 edition of *The War of the Worlds* are reproduced with permission of Random House Inc. The two film posters advertising the 1953 and 2005 'War of the Worlds' films are reproduced by permission of Paramount Pictures. The BBC Audience Research Reports were kindly provided by the BBC Written Archives Centre, Caversham. Some maps have been reproduced from the 1893–4, 1895–6 and 1913 Ordnance Survey maps. Table 1.1 recording the number of editions of *The War of the Worlds* published since 1898 is reproduced by permission of Harold Poskanzer (aka Dr Zeus). Ann Harington kindly allowed me access to Woking's War of the Worlds Steering Group Committee minutes and papers, 1996–8. If any copyright has been inadvertently infringed, the author will acknowledge copyright in any future publication.

PREFACE

Originating during the late 1980s as a small scale local history project focused upon Wells and his brief residence in Woking (1895–6), this study, drawing increasingly upon archival research conducted in both Britain and the USA, expanded gradually into a biography of *The War of the Worlds* as a book. Even so, for an author living a mile or so from both the place where Wells's Martians landed and the site of the first interplanetary battlefield, the local history dimension has always been there, albeit evolving increasingly into a focus upon the Wellsian literary heritage dimension. Indeed, my involvement as the H. G. Wells Society's representative on a Woking Task Group organizing events in 2016 to mark the 150th anniversary of Wells's birth and the 70th anniversary of his death has merely reinforced this aspect.

Jonathan, Catharine, Richard and Ethan have provided an encouraging family environment for undertaking this project. Sadly, my wife, Barbara, passed away midway through the project and hence this book is dedicated also to her memory. This book has benefited from the constructive editorial roles performed for Bloomsbury Academic by David Avital and Mark Richardson, the referees advising on the draft proposal, and to those, especially Keith Williams, reading sections of the manuscript in progress, plus the invaluable role played by Kim Storry and her team at Fakenham Prepress Solutions. I should like to thank also the personal contributions made by Paul Malcolm Allen, chair of the H. G. Wells Society; Pam Arbeeny of the John F. Reed Library, Colorado; Matthew J. Boylan of The New York Public Library; Rosemary and Richard Christophers; John M. Clarke; Damian Collier; Peter Darley; Mark Doyle; Edward J. Epstein; John Hammond; Ann Harington; Andrew Heggie; Simon James; Tony Kremer; Larry McAllister of Paramount Pictures; Louise North; Amber Paranick of the Library of Congress; Diane Parks of Boston Public Library; Patrick Parrinder; Lauren Plosker; Lynn Porteous; Paul Rimmer; Gene Rinkel; David Rymill; Henry F. Scannell of Boston Public Library; Dennis Sears; Michael Sherborne; Linda Shaughnessy; Riette Thomas; Travis Westly of the Library of Congress; Nathan Wilkes; and Keith Williams.

Present-day values of incomes and prices have been calculated using the online Bank of England inflation calculator: http://www.bankofengland.co.uk/education/Pages/resources/inflationtools/calculator/flash/default.aspx. To help readers follow up specific textual references to *The War of the Worlds*, the bracket following each quote from the book records the relevant section, chapter and page numbers in the original 1898 book and the 2005 Penguin edition in the following format: book section: 1898 book page/2005 book page (i.e. II.2: 204/124). Any changes of text from the 1898 book are recorded in square brackets.

Peter J. Beck
Kingston University

LIST OF ABBREVIATIONS

CGI	Computer generated imagery
EST	Eastern Standard Time
H.C.P.S.	Horsell Common Preservation Society
MP	Member of Parliament
NASA	National Aeronautics and Space Administration
OS	Ordnance Survey Maps
PBS	Public Broadcasting Service (USA)

HERBERT GEORGE WELLS: CHRONOLOGY

1866 21 September Born in Bromley, Kent, third son of Joseph and Sarah Wells

1874–80 School at Morley's Academy, Bromley

1880–3 Apprenticed to drapers in Windsor and Southsea and a pharmacist in Midhurst

1883–4 Pupil teacher at Midhurst Grammar School – won scholarship to Normal School of Science, London

1884–7 Attended Normal School of Science – studied under T. H. Huxley; met Isabel Wells; failed to graduate

1886 December Founded and initially edited *The Science Schools Journal*; published 'The Chronic Argonauts' (an early version of *The Time Machine*) in *The Science Schools Journal*

1887–8 Taught at Holt Academy, North Wales; seriously ill after footballing injury; convalesced in the Potteries and then at Uppark

1889–93 Taught at Henley House School, Kilburn and tutored for the University Correspondence College

1890–1 Gained London University B. Sc. Hons in Zoology & Geology plus teacher's diploma

1891 Married Isabel Wells, his cousin

1891 First article 'The Rediscovery of the Unique' published in a major periodical, *The Fortnightly Review*

1893 Gave up teaching because of illness – became a journalist

1893 Published *Textbook of Biology* and co-authored (with Richard Gregory) *Honours Physiography*

1893–4 Left Isabel to live with Amy Catherine Robbins (Jane)

1895 Divorced Isabel (she died in 1931); **May** Moved from London to Woking, Surrey; married Jane (October 1895)

1895 Published *The Time Machine*; *The Wonderful Visit*; *Select Conversations with an Uncle*; *The Stolen Bacillus*

1896 August–October Moved to Worcester Park, Surrey

1896 Published *The Island of Dr Moreau*; *The Wheels of Chance*

1897 Published *The Plattner Story and Others*; *The Invisible Man*; *Certain Personal Matters*; *Thirty Strange Stories*; serialization of *The War of the Worlds*

1898 Serious illness led to move to Sandgate on the Kent coast

1898 Published *The War of the Worlds*

1899 Published *When the Sleeper Wakes*; *Tales of Space and Time*

1900 Moved into Spade House, a new house built at Sandgate

1900 Published *Love and Mr Lewisham*

1901 Published *First Men in the Moon*; *Anticipations*

1927 Death of Jane, his second wife

1943 Awarded DSc by University of London

1946 13 August Died in London

H. G. WELLS: BOOKS PUBLISHED, 1895–1900

Title	Serialized	Published as a book	Price
The Time Machine: An invention	*The National Observer*, March–June 1894 [partial serialization] *The New Review*, January–May 1895	William Heinemann, London: May 1895 Holt, New York: May 1895	UK: 2s 6d [£0.125] 1s 6d pb [£0.075] USA: $0.75
Select Conversations with an Uncle (now extinct) and two other reminiscences	12 conversations plus two short stories printed in the *Pall Mall Gazette*, 1893–4	John Lane, London: May 1895 Merriam, New York: May 1895	UK: 3s 6d [£0.175] USA: $1.25
The Wonderful Visit		J. M. Dent, London: September 1895 Macmillan, New York: September 1895	UK: 5s [£0.25] USA: $1.25
The Stolen Bacillus and Other Incidents	15 short stories published previously in journals, including *Pall Mall Budget, Pall Mall Gazette* and *St. James's Gazette*, 1893–5	Methuen, London: November 1895	UK: 6s [£0.30]
The Island of Dr Moreau	Excerpt based on Chap. XIV in *Saturday Review of Literature*, 19 January 1895 entitled, 'The Limits of Individual plasticity'.	William Heinemann, London: March 1896 Stone & Kimball, New York: August 1896	UK: 6s [£0.30] USA: $1.25
The Wheels of Chance: a holiday adventure [in USA sub-titled *a bicycling idyll*]	*To-Day* May–September 1896	J. M. Dent, London: October 1896 Macmillan, New York: October 1896	UK: 5s [£0.25] USA: $1.50
The Plattner Story and Others	17 short stories published previously in such journals as *The Idler*, *The New Review* and *Pall Mall Budget*, 1894–6	Methuen, London: May 1897	UK: 6s [£0.30]
The Invisible Man	*Pearson's Weekly*, June–July 1897	C. Arthur Pearson, London: September 1897 Edward Arnold, New York: November 1897	UK: 3s 6d [£0.175] USA: $1.25

Title	Serialized	Published as a book	Price
Thirty Strange Stories	30 short stories including all stories from *The Plattner Story*, ten stories from *The Stolen Bacillus*, plus three new stories	Edward Arnold, New York: January 1897	USA: $1.50
Certain Personal Matters	39 essays published principally in the *Pall Mall Gazette*, but also in the *New Budget* and *Black and White*, 1893–5	Lawrence & Bullen, London: October 1897	UK: 3s 6d [£0.175]
The War of the Worlds	*Pearson's Magazine*, April–December 1897 *Cosmopolitan* April–December 1897	William Heinemann, London: January 1898 Harper, New York: March 1898	UK: 6/- [£0.30] USA: $1.50
When the Sleeper Wakes (retitled *The Sleeper Awakes*: 1910)	*The Graphic*, January–May 1899 *Harper's Weekly*, January–May 1899	Harper, London & New York: May 1899	UK: 5s [£0.25] USA: $1.50
Love and Mr Lewisham	*The Times Weekly Edition*, November 1899–February 1900	Harper, London and New York: June 1900	UK: 6s [£0.30] USA: $1.50

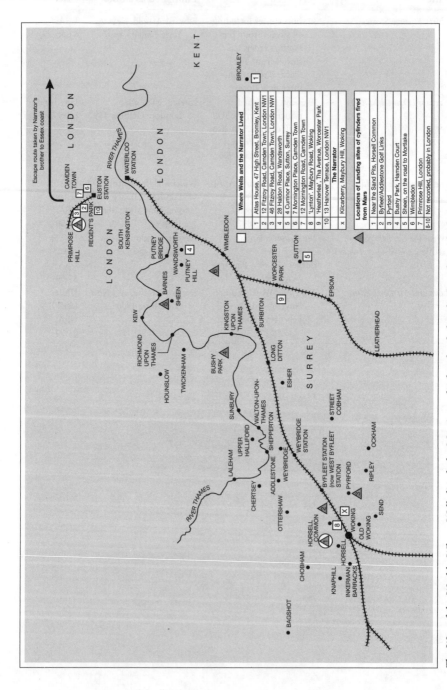

The War of the Worlds: Where Wells lived, the Martian cylinders landed and events happened.

Part I

INTRODUCTION

Chapter 1

H. G. WELLS'S *THE WAR OF THE WORLDS*: AN ENDURING PRESENT-DAY STORY

In August 2012 the USA's National Aeronautics and Space Administration (NASA) successfully landed a robot rover on Mars. For NASA, like most people, the defining question is 'Life on Mars?' Was there once a time when life proved possible there? Unsurprisingly, all stages of the 'Mars Curiosity Project' have attracted extensive worldwide media coverage, particularly given the manner in which myriad works of science fiction have both encouraged and reflected our fascination with the Red Planet, Martians and all that. However, as the *New Scientist* asserted in 2015, the jury is still out on such questions.[1]

The War of the Worlds (1898), H. G. Wells's ground-breaking work of science fiction about a Martian invasion of earth, occupies a prominent place in our thinking about Mars. As a result, Wells is viewed still as a central player in Mars's storyline, as evidenced by his significant role in NASA's online 'Mars chronology'.[2] Moreover, the Press Kit prepared by NASA for the launch of the Mars rover included a section about fiction and reality focused upon the closing decades of the nineteenth century when the discoveries of astronomers like Giovanni Schiaparelli and Percival Lowell combined with the writings of Wells about Mars and Martians to fuel speculation about life on the red planet.[3] Indeed, as NASA's Press Kit recorded, Wells went even further by imagining future scenarios regarding Earth's relationship with Mars: 'On the dark side, H. G. Wells's 1898 novel "The War of the Worlds" portrayed an invasion of Earth by technologically superior Martians desperate for water'.

Today, 'the ghost of H. G. Wells' looms large still over contemporary media debates about the Red Planet.[4] In part, this reflects the enduring fame of *The*

---

1. Jacob Aron, 'What's flying over Mars ... Could it be auroras? Volcanoes? Even aliens?' *New Scientist*, 21 February 2015, p. 10; Stuart Clark, 'Across the Universe: Curiosity rover: why NASA isn't looking for life on Mars', *The Guardian Science Blog*, 5 August 2012, http://www.guardian.co.uk/science/across-the-universe [accessed 5 August 2012].

2. Paul Karol and David Catling, *NASA: Mars Chronology: Renaissance to the Space Age*, 29 October 2003, http://www.nasa.gov/audience/forstudents/9-12/features/F_Mars_Chronology.html [accessed 16 October 2014].

3. NASA, *Mars Science Laboratory Launch: Press Kit*, November 2011, p. 56.

4. Robert Markley, *Dying Planet: Mars in Science and the Imagination* (Durham, NC: Duke University Press, 2005), p. 386; Kenneth Chang, 'On Mars Rover, tools to plumb a methane mystery', *New York Times*, 22 November 2011.

War of the Worlds as a book, but it results also from the way in which Wells's pioneering story has been taken, and continues to be taken, to new audiences across the world – most notably on film by George Pal and Steven Spielberg, on radio by Orson Welles and through music by Jeff Wayne.[5] Moreover, Wells's book, like Orson Welles's broadcast, has even been targeted at a Martian audience, since both featured in 'Visions of Mars', a multimedia collection of literature and art about the Red Planet included in a DVD attached to the deck of NASA's Phoenix lander which arrived on Mars in May 2008.[6] Represented by the Planetary Society as 'the first library on Mars', the silica-glass DVD was designed to withstand the Martian environment for hundreds of years.[7]

Commenting upon the 'Mars Curiosity Project' for *USA Today*, Britt Kennerly reflected on Mars's role in popular culture:

> Mars is cool. No, not that kind of cool, though it gets nippy on a planet with temperatures that can dip to 200 degrees below zero Fahrenheit. Rather, it's an indefinable but unifying sort of cool that for centuries has inspired literature and legend. Sparked music and movies. Blended fact and fantasy in a way that's earned Mars a kind of "Pop Culture King of Planets" crown. Let's get down to Earth: You don't see Neptune or Uranus getting this kind of play.[8]

For Kennerly, Wells played a lead role in stimulating and moulding popular interest in and thinking about the Red Planet: 'Pop culture experts say widespread public interest in the planet really took off after H. G. Wells's "The War of the Worlds" was published in 1898, making plausible – or at least not out-of-this-world – the idea of Martian invaders'. Throughout its lifetime, *The War of the Worlds* has been acknowledged as – to quote Robert Crossley – 'a central text in the cultural history of Mars'.[9] Although it was not the first fictional work written about Mars, the book has proved instrumental in giving the planet global visibility and a central place in popular culture, most notably in serving as a reference point for the media. Significantly during 2013, Indian press coverage of the country's

5. Throughout this book, Orson Welles's name is written in full in order to avoid confusion with the use of 'Wells' for H. G. Wells.

6. The Planetary Society, 'Visions of Mars', 2007, http://www.planetary.org/explore/projects/vom/ [accessed 16 October 2014].

7. The Planetary Society, 'Press Release: Phoenix Takes Image of First Library on Mars', 27 May 2008, http://www.planetary.org/press-room/releases/2008/0527_Phoenix_Takes_Image_of_First_Library_on.html [accessed 16 October 2014].

8. Britt Kennerly, 'Mystery of Mars still attracts space lovers', *Florida Today*, 1 August 2012, http://www.usatoday.com/tech/science/space/story/2012-08-01/mars-mystery-attracts/56650542/1 [accessed 5 August 2012]; Charles E. Gannon, '"One swift, conclusive smashing and an end": Wells, war and the collapse of civilisation', *Foundation: The International Review of Science Fiction* 28 (77) (1999): 44.

9. Robert Crossley, *Imagining Mars: A Literary History* (Middletown, CT: Wesleyan University Press, 2011), p. 115.

'Mars Orbiter Mission', yet another project investigating past Martian habitats for indicators of life, echoed that in the USA. Thus, the *Times of India* foregrounded *The War of the Worlds* as a 'science fiction masterpiece', even quoting from the actual text by way of contextualizing India's interplanetary mission.[10] For the *Hindustan Times*, like *The Indian Express*, popular interest in Mars 'started with a book. In 1898, HG Wells brought Mars into popular culture with his book "The War of the Worlds".[11]

These examples, drawn from media coverage of recent space exploration, viewed alongside ongoing audio-visual adaptations of *The War of the Worlds*, reaffirm Wells's prominent place in contemporary popular culture. Indeed, ever since *The War of the Worlds* was published during the late 1890s, he has proved an influential popular cultural figure, as highlighted by his inclusion as one of the sixty or so people selected to feature on the cover of The Beatles' iconic 'Sergeant Pepper's Lonely Hearts Club Band' music album. Released in 1967, the Grammy Award-winning album, whose cover was designed by Peter Blake and Jann Haworth from an initial sketch by Paul McCartney, has sold over thirty million copies.

The War of the Worlds' *past and present*

The War of the Worlds, together with his other scientific romances, proved instrumental in forging Wells's reputation as a successful British writer reaching large audiences across Britain and the world. Moreover, these books have led Wells to be represented as a key figure, if not *the key figure*, responsible for originating what came to be described subsequently as science fiction.

Written in the late nineteenth century and set during the early twentieth century, *The War of the Worlds* continues to attract audiences during the twenty first century. Serialized in 1897 and published as a book in 1898, this seminal work of science fiction has never been out of print. Over time, it has appeared in an ever increasing number of new print editions (Table 1.1), such as the 2005 Penguin Classic version referenced in this publication alongside the original book. Moreover, the book has been translated into numerous languages, is widely available for downloading on the internet and has been adapted for an ever wider range of media formats to reach new audiences.

Widely praised for its literary qualities, *The War of the Worlds* proved a crucial publication enabling Wells to make his mark in the challenging literary

10. 'Mars in Popular Culture', *Times of India*, 6 November 2013, http://articles. timesofindia.indiatimes.com/2013-11-06/india/43730963_1_mars-attacks-from-venus-from-mars [accessed 10 November 2013].

11. 'Mars, the muse: how Red Planet has inspired Earth', *Hindustan Times* 6 November 2013 http://www.hindustantimes.com/StoryPage/Print/1147655.aspx [accessed 10 November 2013]; 'Mars of the mind', *The Indian Express*, 5 November 2013, http://www. indianexpress.com/news/mars-of-the-mind/1190930/ [accessed 10 November 2013].

Table 1.1 Editions of *The War of the Worlds* published per year

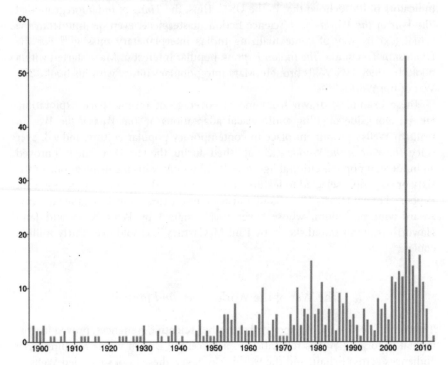

Source: http://drzeus.best.vwh.net/wotw/chron.html [accessed 30 July 2013].

world, particularly by highlighting his skill in making fantasy scenarios appear both engaging and real to readers within Britain and the wider world. For most readers, the story about a Martian invasion launched against Britain was just an excellent read, an exciting page-turner offering a very different type of story from the norm as well as raising such fantasy counterfactuals as 'What if the Martians invaded earth?'. For many its enduring appeal derives from its timeless focus upon the impact of a foreign invasion and war upon present-day society, through a storyline touching upon such perennial themes as complacency about national security; the need to take account of the unexpected; the ferocity of aggressive imperialism; the devastation and mass panic prompted by a sudden invasion; and the impact of science and technology upon warfare. Notwithstanding an understandable amount of scientific and technological anachronism due to subsequent advances in communications, weaponry and knowledge about Mars, *The War of the Worlds* has continually showed its ability to appeal to new and diverse audiences.

For Jeff Wayne, whose musical stage adaptation helps to explain *The War of the Worlds*' continuing visibility and popularity, Wells's storyline still talks to today's world: 'It resonates today ... it's all about conquering or being conquered'.[12] For Robert Silverberg, what keeps *The War of the Worlds* and the other scientific romances in print are Wells's literary skills, soaring imagination and vision of the time to come: 'it is that vision that gives his work continuing life'.[13] Likewise, Jorge Luis Borges, describing Wells as 'an admirable storyteller' writing scientific romances 'for all ages', praised the literary 'excellence' of these 'fantastic exercises': 'Not only do they tell an ingenious story; but they tell a story symbolic of processes that are somehow inherent in all human destinies. ... I think they will be incorporated ... into the general memory of the species and even transcend the fame of their creator or the extinction of the language in which they were written'.[14]

As a child, Wells used books to transport himself away from 'Atlas House', his birthplace in Bromley. Reading about diverse imaginary worlds took the young Wells away from the dark subterranean kitchen, the bug-infested bedrooms and the dingy parlour and carried him to faraway places and time periods. In turn, Wells, the writer of scientific romances, did the same for his many readers, offering them the opportunity to escape for a while from everyday realities to alternative worlds. Wells's scientific romances, most notably *The War of the Worlds*, have always appealed strongly to the young, a point made in 2005 by several respondents for a Mass Observation study about popular attitudes towards science fiction. Typically, one seventy-four-year-old recorded that as a boy he could 'still remember the pleasure of discovering' *The War of the Worlds*, which not only proved a good read, but opened his mind to other worlds beyond earth.[15]

One young reader enthused by the originality and sheer literary brilliance of Wells's early work was George Orwell (1903–50), whose dystopian novel *1984* (1949) was to prove as ground-breaking a text as *The War of the Worlds*.[16] For Orwell the schoolboy, 'There was the joy of waking early on summer mornings and getting in an hour's undisturbed reading (Ian Hay, Thackeray, Kipling and H. G. Wells were the favourite authors of my boyhood) in the sunlit, sleeping dormitory'.[17] As Bernard Crick recorded, Wells's writings, or rather those of the

12. Quoted, Stewart Lee, 'A new theatre of operations', *Sunday Times*, 19 March 2006, p. 27.

13. Robert Silverberg, 'Introduction', in Robert Silverberg (ed.), *The Mirror of Infinity: A Critics' Anthology of Science Fiction* (New York: Harper & Row, 1970), p. viii.

14. Jorge Luis Borges, *Other Inquisitions, 1937–1952* (Austin, TX: University of Texas Press, 1964), pp. 86–8.

15. The Mass Observation Project, Summer 2005 Directive: Part 1: the Universe and Outer Space (MO), SxMOA2/1/75/1, B1654, n.d. (2005), pp. 1–2, Mass Observation Archive, University of Sussex Special Collections, The Keep, Falmer, Brighton (Sussex). See also responses B1509, B2240, F3112, H1745, H2410, P2915, R1418.

16. George Orwell, 'The true pattern of H. G. Wells', *Manchester Evening News*, 14 August 1946.

17. George Orwell, 'Such, Such were the Joys', c. 1946–7 [first published 1952], in Peter Davison (ed.), *Orwell's England* (London: Penguin, 2001), p. 379.

early Wells, stayed with Orwell throughout his life both for what he wrote and for whom he wrote, that is the people, not intellectuals or fellow literary men.[18]

Despite acknowledging the difficulty of assessing any writer's impact, Orwell opined that during the late Victorian and Edwardian years no English writer 'so deeply influenced his contemporaries as Wells'.[19] Indeed, for Orwell, 'Mr Wells has certainly been the most influential novelist of our time, at any rate in the English-speaking world'.[20] What impressed Orwell, was the way in which Wells, 'a true prophet', confronted conventional modes of thought: 'there was need of someone who could state the opposite point of view'.[21] Expressing his 'great admiration' for Wells, Orwell admitted that he proved 'a very early influence on me: "The minds of all of us, and therefore the physical world, would be perceptibly different if Wells had never existed"'.[22]

> Back in the nineteen-hundreds, it was a wonderful experience for a boy to discover H. G. Wells. There you were in a world of pedants, clergymen and golfers, with your future employers exhorting you to "get on or get out", your parents systematically warping your sex life, and your dull-witted schoolmasters sniggering over their Latin tags; and here was this wonderful man who could tell you about the inhabitants of the planets and the bottom of the sea, and who *knew* that the future was not going to be what respectable people imagined.[23]

In this manner, Orwell's commentaries highlight not only Wells's role as a leading figure in popular culture, but also his ability to attract and engage the young often for life. Like Orwell, many other enthusiasts of *The War of the Worlds* – including Brian Aldiss, Timothy Hines, Steve Jones, Dominic Sandbrook, Will Self, Steven Spielberg and Fay Weldon – to quote Brian Aldiss – 'first came upon this novel at a youthful age'.[24]

18. Bernard Crick, *George Orwell: A Life* (London: Secker & Warburg, 1980), p. 68.

19. Orwell, 'The true pattern of H. G. Wells'.

20. George Orwell, 'The Male Byronic', *Tribune*, 21 June 1940, p. 21.

21. Orwell to Symons, 10 May 1948, in Peter Davison (ed.), *George Orwell: A life in letters* (London: Harvill Secker, 2010), p. 406; George Orwell, 'Wells, Hitler and the World State', *Horizon*, (August 1941), in Peter Davison (ed.), *The Complete Works of George Orwell, vol. XII: A Patriot after all, 1940–1941* (London: Secker and Warburg, 1998), p. 540.

22. Orwell to Symons, 10 May 1948, in Davison, *George Orwell: A life in letters*, p. 406; Orwell, 'Wells, Hitler and the World State', pp. 539–40; Patrick Parrinder, *Science Fiction: Its History and Criticism* (London: Methuen, 1980), p. 36. On Wells's irritation with Orwell's *Horizon* article, see Michael Sherborne, *H. G. Wells: Another Kind of Life* (London: Peter Owen, 2010), pp. 332–4. See also John S. Partington, 'The Pen as Sword: George Orwell, H. G. Wells and Journalistic Parricide', *Journal of Contemporary History* 39 (1) (2004): 45–56.

23. Orwell, 'Wells, Hitler and the World State', p. 540.

24. Brian Aldiss, 'Introduction', in H. G. Wells, *The War of the Worlds* (London: Penguin, 2005), p. xv; John C. Snider, 'Interview: Timothy Hines, Pendragon Pictures', *Sci-fi Dimensions*, November 2004, http://www.scifidimensions.com/Nov04/timothyhines.htm

Accessing Wells at second hand

Notwithstanding its strong sense of time and place centred upon late Victorian London and Surrey, themes studied in the next two chapters, *The War of the Worlds* has proved – to quote Patrick Parrinder – 'highly adaptable'.[25] Thus, as detailed in Part III, the story has been reimagined and retold frequently through alternative audio-visual and literary formats normally set in different locations and time periods appropriate to the prevailing moods of the day. The storyline's 'unusual plasticity' means that its alien invasion template, though applied by Wells to late Victorian London and Surrey, could be set anywhere – for example, Boston, Braga, Buffalo, Lisbon, Los Angeles, New York, Providence, Quito, Rio de Janeiro and Santiago have suffered the same fate as London – and in any time period.[26]

In turn, each new adaptation marks recognition of the literary quality and originality of Wells's genre-defining storyline. In particular, they show that Wells's strong sense of time and place was both a strength, such as in terms of enhancing the story's realism and a weakness in enabling Wells's text to be rewritten for alternative locations and periods, just by switching the landing point, the Martians' target and the date of the invasion. In certain cases, like the 2005 Spielberg film, even the Martians were written out of the storyline to be replaced by anonymous alien invaders. Adaptations reflect also the timeless character of a storyline reconfigured repeatedly in different media to reflect contemporary scenarios, such as the threat of world war during the late 1930s in the case of Orson Welles's radio drama, Cold War paranoia during the early 1950s for Pal's film and post-9/11 trauma for Spielberg's film.

In fact, as detailed in Chapter 11, soon after *The War of the Worlds* was serialized, but before its publication as a book, the story was reworked and re-located for publication by two American newspapers, an episode establishing that this process of retelling Wells's original story geographically and/or chronologically possesses a long history across the world. Numerous reworkings, transplantings and updatings of the basic storyline in a wide range of media

[accessed 20 February 2014]; Steve Jones, 'View from the Lab: A century's worth of wisdom since the Martians first landed', *Daily Telegraph*, 18 February 1998; Dominic Sandbrook, 'Classic sci-fi', *The Times*, 15 November 2014; Dominic Sandbrook, 'Tomorrow's Worlds: the unearthly history of science fiction', BBC2, 22 November 2014; Will Self, 'Death on three legs', *The Times*, 23 January 2010; Devin Faraci, 'Interview: Tom Cruise and Steven Spielberg (War of the Worlds)', 29 June 2005, http://www.chud.com/3533/interview-tom-cruise-and-steven-spielberg-war-of-the-worlds/ [accessed 20 February 2014]; Fay Weldon, 'Great Lives: H. G. Wells', *BBC Radio Four*, 8 May 2014.

25. Patrick Parrinder, *Shadows of the Future: H. G. Wells, Science Fiction, and Prophecy* (Liverpool: Liverpool University Press, 1995), p. 87; Thomas C. Renzi, *H. G. Wells: Six Scientific Romances Adapted for Film* (Metuchen, NJ: Scarecrow Press, 1992), pp. 5–9.

26. John Gosling, *Waging the War of the Worlds: A History of the 1938 Broadcast and Resulting Panic* (Jefferson, NC: McFarland, 2009), p. 2.

formats have kept both Wells and *The War of the Worlds* in front of audiences comprising not only readers of books and magazine serials but also cinema-goers, computer games players, music and radio listeners, readers of comic books and graphic novels and television viewers. Other spin-offs include parodies, prequels and sequels. In addition, the repeated referencing of both Wells's original storyline and adaptations based thereupon by a wide range of media results from a process of intertextuality reflecting and reaffirming *The War of the Worlds*' enduring impact upon popular culture.

In the present-day multimedia world, Wells's science fiction classic continues to attract adaptations. Indeed, today *The War of the Worlds* is probably best known through its many and varied contemporary retellings in a growing range of multi-media formats rather than the ground-breaking original written text. Thus, *The War of the Worlds* is accessed increasingly by audiences second-hand through the audio-visual media, especially film, music or television, rather than the written word. For most people, mention of *The War of the Worlds* is most likely to conjure up images of Tom Cruise taking on aliens in Spielberg's Hollywood blockbuster, the fighting machine descending on stage during Jeff Wayne's musical extrava-ganza, or the infamous panic reportedly occasioned by Orson Welles's 1938 radio broadcast. For them, Orson Welles, Spielberg and Jeff Wayne represent their entry points for *The War of the Worlds*.

Familiarity with such alternative spin-offs led Will Self, whose mother told him about listening to the 1938 Orson Welles radio adaptation when growing up in New York, to depict *The War of the Worlds* as 'one of those books that I felt I'd read long before I actually did so'.[27] There is, of course, no reason why those for whom a film, music show or radio broadcast might be the initial point of contact with *The War of the Worlds* should not go on to read the book and then move onto Wells's other writings. Indeed, Table 1.1 suggests that adaptations, such as Orson Welles's radio drama and Spielberg's 2005 film, have played a role in prompting the publi-cation of new editions of the original book. In some cases, they might, like Simon James, the editor of *The Wellsian* (2009–16) and author of a major study of Wells's writing, be encouraged to focus their research on Wells: 'Like many born in the 1970s, my earliest exposure to Wells's words was through Jeff Wayne's musical adaptation of *The War of the Worlds*'.[28] On the other hand, this trend has led to an occasional tendency to gloss over Wells's role as the original author of the story and to treat him as little more than a literary footnote, almost an invisible man. More seriously, the similarity of their surnames has prompted some people to believe that Orson Welles, not H. G. Wells, wrote the original story.

---

27. Self, 'Death on three legs'.

28. Simon J. James, *Maps of Utopia: H. G. Wells, Modernity and the End of Culture* (Oxford: Oxford University Press, 2012), p. xiv.

Wells and science fiction

Born on 21 September 1866, Wells died in London on 13 August 1946, aged seventy-nine. As *The Times'* editorial recorded, Wells, a prolific publisher of books, articles, short stories and book reviews, a writer of both fiction and non-fiction, proved one of the most famous and widely read Englishmen of his time.[29] When writing his autobiography, published in 1934, Wells proclaimed confidently that several million copies of his books were scattered around the world.[30]

But who reads Wells today? Apart from falling out of favour with present-day readers, he does not appear to be a literary figure much studied in history or literature courses in schools and universities, where he has been shunted increasingly towards the margins of literature teaching, except for science fiction studies.[31] This is not to say that his books, or at least his scientific romances, are not still read and studied today, but much of Wells's writing, particularly that published after 1900, has been out of fashion for many years. Claiming that Wells became passé around the time of the First World War, David Lodge pointed to the irony that the Armageddon foreshadowed in such fantasies as *The War of the Worlds* (1898) and *The War in the Air* (1908) prompted a shift in the literary and intellectual world to which Wells failed to attune himself.[32] Also, as James observed, many of the books of the later Wells 'are not, simply, very good', as originality gave way to repetition and art was compromised increasingly by politics.[33]

Within this context, Wells's present-day literary reputation proves somewhat mixed, especially as – to quote Bernard Bergonzi – 'the difficulty of defining what kind of writer he was still remains'.[34] Generally speaking, his scientific romances remain highly regarded, the central element in positive assessments of Wells as a writer and particularly his image as one of the founders of science fiction. As Patrick Parrinder recorded, Wells was and still is 'celebrated as the inventor of the "scientific romance", a combination of adventure novel and philosophical tale in which the hero becomes involved in a life-and-death struggle resulting from some scientific development'.[35] Published predominantly between 1895 and 1901, his scientific romances sold well, attracted critical praise and public visibility, enabling Wells, a new young writer, to establish a fast-growing reputation on both

29. 'Editorial: H. G. Wells', *The Times*, 14 August 1946, p. 5; Patrick Parrinder, 'Biographical Note', in H. G. Wells, *The War of the Worlds* (London: Penguin, 2005), p. xii.

30. H. G. Wells, *Experiment in Autobiography: Discoveries and Conclusions of a Very Ordinary Brain (since 1866)*, II (London: Victor Gollancz and Cresset Press, 1934), p. 729.

31. In 2015 *The War of the Worlds* was introduced as a set book for Pearson Edexcel's GCE A level English Literature.

32. David Lodge, *The Novelist at the Crossroads and Other Essays on Fiction and Criticism* (London: Ark, 1986), p. 205.

33. James, *Maps of Utopia*, p. x.

34. Bernard Bergonzi, 'A global thinker', *The Times Higher Education Supplement*, 3 October 1986.

35. Parrinder, 'Biographical Note', p. ix.

sides of the Channel and the Atlantic. Foregrounding his scientific awareness and knowledge, they showcased Wells's storytelling skills and extraordinary imaginative power by juxtaposing fantastic scenarios with everyday realities.

Indeed, for many commentators, the scientific romances have led Wells to be regarded as 'the Shakespeare of science fiction', the author largely responsible for inspiring and popularizing science fiction, most notably the sub-genres concerning alien invasion and time travel.[36] As A. A. Gill opined when looking back to the origins of the BBC television series about the time travelling 'Doctor Who', 'the idea was a straight steal from H. G. Wells'.[37] Likewise, Wells is viewed as a prime source of inspiration for Gene Roddenberry's *Star Trek* films and television series. For James Broderick, 'If Gene Roddenberry is the father of *Star Trek*, then H. G. Wells should be thought of as the mildly eccentric uncle in the *Trek* family tree.'[38]

Wells was instrumental in taking science to the literary world. Despite proving essentially fantastic products of a highly creative imagination, the scientific romances drew heavily upon his scientific education, informed awareness of contemporary advances in science, strong desire to give practical application to recent scientific research, and ambition to take science to the man in the street. Thus, just as *The War of the Worlds* linked up with recent scientific reports and media speculation about Mars, as detailed in chapter three, so the x-rays, featuring as 'Röntgen vibrations' in *The Invisible Man* (1897), drew inspiration from reports about the experiments of Wilhelm Röntgen, a German physicist, published in *Nature* in January 1896.[39]

Wellsian fantasies as reference points for the real world

Introducing a collected edition of his writings, Wells reminded readers that fundamentally the scientific romances were fantasies, literary products created by his imagination.[40] They were not intended, he stressed, to predict serious possibilities. Perhaps the scientific romances were, and still are, admired mostly for their engaging, fast-moving, innovative and entertaining storylines, but books like *The War of the Worlds*, it is argued, offered far more. As Wells himself admitted, '*The War of the Worlds* like *The Time Machine* was another assault on human

36. Brian Aldiss, *Billion Year Spree: The True History of Science Fiction* (New York: Doubleday, 1973), p. 132.

37. A. A. Gill, 'I don't think we can save this one, Doctor', *The Sunday Times*, 24 August 2014.

38. James F. Broderick, *The Literary Galaxy of Star Trek: An Analysis of References and Themes in the Television Series and Films* (Jefferson, NC: McFarland, 2006), pp. 49–51; Brian J. Robb, *A Brief Guide to Star Trek* (London: Constable & Robinson, 2012), p. 1.

39. H. G. Wells, *The Invisible Man* (London: Penguin, 2005), p. 95.

40. H. G. Wells, *Seven Famous Novels* (New York: Knopf, 1934), p. vii.

self-satisfaction'.[41] For Bernard Bergonzi, among others, *The War of the Worlds* captured the *fin de siècle* angst of late Victorian Britain as Wells – to quote Bryan Appleyard – 'saw through the seductive veneer of modernity to the horrors that might lie beneath'.[42] For I. F. Clarke, *The War of the Worlds*, articulating contemporary forebodings about an uncertain future, 'is still the most remarkable fantasy of imaginative warfare that has so far appeared in the history of the genre. The theme was scientific warfare taken to the limit'.[43]

In this vein over time *The War of the Worlds* has often been represented as possessing a present-day relevance in terms of offering an invaluable reference point, one way of making sense of the contemporary world, as happened in 2011 when Jonathan Jones, *The Guardian*'s art critic, used *The War of the Worlds* to frame his thoughts about London in the wake of serious urban riots. For Jones, the abandoned metropolis seemed an eerie wasteland: 'There was something a bit Wellsian about photographs of riots and looting across London … It all seems uncanny and reminiscent of late Victorian science fiction.'[44]

Seeking to explain the continuing appeal and perceived relevance of a book written and published at the end of the nineteenth century, Stephen Baxter, the best-selling award-winning science fiction author and president of the British Science Fiction Association, represented *The War of the Worlds* as 'a controlling metaphor for the twentieth century'.[45] When researching the history of the Second World War as background for *Time's Tapestry 4: Weaver* (2008), Baxter discovered that 'many eyewitnesses referred to Wells's books as a basis for their experiences: "It's like something out of H. G. Wells"'.[46] For Baxter, *The War of the Worlds* foresaw many aspects of people's experience of war in the twentieth century: 'It is Wells's extraordinary achievement that in the pages of TWOTW [*The War of the Worlds*] he brought together themes that would define the coming century: homeland invasion, defying the tyrant, the convulsive shock of world wars, the loss of innocence, and the possibilities of life in the universe.' The various re-stagings, re-imaginings and fresh explorations of Wells's novel, as detailed in Part 3, highlight this point, as evidenced by the way in which, say, the audio-visual adaptations of Orson Welles, Pal and Spielberg were set in the then present and

41. Ibid., p. ix.

42. Bernard Bergonzi, *The Early H. G. Wells: A Study of the Scientific Romances* (Manchester: Manchester University Press, 1961), pp. 3–4, 12; Bryan Appleyard, 'The plot to hide H. G. Wells's genius', *The Sunday Times*, 26 June 2005.

43. I. F. Clarke, *Voices Prophesying War: Future Wars 1763–1984* (Oxford: Oxford University Press, 1966), p. 99.

44. Jonathan Jones, 'London burning: history just went sci-fi', 8 August 2011, http://www.guardian.co.uk/artanddesign/jonathanjonesblog/2011/aug/08/london-riots-sci-fi-dystopian [accessed 5 September 2011].

45. Stephen Baxter, 'H. G. Wells's *The War of the Worlds* as a controlling metaphor for the twentieth century', *The Wellsian* 32 (2009): 3.

46. Ibid., p. 15.

hence captured the angst and paranoia of the period. As Baxter observed, they prove 'mirrors that expose the themes of the work itself'.[47]

In this vein, Lonna Malmsheimer described Wells's *The War of the Worlds* as 'science fiction with a social history'.[48] Perceived as representing 'the panic model of disaster fiction', the storyline offered a highly visible and accessible reference point for people seeking to articulate their response to serious crises.[49] For Malmsheimer, the focus was the Three Mile Island Incident of March 1979, when the nuclear reactor of the power station at Three Mile Island, Harrisburg, Pennsylvania, went out of control resulting in the mass evacuation of some 144,000 people. Drawing upon extensive oral testimony gained immediately following the emergency, she concluded that when people were projecting responses to an unprecedented disaster their thinking was informed by not only knowledge of past events – unsurprisingly Hiroshima 1945 was often cited – but also familiar fictional narratives.

Two fictional storylines, largely based on the aural and visual media rather than the written word, were cited more often than others: *The China Syndrome* (1979), a film which had just opened in Harrisburg, and 'The War of the Worlds', most notably the 1938 radio and 1953 film versions. According to Malmsheimer, these fictions, though based upon fantasy, possessed metaphoric elements adjudged relevant to a scenario where 'the population is suddenly assaulted with a deadly, little-understood technology by a coldly calculating, but in *War of the Worlds*, alien force':

> Social systems disintegrate under threat; science and government, including the military, fail to understand or deal with the threat. The narrator of the story (a scientist and sometime journalist) survives to report each stage of the annihilation. Only nature can stop this force; in the end the aliens succumb to the earth's bacteria. Both *War of the Worlds* and *The China Syndrome* also dramatize a fearful public powerlessness analogous to that of the Three Mile Island situation.[50]

Malmsheimer foregrounded the testimony of one twenty-year-old, who drew heavily upon his cultural inventory of books and films – reportedly Pal's 1953 film proved a staple feature of American Sunday afternoon television schedules – to make sense of the crisis:

> I could imagine all kinds of fantastic things like … nuclear type holocausts &, that type of thing, being the last few people, just left in an area during evacu-
> ation … imagining what an evacuation would be like … I have never been in

47. Ibid., p. 3.

48. Lonna M. Malmsheimer, 'Three Mile Island: Fact, Frame, and Fiction', *American Quarterly* 38 (1) (1986): 47.

49. Ibid., p. 44.

50. Ibid., p. 47.

one and I have never seen one except we could joke around, some of us, about seeing *War of the Worlds* where people were all fleeing the invading Martians or whatever. They are all fighting each other for cars and all this … Basically that's all people talked about, a week or so.[51]

Wells's science fiction as 'historical fact'

Wells's *The War of the Worlds* proved a major source of inspiration also for Niall Ferguson, when planning his television history 'The War of the World', shown in both Britain and the USA in 2006 and subsequently writing the series' tie-in book. Ferguson, Laurence A. Tisch Professor of History at Harvard University, is one of *TIME Magazine*'s 'TIME 100', public intellectuals adjudged instrumental in shaping present-day thinking through journalism, public lectures and television.

Speaking in New York in September 2006 about the television series and his recently published tie-in book, Ferguson began by asking 'Why is it called "The War of the World"?':

Did I go and see Tommy Cruise in a Steven Spielberg film? No. It was inspired by the original novel H. G. Wells wrote in 1898, *The War of the Worlds*, which, if you remember, describes the destruction of London, rather than New York, in an alien invasion.

As I was reading Wells's extraordinary work of science fiction, it struck me how prophetic it was, because, time and again, the scenes that Wells describes – of a city thrown into turmoil by invaders using powerful technology to destroy buildings and people alike – that vision came true.[52]

A quote from *The War of the Worlds*, centred upon 'the roaring wave of fear' (I.16: 150/92) sweeping through London as the invaders reached the city, the resulting flight of the inhabitants and growing fears of extermination, provided the epigraph for Ferguson's book. In fact, Wells had figured prominently in his thinking already in July 2005, when writing for the *Daily Telegraph* about the 7/7 terrorist attacks launched in London by 'intra-terrestrial invaders'.[53] Quoting from the novel, Ferguson pointed to the way in which *The War of the Worlds* revealed Wells's foresight about future conflicts: 'Part of the reason Wells was so prescient was that he understood how easy it would be for a well-armed invader to plunge London, or any other urban centre, into chaos':

51. Ibid., p. 41.

52. Niall Ferguson, 'The War of the World: Twentieth-Century Conflict and the Descent of the West', *Carnegie Council Public Affairs Program*, 26 September 2006, http://www.carnegiecouncil.org/studio/multimedia/20060926/index.html [accessed 22 February 2012].

53. Niall Ferguson, 'H. G. Wells warned us of how it would feel to fight a "War of the World"', *Daily Telegraph*, 24 July 2005.

It is now more than a century since H. G. Wells published *The War of the Worlds* and once again London is under attack. Though it has titillated generations of cinema-goers – and, courtesy of Steven Spielberg, is doing so once again this summer – Wells's story is much more than just a seminal work of science fiction. It's also a work of astonishing prescience. For so much of what it describes was to happen time and again throughout the 20th century.

For Ferguson, therefore, *The War of the Worlds* is far more than a science fiction story or a Darwinian morality tale. Praising Wells for writing 'a work of singular prescience', Ferguson represented the key developments outlined therein as 'historical fact'.[54] Thus, as argued subsequently also by Baxter, the story offered a metaphor for the twentieth century and after when the nightmarish scenes of death and destruction Wells 'imagined while pedalling around peaceful Woking and Chertsey on his newly-acquired bicycle' became a reality in cities all over the world – not only in London, but also in – to list examples cited by Ferguson – Warsaw, Berlin, Hiroshima, Seoul and Phnom Penh. As Ferguson informed his audience only a few years after the destruction of New York's twin towers in 9/11, 'It suddenly struck me that this was the key *leitmotif* of twentieth-century conflict. And I hardly need to suggest to an audience in New York that that theme is by no means played out.'[55] In his book, Ferguson provided a vivid precis linking the images of Martian power created by Wells's imagination with twentieth-century military realities:

> Invaders approach the outskirts of a city. The inhabitants are slow to grasp their vulnerability. But the invaders possess lethal weapons: armoured vehicles, flame throwers, poison gas, aircraft. They use these indiscriminately and merci-lessly against soldiers and civilians alike. The city's defences are overrun. As the invaders near the city, panic reigns. People flee their homes in confusion; swarms of refugees clog the roads and railways. The task of massacring them is made easy. People are slaughtered like beasts. Finally, all that remains are smouldering ruins and piles of desiccated corpses.[56]

Seeking to understand why the twentieth century, characterized by bloody conflicts and genocide, was 'so astonishingly violent', Ferguson employed a Wellsian analogy to help explain why people emulated the barbarous approach adopted towards humans by the Martians in *The War of the Worlds*: 'The irony is that it didn't need Martians to wreak havoc in so many cities in the world. There was no need for Wells' alien invaders ... what's fascinating is how often it was done as if the victims were aliens.'[57] Pointing to Nazi Germany, Ferguson argued that

54. Niall Ferguson, *The War of the World: Twentieth Century Conflict and the Descent of the West* (New York: Penguin, 2006), pp. xxxiii–iv, 646.

55. Ferguson, 'The War of the World' (Carnegie Council).

56. Ferguson, *War of the World*, pp. xxxiii–iv.

57. Ferguson, 'The War of the World' (Carnegie Council).

'No other regime has come so close to H. G. Wells's nightmare of a mechanized sucking out of human life by voracious aliens.'[58]

Wells's 'Alien Gaze'

Nor are Baxter, Ferguson and Malmsheimer alone in their thinking. Two examples follow, but there are many others. Firstly, Keith Williams repositions *The War of the Worlds* as 'one of the most influential manifestations of the emergence of a critical "postcolonial" vision in the science and culture of the late Victorian period'.[59] For Williams, Wells's book anticipates the total war of 1914–18 and its associated anxieties about imperial domination. This critical 'postcolonial' vision is established in the opening chapter, in which the Martians observe earth – what Williams represents as an 'alien gaze' – as they prepared their invasion plans. Making no secret of his anti-imperial stance, Wells used his Martians to inflict 'scientific terror on the complacent civilisation at the Empire's hub, inverting its relation to distant colonial subjects': '*TWOTW* [*The War of the Worlds*] elaborated the possibility of this emerging alien gaze to allow imperial Britain to look long and hard at itself and the ethics of its foreign policy from the vantage point of another species, a nightmare version of the colonial Other integral to its expansionist ideology'.[60] Wells achieved this effect, Williams argues, by using the anonymous first-person narrator to create 'a double perspective' offering readers the view of not only a victim of war but also an outsider articulating a more critical stance: 'At times I suffer from the strangest sense of detachment from myself and the world about me; I seem to watch it all from the outside' (I.7: 46/32).

Stressing the story's preoccupation with place and the parallels between the Martians and suburbanites, Todd Kuchta argues that *The War of the Worlds*' imperial narrative needs to be studied alongside the growth of suburbia in Britain: '*The War of the Worlds* would have been unthinkable to Wells ... if not for the rise of suburbia'.[61] Kuchta overturns the dominant critical narrative concerning reverse colonization – here the Martian invasion is represented as intended to shock British complacency and to inspire an understanding about imperialism's negative impacts – when arguing that the novel 'is a reflection of what many Britons believed *was* happening to them: that suburbia was threatening to overtake the nation with a race that fused brutal colonizers and brutal savages'.

58. Ferguson, *War of the World*, p. 507.

59. Keith Williams, 'Alien Gaze: Postcolonial Vision in *The War of the Worlds*', in Steven McLean (ed.), *H. G. Wells: Interdisciplinary Essays* (Newcastle: Cambridge Scholars, 2008), p. 49; Keith B. Williams, 'H. G. Wells: The War of the Worlds', *The Literary Encyclopedia*, 8 June 2009, http://www.litencyc.com/php/sworks.php?rec=true&UID=8092 [accessed 9 August 2013.

60. Williams, 'H. G. Wells: The War of the Worlds'.

61. Todd Kuchta, *Semi-Detached Empire: Suburbia and the Colonization of Britain, 1880 to the Present* (Charlottesville, VA: University of Virginia Press, 2010), pp. 36–8, 55.

Biography of the book

'Every book', Leslie Howsam asserted, 'has a history of its own', especially once it meets and travels through the real world.[62] Rather like the characters they portray, books have their own lives, their own distinctive rhythms. Following their completion, they may thrive and achieve fame and fortune; fail and be quite forgotten; or be rediscovered and secure posthumous glory. Against this background, there has emerged growing interest in the biographies of books, as a way for understanding how books 'work', especially how they interact with people and societies. Moreover, as shown by Paul Eggert's *Biography of a Book: Henry Lawson's While the Billy Boils* (2013), such biographies offer also invaluable insights into the course of a country's cultural history.

In brief, these studies focus upon the production, the critical and commercial reception and the reading of books through ever-changing political, socio-economic and cultural contexts:

- the production stage concentrating upon the roles performed by both authors – for example, their sources of inspiration; contextual factors; research methods; and the writing, revising and proofing of the text – and publishers in commissioning, guiding, influencing, publishing and marketing books;
- the reception histories of books, most notably the responses of readers and reviewers when reading, receiving, mediating and interpreting the published tomes; and
- their literary and audio-visual afterlife.

Speaking about his role in editing Princeton University Press's series about 'The Lives of Great Religious Books', Fred Appel admitted that for some books the afterlife proves more prolonged, active and successful than for others. 'Not every book that is born lives a long life. Publishers know all too well that many of them just don't make it past infancy or early adolescence. For one reason or another, they're not taken up by the reading public, don't capture people's imagination, or aren't perceived as original or interesting enough – and they fade.'[63] But some books take on a life of their own and continue to live, particularly those viewed as possessing literary significance and merit, resonating strongly with audiences, or appealing to adapters.

The afterlife of books can take several forms. James Secord employed the concept of 'literary replication' to describe the varying ways in which texts

---

62. Leslie Howsam, *Old Books and New Histories: An Orientation to Studies in Book and Print Culture* (Toronto, ON: University of Toronto Press, 2006), p. viii.

63. Quoted, Ruth Braunstein, 'SSRC. The Immanent Frame: "I would love to read the biography of a book ...", 13 April 2011, http://blogs.ssrc.org/tif/2011/04/13/i-would-love-to-read-the-biography-of-a-book/ [accessed 22 September 2014].

replicate themselves.[64] Thus, books may be reprinted, repackaged and translated countless times, but appear with very different texts, which may or may not have been revised and/or approved by the author and original publisher. Inevitably the reading of books by successive generations of readers and reviewers will differ from that of those at the time of the initial publication. Frequently books, though continuing to have an afterlife through reprints and revised editions, may be adapted for presentation to audiences in alternative audio-visual formats in a manner showing contrasting degrees of accuracy to the original text.[65] Indeed, in today's multimedia world, stories published some time ago will often be accessed initially as well as primarily through non-printed formats, like film, radio and television.

Against this background, this study focuses upon the production and reception histories of Wells's *The War of the Worlds*, which is viewed by many commentators as – to quote I. F. Clarke – 'the best of all his scientific romances'.[66] Moreover, the book has experienced a long, extremely active and increasingly varied afterlife. *The War of the Worlds* has not only proved a best-seller and remained in print, but also appeared in an ever increasing number of new print editions (Table 1.1) and translations.[67] Indeed, the post-2000 period, characterized by a surge in 2005 when over fifty editions were published as spin-offs for Spielberg's film, has witnessed more new editions than ever.[68] Apart from proving a good read, throughout its lifetime the story, such as stressed by Baxter and Ferguson, among others, has been viewed as an invaluable reference point, that is – to quote Williams – 'a topically renewable template', 'a critical method for looking at ourselves', and a prompt to discuss such issues as imperialism, science's impact upon society and the growth of suburbia.[69]

As detailed in Part 3 of this book, *The War of the Worlds*' afterlife is distinguished by the way in which it has continued to flourish across the world during changing times to access and engage vast new audiences through the story's adaptation for a wide range of alternative formats. At times, it seems as if Wells's story is more famous for its numerous reworkings than for the original magazine serialization and book publication. Today, comics, computer games, films, graphic novels, mobile phone apps, music, radio and television take Wells's *The War of the Worlds* to audiences which might otherwise have neither the time, opportunity

---

64. James A Secord, *Victorian Sensation: The Extraordinary Publication, Reception, and Secret Authorship of 'Vestiges of the Natural History of Creation'* (London: University of Chicago Press, 2000), p. 126; Howsam, *Old Books*, pp. 41–5.

65. Sheryl A. Englund, 'Reading the Author in *Little Women*: a biography of a book', *ATQ* 12 (3) (1998): 199–220.

66. Clarke, *Voices Prophesying War*, p. 94.

67. BBC Radio Four, 'Best Seller, 6: The War of the Worlds by H. G. Wells', 19 April 1978. This programme was written by Bernard Bergonzi.

68. '*The War of the Worlds*, years, chronological', *The War of the Worlds Book Cover Collection*, http://drzeus.best.vwh.net/wotw/ [accessed 5 May 2015].

69. Williams, 'Alien Gaze', p. 66; Williams, 'H. G. Wells: The War of the Worlds'.

nor inclination to read the original book. Despite their variable quality and fluctuating degrees of conformity to the original storyline, these adaptations highlight the timeless nature of Wells's creative imagination. Moreover, for those who may not have even encountered his writings before, adaptations provide a possible prompt to move on to sample an engaging piece of literature likely to encourage further explorations of Wells's publications and life story.

Conclusion

In 1901 the death of Queen Victoria brought the Victorian age to an end. The turn of the century proved also a major watershed in Wells's career, as 'the Early Wells', the writer responsible for both a series of scientific romances and an extensive range of journalism and short stories, gave way to the 'Later Wells'. The latter phase is frequently dated as commencing with *Love and Mr Lewisham* (1900), a novel described by Wells as 'a more serious undertaking than anything I have ever done before'.[70] Significantly, *Love and Mr. Lewisham* was represented by *The Bookman*'s reviewer as 'the work of a new Mr. Wells': 'There is the essential difference between this novel by the new Mr. Wells and all that has preceded it … From the realms of fantastic imaginings the author of "The War of the Worlds" has descended to a phase of existence of the earth earthy. "Love and Mr. Lewisham" is lived'.[71]

Despite still returning occasionally to write a scientific romance, such as *The War in the Air* (1908), Wells largely abandoned the literary genre responsible for making his name and fortune for what he represented as 'proper' novels, like *Love and Mr Lewisham*, *Kipps: the Story of a Simple Soul* (1905) and *The History of Mr Polly* (1910), and non-fiction studies, such as *Anticipations of the Reaction of Mechanical and Scientific Progress Upon Human Life and Thought* (1901) and *The Outline of History* (1920), scientific ideological treatises and encyclopaedias. For Wells, the literary life was 'one of the modern forms of adventure', especially as fame brought him as a writer 'the utmost freedom of movement and intercourse'.[72] Basically, he wanted to be viewed as far more than a writer of what came to be called science fiction. In part, his novels reflected increasingly his emerging role and fame as a public intellectual using his writings, not excluding his fiction, and his voice to discuss contemporary political and social issues. As a public figure, Wells met world leaders, including American presidents (Theodore Roosevelt 1906; Franklin D. Roosevelt 1934) and Soviet leaders (Lenin 1920; Joseph Stalin 1934), while rubbing shoulders with Hollywood celebrities like Charlie Chaplin. Significantly, in September 1921 Chaplin, having just finished a film, decided to

70. Wells to Healey, 22 June 1900, David C. Smith (ed.), *The Correspondence of H. G. Wells*, 1 (London: Pickering & Chatto, 1998), p. 356.

71. J. E. H. W., 'The new Mr. Wells', *The Bookman* 18 (107) (August 1900).

72. H. G. Wells, 'My Lucky Moment, *View*, 29 April 1911, quoted Parrinder, *Shadows of the Future*, p. 89.

take a holiday and visit London 'where I hope to meet H. G. Wells and George Bernard Shaw – all the big men of that country'.[73]

During the 1890s Wells reached his audience in print, not by speech. For most commentators, his skills were fundamentally those of a writer, not a speaker. A thin high-pitched voice, likened as ranging between a squeak and a falsetto, meant that he is often represented as an uninspiring public speaker. Looking back to his attendance at a meeting of the Fabian Society during the 1900s, Clement Attlee, who later became British prime minister (1945–51), commented that the platform 'seemed to be full of bearded men', like Sidney Webb and George Bernard Shaw.[74] Attlee asked his brother, 'Have we got to grow a beard to join this show?'. A moustached H. G. Wells was also on the platform. Described by Attlee as 'speaking with a little piping voice', he seemed 'very unimpressive' as a speaker. Even so, during succeeding decades, this did not prevent Wells playing a major role as a public intellectual, attracting an audience, performing an active role in the Fabian Society and making frequent radio broadcasts.[75] Indeed, there are sound recordings in which Wells's voice sounds more normal and less shrill.[76]

Inevitably, many publications by the later Wells, when he was writing more as what Borges depicted as 'a sociological spectator', lost their appeal to readers as soon as the topics covered ceased to engage contemporary interest.[77] Hence a substantial proportion of Wells's post-1900 oeuvre remains largely unread today. By contrast, Wells's scientific romances, published – to quote Bergonzi – 'when he was writing as an artist, and not as a propagandist', have proved far more successful in both literary and commercial terms.[78] For Bergonzi, among others, they are his most creative, original and enduring literary achievement: 'Wells, at the beginning of his career, was a genuine and original imaginative artist, who wrote several books of considerable literary importance, before dissipating his talents in directions which now seem more or less irrelevant'.[79] Today, Wells's public visibility and literary reputation may have dimmed, but *The War of the Worlds*, like his other scientific fantasies, is still read and in print thereby enabling readers to travel through time and space in their minds. Furthermore, the story continues to reach large present-day audiences through the audio-visual media. Notwithstanding the preference of academics to focus upon Wells as a historical and literary subject, there is no denying the fact that today his popular appeal

73. Frank Vreeland, 'Charlie Chaplin, philosopher, has serious side', *New York Herald*, 11 September 1921; David Robinson, *Chaplin: His Life and Art* (London: Collins, 1985), pp. 285–7.

74. Clement R. Attlee, *As it Happened* (London: William Heinemann, 1954), p. 21.

75. David C. Smith, *H. G. Wells: Desperately Mortal. A Biography* (New Haven, CT: Yale University Press, 1986), pp. 295–322; Norman and Jeanne MacKenzie, *The Time Traveller: The Life of H. G. Wells* (London: Weidenfeld & Nicolson, 1973), pp. 201–20.

76. Simon James, 'Digital Wells', Wells Society AGM, 28 June 2014.

77. Borges, *Other Inquisitions*, pp. 86–8.

78. Bergonzi, *Early Wells*, pp. 165–6, 173.

79. Ibid., p. 22.

and impact derives principally from the way in which his writings have been and still are being taken to a diverse range of public audiences through the aural and visual media.

Recent decades have continued to see a widening range of adaptations as well as further editions of the original novel. *The War of the Worlds* storyline, first put in print as a serial in 1897 and then as a book in 1898, is now nearly 120-years-old, but shows no signs of losing either momentum or impact. If anything, the story's appeal has intensified and gained further impetus in 2016, from events marking the 150th anniversary of Wells's birth and the seventieth anniversary of his death. For well over one century *The War of the Worlds*, whether viewed as a serial, book or an audio-visual adaptation thereof, has ensured that Wells has continued to attract, reach, engage and enthuse a wide spectrum of audiences, whether listeners, readers or viewers, across both the world and the age range.[80]

Viewed alongside such books as *The Time Machine* and *The Invisible Man*, *The War of the Worlds*' literary merits and constant ability to link up with present-day issues, particularly at times of communal angst, ensures Wells's 'survival into futurity'.[81] *The War of the Worlds* has proved, and remains, prominent in this process of keeping Wells's name in the public eye as a central figure in popular culture. For David Mattin, '*War of the Worlds* seems to occupy a place all of its own in the modern Western psyche.'[82] As Patrick Parrinder reminded us, *The War of the Worlds* is not only a text but also a secular myth.[83] Apart from inspiring science fiction iconography and providing the template for the alien invasion sub-genre, Wells's storyline retains its massive appeal, its mythical status. For adapters, the story's plasticity means that its 'mythic universality' can be targeted by altering its local particularity in order to make the geographical details of the imagined invasion familiar to various audiences.[84] Thus, ever since 1897 *The War of the Worlds* has been retold and adapted repeatedly for alternative creative forms basically because – to quote Jeff Wayne, one prominent adapter – 'The story of invasion whether it's alien or against one another, is just as current now as it was in the 1890s'.[85]

80. Over time the story has been published in English and in translation as a book targeted at alternative audiences. Abridged editions are available for children of varying reading levels.

81. Nicholas Ruddick, 'Introduction', in Nicholas Ruddick (ed.), H. G. Wells, *The Time Machine: An Invention H. G. Wells* (Peterborough, ON: Broadview, 2001), p. 22.

82. David Mattin, 'Words on worlds: Spielberg's writer', *The Times*, 20 July 2005.

83. Patrick Parrinder, 'How far can we trust the narrator of *The War of the Worlds*?', *Foundation: The International Review of Science Fiction* 28 (77) (1999): 15. See also Self, 'Death on three legs'.

84. Crossley, *Imagining Mars*, pp. 115–16.

85. Michael Took, 'Interview: Jeff Wayne', 2010, http://www.whatsonwales.co.uk/interviews/i/18910/ [accessed 12 January 2012].

Chapter 2

WELLS'S POWERFUL SENSE OF PLACE

In 1934 Wells published his autobiography, a work of personal history, anecdote and confessional typically critiqued by Odette Keun, one of his former lovers, as an enormous exercise in self-justification.[1] For some commentators and reviewers, the two-volume publication offered little that was new, since Wells had already used fiction, not excluding his scientific romances, to write up his life. Indeed, when offering *Love and Mr Lewisham* to publishers in 1896, Wells claimed both to have studied and lived life as would be described therein.[2] Wells was very much an author whose writing employed material mined from his life and relationships: 'No books of mine are autobiographical though of course I use all my experiences'.[3] In particular, places where he resided often proved a prime source of literary inspiration imparting a factional dimension to his work. For John Hammond, literary specialists have paid insufficient attention to the fact that Wells as a writer of fiction was 'in reality a regional novelist' setting his books in specific identifiable localities: 'He was the delineator of a particular region of England – London and the Home Counties – and he rarely strayed far in his novels from the Weald and South Downs which he loved ... Though in his ideas and breadth of vision he ranged far and wide, as a novelist he remained almost exclusively provincial.'[4] Also, as outlined in the previous chapter, Wells's 'preoccupation' with place underpinned Kuchta's thinking about *The War of the Worlds*.[5]

In 2012 the British Library hosted a 'Writing Britain Exhibition: Wastelands to Wonderlands' exploring literature and place, with special reference to the way in which the landscapes of Britain permeated great literary works. In fact, Wells,

---

1. Odette Keun in *Time and Tide*, October 1934, quoted Vincent Brome, *H. G. Wells: A Biography* (London: Longmans, Green, 1951), Preface.

2. Wells to Pinker, n.d. [October 1896], in Bernard Loing, *H. G. Wells à l'oeuvre: les débuts d'un écrivain (1894–1900)* (Paris: Didier Erudition, 1984), p. 433.

3. Wells to Mrs Tooley, n.d. [October–November 1908], WT37–1A–B, H. G. Wells Correspondence, Manuscripts Library, University of Illinois at Urbana-Champaign, Urbana-Champaign, Illinois, USA (UIUC).

4. John Hammond, *An H. G. Wells Companion: A Guide to the Novels, Romances and Short Stories* (London: Macmillan, 1979), pp. 27, 88–94.

5. Kuchta, *Semi-Detached Empire*, p. 37.

merely depicted posing with G. K. Chesterton for a home movie dressed as a suburban cowboy, was assigned a very small part, possibly yet another indicator of his relatively low contemporary profile as a writer. And yet, landscapes in general and those of Southern England in particular figured prominently on Wells's literary map. Notwithstanding the fact that science fiction is by definition remote from any writer's experience, Wells's scientific romances were distinguished by a strong sense of place, which served to:

- impart realism to his fantasy scenarios;
- provide 'a strong structural force' imparting greater cohesion to the narrative;[6]
- reflect his life story, particularly his geographical mobility;
- provide geographical and topographical detail complementing the scientific inputs; and
- underpin his storylines to highlight his love of the fast-disappearing countryside.

Place and fantasy

Like *The Time Machine* and *The Invisible Man*, *The War of the Worlds* is treated today as science fiction, but was described by Wells as a 'scientific romance'. Subsequently, when discussing such writings in theoretical terms, he offered alternative descriptors, including 'fantasias of possibility', 'fantastic stories', 'fiction about the future' and 'futurist romances', but not science fiction.[7]

Wells's success as an author of such books lay in his ability to juxtapose fantasy and normality in innovative and appealing storylines. Recording the inspiration for his early scientific fantasies, Wells claimed:

> I found that, taking almost anything as a starting-point and letting my thoughts play about it, there would presently come out of the darkness, in a manner quite inexplicable, some absurd or vivid little incident more or less relevant to that initial nucleus. Little men in canoes upon sunlit oceans would come floating out of nothingness, incubating the eggs of prehistoric monsters unawares; violent conflicts would break out amidst the flower-beds of suburban gardens; I would discover I was peering into remote and mysterious worlds ruled by an order logical indeed but other than our common sanity.[8]

6. David Y. Hughes, *An Edition and a Survey of H. G. Wells' The War of the Worlds*, Ph.D. diss. (Urbana, IL: University of Illinois, 1962), p. 350.

7. Wells, December 1938, Patrick Parrinder and Robert M. Philmus (eds), *H. G. Wells' Literary Criticism* (Brighton: Harvester, 1980), pp. 226, 246–50; Wells, *Seven Famous Novels*, pp. vii, ix; H. G. Wells, *The War in the Air, and Particularly how Mr Bert Smallways Fared while it Lasted* (London: Collins, 1921), p. 5.

8. H. G. Wells, *The Country of the Blind and Other Stories* (London: Nelson, 1911), p. iv.

This template stressing the interchangeability of settings, explains the 'violent conflicts' set in the 'suburban gardens' of Surrey. Wells's mental map, his world view, comprised many layers, but an influential element was topography; thus, mental maps of places he had lived in or visited provided him with the geographical framework within which to set his tale and apply his imaginative and writing skills.[9] Relating the story of a Martian invasion conducted with highly advanced weapons technology in the peaceful English countryside, *The War of the Worlds* offered readers engaging evocations of place. Despite imagining a war between two worlds launched from another planet, the story's action was firmly rooted in London and Surrey, places that Wells knew well. As the narrator asserted, when returning from Leatherhead to his home at Woking, 'Happily, I knew the road intimately' (I.10: 68/45). Specific references to actual places therein represented an invaluable dramatic device bestowing depth and reality to the fantastic storyline by transporting readers mentally to the events, evoking strong emotional responses on their part and making them feel fully engaged with the conflict.

Mixing fact and fiction, Wells encouraged readers to make the necessary suspension of disbelief required to treat an alien invasion as a real possibility. One section of the book highlighting Wells's skill in using the real world to contextualize fantasy is that where the narrator, having witnessed the awesome display of Martian weaponry on Horsell Common, returned home to Woking where he encountered an everyday scene, the passage of a steam train billowing smoke and a group of people speaking at a gate: 'It was all so real and so familiar ... It was frantic, fantastic! Such things, I told myself, could not be' (I.7: 46/32). That they could be, soon becomes evident. Setting up a series of thunderous confrontations designed to make things palpable for readers and to manipulate their emotions, Wells challenged them to think how they would feel if Martians invaded earth and came towards them firing heat-rays: 'that is where there was a certain slight novelty in my stories'.[10]

Wells was, and still is, often compared to Jules Verne (1828–1905), the author of such works as *20,000 Leagues Under the Sea* (1869), but whereas Verne wrote about actual possibilities of invention and discovery, Wells characterized his scientific romances as 'exercises of the imagination' making use of magic tricks: 'They are all fantasies; they do not aim to project a serious possibility ... They have to hold the reader to the end by art and illusion and not by proof and argument, and the moment he closes the cover and reflects he wakes up to their impossibility.'[11] Representing them as 'fantasias of possibility', Wells described his scientific romances as taking 'some fantastically possible or impossible thing

9. On Wells's mental map, see N. and J. Mackenzie, *The Time Traveller*, p. 28 note. On mental maps in general, see Steven Casey and Jonathan Wright (eds), *Mental Maps in the Era of Two World Wars* (Basingstoke: Palgrave Macmillan, 2008), pp. xii–xiv.

10. Wells, *Seven Famous Novels*, p. viii.

11. Ibid.

into a commonplace group of people', and then writing about their reactions in a serious and reasonable manner:

> The thing that makes such imaginations interesting is their translation into commonplace terms and a rigid exclusion of other marvels from the story. Then it becomes human …
>
> Nothing remains interesting where anything may happen. For the writer of fantastic stories to help the reader to play the game properly, he must help him in every possible unobtrusive way to *domesticate* the impossible hypothesis. He must trick him into an unwary concession to some plausible assumption and get on with his story while the illusion holds … as soon as the magic trick has been done the whole business of the fantasy writer is to keep everything else human and real. Touches of prosaic detail are imperative and a rigorous adherence to the hypothesis. Any *extra* fantasy outside the cardinal assumption immediately gives a touch of irresponsible silliness to the invention.[12]

'Wells's Law', the principle that a science fiction story should not overdo extraordinary assumptions, was formulated to codify Wells's approach.[13]

Woking and The War of the Worlds

For Wells, therefore, an extraordinary tale about an alien invasion had to be set somewhere very real, a place where unusual things did not happen and where better to find such a location than Woking, a suburban town in Surrey where things seemed 'so safe and tranquil' (I.1: 11/12) and 'no one gave a thought to the older worlds of space as sources of human danger' (I.1: 2/7). And yet the area around Woking was not only being watched closely by Martians but also being identified as the landing place and base to launch an invasion of Earth.

The War of the Worlds begins and ends at Woking, the place where the story's narrator lived and where Wells himself resided when writing much of the text. By the time the story was published, Wells had moved on, but what *The War of the Worlds* did was to put Woking and its environs on the map. The Martian invaders landed first near the sandpits on Horsell Common, an extensive sandy heathland located on the north-west outskirts of Woking. Emerging from their cylinder, the Martians soon gave the locals a devastating demonstration of the power of their weaponry before spearheading a relentless assault spreading death and destruction throughout Surrey and London. Mounted in huge mechanical tripods (1.10: 71–2/46; 1.12: 92/58), they destroyed almost everything in their path.

Operating from their base on Horsell Common, the Martians struck the first blows against the nearby town and villages. Woking was laid waste by the tripods,

---

12. Ibid., pp. vii–viii; Wells, *The War in the Air*, p. 5.
13. 'Wells' Law', *Encyclopedia of Science Fiction*, n.d., http://www.sf-encyclopedia.com/entry/wellss_law [accessed 2 May 2014].

with the heat-rays making the town 'a heap of fiery ruins' (I.11: 85/54). Byfleet, Weybridge, Kingston upon Thames and Richmond upon Thames followed suit as the Martians advanced upon London. People across Surrey and beyond panicked and took flight. However, despite entering central London, the Martian invaders failed not because of the efforts of the British military and people but because of their inability to resist Earth's bacteria. Primrose Hill in Camden Town, London, became their final resting place. Returning from London by rail to his home in Woking after the end of the war the narrator recorded the scenes of destruction, 'scorched grays and sullen reds' (I.9: 294/174–5), flowing past the train's windows.

The War of the Worlds was planned, researched and largely written while Wells lived in Woking, where he rented a house located in Maybury Road some ten minutes' walk from the railway station. Residing in Woking clearly inspired Wells, for he brought much of the local area into the storyline – the people and town, the railway station, the trains which ran past the front windows of his house, nearby villages like Horsell and Chobham, the surrounding countryside on which he walked and rode his bike, and the Basingstoke Canal, on which he boated. The first-person reporting role, provided by a narrator, 'The man from Woking' (II.7: 252/151) actively involved in following the invaders into London, helped to engage readers in a seemingly authentic, fast-moving and action-packed series of events. Like Wells, the narrator lived in Maybury, Woking, but in a house occupying a more elevated position – Maybury Hill, a short distance from Maybury Road, seems the most likely location – affording a good view across to the Martian landing site. Apart from repeatedly setting an ever-changing scene for readers, the narrator acted as both an eye witness of key developments and a reporter passing on news and updates provided by others, most notably his brother based in London, the artilleryman and the curate from Weybridge.

Reflecting Wells's life and residential mobility

Wells's emphasis upon place reflected the manner in which his scientific romances incorporated a wide range of geographical and topographical information used to underpin storylines and complement the inputs drawing upon his scientific knowledge and understanding. This wealth of detail about place proved in part a function of Wells's lifestyle, most notably the fact that during the 1880s and 1890s he was constantly moving on from one post to another and hence from one place of residence to another (Table 2.1). Wells got on by getting out, so that the initial phase of his life story was characterized by a series of false starts and subsequent escapes, frequently after only a few weeks to yet another place. Indeed, Wells had so many fresh starts in life that he gave up counting them![14]

For Wells, his search for a better life and a more fulfilling career led him to react against the constraints imposed by his Bromley childhood and drapery appren-ticeships served in Windsor and Southsea. Conversely, for his well-meaning

14. Wells, *Experiment in Autobiography*, I, p. 311.

Table 2.1 Where H. G. Wells lived, 1866–1900

1866–80	KENT, Bromley	Atlas House, 47 High Street
1880	BERKSHIRE, Windsor	25 High Street
	SOMERSET, Wookey	Wookey Elementary School
1881	SUSSEX, Midhurst	South Street
1881–83	HAMPSHIRE, Southsea	13 Kings Road
1883–84	SUSSEX, Midhurst	North Street
1884	LONDON, Camden Town	Edgware Road, Westbourne Park
1884–87	LONDON, Camden Town	181 Euston Road, NW1
1887	NORTH WALES, Wrexham	Holt Academy
1887–88	HAMPSHIRE, Petersfield	'Uppark'
1888	STAFFORDSHIRE, Stoke-on-Trent	18 Victoria Street, Basford
1888	LONDON, Camden Town	Theobald's Road, WC1
1888–89	LONDON, Camden Town	12 Fitzroy Road, NW1
1889–91	LONDON, Camden Town	46 Fitzroy Road, NW1
1891–93	LONDON, Wandsworth	28 Haldon Road, West Hill
1893	SURREY, Sutton	4 Cumnor Place (now 25 Langley Park Road)
1894	LONDON, Camden Town	7 Mornington Place, NW1
1894	LONDON, Camden Town	12 Mornington Road, NW1 (now 12 Mornington Terrace)
1894	KENT, Sevenoaks	'Tusculum Villa', 23 Eardley Road
1894–95	LONDON, Camden Town	12 Mornington Road, NW1 (now 12 Mornington Terrace)
1895–96	SURREY, Woking	'Lynton', Maybury Road (now 'Lynton', 141 Maybury Road)
1896–98	SURREY, Worcester Park	'Heatherlea', 41 The Avenue
1898–99	KENT, Sandgate	2 Beach Cottages, Granville Road;
1899–1900	KENT, Sandgate	'Arnold House', Castle Road
1900–1909	KENT, Sandgate	'Spade House', Radnor Cliff Crescent

mother, it seemed as if her youngest son was not only incapable of sticking at anything but also determined to do his own thing in spite of her best efforts. Wells's fundamental restlessness meant that he did not stay anywhere for very long and was constantly moving on from one place to another, a process facilitated by the fact that until the close of the 1890s he always rented property. This repeated moving on continued even when Wells felt 'launched' as a writer, given the impact of personal and other reasons linked to his health, the breakdown of his first marriage, and his affair and new relationship with Amy Catherine Robbins. Moreover, literary success led him to move up the rental property ladder to something better and adjudged more fitting to his enhanced wealth, status and needs as a writer, most notably more space for writing and entertaining friends and relations plus a larger garden for leisure and relaxation. A keen walker and cyclist, Wells used his various residences to explore the area, especially the surrounding countryside. As a result, he was able as an author not only to draw upon his science education but also to make skilful and imaginative use of actual geographical locations and landscapes well known to him. As discussed above, this proved a vital part of the fantasy-realism formula employed to hook readers.

In turn, Wells's scientific romances offer readers illuminating pictures of late Victorian England based upon first-hand experience of living in or travelling through villages and small towns, particularly those located on the periphery of London. For Wells, 'The colour of life is largely a matter of homes', which he represented as responsible for differentiating and influencing the various phases of his life.[15] Naturally Surrey figured prominently on his fictional literary map, as highlighted by its central role in *The War of the Worlds*. Richmond upon Thames was the home of the "Time Traveller" in *The Time Machine* (1895) and the base for his adventures, such as to Combe Wood and Banstead, places located near Sutton, where Wells lived during 1893. *The Wheels of Chance* (1896), a story written in Woking, was set around a long bicycle ride beginning at Putney near where he lived between 1891 and 1893. Passing through Surrey *en route* to the Sussex coast and Hampshire, the story, which included a fictional heroine resident in Surbiton, offered readers charming portrayals of both the Surrey countryside and places like Ripley, Guildford and Haslemere. Following *The War of the Worlds*, Surrey continued to feature in Wells's writing, even if Woking, having played a starring role in *The War of the Worlds*, was assigned merely a bit part in both *Love and Mr Lewisham* (1900), a book Wells started writing while living there, and *Tono-Bungay* (1909).

Articulating love for the fast-disappearing countryside

For Hammond, Wells's writing showed 'a deep love of rural England' partly because of nostalgia for his boyhood enjoyment of Bromley's fast-disappearing countryside and partly because of his continued love of the relatively unspoiled landscapes of Surrey and Sussex.[16] Surrey, like Kent and Sussex, was a county Wells lived in, knew well, and admired for its countryside and proximity to London.[17] More importantly, he lived in the county for a considerable part of the mid-late 1890s (Table 2.1), a formative period in his emergence as a writer. Thus, he resided in Sutton (1893–4), Woking (1895–6) and Worcester Park (1896–8). Moreover, between 1891 and 1893 he lived in Wandsworth, which had been part of Surrey until 1889 – previously the county stretched as far north as the River Thames in central London and as far east as Rotherhithe and Camberwell – when it was included in the new County of London.

15. G. P. Wells (ed.), *H. G. Wells in Love: Postscript to an Experiment in Autobiography* (London: Faber and Faber, 1984), p. 211.

16. John Hammond, *A Preface to H. G. Wells* (Harlow: Longman/Pearson Education, 2001), pp. 87–9, 135.

17. John Wright, 'H. G. Wells and Surrey', *Surrey County Journal* 1 (3) (1947): 61–2; Humphrey Wynn, 'H. G. Wells and Woking', *Surrey Today*, September 1965, p. 34; David Gurney, 'War, Woking and H. G. Wells', *Surrey County Magazine* 27 (12) (1996): 18.

During the 1880s and 1890s cycling and walking acquainted Wells with much of the county, which he explored through daily excursions, often based upon suburban railway stations, holiday stays and visits to Frank and Fred, his elder brothers, when they were working in Farnham and Godalming.[18] Wells's cycling history is discussed in more detail in Chapter 4, but cycling and walking provided Wells with further material for publication. Writing anonymously as 'an Amateur Nature Lover', in 1893 Wells described walking from Epsom and Ewell across the North Downs to Banstead and Sutton when highlighting the appeal of the countryside in autumn to 'a good Londoner' living in an 'entirely urban' environment.[19] Published in the *Pall Mall Gazette*, the article was re-published with minor textual amendments under Wells's name in *Certain Personal Matters* (1898). For Wells, the aesthetical appeal of the countryside was enhanced by the opportunity to try out the nature-loving skills inspired by Richard Jefferies's *Nature near London* (1883). 'Out Banstead Way' provides an early example of Wells's ability to draw vibrant pictures for readers, and particularly to indicate the distinctive appeal of Surrey's landscape and 'the colours of Autumn'. During the course of the article the red houses, the greens, deep browns, reds, crimson, yellows and greens of the trees give way to the black of the cinder paths around Sutton. Wells offered readers a vivid multi-tinted portrayal of the view from Banstead Down:

> We take our last look at the country from the open down above Sutton. Blue hills beyond blue hills recede into the remote distance; from Banstead Down one can see into Oxfordshire. Windsor Castle is in minute blue silhouette to the left, and to the right and nearer is the Crystal Palace. And closer, clusters red-roofed Sutton and its tower, then Cheam, with its white spire, and further is Ewell, set in a variegated texture of autumn foliage. Water gleams – a silver thread – at Ewell, and the sinking sun behind us catches a window here and there, and turns it into an eye of flame.

Unsurprisingly Wells's deep love of the countryside, inspired principally by his father, led him to resent the way in which London's spectacular growth impacted upon places around its periphery, most notably his birthplace, Bromley. Linked to the capital by train in 1858, Bromley, a small town in Kent with a population of c. 5,000, was seemingly taken over by London. Wells saw the woods and fields of his childhood disappear at an ever increasing rate in the face of 'the deluge of suburbanism', while the resulting 'morbid sprawl of population' shattered the town's identity as a real place in his mind: 'Bromley was being steadily suburbanized ... The country round Bromley was being fast invaded by the spreading

---

18. Ann Laver, 'Herbert George Wells, Godalming and Tono-Bungay', *The H. G. Wells Newsletter* 5 (16) (2008): 15; Wells, *Experiment in Autobiography*, I, p. 156.

19. Anon. [H. G. Wells], 'Out Banstead Way by an Amateur Nature Lover', *Pall Mall Gazette*, 25 November 1893, p. 11.

out of London; eruptions of new roads and bricks and mortar covered lush meadows'.[20]

Inevitably, these personal concerns about the deleterious impact of London's growth surfaced in his fiction. Thus, in *The War of the Worlds* the narrator, when speculating how the people's flight from a London under the Martian attack would look from a balloon, described the way in which the metropolis spread out far and wide into surrounding counties (I.17: 172/104). For many commentators, the fictional destruction of Woking and other towns throughout Surrey by the Martian invaders reflected Wells's antipathy towards the affluent class-ridden suburbs and particularly the threat they posed to the county's much loved countryside. Clearly Wells feared that the fast-growing town of Woking, like Bromley, was being swallowed up by suburbanization.[21] One decade later, writing in *The War in the Air* (1908), Wells glimpsed into the future from an airship to the 'landscape of an industrial civilization' describing a Britain characterized as 'a sprawl of undistinguished population', continuous cities and suburbs, with only a few green fragments.[22]

Nor did Wells forget his birthplace. In *The New Machiavelli* (1911), perhaps his most autobiographical novel, he revisited the fate of Bromley, represented as 'Bromstead'. Writing in the first person, Wells recorded that, when growing up in Bromstead, he became aware of 'an invading and growing disorder' replacing the pastoral world's serene 'old-established' rhythms.[23]

> The whole of Bromstead as I remember it, and as I saw it last – it is a year ago now – is a dull useless boiling-up of human activities, an immense clustering of futilities. It is as unfinished as ever; the builders' roads still run out and end in mid-field in their old fashion; the various enterprises jumble in the same hopeless contradiction, if anything intensified. Pretentious villas jostle slums, and public-house and tin tabernacle glower at one another across the cat-haunted lot that intervenes. Roper's meadows are now quite frankly a slum; back doors and sculleries gape towards the railway, their yards are hung with tattered washing unashamed; and there seem to be more boards by the railway every time I pass, advertising pills and pickles, tonics and condiments, and such like solicitudes of a people with no natural health nor appetite left in them.[24]

Subsequently, Wells used Britling in *Mr Britling Sees it Through* (1916) to reinforce the message: 'You're in London suburbs right down to the sea ... Surrey is full of rich stockbrokers, company promoters, bookies, judges, newspaper proprietors ...

20. Wells, *Experiment in Autobiography*, I, pp. 38, 65, 83–4, 139, 194–5. See also E. L. S. Horsburgh, *Bromley, Kent: From the Earliest Times to the Present Century* (London: Hodder and Stoughton, 1929), pp. 47–53. See Kuchta, *Semi-Detached Empire*.

21. Kuchta, *Semi-Detached Empire*, pp. 36–56.

22. H. G. Wells, *The War in the Air* (London: Penguin, 2005), pp. 103–4.

23. H. G. Wells, *The New Machiavelli* (London: Penguin, 2005), p. 40.

24. Ibid., pp. 41–2.

instantly the countryside becomes a villadom. And little sub-estates and red-brick villas and art cottages spring up.'[25] Even so, Wells's concerns about the impact of London's growth upon the surrounding countryside should be viewed in context. Wells was fascinated by and loved the vast metropolis, where he studied, lived for a substantial part of his life (Table 2.2), was married twice and eventually died.[26] As Wells remarked in his autobiography, in 1935 his move to London's Hanover Terrace proved significant because it marked 'a new phase, the last phase, of my life'.[27]

Conclusion

There is much of Wells, his aspirations, his dashed hopes and pessimism as well as his imaginative powers and scientific knowledge, in *The War of the Worlds*. Indeed, for some commentators he is both the author of the story and the narrator responsible for telling the story. But *The War of the Worlds*, as suggested by the narrator's representation as 'The man from Woking' (II.7: 252/151), was imbued also with a strong sense of place, a point Wells often stressed, such as in the preface to the 1924 Atlantic edition:

> The scene is laid mainly in Surrey in the country round about Woking, where the writer was living when the book was written. He would take his bicycle of an afternoon and note the houses and cottages and typical inhabitants and passers-by, to be destroyed after tea by Heat-Ray or smothered in the red weed. He could sit by the way-side imagining his incidents so vividly that now when he passes through that country these events recur to him as though they were actual memories.[28]

Significantly Orwell's commentary marking Wells's death pointed specifically to the need to acknowledge the enduring impact of local landscapes upon his thinking and writing.[29] Despite having interplanetary conflict as its central theme, *The War of the Worlds*' action was firmly rooted in London and Surrey. Thus, when reading Judith Flanders's study of Charles Dickens and Victorian London, it seemed as if only a slight change of name and time would enable sections of her text to fit Wells's approach to place in his fiction. For Wells, Surrey, like London, 'was a place of the mind, but it was also a real place. Much of what we take today

25. H. G. Wells, *Mr Britling sees it through* (London: Cassell, 1916), pp. 28–9.

26. In 1943 Wells listed his London addresses, but both dates and street names suffer from his fading memory: Wells to Sinclair, 20 September 1943, Smith, *Correspondence of H. G. Wells, IV*, p. 442.

27. Wells, *H. G. Wells in Love*, p. 211.

28. H. G. Wells, *The Works of H. G. Wells*, Atlantic Edition, vol. III (London: T. Fisher Unwin, 1924), pp. ix–x.

29. Orwell, 'The true pattern of H. G. Wells', pp. 136–9.

Table 2.2 H. G. Wells's residences in London

1884	Edgware Road, Westbourne Park	– an overcrowded lodging house owned by the daughter of one of his mother's friends from Midhurst – Wells claimed to have forgotten the address and landlady's name
1884–7	181 Euston Road, NW1	– opposite Euston Station, a lodging house run by his Aunt Mary, the widow of one of his father's brothers – here he met Isabel, Mary's daughter – following the house's demolition, the site is now occupied by the Wellcome Museum
1887–8	North Wales; Uppark; Stoke-on-Trent	
1888	Theobald's Road, WC1	– Wells rented a partitioned-off section of an attic, after spending one night in Judd Street
1888–9	12 Fitzroy Road, NW1	– near Regent's Park and adjacent to railway line running into Euston Station – the apartment was lived in by Wells's Aunt Mary
1889–91	46 Fitzroy Road, NW1	– this apartment, which was lived in by Wells's Aunt Mary, was larger than that at 12 Fitzroy Road.
1891–3	28 Haldon Road, Wandsworth	– following their marriage, Wells and Isabel moved to Wandsworth
1893	Sutton, Surrey	
1893–4	7 Mornington Place, NW1	– Wells returned to Camden Town to live with Amy Catherine Robbins (Jane) after separating from Isabel – rented a ground floor apartment, but moved around the corner because of problems with landlady about co-habitation outside marriage
1894	12 Mornington Road, NW1 (now 12 Mornington Terrace)	– two-room apartment near the London and Birmingham railway line to Euston Station
1894	Sevenoaks, Kent	
1894–5	12 Mornington Road, NW1 (now 12 Mornington Terrace)	– problems with their landlady in Sevenoaks led Wells and Jane to return to the apartment rented earlier in the year – they left for Woking in May 1895 but returned briefly in October 1895 to satisfy the residential qualification required for marriage
1895–1909	Woking & Worcester Park, Surrey; Sandgate, Kent	
1901–30	From 1901 Wells often rented a Central London *pied-à-terre* such as at 6 Clement's Inn, WC2; 126 Warwick Street, W1; Candover Street, Westminster; 52 St. James's Court, Buckingham Gate, SW1; Flat 120, 4 Whitehall Court, SW1; and 614 St. Ermin's, Westminster, SW1. Also he lived abroad, such as in Paris and Grasse.	
1909–12	17 Church Row, West Hampstead	– a large house located in what Nikolaus Pevsner described as 'the best street in Hampstead'
1912–30	Easton Glebe, Dunmow, Essex	
1930–6	47 Chiltern Court, Clarence Gate, Baker Street, NW1	– a flat above Baker Street station with Regent's Park on his doorstep; Arnold Bennett was a fellow tenant.
1935–46	13 Hanover Terrace, NW1	– looked out across Regent's Park

to be the marvellous imaginings of a visionary novelist turn out on inspection to be the reportage of a great observer'.[30] In this sense, Wells's fiction, incorporating real places and actual street names, possessed – to quote Henry James's comment about Dickens – the 'solidity of specification'.[31]

Of course, most present-day audiences access *The War of the Worlds* through audio-visual versions of the story, most notably the films of Pal and Spielberg or the radio broadcast of Orson Welles and hence fail to appreciate, that Wells's original storyline was not set in the USA. A rare exception is Jeff Wayne's musical version, which stays close to Wells's geography. Even so, what is significant is the manner in which audio-visual adaptations, making use of actual places, like Bayonne, Grover's Mill, Los Angeles, New York and Princeton to impart realism to their fantasy storyline, follow Wells by exhibiting and exploiting a strong sense of place.

30. Judith Flanders, *The Victorian City: Everyday Life in Dickens' London* (London: Atlantic, 2012), p. 7.

31. Ibid., p. 12.

Chapter 3

WELLS'S STRONG SENSE OF TIME: CONTEXTUALIZING *THE WAR OF THE WORLDS*

For many readers around the world, *The War of the Worlds* remains a really good read – indeed, it has proved so for well over one century – as well as a key text for those evaluating claims regarding Wells's role in the origins of science fiction literature. More recently, the book's appeal has derived increasingly from its perceived role as a tie-in book for those wanting to read the story inspiring Spielberg's film or Jeff Wayne's music show. For other readers, *The War of the Worlds'* appeal reflects an interest in geography, local history and literary heritage, most notably the way in which the text faithfully maps the late Victorian landscape of London and Surrey enabling readers to time travel back to actual places they know, perhaps where they now live, but in which fantastic events once took place. For academics studying Wells's life and work, with particular emphasis upon his science fiction, *The War of the Worlds* shows how his writing drew upon personal experience, scientific knowledge, creative imaginative skills, and a strong sense of place.[1]

Nor is this all, since the book exhibits a strong sense of time in terms of both pacing the story and contextualizing the content. Thus, Bernard Bergonzi, the author of an influential study of Wells's early fiction, reminds us that *The War of the Worlds* is distinguished by a 'precise sense of time' with 'the hour-by-hour' sequencing of events and 'step by step' updates, producing 'the feeling of intolerably mounting tension'.[2] Wells's use of time to structure and sequence the story is discussed in Chapter 8. Here the focus is placed on the use of time as context, given the manner in which Wells's narrative offers readers a vivid image of late Victorian Britain – to quote Bergonzi – 'at the precise moment of its imagined destruction'.[3]

Fin de siècle

Time proved a central focus of a 1902 lecture delivered by Wells at the Royal Institution. Speaking about 'The Discovery of the Future', Wells stressed the way

---

1. Wells, *Experiment in Autobiography*, I, pp. 143–6, 173–4.
2. Bergonzi, *Early Wells*, pp. 127–9.
3. Ibid., p. 127.

in which his thinking and writing reacted against ongoing trends to strike out in new directions exploring the brave new worlds of the mind.[4] Inevitably, his lecture raised questions about the broader historical and literary context within which Wells grew up, lived and wrote, and particularly the extent to which his scientific romances reflected key themes characteristic of what has been described as the *fin de siècle* period.

Fin de siècle, defined as meaning the end of the century or the end of an era, is a term employed to describe the pessimistic mood increasingly prevalent among many Victorian intellectuals during the 1890s, when their widely shared anxieties about the present-day world were compounded by forebodings about the future. As Bergonzi argued, 'The fin *de siècle* mood produced, in turn, the feeling of *fin du globe* [end of the world], the sense that the whole elaborate intellectual and social order of the nineteenth century was trembling on the brink of dissolution.'[5] A prime source of inspiration for contemporary debates about an impending crisis was Max Nordau's *Entartung* (1892), a study published in translation in February 1895 as *Degeneration* by William Heinemann, the publisher of Wells's *The Time Machine* and *The War of the Worlds*. Offering a powerful antidote to prevailing modes of thought, Nordau pointed to a *fin de siècle* state of mind: 'In our days there have arisen in more highly developed minds vague qualms of a Dusk of the Nations, in which all suns and all stars are gradually waning, and mankind with all its institutions and creations is perishing in the midst of a dying world.'[6]

Wells's fin de siècle *mindset*

Writing about the 'Early Wells', Bergonzi set out future directions for the study of Wells's scientific romances. Challenging traditional approaches espousing the optimistic and utopian character of Wells's literary outlook, he pressed the case for focusing more closely upon the historical and literary context of the 1890s. Wells's attitudes, Bergonzi claimed, had been 'largely formed before the end of the Victorian age', and hence *The War of the Worlds*, like his other scientific romances, should be interpreted as reflecting 'some of the dominant preoccupations of the *fin de siècle* period'.[7] Representing *fin de siècle* and *fin du globe* as 'dominant' elements in Wells's scientific romances, most notably *The War of the Worlds*, as well as in such articles as 'The Extinction of Man', Bergonzi argued that:

> In considering these works, it will be necessary to modify the customary view of Wells as an optimist, a utopian and a passionate believer in human progress.

4. H. G. Wells, *The Discovery of the Future* (New York: B. W. Huebsch, 1913), pp. 5–7.

5. Bergonzi, *Early Wells*, pp. 3–4.

6. Max Nordau, *Degeneration* (London: William Heinemann, 1895), p. 2; John St. John, *William Heinemann: A Century of Publishing, 1890–1990* (London: Heinemann, 1990), pp. 113–14.

7. Bergonzi, 'A Global Thinker'; Bergonzi, *Early Wells*, pp. 3–4.

The dominant note of his early years was rather a kind of fatalistic pessimism, combined with intellectual scepticism, and it is this which the early romances reflect. It is, one need hardly add, a typically fin *de siècle* note.[8]

For Bergonzi, *The War of the Worlds* took its cue, therefore, from the 'qualms' identified by Nordau to the effect that traditional views about humankind's place in the universe were no longer supportable. Tracing Wells's preoccupation with changing values, Victorian complacency and the progressive decay of the existing order back to 'The Chronic Argonauts' (1888), Bergonzi claimed that *fin de siècle* pessimism and dissatisfaction with the existing order underpinned *The Time Machine, The Island of Dr Moreau* and *The Invisible Man*, before becoming the 'predominant' motif in *The War of the Worlds*: 'The theme of *The War of the Worlds*, the physical destruction of society, or at least the dissolution of the social order, was one of the dominant preoccupations of the *fin de siècle* period'.[9]

Significantly, Wells selected a quote by Johannes Kepler (1571–1630) – discussing whether humans were the centre of the universe, he speculated whether other forms of life existed beyond earth – as an epigraph for *The War of the Worlds*. Then Wells commenced the opening chapter by pointing out that, while people adopted an attitude of 'infinite complacency' (I.1: 1/7), 'this world was being watched' by other worlds. As W. T. Stead observed when reviewing the book in April 1898, the storyline raised serious, even unwelcome, questions for readers hitherto anticipating the prospect of indefinite human progress.[10] Painting terrifyingly dark images of the future, *The War of the Worlds*, the product of a pessimistic storyteller full of late Victorian anxieties, confronted contemporary attitudes with images suggesting a vision of the degeneration of life on earth.[11]

Subsequently, Wells proved anxious to protect images concerning his *fin de siècle* mindset, such as in 1939 when asserting that his writings from *The Time Machine* onwards had provided 'the clearest insistence on the insecurity of progress and the possibility of human degeneration and extinction'.[12] Science might mean progress, but, as Wells conceded, this was not guaranteed, especially as scientists might take a wrong turn as envisioned in *The Island of Dr Moreau* or *The Invisible Man*. Unsurprisingly, a few years later he responded sharply to Orwell's accusation concerning his alleged membership of 'a despicable generation' of writers believing that science could save the world. Wells pointed to the fundamental message articulated throughout his career, most notably in his

8. Bergonzi, *Early Wells*, pp. 5, 15, 22, 131; H. G. Wells, 'The Extinction of Man: Some Speculative Suggestions', *Pall Mall Gazette*, 25 September 1894, p. 3.

9. Bergonzi, *Early Wells*, p. 131.

10. W. T. Stead, 'The Book of the Month: The latest apocalypse of the end of the world', *The Review of Reviews* XVII (4) (April 1898): 389–93, 396.

11. Juliet Gardiner, 'The History of the Future: 8: H. G. Wells', *BBC Radio Four*, 19 September 2012.

12. Wells to editor, *The British Weekly*, 26 June 1939, Smith, *Correspondence of H. G. Wells, IV*, p. 227.

scientific romances as well as more recently in *Science and the World Mind* (1942): 'From my very earliest book to the present time I have been reiterating that unless mankind adapted its social and political institutions to the changes invention and discovery were bringing about, mankind would be destroyed'.[13]

Following Bergonzi, much of Wells's thinking, as reflected in the scientific romances, has been attributed to *fin de siècle* themes. However, Brian Aldiss has urged an alternative approach viewing Wells as articulating 'a new way of thinking' rather than merely expressing *fin de siècle* angst.[14] Pointing to Wells's 1902 Royal Institution lecture, Aldiss noted his identification of two contrasting mindsets 'distinguished chiefly by their attitude towards time', particularly regarding the future. Whereas most people scarcely thought about the future, a few think 'constantly and by preference of things to come, and of present things mainly in relation to the results that must arise from them'.[15] For Wells, such people continually attacked and altered the established order of things, 'perpetually falling away from respect for what the past has given us'. From this perspective, Aldiss claimed that *The War of the Worlds* was 'designed to conscript more minds into the futurist category' and hence to release society more and more from the stranglehold of the past.[16] Like the other scientific romances, *The War of the Worlds* confronted readers with the possibility 'of social dissolution, of uncomfortable new worlds opening up, old worlds being bludgeoned down to their knees'. For Aldiss, Wells's 'splendid creativity' offered readers a new way of thinking about their world.

Huxley and Darwinism

When looking back to what he represented as his acquisition of a scientific vision of the world, Wells acknowledged the influence of Thomas Huxley, one of his lecturers at the Normal School of Science; thus, the year 'I spent in Huxley's class was, beyond all question, the most educational year of my life'.[17] Writing from Woking in May 1895, Wells sent Huxley a copy of *The Time Machine*. Reminding Huxley that he was a former student, Wells admitted that his recently published book was in effect putting theory into fictional practice: 'The central idea

13. Wells to *The Listener*, 30 March 1942, Smith, *Correspondence of H. G. Wells, IV*, p. 326.

14. Aldiss, 'Introduction', p. xxv.

15. Wells, *Discovery of the Future*, pp. 5–7; Wells, *Experiment in Autobiography*, II, p. 648.

16. Aldiss, 'Introduction', p. xxv. See also Bergonzi, *Early Wells*, p. 12; Clarke, *Voices Prophesying War*, pp. 93–103.

17. Wells, *Experiment in Autobiography*, I, p. 201; Peter Kemp, *H. G. Wells and the Culminating Ape: Biological Imperatives and Imaginative Obsessions* (Basingstoke: Macmillan, 1996), pp. 1–6.

– of degeneration following security – was the outcome of a certain amount of biological study'.[18]

Huxley, an influential scientific thinker, performed a key role popularizing Charles Darwin's theory of evolution. In May 1893 he encapsulated his thinking in a high profile Romanes lecture entitled 'Evolution and Ethics'. Speaking to a capacity audience in Oxford University's Sheldonian Theatre, he warned against millennial optimism:

> The theory of evolution encourages no millennial anticipations. If, for millions of years, our globe has taken the upward road, yet, sometime, the summit will be reached and the downward route will be commenced. The most daring imagination will hardly venture upon the suggestion that the power and the intelligence of man can ever arrest the procession of the great year.[19]

Permeated with Darwinism, Wells's writings reveal his receptivity to Huxley's thinking. Indeed, when reviewing *The Time Machine*, Clement Shorter asserted that Huxley helped to make Wells a 'product of his age': 'he gives us a fairy tale with a plausible scientific justification'.[20] An early text reflecting Wells's acceptance of Darwinist theory – this provided also an example of his popular scientific writing – was 'The Man of the Year Million', an article published anonymously in the *Pall Mall Gazette* in 1893. Claiming that 'the coming man, then, will clearly have a larger brain, and a slighter body than the present', Wells introduced – to quote David Langford – 'that potent SF image of a far-future man with his overdeveloped head, eyes and brain perched on top of a shrunken, atrophied body – the ultimate Darwinian triumph', such as famously represented by 'Dan Dare's implacable foe the Mekon'.[21]

Despite fearing that people would dismiss such thinking as 'utterly impossible', Wells explored the topic further in 'The Extinction of Man', another short essay appearing in the *Pall Mall Gazette* in 1894:

> Man's complacent assumption of the future is too confident. We think, because things have been easy for mankind as a whole for a generation or so, we are

18. Wells to Huxley, May 1895, Smith, *Correspondence of H. G. Wells*, I, p. 238. Huxley, who died a few weeks later, sent no reply.

19. Thomas H. Huxley, 'The Romanes Lecture', *Oxford Magazine*, May 1893, http://aleph0.clarku.edu/huxley/comm/OxfMag/Romanes93.html [accessed 4 February 2012]; Paul White, *Thomas Huxley: Making the "Man of Science"* (Cambridge: Cambridge University Press, 2003), pp. 166–8.

20. Clement Shorter, 'Review: The Invisible Man', *The Bookman* 13 (1) (October 1897): 19.

21. Anon. (H. G. Wells), 'The Man of the Year Million: a scientific forecast', *Pall Mall Gazette*, 6 November 1893, p. 3; David Langford, 'The History of Mr Wells', *Fortean Times*, 199 (2005), http://www.ansible.co.uk/writing/ft-wells.html [accessed 14 January 2012]. Wells's article was parodied by *Punch* on 25 November 1893. Dan Dare was a character in a popular British comic called *The Eagle*.

going on to perfect comfort and security in the future ... for all we can tell, the coming terror may be crouching for its spring and the fall of humanity be at hand. In the case of every other predominant animal the world has ever seen, I repeat, the hour of its complete ascendancy has been the eve of its entire overthrow.[22]

Even so, Wells proved equally pessimistic about the likely impact of such warnings: 'But if some poor story-writing man ventures to figure this sober probability in a tale, not a reviewer in London but will tell him his theme is the utterly impossible. And, when the thing happens, one may doubt if even then one will get the recognition one deserves.' Then, in 1896 'Intelligence on Mars', an essay published in the *Saturday Review*, reaffirmed the way in which Darwinism provided the principal intellectual framework for Wells's thinking about the future.[23] Thus, he emphasized the role of natural selection when discussing Martians, but acknowledged that their evolution would take a rather different path from man on earth.

Inevitably Huxley's thinking proved an enduring presence in Wells's scientific romances, most notably *The War of the Worlds*. As Bergonzi noted, '*The War of the Worlds* can be seen ... as continuing the Darwinian preoccupation of *The Time Machine* and *Moreau*': 'The Martians made a convenient and plausible superhuman adversary for mankind. But in a sense they can be seen also as a projection of Wells's fin *de siècle* forebodings about the future, combined with the desire to *épater le bourgeois* [shock the bourgeoisie] already apparent in *Moreau*.'[24]

Wells pressed the point in *The War of the Worlds*' opening paragraph, where he depicts the Martians as intellectually superior to man (I.1: 1/7). Then, in the main part of the book the Martians are used to offer images of man's possible evolutionary future. Having 'brightened their intellects' (I.1: 3/8), the Martians possessed a 'great superiority over man' (II.2: 214/129): 'We men, with our bicycles and road-skates, our Lilienthal soaring-machines [gliders], our guns and sticks and so forth, are just in the beginning of the evolution that the Martians have worked out. They have become practically mere brains' (II.2: 214/129). Wells supported this observation by referring to his 1893 'The Man of the Year Million' article, a study written 'in a foolish, facetious tone' (II.2: 210/127): 'It is worthy of remark that a certain speculative writer of quasi-scientific repute, writing long before the Martian invasion, did forecast for man a final structure not unlike the actual Martian condition' (II.2: 210/127).[25]

22. Wells, 'The Extinction of Man'. The quotes here come in part also from the revised version in H. G. Wells, *Certain Personal Matters* (London: Lawrence & Bullen, 1898), pp. 178–9.

23. H. G. Wells, 'Intelligence on Mars', *Saturday Review*, 4 April 1896.

24. Bergonzi, *Early Wells*, pp. 133–4.

25. Wells, 'Man of the Year Million'. As Wells mentioned, this article appeared in the *Pall Mall Budget* – it was published on 16 November 1893 – but was published first in the *Pall Mall Gazette*.

The Darwinist theme is central to the narrator's encounter with the artilleryman on Putney Hill.[26] Responding to the destruction of contemporary society, the artilleryman expressed a crude 'survival of the fittest' doctrine when pushing the case for men to adapt to a new world order: 'Cities, nations, civilization, progress – it's all over. That game's up. We're beat.' (II.7: 257/154). Wells uses the narrator to outline his own position. Admitting that he had not thought previously along such lines, the narrator confessed 'a sense of dethronement' while living 'under the Martian heel' (II.6: 241/144). Hence the artilleryman's views struck a chord. Wells pressed home the message in the 'Epilogue' – yet another section of text added for Heinemann – where the narrator drew lessons from the Martian invasion for present-day society:

> At any rate, whether we expect another invasion or not, our views of the human future must be greatly modified by these events. We have learned now that we cannot regard this planet as being fenced in and a secure abiding place for Man; we can never anticipate the unseen good or evil that may come upon us suddenly out of space. It may be that in the larger design of the universe this invasion from Mars is not without its ultimate benefit for men; it has robbed us of that serene confidence in the future which is the most fruitful source of decadence. (II.10: 300/178–9)

Wells's espousal of Darwinism resulted also in personal conflicts between religious belief and the claims of science. Despite attempting to reconcile Huxley's views with the deeply religious belief pressed upon him by his mother – she dismissed Huxley as 'a notoriously irreligious man' – Wells moved at an early age from theism towards atheism.[27] Wells admitted becoming a 'prodigy of Early Impiety': 'And then suddenly the light broke through to me and I knew this God was a lie.'[28] Writing in 1887, he welcomed news of a friend's 'vigorous Atheism': 'it behoves us who deny, to make it as clear to the world as we can.'[29] Indeed, Annie Meredith, a former girlfriend, reported that in 1887 she broke with Wells 'because he told me he was an atheist & socialist'.[30] Unsurprisingly, *The War of the Worlds*, like his other scientific romances, was used by Wells to expose the bankruptcy of institutionalized religion when confronted by new scientific paradigms. Thus, the

26. This chapter, like the Epilogue, was absent from the 1897 serializations, but added for Heinemann's book: David Y. Hughes and Harry M. Geduld, *A Critical Edition of The War of the Worlds: H. G. Wells's Scientific Romances* (Bloomington, IN: Indiana University Press, 1993), pp. 6–7; Hughes, *Edition and a Survey*, pp. 1–43.

27. Wells, *Experiment in Autobiography*, I, p. 175.

28. Ibid., pp. 47–8, 66–9, 162–7, 175–6, II, p. 540; N. and J. MacKenzie, *The Time Traveller*, pp. 23–4, 42–3, 120–1; H. G. Wells, *First and Last Things: A Confession of Faith and Rule of Life* (London: Archibald Constable, 1908); Sherborne, *H. G. Wells*, pp. 27–8.

29. Wells to A. M. Davies, 31 December 1887, Smith, *Correspondence of H. G. Wells, I*, pp. 76–7.

30. Quoted, N. and J. MacKenzie, *The Time Traveller*, p. 71.

curate, a straw man, a deeply flawed character constantly at loggerheads with the narrator, epitomized religion's perceived inadequacies.[31]

The vogue for scaremongering literature

A further manifestation of the *fin de siècle* mood in Britain, continental Europe and the USA was the vogue for war scare literature.[32] Between 1870 and 1914 the British reading public was subjected to decades of fictional military conflict in which Britain took on a range of adversaries from across the globe as well as through Wells's *The War of the Worlds* from another planet. For Bergonzi, the writings of the so-called 'scaremongers' typified *fin de siècle* mindsets: 'It was felt that the normal life of society had continued too long in its predictable and everyday fashion, and that some radical transformation was overdue, whether by war or natural disaster... The willingness to be shocked was at least as significant as the readiness of others to administer the shocks.'[33]

In effect, scaremongering literature linked the fantasies of imaginary military conflict with the facts of the contemporary world. Indeed, many publications, rooting a fictional storyline in actual places and involving real people in events, adopted a factional character. Significantly, given *The War of the Worlds'* geographical focus, 'The Battle of Dorking', an article published anonymously in May 1871 as the reminiscences of a volunteer, revived the popularity of this type of literature. Written by Lieutenant-Colonel Sir George Tomkyns Chesney (1830–95) – later he became a Member of Parliament (1892–5) – the article appeared in *Blackwood's Edinburgh Magazine*.[34] Writing about a German invasion force moving from the south coast towards London, Chesney's article gave Surrey in general and Dorking in particular a central role in the story. Guildford, Reigate, Surbiton and Kingston upon Thames also featured. Clearly, the theme struck a nerve with the reading public. Seven editions of the magazine were printed to meet demand, while the story, when published subsequently as a pamphlet, sold over 80,000 copies. Reminding readers about the unexpected speed with which Prussia had overcome France in the 1870–1 War to unify Germany, Chesney critiqued Victorian complacency about the resulting threat to British security. Thus, the volunteer used to tell Chesney's story, acted also as the 'lamenting chorus' when looking back on the past failings resulting in a successful Prussian invasion.[35]

For late Victorian and Edwardian Britain, fear of 'a bolt from the blue', a surprise invasion launched from the sea, proved nothing less than a national

31. Hughes and Geduld, *Critical Edition*, pp. 9–15.

32. Clarke, *Voices Prophesying War*, pp. 93–103.

33. Bergonzi, *Early Wells*, pp. 12–13, 135.

34. Anon. [Sir George Chesney], 'The Battle of Dorking: Reminiscences of a Volunteer', *Blackwood's Edinburgh Magazine* 109 (May 1871): 539–72; Roger T. Stearn, 'General Sir George Chesney', *Journal of the Society for Army Historical Research* 75 (1997): 106–18.

35. Chesney, 'The Battle of Dorking', p. 539; Clarke, *Voices Prophesying War*, p. 34;

obsession. Chesney's article was followed by a succession of publications about imaginary future wars, normally involving invasion by the perceived principal foreign adversary of the day – for Britain, the principal threats were seen as emanating from France, Germany, Russia and even the USA – and often resulting in defeat and national humiliation. Many stories appeared first as serials in magazines and newspapers given their proven popularity and ability to boost sales. Recognizing their circulation-boosting value, Alfred Harmsworth, later Lord Northcliffe, serialized Beckles Willson's 'The Siege of Portsmouth' in Portsmouth's *Southern Daily Mail* (June–July 1895) and the stories of William Le Queux in the *Daily Mail*.

Inevitably, Surrey's location proximate to both Aldershot, the headquarters of the British army, and London, meant that the county, as happened with 'The Battle of Dorking', figured prominently in scaremongering literature.[36] For example, one chapter in Le Queux's *The Great War in England in 1897*, a best-seller first serialized in *Answers* (1893) and then published as a book (1894), was entitled 'Fighting on the Surrey Hills'. Here Surrey became 'one huge battlefield', in which key roles were played by Dorking, Farnham, Guildford, Haslemere and Leatherhead.[37] But there was no place for Woking, let alone Horsell, in Le Queux's story. During the 1899–1902 Boer War F. N. Maude returned with *The New Battle of Dorking* (1900), while Le Queux's *The Invasion of 1910* (1906), first serialized in the million-selling *Daily Mail*, ranged widely across Surrey, with the rail network running to and from London depicted as a prime military target.

Notwithstanding their role in selling books, magazines and newspapers as well as the fact that many writers – they included P. G. Wodehouse, the author of *The Swoop! Or How Clarence saved England* (1909) – jumped on the scare-mongering bandwagon, the fundamental purpose of most war scare publications was didactic.[38] Despite repeated government assurances that the country was safe from invasion, the scaremongers continued to raise serious questions about national security by warning about British unpreparedness in the face of 'a bolt from the blue'; the growing military and naval power of rival nations; the impact of changing weapons technology; and the perceived threat posed by foreign espionage activities. They warned about Britain's fate unless immediate action was taken in terms of enhancing home defence, strengthening the army and navy, introducing conscription and establishing a secret service. Writing in the preface of *The Great War in England in 1897* (1894), Le Queux stated that 'In writing this book it was my endeavour to bring vividly before the public the national dangers by which we are surrounded, and the absolute necessity which lies upon England

36. Franco Moretti, 'Geography of "Invasion Literature" (1871–1906)', *Atlas of the European Novel, 1800–1900* (London: Verso, 1999), p. 139.

37. William Le Queux, The *Great War in England in 1897* (London: Tower, London, 1895), p. 303.

38. Clarke, *Voices Prophesying War*, pp. 135–6; Christopher Andrew, *Secret Service* (London: Heinemann, 1985), pp. 34–85.

to maintain her defences in an adequate state of efficiency.'[39] He reiterated this aim in *The Invasion of 1910* (1906): 'The object of this book is to illustrate our utter unpreparedness for war, to show how, under certain conditions, England can be successfully invaded by Germany, and to present a picture of the ruin which must inevitably fall upon us.'[40]

For many commentators, the overtly purposive nature of such publications detracts from their literary qualities. For LeRoy Panek, Le Queux might have attracted a substantial readership – for example, *The Invasion of 1910* was not only serialized in the best-selling *Daily Mail* but also sold over one million copies as a book – and made a lucrative living, but exhibited little talent as a writer: "Today, it takes a determined will and a high tolerance for unrefined and unmitigated twaddle to get through many books by William Le Queux ... They seem silly, inept and warped ... His plotting is execrable, his characters are buffoons, and his style is tedious to the extreme.'[41] Wells's *The War of the Worlds* was one major exception to such criticism. Indeed, for I. F. Clarke, the author of the standard study of scaremongering literature, *The War of the Worlds* is 'the most remarkable fantasy of imaginary warfare that has so far appeared in the history of the genre.'[42]

Wells as a scaremonger

Wells's inclusion of the word 'war' in the title of *The War of the Worlds* gave his story a clear contemporary resonance linking up with ongoing debates about national security conducted by the scaremongers and enabling his story to exploit the popularity of invasion literature.[43] Certainly, *The War of the Worlds* possessed several of the elements expected of any war scare tale. Firstly, the story, adopting a factional approach to enhance its realism, opened by setting out life in the peaceful and safe British countryside, a complacent society giving little or no thought to space in general and the Martians in particular as sources of danger (I.1: 1/7; I.1: 9/11). Typically, the arrival of the first Martian projectile on Horsell Common proved more the subject of curiosity than of fear for the watching crowd. Even then, people believed that the invaders, if harbouring any aggressive intentions, would be easily defeated by British troops. Thus, the narrator, opining that the Martians 'seemed very helpless in that pit of theirs' (I.9: 61/40), dismissed

39. Le Queux, *Great War in England in 1897*, pp. 143, 272, 274, 276.

40. William Le Queux, *The Invasion of 1910: with a full account of the Siege of London* (London: Eveleigh Nash, 1906), pp. vi, ix.

41. LeRoy L. Panek, *The Special Branch: The British Spy Novel, 1890–1980* (Bowling Green, OH: Bowling Green University Popular Press, 1981), p. 15.

42. Clarke, *Voices Prophesying War*, p. 99.

43. Bergonzi, *Early Wells*, pp. 134–5; Michael Moorcock, 'Before Armageddon', in Michael Moorcock and Allan Kausch (eds), *Michael Moorcock: London Peculiar and other Nonfiction* (Oakland, CA: PM Press, 2012), p. 191.

the prospect of a successful invasion: 'A shell in the pit ... will kill them all' (I.7: 49/34).

Secondly, Britain was suddenly invaded, a country unprepared and ill-equipped both physically and psychologically to deal with aggressive well-armed invaders. Thirdly, the invasion was conducted by a ruthless technically advanced and well-armed aggressor prompting panic, flight and the breakdown of society. Fourthly, the destruction and loss of life caused by the invasion, even one which eventually proved abortive, highlighted not only the disruptive and costly impact of war but also the need for urgent action to provide future security against any other potential threat. At the close of the story, Britain survived as an independent country, a feature differentiating Wells's tale from that of Chesney in which Britain was defeated. The Martian invasion proved abortive. But much of London and Surrey had been laid to waste. People's mindsets had been changed radically in a manner highlighting the ephemeral, indeed fragile, nature of the present-day world, the impact of changing technology and the destructive impact of war. Moreover, Wells's focus upon the civilian population, most notably their panic and flight in the face of the invaders' rapid advance, illuminated war's psychological impacts.

But Wells offered readers something more than just another Chesney-type war scare story. Apart from producing a much praised work of literature, his masterstroke was to introduce an interplanetary dimension. *The War of the Worlds'* originality lay in a shift from terrestrial threats to a sudden and unexpected invasion conducted by hostile beings from another world. Hitherto scaremongering stories had concentrated upon a conventional 'bolt from the blue' such as might be launched from the sea by France, Germany or Russia. Wells's 'far-future war fiction' transformed scaremongering literature by moving on to a vivid portrayal of what might be represented as a 'bolt from beyond the blue'![44] As Will Self observed:

> Wells's Martian invasion tale ... was not by any means the first novel to deal with a devastating invasion of Britain by vastly superior forces, nor was it the first to propose the existence of life on Mars, but it was unique – in English at least – in synthesising the two anxieties into what was then dubbed a "scientific romance" ... Ever since the theme of alien invasion has never been off the narrative agenda.[45]

Moreover, Wells's focus upon Mars linked up well with both the scaremongering theme, especially as Mars was the Roman god of war, but also contemporary interest in the Red Planet, as discussed in the next section.

Apart from raising the stakes of any military conflict, the alien invasion theme introduced a fresh set of issues for discussion despite Wells's occasional attempts to play down a didactic purpose by pointing to the essentially creative and

44. Gannon, 'One swift, conclusive smashing', p. 45.
45. Self, 'Death on three legs'.

imaginative nature of his scientific romances. Even so, he became increasingly prone to point to the military insight and prescience of his early fiction, such as evidenced by the role played by heat-rays and poison gas in *The War of the Worlds* or aerial warfare in *When the Sleeper Wakes* and *The War in the Air*. Looking back soon after the end of the First World War to the period when he wrote his scientific romances, Wells recorded his 'vivid realization of some disregarded possibility in such a way as to comment on the false securities and fatuous self-satisfaction of the everyday life – as we knew it then':

> Because in those days the conviction that history had settled down to a sort of jog-trot comedy was very widespread indeed. Tragedy, people thought, had gone out of human life for ever. A few of us were trying to point out the obvious possibilities of flying, of great guns, of poison gas, and so forth in presently making life uncomfortable if some sort of world peace was not assured, but the books we wrote were regarded as the silliest of imaginative gymnastics. Well, the world knows better now.[46]

A few years later, he pointed to the way in which the First World War established the prophetic nature of *The War of the Worlds*, its 'intelligent anticipations', regarding society's need to be ready 'to meet a great crisis': 'The reader will be reminded of phases and incidents in the Great War; the use of poison gas and flight before the tank-like "War Machines"'.[47] Subsequently, Wells changed tack again, when dismissing 'the fiction of prophecy' as 'an ephemeral but amusing art', especially as such stories were rapidly overtaken by events.[48]

When *The War of the Worlds* was first published during the late 1890s, it was of course easy for commentators and readers to dismiss the Martians' superior array of power – the tripods, a flying machine, deadly heat-rays, poison gas and invasive red weed – as pure fantasy intended to arouse astonishment, fear and excitement upon the part of readers. However, what Wells did was to illuminate more effectively than most the fast-changing nature of warfare in an industrial age. In effect, Wells represented the Martians as giving a master-class in conducting a modern war – as he wrote, 'Never before in the history of warfare had destruction been so indiscriminate and so universal' (I.11: 87/55) – by establishing the close link between science, technology and war and particularly by showing how a great industrial nation might be overcome by a powerful and determined invader, exploiting science's military potential. Acknowledging Wells's anxieties about future wars, Clarke commented that:

46. H. G. Wells, 'War of the Worlds: Introduction: An Experiment in Illustration', *Strand Magazine* lix (February 1920), p. 154.

47. Wells, *The Works of H. G. Wells*, III, pp. ix–x. On Wells's powers of prophecy, see Ford Madox Ford, *Mightier than the Sword: Memories and Criticisms* (London: George Allen & Unwin, 1938), p. 164.

48. Wells, 'Fiction about the Future', in Parrinder and Philmus, *H. G. Wells' Literary Criticism*, pp. 246–50.

The warriors may have come from Mars for the purpose of the fiction; but their terrible weapons and the immense destruction they caused might one day emerge from Western industrialism, if science were to create the most lethal possible armoury. The marvels of the poisonous Black Smoke, the Heat Ray, the remarkable Handling Machines, and the tall war vehicles in which the Martians stalked over southern England, calling *ulla, ulla, ulla*, to one another – all came from the immensely fertile imagination of Wells as he thought with a fear (half recognized for what it was) of the destruction that would follow on a full-scale industrialized war.[49]

For his readers during the late 1890s, *The War of the Worlds* took warfare to the limit, especially regarding its impacts upon the civilian population, thereby making the prospect of a Martian invasion launched with heat-rays and so on far more terrifying than it might appear to most present-day readers, already living alongside powerful advanced weaponry.

The way in which the Martians laid waste to much of Surrey and then London offered a vivid example of possible future scenarios. Towns, villages and the countryside suffered. Large numbers of people lost their lives. Viewing the destruction wrought by the Martians across Woking from the window of his house, the narrator was forced to confront for the first time the harsh realities of contemporary warfare: 'And this was the little world in which I had been living securely for years, this fiery chaos!' (I.11: 80/51). Subsequently, Wells reiterated this point by way of shaking readers' complacency, such as when the narrator recorded the transformation of Sheen: 'When I had last seen this part of Sheen in the daylight it had been a straggling street of comfortable white and red houses, interspersed with abundant shady trees' (II.5: 238/143). Subsequently the narrator, standing on piles of smashed brickwork, found himself surrounded by wrecked houses and dead trees: 'I found about me the landscape, weird and lurid, of another planet' (II.6: 240/144). Conceding his limited awareness of recent trends affecting the wider world, the narrator, like the volunteer in Chesney's *Battle of Dorking*, acknowledged his failure to anticipate such a 'startling vision of unfamiliar things' (II.6: 240/144).

Viewed from a literary perspective, *The War of the Worlds* can be represented as Wells's 'own take' on the future-war genre, a story published 'halfway through this craze'.[50] Although Wells emulated the factional approach adopted by Le Queux and company, *The War of the Worlds* stood out and still stands out, within this genre, because the high quality narrative complemented – to quote Bergonzi – 'its greater imaginative intensity and technical superiority'.[51] Thus, whereas most war scare fiction has been deservedly forgotten, Wells's work has survived, remained in print and continued to inspire a wide range of alternative audio, textual and visual adaptations. Despite possessing purposive features reflecting

49. Clarke, *Voices Prophesying War*, pp. 94, 98–9.

50. Roger Luckhurst, *Science Fiction* (Cambridge: Polity, 2005), p. 31.

51. Bergonzi, *Early Wells*, p. 135.

the *fin de siècle* mood, neither *The War of the Worlds'* narrative qualities nor its originality were seriously qualified, let alone submerged, by its functional nature.

One decade later, Wells returned to the topic with *The War in the Air* (1908). The threat was still aerial – a German air attack against New York – but not interplanetary. For Wells, the focus was the threat posed by national complacency and advanced technology like new flying machines. Although Wells might be seen as returning to a successful topic to make money with a rapidly written potboiler – reportedly his fee was £3,000 – the book reflected his belief that, though lacking any specific military expertise, he could make a meaningful contribution to ongoing contemporary debates about national defence, particularly through brainstorming sessions drawing upon his creative imagination and scientific education.[52] Writing in 1909 to Lord Esher, an influential figure in British military circles and a member of the Committee of Imperial Defence, Wells claimed that 'I don't think I know anything at all of military matters, but since warfare is evidently to be waged in the future very largely with novel and untried appliances, I suppose an active and well trained imagination is sometimes able to produce suggestions – my training has I think served to keep my imagination rather too much alive.'[53] Despite Wells's disclaimers about his military expertise, Clarke argued that 'Wells was one of the few writers of his time who had the requisite imagination and technical competence' to understand the rapidly changing science, technology and war equation.[54]

For Brian Aldiss, the military issues raised by The *War of the Worlds* 'remain ever topical.'[55] For example, during the Second World War Aldiss recalled coming across a reprint of the book with a jacket showing searchlight beams in the sky and flames arising from the destroyed city. In his view, the German Luftwaffe seemed as remorseless as were the Martians. Likewise, when overviewing Wells's representation of military strategy and tactics in *The War of the Worlds*, Thomas Gangale and Marilyn Dudley-Rowley described the Martian attack on London as the first blitzkrieg – this tactic, literally meaning lightning war, was employed by Hitler's Germany during the early stages of the Second World War – with their advance into London occurring only eighty-six hours after the first landing on Horsell Common.[56] They claimed also that the Martians launched the first chemical war through the use of the Black Smoke. In this vein, as discussed in the first chapter, Wells has won praise, such as from Ferguson and Williams, for his military prescience. By contrast, Roger Stearn argued that Wells's scientific romances should be excluded when evaluating his status as a military thinker: 'before 1914 Wells, and his reviewers and readers, regarded his non-fiction as the primary vehicle of his thinking ... the message of his non-fiction was taken

52. N. and J. Mackenzie, *The Time Traveller*, p. 234.

53. Wells to Lord Esher, 23 August 1909, WE16 (UIUC).

54. Clarke, *Voices Prophesying War*, p. 100.

55. Aldiss, 'Introduction', p. xviii.

56. Thomas Gangale and Marilyn Dudley-Rowley, 'Strategy and tactics in the *War of the Worlds*', *The Wellsian* 31 (2008): 4.

seriously in a way that his fiction was not'.[57] Wells himself is often quoted by way of making this point; thus, in *Anticipations* (1901), 'a rough sketch of the coming time', he pointed to *The Battle of Dorking* when arguing the case for the superiority of non-fiction over fiction.[58] However, here as elsewhere, Wells is on record over time as articulating conflicting points of view.

Wells's place in 'The Great Mars Boom'

Although he pioneered an interplanetary dimension for war scare literature, Wells's focus upon Mars was not as original as might appear at first sight. Indeed, Mark Hillegas claimed that *The War of the Worlds* might be better interpreted as marking 'the climax', not the start, of the contemporary vogue for Martian fiction. As Hillegas recorded, during the decade or so preceding its publication, Mars proved 'the favourite destination of space travellers', as evidenced by such novels as Hugh MacColl's *Mr. Stranger's Sealed Packet* (1889), Robert Cromie's *A Plunge into Space* (1890) and Robert D. Braine's *Messages from Mars, by the Aid of the Telescope Plant* (1892).[59] However, whereas previous authors tended to focus upon travelling to Mars and offer relatively positive images of Martians, Wells reversed the process by writing about a Martian invasion of earth and depicting the Martians as monstrous would-be conquerors. Nor was Wells alone in this trend. The year 1897, when *The War of the Worlds* was serialized, saw the publication of Kurd Lasswitz's *Auf Zwei Planeten* (1897) in which polar explorers discovered a Martian base at the North Pole.[60] Reportedly, this book, which went untranslated into English until 1971 and hence lacked the literary impact of Wells's story, influenced Wernher von Braun, the German rocket scientist and author of *The Mars Project* (1953).

Following the eighteenth century discoveries of William Herschel, who represented the analogy between Mars and earth as perhaps 'the greatest' of any within the solar system, the planet proved a prime focus for study by astronomers, especially during the closing decades of the nineteenth century. Just as astronomers, like Asaph Hall, Percival Lowell and Giovanni Schiaparelli, turned their telescopes towards Mars, so journalists and fiction writers looked to Mars for engaging stories about a new subject full of creative imaginative possibilities. In particular, the mistranslation of Schiaparelli's identification in 1877 of a lengthy network of 'canali' as canals, not channels, fostered considerable media

57. R. T. Stearn, 'Wells and War; H. G. Wells's writings on military subjects, before the Great War', *The Wellsian* 6 (1983): 1.

58. H. G. Wells, *Anticipations* (London: Chapman & Hall, 1901), pp. 2, 186.

59. Mark R. Hillegas, 'Victorian "Extraterrestrials"', in Jerome Hamilton Buckley (ed.), *The Worlds of Victorian Fiction* (Cambridge, MA: Harvard University Press, 1975), pp. 400, 405; Richard A. Gregory, 'Book review: A journey to the planet Mars', *Nature* 40 (25 July 1889): 291–2.

60. Hughes, *Edition and a Survey*, pp. 306–8, 311–13.

speculation about the existence of intelligent life on Mars responsible for such artificial waterways. Writing in the *Fortnightly Review* in September 1892, Robert S. Ball, an Irish astronomer, remarked that 'The newspapers, crowded as they are with their staple political matters, can still make room for paragraphs, columns, and even for long articles on the phenomena of our neighbouring globe'.[61] During the same year the *New York Times* reported Hall's acknowledgement of the scale of 'general popular interest' being taken in Mars.[62] This surge of public interest, fuelled by speculation about the possibility of life in other worlds, ensured that the 'Great Opposition' of 1892 when Mars was closer to earth than during most oppositions – the planet's distance from Earth varies between 56 million kms (35 million miles) and 399 million kms (249 million miles) – was a newsworthy event in Britain, continental Europe and the USA.

As a result, the 1890s saw a mass media 'feeding frenzy on things Martian'.[63] In many respects, what was depicted in October 1896 by the *Edinburgh Review* as 'the great Mars boom' was driven by the manner in which astronomers often bypassed the usual scientific channels to reach a wider readership directly through newspapers, magazines and books.[64] Publications included Nicolas Camille Flammarion's *La Planète Mars et ses conditions d'habitabilité* (1892), Schiaparelli's 'The Planet Mars' published in *Astronomy and Astrophysics* (1894) and Lowell's' *Mars* (1895). The Martian craze inspired several novels, such as those by Braine and Cromie mentioned above, but generally speaking they proved of variable, frequently limited, literary merit. For Robert Crossley, the author of an authoritative literary history of Mars, Wells, 'the first major literary figure to take up the subject of Mars', produced 'the first literary masterpiece in the tradition of Martian fiction', that is *The War of the Worlds*.[65] At the same time, Mars's status as 'a hot topic' in popular discourse suggests that the popularity of *The War of the Worlds*, especially as measured by sales, was due at least in part to 'the great Mars boom' as much as to Wells's reputation and literary skills.[66] In turn, *The War of the Worlds* was to prove instrumental in keeping the Red Planet in the minds of the general public for well over one century.

Wells had long been interested in the possibility of people living on other planets and inevitably Mars's public visibility framed his mindset when thinking, speaking and writing on the topic. For example, in October 1888, when participating in a student debate held at the Normal School for Science about the habitability of the planets, he had claimed that 'there was every reason to suppose

61. Robert S. Ball, 'Mars', *Fortnightly Review*, September 1892, p. 288, quoted, Steven Mclean, *The Early Fiction of H. G. Wells: Fantasies of Science* (Basingstoke: Palgrave Macmillan, 2009), pp. 91–5.

62. Quoted, Crossley, *Imagining Mars*, p. 65.

63. Ibid., pp. 70–1.

64. Anon, 'New views about Mars', *Edinburgh Review* 184 (October 1896): 368.

65. Crossley, *Imagining Mars*, pp. xii, 110.

66. Ibid., pp. 70–1.

that the surface of Mars was occupied by living beings'.[67] Wells's thinking was influenced also by Ball's lengthy article about Mars published in the *Fortnightly Review* in 1892, as well as by a notice published in *Nature* in August 1894 reporting that Stephane Javelle, based at the Nice Observatory, had observed a 'strange light' on Mars.[68] Wells began to draw the planet increasingly into his thinking and writings. Thus, *Honours Physiography* (1893), a textbook co-written with Richard Gregory, included speculations about both Martians and their canals. Gregory, a friend dating back to Wells's student days now working as an assistant editor for *Nature* from 1893, also followed Mars-related developments closely, as evidenced by his regular published updates in the 'Science and Discovery' section of *The Living Hour* and article about 'Mars in the World' recording the existing state of knowledge regarding, say, canals and signalling.[69] Undoubtedly the two men continued to exchange thoughts and information about the planet.

In April 1896, that is while he was living in Woking writing *The War of the Worlds*, Wells published 'Intelligence on Mars' in the S*aturday Review*, a study reflecting his Darwinist outlook as well as recording his participation in ongoing debates about 'the existence of intelligent, sentient life on the planet Mars' and speculation whether Martians were sending messages to Earth.[70] Then 1897, the year in which *The War of the Worlds* was serialized and the text extended for publication as a book, saw further articles – 'The Crystal Egg' and 'The Star' – reaffirming Wells's preoccupation with Mars, most notably the possibility articulated also in the opening lines of *The War of the Worlds* that Martian astronomers were studying earth through their telescopes.[71]

The Martian theme was, of course, central to *The War of the Worlds*. Indeed, in many respects the opening section in which Wells touched upon media coverage of recent astronomical discoveries reinforced the story's realism by complementing his use of actual places. Thus, the story's opening section, albeit suggesting that earth was under even closer scrutiny by aliens, exploited the contemporary vogue for telescopic observation of Mars, while mention of Mars as a planet marked by 'transverse stripes' (I.1: 7/10) touched upon the much discussed canali. Recent media reports were integrated effectively into the fictional storyline:

> Had our instruments permitted it, we might have seen the gathering trouble far back in the nineteenth century. Men like Schiaparelli watched the red planet …

67. Report of a debate, *Science Schools Journal*, November 1888, p. 58, quoted Bergonzi, *Early Wells*, p. 123.

68. Mclean, *Early Fiction of Wells*, p. 95.

69. Richard A. Gregory, 'Mars as a world', *The Living Age* 225 (2209) (April–June 1900): 21–8. For Gregory's *The Living Hour* articles, see Sir Richard Gregory Papers, University of Sussex Special Collections, The Keep, Falmer, Brighton (Sussex): SxMs14/1/4/1.

70. Wells, 'Intelligence on Mars', p. 345.

71. H. G. Wells, 'The Crystal Egg', *The New Review* 16 (May 1897); H. G. Wells, 'The Star', *The Graphic*, December 1897.

but failed to interpret the fluctuating appearances of the markings they mapped so well. All that time the Martians must have been getting ready.

During the opposition of 1894 a great light was seen on the illuminated part of the disc, first at the Lick Observatory, then by Perrotin of Nice, and then by other observers. English readers heard of it first in the issue of *Nature* dated August 2nd. (I.1: 5/9)

Wells named one character in the story "Lavelle" (I.1: 6/9), undoubtedly after Javelle of the Nice Observatory. Wells's red weed, it has been suggested, might have been inspired by Flammarion's claim that vegetation explained Mars' red colour.

Despite changing course as a writer c. 1900, Wells retained his interest in Mars, such as evidenced by 'The Things that Live on Mars' published in *Cosmopolitan* in 1908. Significantly, given debates about whether or not he had read Lowell's *Mars* (1895) prior to writing *The War of the Worlds*, Lowell is represented therein as 'my friend'.[72] In 1937 Wells returned again to the theme of a Martian invasion in *Star-Begotten: A Biological Fantasia*, even if this appears to have been written as much for money, as much as in response to his longstanding interest in Mars. In March 1935 Jacques Chambrun, Wells's long serving representative in New York, reported that *This Week* had offered $15,000 for a 15,000 word story in 'fantastic vein'.[73] Despite complaining that 'I don't write stories to order', Wells instructed Chambrun to offer a novel called *Star-Begotten*. Published in 1937, *Star-Begotten* even included an element of self-mockery:

> Some of you may have read a book called *The War of the Worlds* – I forget who wrote it – Jules Verne, Conan Doyle, one of those fellows. But it told how the Martians invaded the world, wanted to colonize it, and exterminate mankind. Hopeless attempt! They couldn't stand the different atmospheric pressure, they couldn't stand the difference in gravitation; bacteria finished them up. Hopeless from the start.[74]

Wells took the opportunity also to express reservations about the new literary genre with whose origins he was linked, when complaining that science fiction was full of 'progressive utopias' reflecting 'imaginative starvation', empty sacks 'that won't stand up'.[75]

72. H. G. Wells, 'The Things that Live on Mars', *Cosmopolitan* XLIV (4) (March 1908): 335.

73. Chambrun to Wells, 13 March 1935, Wells to Secretary, n.d., Smith, *Correspondence of H. G. Wells, IV*, p. 25.

74. H. G. Wells, *Star-Begotten* (London: Chatto & Windus, 1937), p. 62. Wells dedicated the book to 'my friend', Winston Churchill, who had first made contact with Wells after the publication of *Anticipations* (1901): Wells to Parsons, 30 April 1937, Smith, *Correspondence of H. G. Wells, IV*, p. 149.

75. Wells, *Star-Begotten*, pp. 170–1.

Debating imperialism

According to Anthony West, '*The War of the Worlds* was primarily an allegory of colonialism, showing the destruction of a primitive society by a technically more sophisticated one with no respect for its values and its culture'[76] In this vein, the book is often interpreted as – to quote Herbert Sussman – an 'anti-imperialist fable', a story 'told from the viewpoint of the oppressed'[77] Paradoxically, Britons, the inhabitants of the country possessing the world's largest overseas empire during the late 1890s, were now depicted as 'the oppressed', the victims of imperialism. From this perspective, *The War of the Worlds* showed British imperialism 'getting its comeuppance', a taste of its own medicine, as the mother country was colonized by technologically superior conquerors from another world indifferent to their sufferings.[78]

The period between 1880 and 1914, when vast amounts of territory in Africa, the Far East and the Pacific were taken over in a relatively short space of time, is often represented as 'The Age of Imperialism'. Having grabbed the largest amount of territory to become the empire upon which the sun never set, Britain proved highly vulnerable to critiques about both its policy and methods. Serialized in the same year as Queen Victoria's Diamond Jubilee, a massive triumphalist celebration of a global empire, Wells's *The War of the Worlds* complemented Rudyard Kipling's 'Recessional', a poem written specifically for *The Times* to mark the anniversary.[79] Whereas Kipling reacted against the celebratory mood to warn about eventual decline and to urge people not to be 'drunk with sight of power', Wells confronted Britons with the other side of the imperialism story, that is Britain as the target for an invasion conducted by Martians in an aggressive and merciless manner resulting in 'utter destruction' (I.1: 4/9).

For Wells, *The War of the Worlds* offered an ideal vehicle for articulating his doubts about imperialism and the harsh suppression of opposition in pursuit of control.[80] His reservations, or what Bergonzi calls his 'guilty conscience', about imperialism's oppressive nature underpinned the opening pages of *The War of the Worlds*.[81] Here Wells critiques the 'ruthless ... war of extermination' (I.1: 4–5/9)

76. Anthony West, 'Letters', *Scientific American* CCLII (October 1960), p. 16, quoted Hughes, *Edition and a Survey*, p. 308.

77. Herbert L. Sussman, *Victorians and the Machine: The Literary Response to Technology* (Cambridge, MA: Harvard University Press, 1968), p. 179.

78. Brett Davidson, '*The War of the Worlds* considered as a modern myth', *The Wellsian* 28 (2005): 45; Crossley, *Imagining Mars*, p. xii; Clarke, *Voices Prophesying War*, pp. 94–6.

79. Denis Judd, 'Diamonds are forever?: Kipling's imperialism', *History Today* 47 (6) (June 1997): 37–8; Rudyard Kipling, 'Recessional', *The Times*, 17 July 1897, p. 13. Writing to his brother, Wells described witnessing the Jubilee naval review at Spithead: Wells to Fred Wells, n.d. [1897], Wells, *Experiment in Autobiography*, I, p. 403.

80. Jacqueline Banerjee, *Literary Surrey* (Headley Down: John Owen Smith, 2005), p. 149.

81. Bergonzi, *Early Wells*, p. 134.

waged against Tasmania's native inhabitants following Britain's takeover during the early nineteenth century. As Wells asked, 'Are we such apostles of mercy as to complain if the Martians warred in the same spirit?' (I.1: 5/9). Tasmania's fate, epitomizing the fate of any people subject to the imperial process, proved a major source of concern for Wells, who mentioned discussing this topic with his brother when recalling what initially prompted him to write *The War of the Worlds*.[82] In turn, he used the Martian invaders, possessing 'intellects vast and cool and unsympathetic' (I.1: 2/7), as a representation of the imperial self to encourage, indeed force, the narrator and through him readers to look at things from the position of those subject to imperialism, and particularly to reappraise the methods employed in the past to conquer and colonize overseas territories. In the end, Earth was saved from Martian domination by a combination of luck and bacteria, but not until after the alien invasion had raised serious questions about present-day mindsets. As the narrator commented, 'Surely, if we have learned nothing else, this war has taught us pity – pity for those witless souls that suffer our dominion' (II.7: 249/149).

Writing about another planet and an alien invasion enabled Wells to advance serious concerns about the contemporary world in a vivid, effective and engaging manner, as recognized by Crossley as well as by Kuchta and Williams: 'Wells' greatest achievement in *The War of the Worlds* is his critical examination of what it means to colonize another world, another species, another race. The popular fascination with Mars furnished him with an opportunity to expose the delusions of grandeur and the moral callousness in England's pursuit of its imperial goal.'[83] Contextualized by the continued advance of Britain's imperial expansion, *The War of the Worlds* made a significant contribution to the growing debate about imperialism, such as pressed soon afterwards by J. A. Hobson's seminal text *Imperialism: A Study* (1902). Pointing to their shared *fin de siècle* cultural legacy, Linda Dryden has pointed also to Wells's influence upon Joseph Conrad's critique of empire as articulated in 'The Heart of Darkness' (1899).[84]

Socialism

For Wells, the late Victorian world showed itself incapable of accommodating a growing range of socio-economic issues within the existing political framework, and yet most people, he complained, 'felt and spoke as if they were in an absolutely fixed world'.[85] What was required in his view was political action ushering in socio-economic reform. Wells made contact with the recently founded Fabian Society

82. Wells, '*War of the Worlds*: Introduction: An Experiment in Illustration', p. 154.

83. Crossley, *Imagining Mars*, pp. 122–3; Kuchta, *Semi-Detached Empire*, pp. 36–8; Williams, 'Alien Gaze', pp. 49–73.

84. Linda Dryden, 'H. G. Wells and Joseph Conrad: A Literary Friendship', *The Wellsian* 28 (2005): 4.

85. Wells, *Experiment in Autobiography*, I, p. 245.

when studying at the Normal School, while delivering a speech to the college's Debating Society in October 1886 criticizing the profit motive, denouncing individualism, attacking *laisser faire* and advocating a new world order, a socialist utopia. Reportedly, Wells came to flaunt the red tie which was then the outward and visible badge of the good socialist.[86] In turn, one of his former girlfriends ended their relationship after learning about his socialist leanings.[87]

However, when writing about Wells's professed socialism, Anthony West stressed the need for a sense of perspective:

> Although he had been calling himself a socialist for years, he had little knowledge of political theory, and none of practical politics. He had started saying that he was a socialist when he was still not much more than a rough draft for the prickly young misfit who serves as the eponymous hero of *Love and Mr. Lewisham*. He hadn't at that stage any idea of what socialism was, beyond that it required a man to go about looking fierce, running down the system, and wearing a red tie. When called on to defend his position, he hadn't been able to do much more than sick up some scrambled stuff that he'd got from a random sampling of the literature of dissent. He had retained what caught his attention or what had fired his imagination, and let the dull bits go.[88]

Certainly, during the 1890s socialism, though surfacing in his scientific romances and other publications, was largely kept in check by Wells, a writer seemingly influenced more by *fin de siècle* pessimism than by a belief that the world could be changed by socialism.[89] Even so, he admitted that socialist ideas stood out more strongly in such books as *The Time Machine* than he had intended.[90]

Social class figured in both *The Wonderful Visit* and *The Wheels of Chance*, but without being pressed too hard on readers. Thus, in *The Wonderful Visit* the angel was far from impressed by class distinctions and private ownership and was even accused of preaching 'Socialist rot'.[91] Likewise, the contrasting social backgrounds of Hoopdriver and the girl in grey proved a central determinant of the storyline of *The Wheels of Chance*, with both going their separate ways at the close of the story. In *The War of the Worlds* society became increasingly atomized in the face of the Martian advance, as highlighted by the breakdown of order, the flight from London and the stress on individualism, as people from all classes

86. Geoffrey West, *H. G. Wells: A Sketch for a Portrait* (London: Howe, 1930), p. 55.

87. Quoted, N. and J. MacKenzie, *The Time Traveller*, p. 71.

88. Anthony West, *H. G. Wells, Aspects of a Life* (London: Hutchinson, 1984), p. 277.

89. Wells to Davies, n.d. [1894], Smith, *Correspondence of H. G. Wells, I*, pp. 213–14; Sherborne, *H. G. Wells*, pp. 107, 120–1.

90. Interview with Wells, n.d., *Weekly Sun Literary Supplement*, 1 December 1895, in David C. Smith, 'A chat with the author of *The Time Machine*, Mr H. G. Wells', *The Wellsian* 20 (1997): 5–6.

91. H. G. Wells, *The Wonderful Visit* (New York: Macmillan, 1895), p. 236.

fought savagely for space in railway carriages or sacked shops for bicycles.[92] Steven McLean pointed also to Wells's critique of private wealth, such as the futile efforts of one man fleeing from the Martians to recover spilt coins (I: 16: 167/101) or the exorbitant charges demanded by the steamboat's crew to take the narrator's brother to Ostend (I: 17: 180/108).

By comparison, the 'Later Wells' engaged far more directly with socio-economic realities in his writing and life. Indeed, Wells sought to do more to advance the cause of socialism by venturing out beyond his writing desk to take on society's problems, such as through active membership of the Fabian Society or assumption of the role of a public intellectual, even if questions have often been raised about the extent to which he lived up to socialist principles in his private life, given his alleged individualistic quest for money and private wealth.[93]

Conclusion

Wells's scientific romances, whether focused upon a Martian invasion of earth or the propulsion of the time traveller into the far distant future, were never totally detached from the real world in which he was living. Indeed, for Brian Ash, 'Perhaps more than any other author of his generation, Wells mirrored his times'.[94] Of course, such a point can be made of most authors – it is difficult to understand any writer without viewing them in their historical setting – but Wells's scientific romances were characterized, indeed distinguished by a strong sense of context.

Reflecting upon, highlighting and exposing aspects of the late nineteenth century British *Weltanschauung* in a vivid and engaging manner, *The War of the Worlds* proves – to quote Brian Aldiss – 'a compendium of many nineteenth-century concerns'.[95] In many respects, Wells can be viewed still as an 'angry young man' – he used such a descriptor for himself – strongly critical of prevailing modes of thought concerning such issues as evolution, imperialism, religion, science and technology.[96] Wells was very much a *fin de siècle* writer, but his mental map, his view of the world, comprised many layers, including also family background, education, political values and the domestic and external environment within which he lived. As a result, *fin de siècle* themes need to be viewed alongside a range of other factors, especially the Mars boom of the 1890s and debates about imperialism.

92. Mclean, *Early Fiction of Wells*, pp. 97–100.

93. Lodge, *Novelist at the Crossroads*, pp. 218–20; Wells, *Experiment in Autobiography*, I, pp. 242–66, II, pp. 656–63; Sherborne, *H. G. Wells*, pp. 49–51, 57–9.

94. Brian Ash, *Who's Who in H. G. Wells* (London: Elm Tree Books, Hamish Hamilton, 1979), p. xiv.

95. Aldiss, 'Introduction', p. xxii.

96. H. G. Wells, 'H. G. Wells', in Albert Einstein et al., *Living Philosophies* (New York: Simon & Schuster, 1931), pp. 80–1; Geoffrey West, *H. G. Wells*, p. 276.

Inevitably, Wells's worldview changed over time in response to variations in both his personal circumstances and the broader historical and literary context. If nothing else, *The War of the Worlds*, written during the mid-late 1890s, was both very much of its time and far ahead of its time figuring still in the storyline for twenty-first century space missions. The Martian invasion forced the narrator, a Wells-like visionary, to confront new post-war realities when returning to his house in Woking, where he read the confident ending of his manuscript abandoned abruptly on the eve of the Martian invasion: "'In about two hundred years,' I had written, "we may expect –'" (II.9: 295/176).[97] Wells hoped that his readers, like the narrator, would appreciate how suddenly and unexpectedly things could change. For Crossley, 'In a decade brimming with illusions about the planet Mars, Wells aimed for a disturbing but intellectually healthy exercise in disillusionment'.[98] Clearly some readers would have shared or been influenced by the manner in which Wells articulated his anxieties about facing an uncertain new century, but for most readers, gripped by an exciting and fast-moving story, such academic debates were, and still are, of little or no concern.

---

97. Langford, 'The History of Mr Wells'.
98. Crossley, *Imagining Mars*, p. xii.

Part II

WRITING AND PUBLISHING *THE WAR OF THE WORLDS*

Chapter 4

WELLS'S PERSONAL SETTING

Writing from Woking in November 1895, Wells sent Grant Richards, the editor of *Phil May's Illustrated Winter Annual*, a brief personal history by way of background for the forthcoming publication of his short story 'The Argonauts of the Air' (Figure 4.1). In brief, Wells recorded how events had pushed him increasingly 'to the writing desk', with *The War of the Worlds*, 'a big scientific story', a priority project.[1]

It's awfully good of you to go writing up a reputation for me, & I very gladly do what you ask of me. I was born at a place called Bromley in Kent, a suburb of the damnedest in 1866, educated at a beastly little private school there until I was 13, apprenticed on trial to all sorts of trades, attracted the attention of a man called Byatt, Headmaster of Newhurst Grammar School, by the energy with wh I mopped up Latin – I went to him for Latin for a necessary examination while apprenticed (on approval, of course!) to a chemist there, became a kind of teaching scholar to him, got a scholarship at the Royal College of Science, S. Kensington (1884) worked there three years, started a students journal, read abundantly in the Dyce & Foster Library, failed my last years examination (geology), wandered in the wilderness of private sch teaching, had a lung haemorrhage, got a London degree B. Sc. (1889) with first and second class honours, private coaching, *Globe* turnovers, article in the *Fortnightly* (1890), edited an obscure educational paper, had haemorrhage for the second time (1893) chucked coaching & went for journalism. *P. M. G.* took up my work, then Henley *(Nobs.)*. Hind *P. M. Budget* set me on to short stories. Found *Saturday Review* when Harris bought the paper. *Review of Reviews* first paper to make a fuss over "Time Machine" – for which I shall never cease to be grateful. *Referee*, next. Brings us up to date.

Books published:
Text Book of Biology. A cram book – and pure hackwork.
(Illustrations grotesquely bad – facts imagined.)
Time Machine

1. Wells, *Experiment in Autobiography*, I, p. 370.

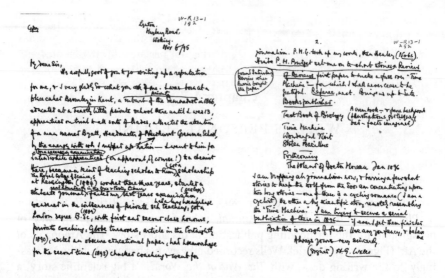

Figure 4.1 Letter from H. G. Wells to Grant Richards, 6 November 1895. A personal history written by Wells and sent to Grant Richards on 6 November 1895 from his home in Maybury Road, Woking.

Source: W-R13-1, Rare Book and Manuscript Library, University of Illinois at Urbana-Champaign, USA.

> Wonderful Visit
> Stolen Bacillus
> *Forthcoming:-*
> The Island of Doctor Moreau. Jan 1896.
>
> I am dropping all journalism now, and barring a few short stories to keep the wolf from the door am concentrating upon two long stories – one of these is a cycling romance (I am a cyclist) the other a big scientific story remotely resembling the "Time Machine". *I am trying to secure a serial publication of these in 1896 – if ever I get them finished.*
>
> But this is enough of facts. Use any you fancy.[2]

Highlighting the fragmented nature of his early life, Wells recorded a series of fresh starts in education and work undertaken in diverse geographical locations

---

2. H. G. Wells to Grant Richards, 6 November 1895, W-R13-1 (UIUC); Grant Richards, *Memories of a Misspent Youth* (New York: Harper 1933), pp. 327–8. Smith transcribes 'beastly' incorrectly as 'beautiful': Smith, *Correspondence of H. G. Wells*, I, p. 250 n.2. On Wells's biography, see also Wells to Mrs Tooley, n.d. [October–November 1908], WT37-1A-B (UIUC); Patrick Parrinder, 'Wells, Herbert George', *Oxford Dictionary of National Biography*, http://www.oxforddnb.com/view/article/36831 [accessed 27 March 2012].

as well as the health issues forcing him to give up teaching and become a professional writer. Descriptors of Bromley as 'a suburb of the damnedest' and his school as 'beastly' – these comments are marked for private information only, not publication – emphasized Wells's desire to get away from his roots. When looking back on his emergence as a writer, Wells was prone to stress the importance of his scientific education, the contributions made to the student journal, the *Science Schools Journal* – that is where 'I really learned to write, so to speak' – and the experience gained working for the educational press, including an 'obscure' journal called *The University Correspondent*.[3] Elsewhere Wells pointed also to the fact that he wrote regularly in the evenings when working as a draper's assistant – 'discussions with myself on religious matters chiefly' – and proved a 'voracious reader', which he represented as 'half the making of a writing-man'.[4]

As a professional writer, Wells opted initially for journalism targeting magazines and newspapers, like the *Pall Mall Gazette* (*P. M. G.*), the *Pall Mall Budget* (*P. M. Budget*) and *The National Observer* (*N. Obs.*), before moving on to fiction. Wells's account establishes how busy he was as a writer with several projects always in progress at any one time. The 'two long stories' mentioned in the note were both completed successfully. Thus, the 'cycling romance' became *The Wheels of Chance* (1896), while 'the big scientific story', entitled *The War of the Worlds*, appeared as a serial and a book in 1897 and 1898 respectively. Despite representing the content as 'facts', there were a few errors. In particular, the publication date of 'The Rediscovery of the Unique' in *Fortnightly*, a landmark event marking the start of his literary career, was 1891, not 1890.[5] Also Wells wrote Newhurst instead of Midhurst.

Whereas he dealt frankly with his health problems in the personal history sent to Richards, Wells omitted any reference to the complex marital issues arising from the rapid breakdown of his marriage, recent divorce and remarriage a few days before sending this letter. Four years earlier, on 29 October 1891, Wells, listed on the marriage certificate as a teacher, married Isabel Mary Wells, his twenty-five-year-old cousin.[6] But he soon realised that the marriage was 'a very great mistake' because of – to quote Wells – 'inalterable' differences in their attitudes and interests, their sexual incompatibility and his reluctance to accept suburban domesticity.[7] Reporting their break-up to his mother, Wells

3. Arthur H. Lawrence, 'The Romance of the Scientist: an interview with Mr H. G. Wells', *The Young Man* 128, August 1897, p. 255.

4. 'A young novelist who has "arrived": A chat with Mr H. G. Wells', *The Sketch Magazine*, 15 September 1897, p. 317.

5. Wells, *Experiment in Autobiography*, I, pp. 223–4.

6. Whereas the actual marriage certificate seen by the author is dated 29 October 1891, Wells claimed in his autobiography that the marriage occurred on 31 October 1891: Wells, *Experiment in Autobiography*, I, p. 337. In fact, writing on 30 October 1891, Wells stated that he had got married the previous day: Wells to Davies, 30 October 1891, Loing, *Wells à l'oeuvre*, p. 408. Following Wells's autobiography, biographies often cite the incorrect date: N. and J. MacKenzie, *The Time Traveller*, p. 88.

7. Wells to Davies, 27 December 1893, Loing, *Wells à l'oeuvre*, p. 409; Wells, *Experiment*

acknowledged that separation was 'almost entirely' his fault, especially as there was also another woman.[8]

During 1892–3 Wells began a relationship with one of his students, Amy Catherine Robbins, who was six years younger than himself. Pointing to his eventual decision to separate from Isabel, Wells claimed that 'I am doing it because I love another woman with all my being, & it seems a hideous thing to me to continue this comfortable life of legal adultery simply because I cannot have the woman I love'.[9] Shortly after Christmas 1893, he left Isabel to live with Amy – Wells affectionately called her 'Jane', this name will be used henceforth, as well as 'Bits' – 'in sin and social rebellion' at lodgings in Camden Town.[10] At first sight, such personal aspects might be deemed irrelevant, but as detailed in this book they impacted upon his writing in varying ways. For example, the need to support his ageing parents as well as his ex-wife and a new partner added to the pressures for literary success, just as Jane was to help Wells's writing by providing much-needed domestic stability alongside active involvement in progressing his writing and managing relations with publishers and agents.

Fearing an early death

By contrast, Wells was far more forthcoming in his personal history about health issues, as evidenced by mention of two haemorrhages, which are symptomatic of tuberculosis, a common cause of illness and death at the time.[11] For the past eight years or so the state of his health had given him serious cause for concern and proved a major determinant upon his mindset, lifestyle, place of residence, career choices and writing. It explained also his recent move from London's polluted environment to Woking, where he arrived in poor health.

While working at Holt Academy in North Wales during 1887, Wells was injured during a game of football, resulting in a crushed kidney and liver damage. Forced to resign his post, he spent a lengthy period convalescing principally at Uppark, a country house near Petersfield where his mother worked as resident housekeeper, and then with friends at Stoke on Trent. Overviewing the parlous

in *Autobiography*, I, pp. 286–7, 300, 360–4; II, pp. 422–3, 426–7. See also Wells to Healey, 11 June 1894, 'Wells, H. G., Letters, Healey Miss 8', *ALS* 1894–8, Harry Ransom Humanities Research Center, University of Texas at Austin, Texas, USA (Ransom).

8. Wells to mother, 8 February 1894, Wells, *Experiment in Autobiography*, I, p. 395.

9. Wells to Davies, 27 December 1893, Loing, *Wells à l'oeuvre*, p. 409.

10. Wells, *Experiment in Autobiography*, I, p. 395; II, p. 462.

11. Parrinder, 'Wells, Herbert George'. On Wells's health, see also Wells to mother [Sarah Wells], n.d. [September 1887], WW29 (UIUC); Wells to Simmons, n.d. [6 September 1887], Smith, *Correspondence of H. G. Wells, I*, pp. 64–5; Wells, *Experiment in Autobiography*, I, pp. 296–8. One of Wells's literary contacts, Stephen Crane, the author of *The Red Badge of Courage* (1895), died in 1900 from tuberculosis aged twenty-eight.

state of his health in November 1887, Wells told friends that he was in effect 'A Wreck'.[12] Wells had been warned by a doctor that he would be 'a confirmed invalid for the rest of my days'. Significantly, in the light of future developments, soon after his footballing accident Wells asserted that 'My only chance now for a living is literature'.[13] Despite hitherto experiencing 'little success' in this sphere, he remained hopeful: 'I think the groove I shall drop into will be cheap noveletteering – Not with my entire approval though; I hanker after essays and criticism – vainly'. In the event, during the late 1880s and early 1890s gradual improvements in his health enabled Wells to complete his degree and teach, but repeated serious bouts of illness reinforced his belief that he was destined for an early death.[14] Thus, in 1893 while convalescing after yet another lung haemorrhage, he expressed fears about seeing 'nothing but a long perspective of relapses to the inevitable end'.[15]

In fact, the 1893 haemorrhage forced him to give up teaching 'for good', since it was now 'outside the range of my possibilities'.[16] Thus, ill health proved instrumental in pushing Wells to pursue his longstanding ambition to become a professional writer seeking to make his mark and to achieve financial security: 'whether I like it or not, I must write for a living now'.[17] Like most aspiring writers, Wells's initial efforts encountered mixed fortunes but, as detailed in the next chapter, he soon established himself as a major new British writer. Certainly, he achieved far more than his initial aspirations, paradoxically in part because the prognosis of an early death led him to write quickly and urgently in order to do as much as he could before he ran out of time. Thus, writing early in 1898, the year in which he was to suffer yet another serious haemorrhage, his somewhat curtailed life expectancy led him to anticipate only 'a dozen good novels at the utmost between me and the grave'.[18] For Patrick Parrinder, such fears impacted heavily upon Wells's writing, especially as they 'quickened his imagination, as is clear from the apocalyptic and visionary starkness of his early scientific romances'.[19]

One further consequence of Wells's second haemorrhage was an urgent need 'to move out of town to some more open and healthy situation'.[20] In August 1893 Wells and Isabel moved from Wandsworth, from where he had commuted daily to the University Correspondence College in central London, to a house with a 'pretty view' in the fresher air of Sutton, where they were 'only about twenty

12. Wells to Davies, n.d. [Autumn 1887], Wells to A. T. Simmons, [December 1887], Smith, *Correspondence of H. G. Wells, I*, pp. 66, 73; Wells, *Wells in Love*, p. 27.

13. Wells to Davies, n.d. [Autumn 1887], Smith, *Correspondence of H. G. Wells, I*, p. 66.

14. Wells, *Experiment in Autobiography*, I, pp. 298–302.

15. Wells to Healey, n.d. [June 1893], Smith, *Correspondence of H. G. Wells, I*, p. 193.

16. Wells, *Experiment in Autobiography*, I, p. 370.

17. Wells to Miss Robbins, n.d. [22 May 1893], Smith, *Correspondence of H. G. Wells, I*, p. 191.

18. Wells to Healey, n.d. [4 January 1898], Wells, H. G. Letters Healey, Miss 8 *ALS* 1894–8 (Ransom).

19. Parrinder, 'Wells, Herbert George'.

20. Wells, *Experiment in Autobiography*, I, p. 370.

minutes' walk from the downs': 'we can go by Banstead and Epsom to Dorking over them all the way'.[21] In the event, the breakdown of his marriage and subsequent co-habitation with Jane resulted in Wells's return to Camden Town during the final days of 1893. However, in 1894 continuing poor health led a doctor to advise Wells to spend the summer in the 'fresh air' at 'country lodgings': 'London got a bit too much for me some weeks ago'.[22] The choice of Sevenoaks saw Wells return to Kent, the county of his birth. At one time, Wells and Jane thought of making the move to Sevenoaks permanent, but the moral qualms of their landlady – her strong disapproval of their lack of marriage lines was compounded by complaints about Wells's use of excessive quantities of lamp-oil when writing late at night – resulted in their return to Camden Town. Even so, the stay at Sevenoaks enabled him to get *The Time Machine* into shape ready for publication.[23] In the event, Wells's return to London proved relatively brief, since in May 1895 the serious deterioration in his health resulted in yet another move to the country.

Escaping from London's fogs

London might have been a great city, the hub of a world power and a vast empire, but during the late nineteenth century it was also a challenging place to live, especially for those like Wells and Jane in poor health. London was crowded, noisy, dirty, smoky, smelly and foggy. Proving increasingly frequent during the Victorian period, London's 'Great Stinking Fogs', a blend of smoke and fog resulting from the domestic and industrial use of coal, peaked in the 1890s when – to quote Arthur Symons, the poet and magazine editor, 'you cannot see a yard beyond your feet'.[24] For Symons, there was 'nothing in the world quite like a London fog ... The grime blackens your face, your eyes smart, your throat is choked with dust. You breathe black foulness and it enters you and contaminates you'.[25] In effect, fog created a black city.[26] Nor were things much better indoors, as recorded in 1886 by a *Punch* cartoon, entitled 'The Winter Art Exhibitions', depicting a fog-bound art gallery in which critics viewed paintings largely indistinguishable through

21. Wells to Davies, 4 August 1893, Wells to Fred Wells, n.d. [August 1893], Smith, *Correspondence of H. G. Wells*, I, pp. 194, 196; Wells to Freddie, n.d. [November 1893], Wells, *Experiment in Autobiography*, I, p. 393. Sutton and the North Downs featured in the 1893 article 'Out Banstead Way by An Amateur Nature Lover' discussed in Chapter 2.

22. Wells, *Experiment in Autobiography*, II, p. 512; Wells to Healey, 16 July 1894, Wells to his father, 10 August 1894, Smith, *The Correspondence of H. G. Wells*, I, pp. 218–19.

23. H. G. Wells, *The Time Machine: An Invention* (New York: Random House, 1931), pp. vii–viii; Ruddick, 'Introduction', p. 27.

24. Arthur Symons, *London: A Book of Aspects* (Minneapolis, MN: Private Printing, 1909), p. 62; Peter Brimblecombe, *The Big Smoke: A History of Air Pollution in London since Medieval Times* (London: Routledge, 2011), pp. 110–12.

25. Symons, *London*, pp. 63–4.

26. Flanders, *The Victorian City*, p. 204.

the gloom.[27] Eventually in 1901 the London County Council commissioned a Meteorological Council inquiry to help – to quote *Nature* – 'deliver London from its insidious enemy'.[28]

Writing during the early 1850s Thomas Miller devoted one whole chapter of *Picturesque Sketches of London* to 'London Fog': 'Such of our readers as have never been in London in November can scarcely imagine what it is to grope their way through a downright thorough London fog. It is something like being imbedded in a dilution of yellow peas-pudding, just thick enough to get through it without being wholly choked or completely suffocated'.[29] The metropolis's 'blackness' was captured vividly by Henry James, who became one of Wells's literary acquaintances. In 'London at Midsummer' (1877), he told the story of a voyage along the Thames from Westminster Bridge to Greenwich on a 'grimy sixpenny steamer' belching a 'carboniferous shower' from its funnel: 'For miles and miles you see nothing but the sooty backs of warehouses, or perhaps they are the sooty fronts ... A damp-looking, dirty blackness is the universal tone. The river is almost black, and is covered with black barges; above the black housetops, from among the far-stretching docks and basins, rises a dusky wilderness of masts'.[30]

Naturally, fog's transformation of the cityscape featured prominently in fiction, such as to set the scene, develop the plot and so on, most notably in the writings of Charles Dickens, perhaps 'the greatest recorder the London streets has ever known'.[31] Thus, *Bleak House* (1852–3) opened with a descriptive section set in central London: 'Fog everywhere. Fog up the river, where it flows among green aits and meadows; fog down the river, where it rolls defiled among the tiers of shipping and the waterside pollutions of a great (and dirty) city'.[32] Dickens's mention of the way the 'rusty-black' fog irritated 'the eyes and throats of ancient Greenwich pensioners, wheezing by the firesides' was echoed in *Our Mutual Friend* (1864–5):

> It was a foggy day in London, and the fog was heavy and dark. Animate London, with smarting eyes and irritated lungs, was blinking, wheezing, and choking; inanimate London was a sooty spectre, divided in purpose between being visible and invisible, and so being wholly neither ... From any point of the high ridge of land northward, it might have been discerned that the loftiest buildings made an occasional struggle to get their heads above the foggy sea.[33]

27. 'The Winter Art Exhibitions', *Punch*, 4 December 1886, p. 274; 'A Rondel in the Fog', *Punch*, 4 December 1886, p. 273.

28. W. N. Shaw, 'The London Fog Inquiry', *Nature* 64 (31 October 1901): 649–50; 'London Fog Inquiry, 1901–02', *Nature* 67 (9 April 1903): 548–9.

29. Thomas Miller, *Picturesque Sketches of London: Past and Present* (London: Office of the National Illustrated Library, 1852), pp. 243–8.

30. Henry James, *Portraits of Places* (Boston, MA: James R. Osgood, 1883), pp. 219–20.

31. Flanders, *The Victorian City*, pp. 203–5.

32. Charles Dickens, *Bleak House* (London: Vintage, 2008), p. 1.

33. Charles Dickens, *Our Mutual Friend* (London: Vintage, 2011), p. 420.

Arthur Conan Doyle was another author using fog to create the appropriate atmosphere for his Sherlock Holmes's stories, while Morley Roberts made fog the cause of London's destruction in an apocalyptic essay published in *The Strand* in 1908.[34]

As one article in *Nature* pointed out millions of people living in the capital were well aware of fog's 'intolerable prevalence' in their locality.[35] In particular, for London's residents, particularly those like Wells and Jane suffering from respiratory complaints, fog, a prime indicator of atmospheric impurities and poor air quality, proved a serious health issue. The problem was even worse for people living near railway lines, such as those passing through Camden Town to Euston, King's Cross and St. Pancras stations. When living in Fitzroy Road between 1889 and 1891 Wells faced problems arising from the steam trains rushing repeatedly past the end of the road to and from Euston as well as the engines waiting to use the coaling station at Chalk Farm night and day 'pouring smoke from their funnels into the acrid air above them'.[36] Camden Shed, near where locomotives waited to blow off their surplus steam and smoke at the end of a journey, stood at one end of Fitzroy Road: 'As a result the atmosphere in the vicinity was often similar to that on a main line station platform, and the dirt which collected everywhere had to be encountered to be believed'.[37] Surrounding houses were bathed in smoke for much of the day, while a sooty corrosive dust covered everything indoors.

Reportedly, Wells complained about the engine smoke, thick sooty layers and noise when he lived in Fitzroy Road, an experience perhaps combining with fog to inspire another literary invention, the Martians's poisonous black vapour and Wells's descriptions in *The War of the Worlds* of views across the metropolis, such as from Putney Hill: 'London was black' (II.7: 271/161). Nor did Wells's lodgings in Mornington Place and Mornington Road offer a healthier environment, since both streets were very close to mainline rail tracks running into and out of Euston Station. Exploring Wells's links with Camden Town, Christopher Rolfe suggested that the 'Martian fighting machines, described by one refugee from Surrey as 'boilers on stilts' (I.14: 128/79–80), were inspired by images of steam engines belching fire and sooty smoke rushing past Wells's lodgings all day.[38]

To some extent, day trips to open parkland in Barnes, Kew, Kingston upon Thames and Richmond upon Thames offered Londoners one way of alleviating conditions; indeed, in *The War of the Worlds* Wells described such places as providing 'the South-Western "lungs"' (I.14: 123/76). As one contributor apprised

34. Nicholas Freeman, *Conceiving the City: London, Literature and Art, 1870–1914* (Oxford: Oxford University Press, 2007), pp. 90–3.

35. Shaw, 'London Fog Inquiry', pp. 649–50.

36. David Thomson, *In Camden Town* (London: Hutchinson, 1983), p. 20.

37. Caroline Ramsden, *A View from Primrose Hill: The Memoirs of Caroline Ramsden* (London: Hutchinson Benham, 1984), p. 25.

38. Christopher Rolfe, 'From Camden Town to Primrose Hill', *Camden History Review* 10 (1982): 4.

readers of the *Illustrated London News*, Surrey's countryside offered much to London's cyclists and walkers prepared to take a brief train ride: 'Many a pleasant and healthful saunter can be taken over elevated downs and breezy commons, or along umbrageous lanes and by the side of silver streams'.[39] Visitors to such places as Guildford, Reigate or Woking, the author claimed, 'would secure pure air and water, healthy food, glorious scenery, and that recuperative restfulness which Dame Nature alone can furbish'. In this vein, during 1897 *The Woking Mail* pointed to the 1896 annual report of Surrey's medical officer of health recording low mortality rates and declining incidence of consumption as 'strong testimony' for the county's role as 'a Health Resort'.[40]

Alternatively, a more radical approach was to move permanently to the surrounding countryside, as highlighted by 'The Hilltop Writers' – they included Grant Allen, Conan Doyle and Richard Le Gallienne – living in and around Haslemere and Hindhead in Surrey.[41] For example, in 1895 Conan Doyle decided to build a house to be called 'Undershaw' at Hindhead to alleviate the ill-health of his wife Touie:

> I met Grant Allen at luncheon, and he told me that he had also suffered from consumption and that he had found his salvation in the soil and air of Hindhead in Surrey. It was quite a new idea to me that we might actually live with impunity in England once more, and it was a pleasant thought after resigning oneself to a life which was unnatural to both of us at foreign health resorts.[42]

Conan Doyle informed his mother about the appeal of an area often described as 'Little Switzerland':

> It is not merely Grant Allen's case which gives us hopes that the place will suit Touie, but it is because its height, its dryness, its sandy soil, its fir trees, and its shelter from all bitter winds present the conditions which all agree to be best in the treatment of phthisis [tuberculosis]. If we could have ordered Nature to construct a spot for us we could not have hit upon anything more perfect.[43]

39. W. H. S. A., 'Rambles in Surrey', *Illustrated London News*, XCV (2622), 20 July 1889, p. 92.

40. 'Surrey as a Health resort', *The Woking Mail*, 29 May 1897, p. 6.

41. W. R. Trotter, *The Hilltop Writers: A Victorian Colony Among the Surrey Hills* (Headley Down: John Owen Smith, 2003), pp. 43–7; Wells to Grant Allen, n.d. [1896], Smith, *The Correspondence of H. G. Wells, I*, p. 274; Richards, *Memories of a Misspent Youth*, p. 329–31; Wells, *Experiment in Autobiography*, II, p. 552.

42. Arthur Conan Doyle, *Memories and Adventures* (Boston MA: Little, Brown, 1924), p. 121.

43. Conan Doyle to Mary, 25 May 1895, in Jon Lellenberg, Daniel Stashower and Charles Foley (eds), *Arthur Conan Doyle: A Life in Letters* (New York: Penguin Press, 2007), pp. 352–3. Touie died in 1906.

During the same year Wells, albeit only moving out as far as Woking, followed Doyle in deciding to leave London for Surrey's countryside.

Wells and cyclomania

When writing his personal history for Grant Allen, Wells proudly admitted that 'I am a cyclist'. In this vein, when looking back from the early 1930s, Wells stressed how different he was from 'the H. G. Wells of 1896, who I find from a photograph wore side whiskers and a cascade mustache and rode about the countryside on a bicycle' (Figure 4.2).[44] Indeed, during 1895–6 Wells is often represented as taking up cycling for the first time, a point reinforced by his frequent assertions to the effect that he was now a cyclist and the fact that the narrator in *The War of the Worlds* – for many commentators, the narrator is Wells – was learning to ride a bicycle (I.1: 1011/12). Moreover, during this period Wells wrote *The Wheels of Chance*, a cycling novel in which Hoopdriver, the central character, meets a clergyman at Ringwood:

> "I myself am a cyclist," said the clergyman, descending suddenly upon Mr Hoopdriver. "We are all cyclists nowadays," with a broad smile.
> "Indeed!" said Mr Hoopdriver.[45]

At the time it was easy to believe that all Britons, not excluding Wells, had just become cyclists as part of the so-called 'cycling craze' sweeping through Britain, continental Europe and the USA following the advent of the 'safety bicycle' in place of high wheelers like the Penny Farthing.[46]

However, Wells's correspondence and publications provides a rather different impression regarding his cycling history. For example, during the late 1880s he conducted a week-long cycling tour of Surrey and Sussex visiting such places as Arundel, Guildford and Reigate.[47] In October 1891 Wells published an account of a summer cycle ride made with his brother passing through Surrey from Petersfield to Crawley.[48] Surrey offered cyclists, especially those riding out from

44. Wells, 'H. G. Wells', *Living Philosophies*, p. 81.

45. H. G. Wells, *The Wheels of Chance & The Time Machine* (London: J. M. Dent, 1935), p. 173.

46. 'Editorial: The Bicycle as a Social Force', *The Times*, 15 August 1898, p. 7; David Rubinstein, 'Cycling in the 1890s', *Victorian Studies* 21 (1) (1977): 47–71. The 'cycling craze' figured prominently in the British media. Examples include 'The Cycling Craze', *Hampshire Telegraph and Sussex Chronicle* (Portsmouth), 23 November 1895, p. 12, 15 February 1896, p. 12; 'The Cycling Craze', *The Sheffield and Rotherham Independent* (Sheffield), 25 March 1896, p. 6; 'The Cycling Craze', *Western Mail* (Cardiff), 27 February 1897, p. 7.

47. Wells to Healey, n.d. [1888–9?], Smith, *Correspondence of H. G. Wells, I*, p. 116.

48. H. G. Wells, 'Specimen Day (from a holiday itinerary)', *Science Schools Journal* (October 1891): 17–20; Sherborne, *H. G. Wells*, p. 79.

Figure 4.2 H. G. Wells in 1895.

Source: H. G. Wells, *Experiment in Autobiography, II* (1934), p. 432.

the metropolis, numerous opportunities for day trips and tours. Located on the well surfaced London to Portsmouth road some six miles south east of Woking, Ripley established itself as the Mecca for cyclists. Like many fellow cyclists, Wells signed the visitors' book of Ripley's 'Anchor Hotel'.[49] In 1892 Wells, having recently joined the *Cyclists' Touring Club*, announced that the Wells had 'become tricycle riders of the most prominent type' undertaking 'several delightful journeys' from their home at Wandsworth to such places as Cheam, Crawley and Reigate.[50] Then in May 1894 Wells published 'On a Tricycle: Cycling and the higher criticism' in the *Pall Mall Gazette*.[51] A short story called 'A Perfect Gentleman on Wheels' narrated a cycle ride through Surrey commencing at Sutton, where Wells lived in 1893, to Brighton.[52] Within this context, it seems that in 1895, when announcing that he was now a cyclist in a manner encouraging the impression that he was taking up the activity for the first time, Wells was in fact recording his switch from a tricycle to the 'safety bicycle' and hence his recent mastery of 'the art of wheeling' on two wheels.[53] A lady-front tandem bicycle enabled Wells and Jane to continue sharing their cycling journeys (Figures 4.3–4.4).[54]

Unsurprisingly, the bicycle played a significant role in Wells's lifestyle. Certainly Wells took pride in telling friends and acquaintances that he was playing his part in what *The Bookman* depicted as 'cyclomania'.[55] For Wells, cycling proved an essential mode of transport as well as a leisure activity highly beneficial to his

49. The Anchor Hotel, Cyclists Book, 1887, entry no. 67, 16 January 1887, entry no. 769, 29 March 1887, SHC 7597/8, Surrey History Centre, Woking, Surrey (SHC); Les Bowerman, 'Early Cycling on the Surrey Roads with particular reference to the "Ripley Road"', *Surrey History* III (4) (1987): 157–60.

50. Wells to Healey, 2 May 1892, Wells to Fred, 15 May 1892, Smith, *The Correspondence of H. G. Wells*, I, p. 182–3; Smith, *The Correspondence of H. G. Wells*, I, p. 182. The Wells's Wandsworth residence had a tricycle house: Wells to Davies, 4 August 1893, Smith, *Correspondence of H. G. Wells*, I, p. 194.

51. H. G. Wells, 'On a Tricycle: Cycling and the higher criticism', *Pall Mall Gazette*, 18 May 1894. This story appeared subsequently in *Select Conversations with an Uncle* (1895).

52. H. G. Wells, 'A Perfect Gentleman on Wheels', *Woman at Home*, April 1897, pp. 673–81. The story was re-published in both the *New York Daily Tribune* on 16 May 1897 and Jerome K. Jerome et al. (ed.), *The Humours of Cycling: Stories and Pictures* (London: James Bowden, 1897), pp. 5–14.

53. Wells, *Experiment in Autobiography*, II, p. 543; Wells to Richards, 6 November 1895, Smith, *The Correspondence of H. G. Wells*, I, p. 250; Wells to Fred Wells, 24 January 1896, Smith, *The Correspondence of H. G. Wells*, I, p. 258. Simon James, the author of a study of Wells and cycling, agrees that this seems the most likely explanation for the seemingly contradictory evidence: Simon James to the author, 21 March 2013. Michael Sherborne, Wells's biographer, reaffirmed that prior to the mid-1890s Wells was a 'tricycle-fiend': Michael Sherborne to the author, 22 March 2013.

54. Wells, *Experiment in Autobiography*, II, pp. 543–6.

55. 'The Wheels of Chance', *The Bookman* 11 (64) (January 1897): 124.

Figure 4.3 Wells and Jane cycling at Woking, 1895.

Source: H.G. Wells, *Experiment in Autobiography, II* (1934), p.536.

health and wellbeing as a writer, as he indicated when replying to one interviewer who asked him why he cycled: 'Do you think it a dignified thing for an author to do?':

'It's a most delightful exercise,' Mr Wells says rather severely. 'The cycle is one of the great blessings which the nineteenth century has brought us. Its value is simply inestimable to nervous men, and I think all writers are more or less troubled with nerves. There's no time to think of anything when you are on the machine. It's all nonsense for people to say that they think out stories and things when they are cycling. It is just the simple fact that you are travelling so rapidly, and – however expert you may be – have to mind what you are doing, which drives away all possibility of thinking of work, and that is the joy of it. All the cobwebs get brushed away from the brain, and you return to your work really refreshed.'[56]

But cycling was far from easy, as Wells recorded after a fifty-mile round trip from Woking to Liss. Apart from fog, the so-called roads were not only badly rutted but

56. Lawrence, 'Romance of the Scientist', p. 256. See also 'A young novelist who has "arrived"'.

Figure 4.4 Picshua: 'Cycling Trip' from Woking, July 1895. Wells's picshua shows the
  Wells going off for a cycling trip, July 1895

Source: H. G. Wells, *Experiment in Autobiography, II* (1934), p. 544.

covered with flints so that he arrived home with a splitting headache.[57] Despite
claiming that when cycling it was impossible to think about work, cycling was
linked closely to his thinking, research and writing. Indeed, he was instrumental
in giving cycling a literary dimension. Thus, the bicycle became not only a writing
tool, a useful way of conducting research for ongoing and future projects, most
notably about their geography, but also a literary device, something to use in his
writing for dramatic or comic effect. For Ruddick, *The Time Machine*, recorded as

---

57. Wells to Simmons, n.d. [1895], Smith, *Correspondence of H. G. Wells, I*, p. 244.

having a saddle, levers and bars perhaps resembling handlebars, might be likened to a tricycle enabling riders to travel through time.[58]

Writing *The Wheels of Chance* (1896) enabled Wells to indulge his love of cycling, draw the activity into the world of literature and exploit cyclomania to sell books. *The Wheels of Chance* drew heavily upon Wells's cycling escapades throughout Surrey and beyond. As Wells acknowledged when referring to 'the worthy Hoopdriver', the book's hero, 'I rode wherever Mr Hoopdriver rode in that story'.[59] Indeed, following one fall, 'I wrote down a description of the state of my legs which became the opening chapter of the *Wheels of Chance*'. Hoopdriver was Wells. Like Wells, he had an 'intensely undesirable life' of servitude as an apprentice draper.[60] Like Wells, Hoopdriver fantasized about becoming an author. Like Wells, Hoopdriver embarked on an ambitious cycling holiday well away from the everyday dull routine of the drapery counter. Moreover, the story reaffirmed Wells's strong sense of place, with Hoopdriver discovering and describing 'charming little' places *en route* to the coast.[61] In turn, his use of real places readily traceable by readers on a map met what *The Bookman* represented as the present-day demand of readers for 'local colour' and delightful pastoral visions.[62] Riding to the New Forest, Hoopdriver gained a greater sense of freedom from dreary everyday life and work. Despite returning to the dull routine of the drapery emporium, Hoopdriver's mindset had been transformed by experiencing another world offering alternative possibilities.

Having helped Wells when planning, researching and writing the geography of *The War of the Worlds*, cycling proved a favoured leisure pursuit while writing the actual story in which the bicycle had a not insignificant place. Wells highlighted the fact that the story's narrator shared his enthusiasm for cycling – 'For my own part, I was much occupied in learning to ride the bicycle' (I.1: 10-11/12) – perhaps having moved on from one of those 'old fashioned tricycles' (I.14: 128/79). The bicycle, though 'the swiftest thing upon the roads in those days', was employed also to highlight the advanced nature of the Martians (II.2: 214/129).[63] Descriptions of the sacking of a cycle shop (I.16: 152/93), the use of cycles to flee London (I.16: 152/93) and images of smashed cycles (II.1: 192/117), played their part in illuminating the destruction and panic resulting from the Martian invasion. Bicycles were of course an essential part of the everyday scene (II.10: 302/180), as evidenced by those used by some members of the crowd viewing the Martian cylinder on Horsell Common (I.3: 19–22/17–18).

58. Ruddick, 'Introduction', p. 24.

59. Wells, *Experiment in Autobiography*, II, p. 543; Wells to Healey n.d. [November 1896], Loing, *Wells à l'oeuvre*, p. 433.

60. Wells, *Experiment in Autobiography*, I, p. 116, pp. 146 *et seq.*

61. Wells, *The Wheels of Chance*, p. 31

62. 'The Wheels of Chance', *The Bookman*, p. 124.

63. Wells, *Experiment in Autobiography*, II, p. 543.

The demand for new writers

Notwithstanding the present-day tendency to associate Wells's stay in Woking with the glittering success of *The War of the Worlds*, it is vital to introduce a sense of perspective. When he took up residence in the town in 1895, Wells, aged twenty-eight, was still making his way, or rather struggling to make a living, as a new young writer. Indeed, looking back in 1931, Wells represented *The Time Machine* as 'the work of an inexperienced writer': 'It seems a very undergraduate performance to its now mature writer'.[64] Nevertheless, during 1895 there were strong indications that his career as a professional writer was beginning to take off, even if serious question marks remained still about his health and life expectancy.

In retrospect, his arrival in Woking can be viewed as occurring at the very moment when he was on the brink of literary success arising from the recent serialization of *The Time Machine* in *The New Review* (January–May 1895) and its impending publication as a book in both London and New York. Encouraged by the success of its serialization, Wells possessed confidence that his first scientific romance would do well as a book, but the story's innovatory nature meant that success could not be taken for granted. Nor should we forget that he was still relatively unknown, as emphasized shortly after *The Time Machine*'s publication by *The Bookman*'s inclusion of Wells in its prestigious series about 'New Writers'. The article illuminated also the impact of health upon his career as a writer:

> Mr H. G. Wells is a comparatively new addition to the ranks of those who live by imaginative writing. Until two years ago he had published nothing except for a few contributions to the educational papers, one short article in the *Fortnightly Review*, some scientific essays, and a concise cram-book in Biology for the London University science examinations. At that time he had abandoned any literary ambitions he may have entertained, and was almost wholly engaged in educational work, and, but for the accident of a violent haemorrhage from the lungs, might still be so engaged. But his lung collapse rendered a more sedentary employment imperative, and he turned to journalism. What he regarded as an overwhelming misfortune proved in the end to be a really very good thing for him.[65]

By implication, if Wells had died in, say, 1893 or 1894, as seemed possible, today he would prove an unknown forgotten writer.

Wells's recognition as a successful young writer, though reflecting his own skills and abilities, was the product also of publishing trends during the mid-1890s, especially the rising demand for new writers and the proliferation of alternative publication possibilities. The period saw the emergence of a new reading public resulting from reforms in the wake of the 1870 Education Act, increased leisure and the rise of public libraries. Furthermore, an explosion of reading materials was facilitated by advances in the printing industry – these included the advent of

---

64. Wells, *The Time Machine* (1931), pp. vii, xi.
65. 'New Writers: Mr H. G. Wells', *The Bookman* 8 (47) (August 1895), pp. 134–5.

cheaper paper and faster typesetting – and publication formats as less expensive single volume books replaced costly three-deckers.[66] Traditionally the purchasing power wielded by Mudie's and other private circulating libraries meant that such three-volume books tended to be the standard format for fiction, especially as such books, normally priced at £1 11/6d (£1.65p), were well beyond the pocket of most people.

However, during the mid-1890s several publishers, especially newcomers like William Heinemann, began to revolutionize the book trade by publishing six shilling (£0.30) single-volume novels targeted at the expanding network of public libraries and the growing middle-class readership.[67] Heinemann, who published Wells's *The Island of Dr Moreau* and *The War of the Worlds* as six shilling novels, asserted that, 'I believe greatly in the single-volume form of publication for popular fiction'.[68] Sales of 400,000 for Hall Caine's *The Manxman*, published by Heinemann as a six shilling book in July 1894, strengthened the case for change, so that by July 1896 *The Bookman* was reporting the 'marvellous' output of six shilling novels – during one week some fifty titles appeared – and the fact that many had 'a good sale'.[69] Cheaper editions soon followed at 3/6d (£0.175) or less, although selected titles were first published at a lower price. For example, in 1895 Heinemann, treating the book as too short for a six shilling novel, priced *The Time Machine* at 2/6d (£0.125) and 1/6d (£0.075) for the cloth and paper versions respectively.

Apart from raising questions about the case for the continued serialization of novels in magazines, a relic of the days when fiction was obtainable initially only in three-volume form, the decline of three-deckers has been interpreted as beneficial for the emergence of what came to be depicted as science fiction.[70] For George Locke, 'the three-decker was not a good medium for the genre', given the standard requirement for 150,000–200,000 words and the modest word length – generally speaking this ranged from 32,400 for *The Time Machine* to 60,000 for *The War of the Worlds* – characteristic of Wells's scientific romances: 'No longer did a novelist desirous of seeing his work in hard covers have to write to a length unsuited to his theme'.[71]

---

66. George Locke, 'Wells in three volumes?: A sketch of British publishing in the 19th Century', *Science Fiction Studies* 3 (3) (1976): 285–6; Guinevere L. Griest, *Mudie's Circulating Library and the Victorian Novel* (Bloomington, IN: Indiana University Press, 1970), pp. 156–202.

67. St. John, *William Heinemann*, pp. 26–9; Troy J. Bassett, 'The Production of Three-Volume Novels, 1863–1897', *Papers of the Bibliographical Society of America* 102 (1) (2008): 61–75.

68. Quoted, St. John, *William Heinemann*, p. 28; Griest, *Mudie's Circulating Library*, pp. 69, 202, 208.

69. 'English Letter, London, April 20 to May 23, 1896', *The Bookman* (USA), III (5) (July 1896): 471.

70. C. K. S., 'A Literary Letter', *Illustrated London News* CXII (3064), 8 January 1898, p. 50.

71. Locke, 'Wells in three volumes?', pp. 283–4. Of course, today science fiction books frequently push well over 100,000 words.

In *The War of the Worlds* Wells acknowledged 'the abundance and enter-prise' (1.1: 10/12) of the contemporary press when narrating the media response to the Martian landing in Woking. During the mid-late 1890s existing newspapers grew, new newspapers like *The Daily Mail* (1896) appeared, weekly and monthly magazines were launched or revamped and entrepreneurs, like Alfred Harmsworth, George Newnes and Arthur Pearson, made their name and fortunes. Unsurprisingly, there was a growing demand for new writers. Nor were such trends confined to Britain, as highlighted by developments across both the Channel and the Atlantic, as well as those in the sphere of translating English language publications. As David Smith commented, 'This was the world in which H. G. Wells hoped to succeed. He began early to throw his material into the literary lion's den'.[72] For Wells, networking with editors and publishers was vital in order not only to secure alternative outlets for his writings but also to exploit well-known names prepared to endorse his talent as an emerging writer. Frequently, the initial contact involved reviewing books anonymously, but then this was used as a foundation for moving on to review under one's own name or to be commis-sioned to write short stories and articles. Key targets included Frank Harris, editor of the *Saturday Review* and William Ernest Henley.

Perhaps the greatest boost to Wells's career derived from the support of Henley. During the late 1880s and early 1890s Henley, the editor of such magazines as *London*, the *Magazine of Art*, *The National Observer* and *The New Review*, was a powerful figure in London's literary circles possessing a global reputation as a – to quote *The Bookman* – 'vigorous stimulant of seedling authors'.[73] As Le Gallienne remarked, Wells was a key member of Henley's 'band of brilliant young literary swordsmen'.[74] Indeed, Henley's serialization of *The Time Machine* was part of the reason why in April 1896 *The New York Times* stated that 'no one who desires to keep in touch with the literary London of his day can afford to miss seeing' *The New Review*.[75]

Apart from Wells, over time Henley's 'band' included Kenneth Grahame, Rudyard Kipling, George Bernard Shaw, Robert Louis Stevenson and W. B. Yeats. As Ernest Mehew observed:

> Henley's editorship has become something of a legend. He had a gift for finding and encouraging new talent and gathered round him a group of what were called his Young Men – nicknamed the 'Henley regatta' by Max Beerbohm ... – who were a little in awe of him. He maintained firm editorial control and imposed his own style and opinions throughout by ruthlessly revising contributions.[76]

72. Smith, *H. G. Wells: Desperately Mortal*, pp. 29, 54–5.

73. 'Chronicle and Comment', *The Bookman* (USA) III (4) (June 1896): 293.

74. Richard Le Gallienne, *The Romantic '90s* (London: Robin Clark, 1993), p. 79.

75. Harold Frederic, 'Henley's art as editor', *The New York Times*, 5 April 1896.

76. Ernest Mehew, 'Henley, William Ernest (1849–1903)', *Oxford Dictionary of National Biography*, Oxford University Press, May 2006, http://www.oxforddnb.com/view/article/33817 [accessed 27 March 2012]; Wells, *Experiment in Autobiography*, II, pp. 532–3;

Recalling that Henley 'made us feel always our importance', Yeats highlighted the manner in which Henley's endorsement and editorial skills advanced his literary career: 'No man among us could do good work, or show the promise of it, and lack his praise ... Henley got the best out of us all, because he made us accept him as our judge and we knew his judgment could neither sleep, nor be softened, nor changed, nor turned aside'.[77] In brief, Henley's 'imprimatur was not only a widely accepted certificate of merit ... it was also an augury of success'.[78]

Nor was recognition of Henley's literary reputation confined to Britain. Writing in *The New York Times* in April 1896, Harold Frederic apprised an American audience about how publications edited by Henley acted as a 'hospitable kinder-garten and nursery for Mr Henley's young men': 'To catalogue the young men whom during these years Henley gathered about him and profoundly influenced would be to recite half the well-known names of the younger writing corps in England'.[79] Among these writers 'still called young' but already well known in the USA, Frederic highlighted Wells. Indeed, Wells recorded that 'Henley, who has helped so many men, was my great helper'.[80] In 1901 Wells, having viewed William Nicholson's recently completed portrait of him as 'A Man of Letters', wrote to Henley in exaggerated terms as someone who would be 'doubly Immortal' and 'shine' in any gallery.[81] Apart from commissioning the serialization of *The Time Machine* for *The New Review* and advising on the text, Henley recommended Wells to Heinemann, who published his first two scientific romances as well as *The War of the Worlds*.

In addition, Wells exploited existing contacts, most notably Richard Gregory, a fellow student and close personal friend with whom he had co-authored a textbook on *Honours Physiography* (1893). In 1893 Gregory became assistant editor of Macmillan's science journal, *Nature* and provided space for Wells's occasional contributions about popularizing science and science education, as well as for reviews of Wells's books, even reviewing some himself. Wells proved

'New Writers', p. 134; Sir John Squire, 'An "unconquerable soul": "W. E. Henley" by John Connell', *Illustrated London News* 215 (5762) (24 September 1949): 452; Grant Richards, *Memories of a Misspent Youth*, p. 158. Reportedly Robert Louis Stevenson based *Treasure Island*'s Long John Silver on Henley, who had worn a wooden leg since the late 1860s. The attempts of Henley's young daughter, Margaret, to refer to J. M. Barrie as her 'friendy' – in fact, it came out as "fwendy-wendy" – allegedly resulted in his use of the name Wendy in *Peter Pan* (1904).

77. W. B. Yeats, *Autobiographies* (London: Macmillan, 1955), p. 128.

78. Yug Mohit Chaudhry, *Yeats, the Irish Revival and the Politics of Print* (Cork: Cork University Press, 2001), p. 152.

79. Frederic, 'Henley's art as editor'.

80. Lawrence, 'The Romance of the Scientist', p. 255.

81. Wells to Henley, 31 October 1901, in John Connell, *W. E. Henley* (London: Constable, 1949), p. 362. Delighted by the letter, Henley sent a signed print of the portrait to Wells, who hung it in his study at Spade House, Folkestone, as visible in Wells, *Experiment in Autobiography*, II, pp. 652–3.

also a willing interviewee and gave considerable time – reportedly in one case the visit lasted seven hours – to interviewers.[82]

Conclusion

During the course of a press interview conducted during late 1895, Wells claimed that 'I am simply a storyteller who happens to be a student of science. If a man writes the best that is in him, he cannot help some of his serious speculations appearing.'[83] In Wells's case, the mid-1890s saw the most intensive period of writing in his whole literary career, including the publication of his first scientific romances. Within a short space of time his career and reputation as a writer within and outside Britain was transformed. In October 1895 the American edition of the *Review of Reviews* reported that *The Time Machine* had proved a best-seller:

> Mr Wells' rise into popularity has been by leaps and bounds. It is not too many months since the *Pall Mall Budget* published his first short stories (stories of so fresh and absorbing a character that I am glad to see that Messrs. Methuen announce their collection in book form [*The Stolen Bacillus and other incidents*], and now "The Time Machine" is the talk of the town.[84]

Soon afterwards, Picaroon, another American reviewer, informed his readers that the literary world was waking up 'to the fact that Mr Wells was a new force in English literature':

> WHEN I say that Mr Wells is the most notable of the younger English writers, and more notable than a good many of the older ones, I am ready to make good my words. There is no man in whom I have greater literary faith; no man from whom better work may be expected. To him more than to anyone else do I look for the cleansing of the English novel, for the effective damming of that stream of crude philosophy and cheap sentiment which has deluged English literature and drama for the last five years. It seems to me that Mr Wells has it in him to write a really great novel; and I would not willingly risk my critical reputation by saying as much for any other writer.[85]

As Picaroon advised, 'He is a man to keep your eye on'.

82. 'A young novelist who has "arrived"'.
83. Smith, 'A chat with the author', p. 8.
84. 'The New Books. Notes from Our London Correspondent', *Review of Reviews* (New York) XII (October 1895): 496–8.
85. Picaroon, 'Portrait of Mr H. G. Wells', *The Chap-Book* (Chicago) 5 (1) (May 1896): 366, 370, 374.

Chapter 5

STRUGGLING FOR RECOGNITION AS A
NEW WRITER

Having decided to become a professional writer, Wells saw himself initially as more of a journalist than an author – this was the occupation recorded on his marriage certificate in October 1895. Inevitably, he experienced the usual ups-and-downs faced by any aspiring writer alongside widespread fluctuations in his earnings. Even so, for Wells, the start of 1895, though characterized by yet another pressing lack of ready cash as well as a recurrence of his longstanding health problems, offered the promise of better things, given the forthcoming British serialization of *The Time Machine* followed by its appearance as a book in both Britain and the USA, plus the publication of two collections of short stories. Expressing optimism about the future, Wells anticipated successfully launching his career as a professional writer, switching from journalism to 'authorship', making his reputation as a promising new writer and releasing himself from the omnipresent pressures of making ends meet.[1]

The struggles of a new writer

During the early phase of his writing career, Wells concentrated upon articles, short stories and book reviews targeted at journals, magazines and newspapers. Like any new writer, he struggled to get material accepted for publication, since he possessed little reputation outside the specialist educational and technical press, especially as much of his early writing was published anonymously.

Suddenly Wells's position was transformed following a radical change of course. Convalescing after another lung haemorrhage in May 1893, Wells was staying on the Sussex coast at Eastbourne. He was smarting still from the uncomprehending reaction of Frank Harris, the editor of *Saturday Review* (1894–8), to his article entitled 'The Universe Rigid'. Reading J. M. Barrie's *When a Man's Single* (1888), Wells believed that he had discovered 'the hidden secret' of writing publishable articles: 'For years I had been seeking rare and precious topics. *Rediscovery of the Unique! Universe Rigid!* The more I was rejected the higher my shots had flown. All

1. Wells, *Experiment in Autobiography*, II, p. 530.

the time I had been shooting over the target'.[2] Returning to his lodgings in Meads Road, Wells followed the advice articulated by Rorrison in Barrie's novel, that is, to tone down philosophical issues in favour of 'chatty articles' about mundane everyday topics: 'I did lower my aim and by extraordinary good fortune I hit at once'. The resulting article 'On the Art of Staying at the Seaside' was sent off to the *Pall Mall Gazette*, accepted by return of post and published within a few weeks.

Further publications followed – over 140 articles, stories, reviews and other items were published in 1894 – and soon he was receiving nearly £15 for one month's contributions.[3] Short stories, though not always easy to place, proved useful in terms of gaining visibility – they helped to 'get my name up' – and networking.[4] When living in Camden Town, Wells and Jane often ventured out after dinner on an 'article hunt' seeking 'unlikely places at unlikely times in order to get queer impressions of them': 'Whenever we hit upon an idea for an article that I did not immediately write, it was put into the topmost of my nest of green drawers for future use'.[5] 'The Universe Rigid' article was never published, but its rejection had proved instrumental in prompting Wells to seriously rethink his strategy as a writer. Moreover, Wells claimed that the article gave him 'a frame' for writing *The Time Machine*.[6]

Nor did Wells's scientific education go to waste in his literary career. Charles Lewis Hind, the editor of the weekly *Pall Mall Budget* commissioned a series of 'Single-Sitting Stories', short stories with a scientific dimension intended to popularize science in a world where educated people showed few qualms when confessing their scientific ignorance and displaying seeming indifference to the issues thrown up by science. Published in June 1894, 'The Stolen Bacillus', Wells's first signed science fiction story, was a comic tale of biological terrorism in which an anarchist, seeking to spread plague through London's water supply, stole and then swallowed what he thought mistakenly was cholera bacillus.[7] In the event, this 'deadly' germ merely turned the skin blue. Providing early evidence of his vivid imagination and capacity for unexpected plot twists, these 'Single-Sitting Stories' record how Wells developed his craft, prepared the ground for his scientific romances and imagined plots suitable for subsequent expansion into larger works. For example, *The Island of Doctor Moreau* followed 'The Stolen Bacillus' by emphasizing the power of scientists to do harm as well as good, while posing questions about the need to exercise their power ethically.

2. Wells, *Experiment in Autobiography*, I, pp. 371–2; 'New Writers', p. 134.

3. Wells, *Experiment in Autobiography*, I, p. 393.

4. Ibid., p. 396.

5. Wells, *Experiment in Autobiography*, II, pp. 510–11.

6. Wells, *Experiment in Autobiography*, I, p. 214.

7. H. G. Wells, 'The Stolen Bacillus', *Pall Mall Budget*, 21 June 1894. For Steven McLean, present-day terrorism gives this story contemporary relevance: Mclean, *Early Fiction of H. G. Wells*, p. 208 note 87. See also Yorimitsu Hashimoto, 'Victorian biological terror: a study of "The Stolen Bacillus"', *The Undying Fire: The Journal of the H. G. Wells Society, The Americas* 2 (2003): 3–27.

In turn, Wells's early science-based short stories were collected together and published by Methuen in November 1895 as *The Stolen Bacillus and other incidents*, thereby highlighting the additional financial return from the re-publication of short stories paying five guineas [£5.25] each when first published. For reviewers, this book highlighted Wells's potential as a writer of stories that were – to quote the *Daily News'* reviewer – 'a blend of science and fantasy': 'The author has a delicate touch, a sprightly vein of humour, and much deftness of method ... Every story is readable, some are strikingly imaginative, and all are adroitly handled.'[8] The *Morning Post's* reviewer was equally positive. Recognizing the literary challenge of writing short stories, this reviewer praised Wells for publishing 'One of the freshest books of "short stories" that have appeared for some time past.'[9] Subsequently, some tales provided a framework for others to develop for publication or adaptation. For example, 'The Flowering of the Strange Orchid', a story about the discovery of a rare carnivorous plant originally published in *Pall Mall Budget* on 2 August 1894, is frequently represented as one source of inspiration for *The Little Shop of Horrors* released as a film (1960; 1986) and produced during the 1980s as a stage musical.[10]

Networking with editors and publishers

Towards the close of 1894 Wells began to write less for the *Pall Mall Gazette* – for much of the year, when he was writing up to ten columns per month at two guineas [£2.20] per column, this journal had proved his 'bread and cheese' – but increasingly, to write for Frank Harris's *Saturday Review*.[11] Apart from continuing to make science intelligible to the layman through short stories, Wells contributed book reviews to the *Saturday Review*. Initially, like most book reviews at the time, they were anonymous, but then published increasingly under his own name. According to Gordon Ray, Wells's exposure to a wide range of contemporary writers – they included Joseph Conrad, Stephen Crane, George Gissing and Thomas Hardy – proved beneficial in terms of shaping his own fiction.[12] For Michael Sherborne, Wells's close engagement with such writers through reviewing helps to explain the intertextual nature of some of his writing and particularly the numerous explicit references made therein to other authors.[13]

As discussed in the previous chapter, Henley played a key role in Wells's career. Wells was first recommended as a promising young writer to Henley, then editor

8. 'Novels', *Daily News*, 8 January 1896, p. 6.

9. 'Books of the Day', *Morning Post*, 19 December 1895, p. 7.

10. Renzi, *Wells*, p. 196. Compare Christopher Fowler, 'Forgotten Authors no. 34: John Collier', *The Independent on Sunday*, 24 May 2009.

11. Wells to his father, 10 August 1894, Wells, *Experiment in Autobiography*, I, p. 396.

12. Gordon N. Ray, 'H. G. Wells's contributions to the *Saturday Review*', *The Library* XVI (1) (1961): 29–30.

13. Sherborne, *H. G. Wells*, p. 101.

of the *National Observer*, by Harry Cust, the editor of the *Pall Mall Gazette*, and H. B. Marriott Watson, the *Pall Mall Gazette*'s literary editor and described by Wells as 'always a firm friend of mine'.[14] Summoned to meet Henley at his home in Barnes, Wells was commissioned to write a serial based upon his 'old idea of "time-travelling"', a heavily 'recast' version of 'The Chronic Argonauts', an article published in the *Science Schools Journal* in April–June 1888.[15] In the event, changes in the ownership and editorial control of the *National Observer* placed the project in jeopardy, since Henley's replacement as editor disapproved of Wells's 'queer wild ramblings' about time travel already published between March and June 1894.[16]

Nevertheless, Wells, apprised of Henley's hopes of setting up a new monthly in which the time traveller story would appear as a serial, continued work rewriting the whole text with a view to enabling readers to travel through time in their minds.[17] Soon Wells received news from Henley about his new monthly, *The New Review*, scheduled to start publication in January 1895. Indeed, one of Henley's first actions as editor was to offer Wells the princely sum of £100 – this amounts to nearly £11,750 in present-day terms – for the serial rights to *The Time Machine*.[18]

Personal, financial and health concerns 1894–5

Although he was receiving the occasional direct approach from publishers by way of recognition of his potential as an emerging writer, Wells was anxious to push forward faster with his literary ambitions. During the closing months of 1894 he was writing two or three articles per week plus a growing number of book reviews for anonymous publication. But Wells wanted more: fame, release from the incessant daily 'grind' of trying to place stories and articles for income to meet his 'responsibilities' and a published book, since hitherto 'no article as yet has created an epoch. So far my greatest success has been a review of an American book (which led the author to ask the publisher for my name)'.[19]

Once again, Henley played a prime role in fulfilling Wells's objectives. Impressed by the 'wonderful' inventions of the draft serial, Henley recommended *The Time Machine* to William Heinemann, *The New Review*'s publisher, for publication as a book.[20] Advising Heinemann on the manuscript, Daniel Conner, the house

14. Wells, *Experiment in Autobiography*, II, p. 517; Connell, *Henley*, pp. 279–81; 'Chronicle and Comment', *The Bookman* (USA) III (4) (June 1896): 293.

15. Wells to Davies, n.d. [March 1894], Smith, *Correspondence of H. G. Wells, I*, p. 214; Wells, *Experiment in Autobiography*, II, p. 515; 'New Writers', p. 134.

16. Wells, *Experiment in Autobiography*, II, p. 517; Sherborne, *H. G. Wells*, p. 94.

17. Anthony West, *H. G. Wells*, p. 216.

18. Connell, *Henley*, pp. 293, 323.

19. Wells, *Experiment in Autobiography*, II, p. 530; Wells to Healey, 18 September 1894, 14 November 1894, 'Wells H. G. Letters Healey Miss 8', ALS 1894–98 (Ransom).

20. W. E. Henley to Wells, 28 September 1894, 26 November 1894, Loing, *Wells à l'oeuvre*, pp. 412, 414.

reader, produced a highly positive report when praising an engaging and 'unquestionably original' work characterized by 'some really fine imaginative writing': 'The whole story is, of course, absurd; but it is extremely ingenious and, in a way, even impressive. Certainly, it is so written as to carry one on, after once starting to read it'.[21] Agreeing to publish *The Time Machine*, Heinemann offered Wells a £50 advance and 15 per cent royalty.

From an early stage of his writing career, Wells, despite preferring a direct personal approach, often made use of literary agents – they included Morris Colles of the Author's Syndicate, James Brand Pinker and A. P. Watt – then a relatively new role in the literary world.[22] In 1894 Wells began using A. P. Watt to secure a contract for a book composed of collected selections of his short stories and articles.[23] As a result, John Lane agreed to publish stories previously printed in the *Pall Mall Gazette* as a book – this appeared as *Select Conversations with an Uncle* – even if Wells expressed irritation with his refusal to accept a larger print run than 650 copies. Subsequently, his anxiety to become visible as an author led Wells to complain about the book's slow progress towards publication – this was eventually published 30 May 1895 – as well as about delays in payment.[24] Watt also secured a contract with Methuen for re-publication of fifteen science-based 'Single-Sitting Stories' which had appeared in the *Pall Mall Budget* and other journals.[25] The resulting book, *The Stolen Bacillus and other Incidents*, was published in November 1895. Impressed by the story's potential, Watt indicated his willingness to help place *The Time Machine* should Heinemann not offer a contract.

However, none of these books appeared in print before May 1895, so that throughout 1894 and early 1895 Wells was still making his way as a writer. Money remained a perennial source of worry. His writing, though showing an 'encouraging successfulness', produced an uncertain and variable flow of income, especially when journals tired of his work or experienced a change of ownership and/or editors.[26] For example, the above-mentioned changes at the *National Observer* led Wells to complain about the 'sudden fall' in his income accruing from the time travel project.[27] He feared always that any withdrawal of support for his writing might prove permanent. At one moment, Wells was earning more money than ever and feeling reasonably prosperous. At another moment, his financial position seemed extremely precarious, with ready cash deemed an

21. Daniel H. Conner, 'The Time Machine', 25 October 1894, Author File: H. G. Wells, William Heinemann Archive, Random House Group Archive & Library, Rushden, Northants, UK (Rushden).

22. On the 'Author's Syndicate', see James L. W. West III, *American Authors and the Literary Marketplace since 1900* (Philadelphia, PN: University of Pennsylvania Press, 1988), pp. 77–80.

23. Wells to his father, 10 August 1894, Wells, *Experiment in Autobiography*, I, p. 396.

24. Wells to Lane, 2 February 1895, Smith, *Correspondence of H. G. Wells, I*, p. 231.

25. A. P. Watt to Wells, 21 December 1894, Loing, *Wells à l'oeuvre*, p. 416.

26. Wells, *Experiment in Autobiography*, II, p. 512.

27. Ibid., p. 516.

urgent necessity and bankruptcy was deemed a distinct possibility. Nor was it just a question of meeting the one guinea [£1.05] per week rent, since Wells was supporting not only Jane and himself, but also his elderly parents and first wife.[28] Thus, during early 1895 he was contributing c. £100 per year to Isabel, who had moved to Hampstead following their separation, plus £60 per year to his parents. Little, if anything, remained for leisure: 'We went very little to concerts, theatres or music-halls for the very sound reason that we could not afford it. Our only exercise was "going for a walk." ... we had no social life at all.'[29] Wells's finances dipped once again in January 1895, in the wake of his divorce, in spite of it being arranged by his cousin upon 'the most economical lines'.

In brief, the budding author, whilst seeking to make his name through writing fiction, had no choice but to maintain his journalism to meet the everyday calls made upon his purse. In fact, the financial pressures were such that in January 1895 Wells agreed to become drama critic of the *Pall Mall Gazette*, an evening newspaper for which he had written several short stories and book reviews. Cust, the editor, summoned Wells to his office by telegram:

> 'Here,' said Cust and thrust two small pieces of coloured paper into my hand.
> 'What are these?' I asked.
> 'Theatres. Go and do 'em.'
> 'Yes,' I said and reflected. 'I'm willing to have a shot at it, but I ought to warn you that so far, not counting the Crystal Palace Pantomime and Gilbert and Sullivan, I've been only twice to a theatre.'
> 'Exactly what I want,' said Cust. 'You won't be in the gang. You'll make a break.'[30]

As Wells warned Cust, he did not understand the theatre and felt out of place there.[31] Even so, Wells, though resenting the cost of purchasing evening dress for the job, admitted seeing some good plays while making useful personal contacts, including George Bernard Shaw, a fellow contributor to the *Saturday Review* and someone he had heard speak at William Morris's Kelmscott House, Hammersmith, during his student days.[32]

Subsequently, 'Sad story of a dramatic critic', first published in the *New Budget* on 15 August 1895, typified the manner in which much of Wells's writing drew upon personal experience. Like Wells, the story's chief character, Egbert Craddock Cummins, was given the job of reviewing plays for a newspaper. Like Wells, Cummins began by informing the editor that he had never been to a theatre in his life:

28. Wells to his parents, 5 February 1895, Wells to Simmons, n.d. [March 1895], Smith, *Correspondence of H. G. Wells*, I, p. 232, pp. 235–6.

29. Wells, *Experiment in Autobiography*, II, pp. 511–12.

30. Ibid., pp. 534–5, 539.

31. Ibid., p. 541.

32. Wells, *Experiment in Autobiography*, I, p. 244.

'But I don't know anything about it, you know.'

'That's just it. New view. No habits. No clichés in stock. Ours is a live paper, not a bag of tricks. None of your clockwork professional journalism in this office.' [33]

Possibly the story, in which Cummins's fiancée became annoyed by his extending range of dramatic affectations resulting from regular daily exposure to the theatre, reflected Wells's fears that he might suffer the same fate. In the event, for Wells, the principal problem arose from his poor state of health. Late winter nights and London's unhealthy environment combined to ensure that his first regular job on a London daily newspaper did not last long: 'I caught a bad cold, streaks of blood appeared again, and once more the impossibility of my moving about in London in all weather was demonstrated'.[34] Resigning as theatre critic, Wells was forced to revisit the question of moving out of the metropolis. Already in 1893, confinement to bed due to a recurrence of his lung problem, prompted Wells to contemplate cutting himself 'adrift from London at last and go somewhere where colds cease from troubling in the winter'.[35] In February 1895 the death of Walter Low, a close friend and collaborator on the *Educational Times*, reinforced fears about his own mortality.[36] Soon afterwards a further 'bed of sickness' meant that a change of residence could be delayed no longer: 'I want a little fresh air and idleness'.[37] While deciding upon a suitable location, Wells and Jane took a short holiday at The Glen Boarding House (now The Royal Glen Hotel) in Sidmouth.[38]

Despite ill-health and renewed fears of bankruptcy, Wells believed that 1895 held the promise of better things, most notably the prospect of passing on from working as a journalist – '"occasional journalist" at that, and anonymous' – to 'authorship' under his own name:

I was now in a very hopeful and enterprising mood. Henley had accepted *The Time Machine*, agreed to pay £100 for it, and had recommended it to Heinemann, the publisher. This would bring in at least another £50. I should have a book out in the spring … And there was talk of a book of short stories with Methuen [*The Stolen Bacillus*]. Furthermore John Lane was proposing to make a book out of some of my articles [*Select Conversations with an Uncle*], though for that I was to get only £10 down. The point was that my chance was plainly coming fast. I should get a press – and I felt I might get a good press – for *The Time Machine* anyhow. If I could get another book out before that amount

33. H. G. Wells. 'The sad story of a dramatic critic', in H. G. Wells, *The Plattner Story and Others* (London: Methuen, 1897), pp. 264, 267–8.

34. Wells, *Experiment in Autobiography*, II, p. 542.

35. Wells to Milne, n.d. [November 1893], Loing, *Wells à l'oeuvre*, p. 409.

36. Wells dedicated *The Wonderful Visit* (1895) to Low.

37. Wells to Simmons, n.d. [March 1895], Wells to his mother, 25 March 1895, Loing, *Wells à l'oeuvre*, p. 418.

38. Wells to his mother, n.d. [1895], Smith, *Correspondence of H. G. Wells, I*, p. 247.

of publicity died away I should be fairly launched as an author and then I might be able to go on writing books.[39]

In Spring 1895 Watt began negotiating with publishers in both Britain and the USA for two projected novels. Dent agreed to publish what became *The Wonderful Visit* – to quote Wells, 'a thing about a Vicar and an angel' inspired in part by F. Anstey's *The Tinted Venus* (1885) – upon the basis of reading the first sixty or so pages.[40] Wells worked hard on this book, which he described as 'a fantastic romance', not a scientific romance, with the aim of completion by early June.[41] In effect, Wells was inverting the story told in *The Time Machine*. Whereas the Time Traveller, an ordinary human being, was transported into a very different future society, *The Wonderful Visit*'s angel, a fantasy creation, was dropped into the present-day world to confront its strange ways. A more challenging storyline meant that *The Island of Dr Moreau*, the other proposal, proved more difficult to place in spite of being categorized like *The Time Machine* as a scientific romance. Commencing work on *Dr. Moreau* during late 1894, Wells published an article 'The Limits of Individual Plasticity' embodying the substance of the story in the *Saturday Review of Literature* on 19 January 1895.

Retreating from London's fogs

In August 1895 an article in *The Bookman*, reported that 'uncertain health' forced Wells 'to live in retirement out of London' at Woking.[42] Admittedly Wells's health, like that of Jane's, was problematic and represented the principal reason for his departure from the metropolis, but the rest of the assertion requires qualification. Wells was not living in retirement. On the contrary, he was writing as hard as ever, as indicated by the fact that the same issue of *The Bookman* announced that Wells, the author of *The Time Machine*, had three more works – *The Island of Dr. Moreau, The Wonderful Visit, The Stolen Bacillus and Other Stories* – scheduled for the coming publishing season.[43] Wells's own descriptor stressing his 'withdrawal to Woking' proves more appropriate.[44]

Wells's health had remained problematic since the late 1880s. Yet another breakdown in his health in February 1895, led him to contemplate moving to a more healthy location in the countryside. Wells's personal life, combined with the strict Victorian moral code regarding adultery and divorce, was another

---

39. Wells, *Experiment in Autobiography*, II, p. 530; Wells to Simmons, n.d. [March 1895], Loing, *Wells à l'oeuvre*, p. 418;

40. Wells to Simmons, n.d. [Spring 1895], WS31 (UIUC); 'The Scientific Novel. A talk with Mr H. G. Wells', *Daily News*, 26 January 1898.

41. Wells to Dent, 1 May 1895, Smith, *Correspondence of H. G. Wells, I*, pp. 236, 239.

42. 'New Writers', p. 135.

43. Ibid., pp. 134–5; 'Literary Gossip', *The Belfast News-Letter*, 5 August 1895, p. 8.

44. Wells, *Experiment in Autobiography*, II, p. 542.

influential factor. News of his divorce from Isabel in January 1895 was covered briefly in several national and provincial newspapers. Much of the coverage proved relatively factual, but some reports were worded in a somewhat emotive manner. Thus, the *Sheffield Evening Telegraph*, headlining its article 'Deserted and Betrayed Wife', recorded that Isabel's petition for divorce was granted on the grounds of adultery by Wells, described as 'an author and journalist' and his 'failure to comply with a decree for the restitution of conjugal rights'.[45] Reportedly, one witness 'stated that the respondent had lived with a lady near Regent's Park London, for some months'.

Against this background, Wells feared that 'In sexual matters my good name will be smirched' in the 'popular mind', even if his current lack of a high public profile meant that any damage would be limited.[46] Moreover, as Wells and Jane had discovered when lodging at Mornington Place, Camden Town and Sevenoaks, society, typified by their landladies and Jane's mother, disapproved strongly of 'our flagrant immorality' in co-habiting outside of marriage'.[47] Nor was Wells's marital 'crisis' glossed over completely by the literary world.[48] Thus, for Wells, a place in the country came to be seen also as a place to lie low for a while in the wake of his divorce, accusations of adultery and continuing co-habitation with Jane outside of marriage.[49] Following his brief convalescent stay at Sidmouth, Wells ruled out any possibility of returning to Sevenoaks given the problems experienced with their landlady in 1894. Instead, he decided to retreat to Surrey, where he 'set about finding a little house in the country'.[50] Apart from taking the opportunity to recuperate further, Wells anticipated that the county's much-loved countryside would provide conducive writing quarters enabling him to follow up *The Time Machine*. Surrey was already well known to Wells, such as through cycling, walking or travelling through the county *en route* to visit his brothers when working in Farnham and Godalming.

Wells chose Woking, some thirty miles from central London. He informed a friend that 'I've just been seeing about a little home at Woking and I shall go there I hope in the course of a month and put in some good work'.[51] There was no possibility that poor health meant retirement as a writer. In Woking he rented 'Lynton', a semi-detached villa in Maybury Road. Facing the railway line, it was a short walk from Woking station. Wells's rent was c. £28 per year.[52]

45. 'Deserted and Betrayed Wife', *Sheffield Evening Telegraph*, 11 January 1895, p. 4.

46. Wells to Davies, 27 December 1893, Loing, *Wells à l'oeuvre*, p. 409.

47. Wells, *Experiment in Autobiography*, II, p. 517; Sue Gosling, 'H. G. Wells' letter goes on display', *BBC News*, 1 February 2011, http://news.bbc.co.uk/local/kent/hi/people_and_places/history/newsid_9373000/9373313.stm [accessed 28 January 2012].

48. Charles Whibley to Henley, 14 January 1895, in Connell, *W. E. Henley*, p. 295.

49. Banerjee, *Literary Surrey*, p. 143.

50. Wells, *Experiment in Autobiography*, II, p. 542.

51. Wells to Tommy [A. T. Simmons], Spring 1895, n.d. WS31 (UIUC).

52. Supplemental Valuation List, Woking, 20 June 1893, n.p. [p. 13], SHC 6198/13/19 (SHC); Valuation List, Woking, 26 August 1895, SHC 6198/13/5a, no. 285 (SHC). The 1895

The two Wokings

Prior to his arrival, Wells gave little away about his reasons for choosing Woking in preference to any other place in Southern England in general or Surrey in particular. However, when asked in late 1895 why he moved to Woking, he responded that 'I am fond of boating, and found it out as I was rowing along the canal. It seemed so quiet and soothing, and indeed I have found it so'.[53] Over time, Woking's appearance and appeal have often been viewed negatively, as typified by Brian Aldiss when commenting about the destruction of the town in *The War of the Worlds* 'desirable though that might be'.[54] By contrast, Alan Crosby, the town's historian, claimed that during the late nineteenth century, Woking possessed many attractions for those seeking to get away from the congestion, noise and pollution of the metropolis: 'The combination of natural beauty, cheap land and easy access to London was rare ... the landscape was delightful – groves of tall scented pines, glades of heather and gorse, and views across green valleys to distant hills and ridges'.[55]

Recently built on land sold off for development by the London Necropolis and National Mausoleum Company, Wells's house typified the fast-growing nature of Victorian Woking. Old Woking, the original village located on the River Wey, was increasingly marginalized by new Woking centred upon the railway station opened in 1838 and built on land sold by the cemetery company and local landowners.[56] Reflecting in 1908 upon the two Wokings, Eric Parker described the countryside attracting Wells and featuring also in *The War of the Worlds*:

> In whatever way you may choose to travel through Surrey, it is difficult to avoid making Woking a centre and a rendezvous. All the trains stop there ... It was that Woking, the Woking of the station, which for many years I imagined to be the only Woking in Surrey. One did not wish for another.
>
> But there is another Woking, and it is as pretty and quiet as the railway Woking is noisy and tiresome. It stands with its old church on the banks of the Wey two miles away, a huddle of tiled roofs and old shops and poky little corners, as out-of-the-way and sleepy and ill-served by rail as anyone could

list recorded H. G. Wells as the occupier. The present-day monetary equivalent of Wells's 1895 annual rent of £28 is £3,288.

53. Smith, 'A chat with the author', p. 8.

54. Aldiss, 'Introduction', p. xvii. Hitherto, I have seen no evidence that Wells knew Woking well or had relatives there. According to one letter in Smith's *The Correspondence of H. G. Wells*, Wells claimed to have spent one month in Woking. But this results from a transcription error misreading 'Wookey', Somerset, where he spent a few weeks as a teacher, as 'Woking: Wells to his Mother', n.d. [c. July 1883], Smith, *The Correspondence of H. G. Wells*, I, p. 25.

55. Alan Crosby, *A History of Woking* (Chichester: Phillimore, 2003), pp. 109–10.

56. Ibid., pp. 70–80; John M. Clarke, *London's Necropolis: A Guide to Brookwood Cemetery* (Stroud: Sutton, 2004), pp. 1–23.

wish. I found it first on a day in October, and walked out from the grinding machinery of the station by a field-path running through broad acres of purple-brown loam, over which plough-horses tramped and turned. It was a strange and arresting sight, for over the dark rich mould there was drawn a veil of shimmering grey light wider and less earthly than any mist or dew. The whole plough land was alive with gossamer and Old Woking lay beyond the gossamer as if that magic veil were meant to shield it from the engines and the smoke.[57]

As Parker acknowledged, Woking offered yet another example of suburban-ization, with the railway linking the town ever more closely to London. Speaking in 1895, Gustav Wermig, the chairman of Woking Council, stressed the impor-tance of Woking's 'good train service' – generally speaking there were up to four trains per hour to London with journey times of thirty-four minutes upwards – as one of 'the chief factors' in the town's development.[58] Another key element was the Necropolis link. Following discussions with Lord Onslow, the Lord of the Manor of Woking and the passage of parliamentary legislation, in 1854 the London Necropolis Company paid £38,000 for 2,200 acres of the common lands of Woking, part of which was to be laid out as a cemetery at Brookwood to relieve the escalating pressure upon London's burial sites. Subsequently, further parliamentary legislation allowed the company to sell off surplus land, thereby preparing the way for the cemetery company to become more of 'a land specu-lation company'.[59]

Advertising literature for land sales provides insights into Woking's perceived attractions. For example, in 1883 sales information for the Cross Lanes Estate highlighted 'the beauties of the neighbourhood', including 'large heath-covered Commons' and the 'exceptionally good' train service to London.[60] It was also asserted that Woking was 'one of the healthiest spots in the country, a fact well known to the leading physicians, who strongly recommend it to their patients'. Such features were echoed a few years later in the auction notice for the Maybury Common Estate, which included the plot on which Wells's house was built. Foregrounding the excellence of Woking's train services, it stressed that villa residences built in Maybury Road would be a short walk from the railway station from which frequent trains reached London within thirty-five minutes.[61] Moreover, the town's rapid growth, it was argued, offered purchasers the prospect of a speculative investment rising in value, particularly given the popularity of owning property available for rent.

57. Eric Parker, *Highways and Byways in Surrey* (London: Macmillan, 1908), pp. 217–18.

58. 'Woking UDC', *Surrey Times*, 17 August 1895, Press Cuttings 1895–1901, SHC 6198/3/80 (SHC); 'Train timetables', *The Woking News*, 27 December 1895, p. 8.

59. Crosby, *History of Woking*, pp. 74, 77–8.

60. Paine & Brettell, 'The charming Freehold Estate "Cross Lanes", Woking, Surrey, 1883', SHC 4363/72, Folder 1 (SHC).

61. Wm. R. Nicholas, 'Sale of Freehold Building land known as the "Maybury Common Estate"', 24 August 1888, SHC 6852/8/2/3, SHC 6852/8/2/4 (SHC).

Thus, Wells arrived in Woking at a time when the town, like his birthplace Bromley, was experiencing what the local council and media represented as 'astounding' growth (Table 5.1) – for *The Woking Mail* this was 'proceeding at a more rapid rate than ever' – and were even predicting that Woking might soon become the largest town in Surrey.[62] There was a new Public Hall, new houses, shops and industries, including electricity and gas companies, with the area centred upon the railway station and Maybury witnessing the greatest advances. Common land and green fields were making way for new housing developments accompanied by the inevitable pressures upon infrastructure. Unsurprisingly, the mid-1890s witnessed repeated coverage by the local press of the consequences of the town's recent growth 'by leaps and bounds': impassable roads in wet weather; lack of footpaths; bridges inadequate for present-day traffic; an incomplete sewerage system; unreliable street lighting; and jerry building.[63] During 1896 the formation of the Woking Improvement Association, reflected the desire of local people for a more effective way of exerting pressure upon the council and other bodies for appropriate timely action upon such issues. At this time, Horsell, which was to play a central role in *The War of the Worlds*, was expanding fast also, but for the purposes of local government was controlled by Chertsey Rural District Council until 1907 when Horsell's ratepayers, attracted by the prospect of linking up with the town's sewerage and drainage system, voted to join Woking.[64]

At the same time, Woking's growth should be viewed in perspective. As John Clarke points out, the 1888 auction of Maybury Common Estate 'proved a failure': 'no plots reached their reserve price'.[65] Subsequently, several lots, presumably including that upon which 'Lynton' was constructed, were sold at or just below the reserve price. Notwithstanding the town's rapid growth, the 1896 Ordnance Survey (OS) map establishes that hitherto the pair of semi-detached villas, one of which was rented by Wells, were the only properties built on the plots auctioned in 1888 in the lengthy section of Maybury Road between Monument Road and King's Road. Nor was the next section of Maybury Road, between King's Road and North Road, heavily built upon as yet with only nine existing houses shown on the 1896 OS map.

In many respects, Woking can be interpreted as offering rural variants of features Wells valued in Camden Town, the principal area favoured by him for

62. 'Woking's Changing Aspect: Some significant signs of progress and prosperity', *The Woking Mail*, 4 September 1897, p. 5; 'Surrey in 1897: Looking Backward', *Surrey Advertiser*, 1 January 1898, p. 2.

63. 'The Woking News: Our Public Roads', *The Woking News*, 22 November 1895, pp. 4–5; 'The Woking News', *The Woking News*, 6 December 1895, p. 4; 'Local Affairs: Woking's Growth', 'Woking's Changing Aspect: Some Significant Signs of Progress and Prosperity', *The Woking Mail*, 4 September 1897, pp. 4–5. On jerry building, see Crosby, *History of Woking*, p. 85; An Ambler, 'The Gentle Art of Cycling', *Macmillan's Magazine*, January 1898, p. 206.

64. Crosby, *History of Woking*, pp. 119–20.

65. Clarke, *London's Necropolis*, pp. 22–3. The cemetery company has not granted access to its archives.

Table 5.1 Population of Woking and Horsell, 1801–1911

Year	Woking	Horsell
1801	2,685	493
1891	12,485	1,021
1901	19,627	2,105
1911	25,673	

Note: Horsell joined Woking in 1907 and hence, its 1911 population of 3,026 is included within Woking's total.

Source: GB Historical GIS/University of Portsmouth, Woking SubD through time |Population Statistics Total Population, *A Vision of Britain through Time*:

http://www.visionofbritain.org.uk/unit/10540410/cube/TOT_POP [accessed: 17 August 2013]; GB Historical GIS/ University of Portsmouth, Horsell AP/CP through time |Population Statistics| Total Population, *A Vision of Britain through Time*: http://www.visionofbritain.org.uk/unit/10187941/cube/TOT_POP [accessed: 17 August 2013].

residence during the past. These included open spaces, proximity to a canal and excellent rail links with central London:

- open spaces: Woking's surrounding countryside proved far more extensive than that offered by Regent's Park and Primrose Hill. The surrounding topography highlighted the prominent part played by nurserying – plant nurseries, like Jackmans of Mayford and Anthony Waterer's Knap Hill Nursery, possessed national and international reputations for growing and exhibiting azaleas, clematis and rhododendrons – so that 'extensive areas around the town were given over to plantations of shrubs and trees, rose gardens and greenhouses, and colourful beds of herbaceous plants'.[66] Apart from nurseries, all around still were open fields, common land and wide heathery spaces. By 1895 two golf courses, Woking Golf Club and the New Zealand Golf Club, had been constructed on heathland.[67] The surrounding rural landscape, including extensive commons and the North Downs, clearly registered with Wells, who utilised them to good effect in *The War of the Worlds*, such as through the use of Horsell Common and the New Zealand Golf Club (named in the story as Addlestone or Byfleet Links) as Martian landing sites and mention of golf caddies as part of the crowd on the common. Likewise, the surrounding countryside, such as 'the flat pineland around Woking where he lives and writes', was recorded also by Wells's commentators and interviewers.[68]

66. Crosby, *History of Woking*, p. 55.

67. Prominent politicians living in Woking included Gerald Balfour (1853–1945), brother of Arthur Balfour, the prime minister (1902–5) and Alfred Lyttelton (1857–1913). Both Balfour and Lyttelton captained Woking Golf Club which was founded in 1893. Lyttelton represented England at cricket and football.

68. Picaroon, 'Portrait of Mr H. G. Wells', p. 367; Smith, 'A chat with the author', p. 7.

- proximity to a canal, with Woking's Basingstoke Canal paralleling Camden Town's Regent's Canal;
- living near a railway line going to a mainline London station – whereas his lodgings in Camden were close to the line travelling into London Euston, Wells's house in Woking faced the track leading to London Waterloo's station. Today his former lodgings in Camden Town face the railway track, but during Wells's period of residence they were separated from the line by a row of houses, now demolished, on the other side of the road.

The principal difference, particularly for someone like Wells suffering from respiratory and related problems, was that Woking did not suffer from London's pollution, and hence provided a healthier living and working environment. Indeed, as *The Woking News* recorded in October 1894, Londoners, unlike the people of Woking, were reconciling themselves to the usual prospect of a prolonged winter characterized by the 'prevalence of fogs in the metropolis'.[69] In effect, Wells, though relishing living in, exploring and working in London, exchanged the noxious fumes, fog and stench of the unhealthy and crowded metropolis for the fresh air, open spaces and rural charms of Woking. The wisdom of his move to North West Surrey, alongside the downside of residence in central London, was brought home to Wells in November 1895 when receiving a letter from Henley in London: 'It's so dark (1.30) [1330 hours] I can scarce see to write; the River is hideous with fog & filthy air'.[70]

Nor was Wells alone among people in the literary world in being attracted to Woking during the late nineteenth and early twentieth centuries, when its literary residents included Henley, Arthur J. Munby, the diarist and poet, George Bernard Shaw (1856–1950) and Sir Charles Dilke (1843–1911), the Liberal Party politician and owner of both the *Athenaeum* magazine and *Notes and Queries*. Although Conan Doyle moved out of London to Hindhead, he knew Woking well. In his correspondence, Conan Doyle wrote about playing golf all day there and cycling with his wife from South Norwood to Woking to visit Kingsley Milbourne during the early 1890s.[71] Having been resident at 'The Firs', near Woking Station, during the mid-1890s Milbourne moved to 'The Rough', Maybury Hill, that is near where Wells lived and almost next door to the house represented as that probably occupied by *The War of the Worlds*' narrator. Moreover, Conan Doyle's writings often portrayed Woking in a positive light. For example, in 1893 a Sherlock Holmes short story, 'The Adventure of the Naval Treaty' published in *The Strand Magazine* (October–November 1893), highlighted Woking's frequent train service to London as well as its 'admirable

69. 'Our London Correspondent', *The Woking News*, 26 October 1894, p. 2.

70. Henley to Wells, 8 November 1895, Loing, *Wells à l'oeuvre*, p. 425.

71. Conan Doyle to Mary Doyle, 29 October 1891, in Lellenberg, Stashower and Foley, *Conan Doyle*, pp. 298–9.

Surrey scenery', 'the fir-woods and the heather of Woking', 'the balmy summer air' and nearby 'pretty' villages like Ripley.[72]

Maybury Hill proved the location also of the residence of Wells's literary mentor, Henley, who spent his final years at 'Heather Brae' located near Milbourne's 'The Rough'. Purchased as a 'country home' with easy access to his London residence and the capital's literary world, 'Heather Brae' was located close to where Wells had lived during 1895-6 and almost adjacent to the house interpreted as that most likely occupied by the narrator in *The War of the Worlds*.[73] Having been in regular contact with Wells since 1894, it is probable that Wells apprised him of the attractions of living in Woking. Certainly, the town's excellent train service to London figured in the decision to move from Worthing in 1901. Writing from Woking in October 1902 to a London-based friend suffering ill health and depression, Henley praised also Woking's healthy environment. 'Can't you try Doctor Brighton?', or writing from Woking, he said: 'Why not try this place of pines and sands (i.e. Woking)?'[74] Following an accident on Coombe and Malden Station in March 1902, when 'a fool-guard' started the train 'before I could board it', Henley used 'Heather Brae' to convalesce after the fall.[75] His recovery proved slow, but in October 1902 Henley and his wife were able to visit an old acquaintance, Alfred Harmsworth, the proprietor of the *Daily Mail* and owner of a large estate nearby: 'We were at Sutton Place on Sunday. *What* a 'ouse, Charles! I came home on a motor, in style!... A. H. and his wife more kind than I can say. In fact, we're delighted to have them for neighbours'.[76] In July 1903 Henley died at Woking, where he was cremated at St John's Crematorium.

Arthur J. Munby (1828–1910), a barrister but better known as a diarist and poet, lived at Wheelers Farm, Pyrford, Woking, between 1878 and 1910 and was buried at St. Nicholas's Church, Pyrford, a church mentioned in *The War of the Worlds*. Apart from frequently extolling the virtues of the local landscape, most notably 'the freshness and quiet, & the sense of infinitude ... that the remote heaths and meadows of the Wey can give', Munby used the area as the setting for *Dorothy: A Country Story*, a lengthy poem published anonymously

72. Arthur Conan Doyle, 'The Adventure of the Naval Treaty', *The Strand Magazine* 6 (34–5) (October–November 1893), pp. 393–4, 466.

73. Connell, *Henley*, p. 370.

74. Ibid., p. 373.

75. Ibid., p. 371. Henley did not fall at Woking Station, as stated in some publications: Iain Wakeford, *Heritage Notes: Maybury Hill* (Old Woking: Wakeford, 2000); 'History of Maybury', Lynch Sales & Lettings, n.d., http://www.housesinwoking.com/GenericPage. aspx?type=AreaProfile&key=history_maybury [accessed 11 May 2015]. Coombe and Malden Station is now named New Malden.

76. Henley to Whibley, 28 October 1902, Connell, *Henley*, pp. 374,376. Impressed by Harmsworth's 'amazing Mercedes' car, Henley wrote a lengthy poem called 'Song of Speed' dedicated to Harmsworth: William Ernest Henley, *Song of Speed* (London: David Nutt, 1903), pp. 9–30.

in 1879.[77] For Munby, Pyrford's appeal, most notably 'its country quiet', was enhanced by Woking's rail links with London, as highlighted by his praise for the view of Newark Abbey from St Nicholas's Church: 'And all this within a few miles, so to say, of London!'.[78] Even so, like Wells, his appreciation of the benefits arising from easy access to the metropolis was qualified by the threat posed by the spread of the suburbs. For Munby, 'The influence of London' was omnipresent. In particular, rumours that the railway line was coming to Ripley led him to articulate 'the state of passionate alarm in which one lives as to all beautiful things near London; fearing every moment that they may be lost forever'.[79]

Wells's 'Trump Card'

For Wells, The Time Machine was central to his personal and literary aspirations, that is to his fundamental desire to move on and to write more substantial literary works: 'the important thing to me is to get the book published'.[80] In many respects, he saw The Time Machine's reception by reviewers and readers as a test of his suitability for a literary career: 'It's my trump card and if it does not come off very much I shall know my place for the rest of my career. Still we live in Hope'.[81]

Serialized in The New Review from January to May 1895 in five monthly instalments, The Time Machine was published as a book by Henry Holt in New York on 7 May 1895. Then, on 29 May 1895, soon after Wells took up residence in Woking, it was published in London by William Heinemann with an initial print run of 10,000.[82] Unlike the American publication, Heinemann's version

77. Arthur J. Munby, though seemingly forgotten by Woking today, is a character worth foregrounding for his poetry, invaluable Victorian diaries and art, collection of photographs of Victorian women and his unconventional personal relationship with (and secret marriage to), Hannah Cullwick, a maid: Derek Hudson, Munby, Man of Two Worlds: the Life and Diaries of Arthur J. Munby 1828-1910 (London: Sphere, 1974), pp. 191, 244; David C. Taylor, 'A. J. Munby in Surrey', Surrey History II (5) (1983): 217–21. Munby's diary also mentions contacts in the early 1890s with Dilke, who lived nearby at Pyrford Rough: Hudson, Munby, pp. 415–16. Munby is commemorated by a brass memorial at St Nicholas's Church.

78. Hudson, Munby, p. 402; quoted, Taylor, 'Munby in Surrey', p. 219. When he began living at Pyrford Munby's diary records the Woking to Waterloo return fare costing 3s 8d [£0.183]: Hudson, Munby, p. 392.

79. Quoted, Taylor, 'Munby in Surrey', p. 218.

80. Wells to Heinemann, 14 May 1895, Smith, Correspondence of H. G. Wells, I, p. 240.

81. Wells to Healey, 22 December 1894, Smith, Correspondence of H. G. Wells, I, p. 226.

82. St. John, Heinemann, pp. 32–3. In late 1895 Wells claimed the sale of 10,000 copies: Smith. 'A chat with the author', p. 5. Responding during the late 1950s to an enquiry from Bernard Bergonzi, Heinemann confirmed the 10,000 print run, but could only provide definite totals of 2,450 in cloth and 6,000 in paper. Reportedly, there was 'no record' about

included textual revisions introduced to give added polish to the serialized text.[83] Offering an early example of his close monitoring of detail, Wells played a proactive role as regards pricing of the book. At one stage Heinemann contemplated marketing the book at 1s 6d (£0.075) 'for a big sale', but Wells, conscious of Heinemann's preference for six shilling novels, found a 15 per cent royalty based upon 6s 0d more attractive. Moreover, he feared that 'an initial publication at a low price involves some risk of the book being scantily reviewed. We appeal I think to a public which reads reviews'.[84] In the event, Heinemann, claiming that the 32,400-word *The Time Machine* fell well short of the length expected of six shilling novels, compromised releasing the book at 2s 6d (£0.125) and 1s 6d (£0.075) for the cloth and paper covered versions respectively.

The monthly instalments serialized in *The New Review*, described by several newspaper reviewers as 'thrilling' and 'the first pages fastened on by regular readers of that popular monthly', attracted widespread attention and praise.[85] Moreover, the influential *Review of Reviews*, referring positively to the serial in successive issues from March onwards, gave both Wells and *The Time Machine* invaluable visibility in the literary world. Acknowledging the quality of this 'very powerful story', the *Review of Reviews* reaffirmed also that that there had been 'no falling off in the thrilling and ghastly interest of the story'.[86] Likewise, highly favourable sentiments were expressed when the story appeared as a book, with Heinemann making extensive use of praise from reviewers – following usual practice, most reviews were anonymous – in press advertisements. For the *Morning Post*'s reviewer, *The Time Machine*, an 'imaginative phantasy', showed that Wells 'possessed a well-developed imagination and the power to turn its workings to good account in the interests of readers'.[87] Such views were echoed by the *Glasgow Herald*'s reviewer, who opined that his 'remarkably brilliant' book 'had qualities approaching to genius, whether it were regarded as pure romance or as philosophical fiction'.[88]

Predictably, Wells was frequently compared to other writers. Thus, *The Review of Reviews* observed that the story was 'admirably done in a manner worthy of

the rest of the print run: J. D. Dettmer, to Bain, 20 June 1958, Author File: H. G. Wells, Heinemann Archive (Rushden).

83. Ruddick, 'Introduction', 'Note on Text', *The Time Machine*, pp. 21, 28–30, 52–3.

84. Wells to Simmons, n.d. [March 1895], Wells to Heinemann, 14 May 1895, Smith, *Correspondence of H. G. Wells, I*, pp. 234, 240.

85. 'The May Magazines', *The Yorkshire Herald*, 6 May 1895, p. 6; 'Books of the Day', *Freeman's Journal and Daily Commercial Advertiser* (Dublin) (7 June 1895): 2.

86. 'The New Review', *Review of Reviews* (London) XI (March 1895): 263; 'The World several millions of years hence: a vision of the fate of man', *Review of Reviews* (New York) XI (June 1895): 701–2; Joseph O. Baylen, 'W. T. Stead and the early career of H. G. Wells, 1895–1911', *Huntington Library Quarterly* 38 (1) (1974): 53.

87. 'Books of the Day, *Morning Post*, 19 December 1895, p. 7.

88. 'Novels and Stories', *The Glasgow Herald*, 3 October 1895, p. 7.

Poe', a view echoed in *Black and White*, among others.[89] For *The Referee*, Wells had produced 'a conception more than worthy of Jules Verne'.[90] These quotes reflect the manner in which Wells, though inevitably compared with Edgar Alan. Poe and Verne, was viewed from an early stage as a distinctive writer producing work which was intensely original, strongly imagined, inventive, exciting and an excellent read. Nor was the scientific dimension overlooked, with some reviewers emphasizing the book's appeal to readers looking for 'excitement and sensation in an altogether untouched direction'.[91] As *The Referee* pointed out, Wells offered readers 'an ingenious application of evolutionary science for the purposes of fiction'.[92] Indeed, *Nature* reaffirmed that *The Time Machine*, 'based so far as possible on scientific data' but without taking science 'too seriously', was well worth the attention of scientists and others interested in science.[93]

Conclusion

As *The Bookman* reported, Wells's *The Time Machine* received 'a very friendly reception in England, where it met with a sale of over 6,000 copies within a few weeks'.[94] Wells proudly informed his mother that 'My last book seems a hit – everyone has heard of it – and all kinds of people seem disposed to make much of me'.[95] Despite experiencing the usual trials and tribulations of any new writer, what he depicted subsequently as serving his literary apprenticeship, Wells retained confidence in his abilities and the eventual fulfilment of his hopes and expectations: 'Someday I shall succeed, I really believe, but it is a weary game'.[96] Although he made modest advances from mid-1893 onwards through the support of editors, most notably Harris and Henley and attracted praise from such writers as Richard Le Gallienne – to quote Grant Richards – 'one of the first to recognise the Wellsian genius', Wells's real move forward came in 1895.[97] Then, he felt that things were starting to happen, with one book, *The Time Machine* and two collections of short stories – *Select Conversations with an Uncle* and *The Stolen Bacillus*

89. *The Review of Reviews* and *Black and White*, quoted in Heinemann's advertisement, *The Times*, 5 August 1895, p. 6; 'Books of the Day', *Freeman's Journal and Daily Commercial Advertiser* (Dublin), 7 June 1895, p. 2.

90. *The Referee*, quoted in Heinemann's advertisement, *The Times*, 28 May 1895, p. 12.

91. 'Books of the Day', *Freeman's Journal and Daily Commercial Advertiser* (Dublin), 7 June 1895, p. 2.

92. *The Referee*, quoted in Heinemann's advertisement, *The Times*, 28 May 1895, p. 12.

93. 'The Time Machine', *Nature*, 52, 18 July 1895, p. 268.

94. 'Chronicle and Comment', *The Bookman* (USA) III (4) (June 1896): 293. In late 1895 Wells claimed the sale of 10,000 copies: Smith. 'A chat with the author', p. 5.

95. Wells to his mother, 13 October 1895, Wells, *Experiment in Autobiography*, I, p. 400.

96. Wells to Davies, n.d. [May–June 1888], Smith, *The Correspondence of H. G. Wells, I*, p. 103; Wells, *Experiment in Autobiography*, I, pp. 372–4.

97. Richards, *Memories of a Misspent Youth*, p. 330, note.

and other Incidents – scheduled for early publication.[98] In particular, as Wells acknowledged, the publication of *The Time Machine*, first as a serial and then as a book, 'first won me recognition as an imaginative writer'.[99]

At last, there promised to be a strong, indeed growing, demand for his work from publishers, journal editors and readers by contrast with a period when he had to work hard to attract and keep an audience for his writing as well as to accept the regular return of rejected manuscripts. Writing shortly before *The Time Machine*'s publication as a book, Wells opined that the story's serialization in *The New Review*, combined with his early science fiction stories, meant that already 'I have indeed a kind of small public of my own in this constituency'.[100] The story's publication as a book vastly expanded Wells's reading public principally comprising – to quote Bernard Crick – 'those whose only university had been the public library', that is the lower middle class and the self-educated working class.[101] In part, Wells's ability to target a wider readership with his first scientific romance resulted also from the ongoing revolution in book, magazine and newspaper publishing in Britain outlined in Chapter 4, as well as from *The Time Machine*'s simultaneous publication across the Atlantic.

The Time Machine did wonders for Wells's image and visibility in London's literary circles. *The New Review*'s serialization won widespread attention – the monthly instalments were extensively advertised in the national and regional press – and attracted good reviews. London's literary world began to notice Wells as a new, indeed distinctive new, writer. As *The Reviews of Reviews* predicted, 'Mr Wells's book is sure to make a sensation'.[102] Writing to his mother, Wells reported the book's impact on London's literati world: 'Already I'm invited out to-night and every night next week except Monday and Friday. I've had letters too from four publishing firms asking for the offer of my next book but I shall, I think, stick to my first connection. It's rather pleasant to find oneself something in the world after all the years of trying and disappointment.'[103] As Richard Gregory observed, following the publication of *The Time Machine* Wells soon 'found himself recognized as a bright star rising above the horizon of the world of letters to radiate a new penetrating light before men'.[104]

The attention shown by the *Review of Reviews*, a monthly magazine edited by William Thomas Stead and published in Britain alongside American and

98. Wells to Healey, 20 February 1895, 'Wells H. G. Letters Healey Miss 8', *ALS* 1894–98 (Ransom).

99. Wells, *Experiment in Autobiography*, I, p. 309.

100. Wells to Heinemann, 14 May 1895, Smith, *Correspondence of H. G. Wells, I*, p. 240.

101. Bernard Crick, 'Introduction', in George Orwell, *George Orwell: Essays* (London: Penguin, 2000), p. ix.

102. *The Review of Reviews*, quoted in Heinemann's advertisement, *The Times*, 5 August 1895, p. 6.

103. Wells to his mother, 13 October 1895, Smith, *Correspondence of H. G. Wells, I*, p. 248.

104. Sir Richard Gregory, 'H. G. Wells: A Survey and Tribute', *Nature* 158, 21 September 1946, p. 406.

Australian editions, was especially significant. Claiming that virtually every book published during the early-mid 1890s passed through his hands when working for the *Review of Reviews*, Grant Richards repeatedly discovered good new writers, who he sought to bring to the attention of his seniors, most notably Stead and Grant Allen.[105] Normally, it proved difficult to make much impact on Stead – 'he had too many demands on his time' – but Richards recalls 'making him read H. G. Wells's *The Time Machine*' while it was being serialized in *The New Review*, thereby resulting in public acknowledgement of this 'remarkable' imaginative story:

> *The Review of Review's* warm praise of that story was some of the earliest that came to Mr Wells's and was either from that of my pen (as I have always thought) or from Stead's own. Myself. I had been led to enthusiasm over this new writer by some stories that appeared in Lewis Hind's *Pall Mall Budget* ... Extraordinary stories they are – of their kind there have been none better.[106]

Indeed, in March 1895 the *Review of Reviews* declared that 'H. G. Wells, who is writing the serial in the *New Review*, is a man of genius'.[107] Such comments helped ensure the success of the resulting book.[108] As Wells admitted, the *Review of Reviews* was the first major publication to give visibility to *The Time Machine*.[109] Reviewers welcomed Wells variously as 'a writer of distinct and individual talent' responsible for 'a fine piece of literature', 'a book of remarkable power and imagination' and a story making impressive and innovative use of science.[110] In this vein, *The Pall Mall Gazette*'s reviewer, highlighted the fact that in 1895 he remained still a 'comparatively new and little known' writer, offered a useful summary of the key qualities identified by fellow reviewers as well as an assessment of the book's significance for Wells as a writer:

> The ingenuity of the reasoning by which The Time Machine is constructed, the invention with which the adventure is pursued, the imagination which marks not only the plot itself, but the subsequent impressive scenes of the world's history – all these stamp the author as a writer of the highest talent. Mr Wells's name is comparatively new and little known. We make bold to prophesy that he is more likely to make a reputation than any young writer of his standing.[111]

105. Richards, *Memories of a Misspent Youth*, p. 157.

106. Ibid., pp. 158, 331; 'The World Several Millions of Years Hence', *The Review of Reviews* (New York), XI (June 1895): 701–2.

107. 'The New Review', *Review of Reviews*, XI (March 1895): 263.

108. Bergonzi, *Early Wells*, pp. 40–1.

109. Wells to Grant Richards, 6 November 1895, W-R13-1 (UIUC); Richards, *Memories of a Misspent Youth*, pp. 327–8.

110. *The Saturday Review* and *The National Observer*, quoted in Heinemann's advertisement, *The Times*, 5 August 1895, p. 6; Ruddick, 'Introduction', pp. 37–9.

111. 'Reviews: A. D. 802,701', *The Pall Mall Gazette*, 10 September 1895, p. 4.

Naturally, Henley, who had predicted, after reading the draft manuscript, that *The Time Machine* 'must certainly make you a reputation', took a close interest in developments, especially as he proved instrumental in its publication as both a serial and a book.[112] As *The New Review*'s serialization of the story came towards a close, Henley, to whom the published book was dedicated, informed Wells that his 'wonderful' story had 'gone some way toward placing its author as a man of letters'.[113] Moreover, the story's serialization had been a good thing for *The New Review* ensuring that its relaunch was a success, as acknowledged by *Vanity Fair*: 'Everything is New about the New Review under Mr. Henley's brilliant editorship'.[114] In turn, Heinemann, *The New Review*'s publisher, benefited from not only publishing the book but also establishing a link with Wells resulting also in securing the rights to *The War of the Worlds*.

Despite Wells's subsequent claim that *The Time Machine* was written in three weeks, the reality proved somewhat different.[115] The lengthy and complex bibliographical history of *The Time Machine* covering numerous rewrites, over a seven year period between 1888 and 1895, led Geoffrey West to represent Wells's first novel as the endpoint and outcome of a lengthy literary apprenticeship.[116] This story, based upon a consummate reworking of time travelling speculations first published as 'The Chronic Argonauts' in 1888 and reworked subsequently in 1894, reaffirmed Wells's narrative and imaginative skills in writing fiction about the future drawing upon his scientific knowledge and understanding. It proves – to quote David Smith – 'a significant and seminal work' showing readers the future through science: 'he provided readers with a masterpiece – not a masterpiece of plot, construction, or even of character, but a masterful marriage of the fictive art and theoretical science'.[117] For Nicholas Ruddick, Wells's 'time machine became a metaphorical vehicle for exploring the future of the human race'.[118] For George Gissing, the book promoted serious thought about the future of humankind.[119]

The success of *The Time Machine*, a story perceived by Wells as a test of his suitability for a literary life, meant that when Wells took up residence at Woking in May 1895 his career as a professional writer was on the launch pad. Whether or not the career of an author, described increasingly as one of Britain's most

112. Henley to Wells, 28 September 1894, Loing, *Wells à l'oeuvre*, p. 413.

113. Henley to Wells, 1 April 1895, Loing, *Wells à l'oeuvre*, p. 419.

114. *Vanity Fair*, quoted in Heinemann's advert, *The Standard*, 29 April 1895, p. 9.

115. For example, see Wells to Lee, 6 August 1904, Smith, *Correspondence of H. G. Wells, II*, p. 40.

116. Geoffrey West, *H. G. Wells*, pp. 287–95; Ruddick, 'Introduction', pp. 22–30; Loing, *Wells à l'oeuvre*, pp. 21–140.

117. Smith, *Wells*, pp. 50, 56–7.

118. Ruddick, 'Introduction', p. 11.

119. George Gissing to Henry Hick, 29 November 1895, in Paul F. Mattheisen, Arthur C. Young and Pierre Coustillas (eds), *The Collected Letters of George Gissing, Vol. 6: 1895–1897* (Athens, OH: Ohio University Press, 1995), p. 63.

promising new writers and attracting greater interest upon the part of editors and publishers would actually take off, depended very much on what happened next. In particular, could Wells build on this initial success with his ongoing and planned projects? Or would he prove a one-book wonder unable to write another scientific romance consolidating his claim to be one of the founders, perhaps even *the founder*, of science fiction? Alternatively, would living in Surrey's countryside help to improve his fragile state of health and avoid the early death he anticipated, while providing an environment conducive to Wells's strong work ethic?

Chapter 6

WELLS'S 'LITERARY FACTORY' IN WOKING

In May 1895 Wells and Jane took up residence in Woking, where they rented 'Lynton', 'a little house in the country' located within easy walking distance of Woking railway station.[1] As ever, money remained tight:

> We borrowed a hundred pounds by a mortgage on Mrs. Robbins' house in Putney and with that hundred pounds, believe it or not, we furnished a small resolute semi-detached villa with a minute greenhouse in the Maybury Road facing the railway line, where all night long the goods trains shunted and bumped and clattered – without serious effect upon our healthy slumbers.[2]

Aged twenty-eight, Wells, as portrayed in Figure 4.2, was described at the time by one contemporary as 'short, well-built, a finely developed head with a striking forehead, bluish eyes that show traces of hard work and a straggling moustache'.[3]

Despite arriving at Woking in ill health, Wells had no intention of slowing down as a writer. Woking was viewed as somewhere to recover his health as well as to move on from divorce, but for Wells the crucial consideration was to 'put in some good work' to launch his literary career.[4] For Wells, success as a writer would provide the financial security enabling him 'to settle down in the world' and support a lifestyle very different from that experienced, or rather suffered, at Atlas House.[5] Significantly, his arrival occurred only days before the scheduled publication of both *The Time Machine* and *Select Conversations with an Uncle*. In the event, positive reviews for *The Time Machine* – Wells especially welcomed Le Gallienne's praise in the *Star* – built upon the strong springboard provided by

---

1. Wells, *Experiment in Autobiography*, II, p. 542; Wells to Tommy [A. T. Simmons], Spring 1895, WS31 (UIUC). Ruddick claims mistakenly that they arrived at Woking in October 1895 and were married there: Ruddick, 'Introduction', p. 21.

2. Wells, *Experiment in Autobiography*, II, pp. 542–3; Wells to Simmons, Spring 1895, WS31 (UIUC). Wells did complain occasionally about the noise from the railway.

3. Picaroon, 'Portrait of Mr H. G. Wells', p. 367.

4. Wells to Tommy, Spring 1895, WS31 (UIUC).

5. Wells to Pinker, n.d. [c. 11 June 1896], Loing, *Wells à l'oeuvre*, pp. 430–2; Wells, *H. G. Wells in Love*, p. 27.

the favourable reception accorded to the story's serialization.[6] Of course, as Wells himself admitted, reviews were one thing. In the end, 'the public has got to buy the thing'.[7] And this they did, with over 6,000 copies of the book being sold in Britain within a few weeks of publication.[8] Moreover, reviews of *Select Conversations with an Uncle* – 'a book of cheerful rambling' reprinting stories previously appearing in the press – were generally positive.

Wells's second marriage

For Wells, the ongoing transformation in his personal fortunes was in part the product of adversity, the need to respond to 'a smashed kidney, a ruptured pulmonary blood vessel, an unsuccessful marriage, and an uncontrollable love affair'.[9] In this vein, Wells saw his stay in Woking as offering the opportunity to impart a semblance of domestic stability following the breakdown of his marriage and recent divorce. In particular, he sought to strengthen his relationship with Jane, or 'Bits' as he often called her, but without necessarily going as far as marriage. In the event, on 27 October 1895 they were married at St Pancras Register Office in London after returning temporarily to their previous lodgings in Mornington Road to fulfil the fifteen-day residential requirement for the civil marriage licence.[10] Marriage was, as Wells remarked, a reluctant response to 'the tart reproaches of the social system': 'Directly the unsoundness of our position appeared, servants became impertinent and neighbours rude and strange'.[11]

Over time Wells drew numerous illustrative sketches or cartoons, what he called 'picshuas', to complement the text of his letters and writings.[12] One Woking 'picshua', entitled 'A Satirical Picshua', contrasted 'Bits as she *finks* she is' – full of high pretensions, Jane floated radiantly like an angel – with 'The real Bits, really a very dear Bits indeed' preoccupied with mundane everyday activities,

6. Wells to Healey, 20 February 1895, Wells H. G. Autograph Letters to Miss Healey, 1888–1905, 35 *ALS* (Ransom); Wells to Tommy [A. T. Simmons], Spring 1895, WS 31 (UIUC); Wells to Healey, 10 June 1895, Wells H. G. Letters to Miss Healey, 1894–8, 8 *ALS* (Ransom).

7. Wells to Healey, 10 June 1895, Wells H. G. Letters to Miss Healey, 1894–8, 8 *ALS* (Ransom).

8. 'Chronicle and Comment', *The Bookman* (USA) III (4) (June 1896): 293. Another American commentator reported that some 12,000 copies were 'rapidly sold': Picaroon, 'Portrait of Mr H. G. Wells', p. 370.

9. Wells, *Experiment in Autobiography*, I, pp. 290–1.

10. Thus, 12 Mornington Road, not their Woking address, was listed on the marriage certificate as their place of residence. See Wells to his mother, 13 October 1895, Smith, *Correspondence of H. G. Wells, I*, p. 248.

11. Wells, *Experiment in Autobiography*, II, pp. 438, 519.

12. Gene K. Rinkel and Margaret E. Rinkel, *The Picshuas of H. G. Wells: A Burlesque Diary* (Urbana and Chicago, IL: University of Illinois Press, 2006), pp. 1–7.

like cycling, eating, gardening, sleeping and walking.[13] Indeed, at Woking, the Wells's conducted many of these suburban pleasures together – 'picshuas' show them taking pride in growing their first marrow or riding their lady-front tandem tricycle (Figure 4.3) – without worrying as much about money as in the past.[14] Wells remarked how quickly the days slipped away, as he spent time not only writing hard and fast but also 'cycling or messing about on the canal or walking' in the fresh air and countryside around Woking.[15]

> Close at hand in those days was a pretty and rarely used canal amidst pine woods, a weedy canal, beset with loosestrife, spiræa, forget-me-nots and yellow water lilies, upon which one could be happy for hours in a hired canoe, and in all directions stretched open and undeveloped heath land, so that we could walk and presently learn to ride bicycles and restore our broken contact with the open air.[16]

Despite claiming that they felt quite isolated socially, Wells admitted broadening the range of their personal and literary contacts: 'By the time of our removal, our circle of acquaintances and friends had increased very considerably. I will not catalogue names but one friendly figure stands out amidst much other friendliness, that once much reviled and now rather too much forgotten writer, Grant Allen.'[17] Other contacts included Richard Le Gallienne, who was renting a house at Hindhead and valued Wells's visit conducted in March 1896:

> He was very comforting … He seemed, if I may say so, quite to "look up" to me as a writer, and his scientific impersonal view of my present situation and the probable future was very helpful to me … [he] said everybody was waiting for a new big book by me, and advised a novel somewhat in the manner of the last *Prose Fancies*.[18]

Apart from welcoming his counsel, Le Gallienne was impressed by Wells as an author and particularly by his business-like attitude: 'He's a very unattached sort of chap – really belongs to no one set, but is just fighting, with a keen business eye, for his own hand, and, therefore, I valued his opinions the more'. Like Wells, Le Gallienne was a keen cyclist and subsequently Wells invited him to visit Woking, possibly travelling by bicycle.[19] Apart from visits by family members, other visitors

13. Ibid., pp. 44–5.

14. Ibid., pp. 45–7; Wells, *Experiment in Autobiography*, II, p. 536.

15. Wells to Healey, 10 June 1895, Wells H. G. Letters to Miss Healey, 1894–8, 8 *ALS* (Ransom).

16. Wells, *Experiment in Autobiography*, II, p. 543.

17. Ibid., p. 546.

18. Richard Whittington-Egan and Geoffrey Smerdon, *The Quest of the Golden Boy: The Life and Letters of Richard Le Gallienne* (London: Unicorn, 1960), p. 297.

19. Wells to Le Gallienne, n.d. (1895–6), Wells H. G. Letters G-Z, *ALS* (Ransom); Trotter, *The Hilltop Writers*, pp. 139–40.

included Sidney Bowkett, a former school friend who had recently returned from working as an actor in the USA and was now resident in Thames Ditton.[20]

Jane's role in Woking's 'Literary Factory'

Wells's relationship with Jane was built upon and reinforced by their 'unreserved co-operation in work and business affairs'.[21] Notwithstanding his serial infidelity, the initial phase of their marriage worked well and provided a strong foundation for Wells's writing, perhaps even explaining the surge in his work during his stay at Woking. Jane made a multi-faceted contribution enabling Wells to advance his career as an author who not only produced engaging creative imaginative work for his readers but also worked fast. In brief, Jane played a central support role for Wells's career as a writer in terms of fulfilling a wide range of roles: companion, wife, homemaker, manager, typist/secretary, literary consultant and critic.

Wells acknowledged that Jane, though 'overshadowed' as a writer, possessed her own 'very distinctive literary personality'.[22] Certainly she played an invaluable role supporting, promoting and enhancing Wells's career, most notably by clearing time and space for his writing, improving and typing up manuscripts and dealing with publishers, editors, agents and translators. As Wells pointed out, Jane expedited and improved the whole process: 'At first I sent my MSS. to be typed by a cousin… but later on my wife learnt to typewrite in order to save the delay of posting and waiting to correct copy, which latter process often necessitated retyping.'[23] Over time Jane's role became far more substantial than that of a secretary typing up drafts and then packing and posting completed manuscripts to publishers and editors: 'She not only typed, she scrutinized my text, watched after my besetting sin of verbal repetitions, and criticized and advised'. In one 'picshua' called 'Waiting for the Verdik' (1899), Wells anxiously awaits Jane's thoughts upon his latest manuscript.[24] Another 'picshua', 'The Narrative Machine' (1905), foregrounded Jane's role as the 'begetter' of his immense 'narrative flow' in terms of listening to his thoughts, supplying ideas, helping to gather research and offering much valued critical advice.[25] One 'picshua', drawn in November 1895 to mark the positive reception accorded to *The Time Machine*, depicts Jane working

20. Sarah Wells's Diaries, 1895, 21 August 1895 (UIUC); Wells, *H. G. Wells in Love*, pp. 58–60.

21. Wells, *Experiment in Autobiography*, II, pp. 461; Banerjee, *Literary Surrey*, p. 146.

22. Wells, *Experiment in Autobiography*, II, p. 462.

23. Ibid., p. 461.

24. G. and M. Rinkel, *Picshuas of H. G. Wells*, p. 192. Like other 'picshuas' mentioned here, 'Waiting for the Verdik' probably typifies previous practice. In one letter, Wells records reading his text out loud to 'Madam' and then making changes: Wells to Pinker, 21 July 1899, Loing, *Wells à l'oeuvre*, p. 448.

25. G. and M. Rinkel, *Picshuas of H. G. Wells*, pp. 196–7.

diligently at the desk surrounded by stacks of work and writing with a large quill pen: 'Got to write his old stories for 'm now'.[26]

In November 1895 Wells used 'The Shop of Authorship' (Figure 6.1), a multi-panelled 'picshua', to overview the whole literary process from writing, through production to sales, readers and reviewers. Wells depicts himself top left writing at a desk, a black cat at his side and with Jane providing support and advice.[27] The next frame shows Jane typing up the manuscripts fluttering down from Wells to her desk. Following the submission of the final text to publishers and the production of proofs, another frame shows Wells and Jane checking and correcting the proofs before the presses roll and the book reaches enthusiastic readers and reviewers. Finally, the authorship cycle ends with Wells carrying a bag of money, the financial reward of literary success. Subsequently Wells used a five-frame 'picshua' entitled 'The Literary Regimen' (1896) to represent the production process of his 'literary factory'.[28]

These 'picshuas', though impressionistic, record Wells's recognition of the manner in which from the mid-1890s onwards Jane, though making a far from insignificant literary input, increasingly assumed the role of office manager-cum-secretary, dealing with an ever growing number of administrative, business, financial and income tax matters, thereby leaving the way clear for Wells to write and to remain extremely productive: 'Quite early in our life together, so soon as I had any money, I began handing over most of it to her… I ceased more and more to look into things, satisfied when she told me that everything was "all right," and, when she died, I found myself half as much again better off than I had ever imagined myself to be'.[29] Depicting 'Bits as a Martian Invader', a 1898 'picshua' inspired by *The War of the Worlds*, Wells recorded how Jane had seemingly taken over his world.[30] Even so, in practice, Wells did not always adopt a 'hands-off' approach concerning his writing, particularly with regard to relationships with editors and publishers.

Working routine

Despite possessing an excellent track record in terms of starting, progressing and completing projects – normally at any one time he would have several future publications in hand at various stages of progress – Wells claimed to enjoy planning and researching stories far more than putting them down on paper. Indeed, in 1897 he admitted that 'I hate writing them'.[31] Whether or not he

26. Ibid., p. 181.

27. Wells, *Experiment in Autobiography*, II, p. 556.

28. Ibid., p. 558.

29. Ibid., p. 462.

30. G. and M. Rinkel, *Picshuas of H. G. Wells*, p. 189, p. 191,

31. 'The Output of Authors', *Pearson's Magazine* 3 (16) (April 1897): 460. This issue carried also the first part of *The War of the Worlds*. See also Wells to the Editor, *Pearson's Magazine*, n.d. [March 1897], Smith, *Correspondence of H. G. Wells, I*, p. 284.

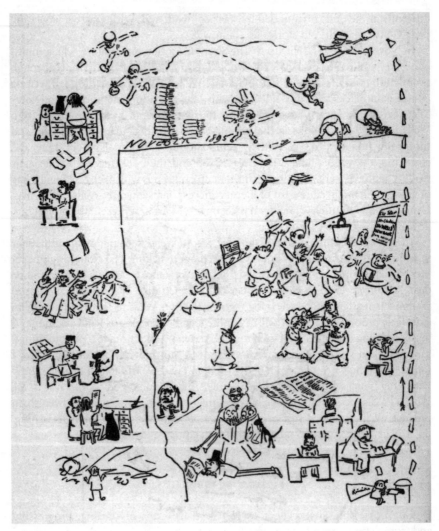

Figure 6.1 Picshua: 'The Shop of Authorship', November 1895. Wells's picshua shows his 'literary factory' at work, November 1895

Source: H.G. Wells, *Experiment in Autobiography, II* (1934), p.557.

really meant this remains debatable, although the perceived financial and other pressures compelling him to keep publishing, probably encouraged a certain negativity towards continually writing towards tight deadlines.

Writing in longhand with pencil or pen on foolscap, Wells claimed that 'I do all my work in M. S. Then it is typed, then I correct it & recorrect it'.[32] Reportedly he tended to 'burn' at least half of what he wrote. The task of making a fair typed copy

32. Wells to Mrs Tooley, n.d. [October–November 1908], WT37-1A-B (UIUC).

of his initial handwritten draft was undertaken increasingly by Jane. This stage was vital in terms of rewriting and firming up the text, since 'Wells' mind usually raced ahead of his pen on first writing.'[33] Few handwritten drafts survive, perhaps indicating that they were usually destroyed. Normally Wells claimed to write about 1,000 words per day, but admitted that while living in Woking he vastly exceeded that figure: 'For six months or more when I was scrambling for a footing among novelists, I must have turned out, Heaven forgive me! about 7,000 words each working day, "Moreau" and "The Wonderful Visit" came in that feverish time.'[34]

According to John Hammond, it was while living at Woking that Wells 'first established his routine of writing letters in the morning, cycling or walking in the afternoon, and getting down to serious literary work after returning from his cycle ride'.[35] Shortly after leaving Woking, Wells sketched out a typical working day in his 'literary factory':

> In the morning I merely revise proofs and typewritten copy, and write letters, and, in fact, any work which does not require the exercise of much imagination. If it is fine, I either have a walk or a ride on the cycle. We also have a tandem bicycle, and sometimes my wife and I take the double machine out; and then, after lunch, we have tea about half past three in the afternoon, and I like my tea extremely strong. It is after this that I do my real work. It is after this cup of tea that I do my work. The afternoon is the best time of the day for me, and, I nearly always work right on until eight o'clock, when we have dinner. If I am working at something in which I feel keenly interested, I work on from nine o'clock until after midnight, but it is on the afternoon work that my output mainly depends.[36]

The insecurities of an increasingly successful new writer

Wells's emergence as a successful new writer attracting increasing recognition from the literary world and building up a substantial readership was not unproblematic. Despite experiencing a generally upward path as a writer, during the mid-late 1890s Wells faced still a series of challenges affecting his life, work, reputation and income:

i)   Did writing fast impact adversely upon literary quality?;
ii) Could Wells maintain his reputation as a writer of engaging scientific romances?;

33. Smith, *Wells*, p. 30; Hughes, *Edition and a Survey*, pp. 16–19.

34. 'The Output of Authors', p. 460; Wells to the Editor, *Pearson's Magazine*, n.d. [March 1897], Smith, *Correspondence of H. G. Wells, I*, p. 284.

35. John Hammond, 'Wells and Woking', *Foundation: The International Review of Science Fiction* 28 (77) (1999): 6. Compare Smith, *Wells*, pp. 30–1.

36. Lawrence, 'The Romance of the Scientist', p. 255; 'Record Portraits: no. XXV H. G. Wells', *The Bromley Record and Monthly Advertiser*, February 1898, p. 22.

iii) Could Wells keep his name visible to readers through a regular cycle of
      published books?;
iv)   Would Wells succeed in getting and keeping his finances on an even keel?;
v)   Would Wells be able to move on to establish himself as a writer of
      mainstream novels?; and
vi)   Would Wells's relationship with publishers remain problematic?

i) Did writing fast impact adversely upon literary quality?

Having welcomed *The Time Machine*, Henley maintained a close watch on Wells's
writing, even adopting a kind of mentoring role. In particular, he soon articulated worries about the productivity of the Woking 'literary factory' when raising
questions about the implications for both Wells's fragile health and writing quality.
Was Wells's anxiety to make his name causing speed of completion to take priority
over qualitative and other considerations? Having set out the issues, Henley urged
him to heed the advice of an 'Elderly Ass':

> You must take a rest and slow ... I believe in your future; & I don't want to see
> it foundered. I believe in your future; & I don't want to see it commonplaced.
> And you really frightened me: you work so easily, & up to a certain level all you
> do is so equal in excellence. But you can do better – far better; & to begin with,
> you must begin by taking yourself more seriously.[37]

What concerned Henley, what he thought should have been 'far better', was Wells's
The Wonderful Visit. Having been accepted by Dent upon the basis of reading
some sixty or so pages, *The Wonderful Visit* was published in London and New
York in September 1895.

Reportedly, the storyline, centred upon the sudden descent of an angel into a
small English village a short distance from the coast, was inspired by a remark
attributed to John Ruskin to the effect that if an angel arrived in England most
people would simply treat it as a new species of bird to be shot or recorded by bird
spotters. Thus, the angel, represented by the local people as a strange bird, was
hunted and shot in the wing by the local vicar, a keen ornithologist. For Wells, the
story, 'a thing about a Vicar and an angel, grotesque and humorous', was intended
to highlight 'the littleness, the narrow horizon' of people's lives.[38] In effect, the story
was used to enable readers to view present-day society, most notably the role of
class and property, in a 'fresh light' through the eyes of an outsider.[39] As Bergonzi
commented, the story, albeit 'an exercise in pure fantasy', gained strength from its

37. Henley to Wells, 5 September 1895, Loing, *Wells à l'oeuvre*, p. 423.
38. Wells to Simmons, n.d. [Spring 1895], WS 31 (UIUC); Wells to Dent, 1 May 1895,
Smith, *Correspondence of H. G. Wells, I*, p. 239; quoted, Bergonzi, *Early Wells*, p. 89.
39. 'Mr H. G. Wells', *The Graphic*, 7 January 1899.

account of contemporary English rural life.[40] In many respects, this descriptive element means that in spite of being a fantasy *The Wonderful Visit* is not listed as one of Wells's scientific romances. Certainly, it lacked their originality, as noted by *The Glasgow Herald's* reviewer when recording previous examples of writers using visitors from another world to critique present-day society.[41] Inevitably, there are other opinions and in 1899, *The Graphic* praised *The Wonderful Visit* as perhaps 'his most promising achievement' to date.[42]

Henley's response to the book proved somewhat mixed. Despite acknowledging that *The Wonderful Visit* was both 'very good reading' and amusing, he claimed that the writing proved 'a little sloppy here and there', possibly because the quality of the prose was being sacrificed for speed of completion:

> I know it should have been better than it is ... And I am moved to suspect that the real fault is the one you've named; that the thing has been too quickly done ... it will succeed ... But I can't help feeling, that it might, & ought to have been very much stronger, more moving, more direct & elemental, than it is.[43]

Henley claimed that Dent, the publisher, wished also that the book 'had been better'.[44] Fearing that dashing books off so quickly risked damaging both his fast growing literary reputation and frail health, he urged Wells to slow down and reduce his workload: 'For Heavens' sake, take care of yourself. You have a unique talent; and – you've produced three books, at least, within the year, & are up to the elbows in a fourth! It is magnificent, of course; but it can't be literature.'[45] Even so, Henley, having been apprised of Wells's future plans, could not resist indicating his pleasure upon learning about *The War of the Worlds'* project, what he represented as 'the Martialist visitation'.

Notwithstanding being always respectful of such expert counsel, Wells refused to rest upon his laurels and heed advice to adopt a slower pace of work. Nor did he keep to the resolution, such as expressed to Grant Richards in November 1895, to concentrate on longer works. Indeed, soon afterwards he was writing to editors and publishers indicating his preparedness to squeeze in extra stories to his busy schedule, especially if a commissioning editor was willing to pay at least six guineas [£6.30] per thousand words for a 3,000 word story.[46] One visitor to 'Lynton' during late 1895 noticed 'a tottering pile of books' awaiting review.[47]

40. Bergonzi, *Early Wells*, p. 89; Smith, *Wells*, p. 63.

41. 'Novels and Stories', *The Glasgow Herald*, 3 October 1895, p. 7.

42. 'Mr H. G. Wells', *The Graphic*, 7 January 1899.

43. Henley to Wells, 5 September 1895, Loing, *Wells à l'oeuvre*, p. 423.

44. Henley to Wells, 8 November 1895, Loing, *Wells à l'oeuvre*, p. 425.

45. Henley to Wells, 5 September 1895, Loing, *Wells à l'oeuvre*, p. 423.

46. See Wells to unknown recipient, 10 January 1896, Smith, Ernest B. misc. 4 *ALS* (Ransom); Wells to unknown correspondent, 13 January 1896, Smith, *The Correspondence of H. G. Wells, I*, pp. 257–8.

47. Smith, 'A chat with the author', p. 9.

Despite his growing fame and wealth and seemingly terminal health condition, Wells continued to work hard and fast. Paradoxically, one reason explaining Wells's heavy workload was the genuine expectation of early death, the belief that he was 'a dying man' and hence the strong conviction to work fast in order to write much of what he wanted to do.[48] During his high intensity periods, Wells was prone to use a metaphor by way of articulating his mindset: 'the dying candle just now is in a taste of flare before the final flicker cometh'.

In a short story entitled 'How I Died', published in Certain Personal Matters in 1897, the central character, 'a doomed man' who had received his 'death warrant' ten years earlier, drew heavily upon Wells's personal expectations of an early death.[49] Even so, like the narrator in 'How I Died', everyday life and growing success as a writer meant that at times Wells, though constantly 'dodging' death, 'quite forgot I was a Doomed Man': 'Another ream of paper; there is time at least for the Great Book still'. At any one time, he had several projects in hand at varying stages of progress: planning, research, writing, editing and finalizing proofs. As he admitted, a 'driving quality' pushed him to keep writing: 'I put too large a proportion of my available will and energy into issues that dominate me. Only in that way do I seem able to get on with these issues that dominate me. I have to overwork – with all the penalties of overworking in loss of grace and finish – to get my work done'.[50]

The fact that Wells continued not only to write as much, indeed more than ever, in defiance of the advice of Henley, among others, but also to plan ambitious future projects suggested that he found Woking a good place in which to combine work and play, a place beneficial for his health, relationship with Jane and writing. His high productivity during 1895–6 establishes that the town provided a supportive environment for Wells the writer in terms of inspiring, planning, researching, contracting, starting, writing and completing articles, short stories, books and reviews for publication in Britain and the USA. Despite his relatively brief stay there, Woking figured at some stage or another in the production of all the scientific romances published before 1900 (Table 6.1) as well as in The Wonderful Visit, The Wheels of Chance and Love and Mr Lewisham. Furthermore, the way in which The War of the Worlds draws heavily upon the local geography raises the question as to whether such a book would ever have been written but for Wells's residence in Woking.[51] Wells's "Woking period' saw the publication also of some one hundred articles, short stories and reviews. Loing's listing thereof extends over three pages.[52]

48. Wells to Healey, 28 April 1888, Smith, The Correspondence of H. G. Wells, I, pp. 98–9.

49. H. G. Wells, Certain Personal Matters (London: Lawrence & Bullen, 1898), pp. 274–8.

50. Wells, Wells in Love, p. 34.

51. Banerjee, Literary Surrey, p. 142.

52. Loing, Wells à l'oeuvre, pp. 551–3.

Table 6.1 Wells's Woking 'Literary Factory'

SCIENTIFIC ROMANCES

Title	What happened while Wells lived at Woking
The Time Machine	Published as a book
The Island of Dr Moreau	Completed; published
The Invisible Man	Started, largely written
The War of the Worlds	Started; completed for serialization
When the Sleeper Wakes	Started
OTHER BOOKS	
Select Conversations with an Uncle	Published (short stories previously published in the press)
The Wonderful Visit	Started; completed; published
The Stolen Bacillus and Other Incidents	Published (short stories previously published in the press)
The Wheels of Chance: A Holiday Adventure	Started; completed; serialized; published as a book
Love and Mr Lewisham	Started

ii) Could Wells maintain his reputation as a writer of engaging scientific romances?

Today, Wells's scientific romances prove central to perceptions of him as a major British author. Within this context *The Island of Dr. Moreau*, his second scientific romance about a mad scientist, is viewed as just another title in the genre, whose long-term success as a book exploring the ethical dimension of science has been matched by its adaptability for film and so on. Moreover, Wells often named it as one of his best works.[53] However, when the book was originally published, its reception proved somewhat lacklustre, especially as compared to that for *The Time Machine*. Negative reviews predominated, with Stead, hitherto one of the most influential literary admirers of Wells's *The Time Machine*, opining that the book 'ought never to have been written'.[54]

Having started writing the book while living in London, Wells began seeking a publisher prior to the release of *The Time Machine*. In the event, the difficulties experienced in placing the story either directly or indirectly through Watt soon apprised Wells of the way in which its storyline about the misuse of science for evil purposes through experiments on animals and humans was viewed as 'a trifle gruesome', a veritable 'festival of 'orrors'.[55] As a result, in August 1895, Wells decided to exploit the success of *The Time Machine* by making a direct approach to Heinemann, its publisher, with a view to publication during late 1895 or early 1896. Following discussions centred principally upon the size of the advance and

53. Lawrence, 'The Romance of the Scientist', pp. 256–7.

54. Stead, 'The Book of the Month', p. 393.

55. Wells to Dent, 2 January 1895, Smith, *Correspondence of H. G. Wells, I*, p. 228; Wells to Healey, n.d. [24 May 1896], WB78/7 (UIUC).

royalty arrangements, on 20 August 1895 Wells signed a contract for the publication of *Dr. Moreau* as a six shilling novel.[56] Having demanded an advance of £100, Wells settled for £75, plus a 15 per cent royalty for the first 5,000 copies and then a 20 per cent royalty on further copies. A royalty of 3d [£0.0125p] would be paid for each copy sold of the colonial edition. No contract for serialization was secured.

More significantly, Heinemann's contract for *The Island of Dr Moreau* confirmed that *The War of the Worlds* was now moving up Wells's writing priorities. Thus, it stipulated that Heinemann would have 'the sole and exclusive right' to publish 'another original work by the said Herbert George Wells entitled at present *The War of the Worlds*'.[57] Royalty arrangements for the latter would be the same as those for the *Moreau* book, while the advance would be equal to the royalties earned by that book during the first year after publication. Revenue from translation rights and continental editions would be divided with two-thirds accruing to the author, the rest to the publisher.

In the event, *The Island of Dr Moreau*, scheduled for publication in January 1896, suffered also from a delayed release date. Writing to his brother Fred in South Africa, Wells pointed to the way in which a disturbed international situation, most notably difficult British–German relations and the Jameson Raid in South Africa, delayed its publication until March: 'Here things have been of the liveliest, war rumours, all the Music Halls busy with songs insulting the German Emperor, fleets being manned, and nobody free to attend to the works of a poor struggling author from Lands End to John o' Groats. Consequently a book I was to have published hasn't been published, and won't until March.'[58] In August, it was published by Stone & Kimball in New York. Despite attracting praise for the narrative's 'daring' and 'imaginative' qualities, Wells's 'biological nightmare' was regarded by most reviewers as far worse than merely 'gruesome'.[59] Rather it was treated as a real shocker, even, as Stead commented in *The Review of Reviews*, a book that should never have seen the light of day.[60] Likewise *The Times*, admitting its hesitancy in reviewing a book with such a 'perverse' storyline, advised readers

56. Wells to Heinemann n.d. [August 1895], Smith, *Correspondence of H. G. Wells, I*, p. 243; Wells to Heinemann, August 1895, Memorandum of Agreement, 20 August 1895, Wells to Heinemann, 30 March 1905, Author File: H. G. Wells, Heinemann Archive (Rushden); Wells to Heinemann, August 1895, Smith, *Correspondence of H. G. Wells, I*, p. 243; St. John, *Heinemann*, p. 33. In 1905 Wells proposed a new agreement with a uniform 15 per cent royalty on the three scientific romances published by Heinemann.

57. Wells to Heinemann, August 1895, Memorandum of Agreement, 20 August 1895, Author File: H. G. Wells, Heinemann Archive (Rushden).

58. Wells to Fred Wells, 24 January 1896, Wells, *Experiment in Autobiography*, I, p. 401.

59. 'Review: The Island of Dr Moreau', *The New York Times*, 16 August 1896; N. and J. MacKenzie, *The Time Traveller*, pp. 125–6; Anthony West, *H. G. Wells*, pp. 230–2.

60. Stead, 'The Book of the Month', p. 393.

that the book should be 'avoided by all who have good taste, good feeling, or feeble nerves'.[61]

Certainly, *The Island of Dr Moreau* rates as the scientific romance most criticized by contemporary reviewers, as highlighted when Wells replied to one correspondent praising the book that 'I'm very glad to find anyone who thinks well of my Moreau'.[62] Some reviewers were prompted to draw comparisons with *Frankenstein*, except that on Moreau's island there were 'nearly 200 horrible monsters instead of one'![63] Significantly, as discussed in Chapter 14, *Island of Lost Souls*, a 1932 film adaptation of Wells's novel, proved equally problematic. But Wells, though disappointed, was not discouraged, given his belief that the book possessed 'the vitality to live through its troubles'.[64] As mentioned above, he often claimed that *The Island of Dr Moreau* was one of his best works, but generally speaking he has proved a lone voice on this point.[65] Unsurprisingly, Wells welcomed the rare supportive review such as appeared in *The Guardian*, a Church of England weekly.[66] Wells claimed, even when he was a new writer, to ignore, even to prove 'impervious', to reviews of his work.[67] In reality, just as he basked in the praise accorded to, say, *The Time Machine*, so he resented critiques targeting *The Island of Dr Moreau*: 'Damn all the silly nonsense about the public! I'm going to do my own work in my own way'.[68]

iii) Could Wells keep his name visible to readers through a regular cycle of published books?

Notwithstanding recent publication successes on both sides of the Atlantic, during the mid- to late-1890s Wells was haunted still by a range of insecurities, especially fears that his popularity might prove somewhat ephemeral. Thus, during the latter part of his stay in Woking, Wells speculated that he might be experiencing merely 'a little boom' and hence would be forced eventually to return to journalism.[69] Inevitably, the hostile reception accorded to *The Island of Dr Moreau* acted as a reality check by showing that media images of him as a skilled and imaginative

61. 'Recent Novels', *The Times*, 17 June 1896, p. 17.

62. Wells to unknown correspondent, [17 December 1896], Smith, *Correspondence of H. G. Wells, I*, p. 279.

63. 'Review: The Island of Dr Moreau', *The New York Times*, 16 August 1896.

64. Wells to unknown correspondent, 17 December 1896, Smith, *Correspondence of H. G. Wells, I*, pp. 279–80.

65. Lawrence, 'The Romance of the Scientist', pp. 256–7.

66. *The Guardian*'s review, dated 3 June 1896, can be interpreted as more critical than supportive: Anthony West, *H. G. Wells*, pp. 231–2.

67. Hughes and Geduld, *Critical Edition*, p. 26.

68. Wells to Pinker, n.d. [1896], H. G. Wells: Letters to J. B. Pinker & Sons, Literary Agents, Vol. 1 [henceforth Pinker, Vol. 1] (Ransom).

69. Wells to Sergeant, [Autumn 1896], Smith, *The Correspondence of H. G. Wells, I*, p. 273.

writer of engaging scientific romances, could not be taken for granted. Indeed, it seemed important to retrieve his reputation in this sphere as soon as possible and particularly to show the literary world that as a writer of scientific romances, he was not a one-book wonder.

Wells placed great emphasis also upon keeping his name before the reading public captivated by *The Time Machine*: 'I shall be forgotten if I don't publishing [*sic*] anything but short stories' in any one year.[70] As a result, during April 1896 Wells reviewed his publications schedule for the next two years. Having set an annual target of two substantial projects, defined as long stories serialized and published as books, he worried about a gap in 1897.[71] For 1896 there was *The Island of Dr Moreau* and *The Wheels of Chance* – the former had already been published, while the latter was scheduled for publication later in the year – but only *The Plattner Story and Others*, a collection of short stories, was listed for 1897. *The War of the Worlds*, viewed by Wells as crucial in re-establishing his image as a writer of well-regarded engaging scientific romances, was pencilled in as a book for publication in 1898 following the completion of magazine serialization in 1897.

Contemplating additional projects likely to do well on the bookstalls in 1897, Wells decided in favour of a story called *The Man at the Coach and Horses*, but retitled *The Invisible Man* for publication. Drawing in part upon his stay during the early 1880s at Midhurst, West Sussex, renamed Bramblehust for the purposes of the story, the tale started in the nearby village of Iping when a stranger, swathed in bandages and excessive clothing, walked into 'The Coach and Horses' public house. By mid-June 1896 Wells, who was still finalizing *The War of the Worlds* for serialization in *Pearson's Magazine*, had already written some 25,000 words to help Pinker, one of his literary agents, to place the story as both a book and a serial.

Whereas Heinemann had published Wells's two previous scientific romances and held the British book rights for *The War of the Worlds*, *The Man at the Coach and Horses* was contracted to C. Arthur Pearson as both a serial and a book. Despite Wells's hopes of securing an American serialization, Pinker failed to sell the serial rights in the USA.[72] Following a further burst of writing during July and August 1896, typically the manuscript was then put aside as Wells commenced work on two new projects – *When the Sleeper Wakes* and *Love and Mr Lewisham* – and left unfinished until February 1897, when he was living in Worcester Park.[73] Then, just prior to serialization, Wells decided 'to take it all to pieces & reconstruct it'.[74] Serialized in *Pearson's Weekly* in June and July 1897, *The Invisible Man* was

70. Wells to Pinker, n.d. [16 April 1896], Pinker, Vol. 1 (Ransom).

71. Wells to Colles, 15 April 1896, 24 ALS, H. G. Wells Correspondence, Beinecke Rare Book and Manuscript Library, Yale University, New Haven, Connecticut, USA (Yale).

72. Wells to Pinker, n.d. [c. 11 June 1896], Loing, *Wells à l'oeuvre*, p. 430.

73. Wells to Healey, n.d. [November 1896], Smith, *The Correspondence of H. G. Wells*, I, p. 278; Anthony West, *H. G. Wells*, pp. 234–7; Wells to unknown American correspondent, 25 November 1897, Loing, *Wells à l'oeuvre*, pp. 436–7.

74. Wells to Edmund Gosse, 2 October 1897, Smith, *The Correspondence of H. G. Wells*, I, p. 290.

published soon afterwards as a book by Pearson in London and Edward Arnold in New York. Significantly, in Britain *The Invisible Man* returned to Woking for printing at Unwin Brothers, who had moved to Old Woking in mid-1896 following a fire at their works in Chilworth.

iv) Would Wells succeed in getting and keeping his finances on an even keel?

Uncertainty about how long his health and success would last, in conjunction with his ever-growing list of financial commitments, meant that an 'assured income' remained a constant factor in Wells's thoughts.[75] Following occasional flirtations with bankruptcy, during the mid- to late-1890s Wells's finances continued to improve (Table 6.2). In January 1896 Wells, though representing himself still as 'a poor struggling author', informed his brother Fred that things were going 'very well altogether ... things are on the move towards comfort', particularly given the success of *The Time Machine* both as a serial and a book: 'I made between five and six hundred last year, and expect to make more rather than less, this year'.[76] Hitherto, he had made regular payments to support his parents, but his enhanced wealth enabled him to fulfil his long expressed desire to do more: 'I've just taken a pretty little house at Liss ... for the old folks'.[77] As Wells recorded in his autobiography, 'Every year for a number of years my income went on expanding in this fashion', thereby enabling him to pay off quickly the costs of his divorce, meet punctually the alimony payable to Isabel, continue supporting his parents, cover his health expenses and 'accumulate a growing surplus'.[78] One Woking 'picshua', dated 1895, showed Jane interviewing and engaging their first servant.[79]

One year later, Wells informed his brother that 1896, when his predicted earnings totalled between £800 and £1,000, more than lived up to expectations: 'next year it will be more and after that still more'.[80] Although the present-day equivalent of his 1896 income is over £125,000, Wells claimed that hitherto his

75. Wells to Pinker, n.d. [16 April 1896], Pinker, Vol. 1 (Ransom).

76. Wells to Fred Wells, 24 January 1896, *Experiment in Autobiography, 1*, pp. 401–2. Table 6.2 suggests that Wells repeatedly underestimated his annual earnings.

77. Wells to Fred Wells, 24 January 1896, Wells to his parents, 5 February 1895, *Experiment in Autobiography, 1*, pp. 400–2.

78. Wells, *Experiment in Autobiography*, I, pp. 375–6.

79. Wells, *Experiment in Autobiography*, II, p. 545. Although this represented a marked step forward for the Wells, the employment of domestic servants was commonplace throughout Victorian society upon the part of the lower middle classes upwards and not necessarily an indicator of great wealth. The picshua included as Figure 4.4 shows a servant waving goodbye to the Wells as they depart for a cycling tour.

80. Wells to Freddy [Wells], 31 December 1896, in Wells, *Experiment in Autobiography*, I, p. 407. See also Lovat Dickson, *H. G. Wells: His Turbulent Life and Times* (London: Readers Union, Macmillan, 1971), p. 72.

Table 6.2 H. G. Wells's annual income, 1893–6

1893	£380 13s 7d [£380.68]
1894	£583 17s 7d [£583.88]
1895	£792 2s 5d [£792.12]
1896	£1,056 7s 9d [£1,056.39]

Source: Wells, *Experiment in Autobiography, 1*, pp. 367, 375.

Note: Wells's 1893 income included teaching fees. The present-day monetary equivalents of Wells's 1895 and 1896 income are c. £93,014 and £125,477 respectively.

success had 'meant more fame than money to me', since he viewed his income more as a symbol of what he had achieved rather than as something enabling an extravagant lifestyle:

> I have been still on the rise of fortune's wave this year, and it seems as though I must certainly go on to still larger successes and gains next for my name still spreads abroad, and people I have never ever seen, some from Chicago, one from Cape Town, and one from far up the Yung T'se Kiang in China, write and tell me they find my books pleasant.

Writing to Pinker in September 1898, Wells indicated his willingness to move on at last from renting to buying a house, given the favourable state of his finances; thus, his estimated literary earnings of £1,600 including £250 for *The War of the Worlds*, meant that he would have about a £1,000 or so in hand.[81]

v) Would Wells be able to move on to establish himself as a writer of mainstream novels?

Despite appreciating the distinctive appeal of his scientific romances and the way in which *The Time Machine* had grabbed the attention of both the literary world and readers, Wells thought increasingly of moving on to mainstream novels, as evidenced during August 1896 when he began writing not only another scientific romance, *When the Sleeper Wakes*, but also a novel entitled *Love and Mr Lewisham*. What he referred to as his 'South Kensington novel' – the storyline of *Love and Mr Lewisham* was to be set around 'the museums and the schools and the streets of Clapham and Chelsea and so forth' – reflected his growing desire to write something perceived as being more 'ample' and prestigious than scientific romances.[82]

81. Wells to Pinker, 20 September 1898, Loing, *Wells à l'oeuvre*, pp. 439–40.
82. Wells to Healey, n.d. [November 1896], WB 78/8 (UIUC); Anthony West, *H. G. Wells*, pp. 234–7.

Fundamentally, Wells wanted to be known principally as a writer of mainstream novels rather than fantastic fiction: 'I finished the *War of the Worlds* in the summer of 1896. Then, said I, let me do something worthy to prove I'm no charlatan'.[83] When sounding out Dent about *Love and Mr Lewisham*, Wells went out of his way to stress that it was not another scientific romance, but rather 'a sentimental humorous story' like *The Wheels of Chance*, which Dent published in 1896.[84] For Wells, the novel's factional element proved a key selling point: 'Mr Wells has not merely studied this /// [blank] of life he will describe in his novel; – he has lived it'.[85]

Wells saw *The Wonderful Visit* (1895) – as previously discussed – and *The Wheels of Chance* (1896) as providing a sound foundation for this particular career direction. Set during the late Victorian 'cycling craze', *The Wheels of Chance* offered readers an engaging carefree story highlighting both the charms of rural Surrey, Sussex and Hampshire and the appeal of cycling. When seeking to interest magazine editors in serializing *The Wheels of Chance*, Wells expressed confidence in the story's appeal to their readers: 'The details of bicycle riding, carefully done from experience, & the passing glimpses of characteristic scenery of the south of England, should, I think, appeal to a certain section of the public'.[86] Stressing that the proposed book possessed 'no "scientific" element', Wells claimed that of his previous work the story most resembles *The Wonderful Visit*.[87] Completed by December 1895, *The Wheels of Chance* was serialized in Jerome K. Jerome's *Today* between May and September 1896 and published as a book in October 1896 by Dent in London and Macmillan in New York. The serial rights were offered initially to Henley, who liked the story but concluded 'it's not for me, I fear'.[88] Instead, he advised Wells to approach Jerome, the founder and editor of *Today*: 'But make him pay for it'.

Reviewing the book, *The Bookman* praised Wells for performing a major feat in terms of writing 'the first bicycle novel readable by such as have not fallen victims to cyclomania'.[89] The storyline won strong praise in the USA, where *The Bookman*'s reviewer opined that the book would take Wells to a large American

83. Wells to Healey, n.d. [4 January 1898], Wells, H. G. Letters Healey, Miss 8 *ALS* 1894–8 (Ransom).

84. Wells to Dent, 12 September 1896, Loing, *Wells à l'oeuvre*, p. 432; 'News Notes', *The Bookman* 13 (76) (January 1898): 113.

85. Wells to Pinker, n.d. [October 1896], Loing, *Wells à l'oeuvre*, p. 433.

86. Wells to Editor, *Blackwood's Magazine*, 29 November 1895, Wells to unknown correspondent, 2 January 1896, in Smith, *Correspondence of H. G. Wells, I*, pp. 250–1, 256–7. Reportedly, *The Wheels of Chance* 'was written from week to week to meet the requirements of serial publication': 'News Notes', *The Bookman* 13 (76) (January 1898): 113.

87. Wells to unknown correspondent, 2 January 1896, in Smith, *Correspondence of H. G. Wells, I*, pp. 256–7; Wells to Harpers, 15 October 1895, Loing, *Wells à l'oeuvre*, p. 426.

88. Henley to Wells, 1 January 1896, Loing, *Wells à l'oeuvre*, p. 426.

89. 'The Wheels of Chance', *The Bookman* 11 (64) (January 1897): 124.

audience.[90] Undoubtedly, for many readers, the book's appeal derived in part from the fact that it offered much more than a good story focused upon cycling, as viewed through the trials and tribulations of Hoopdriver, an apprentice draper on holiday. For more thoughtful readers, *The Wheels of Chance* illuminated broader themes concerning, say, personal liberty, the oppressive nature of retail apprenticeships, class, personal relationships and female cyclists. In effect, Wells pointed to the cultural and socio-economic impact of the bicycle, given the manner in which the plot – to quote Simon James – 'depends on the democratising effects both of new styles of clothing alongside another class-levelling, cheaply produced technological innovation, the safety bicycle'.[91]

Despite building upon such a strong foundation, Wells soon discovered that writing a novel like *Love and Mr Lewisham* made new demands upon him as an author. Although he claimed that the initial section, 'The First Book', was finished by October 1896, he realised the need to extend the scheduled completion date well beyond the initial target date of Christmas 1896: 'Heaven knows when it will get done, for writing fantastic romance is one thing, and writing a novel is quite another'.[92] In the event, *Love and Mr Lewisham* was not published until 1900.

vi) Would Wells's relationships with publishers remain problematic?

For Wells a major irritation concerned his dealings with publishers. Generally speaking, these relationships proved somewhat difficult, often quarrelsome, even fractious and frequently short term. Wells's preoccupation with image and money came increasingly to dominate his dealings with publishers whether conducted directly or indirectly through Jane, or literary agents. In part, Wells sought to use agents to secure an additional edge in his dealings with publishers. As he told one agent, 'I want money to work on. If I can get it through agents I will & if I can't I shall get it my own way'.[93] Agents also proved invaluable in securing and negotiating rights for serialization, publication overseas and translations. Indeed, Wells admitted that James Brand Pinker, who had published his articles when editing *Black & White* in 1894 and acted as launch editor of *Pearson's Magazine*, obtained ten times more for serial and American rights than he could have negotiated for himself. Despite admitting that they fulfilled a useful role, Wells tended also to

90. Mathilde Weil, 'A modern Don Quixote', *The Bookman* (USA) IV (4) (December 1896): pp. 362–3; Lawrence, 'Romance of the Scientist', pp. 256–7.

91. Simon J. James, '*Fin-de-cycle*: romance and the real in *The Wheels of Chance*', in Steven McLean (ed.), *H. G. Wells: Interdisciplinary Essays* (Newcastle: Cambridge Scholars, 2008), p. 41.

92. Wells to Healey, n.d. [November 1896], WB78/8 (UIUC).

93. Wells to Cazenove, n.d. [December 1908], Smith, *Correspondence of H. G. Wells, II*, p. 232. See also Wells to Quilter, (December 1898), Smith, *Correspondence of H. G. Wells, I*, p. 335.

regard literary agents 'with suspicion tinged with derision'.[94] In fact, this was one of the few points upon which he was in agreement with Heinemann, who viewed agents as parasites.[95] Unsurprisingly, Wells's relationships with literary agents often proved equally problematic.

Focusing increasingly upon advances and royalties, Wells adopted a demanding, frequently abrupt, attitude towards publishers and agents in the light of the success of his recent writings and strong conviction in the commercial worth of forthcoming publications. Also, Wells believed that the more he demanded and received, the more effort publishers would make to market his work in order to recoup their investment. Wells's perception of his constantly improving bargaining position *vis-à-vis* publishers, led him to take every opportunity to exploit the situation, such as evidenced when he instructed Pinker to take advantage of the fact that 'War of the Worlds will double our prices'.[96] Typically beginning communications to publishers with, 'What do you offer?', or to literary agents along the lines of 'How much will Pearson give?', Wells demanded higher advances and improved royalty arrangements for books, better payments for serial rights and more money per thousand words for short stories.[97] Little wonder, that at one stage Dent accused Wells of being 'sordid'.[98]

Wells's desire to protect his image as regards readers and reviewers while maximizing sales and revenue, led him to take a close interest also in the pricing of books. Thus, despite fearing that a lower price risked devaluing the book in the eyes of reviewers, Wells agreed to Pearson's suggestion to price *The Invisible Man* at 3s 6d instead of the planned six shillings, in order to enhance sales and income from royalties.[99] Pearson reassured him that 'reports of my travellers' indicated that a cheaper version would sell 'four times as well', especially as the book was deemed rather short for a six shilling novel. Nor was Wells slow in checking publishers' statements of accounts – in fact, frequently this task was undertaken by Jane – and chasing up delayed payments. For example, even when holidaying at Budleigh Salterton during Summer 1897, Wells reminded Pinker that Pearson still owed £150 for the serialization of *The War of the Worlds*.[100]

Against this background, Wells frequently represented publishers as the enemy – at one time, he dismissed them as 'the most stupid human beings' – rather than as allies in reaching out to the reading public: 'I loathe the brainless production

94. Wells to Watt, 5 October 1926, Smith, *The Correspondence of H. G. Wells, III*, pp. 222–3

95. St. John, *Heinemann*, pp. 90–5.

96. Wells to Pinker, n.d. [1897], Pinker, Vol. 1 (Ransom).

97. Wells to Colles, 3 February 1896, 24 *ALS*, Yale; Wells to Dear Sir (Pearson?), n.d. (1895–6), Smith, Ernest B. Misc. (Ransom).

98. Wells to Dent, 17 September 1896, Smith, *Correspondence of H. G. Wells, I*, pp. 269–70.

99. Pinker to Wells, 28 April 1897, Loing, *Wells à l'oeuvre*, p. 434.

100. Wells to Pinker, n.d. [Summer 1897], Pinker, Vol. 1 (Ransom).

of the common publisher intensely'.[101] Typically, in June 1896 Wells told Pinker that he found it a 'devil of a business' dealing with publishers: 'I'm sick of all my present publishers'.[102] In many respects, this comment reflected his recent war of words with Pearson conducted in part through Colles, another of his literary agents, about the serialized version of *The War of the Worlds*, most notably regarding deadlines and the story's length and conclusion.[103] Notwithstanding Wells's somewhat prejudiced take upon him, Pearson – to quote Locke – 'probably did more to advance the cause of SF [science fiction] than any other person at that time', even if his support for science-based fiction was more a function of his desire to boost magazine circulations than for literary reasons.[104] Pearson expected high standards – like any publisher, such pressure was designed to result in a more publishable and popular product – but paid well and ensured that *Pearson's Magazine* reached a large readership. Reportedly, he distributed one million illustrated pamphlets advertising the serialization of *The War of the Worlds*.[105]

Unsurprisingly, Wells had scarcely a good word to say about any of his publishers. Thus, he criticized John Lane for slow progress towards publication of *Select Conversations with an Uncle*, failing to advertise the published book and then delaying payments.[106] Dent, the publisher of *The Wonderful Visit* and *The Wheels of Chance*, was criticized for poor production, unsatisfactory illustrations, a refusal to correct textual errors and insufficient advertising.[107] Nor did William Heinemann avoid incurring Wells's not inconsiderable wrath: 'My transactions with Heinemann have been a lesson to me'.[108] Having agreed in effect to let Heinemann, the publisher of *The Time Machine*, have the next two scientific romances on the understanding that the books would be actively marketed, Wells complained bitterly about Heinemann's 'want of advert and gen neglect' of *The Island of Dr Moreau*. In part, he attributed alleged inaction to unfavourable reviews: 'he disappointed me by funking the "Island" pitifully because the Chronicle slated it'. In turn, arguments about the accuracy of statements of accounts, including alleged overpayments, led Wells to propose cancelling all existing contracts – this would have resulted in *The War of the Worlds* becoming available to offer other publishers – between them, while dropping hints about

101. Wells to Grant Allen, n.d. [1896], Wells to Quilter, n.d. [December 1898], Smith, *Correspondence of H. G. Wells*, I, pp. 265, 335.

102. Wells to Pinker, n.d. [c. 11 June 1896], Pinker, Vol. 1 (Ransom).

103. Wells to Colles, 26 March 1897, H. G. Wells, Autograph Letters (Ransom).

104. Locke, 'Wells in three volumes?', p. 285.

105. Pinker to Wells, 28 April 1897, Loing, *Wells à l'oeuvre*, p. 434.

106. Wells to Lane, n.d. [May–June 1896], Smith, *Correspondence of H. G. Wells*, I, p. 265.

107. Wells to Quilter, n.d. [December 1898], Smith, *Correspondence of H. G. Wells*, I, p. 335.

108. Wells to Dent, 12 September 1896, 17 September 1896, Smith, *Correspondence of H. G. Wells*, I, pp. 268–9. See also his strong critique of Heinemann: Wells to Heinemann, 8 July 1898, Smith, *Correspondence of H. G. Wells*, I, p. 315.

litigation.[109] By way of retaliation, Wells offered the serial and book rights for *The Invisible Man* to Pearson, not Heinemann.

In the event, the contract with Heinemann for *The War of the Worlds* remained in force, but Wells made it clear that the book had to be actively marketed. Also, any future publication would require better terms: 'Otherwise I cut him off for ever'.[110] Inevitably, the publication of *The War of the Worlds* in January 1898 was soon followed by yet another chapter in their fraught relationship, which had not been helped by Wells's irritation with Heinemann's repeated requests prior to publication for more words to justify its price. Despite acknowledging good sales of *The War of the Worlds* accruing royalties of c. £230 in the first five months, Heinemann claimed that sales would have been much higher if 'the book had been longer', as he had requested repeatedly.[111] Seeking to acquaint Wells with bookselling realities, he commented that 'however distasteful such an admission must be to the artist, it is one of the elements which a publisher has to consider, because it affects sales': 'The book had from the purely bookselling point of view a great disadvantage, being looked upon as too little for the money ... it is impossible to get a large public to pay six shillings for a book of 60,000 words if they can get another book of 160,000 words for the same money'. Responding to Wells's complaints about the lacklustre marketing of *The War of the Worlds*, Heinemann defended his sales strategy, which included press adverts, personal visits to libraries and big trade houses and the issuing of instructions to his company's representatives to promote the book: 'we used every legitimate means at our disposal for pushing its sale'. Wells was unimpressed, even confrontational: 'I'm sick of seeing my good honest work fizzle in obscure corners'.[112]

Nor did things improve when Wells asked for an advance of £750 and increased royalties for his next scientific romance *When the Sleeper Awakes*. For Heinemann, Wells's demands were 'out of all proportion to what I consider fair'.[113] Wells gave Heinemann an ultimatum: 'it's £750 or nothing. If you don't intend to publish the book on that scale you are no good to me as a publisher ... Practically then this negotiation is at an end'.[114] Wells took the opportunity also, to press his view of the 'them and us' nature of the relationship between publishers and writers: 'I have been told once or twice that publishing is not philanthropy. But authorship is not solely for the support of the class of publisher'. No contract was concluded with Heinemann for When *the Sleeper Wakes*, which was published by Harper in both London and New York.

Meanwhile, Heinemann retained rights to three scientific romances, but published no further titles written by Wells, even if in 1910 Wells thought about

109. Wells to Heinemann, n.d. [7 August 1897], 19 April 1899, 22 May 1899, Smith, *Correspondence of H. G. Wells, I*, pp. 288, 340–41.

110. Wells to Pinker, n.d. [1896], Pinker, Vol. 1 (Ransom).

111. Heinemann to Wells, 7 July 1898, Pinker, Vol. 1 (Ransom).

112. Wells to Heinemann, 8 July 1898, Pinker, Vol. 1 (Ransom).

113. Heinemann to Wells, 7 July 1898, Pinker, Vol. 1 (Ransom).

114. Wells to Heinemann, 8 July 1898, Pinker, Vol. 1 (Ransom).

returning with *The New Machiavelli*. For St John, Wells offered a vivid example of the fact that 'Heinemann was brilliant at discovering and contracting the up-and-coming authors of his day, too often he failed to hold on to them. Too many moved elsewhere'.[115] On the other hand, Wells, even the early Wells, had his own selfish agenda and hence proved a difficult writer for any publisher to handle. Indeed, Wells's tirades against individual publishers offer useful insights into his character, including an arrogant belief that he knew best, an urgent quest for fame and money, a preoccupation with the financial details of contracts and an anxiety about the pricing and marketing of his publications. As J. B. Priestley opined, Wells was 'not difficult to quarrel with' for he proved highly opinionated, 'Prickly, often intolerant, exasperated and exasperating'.[116]

Conclusion

Apart from planning to publish at least two books every year in terms of keeping his name in the public eye and providing financial security for the wider family, Wells's output included numerous short stories and reviews. Indeed, his workload led several commentators, such as *The New York Times*'s William Alden, to echo Gissing, Henley and Pinker in worrying about possible adverse impacts upon both the quality of his writing and his health.[117] Having praised Wells's 'brilliantly successful' *The War of the Worlds* and admitted looking forward to his future publications, in March 1898 William Alden expressed the hope that 'someone would prevail upon him to do less work':

> Naturally he wishes to take advantage of his present popularity, but by writing two or three books every year he will not only do himself injustice, but will overstock the market. I am ready to read anything Mr Wells will write, but for his own sake he ought to do less work than he has been doing for the last three years.[118]

Conceding occasional instances of hasty execution, Wells began gradually to agree with such thinking, even admitting to the constraints exerted by the relentless pressure to deliver the goods and meet deadlines. For example, when preparing a revised edition of *When the Sleeper Wakes* for publication in 1910, he took the opportunity not only to improve what he regarded as one of his 'least satisfactory' books, but also to amend the title to *The Sleeper Awakes*. Wells used the preface to look back upon his earlier work:

115. St John, *Heinemann*, p. 75.

116. J. B. Priestley, 'Right or wrong. H. G. Wells was a major prophet of this age: He saw the shape of things to come', *Daily Mail*, 14 August 1946.

117. N. and J. Mackenzie, *The Time Traveller*, p. 133.

118. William L. Alden, 'London Literary Letter', *The New York Times*, 19 March 1898, 23 April 1898.

Like most of my earlier work, it was written under considerable pressure; there are marks of haste not only in the writing of the latter part, but in the very construction of the story … I was at that time overworked, and badly in need of a holiday. In addition to various necessary journalistic tasks, I had in hand another book, *Love and Mr Lewisham*.[119]

Of course, most writers revisiting a previous book will see the scope for improvements and changes, even in the case of books, like *When the Sleeper Wakes*, generally well-reviewed upon their original publication. The fact is that throughout the period 1893–1900, Wells viewed himself as writing under great pressure in order to launch his career as a professional writer, make his reputation, keep his name in front of the reading public and achieve financial security. As a result, he overworked, wrote fast, pursued several projects at the same time, took too few holidays, employed literary agents and adopted a somewhat fraught 'us and them' relationship with publishers and magazine editors.

Looking back in his autobiography, Wells asserted that living in Maybury Road, proved 'a fairly cheerful adventure' for Jane and himself: 'We lived very happily and industriously in the Woking home'.[120] In fact, soon after taking up residence there, Wells, who had recently described himself as 'in a gorgeous state of cockiness just now', admitted it was 'a good time' for him as a writer.[121] Even so, he took nothing for granted. Soon after his arrival *The Time Machine* appeared as a book and proved instrumental in launching Wells's literary career, providing a strong foundation for Wells's 'literary factory' and marking Wells's freedom from the burdens imposed by the drapery counter, pharmacy indentures and teaching. Today, Wells's time in Woking is associated almost exclusively with *The War of the Worlds*. In reality, the Woking years proved an extremely productive period for Wells the writer, as he himself admitted: 'There I planned and wrote the *War of the Worlds*, the *Wheels of Chance* and the *Invisible Man*.'[122] In fact, there was much more, as he completed work on *The Wonderful Visit* and *The Island of Dr Moreau*, began writing *When the Sleeper Wakes* and *Love and Mr Lewisham* and wrote numerous articles, short stories and book reviews. But the principal and most enduring products of Woking's literary factory were the scientific romances. In particular, they established Wells's ability to write engaging stories for his fast-growing band of readers while exploring themes possessing an enduring contemporary resonance, including – to quote Ruddick – 'the complex nature of time; the uncertain relation between biological evolution and social progress; and the ultimate meaning of human life in the context of the universe as understood by science'.[123]

119. H. G. Wells, *The Sleeper Awakes* (London: Penguin, 2005), p. 3.

120. Wells, *Experiment in Autobiography*, II, pp. 542, 546.

121. Wells to Tommy [A. T. Simmons], Spring 1895, WS 31 (UIUC); Wells to Healey, 10 June 1895, Wells H. G. Letters to Miss Healey, 1894–8, 8 *ALS* (Ransom).

122. Wells, *Experiment in Autobiography*, II, p. 543.

123. Ruddick, 'Introduction', p. 11.

Chapter 7

WRITING *THE WAR OF THE WORLDS*

Following *The Time Machine*'s successful serialization and launch as a book, Wells began to see himself increasingly as a writer rather than a journalist. Scaling down his journalism, Wells prioritized writing scientific romances at least for the time being: 'it seems to me pseudo-scientific romance is the line for me to take just now'.[1] This meant completing *The Island of Dr Moreau*, a story started and 'hacked' around a good deal before leaving Camden Town and then moving on to the 'big scientific story remotely resembling "The Time Machine"', that is *The War of the Worlds*.[2] Even so, in practice, Wells could never quite shake off his journalistic past, nor forego the opportunity for extra income by seeking and accepting commissions for articles, books, reviews and short stories.[3] Nor did the concentration upon scientific romances prevent him harbouring ambitions to write what he saw as mainstream fiction.

In many respects, *The War of the Worlds,* was to prove even more successful than Wells's previous scientific romances. It was the first to be serialized and published as a book on both sides of the Atlantic, and was – and still is – viewed by many commentators, reviewers and readers as his most engaging, influential and enduring work to date. The story, though largely written during 1895–6, was not published until 1897–8, when the serial and book versions reinforced the impact made already by Wells upon the literary world and the reading public during an extremely brief time period by *The Time Machine, The Wonderful Visit, The Island of Dr Moreau, The Wheels of Chance* and *The Invisible Man*. Taken together, these books made Wells's name and fortune. Far from appearing still as an up-and-coming writer, Wells could well claim to have arrived.

1. Wells to Healey, 10 June 1895, Wells H. G. Letters to Miss Healey, 1894–8, 8 *ALS* (Ransom).

2. Wells to Simmons, n.d. (March 1895), Smith, *Correspondence of H. G. Wells, I*, p. 236; Wells to Grant Richards, 6 November 1895, W-R13-1 (UIUC).

3. The extent of Wells's journalism is indicated by Loing's four-page listing: Loing, *Wells à l'oeuvre*, pp. 550–4.

The inspiration for The War of the Worlds

When leaving London in May 1895, Wells, it seems, had nothing specific in mind regarding *The War of the Worlds*'s project, even if he implied that the fundamental inspiration for the story was already in his head from the early 1890s. What proved instrumental, Wells recorded, was a conversation while out walking with his brother Frank about 'some disregarded possibility', a point recognized when he dedicated the resulting book, 'To my brother Frank Wells, this rendering of his idea'.[4] Generally speaking, this undated exchange has been represented as taking place somewhere in the Surrey countryside, a view reflecting the fact that Wells was researching and writing the story while living in Surrey, the county's prominent role in the actual story and an assertion made by Wells himself in 1920:

> The book was begotten by a remark of my brother Frank. We were walking together through some particularly peaceful Surrey scenery. "Suppose some beings from another planet were to drop out of the sky suddenly," said he, "and begin laying about them here!" Perhaps we had been talking of the discovery of Tasmania by the Europeans – a very frightful disaster for the native Tasmanians! I forget. But that was the point of departure.[5]

The mention of Tasmanians, reveals also Wells's preoccupation with the sins of British imperialism, a point made in the opening pages of the book (I.1: 4–5/9).

Confusingly, Wells is also on record as asserting that this exchange with Frank took place elsewhere, that is on London's Primrose Hill, another location figuring prominently in the story and close to where he had been lodging prior to his move to Woking. Moreover, this version gains additional credence, from the fact that it was published in a newspaper interview conducted in 1898 shortly after the book's publication:

> 'The War of the Worlds' originated in a remark made to me some years ago by my brother, as we were walking on Primrose Hill one day, about the bombardment of some village in the South Seas. 'How would it be with us', he said, 'if some creatures of a vastly superior power came down upon us and behaved like a drunken man-of-war's crew let loose among some gentle savages?'[6]

---

4. Hughes and Geduld, *Critical Edition*, p. 1; 'The Scientific Novel'. The dedication, though included in the edition edited by Martin Danahay, *The War of Worlds* (Peterborough, ON: Broadview Press, 2003), p. 39, is not reproduced in the 2005 Penguin Classic edition.

5. Wells, '*The War of the Worlds*: Introduction: An experiment in illustration', p. 154; Hughes and Geduld, *Critical Edition*, p. 1; Charles E. Gannon, *Rumors of War and Infernal Machines: Technomilitary Agenda-setting in American and British Speculative Fiction* (Lanham MD: Rowman & Littlefield, 2005), p. 102.

6. 'The Scientific Novel'.

Wells's mention of 'some years ago', suggests that the exchange took place during the early to mid-1890s, while the reference to 'the 'South Seas' reaffirms his anti-imperial stance.

Nor are these the only recorded explanations. Writing a biography of his father – his mother was Rebecca West, one of Wells's many mistresses – Anthony West offered yet another scenario linked to *The Time Machine* and particularly to the Time Traveller's recognition of the evolutionary conflict, represented by the inhuman Morlocks:

> The seed idea for *The War of the Worlds* is to be found in *The Time Machine*, in the passage that describes the fears that crowded in on the Time Traveller as he hurtled into the future: suppose that, in the enormous interval between the *now* of his departure and that of his arrival, some eight hundred thousand years further on, mankind had undergone substantial evolutionary changes and had "developed into something inhuman, unsympathetic, and overwhelmingly powerful?".[7]

Developing this hypothesis in *The War of the Worlds*, West argues that Wells introduced 'a fresh element' centred upon the arrival on Earth of alien invaders, Martians far ahead of earthlings. Hitherto, West's scenario has made little impact on Wellsian literature.

When looking back in 1920, Wells took the opportunity also to contextualize *The War of the Worlds* in a broader manner touching upon points discussed already in Chapters 3 and 4, while introducing a gloss reflecting the passage of time, hindsight and the experience of living through the First World War:

> In those days I was writing short stories, and the particular sort of short story that amused me most to do was the vivid realization of some disregarded possibility in such a way as to comment on the false securities and fatuous self-satisfaction of the everyday life – as we knew it then. Because in those days the conviction that history had settled down to a sort of jog-trot comedy was very widespread indeed. Tragedy, people thought had gone out of human life for ever. A few of us were trying to point out the obvious possibilities of flying, of great guns, of poison gas, and so forth in presently making life uncomfortable if some sort of world peace was not assured, but the books we wrote were regarded as the silliest of imaginative gymnastics. Well, the world knows better now.[8]

In a press interview conducted in January 1898, Wells admitted having 'a second idea' a few years after forming his initial thoughts about an alien invasion.[9] This concerned the vision of 'an empty and depopulated London', a scenario 'suggested

7. Anthony West, *H. G. Wells*, pp. 232–3. The quoted section is from H. G. Wells, *The Time Machine* (London: Penguin, 2005), p. 22.
8. Wells, '*The War of the Worlds*: Introduction: An experiment in illustration', p. 154.
9. 'The Scientific Novel'.

to me almost simultaneously by a friend in conversation and by a wild whirling book I chanced upon, "A Sensational Trance" by Mr Dawson', a book Wells read soon after his arrival in Woking. Exploring the extravagant imaginings of a man falling into a trance, Forbes Dawson's book, published in July 1895 to mixed but generally unenthusiastic reviews, imagined a dead London.[10] Attracted by the project's literary possibilities, most notably affording the writer 'fine effects', Wells explored alternative ways of 'how to get London still and empty': 'First a pestilence, only that wouldn't do it quickly enough: and total depopulation would make it impossible for the one odd, immune man. That left flight: and then, thinking it all over, came my brother's old idea of creatures from another planet'.[11] But from which planet? For Wells, a walk on Horsell Common in Woking, proved crucial in helping to structure his initial thoughts:

> At that time I was living in Woking, and one day walking on Horsell Common there came to me suddenly a vivid picture, clean into my head, of the invaders just arrived in one of those inter-planetary cylinders which I borrowed from their inventor, Jules Verne. What planet should I choose? came next. Well, Mars, of course, as being the only one at all like the earth, older than the earth, and so likely to contain more advanced creatures. From that other facts followed necessarily.

The choice of Mars was undoubtedly influenced also by the manner in which Mars had not only emerged as a serious topic of contemporary interest on both sides of the Atlantic – the Mars boom was discussed in Chapter 3 – but also figured in Wells's recent journalism. Jules Verne did not write much about Mars, but a brief reference to his writings in a local Woking paper during August 1895 might have acted as an additional prompt.[12]

As Wells's leading ideas evolved and came together, 'All that remained was to write the story'.[13] Whatever the actual sources of inspiration for *The War of the Worlds* – the 1898 *Daily News* interview might be taken as providing a more authoritative guide than the 1920 article to Wells's thinking when writing the book – Wells was firming up his intentions by late summer and early autumn 1895, when he began to make contact with publishers and editors in Britain and the USA. In Britain, the book version was contracted along with *The Island of Dr Moreau* to Heinemann, in August 1895. Representing the story as 'a scientific romance on the lines of my *Time Machine* & *Island of Doctor Moreau*', Wells told an American publisher that *The War of the Worlds* would be 'less "difficult" than the former, less horrible than the latter & longer & more elaborately finished than

10. 'Fiction', *Saturday Review of Politics, Literature, Science and Art*, 17 August 1895, p. 216. 'New books', *The Pall Mall Gazette*, 26 August 1895.

11. 'The Scientific Novel'.

12. 'Art and Literature', *The Woking News and North-West Surrey Gazette*, 2 August 1895, p. 2.

13. 'The Scientific Novel'.

either'.[14] At this time, *The Island of Dr Moreau* was still in press, and hence had yet to arouse the controversial reception outlined in the previous chapter.

Wells's initial thinking about the project's imaginative possibilities was given substance through research conducted when walking and cycling in and around Woking, just as when a schoolboy he used to imagine 'early war fantasies' making Bromley 'one of the greatest battlegrounds in history'.[15] Thus, in Woking, he 'would take his bicycle of an afternoon and note the houses and cottages and typical inhabitants and passers-by, to be destroyed after tea by Heat-Ray or smothered in the Red Weed' by 'my Martians'.[16] Nor, he told Elizabeth Healey, would his fictional invaders confine their actions to Woking – they would also destroy South Kensington where he went to college: 'I'm doing the dearest little serial for Pearson's new magazine, in which I completely wreck & destroy Woking – killing my neighbours in painful and eccentric ways – then proceed via Kingston and Richmond to London, which I sack, selecting South Kensington for feats of peculiar atrocity.' [17]

The Necropolis factor

Seeking to explain at least in part why when living in Woking Wells wrote a book centred upon an apocalyptic vision of mass destruction and numerous deaths, Jacqueline Banerjee pointed to the town's 'unique and rather morbid' origins: 'Long before Wells came to live here, this ordinary-looking mid-Surrey town was renowned, in fact, notorious, for its connection with death'.[18] For Wells, Banerjee argued, the Necropolis cemetery and the local crematorium gave Woking a strong connection with death, particularly by burning. Thus, *The War of the Worlds* features dreadful fires characterized by a 'sharp resinous twang [tang] of burning' (I.11: 79/51) reducing the whole area below the narrator's house in Maybury, into 'a valley of ashes' (I.11: 86/55), a charnel house of burnt corpses.

During the late Victorian period, Woking acquired national, even global, media visibility regarding both burial and cremation in terms of possessing not only the 500-acre London Necropolis cemetery, the largest burial ground in the country, but also Britain's first-ever crematorium.[19] For example, throughout the mid- to late-nineteenth century the 300,000 plus readers of the *Illustrated London*

14. Wells to Harpers, 15 October 1895, Loing, *Wells à l'oeuvre*, p. 424.

15. Wells, *Experiment in Autobiography*, I, pp. 101–2.

16. Wells, *The Works of H. G. Wells*, III, pp. ix–x; Wells, *Experiment in Autobiography*, II, p. 543.

17. Wells to Healey, n.d [May 1896], WB78/7 (UIUC). In Wells's 'Argonauts of the Air' (December 1895), a flying machine crashes into the Royal College of Science at South Kensington.

18. Banerjee, *Literary Surrey*, p. 147.

19. Local histories often record 400 acres, but the company's brochure states 500 acres: *The London Necropolis Company*, November 1898, p. 4, SHC 6852/7/1/5 (SHC).

News received a steady flow of reports regarding both projects.[20] Other Woking-based topics attracted occasional media coverage – these included the Royal Dramatic College and its successor body, the Oriental Institute, the Shah Jahan Mosque, golf, Jackmans and Waterers plant nurseries and shooting at Bisley – but at the national level Woking's image was linked most closely to the cemetery and crematorium, ongoing debates about cremation and media reports about the funerals and cremations of famous people.

Revealingly, during the 1890s and 1900s Woking football club, founded in 1889, was nicknamed 'the Cremators'.[21] Reportedly, in 1908 when lowly Woking football club reached the last sixty-four in the FA Cup against Bolton, one northern athletic journal previewed the game: 'Bolton Wanderers will introduce a new combination to Lancashire. They are called Woking, a town where they cremate the great dead. Next Saturday evening the mortal remains of Woking will be consigned south, but they will not be subjected to a fiery ordeal. They will pass through the furnace of Burnden.' Bolton triumphed 5–0 in a match giving renewed visibility to Woking's national image as a town associated with death.

Largely developed on land sold off by the London Necropolis Company, the Victorian town of Woking was – to quote Alan Crosby – 'unique in the means of its birth and development: there were many railway towns, steel towns, canal towns and mining towns, but nowhere else in Europe was a cemetery town'.[22] In turn, the Cremation Society, founded in 1874, selected Woking as the site for Britain's first-ever crematorium, which was constructed at St John's on land purchased from the London Necropolis Company. In part, the society's decision was influenced by the pre-existing train service suitable for conveying the dead between London and Brookwood. Notwithstanding initial local opposition to the construction of a crematorium and the more fundamental problem of selling the case for cremation to both the government and society as a whole, the initial cremations took place at St John's Crematorium in 1885.[23] During the early 1890s, over one hundred cremations per year were taking place there. By 1905, when

20. 'Woking Cemetery', *Illustrated London News* XXI (579–80) (18 September 1852): 214; 'The London Necropolis and National Mausoleum', *Illustrated London News* XXI (598) (18 December 1852), p. 548; 'The Great Cemetery at Woking', *Illustrated London News* XXVIII (795–6) (25 April 1856): 462, 464; 'A Visit to Woking Cemetery', *Illustrated London News* XXXIII (928) (24 July 1858): 77; 'Home News' [on cremation], *Illustrated London News* XCVIII (2701) (24 January 1891): 98. The crematorium was covered regularly in Andrew Wilson's 'Science Jottings', referenced below.

21. Mark Doyle, 'The burning question is, why the Cremators?', Woking *Football Club Programme*, 9 December 2006; Mark Doyle, 'How the Cremator name came to be', *Woking News and Mail*, 12 December 2013, p. 38. During the early twentieth century, the team became increasingly known by its present-day nickname 'The Cardinals'.

22. Crosby, *History of Woking*, p. 77.

23. Ibid., pp. 100–1; 'The Crematory at Woking', *The Sanitary Record*, 24 January 1879, p. 49, SHC PX/160/56 (SHC).

it had been joined by a further twelve crematoria dotted across the country, the crematorium at Woking had conducted 2,888 cremations.[24]

Nor were such images lost on Wells, who reportedly confessed to be fascinated by what Arthur Mee represented as the 'great camp of the dead' at nearby Brookwood.[25] When looking back to his move in 1895, Wells recalled that 'Woking was the site of the first crematorium but few of our friends made more than five or six jokes about that'.[26] Wells's interest in the application of science suggests that he was likely to be aware of such columns as Andrew Wilson's 'Science Jottings', published during the 1890s and 1900s in the *Illustrated London News*, where he wrote supportively about cremation and highlighted Woking crematorium's central role.[27] Moreover, media coverage of the burials and/or cremations of famous people and others possibly known to Wells – the first wife of Richard Le Gallienne was cremated at Woking in 1894 – repeatedly reinforced the Woking linkage.[28] Shortly after Wells took up residence in Maybury Road, Friedrich Engels (1820–95), the author of The *Condition of the Working Class in England* (1844) and Karl Marx's collaborator on *The Communist Manifesto* (1848), was given a high profile funeral attracting a large cosmopolitan gathering, including Marx's daughters.[29] Leaving the Necropolis Company's station at London Waterloo, a special train conveyed Engels's body and mourners to the company's station at Brookwood. The body was then taken by horse and carriage to the crematorium

24. Andrew Wilson, 'Science Jottings', *Illustrated London News* CXXX (3536) (26 January 1907): 146.

25. Arthur Mee, 'Brookwood', *The Kings' England: Surrey: London's Southern Neighbour* (London: Hodder and Stoughton, 1938), pp. 332–3; Clarke, *London's Necropolis*, p. 62. Having selected a plot in a section reminding her of a private park, Rebecca West, one of Wells's lovers, was buried at Brookwood in 1983.

26. Wells, *Experiment in Autobiography*, II, p. 542.

27. Andrew Wilson, 'Science Jottings', *Illustrated London News* C (2758) (27 February 1892), p. 272.

28. Charles Bradlaugh, founder of the National Secular Society and mentioned in Wells's *Experiment in Autobiography*, I, p. 184, and Sherborne's biography (pp. 46, 57, 61), was buried at Brookwood in February 1891. He was admired by Wells for seeking to change the world through his advocacy of such causes as atheism and birth control. Mourners included David Lloyd George, John Morley and a young Mahatma Gandhi: John M. Clarke, *The Brookwood Necropolis Railway*, 4th edn (Usk: Oakwood Press, 2006), pp. 113–16. W. E. Henley was cremated at Woking in 1903.

29. 'Engels' funeral – yesterday', *Reynolds's Newspaper*, 11 August 1895; 'Obituary: The Late Friedrich Engels', *The Times*, 12 August 1895, p. 10; 'Personal', *Illustrated London News* CVII (2939) (17 August 1895), p. 198; Gareth Stedman-Jones, 'Friedrich Engels', *Oxford Dictionary of National Biography*, Oxford University Press, 2004; online edn, September 2010, http://www.oxforddnb.com/view/article/39022 [accessed 27 March 2012].

at St Johns.[30] A few years later, in April 1898, Eleanor Marx, Marx's daughter, was cremated at Woking.[31]

However, by the mid-1890s the local media and a growing number of Woking residents began to view the town's close identification with death in general and the cemetery company in particular as a serious drag upon the town's image and future development. Quite apart from lobbying Woking Council for improved local infrastructure, the Woking Improvement Association pressurised the London Necropolis Company to downplay the cemetery's Woking location in its advertising, since the cemetery was over three miles distant from the town centre and the company's trains ran straight into a private station within the cemetery.[32] Reporting the association's concerns and actions, in July 1897 *The Woking Mail* published a supportive editorial arguing that 'it seems hard that Woking should have to suffer for something with which it has absolutely nothing to do':

> A petition has, on their initiative, just been forwarded to the London Necropolis Company, praying that the name of Woking may be omitted in future from all the company's advertisements ... The injury done to Woking, particularly as a growing residential neighbourhood, by the association of the name with interments, is unquestioned and considerable. The general public, not being acquainted with the facts, have been led exclusively to connect Woking with burials and cremations. In this light the town would appear, even to the most practical, to offer serious drawbacks as a place of residence; while sentimental folk would turn from the bare contemplation of the idea with a shudder.

The editorial argued that the company, being large landowners, would benefit from the town's further growth boosted by the removal or scaling down of its negative image. In fact, the extent to which the link with the cemetery and cremation hindered the town's growth remains uncertain, especially as demographic data (Table 5.1) challenge the pessimistic assumptions articulated by the Woking Improvement Association and *The Woking Mail*.

Significantly this campaign came at the very moment *The War of the Worlds* was being serialized by *Pearson's Magazine* – extracts were published between April and December 1897 – detailing death and destruction in Woking. Neither the London Necropolis Company, Brookwood Cemetery nor Woking Crematorium featured in the story, but it seems possible that the association's campaign was inspired at least in part by the magazine serial. The large circulation of *Pearson's Magazine* implies that many Woking residents must have seen the serial, but its impact is not revealed in local newspapers. In the short term Woking's destruction

30. Clarke, *Brookwood Necropolis Railway*, pp. 117–18.

31. Ibid., p. 118; Clarke, *London's Necropolis*, p. 271 n.18.

32. 'Editorial: Local affairs: The Improvement Association', *The Woking Mail*, 10 July 1897, p. 4. At its general meeting held in October, the association reported that the company met the petition 'in a most friendly spirit'. Early action was anticipated: 'Woking Improvement Association', *The Woking Mail*, 9 October 1897, p. 5.

in *The War of the Worlds* can be interpreted as reinforcing the images of the town Woking critiqued by the Woking Improvement Association and *The Woking News and Mail*, but over time the town's linkage with Wells in general and *The War of the Worlds* in particular has proved highly positive, especially as the story's page-turning nature and popularity pushed aside negative features. Wells went on to become one of the leading British authors and acquire a global literary reputation from which Woking could only benefit. Thus, *The War of the Worlds* took Woking's name across Britain and the wider world both as a book and through the story's adaptation into alternative audio-visual formats.

Writing The War of the Worlds *as a serial and as a book*

Generally speaking, Wells wrote at speed and proved capable of completing a book quickly.[33] However, in practice the history of writing any one book often proved somewhat extended, on account of his tendency to have several projects in progress at any one time and repeatedly to start and stop writing individual stories. As Wells recalled, *The War of the Worlds* and *The Invisible Man* were written 'in intermittent periods of spontaneousness. They were often dropped in the midst of other work, then toiled at, taken to pieces and put together in all sorts of ways'.[34] In fact, *The War of the Worlds* was written – to quote David Hughes and Harry Geduld – 'in three spurts':

1 developing the text, late summer and autumn 1895;
2 'intense composition' completing the serialized manuscript, first half of first half of 1896; and
3 rushed revisions and additions for the book, the final quarter of 1897.[35]

Much of the text, particularly that serialized in 1897, was completed by mid-1896, that is while Wells was living in Woking. The third phase, when the story was already being serialized, occurred when Wells was resident in Worcester Park and involved making amendments and additions to the serialized text. By the time the book was published in January 1898, *The War of the Worlds*'s project had extended over a period of two and a half years, but still compared favourably with the *Time Machine* whose bibliographical history extended over seven years.[36] Lest Wells might be adjudged guilty of not pushing ahead with the project as quickly as he might have done, it is important to stress two key constraints: the fragile state of his health, including the constant need to maintain a balance between work and

33. Hughes, *Edition and a Survey*, pp. 16–17.
34. Wells quoted, 15 April 1906, Geoffrey West, *H. G. Wells*, p. 128.
35. Hughes and Geduld, *Critical Edition*, pp. 1, 9; Hughes, *Edition and a Survey*, pp. 8–16.
36. Ruddick, 'Introduction', p. 22.

leisure; and the fact that throughout this period he was working on several other publications, which at times assumed priority over *The War of the Worlds*.

Phase 1: Late summer and autumn 1895

In September 1895 Henley remarked that Wells, who had contracted the book rights to Heinemann the previous month, appeared not only to possess a 'strong' idea about what he called 'the Martialist visitation' but also to be 'working it out with so much gusto': 'I have great hopes of it'.[37] Just over one month later, Wells indicated that this 'scientific romance', totalling some 75,000 words, would be ready 'early in 1896', possibly sooner.[38] Meanwhile, he was attempting to sell the American book and serial rights, while employing Morris Colles of the Author's Syndicate to place the British serial rights.[39]

Phase 2: First half of 1896

In the event, Wells's hopes of completion early in 1896 proved abortive; indeed, in January 1896 he felt able only to send Colles a 'sketch' of the story as a basis for negotiation.[40] Reflecting a growing tendency to take revenge on publishers and editors who had rebuffed him at some stage in the past, Wells instructed Colles not to offer the serial to either the *Graphic* or even Henley's *New Review*, since both had refused to serialize *The Wheels of Chance*.[41] His key target was C. Arthur Pearson's *Pearson's Magazine*, which began publication in 1896.

Following a break in working on the manuscript during late 1895, Wells devoted 'a whole half year' at the start of 1896 to the story targeted initially for serialization.[42] By this stage, the projected 75,000 words had been reduced to 60,000 words, but even this was well in excess of the 40,000 word norm for serialized articles. Despite telling Colles that he could not be hurried because 'these things require days of thought and intervening days', Wells worked hard and fast on the story.[43] Confident about the story's potential, he promised Colles that 'I won't let anything stand in the way of my doing my very best on this thing'.[44] Following the somewhat negative reception accorded to *The Island of Dr Moreau*,

37. Henley to Wells, 5 September 1895, Loing, *Wells à l'oeuvre*, p. 423.

38. Wells to Harpers, 15 October 1895, Loing, *Wells à l'oeuvre*, p. 424.

39. Wells to Colles, 2 January 1896, Loing, *Wells à l'oeuvre*, pp. 426–7.

40. Wells to Colles, 22 January 1896, H. G. Wells, Autograph Letters (Ransom).

41. Wells to Colles, 26 January 1896, Smith, *Correspondence of H. G. Wells, I*, p. 260.

42. Wells to unknown American correspondent, 25 November 1897, Loing, *Wells à l'oeuvre*, p. 436.

43. Wells to Colles, 26 March 1896, 24 *ALS* (Yale).

44. Wells to Colles, 22 January 1896, H. G. Wells, Autograph Letters (Ransom); Wells to Colles, 3 February 1896, 24 *ALS* (Yale).

it became even more important for *The War of the Worlds* to be well received by editors, reviewers and readers. Early in March, Wells warned Colles that the draft to be sent for review by Pearson was provisional – for example, the text was 'not revised' and some sentences were sheer nonsense because of 'my abominable handwriting' – and hence should be treated as no more than a rough guide.[45]

Despite indicating his satisfaction at the story so far, Pearson wanted to see the rest of the narrative, especially 'the finish of the story', as soon as possible. Excessive word length proved another issue. Welcoming news of Pearson's relatively positive response, Wells sketched a 'picshua' at the bottom of Colles's letter detailing Pearson's demands.[46] Wells showed Pearson saying 'Very nice tale so far. But do you mind taking the end out of your ink pot before I decide'. Producing the end of his 'tail', Wells faced the prospect of rejection from Pearson. On the reverse side of the letter, Wells sketched out an alternative scenario. It was, Wells conceded, 'vain-glorious to the utmost degree' in the sense that he drew Jane dipping the author's tail back into the ink pot under Pearson's watchful eye. Jane withdrew the tail with a revised manuscript to which Pearson made three large cuts on his 'serial chopping block'. Returning home with a bandaged tail, Wells depicted himself as a cat, proudly carrying home to Jane a sack marked £200.

Wells's pleasure regarding Pearson's response was qualified by irritation with his 'demands to see all the story, and restrictions as to length, & so forth', due to pressure on space in his new magazine.[47] As a result, at one stage, Wells contemplated offering the serial rights to Jerome K. Jerome, the editor of *To-day*, who was going to serialize *The Wheels of Chance* and had already indicated an interest in publishing *The War of the Worlds*.[48] In the end, Wells decided to stay with Pearson and on 26 March 1896 sent him a revised manuscript described as still 'in the immaturest state'.[49] Pearson was suitably impressed, so that in April Wells contracted the serial rights to *Pearson's Magazine*. Having promised to submit 'complete & finished copy' by 1 August 1896, Wells agreed to 'ruthlessly cut down' his manuscript to fit nine instalments totalling some 50,000 words, but warned Pearson that his demands meant cutting out 'some magnificent fighting'. Eventually the story was completed in Summer 1896 and ready for serialization in 1897.[50]

Wells's growing focus upon Mars was shown also by his unsigned article 'Intelligence on Mars' published in April 1896 by *The Saturday Review* and possibly composed while writing the initial sections of *The War of the* Worlds.[51]

45. Wells to Colles, 5 March 1896, 24 *ALS* (Yale).

46. Colles to Wells, 14 March 1896, Wells, *Experiment in Autobiography*, II, pp. 553, 555.

47. Wells to Colles, n.d. [March 1896], Loing, *Wells à l'oeuvre*, p. 427; Wells to Elizabeth Healey, May 1896, quoted Rinkel and Rinkel, *The Picshuas of H. G. Wells*, p. 185.

48. Wells to Colles, n.d. [19 March 1896], H. G. Wells, Autograph Letters (Ransom).

49. Wells to Colles, 26 March 1896, 24 *ALS* (Yale).

50. Wells to Healey, n.d. [4 January 1898], Wells, H. G. Letters Healey, Miss 8 *ALS* 1894–8 (Ransom).

51. Wells, 'Intelligence on Mars', pp. 345–6; Hughes, *Edition and a Survey*, pp. 285–6 n.19.

Typically, when finalizing the serialized text, Wells had already commenced work on another scientific romance – the story was published as *The Invisible Man* – targeted to fill the gap in his books schedule for 1897. Despite initial hopes that *The War of the Worlds* might be published as a book in September 1897, 1898 seemed more likely.[52] Indeed, by June 1896 he had already written some 25,000 words to be used for selling book and serial rights for *The Invisible Man*. Following further work, the manuscript for *The Invisible Man* was put aside in August 1896 and finished during the early weeks of 1897.[53] Irritated by Colles's apparent assumption that he would deal also with American rights, Wells began employing Pinker to place the book and serial rights for *The War of the Worlds* in the USA, where *Cosmopolitan* and Harper took up the serial and book rights respectively.[54]

Phase 3: The final quarter of 1897

While the closing stages of *The War of the Worlds* were being serialized in *Pearson's Magazine* and *Cosmopolitan*, Wells returned to the story to prepare the manuscript for publication as a book. Paradoxically, whereas Pearson had pressurised Wells to get rid of words from an overlong serial, Heinemann complained that the manuscript was 'very short' for a book and hence pressed Wells for more words to meet the purported expectations of readers: 'The plain man wants a certain amount of reading for his six shillings'.[55] On 25 November 1897 Wells indicated that he had been 'rewriting' *The War of the Worlds* for at least the past month, preparing, improving and adding text to the serialized manuscript.[56] Responding somewhat reluctantly to Heinemann's demands, Wells added extra text including the artilleryman episode on Putney Hill of c. 5,000 words (II.7), 'several pages' describing the Martians at Sheen, plus the Epilogue (II.10).[57] Moreover, he took the opportunity to make minor changes, such as inserting a sentence critiquing Warwick Goble's illustrations accompanying the serialized text in both *Pearson's*

52. Wells to Pinker, n.d. (June 1896), Loing, *Wells à l'oeuvre*, pp. 430–1.

53. Wells to unknown American correspondent, 25 November 1897, Loing, *Wells à l'oeuvre*, p. 436.

54. Wells to Pinker, n.d. [1896], Pinker, Vol. 1 (Ransom); Hughes and Geduld, *Critical Edition*, p. 7; A. D. 'An interview with Mr J. B. Pinker', *The Bookman* 14 (79) (April 1898): 9–10; Wells to Colles, n.d., 8 June 1896, 11 July 1896, 26 March 1897, 24 *ALS* (Yale).

55. Sydney Pawling, Heinemann, to Wells, 2 January 1897, William Heinemann to Wells, 13 October 1897, quoted Hughes and Geduld, *Critical Edition*, pp. 5–6; 'News Notes', *The Bookman* 13 (76) (January 1898), p. 113.

56. Wells to unknown American correspondent, 25 November 1897, Loing, *Wells à l'oeuvre*, p. 436; Hughes, *Edition and a Survey*, p. 9.

57. Hughes, *Edition and a Survey*, p. 3; David Y. Hughes, '*The War of the Worlds* in the Yellow Press', in Hughes and Geduld, *Critical Edition*, p. 285.

Magazine and *Cosmopolitan* as doing 'a lot of harm' to the story.[58] Wells used the narrator to warn readers that the drawings reproduced in 'one of the first pamphlets to give a consecutive account of the war' were 'no more like the Martians I saw in action than a Dutch doll is like a human being' (II.2: 204–5/124): 'To my mind, the pamphlet would have been much better without them'.

Overviewing the whole process, Hughes concluded that Wells wrote *The War of the Worlds* 'desultorily over a period' from the summer of 1895 to late 1897 recasting and reorganizing his text, such as by changing the locations of various scenes.[59] For example, in the published text the narrator was imprisoned in a house at Sheen in place of Byfleet, while the naval battle was shifted from the Solent to the east coast. Moreover, Wells lengthened the story, principally by injecting fresh chapters into the main body of the story containing new episodes, like the battle at Weybridge, additional characters like the curate, extra scenes, such as the panic and flight from London and extended commentary, such as that concerning the Artilleryman on Putney Hill.

Publication

Writing at the close of 1896 Wells indicated that he expected 'great things' from the serialization of *The War of the Worlds* in the new year.[60] Between April and December 1897 the story was serialized simultaneously by *Pearson's Magazine* and *Cosmopolitan* in nine monthly parts (Table 7.1). Priced at ten cents [$0.10] per copy, Cosmopolitan had a nationwide circulation across the USA of 300,000, while sales of the sixpenny [£0.025] *Pearson's Magazine* fluctuated between 200,000 and 400,000.[61] Wells's story appeared also in the collected volumes of *Pearson's Magazine* published at the close of the year.

Widely advertised in the press as another work by the 'Author of "The Time Machine"' – *The Island of Dr Moreau* was conspicuous by its absence from most adverts – *The War of the Worlds* was published as a book in Britain by William Heinemann in January 1898 with a reported initial print run of 10,000.[62] Significantly, the published book, like *The Invisible Man*, retained a strong link with Surrey through the production process. Thus, *The War of the Worlds* was printed at Guildford by Billing and Sons, a firm based in Woking until 1856. Harpers published the book in the USA two months later. While finalizing the book manuscript during late 1897, Wells agreed to requests made by two

58. Wells to Pinker, 15 November 1898, Pinker, Vol. 1 (Ransom).

59. Hughes, *Edition and a Survey*, p. 43.

60. Wells to Fred Wells, 31 December 1896, Wells, *Experiment in Autobiography, I*, p. 408.

61. Matthew Schneirov, *Dream of a New Social Order: Popular Magazines in America 1893–1914* (New York: Columbia University Press, 1994), pp. 11, 82, 87; *The Waterloo Directory of Nineteenth Century Periodicals*, quoted The Newspaper Library, British Library, to the author, 1 October 2013.

62. 'News Notes', *The Bookman* 13 (76) (January 1898), p. 113.

Table 7.1 Serialization of *The War of the Worlds* in *Pearson's Magazine* and
Cosmopolitan, 1897

1897	*Pearson's Magazine* (UK)		*Cosmopolitan* (USA)	
1 April	Vol. 3 (16)	pp. 363–73	Vol. 22 (6)	pp. 615–27
2 May	Vol. 3 (17)	pp. 487–96	Vol. 23 (1)	pp. 3–9
3 June	Vol. 3 (18)	pp. 599–610	Vol. 23 (2)	pp. 215–24
4 July	Vol. 4 (19)	pp. 108–19	Vol. 23 (3)	pp. 251–62
5 August	Vol. 4 (20)	pp. 221–32	Vol. 23 (4)	pp. 391–400
6 September	Vol. 4 (21)	pp. 329–39	Vol. 23 (5)	pp. 541–50
7 October	Vol. 4 (22)	pp. 447–56	Vol. 23 (6)	pp. 601–10
8 November	Vol. 4 (23)	pp. 558–68	Vol. 24 (1)	pp. 79–88
9 December	Vol. 4 (24)	pp. 736–45	Vol. 24 (2)	pp. 162–71

American newspapers – first the *New York Journal* and then the *Boston Post* – for secondary newspaper rights to the serialized text first published in *Cosmopolitan*.[63]

Variations between the texts serialized during 1897–8 and published as books in 1898 highlight the fact that there is no one version of *The War of the Worlds*. Whereas the book published in New York by Harpers was based on the text serialized by *Cosmopolitan* and *Pearson's Magazine*, Heinemann's publication, like the versions published by newspapers in Boston and New York, included the extra text, most notably the artilleryman episode and 'The Epilogue', added somewhat grudgingly by Wells in response to Heinemann's demands for more pages. Subsequently Wells 'continued to tinker with the text', but 'made no further important revisions or additions', with the 1924 Atlantic edition treated as the definitive text used for reprints.[64] Over time the book has often been re-published in special editions, such as for the military during the Second World War or for the educational market. Thus, from 1951 onwards Heinemann, acting with the permission of Marjorie Wells, published a revised text – basically this involved toning down the gory passages – for schools.[65]

From the start a further source of revenue – this highlighted also the manner in which Wells's scientific romances took his name around the world – derived from translations (Table 7.2), such as into Dutch (1899), French (1900), Italian (1901), German (1901) and Spanish (1902).[66] For example, the German and Spanish

63. Hughes and Geduld, *Critical Edition*, p. 6.

64. Hughes, *Edition and a Survey*, pp. 3–5; Hughes and Geduld, *Critical Edition*, pp. ix, 1–9, 43–4; Patrick Parrinder, 'Note on the Text', in H. G. Wells, *The War of the Worlds* (London: Penguin, 2005), pp. xxxii–vi.

65. Marjorie Wells to Miss Callender, Heinemann, 6 October 1949, Anon, minute, n.d. [1961?], Author File: H. G. Wells, Heinemann Archive (Rushden); Hughes, *Edition and a Survey*, p. 4. Today, editions are available targeted at varying age groups.

66. Patrick Parrinder and Paul Barnaby, 'Timeline: European Reception of H. G. Wells',

rights of *The War of the Worlds* were assigned to *Das Wissen für Alle* and Don J. del Perojo of Madrid in 1900 and 1901 respectively.[67] In February 1898, Wells signed an agreement awarding the continental rights of *The War of the Worlds* in English to Bernard Tauchnitz, the Leipzig-based publisher of the 'Tauchnitz Collection of British Authors' for £35.[68] Tauchnitz had been publishing the works of British and American authors since the early 1840s in a way recognizing copyright and making payments to the author, given the fact that copyright was not always respected during this period in many countries, not excluding the USA.[69] When he travelled to the Soviet Union in 1920, Wells discovered that many of his books, including *The War of the Worlds* (1899), had been published in unauthorized Russian translations soon after publication in Britain.

The timeline of translations (Table 7.2) suggests that *The War of the Worlds* proved the catalyst responsible for creating large-scale interest in his work among readers and publishers on the continent and hence prompting sufficient interest in Wells's work to justify the extra costs of publication in translation. Although *The Stolen Bacillus and other Incidents* and *The Island of Dr Moreau* appeared in Swedish (1897) and Danish (1898) respectively, the real surge in translations of Wells's work occurred in 1899 with four foreign language versions of *The War of the Worlds* and the initial three translations of *The Time Machine*. By the time of the outbreak of the First World War in 1914, his scientific romances had been translated into several foreign languages. *The Invisible Man* and *The War of the Worlds* led the way with thirteen and eleven translations respectively. Other totals were *First Man in the Moon*: nine; *The Time Machine*: eight; *When the Sleeper Wakes*: eight; and *The Island of Dr Moreau*: seven. Wells's other novels fared less well. By 1914 *The Wonderful Visit* and *The Wheels of Chance* had only been translated into French and Spanish.

Apart from being a very visual writer capable of both conjuring up vivid fantastic images for readers and representing his thoughts through picshuas, Wells had strong feelings about the illustrations employed to support his work, as evidenced by his above-mentioned critique of Goble's illustrations used for the story's serialization. Writing in 1920, Wells recorded that just as he had used his imagination to write *The War of the Worlds*, so his story had encouraged several 'imaginative people' to draw Martians; 'The story from first to last has provoked quite a number of gifted illustrators'.[70] Those impressing Wells included York

in Patrick Parrinder and John S. Partington (eds), *The Reception of H. G. Wells in Europe* (London: Thoemmes Continuum, 2005), pp. xxiii–xl; Patrick Parrinder, 'Introduction', in Parrinder and Partington (eds), *The Reception of H. G. Wells in Europe*, pp. 1–7; Smith, *Wells*, pp. 54–5, 75.

67. Marjorie Wells to P. Zsolnay, 16 December 1951, J. M. Pinker to Perojo, 13 February 1901, Author File: H. G. Wells, Heinemann Archive (Rushden).

68. Vertrag [Contract], 24 February 1898, Author File: H. G. Wells, Heinemann Archive (Rushden).

69. Wells to Colles, 2 January 1896, Loing, *Wells à l'oeuvre*, pp. 426–7.

70. Wells, '*The War of the Worlds*: Introduction: An experiment in illustration', p. 154. On the problem of illustrating Wells's novel, especially Wells's complaints about

Table 7.2 Translations of *The War of the Worlds*

1898	Russian [unauthorized]
1899	Dutch, Hungarian, Norwegian, Polish
1900	French
1901	German, Italian
1902	Spanish
1903	Czech (Bohemia)
1906	Swedish
1912	Danish
1921	Ukrainian
1923	Croatian
1924	Lithuanian
1933	Estonian
1934	Irish, Portuguese, Slovenia
1951	Serbian
1953	Romanian (Yugoslavia)
1956	Ukrainian
1964	Bulgarian
1970	Latvian, Moldovan
1973	Greek
1979	Finnish
1986	Catalan (Spain)
1989	Macedonian
1991	Basque (Spain)

Source: Patrick Parrinder and Paul Barnaby, 'Timeline: European reception of H. G. Wells', in Patrick Parrinder and John S. Partington (eds), *The Reception of H. G. Wells in Europe* (London: Thoemmes Continuum, 2005), pp. xxiii–xl.

Powell, R. A. M. Stevenson, Alvim-Corrêa and M. Briede. Moreover, whereas in the 1898 Heinemann text Wells had criticized Goble's sketches, in a 1920 *Strand Magazine* article Wells acknowledged that the illustration of his story 'was done very well by Mr Warwick Goble, during its first magazine publication'.[71] Indeed, a few years earlier Wells had agreed to the use of Goble's illustrations in a proposed new edition of the book.[72]

representing the tripods as 'kettles on camera stands', see Hughes, *Edition and a Survey*, p. 298 n.91; Michael Livingston, 'The tripods of Vulcan and Mars: Homer, Darwin, and the fighting machines of H. G. Wells's *The War of the Worlds*', *The Wellsian* 32 (2009): 54–60.

71. Wells, '*The War of the Worlds*: Introduction: An experiment in illustration', p. 154.

72. Catherine Wells to Heinemann, 9 April 1916, Author File: H. G. Wells, Heinemann Archive (Rushden).

Reception

The War of the Worlds was widely reviewed across both Britain and the USA. Generally speaking, the book was well received by reviewers, many of whom wrote anonymously in line with contemporary practice. Like *The Time Machine*, *The War of the Worlds* gained much praise when serialized in 1897; thus, the *Illustrated London News* recorded that the story 'had a very distinct success as it appeared in *Pearson's Magazine*'.[73] But *The War of the Worlds* did even better as a book, with some reviewers rating as 'the best story he has yet produced'.[74] For the *Academy*'s reviewer, 'Mr Wells has done good work before, but nothing quite so fine as this'.[75] When advertising *The War of the Worlds* in the press, Heinemann found it easy to find positive reviews to use. Although such quotes were taken out of context for promotional purposes, many would see the assessments as informed literary evaluations rather than journalistic hyperbole.

Firstly, the book was welcomed as the striking product of a writer combining an imaginative mind with scientific knowledge and understanding, so that scientific material was 'cleverly woven into the web of fiction'.[76] In particular, reviewers highlighted the story's originality, most notably representing Mars in 'a new light' through the 'daring' concept of an alien invasion of earth, offering a 'distinctively clever' mode of destruction of the Martians and depicting the impact of a ruthless enemy's attack upon a large city.[77] Thus, the story's central theme was seen as building cleverly upon contemporary speculation about both life on other worlds, especially Mars and invasion scares: 'No astronomer, no physicist, can take it upon himself to declare that it is absolutely certain that this planet will never be invaded from a foreign world'.[78]

Once again, Wells's skills as a writer of scientific romances won high praise for making a fantastic event both believable and highly engaging for readers. Reviewing the book for *Harper's Weekly* in the USA, Sidney Brooks admired Wells's writing style: 'Much of its strength is the contrast between the tale itself and Mr Wells' manner of telling it. He has a complete check over his imagination,

---

73. C. K. S., 'A Literary Letter', *Illustrated London News* CXII (3064) (8 January 1898), p. 50.

74. *Speaker*, 5 February 1898, p. 174, *Spectator*, 29 January 1898, p. 168, quoted Bergonzi, *Early Wells*, p. 123.

75. 'Review', *Academy* liv, 29 January 1898, pp. 121–2, in Patrick Parrinder (ed.), *H. G. Wells: Critical Heritage* (London: Routledge, 1972), p. 70. This might have been written by Lewis Hind, the editor: Wells to father, 18 December 1898, Wells, *Experiment in Autobiography*, I, p. 408.

76. *Academy*, 29 January 1898, in Parrinder, *Wells: Critical Heritage*, p. 73.

77. Ibid., p. 72; 'Review', *The Critic* (USA), xxix, 23 April 1898, p. 282, in Parrinder, *Wells: Critical Heritage*, p. 69; Richard A. Gregory, 'Review', *Nature*, lvii, 10 February 1898, pp. 339–40, in Parrinder, *Wells: Critical Heritage*, p. 75.

78. 'Review', *Saturday Review*, 29 January 1898, p. 146, quoted, Mclean, *Early Fiction of H. G. Wells*, p. 90.

and makes it effective by turning his most horrible fancies into language of the simplest, least startling denomination.' [79] The *Daily News'* reviewer praised Wells's 'power of vivid realization': 'The imagination, the extraordinary power of presentation, the moral significance of the book cannot be contested'.[80] For many reviewers, the gripping and thrilling narrative engaged them from an early stage and prompted them to keep turning the pages. *The Spectator's* John St Loe Strachey praised Wells's 'literary workmanship', particularly his 'very remarkable gift of narration': 'There is not a dull page in it': 'One reads and reads with an interest so unflagging that it is positively exhausting. *The War of the Worlds* stands, in fact, the final test of fiction. When once one has taken it up, one cannot bear to put it down without a pang. It is one of the books which it is imperatively necessary to sit up and finish.'[81]

Moreover, Wells's use of reportage and placement of the story in actual geographical locations won much praise from the *Academy's* reviewer, among others, for creating 'an atmosphere of actuality' by making the impossible seem possible.[82] Strachey agreed and pointed to the way in which 'The vividness of the local touches, and the accuracy of the geographical details, enormously enhance the horror of the picture':

> Mr Wells ... brings the awful creatures of another sphere to Woking junction, and places them, with all their abhorred dexterity, in the most homely and familiar surroundings. A Martian dropped in the centre of Africa would be comparatively endurable .... When the Martians ... land on a peaceful Surrey common, we come to close quarters at once with the full horror of the earth's invasion. Those who know the valleys of the Wey and the Thames, and to whom Shepperton and Laleham are familiar places, will follow the advance of the Martians upon London with breathless interest.[83]

Naturally, *The War of the Worlds* was not without its critics questioning, say, the alleged lack of human interest, the detailed focus upon the macabre, and Wells's writing style.[84] For example, Strachey, though generally highly appreciative of the book, was very critical of Wells's characterization of the curate. Reviewing the

79. Sidney Brooks, *Harper's Weekly*, quoted Hughes and Geduld, *Critical Edition*, pp. 25–6;

80. 'More News from Mars: a "scientific shocker"', *Daily News*, 21 January 1898. Extracts from this review were used in Heinemann's advert in *The Times*, 25 January 1898, p. 12.

81. John St Loe Strachey, 'Books: *The War of the Worlds*', *The Spectator*, lxxx, 29 January 1898, pp. 168–9. Strachey's review was published unsigned.

82. *Academy*, 29 January 1898, in Parrinder, *Wells: Critical Heritage*, p. 71.

83. Strachey, 'Books: *The War of the Worlds*', p. 168.

84. For individual reviews, see William J. Scheick and J. Randolph Cox (eds), *H. G. Wells: A Reference Guide* (Boston, MA: Hall, 1988), pp. 10–13. The more critical reviews reprinted include items 92 (*Toledo Blade*, 30 April 1898), 97 (*Critic*, 23 April 1898), 99 (*Chicago Tribune*, 9 April 1898), 108 (*Dial*, 1 June 1898), 111 (*The Times*, 18 April 1898).

book for the *Bookman*, Clement Shorter worried about Wells's pessimism.[85] The *Daily News* reviewer complained that Wells offered too much 'cheap horror' in the vein of his 'nightmare creation, "The Island of Dr Moreau"': 'There are episodes that are so brutal, details so repulsive, that they cause insufferable distress to the feelings. The restraint of art is missing.'[86]

Perhaps the most negative review appeared in the *Athenaeum*, where the anonymous reviewer – in fact, he was known to be the historian Basil Williams – complained that 'the narrator sees and hears exciting things, but he has not the gift of making them exciting to other people'.[87] More revealing, at least about the reviewer's prejudices, was Williams's barb about the story's 'vulgar and commonplace' nature imbued with 'too much of the young man from Clapham attitude'. Williams was also one of those drawing what Wells represented as the dreaded comparisons with Daniel Defoe, Edgar Allan Poe, Jonathan Swift, Jules Verne and so on. Fearing also that Wells wrote 'too much', Williams echoed Henley, among others, in suggesting that Wells was prioritizing quantity and sales over literary quality and should worry about his reputation!

The book's sales and impact both at the time and ever since publication suggest that Williams was not only out of step with most reviewers but also got things very wrong. Writing to Wells about the reviews, George Gissing dismissed such reviewers as 'beastly creatures'.[88] By way of response, Wells claimed that 'The *Athenaeum* review doesn't matter a damn. I know it's spiteful & unjust, it irritates reviewers elsewhere into unseemly praise, & it makes no impression on sales … And for the most part I have had reviews which only my regard for your regard of our native language prevents my calling phenomenal.'[89] These remarks reaffirm yet again that contrary to what he claimed, Wells did not ignore reviews.

A contemporary parody: The War of the Wenuses

One example of *The War of the Worlds*'s contemporary literary impact and – to quote Alden – 'the wide popularity of Mr Wells's book' was provided in March 1898 by the publication of *The War of the Wenuses*.[90] The co-authors, C. L. Graves

85. Clement Shorter, 'Mr Wells "War of the Worlds"', *The Bookman* (USA) VII (3) (May 1898): 246–7. This was published in the British Bookman in March 1898: 14 (78) (March 1898): 182–3.

86. 'More News from Mars'.

87. Basil Williams, *Athenaeum*, 5 February 1898, p. 178, in Parrinder, *Wells: Critical Heritage*, p. 67.

88. Gissing to Wells, 18 February 1898, in Paul F. Mattheisen, Arthur C. Young and Pierre Coustillas (eds), *The Collected Letters of George Gissing, Vol. 7: 1897–1899* (Athens, OH: Ohio University Press, 1995), pp. 63–4.

89. Wells to Gissing, n.d. (23 February 1898), in Mattheisen, Young and Coustillas, *The Collected Letters of George Gissing, Vol. 7*, p. 67.

90. William L. Alden, 'London Literary Letter', *The New York Times*, 19 March 1898.

and Edward Verrall Lucas, dedicated their parody, represented as an 'Outrage on a fascinating and convincing romance', to Wells. Offering a 1890s variant on the saying that 'men come from Mars and women from Venus', Graves and Lucas replaced a 'v' with a 'w', as with their book's title, 'from an inordinate affection for that letter'.[91] The story began with an amusing take on Well's famous opening paragraph:

> No one would have believed in the first years of the twentieth century that men and modistes on this planet were being watched by intelligences greater than woman's and yet as ambitious as her own. With infinite complacency maids and matrons went to and fro over London, serene in the assurance of their empire over man. It is possible that the mysticetus does the same. Not one of them gave a thought to Wenus as a source of danger, or thought of it only to dismiss the idea of active rivalry upon it as impossible or improbable. Yet across the gulf of space astral women, with eyes that are to the eyes of English women as diamonds are to boot-buttons, astral women, with hearts vast and warm and sympathetic, were regarding Butterick's with envy, Peter Robinson's with jealousy, and Whiteley's with insatiable yearning, and slowly and surely maturing their plans for a grand inter–stellar campaign.[92]

Following Wells's use of actual locations 'for verisimilitude', Graves and Lucas, though switching the story's focus away from Surrey to London, adopted a somewhat exaggerated street-by-street approach.[93] Like Wells, Graves and Lucas employed a narrator, resident in Kensington and Chelsea, to provide the background – 'It all seemed so safe and tranquil. But the Wenuses were even then on their milky way' – and then relate what happened after the Wenuses landed in Kensington Gardens.[94] Maybury, Woking and Surrey are mentioned, but only in a relatively marginal way, such as through mention of a young shopman from Woking or a woman living at Maybury tenements. Also the crowd watching the Wenuses' missile in Kensington Gardens was compared unfavourably to that in Woking: 'Scientific knowledge has not progressed at Kensington by the same leaps and bounds as at Woking. Extra-terrestrial had less meaning for them than extra-special'.[95]

The book included also occasional references to Wells's other writings. For example, the narrator, representing himself as an 'indivisible man', described a night-time *Wheels of Chance*-type bicycle ride with his wife: 'she rode very badly.

91. C. L. Graves and Edward Verrall Lucas, *The War of the Wenuses* (Bristol: Arrowsmith, 1898), p. 4.

92. Graves and Lucas, *War of the Wenuses*, p. 4. Modistes were designers and makers of women's fashions. Butterick's published sewing patterns, while Peter Robinson and Whiteley's were leading department stores.

93. Ibid., p. 6.

94. Ibid., p. 5.

95. Ibid., p. 7.

I told her the names of all the stars she saw as she fell off her machine. She had a good bulk of falls.[96] Another character was called Hoopdriver, the cycling hero of the *Wheels of Chance*. Wells and Heinemann [Winymann], the publisher of *The War of the Worlds*, were also mentioned, as was another of Wells's books *The Wonderful Visit*:

> Then came the night of the first star. It was seen early in the morning rushing over Winchester ... Trelawny, of the Wells' Observatory ... watched it anxiously. Winymann, the publisher, who sprang to fame by the publication of *The War of the Worlds*, saw it from his office window, and at once telegraphed to me: "Materials for new book in the air." That was the first hint I received of the wonderful wisit.[97]

Conclusion

Over time, *The War of the Worlds* has sold in large numbers in Britain and the wider world. Detailed accounts and sales figures for the book remain closed, but there are occasional insights regarding sales, particularly given Wells's close focus on adherence to contractual terms and repeated querying of royalty statements. Looking back ten years on from its initial publication, Wells recorded that *The War of the Worlds* sold some 6,000 copies at its original price of six shillings – a contracted royalty of 15 per cent on the first 5,000 copies and then 20 per cent on further copies would return some £4,700, over £500,000 in present-day terms – but advised that it was impossible to calculate sales in cheaper editions.[98] Soon afterwards, he agreed to Heinemann's proposal to publish *The War of the Worlds* in its forthcoming seven-penny novel series, due for publication in 1912 with a penny royalty.[99] In 1934 Heinemann published a 3s 6d edition, which sold 624 copies during the year.[100]

Despite Wells's tendency to devalue his scientific romances through his anxiety to become a mainstream novelist, *The War of the Worlds*, like the other scientific romances, has proved instrumental in ensuring that he possesses a present-day reputation and visibility as an original, distinctive and inspirational writer. *The War of the Worlds* was an instant hit, attracting much praise when it was first published. Moreover, in today's world, commentators continue to echo Bergonzi, who during the early 1960s praised *The War of the Worlds* as 'Wells's finest piece

96. Ibid., p. 5.

97. Ibid., p. 6.

98. Wells to Cazenove, 10 November 1908, Smith, *Correspondence of H. G. Wells, II*, p. 231.

99. Wells to Heinemann, n.d. [1911–12], Author File: H. G. Wells, Heinemann Archive (Rushden).

100. Mrs G. P. Wells to Heinemann, 2 April 1935, Author File: H. G. Wells, Heinemann Archive (Rushden).

of sustained imaginative writing'.[101] In his literary history of Mars, Robert Crossley described *The War of the Worlds* as a 'literary masterpiece in the tradition of Martian fiction'.[102] Moreover, the book is selected regularly by well-known writers – they have included Brian Aldiss, Dominic Sandbrook and Will Self – as meriting a place on lists of the best science fiction studies by way of reaffirming Wells's description of the book as a reference point, 'a corners shaking affair'.[103] Also, as detailed in Part III of this book, the storyline lives on in today's multimedia world through a wide range of film, musical, radio, television and other adaptations.

One element widely admired today by many readers is the story's opening paragraph. Moreover, its present-day impact has been accentuated by the manner in which it is used, albeit in an updated and truncated form, in audio-visual spinoffs of the story and spoken by leading actors like Richard Burton, Morgan Freeman, Sir Cecil Hardwick and Liam Neeson. Like many readers, Brian Aldiss was impressed by 'that magnificent paragraph with which *The War of the Worlds* opens', for it hooked him, like many others, straight away:

> But I do not recall any sentence which ever had such awesome effect on me as one sentence in that first paragraph of *The War of the Worlds:* "Yet across the gulf of space, minds that are to our minds as ours are to those of the beasts that perish, intellects vast and cool and unsympathetic, regarded this earth with envious eyes, and slowly and surely drew their plans against us." Had there ever been such an opening statement, labyrinthine yet pellucid, before? No latinate long words here, designed to impress; the longest word is that readily comprehensible understatement of an adjective, 'unsympathetic'.
>
> So the curtain comes up on the drama, and already the seeds of Wells's clever denouement have been planted.[104]

Against this background, the next chapter examines how Wells sought to meet readers' expectations.

---

101. Bergonzi, *Early Wells*, p. 123.

102. Crossley, *Imagining Mars*, p. xii, p. 110.

103. Wells to Pinker, n.d. [1898], Pinker, Vol. 1 (Ransom); Dominic Sandbrook, 'Classic sci-fi', *The Times*, 15 November 2014; Dominic Sandbrook, 'Tomorrow's Worlds: the unearthly history of science fiction', BBC2, 22 November 2014; Self, 'Death on three legs'; Aldiss, 'Introduction', p. xxix.

104. Aldiss, 'Introduction', p. xv.

Chapter 8

THE WAR OF THE WORLDS:
STORYLINE AND METHODOLOGY

In *The Time Machine* 'The Time Traveller' invades the future. By contrast, in *The War of the Worlds*, the Martians, represented as a possible indicator of the future evolution of humankind, invade the present, or rather the very near future.[1] What Wells offered readers was an 'apocalyptic' storyline – to quote David Y. Hughes and Harry M. Geduld – 'unveiling a predestined future cataclysm of extra human proportions which destroys the world as we know it but eventuates in the triumph of good over evil'.[2]

The storyline

Despite the global dimension implicit in its title, *The War of the Worlds* possessed a much more confined geographical focus concentrated upon Southern England, most notably London and Surrey but with a side excursion to Essex. Having begun in Woking, where Wells planned and wrote *The War of the Worlds*, the Martian invasion ended on Primrose Hill in London. Nestling between Camden Town and Regents Park, Primrose Hill was located in an area where Wells had been living on and off for several years, including the period immediately preceding his move to Woking. Nor did the story cover a lengthy conflict, since the interplanetary war lasted less than two months.

The story is told by a narrator, who reports a conflict which took place some six years earlier (I.1: 6/9) and sets out events as happening in several distinct stages:

i. **prelude to invasion** – the starting point of *apparent* normality;
ii. **alien invasion and conquest**; abortive military resistance to the powerful and seemingly unstoppable Martian invaders; panic and flight; conquest;
iii. **the invasion's failure**;
iv. **aftermath**.

---

1. John Batchelor, *H. G. Wells* (Cambridge: Cambridge University Press, 1985), p. 23.
2. Hughes and Geduld, *Critical Edition*, p. 9.

i) Prelude to invasion

Writing in the mid-1890s, Wells set the story as occurring in the near future. The text's mention of specific days, months and time lapses reflects Wells's strong sense of time, a feature introduced in Chapter 2 and elaborated below. Despite stating that the events took place 'early in the twentieth century' (I.1: 2/7), Wells failed to specify an actual year perhaps to reflect the timeless nature of his story. Even so, as discussed below, many commentators have sought to date the Martian invasion more precisely.

The War of the Worlds exhibits also Wells's sense of place with events occurring in specific geographical locations. The story begins at Woking, a fast-growing town in Surrey some thirty miles south west of London. Apart from being the place where the story's narrator was living, Wells uses the town to contextualize the story and particularly to illuminate the present-day mood of Britain. Fostering an impression of apparent normality, alongside present-day complacency about national security, the opening pages set out the calm before the storm by way of providing readers with a reference point for what happens next. The initial section touches also upon contemporary interest in other worlds, especially Mars, which was reportedly growing colder and dying (I.1: 2–3/8–9). The Martians needed a new home and Earth becomes their target. The Martian strategy was clear: strike suddenly at the heart of Britain, a global power with a vast empire; conquer Britain quickly; and then move on to take over the world.[3]

ii) Alien invasion and conquest

The Martian invasion has three stages:

a. The despatch of cylinders from Mars carrying fighting machines;
b. The establishment of a military stronghold on Horsell Common to provide the basis for an offensive targeted at London; and
c. The rapid Martian advance on London, the principal British target.

a) The despatch of cylinders from Mars

The Martians launched cylinders carrying Martians and their weaponry targeted at Britain by way of preparing the ground for invasion (Table 8.1). Appearing through telescopes as reddish flashes jetting out from Mars and subsequently falling to earth like stars, cylinder followed cylinder at daily intervals for ten days (I.1: 9–10/11–13; I.3: 107/67; I.10: 73/47; II.7: 254/152). The initial cylinder landed near the sandpits on Horsell Common, located about two miles north of Woking. Subsequently, other cylinders fell nearby in Addlestone and Pyrford. Three more

---

3. Gangale and Dudley-Rowley, 'Strategy and tactics', pp. 4–5, 13.

fell nearer London in a triangle bounded by Bushy Park, Sheen and Wimbledon. A seventh cylinder landed on Primrose Hill, Camden Town, in London.

Nothing is recorded in the published texts about the fate of the other three cylinders, although Wells specified their locations in an earlier unpublished version of the manuscript: 'Ten cylinders in all had fallen upon the earth, all of them falling into the county of Surrey except the ones at Hounslow & Hampton Court. The furthest south was the one at Merrow, the most easterly that at Wimbledon, the westward one fell at Bagshot.'[4] For Hughes, their subsequent omission reflected Wells's desire to avoid dispersing the story's focus. Mention of Wimbledon as the most easterly location implies that initially Primrose Hill – this lies further east than Wimbledon – was not listed as a landing site. In the published story, Woking is the most westerly location, thereby suggesting that in a previous draft Bagshot might have been the site of the first landing.

Having seen what he thought must be a meteorite land nearby, Ogilvy, an astronomer living at Ottershaw a few miles north of Woking, discovers the first cylinder 'not far from the sand-pits' (I.2: 13/13) on Horsell Common. Moreover, he soon links 'The Thing' with the flashes upon Mars seen on his telescope, a view echoed by the narrator when arriving at the site a few hours later: 'it was quite clear in my own mind that the Thing had come from the planet Mars' (I.3: 21/18). At first, the Martians, or rather their cylinder, are more the object of typical British curiosity than an invader to be feared. In many respects, this stage is used by Wells to juxtapose impressions of normality and peacefulness with the prospect of encountering the unexpected, whose impact is further enhanced by rooting mind-blowing events in real places. Thus, Woking and surrounding villages represent late Victorian Britain wherein people were 'sleeping in peace' (I.1: 9/11) and going about their everyday business, taking excursions, learning to ride bicycles and so on. Everywhere 'It seemed so safe and tranquil' (I.1: 11/12). No one gave any thought to 'the Thing that was to bring so much struggle and calamity and death to the earth'; (I.1: 8/11). Viewing the cylinder on Horsell Common, the local people show no fears about its presence. Nor initially did the British media.

Table 8.1 Locations of landing sites of cylinders fired from Mars

Cylinder 1:	Near the Sand Pits, Horsell Common (I.2: 13/13);
Cylinder 2:	Byfleet/Addlestone Golf Links (I.8: 55/37; I.9: 57/38; I.13: 108/68);
Cylinder 3:	Pyrford (I.10: 70–3/45–7; I.13: 108/68);
Cylinder 4:	Bushy Park, Hampton Court (I.15: 146/89);
Cylinder 5:	Sheen, on the road to Mortlake (I.17: 175/105; II.1: 196–200/119–21; II.2: 201–3/122–3);
Cylinder 6:	Wimbledon (I.17: 175/105; II.9: 293/175);
Cylinder 7:	Primrose Hill, London (I.17: 177/106);
Cylinders 8–10:	Not recorded, but probably in and around London.

4. Hughes and Geduld, *Critical Edition*, p. 260; Hughes, *Edition and a Survey*, pp. 42–3, 60. Hampton Court, though historically part of Middlesex, is now placed within Surrey. Merrow is located between Ripley and Guildford.

b) *The establishment of a military stronghold on Horsell Common*

At a very early stage, the Martians give a vivid demonstration of their hostile intentions and the advanced nature and power of their weaponry, when deploying heat-rays against a deputation, whose members included Ogilvy and the Astronomer Royal, attempting to make contact. Having witnessed the deputation's incineration, the narrator described the way in which flames and death leapt from person to person on Horsell Common: 'It was sweeping round swiftly and steadily, this flaming death, this invisible, inevitable sword of heat' (I.5: 35/26). Fleeing from what he represented as the massacre on Horsell Common (I.6: 39/28) – at least forty people perished – the narrator felt surrounded by 'the invisible terrors of the Martians; that pitiless sword of heat seemed whirling to and fro' (I.7: 44/31). Preparing for the advance on London, the Martians built up an encampment on Horsell Common, with the contents of the second and third cylinders – these had landed a few miles away – being transferred to the pit on the common (I.13: 108/68). Reporting that the Martians worked hard into the night, the narrator claimed that a towering pillar of dense smoke arising from the encampment could be seen from the North Downs about Merrow and Epsom.

The Martian invasion catches the whole country unprepared. Hitherto, national security had been taken for granted, particularly given Britain's great power status, island location, vast empire and naval power. Indeed, even the narrator dismisses the Martian threat, such as when opining that a shell fired into the pit on Horsell Common would stop them in their tracks (I.7: 47–8/33–4). However, for an invader from another planet, Britain's large navy and insular location prove no obstacle. When ready, the technologically advanced invaders from the 'Red Planet' use giant tripods, fighting machines, to sweep through Surrey towards London, devastating everything in their path with heat-rays, deadly Black Smoke and red weed. Despite the efforts of army units despatched from nearby barracks and Aldershot, conventional military means fail to halt the Martians' progress and eventual advance towards London. In the face of the Martian heat-rays and black smoke, organized opposition ends: 'After that no body of men would stand against them, so hopeless was the enterprise' (I.15: 148/90). For readers, the narrator reported the resulting devastation, burnt houses, wrecked trains, the countryside on fire, the smell of burning and dead bodies. Woking was soon destroyed, then Weybridge, Shepperton, Kingston upon Thames and so on, as the Martians, though suffering occasional losses, advance relentlessly upon the metropolis. Fearing a damaging struggle for control of London, the narrator contemplates leaving Britain for France (I.12: 88/56).

Wells conveyed the impression of everyday normality as long as possible by way of contrast with the deadly nature of the rapid Martian advance. Thus, even after the massacre on Horsell Common, much of Britain and the world was still going about everyday life as usual: 'In the rest of the world the stream of life still flowed as it had flowed for immemorial years. The fever of war that would presently clog vein and artery, deaden nerve and destroy brain, had still to develop' (I.8: 54/37). Suddenly, the situation was transformed by news of both the rapid and devastating nature of the Martian advance and the flight of people 'as blindly as a flock of sheep' (I.6: 42/30) in the midst of the terror and darkness. Vivid images show the resulting disintegration of government and society (I.16: 150–1/92) as well as the scenes of destruction left by the invaders, even if the Martians' sparing use of the heat-ray suggests that they wanted the 'complete demoralisation and the destruction of any opposition' rather than its extermination (I.17: 174/105). Thus, the narrator speculates that perhaps 'they did not wish to destroy the country, but only to crush and overawe the opposition they had aroused' (I.15: 147/90).

c) The rapid Martian advance on London

Gradually, London, 'the greatest city in the world' (I.16: 150/92), woke up to the fact that 'the Martians are coming!' (I.14: 131/81; I.16: 164/100). The resulting 'roaring wave of fear' (I.6: 150/92) saw panic, mass exodus from London and the breakdown of society: 'And this was no disciplined march; it was a stampede – a stampede gigantic and terrible – without order and without a goal, six million people, unarmed and unprovisioned, driving headlong. It was the beginning of the rout of civilisation, of the massacre of mankind' (I.7: 173/104). In this vein, Wells uses the narrator's London-based brother to offer readers not only an account of what was happening in and around London but also the experience of flight through Essex in the face of a deadly invader, the resulting fear and chaos, the uncertainty about what to do, the breakdown of law and order, profiteering and so on.

The breakdown in communications meant that the narrator experienced difficulty in following what was happening, most notably the actual extent of the Martian invasion. Having conquered London and Southern England, had they moved north? Were they active across the Channel launching attacks against, say, Paris and Berlin? (II.6: 265/147). Notwithstanding the global dimension implied by a title like *The War of the Worlds* or the header employed for Book II, 'The Earth Under the Martians', the Martian invaders never got further than London and Southern England. Presumably, the Martians would have targeted further cylinders at other parts of the world once they had completed subjugating Britain. Then Britain could have been used as both a base for further conquests, such as through the use of their flying machines (I.17: 187/112; 2.7: 253/152; 2.8: 284/169) and an example to deter further resistance to the Martian invasion.

iii) The invasion's failure

In the end, the all-powerful, seemingly unassailable Martians were defeated by natural bacteria, 'our microscopic allies' (II.8: 283/168), not British military resistance or the British people. The Martians prove powerless against the forces of nature. Despite allegedly scrutinizing and studying Britain closely prior to the invasion, ultimately the Martians failed because of serious intelligence errors, particularly in overlooking the impact of terrestrial bacteria.[5] Having eliminated micro-organisms from their own planet, their bodies were attacked by bacteria to which natural selection has rendered humankind immune. Likewise, the red weed which spread so quickly on land and in water lacked the resistance against bacterial disease possessed by terrestrial plants (II.6: 242–3/145).

As a result, the Martian invaders were repulsed. Britons and the rest of humankind were saved. For many readers, this proved a clever, but somewhat surprising outcome, even if it meant that the story had a happy ending, or at least a semi-happy ending given the solemn tone of the epilogue and the serious questions raised for the future by the Martian invasion. For some commentators, the rushed, even anti-climactic finale, especially the absence of a pulsating action-packed decisive battle, highlighted the fact that science fiction books 'are often better at setting up stories than choreographing them through to a neat resolution'.[6] The crucial role played by bacteria in determining the outcome of the struggle was clearly a function of Wells's scientific education, particularly his appreciation of the power of germs, such as demonstrated already in his 'Stolen Bacillus' story. Moreover, this solution to the problem of defeating the invaders, contrasted with another science-based possibility floated earlier in the book regarding the problems faced by Martians in coping with earth's gravity (I.7: 48–9/33–4).

iv) Aftermath

The Martians had been repulsed. The fate of civilization and that of the human race was no longer at issue, *at least for the time being*. But the prospect of a future invasion remained. Britain was safe for now, but London and parts of Southern England were devastated, as highlighted by the narrator's account of the blackened ruins of 'Dead London' (II.8). Fires continued to glow red. The face of 'London was black' (II.7: 271/161).

At the same time, the invasion, despite its eventual failure, had shown Britain's vulnerability, thereby linking Wells's story to scaremongering literature challenging both repeated government reassurances about British security and the superpower imagery typified by Queen Victoria's 1897 Diamond Jubilee celebrations.[7] Significantly, the latter were sandwiched during the period between Wells's completion of the serialized text and revision of the manuscript for publication as a book. Admittedly, the Martians represented 'a most unconventional and otherworldly foe', but despite being a major global power Britain's army and navy was overstretched across the empire and home defence measures were virtually non-existent: 'Britannia ruled the waves, but the waves were no barrier

---

5. Gangale and Dudley-Rowley, 'Strategy and tactics', pp. 10, 30–1.

6. Sukhdev Sandhu, 'Close encounter of the wrong kind', *Daily Telegraph*, 1 July 2005.

7. Judd, 'Diamonds are forever?', p. 38.

at all to the Martians'.[8] London, like the rest of the country, woke up too slowly to the danger.

For Wells, a key worry centred upon the pace of change in the sphere of weapons technology. Martian heat-rays, Black Smoke and Red Weed, alongside speculation about a Martian flying machine (II.7: 253/152), stressed the need for Britain to be fully prepared, equipped with the latest military technology and well-funded. Britons were reminded also of the deadly impact of modern war upon society and the civilian population and hence the need to deal with both its physical and psychological impacts: 'Never before in the history of the world had such a mass of human beings moved and suffered together' (I.17: 173/104). Returning home to Woking, the narrator was re-united with his wife in what Crossley critiqued as a 'flawed' scene 'stale with banality': 'A made-for-TV movie could have done no worse'.[9] The narrator recalled news about the arrival of the Martians and what had happened since he had left home to monitor the invasion (II.9: 295–6/176). His tone was sombre, certainly not triumphant.

The narrator's role

Unlike many science fiction stories centred upon a Doctor Who-type hero, Wells's *The War of the Worlds* was peopled chiefly by anonymous characters. Obviously, there were exceptions, like Ogilvy the astronomer and Henderson the journalist, but rather like, say, Stephen Crane's *The Red Badge of Courage* (1895), the leading characters – the narrator, his brother, the artilleryman and the curate – have no name. Nor does Wells attempt much character development in terms of creating fully rounded people. In brief, the central characters are employed basically to fulfil a role and particularly to offer a range of contrasting voices. In turn, their anonymous generalized nature contrasts strongly with the story's specificity regarding time and place.[10]

As outlined above, the story's key figure was the narrator, a literary device favoured by Wells already in *The Time Machine*, *The Wonderful Visit* and *The Island of Doctor Moreau*. Having adopted a third person perspective in *The Invisible Man*, Wells returned to the first person approach in *The War of the Worlds*, where the narrator performs a central linking role. Introduced as a writer of 'speculative philosophy' (II.10: 297/177) lacking scientific expertise, the narrator relates the story as a traumatized shell-shocked survivor of a Martian invasion which had occurred some six years earlier (I.1: 6/9). Remaining deliberately characterless, his fundamental function was to report the dramatic events taking place around him.[11] In particular, this technique offered readers a strong sense of immediacy regarding the events unfolding on the page.

8. Gangale and Dudley-Rowley, 'Strategy and tactics', p. 11.

9. Robert Crossley, *H. G. Wells* (Mercer Island, WA: Starmont House, 1986), p. 49.

10. Bergonzi, *Early Wells*, p. 126.

11. Lodge, *The Novelist at the Crossroads*, p. 215.

In addition, the use of a narrator offered Wells the opportunity to play an active role in his fiction. Like Wells, when writing *The War of the Worlds*, the narrator lived in Maybury. Like Wells, the narrator was married and had recently become a cyclist (I.1: 11/12). As the narrator approached central London, he encountered a scruffy looking character on Putney Hill:

> "Where do you come from?", he said …
> He looked at me doubtfully, then started …
> "It is you," said he. "The man from Woking" (II.7: 251–2/151).

Unsurprisingly, the narrator, 'The man from Woking', is often interpreted as Wells himself. Obviously, there are differences – for example, whereas Wells had two older brothers, the narrator's brother is younger – but similarities in their circumstances have encouraged commentators to view the narrator as Wells, a point accentuated in the book's text when the narrator is used to articulate his personal criticism of Goble's illustrations published with the story's serialization (II.2: 205/124). As narrator, Wells took the opportunity also to mention one of his own essays, 'The Man of the Year Million', published in 1893 speculating about the Martians and the future of humanity (II.2: 210/127).[12]

Seeking to link up again with his wife, learn 'whither the Surrey people had fled' (II.7: 250/150) and to monitor the Martian advance, the narrator made his way, albeit not without serious difficulties, delays and diversions, from Woking towards London. The narrator claims to be an eyewitness offering readers a relatively full, informed and reliable account of the war: 'no surviving human being saw so much of the Martians in action as I did' (II.2: 213/128). In particular, he represents himself as one of the first discoverers of the dead Martians (II.9: 288/172). Obviously, questions have been raised about not only the extent of his knowledge but also his reliability, expertise and objectivity, since he was neither technically trained nor always at the centre of the action.[13] Frequently, the narrator is heavily reliant on hearsay evidence, such as provided by the man from Street Cobham about the Black Smoke (I.15: 145/89), or the artilleryman recording how the Martians left Woking in ruins with only a few people remaining alive (I.11: 83–6/52–4). Later, when they met up again on Putney Hill, the artilleryman updated the narrator about developments in central London (II.7: 268/160). Another problem concerned the narrator's reliance upon gossip and speculation given the lack of hard information consequent upon the breakdown of communications and the chaos of war. Finally, the narrator was writing his account six years after the invasion (I.1: 6/9), thereby prompting questions about faulty memory and selective recall.

For a brief period in the story, the narrator shares his reporting role with his brother, a medical student based in London. This allows Wells to link events in

---

12. Wells, 'Man of the Year Million'.

13. Parrinder, 'How far can we trust the narrator?', p. 15; James, *Maps of Utopia*, pp. 46–7.

and around Woking with the wider picture as well as to indicate the time taken by the metropolis to wake up to the Martian threat. Thus, an entrenched belief in the capital's safety and security (I.14: 119–121/74–5) is suddenly eroded as news comes through of the events in Woking, the serious disruption of train services to and from London Waterloo, the subsequent destruction of Kingston upon Thames, Wimbledon and Richmond upon Thames and the arrival of the first refugees from Surrey: 'The first breath of the coming storm of Fear blew through the streets. It was the dawn of the great panic. London, which had gone to bed on Sunday night stupid [oblivious] and inert, was awakened, in the small hours of Monday morning, to a vivid sense of danger' (I.14: 133/82).

Devoting two chapters to the brother's flight from London enabled Wells to expose readers to the experience of escaping the unknown dangers of the Martian invasion – the experience of being told that 'the Martians are coming' (I.14: 131/81) and of being one of the 'black dots' visible to a balloonist flying above London (I.17: 172/104) – as well as to events at sea. Having fled across the sea to Belgium, the narrator's brother figures no more so that subsequent events in London are covered by the narrator himself. Finally, the narrator writes of his return to Woking, including the reunion with his wife, with Wells using the narrator to reflect upon the invasion and its implications for Britain.

Reportage on war

For both readers and reviewers, the page-turning nature of *The War of the Worlds* results in part from Wells's skilful use of reportage to impart a sense of immediacy and action. In part, Wells drew upon his experience as a journalist, but for Hughes, Strachey and Michael Sherborne, his approach was modelled upon that adopted by Daniel Defoe for his factional publication *A Journal of the Plague Year* (1722), which purports to be an eyewitness's account of the Great Plague of 1665.[14] In particular, the reporting role assigned to the narrator enabled a wide-ranging event to be viewed in depth from a more limited angle in terms of relating what he saw, heard, was told, read, felt and thought. As discussed in Part III, this reportage approach has been emulated in the interests of realism by several audio-visual adaptations, most notably by Orson Welles's 1938 radio drama and Steven Spielberg's 2005 film.[15]

The book begins with the narrator setting the scene, with special reference to the complacent nature of pre-invasion British society, as highlighted when the narrator fled towards home to escape the Martian heat-rays on Horsell Common. Passing people at the gate of a house in Woking, the narrator experienced diffi-culty in convincing locals about the fantastic things happening nearby:

14. Hughes, *Edition and a Survey*, pp. 349–52; Strachey, 'Books: *The War of the Worlds*', p. 168; Sherborne, *H. G. Wells*, p. 126.

15. Josh Friedman and David Koepp, *War of the Worlds: The Shooting Script* (New York: Newmarket Press, 2005), pp. 141, 146.

"People seem fair silly about the common," said the woman over the gate.
   "What's it all abart?"
"Haven't you heard of the men from Mars?" said I – "the creatures from
   Mars?"
"Quite enough," said the woman over the gate. "Thenks"; and all three of them
   laughed.
I felt foolish and angry. I tried and found I could not tell them what I had
   seen. They laughed again at my broken sentences.
"You'll hear more yet," I said, and went on to my home (I.7: 47/32).

Subsequently, the narrator covers fast-moving events rather like a war correspondent submitting regular reports for a newspaper based on what he had
witnessed personally or been told by others. Chapter headers – these include
'The Heat–Ray in the Chobham Road', 'The Destruction of Weybridge and
Shepperton' or 'The Exodus from London' – read like newspaper headlines. For
Bergonzi, Wells's reportage method, undertaken 'in an intensely visual fashion
that frequently anticipates cinematic techniques', imparts a sense of journalistic
immediacy conjuring up vivid images for his readers.[16] For example, the narrator
gives readers an on-the-spot running commentary of events on Horsell Common
as the cylinder opened and the Martians emerged: 'Those who have never seen
a living Martian can scarcely imagine the strange horror of its appearance' (I.4:
28/21). Having informed readers what Martians looked like, the narrator detailed
his personal reactions, with his first glimpse filling him with 'disgust and dread'
(I.4: 28/22), even making him feel nauseous (II.2: 205/124). Subsequently, the
narrator was able to build upon this initial 'transient impression' (II.2: 205/124),
'the most unearthly creatures it is possible to conceive' (II.2: 205/124), to sketch
out a detailed description extending across several pages (II.2: 205–16/124–30).
Also, he outlined vividly popular responses to developments, such as on Horsell
Common or at Shepperton where the crowd was 'horror-struck' (I.12: 99/62)
by the Martians' advance: 'There was no screaming or shouting, but a silence'
(I.12: 99/62).
   Soon after the fighting began, the narrator offered a highly visual portrayal
of the scene, as viewed from an upstairs window of his house in Maybury, in a
section in which Wells draws upon memories of his 1888 stay in the Potteries at
Stoke-on-Trent:

I closed the door noiselessly and crept towards the window. As I did so, the
view opened out until, on the one hand, it reached to the houses about Woking
Station, and on the other to the charred and blackened pine-woods of Byfleet.
There was a light down below the hill, on the railway, near the arch, and several
of the houses along the Maybury road and the streets near the station were
glowing ruins. The light upon the railway puzzled me at first; there was a black
heap and a vivid glare, and to the right of that a row of yellow oblongs. Then I

16. Bergonzi, *Early Wells*, pp. 126–7.

perceived this was a wrecked train, the fore-part smashed and on fire, the hinder carriages still upon the rails.

Between these three main centres of light, the houses, the train and the burning country towards Chobham, stretched irregular patches of dark country, broken here and there by intervals of dimly glowing and smoking ground. It was the strangest spectacle, that black expanse set with fire. It reminded me, more than anything else, of the Potteries seen at night. (I.11: 79–80/51).

In turn, the narrator's reaction to such images pushed readers to appreciate the resulting transformation in people's mindsets: 'And this was the little world in which I had been living securely for years, its fiery chaos!' (I.11: 80/51).

Then, as the narrator moves on from Woking, the story becomes more of a road novel, as the narrator is drawn inexorably towards London. As a result, he repeatedly abandoned plans to join his wife in Leatherhead before escaping across the Channel. Crossing Surrey on foot and by boat, the narrator had several near escapes from death, most notably at Shepperton (I.12: 106/66), and then was effectively imprisoned in a house at Sheen. Finally, he decided to go on into London to learn what had happened there (II.7: 271–2/162). Having discovered the dead Martians, the narrator returned home to Woking reporting the destruction, highlighting the need for large-scale reconstruction and articulating post-invasion mindsets.

The story's strong sense of time

Chapter 3 illuminated the way in which *The War of the Worlds* needs to be studied in context. However, time is also important in another way in terms of sequencing the flow of fast-moving events. The reader's perception of ever-increasing chaos and crisis and consequent desire to read 'what happens next?', is enhanced by the novel's emphasis upon real time by both the hour and the day. One example follows:

About three o'clock there began the thud of a gun at measured intervals from Chertsey or Addlestone. I learnt that the smouldering pine-wood into which the second cylinder had fallen was being shelled, in the hope of destroying that object before it opened. It was only about five, however, that a field-gun reached Chobham for use against the first body of Martians.

About six in the evening, as I sat at tea with my wife in the summer-house talking vigorously about the battle that was lowering upon us, I heard a muffled detonation from the common, and immediately after a gust of firing. Close on the heels of that came a violent, rattling crash, quite close to us, that shook the ground; and starting out upon the lawn, I saw the tops of the trees about the Oriental College burst into smoky red flame, and the tower of the little church beside it slide down into ruin. The pinnacle of the mosque had vanished (I.9: 61/40–1).

Nor was the narrator's house exempt. Soon afterwards a piece of its chimney fell into the flower bed by his study window.

The War of the Worlds' use of time, as reflected by mention of the time of the day, the days of the week and the lapse of time between events, enhanced the realism of a story helped also by reference to actual geographical places. At the same time, Wells's failure to specify the exact dates of the Martian invasion gives his storyline an ageless quality attractive to readers as well as to those adapting the story for alternative audio-visual formats. Whether or not Wells wrote with a specific month and year in mind remains uncertain, but this has not prevented speculation about possible dates making use of clues scattered through the story. For instance, Wells writes that the invasion took place in 'terrible June' (II.3: 219/132; I.17: 172/104) during the course of a 'hot, dry summer' (I.9: 56/38; II.6: 242/145), but no year is specified (I.17: 172/104). However, the narrator's mention of 'early in the twentieth century' (I.1: 2/7) rules out dates during the 1890s, even if this has not prevented 1898 and 1899 being frequently cited as the likely date.[17] Also relevant, given the varying orbits of earth and Mars and hence their varying distances from each other, are textual references to the fact that Mars was forty million miles away (I.1: 7/10) and 'approached opposition' (I.1: 6/9), the period when Earth and Mars approach each other most closely.[18] Opposition occurs when earth and Mars are lined up on the same side of the Sun, and hence nearest to each other, whereas conjunction arises when they are on opposite sides of the sun and hence, furthest apart.

Drawing upon such evidence, Thomas Gangale and Marilyn Dudley-Rowley dated the Martian invasion represented in *The War of the Worlds* as taking place in June 1907, when Wells would have known that Mars was scheduled to come within thirty-eight million miles of earth.[19] In addition, they proposed a detailed chronology, which serves as both an invaluable speculative framework for ongoing debates and a useful summary of the day-to-day progression of events (Table 8.2). Hughes suggests July 1907.[20]

A strong sense of place

The War of the Worlds reflects the manner in which – to quote Norman and Jeanne Mackenzie – 'Wells ... explicitly linked his destructive fantasies with his keen topographical sense'.[21] As Iain Sinclair commented, the listing of place-names

17. See examples listed in Thomas Gangale and Marilyn Dudley-Rowley, 'When was the War of the Worlds?', *The Wellsian* 29 (2006): 2–4.

18. Ibid., pp. 2–3.

19. Ibid., pp. 5–11; Thomas Gangale and Marilyn Dudley-Rowley, '*The War of the Worlds*: an after action report', *The Wellsian* 30 (2007): 37–9.

20. Hughes, *Edition and a Survey*, pp. 284–5 n.15.

21. N. and J. Mackenzie, *The Time Traveller*, p. 28; Wells, *Experiment in Autobiography*, I, pp. 100–1.

Table 8.2 Chronology of the Martian Invasion

	1907
13 May Monday	Martians launch the first cylinder towards earth – nine more cylinders follow daily from 14 May onwards
22 May Wednesday	Martians launch the tenth and final cylinder
14 June Friday	Having landed on Horsell Common, near Woking, the first cylinder is discovered by Ogilvy at 0500 hours.
14–15 June Friday–Saturday	Battle of Horsell Common, the Battle of Woking, with the narrator and his wife fleeing their home
16 June Sunday	Battle of Weybridge
17–18 June Monday–Tuesday	The Martians enter London; exodus from London
19 June Tuesday	The seventh cylinder lands on Primrose Hill, the Martians' new headquarters; Battle of Blackwater involving *HMS Thunder Child*
3 July Wednesday	The narrator encounters the artilleryman on Putney Hill
4–5 July Thursday–Friday	The narrator enters London and discovers dead Martians on Primrose Hill
12 July Friday	The narrator returns to Woking to be reunited with his wife
	1913
April	The narrator completes his account of the Martian invasion

Sources: Thomas Gangale and Marilyn Dudley-Rowley, 'When was the War of the Worlds?', pp. 15–20; Thomas Gangale and Marilyn Dudley-Rowley, '*The War of the Worlds*: an after action report', pp. 38–56.

becomes 'a litany of significance', since the story's impact upon readers has proved in part a function of 'its topographic verisimilitude, its forensic examination of the comfortably mundane, the complacency of Surrey suburbia, railway towns surrounded by golf links, tame heathland, somewhere to walk'.[22] As discussed above, *The War of the Worlds* displays also an interesting correlation between geography and Wells's 'casual intimacy' with the area around his places of residence. Thus, the story starts at Woking where he was living when thinking out and writing the story and ends at Camden Town where he had been living for several years prior to his move to Woking.

Certainly *The War of the Worlds* benefited from Wells's proven skills in juxtaposing the fantastic with everyday realities. Writing *The Time Machine* taught him an invaluable lesson guiding subsequent projects: 'I had realized that the more impossible the story I had to tell, the more ordinary must be the setting, and the circumstances in which I now set the Time Traveller were all that I could

22. Iain Sinclair, 'Woking at War', *The Guardian*, 26 June 2004.

imagine of solid upper-middle-class comfort'.[23] For Wells, 'The technical interest of a story like *The War of the Worlds* lies in the attempt to keep everything within the bounds of possibility. And the value of the story to me lies in this, that from first to last there is nothing in it that is impossible'.[24] As he elaborated, 'there may be life in Mars', or there might not. Likewise, 'intelligence may have gone farther there than on this planet', but might not: 'All the possibilities and impossibilities of the case I worked out very carefully before I began the story'. Responding to an interviewer asking about the scientific foundation for *The War of the Worlds* serial, Wells admitted that it was 'a story of a possibility':

> Like "The Invisible Man", it is a piece of realism. It may seem incredible to a large number of people not familiar with the ascertained facts about Mars and its relation to the earth; but to anyone acquainted with the possibilities modern science opens out it will, I am afraid, seem only very sober fiction indeed. If ever anything of the sort did happen, it would probably be a great deal worse than anything I have imagined in that story.[25]

From this perspective, Wells appreciated that the impact of his prose was accentuated by the way in which fictional, indeed fantastic, events concerning an alien invasion take place in real locations and involve local landmarks, that is 'by making all the earthly side of it as commonplace and familiar as possible'. Thus, the Martians provided the fantasy. Horsell Common, Woking, Surrey and London gave the story a sense of reality. By letting an unknown threat loose upon actual locations in the British countryside, suburbia and the metropolis, Wells engaged the attention of readers, especially by allowing them to follow events step-by-step on maps. Day excursions, holidays and residence meant that Wells knew Surrey well. Drawing also upon topographical research conducted across the county when living at Woking, he made strange, indeed fantastic, events convincing enough to hook readers. Thus, his narratives describing the Martian destruction of, say, Woking, Weybridge and Shepperton benefited from detailed geographical descriptions:

> We remained at Weybridge until midday, and at that hour we found ourselves at the place near Shepperton Lock where the Wey and Thames join... The Wey has a treble mouth, and at this point boats are to be hired, and there was a ferry across the river. On the Shepperton side was an inn with a lawn, and beyond that the tower of Shepperton Church – it has been replaced by a spire – rose above the trees (I.12: 96/60).

From Surrey, the story moved into London, with the flight of the narrator's brother across to the continent briefly extending the book's geographical spread

23. Wells, *Experiment in Autobiography*, II, p. 516.
24. Wells, '*The War of the Worlds*: Introduction: an experiment in illustration', p. 154.
25. 'A young novelist who has "arrived"'.

into Essex and the coast. Wells's coverage of the London-centred part of the conflict was equally strong topographically, since the metropolis was a place he knew well from residence (Table 2.1), visits to relatives living in Primrose Hill, and walking.[26] Primrose Hill in Camden Town figured prominently during the closing stages of the story. Here the seventh Martian cylinder landed, the Martians set up camp and the invaders made their last stand as they succumbed to natural bacteria.

Notwithstanding the book's title, the actual conflict described in the story did not stray far beyond London and Surrey, except when the narrator was speculating about whether the Martians were also attacking Berlin and Paris (II.6: 245/147) or reporting how news of the Martians' abortive invasion was flashed across Britain and the world (II.9: 288–9/172). But why did Wells not call the book *The War of Woking* or *The Martians Invade Woking*?[27] After all, Woking was the first place to be affected, targeted, attacked and destroyed by the Martians. However, for Wells, the story represented something far more grandiose than a mere local event. Popular fictional writers target an audience and naturally a Woking-centred title would have lacked the contemporary global resonance of *The War of the Worlds*, especially for an author seeking both a national and worldwide audience and setting his story in the broader contemporary context.

Conclusion

Wells sent a copy of *The War of the Worlds* to Isabel, his former wife. Thanking him for sending the book, she described the changes made for the book as 'a great improvement' over the text serialized in *Pearson Magazine*. Isabel asked, 'Where in the world of all that's wonderful do you get your ideas from? And you make them so terribly realistic too. It is marvellous'.[28] What Isabel did was to put her finger upon the principal factors explaining Wells's success in reaching and engaging a large and expanding audience and impressing the literary world with his scientific romances. For Wells, the author, the key task was to engage readers faced for the first time with a story about invaders from another world, that is to make a fantastic story realistic, such as through reportage, an emphasis upon place and time and curbing the narrative excesses, while making full use of the

26. Wells to Davies, 31 December 1887, Smith, *Correspondence of H. G. Wells, I*, p. 77. See also Wells to Healey, 28 February 1888, 28 April 1888, Smith, *Correspondence of H. G. Wells, I*, pp. 84, 98.

27. Brian Aldiss, 'The referee of *The War of the Worlds*', *Foundation: The International Review of Science Fiction* 28 (77) (1999): 8. Discussing why Wells did not use a title like *The War of Woking*, Aldiss wrote somewhat mischievously: 'Because his intentions were more grandiose than merely the destruction of Woking, desirable though that might be': Aldiss, 'Introduction', p. xvii.

28. Isabel to Wells, n.d. [February 1898], Smith, *Correspondence of H. G. Wells, I*, p. 301.

vitality and power of his visual imagination. Another avid admirer, 'always power-fully impressed' by Wells's scientific romances, was Joseph Conrad: 'Your books take hold of one with a grasp that can be felt'.[29] For Conrad, Wells was the 'Realist of the Fantastic!'

29. Conrad to Wells, 25 May 1896, Smith, *Correspondence of H. G. Wells, I*, p. 264; Conrad to Wells, 4 December 1898, in Georges Jean-Aubry (ed.), *Joseph Conrad: Life and Letters, I* (New York: Doubleday, Page, 1927), p. 259; Wells, *Experiment in Autobiography*, II, pp. 615–23. In 1907 Conrad dedicated *The Secret Agent* (1907) to Wells: Martin Ray, 'Conrad, Wells and *The Secret Agent*: paying old debts and settling old scores', *The Modern Language Review* 81 (3) (1986): 560. Their literary friendship did not last, as reflected by Wells's unflattering caricature of Conrad as the incompetent and corrupt captain in *Tono-Bungay* (1909).

Chapter 9

LEAVING WOKING FOR WORCESTER PARK

During late Summer 1896 Wells moved across Surrey to Worcester Park, near Kingston upon Thames. The exact date of his move remains uncertain, since the principal sources recording that 'On Wednesday next we move to Heatherlea', the name of his new home in The Avenue, are undated.[1] However, Wells's mention of having recently read Grant Allen's story 'The Episode of the Diamond Links' in July's *Strand Magazine* indicates he moved houses during or after July 1896, but most probably between August and October 1896.[2]

Why move from Woking?

At first sight, Wells's departure from Woking after a relatively brief stay of just over one year, might be interpreted as reflecting an anxiety to get away from the town as soon as possible. For some commentators, this impression is reinforced by the fact that *The War of the Worlds* recorded Wells's fictional destruction of the town, with the Martians leaving Woking as 'a heap of fiery ruins' and 'smouldering pine-woods' (I.11: 85/54–5). All that remained were 'countless ruins of shattered and gutted houses and blasted and blackened trees' (I.11: 86–7/55). Only 'a few people' (I.11: 85/54) were left alive. However, the rest of Surrey, a county much admired by Wells for its countryside and ambience, suffered the same fate. Likewise, his chapter entitled 'Dead London' showed that another area which Wells loved and where he spent much of his life, fared even worse, 'a city condemned and derelict' (II.8: 275/164). Looking down from Primrose Hill, the narrator surveyed the destruction – he saw many dead bodies and 'the blackened skeletons of houses' (II.8: 287/170) – wrought upon Camden Town by the invaders.

In fact, Wells's choice of Woking as a place typifying late Victorian Britain gave the fast-growing town national, even global, visibility and played a major

1. Wells to Grant Allen, n.d., [1896], Smith, *The Correspondence of H. G. Wells, I*, p. 274; Richards, *Memories of a Misspent Youth*, p. 329.

2. Grant Allen, 'The Episode of the Diamond Links', *Strand Magazine* 12 (July 1896), pp. 97–106. Subsequently, this story was published as part of Grant Allen's *An African Millionaire* (1897).

role in transforming its image. Henceforth, Woking became more the place where fantastic things had happened following a Martian invasion and less a town associated with death through burials and cremations. Moreover, for Wells, life in Woking had proved not only highly productive for his writing and financially lucrative, but also extremely good for his health, general wellbeing and relationship with Jane. For Wells, Woking proved – as he told one interviewer in late 1895 – 'a pleasant and wholly respectable place'.[3] Having arrived in Woking in poor health, Wells, though still believing that he faced an early death, left the town in much better shape, so that nearly two years passed before he suffered another serious health scare. The fact that Wells lived until the age of seventy-nine, was clearly helped by the manner in which his stay there checked the harm inflicted previously by London's heavily polluted atmosphere.

Nor should the brevity of Wells's residence be viewed necessarily as evidence of a desire to get away from Woking. Table 2.1 shows that during the 1880s and 1890s Wells stayed nowhere very long, a residential mobility facilitated by his preference to rent rather than to own property. Indeed, soon after his arrival, Wells opined that he would not remain long in the town.[4] Hence his relatively brief sojourn in Woking was typical, not a significant departure from the norm reflecting strong dislike for the town, even if he admitted feeling uneasy in a commuter town seemingly unsympathetic to a writer's lifestyle: 'I fancy that the people of Woking regard me with suspicion. I don't go to town by a ten o'clock train, and I don't return to dinner at night. Not to do these things is to loaf. A season ticket is the outward mark of respectability and business habits!' Even so, his stay proved relatively lengthy when viewed against the fact that in 1896, he was making his sixth move in less than three years.[5] From this perspective, the switch from Woking to Worcester Park, where his stay was to prove equally brief, was merely another chapter, albeit one of the more successful chapters, in his life story.

Furthermore, by the mid-1890s Wells's residential mobility was less a matter of exploring a new career direction but increasingly a function of his achievements as a writer. Literary success brought money (Table 6.2) and the ability to move up the property ladder to something better and adjudged more fitting to his enhanced wealth, status and needs as a writer. Aspects prioritized by Wells, included more space for writing, including a dedicated study; improved domestic facilities, most notably modern plumbing; and a large garden for leisure and relaxation. Even so, despite a fast-rising income, Wells continued to rent accommodation until 1899 when he decided to become a property-owner while living in Sandgate, Kent. Whereas previously Wells had never stayed in any one place for very long, house ownership led him to stay at Sandgate for almost ten years until moving back to London in 1909, to Church Row, described by Nikolaus Pevsner as 'the best street

3. *Weekly Sun Literary Supplement*, 1 December 1895, quoted Smith, 'A chat with the author', p. 8.

4. Quoted Smith, 'A chat with the author', p. 8.

5. Sherborne, *H. G. Wells*, p. 115.

in Hampstead.[6] As Christopher Rolfe observed, Wells used London's geography in the semi-autobiographical *Tono-Bungay* (1909) to reflect his socio-economic progression from the 'shabby impecuniosity' of lodgings in Camden Town during the mid-1890s to 'Crest Hill', Hampstead, in 1909.[7]

For Wells, the prime drawback of Woking centred upon 'Lynton', his house in Maybury Road. Despite having a dining room, drawing room and three bedrooms, Wells came to regard the house as increasingly cramped and hence to fall far short of a property offering a 'pleasant well-lit writing room'.[8] Reportedly, he had to clear away his drafts from the dining table for each meal.[9] Wells expressed a preference also for 'a comfortable bedroom … free from distracting noises', predominantly those emanating from the steam trains passing by across the road to and from the nearby station.[10] Moreover, by mid-1896 more room was required for Jane's mother who had fallen ill: 'for a time it was necessary that she should live with us, so that we had to move to a larger house at Worcester Park'.[11] Thus, having moved in May 1895 from a small apartment in Camden Town to 'Lynton', a semi-detached villa with a modest sized garden and greenhouse, Wells was now trading up to a large detached house with an extensive garden and an annual rental of £65, more than double that paid for 'Lynton'.

'Heatherlea' in Worcester Park

In June 1896 the Wells's viewed 'Heatherlea', a detached Victorian house located in The Avenue, Worcester Park.[12] Reportedly Pinker, one of his literary agents, already lived nearby at 'The Oaks', and hence it seems probable that he helped Wells to find a property in Worcester Park, a place away from the hurry and bustle of the metropolis and yet near enough to London to enable Wells to attend meetings and literary events.[13] Although it failed to match Woking's train service, Wells claimed that Worcester Park had 'an excellent but infrequent service of

6. Quoted, 'Writers' houses by Paul Hogarth: 10; H. G. Wells's house', *Illustrated London News* 268 (6987) (25 October 1980), p. 87.

7. Rolfe, 'From Camden Town to Crest Hill', p. 4; H. G. Wells, *Tono-Bungay* (London: Penguin, 2005), p. 232. On the sub-division of large houses into lodgings as in Mornington Terrace, see Wells, *Tono-Bungay*, pp. 89–90.

8. Wells, *Experiment in Autobiography*, I, p. 19.

9. A. West, *H. G. Wells*, p. 232.

10. Wells, *Experiment in Autobiography*, I, p. 19.

11. Wells, *Experiment in Autobiography*, II, p. 546.

12. Wells to Pinker, 21 June 1896, Pinker, Vol. 1 (Ransom).

13. Wells to Grant Allen, n.d., in Richards, *Memories of a Misspent Youth*, p. 329; 'Record Portraits: no. XXV H. G. Wells', p. 22; David Rymill, 'History: pens and paintbrushes in Worcester Park', *Worcester Park Life* 29 (October 2010), p. 7; David Rymill to the author, 22 April 2013; N. and J. Mackenzie, *The Time Traveller*, p. 114. Pinker's prior residence requires further research.

trains to Waterloo'.[14] Moreover, 'Heatherlea' was out of earshot of the trains in spite of being within easy walking distance of the station. Worcester Park was already known to Wells, having figured in 'Argonauts of the Air' (1895).

Following the opening of Worcester Park station in 1859 on the Wimbledon–Epsom line, the Landed Estates Company developed the surrounding area as 'a genteel suburb' of large detached villas aimed principally at professional classes wishing – to quote one resident living in the area during the late Victorian period – 'to have a home in the real country, and go to their daily work in London'.[15] But the project developed slowly and when Grant Richards and the journalist George Steevens visited Wells, they found 'a sparsely populated and uninspiring suburb'.[16] Or, as Wells wrote in *Ann Veronica: A Modern Love Story* (1909), Worcester Park, renamed "Morningside Park" in the novel, 'was a suburb that had not altogether, as people say, come off': 'There was first the Avenue, which ran in a consciously elegant curve from the railway station into an undeveloped wilderness of agriculture, with big yellow brick villas on either side'.[17] Morningside Park was home, Wells wrote, to 'business men, solicitors, civil servants, and widow ladies'.[18] Writers and literary agents might be added to this list, given the presence of Pinker and Wells.

'Heatherlea' had two large rooms downstairs and a visitor's room. There was a study upstairs plus six bedrooms located on two floors.[19] What impressed Wells most was the garden. Following his viewing, Wells described 'Heatherlea' as 'a picturesque and unsanitary house in the early Victorian style standing in its own grounds of a half a quarter of an acre' in a district where oak trees grew 'luxuriantly': 'It's a ripping garden, but the house isn't much'.[20] One interviewer recorded the garden's appeal for Wells:

'It's a good roomy garden, too,' he [H. G. Wells] tells me, as we wend our way down the stairs, 'and I always work in the open as much as I possibly can;' and

14. Wells to Grant Allen, n.d. [1896], in Richards, *Memories of a Misspent Youth*, p. 329.

15. Sir Alexander Harris, quoted David Rymill, *Worcester Park & Cuddington: A Walk through the Centuries* (Worcester Park: Buckwheat Press, 2000), p. 31. See also, pp. 2, 11–12, 28. For contemporary photographs of The Avenue, see SHC 6348/Box 4 (SHC), which includes also a postcard sent from Worcester Park in 1903.

16. Richards, *Memories of a Misspent Youth*, p. 215. Steevens covered the Boer War as the *Daily Mail*'s war correspondent.

17. H. G. Wells, *Ann Veronica* (London: Penguin, 2005), p. 6.

18. Ibid., p. 10. According to the 1901 census, the occupier of 'Heatherlea' was William Walker, a member of the Stock Exchange.

19. 'Heatherlea', Report ref. no. 41, n.d. [1910], Valuer's Field Book, Parish of Cuddington, IR58/80995, British government records: Land Valuation Survey: land value and ownership 1910–15: The National Archives, Kew, London (TNA). In 1910 the owners, who had purchased the house for £675 in 1890, were now the occupiers. The current estimated house value and annual rental were £700 and £65 respectively.

20. Wells to Pinker, 21 June 1896, Pinker, Vol. 1 (Ransom); Wells to Grant Allen, n.d. [1896], in Richards, *Memories of a Misspent Youth*, p. 329.

I soon find that this description of the garden is a true one. We pass over two shady lawns, until we get to the extreme end of it, where we take our seats, with the branches of some fine oak trees waving over our heads.[21]

Reportedly, the Wells employed a servant plus a gardener for one day per week. Wells's description of 'Heatherlea' as an 'unsanitary house' reflected his growing preoccupation with household plumbing and unpleasant memories of the short-comings of several past residences in this regard. Indeed, after viewing the house, he sent a Woking-based plumber 'to stethoscope it'.[22] Clearly action was taken, as evidenced in 1910 when the Land Valuation Survey recorded that 'Heatherlea' possessed 'modern drainage', with all four first floor bedrooms possessing low basins.[23]

Wells's 'new way of life'

Wells represented 'Heatherlea' as inaugurating 'my new way of life'.[24] In reality, it was merely another chapter in his life story characterized by successive new starts. Moving fifteen or so miles across Surrey to Worcester Park reflected his desire to make yet another fresh start in a larger house, adjudged more appropriate to his growing status as a writer and his increasing wealth. For example, he took great pride in showing interviewers his study: '"This is my first study," Mr. Wells tells me, -"never had a house big enough before to enable me to indulge in the luxury."'[25] Large areas of space downstairs plus a substantial garden, enabled the Wells to keep open house on Saturday afternoons and to entertain literary and other friends, like Dorothy Richardson, one of Jane's former school friends, who portrayed Wells's new lifestyle in her novels, most notably *The Tunnel* (1919).[26] Apart from Grant Richards, literary visitors included George Meredith and George Gissing.

21. Lawrence, 'Romance of the Scientist', p. 256.

22. Wells to Pinker, 21 June 1896, Pinker, Vol. 1 (Ransom).

23. 'Heatherlea', Report ref. no. 41, n.d. [1910], Valuer's Field Book, Parish of Cuddington, IR58/80995 (TNA). Noting that the wall had been 'tied', the valuer suggested that 'probably the house has been underpinned'. One letter sent by Wells to Grant Allen was accompanied by two sketches suggesting possible subsidence: Wells to Grant Allen, n.d., [1896], Smith, *The Correspondence of H. G. Wells, I*, p. 264.

24. Wells, Experiment *in Autobiography*, II, p. 557.

25. Lawrence, 'Romance of the Scientist', pp. 254–5. By contrast, Grant Richards, a visitor to 'Heatherlea', claimed somewhat surprisingly that Wells 'had not then crossed the threshold of prosperity': Richards, *Memories of a Misspent Youth*, p. 215.

26. Wells, *An Experiment in Autobiography*, II, p. 557; Banerjee, *Literary Surrey*, p. 152; N. and J. Mackenzie, *The Time Traveller*, pp. 135–6. In *The Tunnel* (1919), the heroine, Miriam Henderson, encounters the world of art and literature when she visits her school friend Alma and her husband, Hypo Wilson, who are modelled on Jane and Wells respectively.

Wells and Gissing

Following their first meeting in November 1896 at an Omar Khayyám Club dinner held at Frascati's Restaurant, Oxford Street, in London, Wells invited Gissing, a resident of nearby Epsom and author of such books as *New Grub Street* (1891) and *The Odd Women* (1893), to visit his 'charming house (a little defective as to the roof & water pipes) & picturesque (if insanitary) surroundings at Worcester Park'.[27] Pointing to the possibility of walking, catching the train, or cycling from Epsom, Wells enclosed a recent press item reporting the success of *The Wheels of Chance*, while adding that 'There is accommodation for bicycles'. Concerned about Gissing's health and lack of exercise, Wells 'tried to make him a cyclist': 'I thought it might be pleasant to explore Surrey and Sussex with him'.[28] But Gissing proved a hopeless pupil: 'It was curious to see this well-built Viking, blowing and funking as he hopped behind his machine. "Get on to your ironmongery," said I. He mounted, wabbled a few yards and fell off shrieking with laughter. "Iron-mongery!" he gasped. "Oh! riding on ironmongery!" and lay in the grass at the roadside, helpless with mirth.'

This episode highlights the central role occupied still by cycling in Wells's life. Apart from keeping his figure within bounds 'by the most strenuous bicycle riding', Wells treated the bicycle as an invaluable means of transport, such as to visit his parents, friends, Isabel, his ex-wife living at Twyford, and literary acquaintances.[29] Recording Wells's enthusiasm for cycling and receptive attitude towards new things, Grant Richards mentioned that just prior to his visit to 'Heatherlea' the Wells had taken delivery of a tandem safety bicycle – what Wells described as 'the double machine' – on which they rode to Clapham Common to return his visit.[30] Nor was Wells's cycling confined to the local area. In April 1897, Wells and Jane reprised their 1895 long distance cycle ride from Woking to the West Country to stay with Gissing at Budleigh Salterton, a round trip of nearly 350 miles. Planning to take some five days to get there from Worcester Park and

27. Wells to Gissing, 25 November 1896, in Mattheisen, Young and Coustillas, *The Collected Letters of George Gissing*, 6, pp. 197–8; Wells to Gissing, 30 November 1896, Smith, *The Correspondence of H. G. Wells*, I, p. 277. See also 'George Robert Gissing (1857–1903)', n.d., http://www.epsomandewellhistoryexplorer.org.uk/Gissing.html [accessed 10 January 2012]. In August 1897 Wells published a literary commentary entitled 'The Novels of Mr. George Gissing' in the *Contemporary Review*.

28. Wells, *Experiment in Autobiography*, II, p. 568. Wells used a series of picshuas to show his friend Davies how to ride a bike: Wells to Davies, Spring 1897, Smith, *The Correspondence of H. G. Wells*, I, pp. 286–7.

29. Wells to Fred Wells, n.d. [July 1896], Wells, *Experiment in Autobiography*, I, pp. 403, 405; Wells, *Experiment in Autobiography*, II, pp. 431–2.

30. Richards, *Memories of a Misspent Youth*, pp. 215–16; Lawrence, 'Romance of the Scientist', p. 255. Presumably this refers to the type of tandem bicycle developed during the mid-1890s as an advance on the lady-front tandem machine the Wells's rode at in Woking (Figure 4.3).

then to stay for a fortnight, Wells asked Gissing, who was in Devon to improve his health as well as to get away from his wife, to book accommodation for 'two dirty cyclists'.[31] But even on holiday Wells could never forget work, as evidenced by his ongoing exchanges with Pinker about *When the Sleeper Wakes*.[32]

Gissing spoke frequently and fondly of Italy. The Wells, neither of whom had yet crossed the Channel, were impressed and agreed to join Gissing in Rome the following Spring for a 'daring adventure "abroad"' scheduled from 7 March to 11 May 1898: '"Abroad" was a slightly terrifying world of adventure for us. And we were not going to just nibble at the continent. We were going straight through, at one bite, to Rome'.[33] Complaining about his 'perpetual catarrh', Wells looked forward to the trip also as offering the opportunity to get away from Britain's 'damned climate'.[34] Gissing advised the Wells to prepare for the trip, such as by learning a few Italian words and phrases and reading up about the Romans.[35] One of Wells's picshuas shows the couple surveying a vast map of Rome. Determined to do as the Romans do, Wells wore a toga and was shown checking his appearance in the mirror.[36] In Rome, where the Wells undertook a fair amount of sightseeing on foot and were joined for a time by Conan Doyle, Gissing proved an inspiring and enthusiastic guide.[37] Apart from spending a month in Rome with Gissing, the Wells went off on their own to visit Amalfi, Capri, Naples and Pompeii.

Following his return from Italy, Wells found it difficult to get back to work: 'I ascribed a general sense of malaise, an inability to stick to my work – I was then writing *Love and Mr Lewisham* – to want of exercise'.[38] As a result, in July 1898, Wells and Jane began yet another long-distance cycling tour to Kent, but the trip was soon cut short at Seaford where Wells fell seriously ill again for the first time since 1893.[39] Wells travelled by train to New Romney to consult Henry Hick, Medical Officer of Health for Romney Marsh and a friend of Gissing. At one stage, Hick feared for his life, but Wells, though 'so sorely ill', pulled through yet again.[40]

31. Wells to Gissing, 19 April 1897, Smith, *The Correspondence of H. G. Wells, I*, p. 285.

32. Wells to Pinker, 29 April 1897, 14 May 1897, Loing, *Wells à l'oeuvre*, pp. 434–5.

33. Wells, *Experiment in Autobiography*, II, pp. 565, 568; Patrick Parrinder, 'The Roman Spring of George Gissing and H. G. Wells', *The Gissing Newsletter* XXI (3) (July 1985): 1–3.

34. Wells to Gissing, 1 January 1898, quoted, N. and J. MacKenzie, *The Time Traveller*, p. 134.

35. Gissing to Wells, 18 February 1898, Wells to Gissing, n.d. (23 February 1898), in Mattheisen, Young and Coustillas (eds), *The Collected Letters of George Gissing, 7*, pp. 63–4, 67.

36. Wells, *Experiment in Autobiography*, II, p. 566.

37. Wells spent Christmas 1903 at 'poor Gissing's deathbed': Wells to Baxter, 12 January 1904, HGW 1245/1/1, H. G. Wells Collection: Bromley Local Studies and Archives, Bromley Central Library, Bromley, Kent, UK (BRO). Gissing died on 28 December 1903.

38. Wells, *Experiment in Autobiography*, II, p. 582.

39. Ibid., pp. 582–4; 'News Notes', *The Bookman* 14 (84) (September 1898), p. 149.

40. Wells to Pinker, 20 September 1898, Loing, *Wells à l'oeuvre*, pp. 439–40.

However, Hick advised Wells to move to the south coast for health reasons. Regretting that he had ever taken the house at Worcester Park, Wells agreed that it would be suicide to winter again at 'Heatherlea': 'According to the best advice available, a long period of invalidism was before me. I had to reconcile myself to complete exile from London, and contrive to live in dry air with no damp in the subsoil and in as much sunshine as possible.'[41] Thus, when writing to Elizabeth Healey, Wells described his departure from Worcester Park as due to 'some obscure geological reason'.[42] Turning away from London's suburbia, Wells sought open sky, sea air and nearby countryside.[43] Fearing that his cycling days were over, Wells even gave away his bicycle. In 1899 his *Who's Who* entry for recreational interests replaced cycling, the previous year's entry, with 'detailed descriptions of his various illnesses, and architecture'.[44]

Leaving Jane to oversee the move, Wells never visited 'Heatherlea' again. As a result, his residence in Worcester Park proved yet another short chapter in his life, albeit nowhere as productive as that in Woking. Indeed, Wells's stay, though successful in terms of his pursuit of an active social life and growing literary recognition, was characterized by what Wells depicted as a 'long silence' regarding publications extending over 'a year or more'.[45] But this did not mean a complete absence of publications. It was more a case of a marked change of pace downwards. Thus, his stay saw the completion of *The Invisible Man* for publication as a serial and a book, the writing of additional text for the book version of *The War of the Worlds*, continued work on *When the Sleeper Wakes* and *Love and Mr Lewisham*, but both progressed slowly, and a considerable but declining number of book reviews, principally for *The Saturday Review* and the *Daily Mail*. Written 'in the vein of the *Time Machine*', *When the Sleeper Wakes* was first serialized in *The Graphic* magazine (1898–9) and then published 'a good deal' altered as a book in 1899.[46] Subsequently, in 1910 Wells, conceding that he had 'scamped the finish', made substantial textual changes for a revised edition re-titled 'in better English' as *The Sleeper Awakes*.[47] *Love and Mr Lewisham*, 'a moral novel' based on Wells's

41. Wells to his mother, n.d. [September 1898], Wells, *Experiment in Autobiography*, II, p. 592.

42. Wells to Healey, n.d. [late 1898], Wells H. G. Autograph Letters to Miss Healey, 1888–1905, 35 *ALS* (Ransom).

43. A. West, *H. G. Wells*, p. 245.

44. G. West, *H. G. Wells*, p. 138.

45. Wells to his father, 18 December 1898, Wells, *Experiment in Autobiography*, I, pp. 408–9; Wells to Gissing, n.d. [c. 1 January 1898], Loing, *Wells à l'oeuvre*, p. 437.

46. Wells to his father, 18 December 1898, Wells, *Experiment in Autobiography*, I, pp. 408–9. *When the Sleeper Wakes* did attract critical reviews; thus, for one American reviewer, it compared unfavourably with *The War of the Worlds*: 'the action drags, the descriptions are complicated and uncommonly tiresome': 'Observations', *The Courier* (Lincoln, Nebraska), 11 March 1899, p. 2.

47. Wells, *Experiment in Autobiography*, II, p. 582.

trials as a young teacher trapped in an unsuitable marriage to Isabel, was not published as a serial and a book until 1900.[48]

Changing course

The house hunt on the Kent coast proved somewhat challenging. Wells's search focussed principally upon Sandgate, near Folkestone, Kent. Placing a high priority on good plumbing, especially a decent bathroom, Wells complained 'Not a house to be got – not what's fit for me to live in nowadays – not one'.[49] In the end, he rented Beach Cottage, a furnished property with 'a back door slap upon the sea' in Sandgate's Granville Road as a temporary measure.[50] Then, in March 1899, he moved a short distance along the coast to Arnold House, a semi-detached villa in Castle Road, with a garden running down to the beach.

Eventually, Wells decided to build 'a house of my own', which 'seemed as good a use for savings as I could imagine'.[51] Following a lengthy period of renting property, Wells's decision to purchase his own house reflected growing confidence in his literary career and the state of his finances, which were 'some hundreds of pounds on the solvent side'.[52] Thus, he decided to build a house at Sandgate, a location intended to improve his health, extend what he feared still was a very limited life span and raise a family.[53] For Wells, Sandgate, whose blue skies contrasted with the 'thick fogs in London', proved 'the most habitable place' he had ever lived in: 'For an elderly invalid (as I am practically) it is incomparable'.[54] When C. F. A. Voysey was designing what came to be called Spade House, Wells's health issues, alongside his usual preoccupation with domestic plumbing, proved paramount. In particular, Wells's fears that he would soon have to 'be wheeled from room to room' in a bath-chair, led him to specify that bedrooms, living rooms and his study must all be located on one floor.[55] Writing towards the end of the building work on Spade House, Wells welcomed the fact that 'it's all my own ... and it's all paid for & it's worth £2000'.[56] For Henry James, it was Wells's 'treasure house

48. Wells to Healey, December 1898, WB78/10 (UIUC); Wells to Gissing, n.d. [c. 1 January 1898], Loing, *Wells à l'oeuvre*, p. 437; Wells, *Experiment in Autobiography*, I, pp. 171, 408.

49. Wells to Tommy (Simmons), October 1898, WS31 (UIUC).

50. Wells to Healey, n.d. [1898], Wells H. G. Autograph Letters to Miss Healey, 1888–1905, 35 *ALS* (Ransom).

51. Wells, *Experiment in Autobiography*, II, pp. 597, 638–9.

52. Ibid., p. 596.

53. N. and J. MacKenzie, *The Time Traveller*, pp. 148–50. Wells was buying a house also for his wife's mother, who had lived with them in Worcester Park.

54. Wells to Healey, n.d. [December 1899], WB77-6a (UIUC); Wells to Dunn, 16 February 1900, Smith, *The Correspondence of H. G. Wells*, I, p. 355.

55. Wells, *Experiment in Autobiography*, I, pp. 299–300, II, p. 639.

56. Wells to Fred Wells, 25 October 1900, Smith, *The Correspondence of H. G. Wells*, I,

on the sea shore'.[57] For Gissing, whose own financial shortcomings gave added point to his comment, the new house reflected the literary success of Wells, who was 'wonderfully prosperous': 'He has built himself a beautiful house at Sandgate (near Folkestone), where, sitting at his ease, he communicates with London by telephone! That kind of thing will never fall to me.' [58] Headed notepaper listed Wells's telephone number at a house employing four servants and a gardener.[59]

At Sandgate, Wells networked with literary figures – they included Joseph Conrad, Ford Madox Ford (then Ford Madox Hueffer), Henry James and Stephen Crane – living nearby or visiting the area.[60] Furthermore, he became increasingly active, such as buying another bike to take up cycling again, walking and learning to swim.[61] As he informed one correspondent in 1908, despite lengthy periods of illness over the years his health was now 'very sound'.[62] His 'favourite exercise' was taking long walks of twenty miles or so, for instance, in 1902 when vacationing in Switzerland he walked to the summit of the St Gotthard Pass. Also he conducted lengthy cycle tours, such as to Brighton, Worthing and Petersfield as well as Paris (1900), and played tennis 'ardently but badly'. Looking back on his life, Wells confronted the media and public 'legend of permanent ill health': 'Early struggles, saddened life, permanent bad health, jaundiced outlook'.[63] As he asserted, 'All nonsense Madam'. Thus, during the 1900s his life-threatening health problems began to dissipate and to become increasingly a thing of the past. The central health problem, it seemed, had been resolved in 1898 when 'the offending kidney had practically taken itself off and there was nothing left to remove': 'Thereupon I began to recover and after a few years of interrogative suspense and occasional pain not even a reminiscent twinge remained of my left kidney'.[64]

Eventually, Wells tired of Sandgate – it proved too healthy and too monotone – and in 1909 moved the family home to Hampstead. As a result, he returned to London, the city he loved, the place to do things, to see people and to meet 'friendly women'.[65] Henceforth, Wells based himself in London, albeit at times

p. 365. When selling Spade House in 1909, Wells asked for £3,200: Wells to Jones, 24 May 1909, Smith, *The Correspondence of H. G. Wells, II*, pp. 240–1.

57. Quoted, N. and J. MacKenzie, *The Time Traveller*, p. 149.

58. George Gissing to Bertz, 17 March 1901, in Mattheisen, Paul F., Young, Arthur C. and Coustillas, Pierre (eds), *The Collected Letters of George Gissing, Vol. 8: 1900–1902* (Athens, OH: Ohio University Press, 1996), p. 147.

59. Wells to Editor, *Labour Leader*, n.d. [February 1908], Smith, *The Correspondence of H. G. Wells, II*, p. 210.

60. N. and J. Mackenzie, *The Time Traveller*, pp. 140–7.

61. Wells, *Experiment in Autobiography*, II, pp. 597–8.

62. Wells to Mrs Tooley, n.d. [October/November 1908], WT–371A–B (UIUC); Wells, *Experiment in Autobiography*, II, pp. 597–8, 639; Wells to Healey, 24 May 1900, Wells to Edith Nesbit, 5 August 1901, Smith, *The Correspondence of H. G. Wells, I*, pp. 355, 381–2.

63. Wells to Mrs Tooley, n.d. [October/November 1908], WT–371A–B (UIUC).

64. Wells, *Experiment in Autobiography*, II, p. 584.

65. Wells, *H. G. Wells in Love*, pp. 82, 84.

living in various *pieds à terre* and abroad, while maintaining a family home at Hampstead and then at Dunmow, Essex, until Jane's death in 1927. In 1935 Wells purchased a large property in Hanover Terrace, a row of houses designed by John Nash overlooking the Outer Circle of Regent's Park. Over forty years earlier, Wells had lived on the other side of Regent's Park while making his way in the world: 'Now he was back, in another century, ageing, famous and positioned on the affluent west side'.[66] Despite representing this move as ushering in what he viewed as the final phase of his life – 13 Hanover Terrace was a house to die in – Wells welcomed the house's garden and view over Regent's Park, as wealth enabled him to bring the much loved countryside to London: 'It is more like a place in the country than a home in London'.[67]

Wells never lived in Surrey again. That chapter of his life was over after he left Worcester Park in 1898. Obviously he returned occasionally to Surrey in his memory and imagination – as mentioned in previous chapters, the county's locations continued to feature frequently in his writing – as well as in real life, such as to see people, to write or to attend Henley's funeral at Brookwood. During 1910–11, he spent two weeks at Cochet Farm, Haslemere. Ostensibly, the stay was for work, that is to write *Marriage* (1912), but in reality Wells wanted a base near Fernhurst, where Elizabeth von Arnim, his new lover, was staying with her sister.[68] Looking back, Wells claimed that 'I forget now how far this proximity was arranged', but the countryside location ensured that the couple 'soon came to an easy understanding'![69]

Wells and women

Wells's 'easy understanding' with von Arnim, reflected another feature of his post-1900 lifestyle, a long history of affairs, the majority extra-marital, and mistresses. Unsurprisingly, biographers have focused increasingly upon this dimension partly because it boosts book sales and partly because it attracts media interest. More importantly, this topic helps us to understand Wells the writer, a novelist who wrote frequently from experience. Indeed, David Lodge's factional biography, *A Man of Parts* (2011), illuminates the way in which sex and women figured prominently in Wells's thinking and life.[70] Moreover, Wells used his literary earnings to support an active extra-curricular love life, given the heavy costs incurred in maintaining *pied-à-terres* in London for romantic liaisons,

66. Sherborne, *H. G. Wells*, p. 314.

67. Wells to Freddy (Wells), 15 July 1936, Smith, *Correspondence of H. G. Wells, IV*, p. 89; Wells, *H. G. Wells in Love*, p. 211. Reportedly such houses now sell for well over £10 million.

68. Trotter, *The Hilltop Writers*, pp. 216–17. For an illustration of Cochet Farm, see Charles Bone, *The Authors Circle* (Godalming: Tremlett's Books, 1998), p. 43.

69. Wells, *H. G. Wells in Love*, p. 88.

70. David Lodge, *A Man of Parts: A Novel* (London: Harvill Secker, 2011), Preface; David Lodge, *Lives in Writing: Essays* (London: Harvill Secker, 2014), pp. 223–56.

entertaining and supporting mistresses and covering the expenses of children arising from his affairs with Amber Reeves (1909) and Rebeca West (1914).[71]

Nor was Wells as circumspect in his extra-marital affairs as he might have been; thus, his adulterous behaviour became a source of gossip for the literary world. Indeed, Wells even devoted one whole volume of his three-volume autobiography to the topic. Introducing the third volume as a *Postscript* written between 1934 and 1942, he described it as an 'intimate diary' exploring 'my amatory life', belief in and practice of free love and revolt against the present-day sexual code: 'I have done what I pleased; so that every bit of sexual impulse in me has expressed itself'.[72] In accordance with Wells's wishes, the exposé remained unpublished until after both his death and the deaths of the women concerned. In 1984 *H. G. Wells in Love*, edited by his eldest son George Wells and published posthumously a half-century after the first two volumes and thirty-eight years after his death, added a hot new chapter to Wells's life story.

According to Wells, marriage to two wives, seemingly incapable of making their alliance 'an intense sexual relationship', led him to indulge increasingly in what he described as 'an enterprising promiscuity', allegedly tolerated by Jane through what Wells represented as a '*modus vivendi*'.[73] Thus, he conducted numerous '*passades*' with a succession of women.[74] Wells sought to rationalize his attitude towards marriage and women, by highlighting the incompatibility of what he represented as his 'Lover-Shadow' – his constant drive for romantic love and 'to *get* girls and women' – with marriage.[75] He acknowledged also, the way in which contact with rakish braggarts like Sidney Bowkett and Frank Harris reinforced his coarser thoughts.

Wells's women were too numerous to list, but over time included several journalists and writers: Martha Gellhorn, Odette Keun, Amber Reeves, Dorothy Richardson, Elizabeth von Arnim and Rebecca West; Margaret Sanger, an American birth control activist; and Moura Budberg.[76] The latter, the great-great

71. Wells, *H. G. Wells in Love*, pp. 82, 84.

72. Ibid., pp. 53, 201, 210; Amelia Hill, 'The secret loves of H. G. Wells unmasked', *The Observer*, 7 January 2001. On the writing of the third volume, see Wells, *Wells in Love*, pp. 15–20.

73. Wells, *Experiment in Autobiography*, II, pp. 424–5, 435. But he fails to address the question of why he married two such women.

74. Strictly defined, a *passade*, represented by Wells as 'a stroke of mutual attraction', is a brief liaison, whereas Wells's relationships often proved far from brief: Wells, *Experiment in Autobiography*, II, p. 465.

75. Wells, *Experiment in Autobiography*, I, pp. 105–7; Wells, *H. G. Wells in Love*, p. 51 *et seq.*, pp. 60, 64; Andrea Lynn, *Shadow Lovers: The Last Affairs of H. G. Wells* (Boulder, CO: Westview Press, 2001), pp. xxi–xxiii.

76. A. West, *H. G. Wells*, p. 21. One of Wells's early conquests was Rosamund, the teenage step daughter of Edith Bland, aka E. Nesbit, the author of *The Railway Children* (1906): Sherborne, *H. G. Wells*, pp. 182–3. The nature of Wells's relationship with Gellhorn remains debatable: Lynn, *Shadow Lovers*, pp. 329–440.

-aunt of Nick Clegg, the British deputy Prime Minister (2010–15), was linked also with Bruce Lockhart and Maxim Gorky and suspected by the British authorities of espionage.[77] Generally speaking, Wells's women were often much younger than him and seemingly known to Jane. Wells claimed that his philandering did not really start until c. 1900: 'It was only when Spade House was building, that I found myself trying definitely to *get* anyone'.[78] During the mid-late 1890s, this was less of a problem when he was enjoying the early period of his relationship with Jane, including their marriage, writing hard and fast and seemingly less inclined to stray. However, some commentators suspect that Wells's 'amorous deviations from Jane' started before 1900.[79] For example, when living at Woking, Wells admitted hoping to encounter women while cycling around the Surrey countryside and lusting after Nell de Boer, the 'vividly pretty blue-eyed' wife of his former school friend and cycling companion Sidney Bowkett.[80] Indeed, in *Man of Parts*, David Lodge depicts their relationship as Wells's first act of adultery since marrying Jane in 1895.[81] Wells also coveted Dorothy Richardson, a regular visitor to his Worcester Park home, but reportedly their affair only commenced during the 1900s.

Nor did Wells's sex drive dim radically in later life. During the mid-1930s, when working with the filmmaker Alexander Korda on *The Shape of Things to Come* (1936), Wells pointed to the difficulty of writing unless having sex at least twice a day.[82] For Wells, sex was as good, if not better, than any other way of avoiding writers' block. When looking back on his own relationships with women, Charlie Chaplin quoted Wells, a long-time friend who often stayed with him when visiting the USA, as an authority on the subject: 'As H. G. Wells said: "There comes a moment in the day when you have written your pages in the morning, attended to your correspondence in the afternoon, and have nothing further to do. Then comes that hour when you are bored; that's the time for sex".[83] Or rather, as one reviewer commented, Wells was 'as randy as a goat, and … decided to enjoy whatever and whoever came his way', particularly upon the part of women attracted by his wealth and celebrity status, or viewing him as someone to help their writing ambitions.[84] For David Langford, Wells had 'an ego

77. Jonathan Calder, 'The story of Clegg's aunt', *New Statesman*, 19 November 2007, http://www.newstatesman.com/politics/2007/11/moura-budberg-british-gorky [accessed 30 August 2012]; Deborah McDonald and Jeremy Dronfield, *A Very Dangerous Woman: The Lives, Loves and Lies of Russia's Most Seductive Spy* (London: Oneworld, 2015).

78. Wells, *Wells in Love*, p. 61.

79. Michael Sherborne, 'Book Review', *The Wellsian* 30 (2007): 58.

80. Wells, *Wells in Love*, pp. 59, 61; Wells, *Experiment in Autobiography*, I, pp. 105–7.

81. Lodge, *A Man of Parts*, pp. 110–11, 237–8.

82. Quoted David Thomson, 'Film Studies: Science vs imagination: the cinematic vision of H. G. Wells', *The Independent*, 8 May 2005.

83. Charles Chaplin, *My Autobiography* (London: Penguin, 2003), p. 354.

84. Robert Douglas-Fairhurst, 'Scratching an endless itch', *Daily Telegraph*, 8 May 2010.

the size of a planet and a sexual appetite to match'.[85] According to Andrea Lynn, Wells's consciousness of his working-class background encouraged him to pursue 'trophy women' decades younger than he, in a desperate attempt to gentrify himself and attain spiritual fulfilment.[86] For John Miller, 'Wells treated the women in his life shabbily. He cheated on his wives and impregnated his mistresses'.[87] Alternatively, as claimed by Brian Aldiss, Wells just 'wanted to be happy' and as a result 'he tried to make the women with whom he so regularly got himself involved happy too'.[88] Typically, when conducting his affair with von Arnim, Wells recalled walking through the countryside. During a break, they read a letter in *The Times* from Mrs Humphry Ward denouncing the moral tone of the younger generation: 'Having read it aloud, we decided we had to do something about it. So we stripped ourselves under the trees … and made love all over Mrs Humphry Ward. And when we had dressed again we lit a match and burnt her. *The Times* flared indignantly.'[89]

Despite spending much time chasing after and being pursued by women, Wells, a self-confessed 'Don Juan among the intelligentsia', advocating and actively practising a more liberated attitude towards sexual behaviour, did not normally allow his repeated romantic entanglements to interfere with his writing commitments: 'I liked my work and my success, and I did not want my reputation to be clouded or my work disordered.'[90] Significantly, in 1898, when living in Worcester Park, Wells even advised an aspiring writer about the need to be 'sure of freedom from the snare of romance & sexual attraction that may suddenly turn your dearest ambitions to empty vanities … It goes without saying you must if you start to be an author stay celibate until you succeed.'[91]

Notwithstanding his serial womanizing and philandering, Wells stayed married to Jane, whom he idolized, treated as his sheet anchor, represented as part of 'a complete and happy unison' and refused to divorce.[92] For Wells, his relationship with Jane, housewife, mother of their two children, devoted companion, secretary and business manager, was non-negotiable.[93] She remained an essential part of his life, even – to quote Anthony West – 'the balance wheel of his existence'.[94] As Wells recorded: 'She had always regarded my sexual imaginativeness as a sort of

85. Langford, 'The History of Mr Wells'.

86. Lynn, *Shadow Lovers*, pp. 217, 368.

87. John J. Miller, 'Badly wrong in the *War of the World* views', *Wall Street Journal*, 21 June 2005.

88. Brian Aldiss, '*In the Days of the Comet*: an introduction', *The Wellsian* 8 (1985): 1.

89. Wells, *H. G. Wells in Love*, p. 89.

90. Wells, *Experiment in Autobiography*, II, p. 465; Wells, *H. G. Wells in Love*, p. 58.

91. Wells to Redfern, n.d. [February 1898], Smith, *Correspondence of H. G. Wells*, I, p. 306.

92. Wells, *H. G. Wells in Love*, p. 58. On Wells's unconventional relationship with Jane, see Katie Roiphe, *Uncommon Arrangements: Seven Marriages* (New York: Dial, 2007), pp. 27–63.

93. Wells fathered at least two, some claim five, illegitimate children.

94. A. West, *H. G. Wells*, p. 21.

constitutional disease; she stood by me patiently, unobtrusively waiting for the fever to subside. Perhaps if she had not been immune to such fevers I should not have gone astray.'[95] When she fell ill with cancer, Wells rushed home and stayed with her until her death. Reportedly, he was so grief-stricken at the funeral, that the ceremony became an ordeal for his fellow-mourners. As Norman and Jeanne Mackenzie remarked, the marriage failed in the conventional sense: 'And yet, in a different sense, it had succeeded, and survived to the end'.[96]

Conclusion

Writing to Elizabeth Healey in May 1900 Wells indicated that the decision to build his own house at Sandgate represented yet another phase in his life, a new stage reflecting a willingness to settle down, contain his restlessness, accept suburban domesticity, scale down the exhausting pace of his writing and terminate his predisposition to move repeatedly from one place to another: 'Uneventful events constitute my days, I have got to the middle period of life … The first excitement of the start is quite over. We never see a press cutting, insult interviewers, avoid literary dinners … Also we are building ourselves a home. Every symptom in fact of incipient Middle Age.'[97]

Overviewing Wells's frequent changes of residence during the 1890s, Smith pointed to the manner in which his moves within Camden Town and then onto Sevenoaks, Woking, Worcester Park and Sandgate, marked the rapid changes characterizing his life and career: 'Each of these geographical moves was a step upward socially and psychologically, but all of them also had as a goal the need to make Wells's life easier as he advanced in his profession'.[98] Wells was never satisfied with what he had and where he was and hence stayed nowhere for very long and was constantly moving on, as both a person and a writer.

During the late 1890s Wells's decision to join the property-owning classes in yet another place of residence, was part of a package of actions and developments whose impact became increasingly apparent during the next decade: the assumption of a new life style as a family man with two sons born in 1901 and 1903, improved health and the removal of fears of an early demise, serial womanizing and the adoption of the role of a public intellectual. Moreover, his mindset continued to change, especially his thinking about the future.[99] But the principal change of course concerned Wells as a writer, the emergence of the 'Later Wells'. During the mid-1890s, Wells sought to escape the everyday pressures

95. Wells, *H. G. Wells in Love*, p. 82. Wells used the prologue of this book to tell Jane's story, Wells, *H. G. Wells in Love*, pp. 23–47.

96. N. and J. Mackenzie, *The Time Traveller*, p. 354.

97. Wells to Healey, 24 May 1900, Smith, *The Correspondence of H. G. Wells*, I, p. 355.

98. Smith, *Wells*, p. 30.

99. H. G. Wells, *The Future in America: A Search After Realities* (London: George Bell, 1906), pp. 9–15.

of journalism by writing what he represented as 'a succession of striking if rather unfinished books'.[100] In fact, notwithstanding their uneven quality and relative brevity, several of the resulting scientific romances, like *The Time Machine* and *The War of the Worlds*, were substantial and highly regarded literary works. Then, during the late 1890s and early 1900s Wells switched increasingly from scientific romances based on fantastical imaginings towards longer and 'more "finished"' works like *Love and Mr Lewisham* set in the present as well as onto non-fiction. Wells might have moved on – now he wanted to write novels, not science fiction – but for most readers his scientific romances remained his most lasting and popular contribution to world literature in general and science fiction in particular. Moreover, as highlighted in Part 3, they have proved most attractive for those seeking to adapt Wells's writing for alternative audio-visual media.

100. Wells to unknown American correspondent, 25 November 1897, Loing, *Wells à l'oeuvre*, p. 436.

PART III

TAKING WELLS'S *THE WAR OF THE WORLDS* TO THE WORLD IN AN EVER-EXPANDING RANGE OF MULTIMEDIA ADAPTATIONS

Chapter 10

THE WAR OF THE WORLDS' MULTIMEDIA AFTERLIFE

On 31 October 1938 Wells's *The War of the Worlds*, or more specifically Orson Welles's radio version thereof, was front page news across the USA. Reportedly, his radio play broadcast the previous evening about a fictional Martian invasion of the USA scared the nation causing mass panic and hysteria. In particular, the realistic manner in which the storyline was presented, that is through a series of news reports and bulletins, fooled many listeners into believing that what Wells had fantasized as happening throughout Surrey and London some four decades earlier, was now actually occurring across the Atlantic. Life, it seemed, was imitating art, as recognized by the *New York Times'* front page headline: 'Radio Listeners in Panic, Taking War Drama as Fact'.[1]

Inevitably, the media took the story across the USA and around the world. In turn, the programme's notoriety and media visibility ensured that Orson Welles's pioneering drama soon acquired mythical status for inspiring more public fear and controversy than any other radio broadcast. For nearly eighty years this episode, as elaborated in Chapter 12, has held a central place in popular culture and media history.[2] In 2013 numerous press articles and radio/television programmes marked the 75th anniversary of the original broadcast by way of reaffirming its enduring place, and especially its role as a high profile reference point, in media history, popular culture and the public memory within and outside the USA. Indeed, over time Orson Welles, like Wells, has had many emulators, whose radio adaptations staged in the local geography of Brazil, Chile, Ecuador and Portugal as well as in the USA once again and discussed in Chapter 13, have reinforced the global visibility of *The War of the Worlds* and extended its geographical impact.

Apart from keeping *The War of the Worlds* in the public eye and reaffirming the storyline's enduring appeal and impact, such adaptations have repeatedly

---

1. *New York Times*, 31 October 1938, p. 1.

2. Susan J. Douglas, *Listening In: Radio and the American Imagination* (Minneapolis, MN: University of Minnesota Press, 2004), p. 165; 'Press and Public divided in reaction to Mars program', 'Editorial: Well, Wells, Welles', *Broadcasting* 15 (10) (15 November 1938): 14–15, 28, 40; Marshall McLuhan, *Understanding Media: The Extensions of Man* (London: Ark, 1987), pp. 299–300.

rewritten the original text. Based loosely upon Wells's book, Orson Welles's radio play updated the timing of the Martian landings from the early 1900s to 1939 and radically reworked the invasion's geography. Despite being frequently represented as a pioneering one-off episode, the 1938 broadcast was in fact – to quote Crossley – part of a longstanding trend: 'In shifting the locale from London and its suburbs to New York City and rural New Jersey, Orson Welles was participating in a century-long series of adaptations of Wells's novel that paid homage to its mythic universality, by altering its local particularity in order to make the geographical details of the imagined invasion familiar to various audiences.'[3]

From this perspective, Orson Welles's programme proved merely another chapter, albeit an influential and highly visible chapter, in an ongoing story (Table 10.1). In fact, this trend began much earlier in the USA, that is during late 1897 soon after the American serialization of *The War of the Worlds* by *Cosmopolitan* but *before* the story's publication as a book in 1898. Thus, as detailed in Chapter 11, between December 1897 and February 1898 Wells's story was serialized in the *New York Evening Journal* and the *Boston Post*, but rewritten as taking place in geographical locations familiar to their respective readerships. Then, in 1938 came Orson Welles's broadcast with yet another switch of place, plus an innovatory change of period. Subsequently, Wells's story was 'Hollywoodized' – once again, as analysed in Chapter 14, this process involved shifting sites and dates – by George Pal and Steven Spielberg in 1953 and 2005 respectively. One significant exception to this trend, is Jeff Wayne, whose musical adaptations are studied in Chapter 15.

Today, *The War of the Worlds'* storyline, as outlined in Chapter 8, seems familiar. But this is largely because Wells's original template about an alien invasion has enthused and inspired so many other people. For example, within days of *The War of the Worlds'* publication, J. M. Barrie, the author of *Peter Pan* (1904), moved on swiftly from praising the book to confessing that he had lain awake all night exploring the story's dramatic possibilities for the theatre.[4] Displaying a realistic grasp of the difficulties of adapting the book as a stage play, Wells eventually persuaded Barrie to drop the idea. The two men celebrated by watching a cricket match. However, many others have not been so easily dissuaded, as evidenced by succeeding chapters. Repeatedly re-imagined in an ever-growing range of multimedia formats (Table 10.1), the original storyline has been taken to new audiences across the world ever since the late 1890s. More importantly, for most people such adaptations have proved increasingly their first point of contact with Wells's writings in general and *The War of the Worlds* in particular. Certainly, this was the case for several present-day Wellsian experts. For Stephen Baxter, 'George Pal's 1953 movie, re-shown on TV many times, was my own first introduction to H. G. Wells and his works.'[5] Will Self came to the story through his mother's reminiscences about the Orson Welles broadcast, while

3. Crossley, *Imagining Mars*, pp. 115–16.

4. Smith, *Wells*, pp. 67, 509 n.11.

5. Baxter, 'Wells', p. 3.

Table 10.1 Wells's *The War of the Worlds*: Reaching different audiences over time through multimedia formats

Date	Format	Title	Publication	Where set
1897	Magazine Serialization	'The War of the Worlds'	*Pearson's Magazine*, UK	Britain
1897	Magazine Serialization	'The War of the Worlds'	*Cosmopolitan*, USA	Britain
1897–8	Newspaper Serialization	'Fighters from Mars, or the War of the Worlds'	*New York Evening Journal*, USA	USA
1898	Newspaper Serialization	'Fighters from Mars: the War of the Worlds in and near Boston'	*Boston Post*, USA	USA
1898	Book	*The War of the Worlds*	William Heinemann, London; Harper, New York	Britain
1927	Magazine	*The War of the Worlds*	*Amazing Stories*	Britain
1938	Radio	'The War of the Worlds'	Orson Welles's Mercury Theater on the Air, CBS, USA	USA
1944	Radio	'La Guerra de los Mundos'	*Radio Cooperativa Vitalicia*, Santiago, Chile	Chile
1949	Radio	'La Guerra de los Mundos'	*Radio Quito*, Quito, Ecuador	Ecuador
1950	Radio	'The War of the Worlds'	BBC, London	Britain
1953	Hollywood Film	*The War of the Worlds*	Paramount Pictures George Pal	USA
1955	Comic	*The War of the Worlds*	*Classics Illustrated*, no. 124	Britain
1955	Radio	'The War of the Worlds'	Lux Radio Theater, NBC, USA	USA
1967	Radio	'The War of the Worlds'	BBC, London	Britain
1978	Music Album	*Jeff Wayne's Musical Version of The War of the Worlds*	Jeff Wayne/CBS	Britain
1983–5	Television	'V'	Warner Brothers/NBC	USA
1988–90	Television	'War of the Worlds'	Hometown Films/ Paramount	USA
2004	Graphic Novel	*The League of Extraordinary Gentlemen*, Vol. II	Alan Moore & Kevin O'Neill	Britain
2005	Hollywood Film	*War of the Worlds*	Paramount Pictures & DreamWorks Steven Spielberg	USA
2005	Graphic Novel	*The War of the Worlds*	Best-Sellers Illustrated	USA
2005–16	Music Stage Show	*Jeff Wayne's Musical Version of The War of the Worlds*	Jeff Wayne/Live Nation	Britain

Date	Format	Title	Publication	Where set
2012	Music DVD/ CD	*Jeff Wayne's Musical Version of The War of the Worlds: The New Generation*	Jeff Wayne/CBS/Sony	Britain
2012	Film	*War of the Worlds: The True Story*	Timothy Hines, Pendragon Pictures	Britain
2012	Film	*War of the Worlds: Goliath*	Tripod Entertainment	USA

Jeff Wayne's musical version provided the entry point for Simon James, one-time editor of *The Wellsian*.[6]

The War of the Worlds' *literary afterlife*

Today Wells, widely acknowledged as one of the founders of science fiction, remains a major source of inspiration for science fiction authors, particularly those writing in the alien invasion and time travel sub-genres. *The War of the Worlds* has proved central for alien invasion writers; thus, Wells's story has been imitated and copied, parodied and lampooned, given prequels and sequels and inspired alternative storylines. As Self remarked, the book was an immediate hit, 'spawning bowdlerisations and unauthorised sequels within months. Ever since, the theme of alien invasion has never been off the narrative agenda'.[7] In turn, the endless metamorphoses of Wells's original storyline, highlight its plasticity and perceived resonance to a wide range of narratives, historical periods and geographical settings, most notably the manner in which its themes prey on present-day fears and anxieties and the ease with which the story's location and time can be varied for specific target audiences.

Over time, many writers – they are too numerous to name – have offered varying twists on *The War of the Worlds*.[8] They include John W. Campbell ('Who Goes There?', *Astounding Stories*: August 1938); Robert A. Heinlein (*The Puppet Masters*: 1951); Arthur C. Clarke (*Childhood's End*: 1953); John Wyndham (*The Kraken Wakes*: 1953); Kevin Anderson (*War of the Worlds: Global Dispatches*: 1996); Robert Silverberg (*The Alien Years*: 1999); Douglas Niles (*War of the Worlds: New Millennium*: 2005); Tony Wright (*The War of the Worlds: Aftermath. Based on characters created by Herbert George Wells*: 2010); and Robert Reginald (*Invasion! Earth vs. the Aliens* [formerly *War of Two Worlds*]: 2007; *The Martians Strike Back*: 2011). Like Wells's *The War of the Worlds*, many of the resulting texts have provided the basis for a film – for example, Campbell's novella 'Who Goes

6. James, *Maps of Utopia*, p. xiv; Self, 'Death on three legs'.
7. Self, 'Death on three legs'.
8. See Baxter, 'H. G. Wells', p. 5.

There?' was filmed as 'The Thing from Another World' (1951) and 'The Thing' (1982; 2011) – or an alternative multimedia adaptation.

As indicated above, frequently authors have used book titles as well as forewords or dedications specifically to acknowledge their debt to Wells for inspiring and framing their work.[9] In some cases, Wells himself even makes an appearance in the story. For Kevin Anderson, Wells returns as a book editor. Anderson's prime objective was to place the Martian invasion, as represented in Wells's *The War of the Worlds*, in the broader international context. As a result, he commissioned individual authors to imagine how several well-known people – they include Joseph Conrad, Henry James, Pablo Picasso, Theodore Roosevelt and Jules Verne – might have viewed the interplanetary war depicted in Wells's text. Anderson contributed a chapter on Percival Lowell, the astronomer. In turn, the resulting anthology, *War of the Worlds: Global Dispatches* (1996), was represented as edited by Wells. Thus, in the foreword the fictional Wells recorded that 'My own chronicle of the Martian invasion that took place at the turn of the century is well known … In this retrospective, however, I have compiled several reports from other notables whose experiences during the Martian attacks may prove interesting and enlightening to students of mankind's first interplanetary war.'[10] Significantly, Anderson dedicated the book to not only Wells but also George Pal and Jeff Wayne, 'whose separate versions of THE WAR OF THE WORLDS have proved immensely inspirational to me, each in their own way'.[11]

Like any multi-authored work, Anderson's book proves variable in quality, but the text is of interest in adopting a broader perspective upon a story represented by Wells as a war for the control of earth, but actually written in a manner confining the interplanetary battlefield to Southern England. Anderson took the opportunity also to re-publish an amusing take upon Wells's original narrative by Howard Waldrop, who rewrote *The War of the Worlds* from the perspective of Lindley, a Texan sheriff. Unsurprisingly, Sheriff Lindley when learning about a Martian landing in Texas taking place alongside that in Britain, was shocked: 'You telling me Mars is attacking London, England, and Pachuco City, Texas?'.[12] In the event, the Martian invaders faced an uncompromising Sheriff Lindley, for attacking citizens within his area of jurisdiction: 'This just won't do'. Even worse, he exclaimed, 'they killed my horse'. Subsequently, Anderson, writing as Gabriel Mesta, explored Wells's thinking through *The Martian War: A Thrilling Eyewitness*

9. For example, see dedications in Robert Reginald's *Invasion! Earth vs. the Aliens* (Rockville, MD: Wildside Press, 2007); Kevin J. Anderson (ed.), *War of the Worlds: Global Dispatches* (New York: Bantam, 1996), p. 5; Gabriel Mesta, *The Martian War: a Thrilling Eyewitness Account of the Recent Invasion as Reported by Mr H. G. Wells* (New York: Pocket Books, 2005), Acknowledgements.

10. 'Foreword', Anderson, *War of the Worlds: Global Dispatches*, pp. 1–2.

11. Anderson, *War of the Worlds*, p. v.

12. Ibid., pp. 106, 108. This story was first published as Howard Waldrop, 'Night of the Cooters', *Omni* 9 (7) (April 1987): 84–91.

Account of the Recent Invasion as Reported by Mr H. G. Wells (2005) by using him to retell the Martian invasion.[13]

Wells made an appearance also in Christopher Priest's *The Space Machine* (1976). Conflating *The Time Machine* and *The War of the Worlds*, this book, written as a tribute to Wells, can be viewed variously as a prequel, a parallel text and a sequel in the sense that its heroes travelled to Mars during the pre-invasion phase and then returned to land in Surrey in the midst of the Martian invasion described by Wells.[14] Apart from stressing the Wellsian link through his book's title, Douglas Niles's *War of the Worlds: New Millennium* (2005) typifies the longstanding tendency of science fiction writers to update and relocate Wells's storyline.[15] Upgrading the Martian invasion with present-day nuclear weapons technology, Niles replaced Woking as the Martian landing site with an American location in rural Wisconsin. Also worthy of note are George H. Smith's *The Second War of the Worlds* (1976) in which the Martians, having been repelled from Earth, attack an alternative world, and Eric Brown's *'Ulla, Ulla'* (2002), a short story recounting the first manned Martian expedition.[16] David Cian's *Megawar* (2005) is a futuristic novel set in 2038, a world which had experienced two Martian invasions, those described in Wells's 1898 'classic work of fiction' and Orson Welles's 1938 radio programme – this broadcast is represented as covering up 'a real incident' – and now facing yet another Martian invasion, originating near Lake Michigan in the USA.[17]

Comics and graphic novels

Other popular fictional explorations constructing alternative narratives of *The War of the Worlds* include comics and graphic novels, which have often been published and/or re-published to take advantage of the interest generated by a recent film, radio or television adaptation.[18] Exploiting the story's ability to conjure up a wide range of vivid imagery in readers's minds, comics and graphic novels have proved important in taking the story to a wider audience, particularly to young readers, while offering a highly effective and engaging way of crossing linguistic boundaries and reaching those reluctant to read a book. Inevitably, they exhibit varying degrees of conformity to the original text. Whereas some comics and graphic novels have followed Wells's storyline relatively closely, others have

13. Mesta, *The Martian War*.

14. Christopher Priest, *The Space Machine* (London: VGSF, 1988), pp. 288–9.

15. Douglas Niles, *War of the Worlds: New Millennium* (New York: Tor, 2005).

16. George H. Smith, *The Second War of the Worlds* (New York: Daw, 1976); Eric Brown, 'Ulla, Ulla', in Mike Ashley (ed.), *The Mammoth Book of Science Fiction* (New York: Carroll & Graf, 2002), pp. 1–26.

17. David Cian, *Megawar* (New York: ibooks, 2005), Prologue.

18. This section glosses over the uncertain boundary between comics and graphic novels, especially as the distinction is often made on marketing grounds.

opted to re-imagine and reinvent the story, to fit different time periods and places as well as to offer prequels, sequels and so on.[19]

Perhaps the most significant adaptation for a comic occurred in 1955 when *The War of the Worlds* appeared as part of the *Classics Illustrated* comic series published in the USA. The story, set in late Victorian Britain, features London as well as Leatherhead. But neither Horsell nor Woking is mentioned; thus, the textual captions accompanying the story's images mention 'the sandpit', but not Horsell Common and the narrator's home 'near London', but not Woking.[20] The comic itself is well-illustrated, has an iconic picture of a tripod on the front cover and offers readers an engaging edited version of the original story. Like books, comics have occasionally made Wells one of the characters in the story. For example, during the late 1980s Caliber Comics published *The Searchers*, a series placing famous authors – apart from Wells, they included Jules Verne, Edgar Rice Burroughs and Conan Doyle – in adventures bringing their fictional creations to life.

In their graphic novel *The League of Extraordinary Gentlemen* (2002–3), Alan Moore and Kevin O'Neill employ classic literary characters from books written by Wells and other authors to tell epic stories set in Victorian Britain.[21] Here the disparate League of Victorian Age superheroes, take on the task of defending the nation against an alien invasion launched from Mars and dated as landing on Horsell Common in Summer 1898. Moore and O'Neill largely retold Wells's *The War of the Worlds* in its original geographical setting centred upon Surrey – Horsell Common, Maybury, Woking and Chobham are all mentioned – and London.[22] Indeed, at one point, Dr Henry Jekyll/Edward Hyde exclaimed that it seemed a 'Long way to come just to conquer Woking'.[23] Several people in the

19. For a fuller account of adaptations in comics, see John Gosling's three-part study beginning, http://www.war-ofthe-worlds.co.uk/comics_mars.htm [accessed 12 March 2015]. Examples of sequels published in comics include Marvel Comics's *Killraven* (1973), published in *Amazing Adventures*, describing a second Martian invasion of earth one hundred years after that written about by Wells, and Eternity Comics's *Sherlock Holmes in the case of the Missing Martian* (1990), a story set in 1908 in which Holmes and Watson are engaged in a race against time to discover the meaning of a bizarre theft from the British museum. The *Killraven* series is available in *Essential Killraven Vol. 1* (New York: Marvel Comics, 2005).

20. 'The War of the Worlds', *Classics Illustrated* 124 (1955): 3, 4–6, 10.

21. Alan Moore and Kevin O'Neill. The *League of Extraordinary Gentlemen*, II (La Jolla, CA: America's Best Comics, 2003). On individual graphic panels, see Jess Nevins, A *Blazing World: The Unofficial Companion to the Second League of Extraordinary Gentlemen* (Austin, TX: MonkeyBrain Books, 2004).

22. One image named the inn near Horsell Common where the League's members stayed overnight as 'The Bleak House'. Despite existing in the mid-1890s, it was not mentioned in Wells's book. The inn, located on the main Woking–Chertsey road, is now called 'Sands at The Bleak House'. Moore and O'Neill's *League of Extraordinary* Gentlemen has no page numbers, but this image is listed as p. 43, panel 4 in Nevins, *Blazing World*, p. 42.

23. According to Nevins, this is p. 48, panel 2: Nevins, *Blazing World*, p. 46.

story – they include Teddy Prendrick and Dr Moreau from *The Island of Dr Moreau* and Hawley Griffin from *The Invisible Man* – are based on characters from Wells's other books. In addition, Ian Edginton and D'Israeli published two graphic novels set in Britain after the Martian invasion covered in Wells's *The War of the Worlds*. *Scarlet Traces*, published in 2003, was followed by *Scarlet Traces: The Great Game*, a sequel taking the story on another thirty years, when a resurgent Britain launched a counter-invasion against Mars.[24]

Frequently, stories published in comics and graphic novels have linked up with *The War of the Worlds* by referencing Orson Welles's radio broadcast, a trend reflecting the programme's prominent place in popular culture, its enduring impact upon people's mindsets since the late 1930s and the fact that most comics originate in the USA.[25] Indeed, the first such reference was in the initial issue of the *Batman* comic in April 1940, when one listener dismissed a radio announcement as a hoax, like 'that fellow who scared everybody with that story about Mars the last time'.[26] One decade later, Orson Welles himself figured in the *Superman* comic when helping Superman avert a Martian invasion.[27] Yet another comic superhero, Spider Man, has also featured battling Martian tripods.[28]

The War of the Worlds' *active multimedia afterlife*

Table 10.1 highlights the fact that Wells's *The War of the Worlds* has possessed not only an active literary afterlife, but also an even more active multimedia afterlife, especially with regards to the film, music, newspaper, radio and television adaptations studied in Chapters 11–15. Nor does Table 10.1 comprise a complete list of linked outputs. For example, during September 1931 weekly *War of the Worlds'* fireworks displays based upon 'incidents' from the story, were held at London's Crystal Palace with Wells's approval.[29] The display's headline item showed London under the Martian attack, with the whole scene turning red 'in representation of the poisonous aftermath'.

24. Ian Edginton and D'Israeli, *Scarlet Traces* (Milwaukie, OR: Dark Horse Comics, 2003); Ian Edginton and D'Israeli, *Scarlet Traces: The Great Game* (Milwaukie, OR: Dark Horse Books, 2007).

25. Examples include *Secret Origins: The Crimson Avenger*, issue 5, DC Comics, August 1986; *The Shadow Strikes: "To Cloud Men's Minds"*, issue 7, DC Comics, 1990.

26. *Batman* 1 (April 1940), *The Batman Chronicles, 1* (New York: DC Comics, 2005), p. 141.

27. *Superman* 62 (January/February 1950), in *Superman from the Thirties to the Seventies* (New York: Bonanza Books, 1971), pp. 210–21; *Superman: War of the Worlds*, DC Comics, October 1998.

28. *Adventures in Reading: The Amazing Spiderman*, Issue 1, Marvel Comics, June 1990.

29. Sir Henry Buckland to Wells, 4 May 1931, Wells, n.d., B570 (UIUC); 'Entertainment' Advertisements, *The Times*, 9, 16, 23 September 1931.

The story's subject matter, most notably its massive potential for vivid imagery, has made *The War of the Worlds*, including recent audio-visual adaptations thereof, an increasingly attractive focus also for exploitation as the basis for bubblegum and cigarette cards, computer games, mobile phone apps and e-books.[30] Enabling users to explore alternative scenarios, such developments have brought a whole new dimension to retelling and rewriting the original story, introducing new audiences to both Wells and *The War of the Worlds* storyline and tapping into contemporary popular culture.

For example, in October 2010 Smashing Ideas, a digital media agency targeting the youth market with 'immersive and interactive entertainment', announced the release of *The War of the Worlds* as an enhanced e-Book for iPads costing $3.99:

> *The War of the Worlds for iPad* by Smashing Ideas is a stunning rendering of a novel that has been in continuous publication for more than one hundred years. We are excited to unveil this classic Sci-Fi tale as our first original eBook. Adding modern, digital elements like real-time physics accompanied by our own illustrations really enhances the reading experience.[31]

Claiming to provide 'a unique, engaging experience', the e-Book takes readers back to early twentieth century London under siege, while allowing them to follow the narrator through the story.[32] Features advertised include:

- '27 interactive, visually stunning pages integrated with text from the original 1898 publication';
- the ability to touch-swipe the Martian cylinders towards Earth to begin the invasion, target the tripod's heat-ray and throw canisters emitting thick deadly Black Smoke;
- and interactive elements allowing readers to act as either a Martian or a human.

In October 2011 Paramount, the company responsible for both the 1953 and 2005 Hollywood film adaptations, released *The War of the Worlds* for Microsoft's

30. John L. Flynn, *War of the Worlds from Wells to Spielberg* (Owings Mills, MD: Galactic, 2005), pp. 163–8. Reportedly, the set of bubblegum cards entitled *Mars Attacks!* inspired Tim Burton's 1996 film of the same name: Flynn, *War of the Worlds*, p. 167. Note the cards issued by Cult-Stuff (2013): http://cult-stuff.com/?p=42492 [accessed 26 May 2014].

31. The Business Journals: Press Release, 'The War of the Worlds App now available for the iPad', 5 October 2010, http://www.bizjournals.com/prnewswire/press_releases/2010/10/05/SF76500 [accessed 4 June 2012]. See https://itunes.apple.com/gb/album/war-worlds-30th-anniversary/id318725185 [accessed 4 June 2012].

32. 'The War of the Worlds for iPad', http://itunes.apple.com/us/app/the-war-of-the-worlds-for-ipad/id394767503?mt=8 [accessed 4 June 2012].

Xbox.[33] Narrated by Patrick Stewart, who had starred in *Star Trek: The Next Generation* and set in Britain, the game follows the exploits of an unknown everyman struggling to escape the Martian attack on London and rescue his family in the face of the Martian invaders. Several computer games, including versions for the *iPhone* and the *iPad*, have been specifically developed around Jeff Wayne's musical adaptation, as outlined in Chapter 15.[34]

Transforming the story's chronology and geography

Preceding sections establish that one consequence of the continuing migration of *The War of the Worlds* from Wells's original printed text to alternative multimedia formats, has been the frequent sweeping aside of the chronological and geographical frameworks constructed by Wells's imagination. Thus, the original locations in London and Surrey, have often been discarded in the interests of ensuring local realism and relevance for the intended audience, with those living in the USA often proving their prime target. An associated trend has been that of modernization, most notably in terms of updating the time period and weapons technology to the present-day. In some cases, key elements in the original story have often been changed, as happened with Spielberg's 2005 film, in which even the Martians dropped out of the story to be replaced by anonymous aliens.

Generally speaking, commercial imperatives arising from box office returns, newspaper circulations, radio listening/TV viewing figures and so on have invariably overridden literary sensitivities. Targeting principally American audiences, Hollywood tells American-centred stories. No author, not even one of Wells's global stature, proves safe from creative movie rewrites bearing little or no resemblance to the original text, particularly given Hollywood's traditional indifference to the sensibilities of other nations and cultures.[35] Unsurprisingly, Hollywood versions of *The War of the Worlds* (1953; 2005), like its steady output of alien invasion films such as *Independence Day* (1996), *Mars Attacks* (1996) and *Deep Impact* (1998), have treated the USA as the primary invasion target. For most adapters, the USA is where the interplanetary action is today. One prominent exception to this Americanizing trend is Jeff Wayne. Despite his New York roots, he remained true to Wells's original geography and time period for his best-selling music album and spectacular stage show.

Notwithstanding Jeff Wayne's efforts, most audiences, whether cinemagoers, radio listeners, readers, or television viewers, have not always appreciated that the original story of *The War of the Worlds* is centred upon London and Surrey and set

33. 'The War of the Worlds Game', 2011 http://www.paramount.com/games/the-war-of-the-worlds/details [accessed 4 June 2012].

34. 'The War of The Worlds: Adventure' https://itunes.apple.com/gb/app/war-worlds-adventure/id508815392?mt=8 [accessed 4 June 2012].

35. Peter J. Beck, *Presenting History: Past and Present* (Basingstoke: Palgrave Macmillan, 2012), pp. 195–6.

during the early twentieth century.[36] Naturally places like Woking, Weybridge and even Kingston upon Thames, though recognizable to many Britons, would mean little to either their American counterparts or most overseas audiences. Even Britons would struggle with Byfleet, Horsell Common, Ottershaw and Pyrford, central places in the story's initial stages. For George Pal, Steven Spielberg and Orson Welles, among others, present-day American locations situated in, say, California, New Jersey and New York State were adjudged essential, if their target audience was to be accessed and engaged by the story, most notably through a sense of living through fast-moving events taking place in familiar geographical settings. In turn, the fact that alien invasions set within the Wellsian framework have been focused principally upon the USA, has allowed it to keep notching up victories over Martian and other alien invaders. Indeed, the repeated threat posed to the USA by such interplanetary invasions, led one reviewer of Spielberg's *War of the Worlds* film to represent the Martian attack upon Woking narrated in Wells's book as 'a ghastly map-reading error for which many tentacles presumably rolled'.[37]

Conclusion

Over one century on from the story's original publication during the late 1890s, *The War of the Worlds*' literary afterlife shows no signs of losing momentum. The book remains in print, most notably as a Penguin Classic, is easily accessible for downloading on the internet, is the focus for numerous websites, and has been widely translated.[38] Nor has the passage of time diminished the storyline's ability to inspire an extensive range of audio, graphical, musical, visual and other spin-offs imparting further dimensions to the story's afterlife. Indeed, the expiry of copyright at the end of 2016 on Wells's publications seems likely to ensure that this trend will continue – for example, 2017 will see a sequel to *The War of the Worlds* penned by Stephen Baxter – but most probably at an ever faster pace. Moreover, some adaptations, most notably Orson Welles's radio broadcast, have acquired both a life of their own and a distinctive place in popular culture.

36. In 1944 an article in the US-based *Newsweek* about a Chilean radio programme based on *The War of the Worlds* claimed incorrectly that Orson Welles' 1938 broadcast 'changed the locale of the story from Wales to Princeton': 'Those Men from Mars', *Newsweek*, 27 November 1944, p. 89.

37. James Christopher, 'Mars attacks – and it's a blast', *The Times*, 30 June 2005. Despite Christopher's title, the invaders in the film were unidentified aliens.

38. Selective examples of internet coverage include John Gosling's, http://www.war-ofthe-worlds.co.uk/; http://www.war-of-the-worlds.org/; http://drzeus.best.vwh.net/wotw/ (*The War of the Worlds* book covers); http://www.sfsite.com/; http://www.isfdb.org/cgi-bin/ea.cgi?65; and http://www.fantasticfiction.co.uk/w/h-g-wells/war-of-worlds.htm

Turning a fictional story into a film, a stage play, a live music show or a drama for radio or television is never easy. Each format makes its own distinctive demands and will impact upon the original in varying, often extensive, ways. As Hilary Mantel pointed out when discussing the transformation of *Wolf Hall*, her best-selling Man Booker prizewinning historical novel, into a play for the Royal Shakespeare Company, 'The old structure has got to be taken down and the new one put in its place'.[39] Creative decisions will be taken to heighten the dramatic effect, so that some characters, events and places may be lost or altered. The chronology might also be changed, particularly updated to reflect present-day mindsets. New possibilities, unrealized in the original book, might be introduced to take advantage of opportunities offered by audio-visual formats, including the latest digital technology.

As a result, what emerges frequently, is not so much an adaptation of the original story as a new version of the material reflecting not only the nature of the alternative format but also the fact that rewrites, like the original story, prove a function of present-day attitudes, anxieties and ideological preoccupations. Over time, therefore, *The War of the Worlds* has often been used in adaptations by successive generations to reflect contemporary preoccupations: the media wars and Spanish–American tensions of the late 1890s, in the case of the American press versions of 1897–8; the breakdown of international order during the late 1930s for Orson Welles's radio broadcast; the Cold War and 'red scare' of the early 1950s, when the first Hollywood film adaptation was made; and 9/11 terrorism for Spielberg's 2005 film. Much may be lost, but much might also be gained, particularly in terms of engaging audiences.

For authors, the kudos and money resulting from the adaptation of their books has to be balanced against a natural tendency to be protective of their original text. Subsequent chapters show that Wells, though welcoming the way in which adaptations of his scientific romances yielded an additional revenue stream, attracted new audiences and enhanced his visibility as a writer, was often angered by the failure of adapters to adhere to their contracts and their tendency to play fast and loose with his original chronology and/or geography. Generally speaking, Wells adopted an uncompromising attitude regarding their infractions, even if in practice his bark often proved worse than his bite. Moreover, the period since his death in 1946, has seen an ever-growing number of adaptations of *The War of the Worlds* covering an extending range of formats. Obviously, the copyright and other implications of this process have been followed closely by the administrators of Wells's estate – this point was highlighted by the 2002 court case discussed in Chapter 14 – but undoubtedly Wells would be pleased about the way in which such adaptations have kept his name to the fore across the world. For example, Spielberg's film, released in 2005, prompted not only new print editions of the book (Table 1.1) but also several radio and television programmes focused on Wells in general and *The War of the Worlds* in particular. Acknowledging the fact that Wells was 'currently enjoying a revival in popularity thanks to the

39. Tanya Gold, 'Hilary Mantel', *Sunday Times Magazine*, 8 December 2013, p. 37.

new *War of the Worlds* movie', BBC Radio Four's 'H. G. Wells and Me' brought together Jonathan Ross, Roy Hattersley and Patrick Moore to discuss his role as the godfather of science fiction.[40]

Meanwhile, the repeated adaptation of Wells's storyline has allowed successive generations across all age groups and countries, the opportunity to access a classic science fiction story and in particular, to discover that once upon a time Britain, not the USA, was the Martians's primary target.[41] Ever since *The War of the Worlds* first appeared in print in 1897, presenters working in the audio, literary and visual media have found it relatively easy to amend the story's place names and time period to suit their specific agendas. Wells's alien invasion formula, was both easily replicated and readily transferable to a different time period and locality. Such fundamental alterations were facilitated also by the story's somewhat loose narrative structure arising from the central role performed by the narrator.[42] When filming the first Hollywood film version of Wells's book, George Pal was well aware of the adapter's fundamental problem: 'Whenever a Hollywood producer brings out a new motion picture in which he has tampered with the plot of a well-known novel or play, he's inviting criticism. We took that risk when we made the H. G. Wells classic, "War of The Worlds".'[43] Confidence in the resulting film led Pal, who later filmed *The Time Machine* (1960), to believe that Wells would approve of the way in which he had used his 'imagination and ingenuity' in his adaptation: 'I'll wager that if I could climb into the Time Machine which Wells wrote about in another story and flash back fifty-six years for a conference with the gentleman, he'd have approved the changes.'[44] Of course, the original author was not the only person for adapters to keep in mind. Wellsian enthusiasts familiar with the book, are not always easy to win over. Thus, Spielberg's film prompted one elderly British enthusiast of Wells's scientific romances to critique the trend to rewrite his stories:

I remain such a fan of Wells that I get angry when people waffle on about the American film versions of his great books and how good they are! How on earth can you transplant the coming of the killer tripods from Woking to some place in the United States and still expect the same sense of disaster that struck sedate Victorian England in The War of the Worlds.[45]

However, this chapter, like those that follow, suggests that such adaptations are part of a seemingly unstoppable trend. The ever-widening range of Wellsian

40. BBC Radio Four, 'H. G. Wells and Me', 20 March 2005.

41. John Lanchester, 'Making War on Woking: H. G. Wells Memorial', *Daily Telegraph*, 30 January 1999, p. A5.

42. Hughes, 'The War of the Worlds', p. 285.

43. George Pal, 'Filming "War of the Worlds"', *Astounding Science Fiction* LII (2) (October 1953), p. 100.

44. Pal, 'Filming "War of the Worlds"', p. 102.

45. The Mass Observation Project, Summer 2005 Directive: Part 1: the Universe and Outer Space, SxMOA2/1/75/1, B1654, aged 74, n.d. [2005], p. 1 (Sussex).

spin-offs might irritate many fans, but they prove a tribute to the quality and timeliness of Wells's scientific romances in general and *The War of the Worlds* in particular. In turn, the resulting films, music shows and radio plays have made the book a cultural landmark in its own right and reaffirmed its status as a seminal science fiction text. As Stephen Leslie remarked at the time of the release of Spielberg's 2005 film, none of these futuristic presentations could exist 'without a dead Englishman', H. G. Wells, whose inspirational role was acknowledged on posters and adverts used to promote the film.[46]

46. Stephen Leslie, 'What have the Brits done for sci-fi?', *The Times*, 21 April 2005.

Chapter 11

WELLS'S MARTIANS INVADE BOSTON AND NEW YORK: SERIALIZING *THE WAR OF THE WORLDS* IN AMERICAN NEWSPAPERS, 1897-8

Despite the prominent role accorded to his 1938 radio programme in the literature about *The War of the Worlds'* afterlife, Orson Welles was not the first to rewrite – or, in Wells's eyes, to be guilty of the unauthorized rewriting of – the original story. Indeed, the practice dates back to late 1897 and early 1898 when Americanized versions of the story appeared in newspapers in Boston and New York soon after its serialization in Britain and the USA, *but before* the story appeared as a book (Table 11.1). Having first crossed the Atlantic as a serial for *Cosmopolitan* in April 1897, *The War of the Worlds* made three more landfalls in the USA during the next twelve months, firstly as serials in *The New York Evening Journal* and then *The Boston Post/Boston Sunday Post* and finally as a book published by Harpers in New York.

This episode offered an early indication of *The War of the Worlds'* potential for adaptations, particularly those set in alternative geographical locations known to the target audience, alongside the way in which such rewrites possessed an overt present-day resonance reflecting contemporary national contexts. Thus, serialized versions published in the *Boston Post* and the *New York Evening Journal* used American locations, especially iconic heritage sites, to provide realism and local colour in order to engage readers and boost sales at a time of newspaper

Table 11.1 *The War of the Worlds* in the USA, 1897-8

Date	Format	Title of Publication
1897 April–December	Serial	*The Cosmopolitan:An Illustrated Monthly Magazine*: Irvington-on-the-Hudson, USA
1897-8 15 December 1897– 7 January 1898	Serial	*New York Evening Journal*
1898 9 Jan–3 February	Serial	*Boston Sunday Post and Boston Post*
1898 March	Book	Harper, New York

circulation wars, as well as strong public interest in scaremongering literature, the possibility of war with Spain and all things linked to Mars.

Selling the serialization rights

In 1896 Wells, acting through his literary agents, sold the serial rights for *The War of the Worlds* for simultaneous publication in 1897 by *Pearson's Magazine* in Britain and *The Cosmopolitan: A Monthly Illustrated Magazine* in the USA (Table 7.1). In turn, the positive reception accorded to *Cosmopolitan's* serialization in the USA fostered the belief that Wells's story would work also for American newspapers anxious to boost their circulations in the ongoing battle for readers.[1] For Hughes, the *New York Journal's* interest in Wells's story reflected in part a belief in the commercial prudence of following the lead of John Brisben Walker, the *Cosmopolitan's* editor: 'As editor of *Cosmopolitan*, he had achieved a spectacular success because, as one admirer put it, "he has introduced the newspaper ideas of timeliness and dignified sensationalism into periodical literature." If Walker liked the story for his audience, it was probably a good choice for the similar, if much less literate, audience of the sensational newspapers.'[2] As Wells commented after meeting Brisben Walker when visiting the USA in 1906, magazines and newspapers tended to complement each other in terms of their target markets; thus, whereas *Cosmopolitan's* readership was nationwide, American newspapers served a more localized audience.[3] Moreover, Wells's story, though focused upon an interplanetary conflict, was viewed as highly relevant at a time of growing talk of war between the USA and Spain over Cuba. Wars were always good for the sales of newspapers: 'While war with Spain was only a splendid possibility, here was a war indeed'.[4]

As a result, in November 1897 William Randolph Hearst's *New York Journal* sought permission to serialize the story in its evening edition. Anxious to reinforce his growing reputation across the Atlantic, Wells readily agreed. Like any writer, especially any up-and-coming author, he was anxious to do well in the USA's lucrative book market and particularly to build upon the good reviews and reasonable sales of his previous books therein and the occasional publication of his short stories in such newspapers as *The New York Times*.[5] However, Wells stipulated that no textual alterations should be made without his consent and that

1. W. Joseph Campbell, *The Year that Defined American Journalism: 1897 and the Clash of Paradigms* (New York: Routledge, 2006), pp. 50–1; Ben H. Procter, *William Randolph Hearst: The Early Years, 1863–1910* (New York: Oxford University Press, 1998), pp. 95–134.

2. Hughes, 'The War of the Worlds', p. 282. Re. the 'admirer', see Frank Luther Mott, *A History of American Magazines, 1885–1905* (Cambridge, MA: Harvard University Press, 1957), p. 482.

3. H. G. Wells, *The Future in America*, pp. 287–8.

4. Hughes, 'The War of the Worlds', p. 283.

5. H. G. Wells, 'The Rajah's Treasure', *The New York Times*, 6–8 July 1896; H. G. Wells,

serialization must be approved by the American publisher of the forthcoming book version.[6] Significantly, Wells instructed his typist to send the *New York Journal* the extra text, most notably the artilleryman episode, added in response to Heinemann's demands for more words.[7] Thus, these significant additions to the text already published in *Pearson's Magazine* and *Cosmopolitan* were sent to the USA and first appeared in a New York newspaper. Subsequently, on 26 December 1897, that is just eleven days after the *New York Journal* began serializing the story, the *Boston Post* successfully requested approval for the reproduction of the serial, 'as New York Journal'.[8]

In the event, the whole episode prompted considerable irritation upon the part of Wells, given the failure of both American newspapers to adhere to the agreed terms. Admittedly, their respective versions conformed to his story's basic narrative framework: a peaceful setting, a Martian invasion, the Martians' aggressive advance upon a large metropolis, mass destruction and panic and the eventual defeat of the invaders by natural bacteria. Nor was there any change of chronology, since both newspapers stated that the invasion occurred early in the twentieth century.[9] But neither newspaper sought Wells's approval for their plans to rework the geographical details to locations more familiar to their respective readerships, let alone to add and delete substantial amounts of text as well as to include numerous illustrations.

Americanizing The War of the Worlds

Inevitably, the promotional advertising conducted by both newspapers prior to serialization was subject to the usual exaggerated language characteristic of the press, but did offer recognition of the pioneering and unique nature of Wells's story. For the *New York Evening Journal*, *The War of the Worlds*' serial was trailed variously as the 'greatest story of modern times' and based upon 'the most interesting novel of modern times'.[10] For the *Boston Post*, this 'Startling,

'In the Abyss', *The New York Times*, 7–10 August 1896. Both introduced Wells as the author of *The Time Machine*.

6. Wells to the Editor, *Critic*, 21 January 1898, in Hughes, 'The War of the Worlds', pp. 281–2; Hughes, *Edition and a Survey*, p. 2.

7. Hughes and Geduld, *Critical Edition*, p. 6.

8. Wells to the Editor, *Critic*, 21 January 1898, in Hughes, 'The War of the Worlds', p. 282.

9. H. G. Wells, 'Fighters from Mars or The War of the Worlds', *New York Evening Journal*, 15 December 1897, p. 11; H. C. (*sic*) Wells, 'Fighters From Mars: The War of the Worlds in and near Boston', *Boston Sunday Post*, 9 January 1898, p. 15.

10. 'War of the World's (*sic*)', *New York Evening Journal*, 13 December 1897; 'Fighters from Mars' advert, *Boston Post*, 3 January 1898, p. 8; Steven Mollmann, 'The War of the Worlds in the Boston Post and the rise of American imperialism: "Let Mars Fire"', *English Literature in Transition, 1880–1920* 53 (4) (2010): 395. As noted by Hughes and Mollmann, few libraries carry the relevant issues of the *New York Evening Journal*: Hughes, *Edition*

Thrilling, Extraordinary' tale was represented as 'Absolutely unlike any story ever before written'.[11] Obviously, such positive descriptors would have been welcomed by Wells.

Whereas New Yorkers read about Martians landing near Irvington-on-the-Hudson, a small riverside town of c. 2,300 people located between Tarrytown and Dobbs Ferry some twenty miles north of Manhattan and then attacking New York . City, Bostonians followed the Martian advance from Concord, Massachusetts, through Lexington and onto Boston. Instead of being set in and around London and Surrey, the action centred on the USA, with every British location being replaced by a suitable American variant. Surrey was pushed aside by Massachusetts, New Jersey and New York State. Horsell Common and Woking were replaced by Irvington-on-the-Hudson and Concord. Wells's narrator, 'The man from Woking', became 'The man from Irvington' or 'The man from Concord'.[12] New York City and Boston, not London, proved the Martians' principal targets. There was no indication that the story had ever been set anywhere else, let alone in Britain.

The *Boston Post*'s selection of Concord, though encouraged by its proximity to Boston, undoubtedly reflected its central role in the 1776–83 American War of Independence against the British, given the serialization's occasional textual references to this earlier struggle. For American readers, the story's impact was enhanced by representing the Martians as following the same route from Concord to Lexington as that taken by British troops in 1776. By contrast, Irvington-on-the-Hudson, though a convenient base for launching an attack upon New York, lacked the historical gravitas of Concord and Lexington, since it had performed only a marginal role in the conflict against the British.[13] Perhaps the *New York Evening Journal*'s choice resulted principally from the fact that a recently constructed neoclassical building in Irvington-on-the-Hudson, had just become the new headquarters of *Cosmopolitan*, the magazine originally serializing *The War of the Worlds* in the USA, following its move from New York City.

Table 11.2 highlights the manner in which the initial part of Wells's story, as serialized originally by *Pearson's Magazine* and *Cosmopolitan*, was rewritten and re-located geographically for readers of the *New York Evening Journal* and the *Boston Post/Boston Sunday Post*.

and a Survey, pp. 3, 44 n.2, 45 n.4, 46 n.10; Mollmann, 'The War of the Worlds', pp. 388–9; Steven Mollmann, 'Fighters from Mars, or The War of the Worlds in and near Boston 21', April 2009, http://steve-mollmann.livejournal.com/124003.html [accessed 6 February 2012]. Several libraries, like the New York Public Library, listed as holding these issues, do not actually hold the relevant copies. The Newspaper Library of the Library of Congress, though experiencing difficulty tracking down the issues, seems to be a rare source. The *Boston Post* serial is held by Boston Public Library.

11. 'Fighters from Mars' advert, *Boston Post*, 3 January 1898, p. 8.

12. Wells, 'Fighters from Mars', *New York Evening Journal*, 5 January 1898, p. 6; Wells, 'Fighters from Mars', *Boston Sunday Post*, 29 January 1898, p. 5.

13. Barbara Dodsworth, *The Foundation of Historic Irvington* (Irvington-on-the-Hudson, NY: The Foundation for Economic Education, 1995), pp. 11–12.

Table 11.2 Americanizing Wells's *The War of the Worlds*

Pearson's Magazine, Vol. 3 (16) (April 1897): 365–70 *Cosmopolitan*, Vol. 22 (6) (April 1897): 617–22	*New York Evening Journal*, 15 December 1897, p. 11	*Boston Sunday Post*, 9 January 1898, p. 15
I might not have heard of the eruption at all had I not met Ogilvy, the well-known astronomer of Ottershaw.	I might not have heard of the eruption at all had I not met Ogilvy, the well-known amateur astronomer of Irvington-on-the-Hudson.	I might not have heard of the eruption at all had I not met Ogilvy, the well-known amateur astronomer of Concord, Mass.
Then came the night of the first falling star. It was seen early in the morning rushing over Winchester eastward, a line of flame, high in the atmosphere.	Then came the night of the first falling star. It was seen early in the morning, rushing over northern New Jersey eastward, a line of flame, high in the atmosphere.	Then came the night of the first falling star. It was seen early in the morning, rushing over northern New Jersey eastward, a line of flame, high in the atmosphere.
Many people in Berkshire, Surrey, and Middlesex must have seen the fall of it, and, at most, have thought that another meteorite had descended.	Many persons in the towns and villages along the Hudson must have seen it fall and have thought that another meteorite had descended.	Many persons in the towns and villages of Middlesex county [New Jersey] must have seen the fall and have thought that another meteorite had descended.
Ogilvy, who had seen the shooting star, and who was persuaded that a meteorite lay somewhere on the common between Horsell, Ottershaw, and Woking, rose early with the idea of finding it. Find it he did soon after dawn and not far from the sand-pits. An enormous hole had been made by the impact of the projectile.	Ogilvy – who had seen the shooting star and who was persuaded that a meteorite lay somewhere in the fields north of Irvington – rose early with the idea of finding it. Find it he did soon after dawn, and not far from the sand pits. An enormous hole had been made by the impact of the projectile.	Ogilvy – who had seen the shooting star and who was persuaded that a meteorite lay somewhere in the fields above the Lexington road – rose early with the idea of finding it. Find it he did soon after dawn, and not far from the Lexington line. An enormous hole had been made by the impact of the projectile.
Something within the cylinder was unscrewing the top! ... Ogilvy ... set off running wildly into Woking ... He met a waggoner and tried to make him understand, but the tale he told and his appearance were so wild – his hat had fallen off in the pit – that the man simply drove on. He was equally unsuccessful with the potman who was just unlocking the doors of the public house by Horsell Bridge.	Something in the cylinder was unscrewing the top! ... Ogilvy ... set off, running wildly toward Irvington ... He met a wagon driver and tried to make him understand, but the tale he told and his appearance was so wild – his hat had fallen off in the pit – that the man simply drove on. He was equally unsuccessful with the porter who was just unlocking the doors of the road house by the bridge.	Something in the cylinder was unscrewing the top! ... Ogilvy ... set off, running wildly toward Concord ... He met a wagon driver and tried to make him understand, but the tale he told and his appearance were so wild – his hat had fallen off in the pit – that the man simply drove on. He was equally unsuccessful with the porter who was just unlocking the doors of the road house.

Pearson's Magazine, Vol. 3 (16) (April 1897): 365–70 Cosmopolitan, Vol. 22 (6) (April 1897): 617–22	New York Evening Journal, 15 December 1897, p. 11	Boston Sunday Post, 9 January 1898, p. 15
He saw Henderson, the London journalist, in his garden … "Henderson," he called, "you saw that shooting star last night?" "Well?" said Henderson. "It's out on Horsell Common now."	He saw Henderson, the journalist, in his garden … "Henderson," he called, "you saw that shooting star last night?" "Well?" said Henderson. "It's out on the sand pits now."	He saw Henderson, the journalist … "Henderson," he called, "you saw that shooting star last night?" "Well?" said Henderson. "It's out on the sand pits now."
The early editions of the evening papers had startled London with enormous headlines: "A MESSAGE RECEIVED FROM MARS," "Remarkable story from Woking," and so forth.	The early editions of the evening papers had startled New York with enormous headlines: "A Message Received From Mars."	The early editions of the evening papers had startled Boston with enormous headlines: "A Message Received From Mars."
The above extracts appeared with minor changes in the book published by Heinemann in January 1898, pp. 6–21 (Penguin 2005 edition, pp. 13–18).		

Nor did either newspaper warn Wells about their intention to undertake substantial textual amendments and additions. Indeed, not even Wells's title was safe. Thus, the *New York Evening Journal* downgraded his choice to a sub-title when introducing a revised main title presumably adjudged to mean more to its readers by exploiting the Mars boom: 'Fighters from Mars, or The War of the Worlds'. Likewise, on 9 January 1898 readers of the *Boston Sunday Post* opened their newspapers to find the initial instalment of Wells's story re-titled 'Fighters From Mars: The War of the Worlds in and near Boston'.

More seriously from Wells's point of view, chapters, such as Chapters 3 and 4 in Book 1, were often merged. The original text was frequently truncated and extended seemingly to ensure a stronger focus upon death and destruction.[14] Significantly, advance advertisements for the serials emphasized this very point, such as by pointing to the advanced nature, power and destructiveness of the Martians' machinery of war; thus, the *Boston Post* advertised the forthcoming serial with an illustration depicting a fighting machine destroying Boston's

14. According to Hughes, the *Boston Post* was responsible for most additions, whereas deletions were largely the work of the *New York Evening Journal*: Hughes, 'The War of the Worlds', p. 283.

Destruction of the Boston City Hall, by the Strange Visitors From Mars,

Figure 11.1 Advertisement for the *Boston Post*'s 'Fighters from Mars', January 1898. The Martians are shown destroying Boston's City Hall in an illustration used to advertise the *Boston Post*'s forthcoming serialisation of *The War of the Worlds*.

Source: Advert for 'Fighters from Mars: The War of the Worlds in and near Boston', *Boston Post*, 3 Jan.1898, p.8.

City Hall (Figure 11.1).[15] Possessing a very different agenda to Wells, the two newspapers published versions of the story which had – to quote Hughes – 'the effect of diminishing the artistic (novelistic) side of the work in favor of a sort of directory of terrors'.[16] For Hughes, the Martians attacking Boston displayed 'indiscriminate, unimaginative bloodthirstiness'.[17] In brief, the newspaper serializations, emphasizing the narrator's 'more bloodcurdling adventures', told a fantastic fast-moving adventure story set in the USA, full of local colour and advanced military technology, but short on 'the "padding" of commonplace observation, speculation and dialogue'.[18] Thus, the *Boston Post* used the narrator's encounter with the artilleryman (II.7) principally to offer readers a mass of 'hackneyed detail' regarding

15. 'Fighters From Mars' advert, *Boston Post*, 3 January 1898, p. 8.
16. Hughes, 'The War of the Worlds', p. 285.
17. Hughes, *Edition and a Survey*, p. 3.
18. Hughes, 'The War of the Worlds', p. 285.

the destruction of Boston, Concord and Lexington, rather than to follow Wells in debating broader issues.[19]

As a result, both newspapers' narratives about the actual Martian invasion proved far longer, more detailed and bloodier than the comparable accounts in Wells's original text. For example, on Christmas Eve 1897 New Yorkers read about the mass exodus from New York in the face of the Martian advance on the city following the destruction of Brooklyn Bridge.[20] On Christmas Day the storyline, written deliberately to cover famous downtown buildings and places detailed the resulting devastation. An accompanying illustration showed the destruction of City Hall:

> The Martians ranged over New York destroying what they would.
>
> They threw down St. John's Cathedral on Morningside Heights … They left the Columbia University Buildings a jumble of granite and bricks and mortar … They knocked a gap in the wall of the reservoir in Central Park and the park was flooded …
>
> One of the tall ornate steeples of St. Patrick's Cathedral was truncated midway from the base… The tower of Madison Square Garden was razed to the ground… City Hall was reduced to ruins, only the majestic steps remaining upright, like a gravestone, to mark its place.[21]

Following this tale of wanton destruction by the Martians, the text posed a question for readers: 'Were the ruins of New York to be one of the gravestones of the human race?'

Some four weeks later the Martians gave downtown Boston the same treatment on the pages of the *Boston Post*. An early target for their 'deadly' heat-ray was Bunker Hill monument, which fell with 'a fearful crash' towards Monument Street tearing through a dozen houses, while the Martians moved on to burn Mystic Wharf.[22]

> As they [the Martians] advanced across the Charles River they destroyed the bridges, burning all the shipping within reach … The roof of the Union station itself fell in one solid piece as the heat ray glanced along the iron girders supporting it … In Copley Square they gave full sway to their fearfully destructive powers. The leaning tower of the New Old South Church toppled over and cracked against the Public Library, which a moment later collapsed itself … The heat ray swept around the circle, and the Art Museum, Trinity Church and all the other buildings in the square were simply masses of debris in a few moments.

19. Ibid., p. 286; Wells, 'Fighters from Mars', *Boston Post*, 29 January 1898, p. 5; 30 January 1898, p. 13; 31 January 1898, p. 5; Mollmann, 'The War of the Worlds', pp. 396–7; Hughes, 'The War of the Worlds', p. 286.

20. Wells, 'Fighters from Mars', *New York Evening Journal*, 24 December 1897, p. 9.

21. Wells, 'Fighters from Mars', *New York Evening Journal*, 25 December 1897.

22. Wells, 'Fighters from Mars', *Boston Post*, 22 January 1898, p. 5.

The most serious loss of life concerned the thousands of Bostonians seeking shelter in the subway, where the use of poison gas meant that 'not one escaped alive'.

The less literary and more sensationalist agenda of both newspapers was reflected also by the extensive use of vivid illustrations elaborating the Martian horrors and destruction inflicted upon Boston and New York, particularly upon specific heritage locations and well known buildings. Thus, the fate of the City Halls in both Boston and New York, took centre stage in the vivid illustrations used in the newspapers serials. Such an image was used also by the *Boston Post* in adverts promoting the serial: 'It took the savage visitors from Mars but a few minutes to tear down Boston's City Hall'.[23] Although some illustrations were 'largely free-hand emasculations' of those produced by Goble and Cosmo Rowe for *Cosmopolitan* and *Pearson's Magazine*, several were original because they depicted scenes fabricated to fit the local geography and hence absent from the original stories serialized in these magazines.[24]

Wells as a victim of 'yellow journalism'

The *Boston Post* and the *New York Evening Journal*, albeit often accused of publishing pirated versions of Wells's original story, were not guilty of piracy in terms of reproducing material without permission. Having contacted Wells, both newspapers received his written approval for the re-publication of the serialized text. Hearst Publications also sent Wells twenty-one guineas (£22.05) for the *New York Evening Journal's* serialization.[25] Thus, John Gosling is incorrect when claiming that the *Boston Post* 'unofficially reproduced' *The War of the Worlds*, and that Wells never 'saw a cent in compensation'.[26] What the two newspapers were guilty of was failing to abide by the terms of the original arrangement allowing the story's reproduction subject to Wells's approval of any textual alterations. However, Gosling is correct when critiquing 'the brutal butchery' of Wells's work and the newspapers' 'sharp business practices' and observing that Wells was 'blissfully unaware of the skulduggery taking place in his name'.

In brief, Wells was yet another victim of 'yellow journalism' and ongoing newspaper circulation wars.[27] During the mid-late 1890s American newspaper publishers and editors chased larger circulations with dubious business practices and over-sensational content, without too much regard being paid to ethical, literary and other standards, a feature summed up by the term 'yellow press'. For

23. 'Fighters from Mars' advert, *Boston Post*, 3 January 1898, p. 8; Wells, 'Fighters from Mars', *Boston Post*, 22 January 1898, p. 5.

24. Hughes, *Edition and a Survey*, p. 44 n.2.

25. Hughes and Geduld, *Critical Edition*, p. 6.

26. Gosling, *Waging the War of the Worlds*, pp. 17–18. Overlooking the *New York Evening Journal's* serialization, Gosling stated also that the *Boston Post* was 'the first' to reinvent Wells's story.

27. Hughes, 'The War of the Worlds', p. 287.

Hearst's *New York Evening Journal*, the chief rival was Joseph Pulitzer's New *York World* (Tables 11.3–11.4). For the *Boston Post* and the *Boston Sunday Post*, the serialization of Wells's story was part of an ongoing effort to close the gap with its principal competitors, that is the morning and Sunday editions of the *Boston Globe* and *Boston Herald* (Tables 11.5–11.6). Tables 11.3 and 11.5 highlight also the tendency of newspapers to exaggerate their circulation figures. By contrast, directories like *Ayer's Annual* adopted a more rigorous approach regarding data and hence tended to publish lower totals than those claimed by newspapers.[28] Indeed, the 1899 edition of Ayer's Annual published no figures for *The New York Evening Journal* because of doubts concerning the accuracy of the data.[29]

Apart from being viewed by both newspapers as a great story capable of attracting additional sales and retaining existing readers, the scaremongering properties of Wells's story possessed a strong contemporary resonance at a time of growing tensions between the USA and Spain over Cuba. Thus, when the story was being serialized, fears that Spain was preparing for war with the USA, then still an emerging power on the world stage, were reflected by such headlines in the *Boston Post* as 'Let Spain fire' and 'Spanish fleet for Havana'.[30] In the event, the Spanish–American war did not start until April 1898, but for Steven Mollmann the response of Americans to the coming of war 'was prefigured by the *Boston Post*'s adaptation of *The War of the Worlds*', most notably as demonstrated by its pre-war coverage of an attack on Boston.[31]

Wells's complaints about giving his story 'local colour'

In the past, Wells had often expressed concerns about infringements of copyright when placing his work in the USA.[32] In January 1898 receipt of a 'startling cutting' from the *Boston Post* supplied by the Author's Clipping Bureau gave substance to his worst fears. Representing himself as a 'remote Englishman' living on the other side of the Atlantic in Worcester Park, Wells used an open letter addressed to the editors of the *Critic* journal in the USA to express his strong displeasure at the unauthorized rewriting of his work. He made clear his annoyance, indeed indignation, about the way in which the *Boston Post* specifically acknowledged his copyright, but then abused his approval of serialization by making unauthorized changes to *his story*.[33]

28. *N. W. Ayer & Sons American Newspaper Annual containing a Catalogue of American Newspapers 1898, Part 1* (Philadelphia, PA: N. W. Ayer, 1898), pp. 13–16.

29. *N. W. Ayer & Sons American Newspaper Annual containing a Catalogue of American Newspapers 1899, Part 1* (Philadelphia, PA: N. W. Ayer, 1899), pp. 21, 571.

30. *Boston Post*, 20 January 1898, 28 January 1898, quoted, Mollmann, 'The War of the Worlds', p. 399.

31. Mollmann, 'The War of the Worlds', p. 402.

32. Wells to Harpers, 15 October 1895, Wells to Authors' Syndicate, 2 January 1895, Loing, *Wells à l'oeuvre*, pp. 424, 426.

33. Wells to the Editor, *Critic*, 21 January 1898, in Hughes, 'The War of the Worlds', pp. 281–2.

Table 11.3 *The New York Evening Journal's* circulation, as advertised by the *New York Journal*, 1898

	Morning edition	**Evening edition**
The New York Journal	300,000	275,000

Source: Advert, *N. W. Ayer & Sons American Newspaper Annual containing a Catalogue of American Newspapers 1898, Part 1* (1898), p. 1381.

Table 11.4 Leading New York daily newspapers' circulations, as reported by *Ayer's American Newspaper Annual*, 1898

	Morning edition	**Evening edition**	**Sunday edition**
The New York Evening Journal		309,427	425,000
New York World	370,000	300,000	500,000

Source: *N. W. Ayer & Sons American Newspaper Annual containing a Catalogue of American Newspapers 1898, Part 1* (1898), p. 571.

Table 11.5 The *Boston Post* and *Boston Sunday Post's* circulation, 1897–8, as claimed by the *Boston Post*

	December 1897	**January 1898**	**February 1898**
Boston Post	121,806	122,681	133,209
Boston Sunday Post	115,321	116,036	118,001

Source: *Boston Post*, 31 January 1898; 1 February 1898; 18 March 1898.

Table 11.6 Leading Boston daily and Sunday newspapers' circulations, as reported by *Ayer's American Newspaper Annual*, 1898

	Daily edition	**Sunday edition**
Boston Journal	77,210	53,103
Boston Post	76,303	88,278
Boston Herald	146,441	144,404
Boston Globe	198,566	244,500

Source: N. W. Ayer & Sons *American Newspaper Annual 1898, Part 1* (1898), pp. 339–45.

Protesting about the switch of 'my story' to New England where it showed how the 'strange voyagers from Mars visited Boston and vicinity', Wells disavowed any responsibility for 'this novel development' employed to give 'local colour' to the storyline: 'This adaptation is a serious infringement of my copyright and has been made altogether without my participation or consent. I feel bound to protest in the most emphatic way against this manipulation of my work in order to fit it to the requirements of the local geography.' Contrary to what was agreed, 'I find too late that my story has been flaunted before the cultivated public of Boston disguised and disarrayed beyond my imagining … I fail to see how a rag of conviction can remain in it after this outrage.' Surprisingly, Wells's open letter failed to mention the illustrations, particularly given his complaints about those appearing in *Pearson's Magazine* and *Cosmopolitan*.

Despite mentioning his contacts with Hearst Publications, Wells's specific focus upon the *Boston Post* implies that hitherto he appeared unaware of the liberties taken with his story by the *New York Evening Journal*. Nor did he appear to notice that the *Boston Post*'s printed acknowledgement of his copyright at the start of each instalment read 'H. C. Wells', an error probably resulting from the *Boston Post*'s reliance upon the basic framework of the *New York Evening Journal*'s text, which soon lapsed for some unexplained reason from 'H. G. Wells' to 'H. C. Wells'. Significantly, early in January 1898 the *Boston Post* exploited Wells's permission to boost sales of the forthcoming serialization by emphasizing the fact that 'Right of Exclusive Reproduction in this part of the country secured by cable from the author, Mr H. G. Wells'.[34]

For the literary world in general and individual writers in particular, the controversy possessed wider significance. During this period American newspaper publishers often proved somewhat lax regarding copyright, as evidenced by not only the unauthorized alteration of existing texts to fit the perceived needs of an American audience in order to boost sales, but also the frequent reproduction of published works without the author's approval. Indeed, William L. Alden, an American author responsible for the 'London Literary Letter' published in the *New York Times*, moved on from seconding Wells's protest against the 'enterprise' of two American newspapers to opine that all writers would sympathize with Wells's predicament in the face of such bowdlerizing: 'If it can be permitted in the case of Mr Wells, no author will be safe. We shall have editions of Shakespeare with a Yankee Merchant of Venice crossing Charlestown Bridge, and editions of Milton [John Milton's *Paradise Lost*: 1667], with the scene of the great debate in the first book laid in Chicago.'[35]

A contemporary sequel: Earth strikes back at Mars

Apart from marking an illuminating chapter in the history of Wells's *The War of the Worlds* and yellow journalism in the USA, this episode saw another interesting development, the commissioning and publication of a sequel. The apparent success of their serialization of *The War of the Worlds*, combined with continuing media and public interest in Mars, led both the *New York Evening Journal* and the *Boston Post* to build upon the commercial momentum generated by Wells's story.

34. 'Fighters from Mars' advert, *Boston Post*, 3 January 1898, p. 8.
35. William L. Alden, 'London Literary Letter', *The New York Times*, 12 March 1898.

Thus, they commissioned Garrett P. Serviss, a science journalist, to write a sequel based on the Earth strikes back theme.

Centred upon Thomas Edison, the famous inventor, Serviss's serialization was entitled '*Edison's Conquest of Mars*'. Responding to evidence that the Martians, undeterred by their recent abortive invasion related in 'Fighters from Mars', were preparing yet another assault upon earth, a counterattack was launched from the eastern USA. For Crossley, Serviss's serial is interesting as an instant response to Wells's story: 'As fiction it is hackwork; as a commentary on The War of the Worlds it is astonishingly impervious to Wells's anti-imperialist motive; but as an example of how cultural and national values get drawn into the Martian myth it is both instructive and appalling.'[36]

Significantly, plans for the projected sequel led the *Boston Post* to omit chunks of the closing section of 'Fighters from Mars'. In part, this resulted from a desire to commence serializing the sequel as soon as possible, especially as the ongoing serialization of 'The Fighters from Mars' had passed beyond the story's more exciting stages. In part, this reflected the fact that the planned sequel, centred upon Earth's retaliation, rendered redundant the section of Wells's text in which the narrator drew lessons from the Martian invasion regarding, say, the transformation in humanity's outlook about the present and future, the removal of complacency about the future and the need to be prepared for a further attack. As Mollmann commented, 'When the war of the worlds happens in England and London is destroyed, the reaction of the English is to watch the skies and wait and hope. But when the war of the worlds happens in the United States and Boston is destroyed, the reaction of the Americans is to take the fight to Mars.'[37] Whereas Wells's story critiqued imperialism, Serviss's sequel – this was not published as a book until 1947 – was underpinned by not only the need for a state to respond strongly to an external threat but also acceptance of the USA's emergence on the world, indeed the interplanetary stage, by becoming an imperial power. Indeed, this soon happened in reality when the 1898 Spanish American War led the USA to take control over Cuba, Puerto Rico and the Philippines.

Conclusion

Even before its publication as a book in 1898, the serialization of *The War of the Worlds* by the *New York Evening Journal* and the *Boston Post* offered further recognition of the story's vivid and engaging nature and ability to appeal to a wide readership. Indeed, *The Boston Post* reported feedback indicating that this 'great story is exciting much interest and is being eagerly read by the public', such as indicated when one 'excited' reader from Concord invaded its editorial

---

36. Crossley, *Imagining Mars*, p. 124.
37. Mollmann, 'The War of the Worlds', p. 403.

offices.[38] The whole episode highlighted also *The War of the Worlds*' potential for adaptation, a task facilitated by the story's somewhat loose structure arising from the central role performed by the narrator, in describing what he witnessed or was told. Both newspapers found it easy to switch the geography to give the text 'local colour'. Neither the *New York Evening Journal* nor the *Boston Post* changed the timing of the Martian invasion, since the prospect of war between the USA and Spain meant that it suited both papers to keep Wells's original chronology.

Wells's complaints about American newspaper spin-offs, or rather what he viewed as rip-offs, showed that re-publication outside Britain, even when receiving his approval, was problematic, since varying editorial standards and agendas raised the risk of unapproved changes of geography and content to suit commercial priorities. Thus, 'The *Cosmopolitan* version was manipulated by the *Journal*; the *Journal* version in turn was manipulated by the *Post*'.[39] Apart from seeking to uphold his rights as an author and to reaffirm his deep-seated antipathy towards editors and publishers, Wells feared that any re-jigging of his storyline would hit sales of *The War of the Worlds* when published in the USA as a book in March 1898. On the other hand, it might be argued that serialization in two American newspapers, especially those serving Boston and New York, provided a solid foundation for sales of all his scientific romances, including the forthcoming publication of *The War of the Worlds*. Having been given visibility across the whole of the USA for nine months by *Cosmopolitan*, a literary magazine claiming 'the largest clientele of intelligent, thoughtful readers possessed by any periodical' and a nationwide circulation of 300,000, Tables 11.3–11.6 establish that the two newspaper serializations reached substantial popular audiences, totalling c. 300,000–400,000 per day, in and around two major urban centres for several weeks.[40]

Undoubtedly, some readers of *The War of the Worlds*, as published in the *Boston Post* and the *New York Evening Journal*, would have been encouraged to buy the book when it was published by Harper in the USA in March 1898. One wonders how such readers felt when finding a very different text, a story set in London and Surrey and not in Boston and Massachusetts or New York and New York State. Nor was the book, which lacked also the extra sections of text written by Wells for Heinemann and sent to the *New York Evening Journal*, illustrated sensationally like the newspaper versions. As stressed throughout this study, there exists no one version of *The War of the Worlds*. In fact, as indicated in this chapter, by early 1898 the story had not only reached the USA, but also was available already in four different versions. What all had in common, though, was a strong sense of time and place, whether the action was set in Britain or the USA. Moreover, the two American newspaper adaptations published in 1897–8 were historically significant in setting a precedent and foreshadowing yet another version of *The War of the Worlds*, that is Orson Welles's 1938 radio script.

38. '"Can't fool me." *Post* visitor refuses to believe in The Fighter from Mars', *Boston Post*, 16 January 1898, p. 1.

39. Hughes, 'The War of the Worlds', p. 283.

40. Advertisement, Cosmopolitan, *Ayer American Newspaper Annual 1898, Part 1*, p. 1425.

Chapter 12

WELLS'S MARTIANS INVADE THE USA YET AGAIN: ORSON WELLES'S 1938 *THE WAR OF THE WORLDS* BROADCAST

In 1955 Orson Welles (1915–85), the famous Hollywood actor and producer, appeared in BBC Television's 'Orson Welles' Sketchbook', a series looking back on his life and illustrious career. Unsurprisingly, his infamous 1938 *War of the Worlds* broadcast, responsible for propelling the twenty-three-year-old actor to national, indeed global, celebrity status, took up one whole programme. Orson Welles reminded viewers about the mass panic and hysteria caused across the country when he sent Martians 'to America, via the radio, in something called *The War of the Worlds*.'[1] Nor, he added, was the resulting panic confined to a few people. Worried listeners, Orson Welles reported, phoned the police, government departments and the media for information and help. Many people took flight. Some made for a local church. Others sought to protect themselves from gas attack: 'It [panic] was in fact nationwide!... there wasn't a phone you could get to... really, anywhere in the States, the highways were jammed with cars going one way or another, those people who were in the cities were going to the hills, and those people who were in the hills were going to the cities.' In brief, large numbers of Americans, he alleged, had been terrorized by their radios, or rather by his dramatized version of Wells's *The War of the Worlds*.

Apart from securing massive media coverage at the time, this controversial episode became embedded in the American national memory, thereby guaranteeing Orson Welles a prominent place in the history of popular culture. Exploiting the resulting fame, he used the 1955 BBC television programme, like other media opportunities, to reinforce his image as 'the Man from Mars', 'the man who panicked America'.[2] Reaffirming that the reported panic and hysteria actually happened, Orson Welles took pains to dispute claims that the resulting terror was

1. 'Orson Welles' Sketchbook: Episode 5', BBC TV, 21 May 1955, http://www.wellesnet.com/sketchbook5.htm [accessed 12 February 2014].

2. Simon Callow, *Orson Welles, Vol. 2: Hello Americans* (London: Penguin, 2007), p. vii. See also when Orson Welles appeared in 'Frost over America', BBC TV, 22 July 1970, http://www.wellesnet.com/frostwelles-houseman-koch-talking-about-the-war-of-the-worlds/ [accessed 25 May 2015].

merely a good media story, a myth, given credibility through repeated retelling over time. Indeed, he went on to challenge any doubters, by offering viewers a series of engaging anecdotes. 'Some of them', he conceded, 'may seem hard to believe, but they're all verified' by 'a very scholarly book Princeton University got out on the subject of mass hysteria.'[3] The 'scholarly book' mentioned, Hadley Cantril's *The Invasion from Mars: A Study in the Psychology of Panic* (1940), is discussed below.

Despite Orson Welles's assertion, none of the stories cited below appeared in Cantril's book, a point suggesting that they were more products of his showmanship and vivid imagination than fact. Moreover, excessive stress upon the truthfulness of any assertion always raises a red warning marker. Even so, they made good stories for a popular audience, thereby highlighting the manner in which the whole episode inspired a range of engaging narratives. There were phone calls, Orson Welles recalled, from people asking the police and officials for advice after claiming that Martians had just landed in their backyards! Reportedly, US Navy sailors on shore leave in New York harbour were recalled for active duty 'to defend America against the Martians'. He related also an amusing story about a 'very select and elegant and exclusive dinner party' celebrating Halloween on Long Island, where those present, allegedly took news of the invasion in a more restrained manner than most of their fellow Americans. Once again, Orson Welles prefaced the tale by stating that 'this is a really true story, I must ask you to believe that'.

> Lot of grand people sitting at dinner, and about halfway through dinner, the butler arrived, serving the next course, and said to the host, in an undertone, which carried around the table, "I beg pardon, sir, but, eh, New Jersey has just fallen." Passed the next plate.
>
> Everyone was very contained and polite ... nobody panicked. And they waited till the next course, and the butler came around again, and the host said, "Meadows," or whatever his name was, "Eh, what was that you said, Meadows, you said, uh... where'd you hear that?" Meadows said "On the radio, sir," And the host said "Exactly what happened?" And Meadows said "Well, I believe sir, that the greater part of the Atlantic seaboard has capitulated." Passed another plate. Of course, everybody assumed it must be the Communists or something; third round of whatever it was – by the time the baked Alaska came, host said "Meadows, um ... have you ascertained who it is that's attacking us?" And Meadows said "I believe it's interplanetary, sir," And at this point, according to my informant, who is highly placed and should be believed, at this point they looked out the window, and there was a falling star. Now I can't vouch for that part of the story, but anyway that's what's told.

Notwithstanding Orson Welles's assertions, the initial assumption of an invasion by Communists reflected more a 1950s Cold War context than that characteristic of the late 1930s.

3. 'Orson Welles' Sketchbook'.

The 1938 radio broadcast

Forty years on from its publication as a book, Wells's *The War of the Worlds* secured massive media and public visibility across the USA, indeed the world, through Orson Welles's radio drama broadcast in the USA on 30 October 1938 at 2000 hours Eastern Standard Time (EST). Selected specifically to mark Halloween, Orson Welles's play was part of a regular series of Sunday night programmes staged by the 'Mercury Theatre on the Air', whose radio dramas, adapted from the original novels, were broadcast nationwide by CBS (Columbia Broadcasting System) from its studios on Madison Avenue in New York City.[4] One week earlier, the series featured Jules Verne's *Around the World in Eighty Days*. Some six million people tuned in to 'The War of the Worlds' broadcast, but a much larger audience of approximately thirty million were listening to NBC's comedy programme, 'The Chase and Sanborn Hour' starring Edgar Bergen, the ventriloquist and Charlie McCarthy, his dummy.[5] The fact that far more Americans were tuned in to another radio station prompted Richard Hand to point to the need to view claims concerning the national impact of Orson Welles's drama in a broader perspective, even if an audience of six million must still be treated as substantial and hence capable of exerting significant consequences across the country.[6]

Dramatizing a Martian landing in the USA, the radio play, it appears, led many listeners to treat it as a news report of an actual alien invasion, thereby prompting large scale panic and hysteria. In New York's Times Square, the Moving News sign read "ORSON WELLES FRIGHTENS THE NATION".[7] Soon after the programme finished, Walter Winchell went on the air for his regular *Jergens Journal* broadcast at 2100 EST. His declaration, though intended to reassure anxious listeners, merely accentuated the scale of the problem: 'Mr and Mrs North America, there is no cause for alarm. America has not fallen. I repeat: America has not fallen.'[8] At 2230 EST, 2330 EST and midnight EST network radio carried announcements stressing the fictional nature of events seemingly treated at some stage by many listeners as factual:

> For those who tuned in to Orson Welles and the Mercury Theater on the Air
> broadcast from 8-9 EST tonight and did not realise that the program was merely

4. John Houseman, *Run Through: A Memoir* (New York: Simon & Schuster, 1972), pp. 390–406; John Houseman. 'The War of the Worlds', *The Times*, 27 January 1973, p. 8; Simon Callow, *Orson Welles, Vol.1: The Road to Xanadu*, (London: Vintage, 1996), pp. 399–408; Paul Heyer, *The Medium and the Magician: Orson Welles, The Radio Years, 1934–1952* (Lanham, MD: Rowman & Littlefield, 2005), pp. 81–90.

5. Hadley Cantril, *The Invasion from Mars: A Study in the Psychology of Panic* (New York: Harper Torchbooks, 1966), p. 56.

6. Richard J. Hand, *Terror on the Air!: Horror Radio in America, 1931–1952* (Jefferson, NC: McFarland, 2006), pp. 6–7.

7. Callow, *Orson Welles, 1*, p. 404.

8. Quoted, Robert J. Brown, *Manipulating the Ether: Power of Broadcast Radio in Thirties America* (Jefferson, NC: McFarland, 2004), p. 217.

a modernized adaptation of H. G. Wells' famous novel, *War of the Worlds*, we are repeating the fact which was made clear four times in the program, that, while the names of some American cities were used, as in all novels and dramatizations, the entire story and all its incidents were fictitious.

Even so, the next morning's American newspapers provided readers with vivid images of mass terror and mayhem across the USA. Typical front page headlines, reported that 'Attack from Mars in Radio Play Puts Thousands in Fear' (*New York Herald Tribune,* 31 October 1938), 'Radio Listeners in Panic, Taking War Drama as Fact' (*New York Times,* 31 October 1938), 'Fake Radio "War" Stirs Terror Though U. S.' (*New York Daily News,* 31 October 1938), 'U.S. Probes "Invasion" Broadcast; Radio Play Causes Wide Panic' (*New York Post,* 31 October 1938) and 'Radio Fake Scares Nation' (*Chicago Herald and Examiner,* 31 October 1938). The *New York Daily News* reported 'unbelievable scenes of terror in New York, New Jersey, the South and as far west as San Francisco.'[9] Reportedly, the programme's apparent realism – apart from setting the story in actual places, like Princeton and New York, clever use of special news bulletins and sound effects enhanced the drama's credibility – led many listeners to believe that the USA was actually being invaded. Typical reactions, as recorded by Cantril, included 'I just naturally thought it was real. Why shouldn't I?', especially as 'it didn't sound like a play'.[10] Newspaper offices and police stations, the press recorded, were flooded with calls from people asking what to do, where to go, and how to protect themselves from a gas attack.[11] Many people, it was reported, required medical treatment for shock and hysteria. Reportedly, the receipt of some 2,000 telephone calls in two hours paralysed the city of Trenton's municipal operations, especially its fire and police departments.[12] Echoing newspaper headlines, *Universal Newsreel*'s coverage of the episode for cinema audiences was entitled 'Radio Station's "Attack by Mars" panics thousands'.[13]

The New York Times, whose front page headline reported 'Radio Listeners in Panic, Taking War Drama as Fact', provides a typical example of press coverage:

> A wave of mass hysteria seized thousands of radio listeners… last night when a broadcast of a dramatization of H. G. Wells' fantasy, *The War of the Worlds,* led thousands to believe that an interplanetary conflict had started with invading Martians spreading wide death and destruction in New Jersey and New York.
>
> The broadcast, which disrupted households, interrupted religious services, created traffic jams and clogged communications systems, was made by Orson

9. *New York Daily News,* 31 October 1938.

10. Quoted, Cantril, *Invasion from Mars,* pp. 67, 70.

11. Gosling, *Waging the War of the Worlds,* pp. 49–55.

12. City Manager of Trenton, New Jersey, to Federal Communications Commission, 31 October 1938, quoted Gosling, *Waging the War of the Worlds,* p. 61.

13. 'Radio Station's "Attack by Mars" panics thousands', *Universal Newsreel,* 31 October 1938.

Welles ... at least a score of adults required medical treatment for shock and hysteria.

In Newark, in a single block at Heddon Terrace and Hawthorne Avenue, more than twenty families rushed out of their houses with wet handkerchiefs and towels over their faces to flee from what they believed was to be a gas raid. Some began moving household furniture.

Throughout New York families left their homes, some to flee to near-by parks. Thousands of persons called the police, newspapers and radio stations here and in other cities of the United States and Canada seeking advice on protective measures against the raids ...

Despite the fantastic nature of the reported "occurrences", the programme ... caused fright and panic throughout the area of the broadcast.[14]

Individual case studies reinforced the *New York Times*'s narrative of mass terror and hysteria:

Samuel Tishman of 100 Riverside Drive was one of the multitude that fled into the street ... 'I came home at 9.15 p.m. just in time to receive a telephone call from my nephew who was frantic with fear. He told me the city was about to be bombed from the air and advised me to get out of the building at once.'

'I heard that broadcast and almost had a heart attack,' said Louis Winkler of Clay Avenue, the Bronx.' I didn't tune it in until the programme was half over, but when I heard the names and titles of Federal, State and municipal officials and when the "Secretary of the Interior" was introduced, I was convinced it was the McCoy [the genuine article]. I ran out into the street with scores of others, and found people running in all directions. The whole thing came over as a news broadcast'.

Nor did interest in the story disappear overnight. The sheer volume of press coverage across the USA, where the story dominated the next day's front page headlines and then featured in some 12,500 press articles over the ensuing three-week period, and the rest of the world is testament to the immense interest generated in the story as well as to the realism of Orson Welles's fictional radio drama.[15] Whereas British national and provincial newspapers, albeit somewhat bemused by the stories of mass panic and hysteria, gave considerable space and prominence to the broadcast and its alleged impact upon large numbers of listeners, they proved relatively restrained in their commentaries. By contrast, the government-controlled press in Hitler's Germany could not resist exploiting the episode for the purposes of propaganda. Thus, on 1 November 1938 the *Völkischer Beobachter*, the Nazi Party's official newspaper, used a report headlined 'Die Folgen der dauernden Kriegshetze: Mars alarmiert Amerika' ['The result of constant warmongering: Mars alarms America'] to expose the decadence of

14. *New York Times*, 31 October 1938.
15. Cantril, *Invasion from Mars*, pp. 61–2.

the democracies as well as to attack American press coverage of Nazi Germany in general, and the recent Munich crisis in particular.[16] The resulting 'artificial war mentality' and 'terror-psychosis' spread by Jewish interests, the *Völkischer Beobachter* alleged, were instrumental in causing fears of an enemy invasion from Mars and mass panic.

Subsequently, the 'night that panicked America' acquired landmark status, as highlighted by the way in which from an early stage both Orson Welles and the actual broadcast were incorporated into alien invasion stories by comics, films, graphic and other novels, the press as well as radio and television programmes. The 1938 broadcast, which figures prominently in NASA's 'Mars chronology', has been celebrated at the time of significant anniversaries, such as in 1988 and 2013.[17] The episode has attracted considerable interest within academia, most notably in terms of studying adaptations of Wells's book and the power and enormous reach of radio, then still a relatively new branch of the media. To some extent, the programme, though reflecting – to quote Cantril – 'the combined talents of H. G. Wells and Orson Welles', has acquired a life of its own as 'the greatest hoax of the twentieth century'.[18] Frequently taking centre stage in present-day discussions about *The War of the Worlds*, it has often pushed Wells and his book to the wings. Indeed, for many people, Orson Welles, not H. G. Wells, is frequently represented as the person responsible for writing *The War of the Worlds'* storyline, a confusion explained in part by the similarity of their surnames and in part by the growing tendency of people to access the story initially through audio-visual formats rather than through literature.

Writing the radio script for The War of the Worlds

Responding to Orson Welles's proposal to mark Halloween with a scary drama, John Houseman, the co-founder and co-producer of the Mercury Theatre on the Air, suggested Wells's *The War of the Worlds*. However, Howard Koch, the programme's scriptwriter, was unimpressed, as recorded by Houseman: 'Under no circumstances, he declared, could it be made interesting or in any way credible to modern American ears'.[19] Koch's secretary agreed: '"You can't do it, Houseman", she whined, "Those old Martians are just a lot of nonsense! It's all too silly! We're going to make fools of ourselves! Absolute idiots!"'. How wrong they were.

Despite such personal reservations about the topic, the period witnessed an apparent renewal of interest in all things Martian. Recent Martian-centred fiction

16. Gosling, *Waging the War of the Worlds*, pp. 96–7.

17. Karol and Catling, *NASA: Mars Chronology*.

18. Cantril, *Invasion from Mars*, p. vii; Robert E. Bartholomew and Benjamin Radford, *The Martians Have Landed!: A History of Media-Driven Panics and Hoaxes* (Jefferson, NC: McFarland, 2011), p. 16.

19. Houseman, *Run Through*, p. 393; John Houseman, 'The Men from Mars', *Harper's Magazine* (December 1948), p. 76.

included Stanley Weinbaum's much acclaimed short story entitled *A Martian Odyssey* (1934) and its sequel *Valley of Dreams* (1934), plus C. S. Lewis's *Out of the Silent Planet* (1938). Even Wells himself returned to the topic in 1937 with *Star-Begotten: A Biological Fantasia*. More influentially for American audiences, in March 1938 *Flash Gordon's Trip to Mars*, a fifteen-part serial starring Buster Crabbe, opened in cinemas across the USA, thereby ensuring that images of Mars impacted upon large numbers of Americans during the period leading up to the CBS radio drama.

Regardless of Koch's initial reluctance, Orson Welles and Houseman pressed on with the project. Despite his assertion that, excepting the concept of a Martian invasion and descriptions of Martians and their war machines, 'practically nothing' could be used from the original novel, the resulting script was more indebted to Wells's text than claimed later by Koch.[20] Moreover, Koch's initial reservations about the story's dramatic possibilities were soon alleviated. Indeed, he recalled relishing the prospect of using the Martians to lay waste to New Jersey and New York State: 'eventually I found myself enjoying the destruction I was wreaking like a drunken general'.[21] Like the American newspaper adaptations discussed in the previous chapter, the story was switched to an American locale, except in this case Grover's Mill and Princeton, New Jersey, took over the role played in Wells's book by Horsell Common, Ottershaw and Woking. New York City replaced London as the Martians' principal target. As Orson Welles remarked when challenged subsequently at the press conference about the changed locations of the original book, 'H. G. Wells used real cities in Europe, and to make the play more acceptable to American listeners we used real cities in America'.[22]

The key innovation as regards adaptations of *The War of the Worlds* was the change of chronology. Updating the setting to the end of October in 'the 39th year of the twentieth century', the production modernized (and Americanized) the dialogue and language to ensure that the story flowed and engaged a present-day American radio audience. Wells's anonymous narrator and Ogilvy were subsumed into a character named Professor Richard Pierson, an astronomer based at the

---

20. Howard Koch, *The Panic Broadcast: Portrait of An Event* (Boston, MA: Little, Brown, 1970), p. 13; Gosling, *Waging the War of the Worlds*, pp. 32–40. Hughes listed eleven derivative elements from the original text: David Y. Hughes, 'Radio and Film Adaptations', in Hughes and Geduld, *Critical Edition*, p. 243.

21. Koch, *The Panic Broadcast*, p. 15.

22. 'The aftermath: Orson Welles "The War of the Worlds" Halloween press conference', 31 October 1938', extract from *Radio Guide Magazine*, n.d., http://www.wellesnet. com/?p=296 [accessed 25 May 2015]. In fact, Orson Welles had form in rewriting the geography of major texts. Two years earlier he had directed an all-black actor production of Shakespeare's Macbeth set in nineteenth Century Haiti, not Scotland: Paul Heyer, 'America under attack 1: A reassessment of Orson Welles' 1938 *War of the Worlds* Broadcast', *Canadian Journal of Communication* 28 (2003): 150–1.

Princeton Observatory, New Jersey.[23] Apart from taking the role of Pierson, Orson Welles, speaking in his capacity as Director of the Mercury Theatre, delivered also the play's introduction. The artilleryman, scripted as the 'Stranger', became a former National Guardsman encountered by Pierson just before reaching New York City. There was no place for Wells's curate.

The radio play that panicked America

The infamous radio play began with Orson Welles, introduced as the Director of the Mercury Theatre, narrating a slightly modified version of the opening paragraph of Wells's book, with the emphasis being placed upon people's 'infinite complacence' as well as the vast, cool intellects regarding the earth 'with envious eyes' and making plans accordingly.[24] In addition, he provided context to give the play a strong modern-day resonance when stating that it was set in 1939, by acknowledging the USA's continuing recovery from the Great Depression and referring implicitly to the Munich Crisis of September 1938 when the fate of Czechoslovakia brought the world to the brink of war: 'It was near the end of October. Business was better. The war scare was over. More men were back at work. Sales were picking up'.

Then the drama switched to a radio station, whose broadcast set the scene for listeners by stressing normality through a weather forecast provided by the Government Weather Bureau and a programme of dance music from the Park Plaza Hotel in downtown New York. Soon afterwards the programme was interrupted by a news flash reporting the sighting of gas explosions on Mars by Chicago's Mount Jennings Observatory. Tension was built up through a succession of increasingly frequent news updates and an on-the-spot interview conducted by Carl Phillips, the radio station's reporter, with Princeton Observatory's Professor Richard Pierson. Then another news flash announced the landing of a flaming object, possibly a meteorite, at Grover's Mill, a rural hamlet some eleven miles from Princeton. Subsequently Phillips and Pierson offered listeners a descriptive on-the-spot report from the landing site on the Wilmuth farm. Having inter-viewed the farmer about the landing of 'this thing' on his property, Phillips described 'the fantastic scene' – the growing police presence, the arrival of hundreds of onlookers in cars and so on – before announcing that the top of the metal cylinder was being unscrewed. Reporting that strange creatures were emerging from the pit made when the cylinder landed, Phillips stated that a jet

23. Reportedly, the network censor, though accepting actual place names, required changes to institutional names. Thus, Princeton University Observatory became Princeton Observatory just as the Columbia Broadcasting Building was renamed Broadcasting Building: Gosling, *Waging the War of the Worlds*, p. 39.

24. The radio programme is widely available on CD/DVD and online. The script has been reproduced in several publications, including Koch, *The Panic Broadcast*, pp. 33–80; Gosling, *Waging the War of the Worlds*, pp. 193–218; Cantril, *Invasion from Mars*, pp. 4–44.

of flame sprang from the pit, spreading everywhere, and coming his way some twenty yards to his right. Then, listeners heard the crash of a microphone followed by silence. Eventually, an announcer came on air to report the loss of contact with Grover's Mill and to introduce a piano interlude.

Subsequently, further cylinders were reported as 'falling all over the country', such as south of Morristown, New Jersey and then at Buffalo, Chicago and St Louis. Using fighting machines, heat-rays and poisonous Black Smoke and proving impervious to conventional weapons – machine guns, field artillery and bomber aircraft failed to halt the Martian advance – the Martians laid waste to New Jersey before marching on to New York. The impact of the drama was heightened by a series of announcements and news bulletins covering a wide range of locations in New Jersey and New York City, reporting not only the death of Phillips, an early victim of the heat-ray, but also numerous casualties and mass panic as people fled the advancing Martians. Listeners were taken also to Washington DC for a statement delivered by the Secretary of the Interior. Significantly, one interchange during the military's abortive efforts to halt the Martians involved a bomber aeroplane commander flying over Bayonne, New Jersey, which was to prove the central location in Spielberg's 2005 film. In the end, the USA was saved not by military force – indeed, the radio announcer reported that 'No more defenses. Our army wiped out … artillery, air force, everything wiped out' – but, as happened in Wells's original story, by natural bacteria to which the Martians lacked immunity.

Towards the close of the programme, Pierson, who was now back in Princeton, looked back on the invasion which he had somehow survived by hiding in an empty house near Grover's Mill, before deciding to move on to monitor the fate of New York City. Leaving the Holland Tunnel, Pierson recalled making his way up Canal Street, reaching Fourteenth Street, standing in Times Square and then walking along Broadway. Rushing into Central Park, he saw the remains of the Martians, who had been killed by the bacteria against which their systems were unprepared. Their fighting machines were silent: 'great metal Titans, their cowls empty, their steel arms hanging listlessly by their sides'. Following a brief specu-lation about whether or not the Martian incursion was a dream, a reprieve, or a sign of humanity's increased vulnerability, Pierson pointed to the nearby museum at Princeton displaying a former Martian fighting machine.

Finally, Orson Welles signed off 'out of character', to reassure listeners that in reality the programme was merely a 'holiday offering' annihilating the world 'before your very ears'. In brief, it was 'The Mercury Theatre's own radio version of dressing up in a sheet jumping out of a bush and saying Boo!': 'So good-bye everybody, and remember, please, for the next day or so, the terrible lesson you learned tonight. That grinning, glowing, globular invader of your living room is an inhabitant of the pumpkin patch, and if your doorbell rings and nobody's there, that was no Martian … it's Halloween.'

The post-broadcast press conference

In the event, as outlined above, the next day's newspapers published across the USA offered readers a rather different view of what people had heard on their radios. Far from treating the broadcast as a harmless escapist radio play, as urged by Orson Welles's closing address, many listeners, the press reported, regarded the programme as news, as fact not fiction. Mass panic and hysteria resulted, or so the press reported.

The resulting furore forced Orson Welles to address a press conference in order to play down the nationwide controversy generated by his Halloween spoof broadcast. Unsurprisingly, the press conference, held the next day, attracted the world's media. Stating that he was 'terribly shocked by the effect it's had', Orson Welles, described as looking tired, red-eyed and unshaven, moved on to express deep regret 'over any misapprehension that our broadcast might have created among some listeners'.[25]

> It came as rather a great surprise to us that the *H. G. Welles* [sic] *classic* [author's emphasis] – which is the original for many fantasies about invasions by mythical monsters from the planet Mars – I was extremely surprised to learn that a story which has become familiar to children through the medium of comic strips and many succeeding novels and adventure stories, should have had such an immediate and profound effect on radio listeners. [26]

Claiming to have been swept along by the script in a manner preventing him from anticipating possible impacts upon the audience, Orson Welles said he was bewildered by listeners' alleged reactions, given the play's clear status as fiction. Four factors, he argued, emphasized the broadcast's fictional nature:

- firstly, the broadcast was performed as an event occurring in the future, that is in October 1939 as announced at the start of the broadcast;
- secondly, the broadcast was part of a scheduled series of weekly Mercury Theatre radio dramas;
- thirdly, it was announced at the start, during the mid-programme intermission and afterwards that the play was 'an original dramatization' of Wells's classic novel; and

25. 'The aftermath: Orson Welles "The War of the Worlds" Halloween press conference'; 'FCC to scan script of "War" Broadcast', *New York Times*, 1 November 1938; W. Joseph Campbell, *Getting it Wrong: Ten of the Greatest Misreported Stories in American Journalism* (Berkeley, CA: University of California Press, 2010), pp. 29–30, 200 nn.11–12: Alan Gallop, *The Martians are Coming!: The True Story of Orson Welles' 1938 Panic Broadcast* (Stroud: Amberley, 2011), pp. 79–83.

26. 'The aftermath: Orson Welles "The War of the Worlds" Halloween press conference'. The online transcript misspelling Wells's name, http://www.wellesnet.com/?p=296 needs to be checked against the original source, but hitherto the latter has proved unobtainable.

- fourthly, Martians have always been treated as synonyms for make-believe: 'For many decades "The Man From Mars" has been almost a synonym for fantasy'.

Explaining the 'tidal wave of panic' caused by the broadcast

Inevitably, the programme prompted numerous commentaries and reactions. Quite apart from press conferences, there were post-mortems, inquiries and threats of legal action.[27] In the event, none of these threats went to court, but broadcasters were instructed to avoid simulated news bulletins in radio dramas adjudged likely to alarm listeners.

The alleged ability of an imaginative 60-minute play telescoping a series of events taking place over time and long distances to terrorize numerous Sunday night homes was striking. Many commentators, most notably Hadley Cantril, have attempted to explain what Houseman described as the resulting 'tidal wave of panic'.[28] Perhaps listeners were gullible – many letters published in newspapers expressed surprise that people could be so influenced by a radio drama – but the problem was prompted in part by 'dialitis' or 'dial surfing', the fact that many listeners switched radio stations and tuned into the play in mid-programme.[29] Reportedly, many listeners reached for the dials when a vocalist came on in NBC's 'The Chase and Sanborn Hour' and suddenly found themselves listening on CBS to what appeared to be a news broadcast about an invasion of the USA. Thus, having missed the initial warnings about the fictional nature of the programme, they were confronted immediately by news bulletins reporting on-the-spot stories of fighting in their backyards and then had seemingly taken flight by the time reassuring messages were delivered in mid-programme and at the end of the broadcast.

The play's mention of a recent war scare highlights the need for any explanation to take account of the contemporary context, most notably the unsettled international scene, widespread public angst in the wake of the Munich Crisis and the repeated war scares posed by Hitler's Germany, Mussolini's Italy and Hirohito's Japan. After all, only a few weeks earlier Americans had been glued to their radios listening to news broadcasts about the Munich Crisis, which had brought Europe and the wider world to the brink of war over Czechoslovakia. As a result, it seemed easy to interpret the dramatized extra-terrestrial invasion as merely moving on from recent terrestrial war scares, particularly given the reportage method employed by Orson Welles's play and people's apparent inexperience concerning the new medium of radio.

In many respects, the programme's impact resulted from not only its contemporary resonance, but also the realistic qualities of Wells's original story line and

27. Heyer, 'America under attack', p. 160.
28. Houseman, *Run Through*, p. 398.
29. Heyer, *The Medium and the Magician*, p. 82.

the play's technical brilliance as radio drama.[30] The whole show was produced in the studio, but the way in which it was presented encouraged listeners to believe that announcers, astronomers, orchestras and reporters were broadcasting from diverse locations. For an American audience, the impression of reality, reinforced by the way in which the fast-moving drama touched many towns and cities across New Jersey and New York State, was enhanced through the vivid, indeed revolutionary, mode of production. It was easy for listeners to suspend their disbelief at the pace and scale of events. As one such listener commented in a letter published in the *New York Times*, CBS must be commended for a 'brilliant dramatization'.[31] One Washingtonian, though admitting that 'I am one of the many thousands whose (to quote a famous newspaper writer) "incredible stupidity, lack of nerve, and ignorance" found cause for alarm while listening' to the broadcast, used a letter to *The Washington Post* to praise Orson Welles for a gripping and well produced radio drama: 'I would like to congratulate him for what I consider one of the greatest radio presentations ever heard on the air. It was a darn good show.[32]

In effect, the play was – to quote Houseman – 'a magic act', employing smoke and mirrors to engage an invisible radio audience living through anxious times in the drama.[33] Speaking in 1955, Orson Welles admitted that the reportage format was adopted deliberately to encourage, even convince, listeners to blur the distinction between fiction and reality, thereby treating the drama as fact transpiring in real time:

> I think because we were criticized a good bit by our sound effects people for dabbling in science fiction we made a special effort to make our show as realistic as possible, that is we reproduced all the radio effects, not only sound effects, but ... well, we did on the show exactly what would have happened if the world had been invaded.[34]

Simulating the style of contemporary news reporting familiar to radio audiences during recent serious international events, the drama's apparent authenticity led many listeners to misframe a science fiction script, deliberately coded for dramatic purposes to encourage listeners to suspend their disbelief, as a genuine

30. James B. Gilbert, 'Wars of the Worlds', *Journal of Popular Culture* 10 (2) (1976): 330–1.

31. Letter, Alvin Bogart, Cranford, NJ, *The New York Times*, 2 November 1938, p. 22.

32. Letter, T. Owen Miller, Washington DC, *The Washington Post*, 10 November 1938, quoted Mark Jones, 'Washingtonians react to the *War of the Worlds*', 29 October 2013, *Boundary Stones: WETA's Local History Blog*, http://blogs.weta.org/boundarystones/2013/10/29/washingtonians-react-war-worlds [accessed 14 February 2014]. The 'famous newspaper writer' quoted was Dorothy Thompson: Dorothy Thompson, 'On the Record', *New York Herald Tribune*, 2 November 1938.

33. Houseman, *Run Through*, p. 400; John Houseman, *Unfinished Business: A Memoir* (London: Columbus, 1986), p. 197.

34. 'Orson Welles' Sketchbook'.

news report about actual events taking place over a lengthy period of time and considerable distances. As Malmsheimer argued, 'A significant number of people reacted in ways consistent with expectable behaviour in the warning stages of actual disasters. In short, because they misframed a fiction which, for dramatic purposes, had been coded to mislead, they reacted "irrationally".[35]

Representing himself as 'an astonished contributor' to a 'bizarre' chain of events, Koch provided an apt summary of the problem: 'In the course of forty-five minutes of actual time – as differentiated from subjective or fictional time – the invading Martians were presumably able to blast off from their planet, land on the earth, set up their destructive machines, defeat our army, disrupt communications, demoralize the population and occupy whole sections of the country. In forty-five minutes!'[36] One moment Phillips and Pierson were talking in the observatory at Princeton. The next minute they were providing an on-the-spot report from Grover's Mill, over ten miles away. Dorothy Thompson's commentary published in the *New York Herald Tribune*, a few days after the broadcast, pointed to another 'impossibility': 'Listeners were told that "within two hours three million people have moved out of New York" – an obvious impossibility for the most disciplined army moving exactly as planned, and a double fallacy because only a few minutes before, the news of the arrival of the monster had been announced.' [37] Apart from the adroit deployment of music – Flynn argued that for listeners the orchestral interludes seemed to last longer than they actually did – the drama made effective use of both sound effects and dead air, complete silence, such as after the Martians unleashed their heat-ray for the first time.[38]

Regardless of the resulting controversy, the Mercury Theatre series as a whole and 'The War of the Worlds' drama in particular, served not only to boost Orson Welles's national and international profile as a young actor and director, but also to sharpen his skills as a self-publicist exploiting the massive public and media interest in the programme. Inevitably, he won applause also for his 'media sense' and skills in pushing radio's dramatic possibilities by pioneering a news reporting format as – to quote from his post-broadcast press conference – 'a legitimate dramatic form' of *radio verité* for plays.[39] Of course, within a few years, his first film, *Citizen Kane* (1941), made his name in Hollywood and beyond. Both at the time and during succeeding decades, Orson Welles took pains to claim credit for the programme's impact when representing himself as the man who scared Americans. Indeed, notwithstanding Koch's role as the play's scriptwriter, Orson Welles claimed repeatedly it was *his script*. At times, this led to messy disputes

35. Malmsheimer, 'Three Mile Island', p. 47.

36. Koch, *The Panic Broadcast*, pp. 11–12.

37. Thompson, 'On the Record'.

38. Flynn, *War of the Worlds*, p. 37.

39. 'The aftermath: Orson Welles "The War of the Worlds" Halloween press conference'; Heyer, 'America under attack', pp. 150–4.

over the issue, such as when Hadley Cantril credited Koch, not him, as the scriptwriter.[40]

Even so, Orson Welles sought to neutralize some of the concern articulated at the press conference by pointing to the fact that he was not the first to adopt such an approach: 'The technique I used was not original with me, or peculiar to the Mercury Theater's presentation.'[41] Although he failed to cite actual precedents, commentators have pointed to Ronald Knox's 'Broadcasting the Barricades', a January 1926 BBC Radio programme employing a news reporting style to make out that Britain was erupting into revolution.[42] However, it remains uncertain whether Houseman, Koch or Orson Welles was aware of Knox's hoax, even if, as indicated below, the BBC programme was reported in the American press at the time. For Orson Welles, the news broadcasting style adopted for radio plays by Archibald MacLeish was probably a more powerful factor. Indeed, he had played the part of the radio announcer in MacLeish's much acclaimed 1937 radio drama 'Fall of a City'. MacLeish's 'Air Raid', a play broadcast by CBS (1938) on 27 October 1938 during the week preceding 'The War of the Worlds', is often cited as influential in terms of using a reportage format, since it was broadcast while the Mercury Theatre's drama was in preparation and the script being finalized.[43]

Commenting on the alleged panic of British listeners to Knox's hoax BBC broadcast in 1926, a columnist writing for the *New York Times* pointed out that 'Large numbers of people were filled with anxiety' by way of opining smugly that 'Such a thing as that could not happen in this country'.[44] Unsurprisingly, in 1938 there was a certain amount of *schadenfreude* upon the part of the British press, such as displayed by *The Times* about what it represented as 'a Wells fantasy in America': 'America today hardly knows whether to laugh or to be angry. Here is a nation which, alone of big nations, has deemed it unnecessary to rehearse her protection against attack from the air by fellow beings on this earth and suddenly believes itself – and for little enough reason – faced with a more fearful attack from another world.'[45] One month on from the radio broadcast, *The Times*'s New

40. Callow, *Orson Welles, 1*, p. 406; Cantril, *Invasion from Mars*, pp. xiv–xv.

41. 'The aftermath: Orson Welles "The War of the Worlds" Halloween press conference'.

42. Raymond Snoddy, 'The Riot that Never Was', *BBC Radio Four*, 16 June 2005; Gosling, *Waging the War of the Worlds*, pp. 80–2.

43. Gosling, *Waging the War of the Worlds*, pp. 36–7; Callow, *Orson Welles, 1*, pp. 399–400.

44. '"We Are Safe From Such Jesting"', *New York Times*, 19 January 1926; Gosling, *Waging the War of the Worlds*, p. 81.

45. 'Panic caused by broadcast: a Wells fantasy in America', *The Times*, 1 November 1938. However, by 1938 the British press seemed to have forgotten Knox's broadcast: Snoddy, 'The Riot that Never Was'. Nor did the British press recall the relevance of one of Wells's often-quoted remarks both online and in history texts, critiquing the isolationist stance adopted by the USA: 'Every time Europe looks across the Atlantic to see the American eagle, it observes only the rear end of an ostrich'. Like many quotes attributed to Wells, this proves difficult to reference, let alone to establish whether or not he ever said it:

York correspondent could not resist reporting that Orson Welles had acquired 'the curious distinction of being the only radio actor ever to scare a nation into fits'.[46] Indeed, 'Some denizens of New Jersey are said to be still looking for Martians under the fallen autumn leaves'!

H. G. Wells meets Orson Welles

Throughout his life Wells welcomed projects taking his writing to new audiences, especially as most promised to enhance his name and public visibility, add a further revenue stream through the sale of rights and lift sales of all his publications. Believing that a new medium like radio was perfectly capable of working with the literary world – indeed, he saw radio, like film, as a force for good, as regards both the spoken and written word – Wells, an experienced broadcaster, had been only too happy to give Orson Welles permission for the proposed radio dramatization.[47]

Following the broadcast and particularly the receipt of news about the scriptural alterations made to the storyline, Jacques Chambrun, his literary representative in New York, announced that Wells was unhappy about the 'unwarranted' infringement of what was represented as his 'overriding copyright as author of the original story'.[48] Wells's secretary complained to CBS that 'Mr Wells was not informed ... that any adaptation was intended: Mr Wells believed that he was merely giving permission for a reading of the novel'.[49] For Wells, the changes, including those of location, made by the play's script represented an unauthorized 'complete rewriting' of the novel and resulted in 'an entirely different story'.[50] For Wells, there was of course a sense of *déjà vu*, given what had happened some forty years earlier concerning adaptations published by the *Boston Post* and *New York Journal*. As a result, he advised, that in future it might be preferable to deal with him direct concerning adaptations rather than through an agent.[51]

see Simon James, 'When I see a quotation on the internet: Wells, the bicycle and the human race', *H. G. Wells Society Newsletter* 27 (Spring 2014): 2–3.

46. 'New York Stage: Playgoers without new plays', *The Times*, 29 November 1938.

47. Wells to Evans, 3 February 1936, Smith, *Correspondence of H. G. Wells, 4*, p. 61; 'FCC to scan script of "War" Broadcast', *New York Times*, 1 November 1938. Later Wells gave permission to publish the programme's script, as based upon his book, in Cantril's book: Cantril, *Invasion from Mars*, pp. xv, 3.

48. Mrs G. P. Wells to Joseph La Gattuta, 14 November 1938, WL4 (UIUC); Chambrun to Wells, 31 October 1938, Smith, *Correspondence of H. G. Wells, 4*, p. 204.

49. Mrs G. P. Wells to Kathryn Campbell, CBS, 15 November 1938, WC64 (UIUC). According to Heyer, the contract concluded between CBS and Wells placed no restrictions on how the work should be adapted for radio: Heyer, 'America under attack', p. 161.

50. 'Mr Wells "deeply concerned"', *The Manchester Guardian*, 1 November 1938; 'FCC to scan script of "War" Broadcast', *New York Times*, 1 November 1938.

51. Mrs G. P. Wells to Kathryn Campbell, *CBS*, 15 November 1938, WC64 (UIUC).

Perhaps also, given his increasing tendency to interpret the early scientific romances less as creative imaginative works but more as having a message, Wells was angered by the way in which Orson Welles had transformed what he regarded as a serious political allegory into a spoof Halloween broadcast. Moreover, it is probable that Wells feared that many listeners might have been confused into thinking that Orson Welles, whose surname was pronounced in the same way as Wells, had actually written the novel, so that the radio drama accurately reproduced the original story. 'Deeply concerned' about being drawn into the resulting media storm, he demanded a retraction.[52] Reportedly, Wells received an apology and compensation from CBS.[53]

Notwithstanding such expressions of concern, the episode brought Wells and his story global visibility adjudged likely to boost his name and sales of *The War of the Worlds,* in not only the USA, but also across the world. Massive public interest in the controversy resulted in the appearance of new editions of *The War of the Worlds* in the USA, among other countries. Thus, in 1939 Grosset & Dunlap, a New York-based publisher, re-issued 'The book that terrified the nation over the Air!', with a cover reproducing press headlines about the alleged panic caused by the broadcast. Dell Publishing, based also in New York, published a 48-page edition specifically acknowledging that – to quote from the book's cover – 'When they told it on the radio … it terrified the whole country' (Figure 12.1).[54]

In Autumn 1940, that is prior to the USA's entry into the ongoing Second World War, Wells undertook what proved his final speaking tour of the USA. During the course of his visit he met Orson Welles, who was just finalizing the film *Citizen Kane,* when they were interviewed together by KTSA Radio at San Antonio, Texas. In the event, Wells expressed no resentment about the liberties taken with his book in the radio broadcast produced by 'my little namesake', who – to quote Wells – 'carries my name with an extra "e"'.[55] On the contrary, as recorded by Orson Welles's biographer, 'they shared a good chortle over *The War of the Worlds* broadcast'.[56] Even so, Wells used the occasion to express scepticism about the uproar claimed for the radio broadcast: 'Are you sure there was such a panic in America?' Wells argued that, 'You aren't quite serious in America yet.

52. 'Mr Wells "deeply concerned"', *The Manchester Guardian*, 1 November 1938.

53. Hughes, 'The War of the Worlds', p. 244; Smith, *Wells*, p. 76.

54. Later, Orson Welles claimed that the episode created a personal interest in sci-fi: Orson Welles, 'Can a Martian help it if he's colored green?', in Orson Welles (ed.), *Invasion From Mars: Interplanetary Stories, Selected by Orson Welles* (New York: Dell, 1949), pp. 5–7.

55. 'H. G. Wells meets Orson Welles', KTSA Radio, San Antonio, 28 October 1940, *The Mercury Theatre on the Air,* http://www.mercurytheatre.info/ [accessed 19 February 2012]; John S. Partington, 'Review of John Gosling's *Waging the War of the Worlds*', *Kritikon Litterarum* 37 (2010): 271–2; Callow, *Orson Welles, 1*, pp. 520–1; Gosling, *Waging the War of the Worlds*, pp. 95–6. Reportedly, during the late nineteenth century, Orson Welles's father, Richard, added an 'e' to his surname, to emphasize 'his independence' of his family: Callow, *Orson Welles, 1*, p. 6.

56. Callow, *Orson Wells, 2*, p. 48.

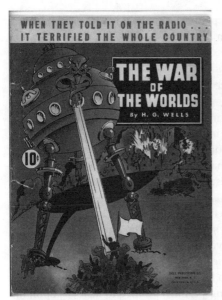
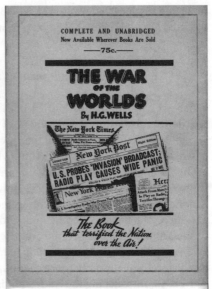

Figure 12.1 Dell's 1938 edition of *The War of the Worlds*. Dell uses the controversy generated by Orson Welles's 1938 radio broadcast to publish and promote a new edition of *The War of the Worlds*.

Source: H.G. Wells, *The War of the Worlds* (NY: Dell, 1938).

You haven't got the war under your chins and in consequence you can still play with ideas of terror and conflict'. Responding to Wells's efforts to downplay the radio drama's contemporary impact, Orson Welles expressed pleasure in pointing to the attention the programme attracted within and outside the USA, even claiming that 'Hitler made a good deal of sport of it' in a speech at Munich. For Gosling, this claim was more a case of Orson Welles, 'the great showman' injecting 'a colorful embellishment into the story' and working the mythology already beginning to surround the programme, a trend accentuated by the publication in April 1940 of Cantril's study thereof.[57]

As demonstrated by his appearance on BBC television in 1955, Orson Welles proved instrumental in upholding the version of events offered by the American media, about the way in which his CBS broadcast terrorized large numbers of people across the nation. Appreciating the fact that the episode transformed both his career and image, Orson Welles continued to exploit his persona as the man who scared America, just as audiences, like the media, came to identify him closely with *The War of the Worlds* and to use it as a reference point for his work.[58] For Orson Welles, the meeting at San Antonio represented a case of 'a man from England' meeting 'the man from Mars'.[59] Typically, one publication, when

57. Gosling, *Waging the War of the Worlds*, p. 96.
58. Callow, *Orson Welles, 1*, pp. 408–9. Callow, *Orson Welles, 2*, p. 158.
59. 'H. G. Wells meets Orson Welles'.

reporting his speech delivered at a 1943 political rally held in Upper Manhattan, depicted Orson Welles as 'The Man from Mars'.[60]

Upholding and enhancing the narrative of terror and fear

When seeking authentication for both images of mass panic and hysteria and anecdotes concerning the reactions of individual Americans to his broadcast, Orson Welles cited the academic study conducted by Hadley Cantril, a researcher based at Princeton University.[61] Thus, what was already a very good story written up in the media was increasingly represented as receiving academic validation from a member of an Ivy League university. For the man and women in the American street, therefore there seemed no reason to challenge the original narrative, which gained momentum and strength over time through repetition in comics, film, newspapers, radio and television.

The Invasion from Mars: A study in the psychology of panic, a report produced by a Princeton University research group led by Hadley Cantril, was published in April 1940. Introducing the study's findings, Cantril pointed to its focus upon the psychological causes for the 'widespread panic' occasioned by the broadcast: 'On the evening of October 30, 1938, thousands of Americans became panic-stricken by a broadcast purported to describe an invasion of Martians which threatened our whole civilization. Probably never before have so many people in all walks of life and in all parts of the country become so suddenly and so intensely disturbed as they did on this night.'[62] In brief, the research priority was to investigate why people panicked – 'to discover the causal factors for panic behavior' and 'why did they [people] become so hysterical' – not to question whether or not the panic and hysteria reported by the media actually occurred.[63]

As reaffirmed by its introductory section, Cantril's report assumed uncritically that the programme caused mass panic and hysteria: 'This broadcast ... created the panic'.[64] The report was used to reinforce this assertion:

> Much to their surprise the actors learned that the series of news bulletins they had issued describing an invasion from Mars had been believed by thousands of people throughout the country. For a few horrible hours people from Maine to California thought that hideous monsters armed with death rays were destroying all armed resistance sent against them; that there was simply no escape from disaster; that the end of the world was near. Newspapers the

60. 'Plain talk by the Man from Mars', *Trade Union Press*, n.d. [1943], quoted Callow, *Orson Welles, 2*, pp. 176–7. Paul Robeson was a fellow speaker.

61. 'Orson Welles' Sketchbook'.

62. Cantril, *Invasion from Mars*, p. ix.

63. Ibid., pp. 189, 197.

64. Ibid., p. 44.

following morning spoke of the "tidal wave of terror that swept the nation". It was clear that a panic of national proportions had occurred …

Long before the broadcast had ended, people all over the United States were praying, crying, fleeing frantically to escape death from the Martians. Some ran to rescue loved ones. Others telephoned farewells or warnings, hurried to inform neighbors, sought information from newspapers or radio stations, summoned ambulances and police cars. At least six million people heard the broadcast. *At least a million of them were frightened or disturbed* [author's italics].

For weeks after the broadcast, newspapers carried human-interest stories relating the shock and terror of local citizens.[65]

Supporting evidence, comprising material yielded by 135 interviews conducted with named individuals, correspondence, questionnaires and newspaper clippings, reinforced the impression of 'shock and terror' of large numbers of Americans.[66] However, the report conceded that not all listeners panicked: 'Several listeners soon related the story to H. G. Wells. A few had read *War of the Worlds*.'[67] But only a few people, it appeared, recognized that the radio broadcast was the Mercury Theatre's dramatization of his text, not a news report of an alien invasion:

I turned the radio on to get Orson Welles, but the announcement that a meteor had fallen sounded so much like the usual news announcements that I never dreamt it was [Orson] Welles. I thought my clock was probably fast … When the machine started to come apart *I couldn't imagine what it was,* but when the queer forms began to come out it *flashed over me suddenly* that this was the Orson Welles program, and I remembered that it was called *The War of the Worlds*.[68]

Nor did Cantril's position change over time. Writing the preface for a 1966 reprint of his original book – in part, the need for a reprint reflected its widespread use as a student textbook – Cantril reaffirmed his fundamental conclusion that 'at least a million Americans became frightened and thousands were panic-stricken'.[69] Foregrounding narratives of terror and fear, Cantril's publication gave academic credibility to the press headlines of October 1938, thereby giving them added substance in the public mind and popular culture. For Orson Welles and the media, Cantril's book, including his Princeton affiliation, was readily cited by way of legitimizing the storyline, particularly responding to sceptics.

65. Ibid., pp. 3, 47, 57–63, 189–206.
66. Ibid., pp. 47–55.
67. Ibid., p. 89.
68. Ibid., p. 89.
69. Ibid., p. vi.

Orson Welles's legacy

Commenting upon Cantril's report, Jefferson Pooley and Michael Socolow observed:

> His scholarly book validated the popular memory of the event. He gave academic credence to the panic and attached real numbers to it. He remains the only source with academic legitimacy who claims there was a sizeable panic. Without this validation, the myth likely would not be in social psychology and mass communication textbooks, as it still is today … Though you may have never heard of Cantril, the War of the Worlds myth is very much his legacy.[70]

Notwithstanding the challenge provided by the rise of television and an ever-expanding multimedia world, Orson Welles's 1938 radio broadcast has retained its place in the popular consciousness, especially in the USA. Images linking Orson Welles's 'The War of the Worlds' with mass panic and hysteria, have continued to feature in the media, the minds of the general public and academia, by way of not only marking the programme's perceived significance but also underpinning the narratives of terror and fear articulated repeatedly by Cantril and Orson Welles.

Selected examples include:

- the incorporation of the 1938 programme into the narrative of mainstream comics – these included *Batman* (issue no. 1 : 1 April 1940), *Superman* (issue 62: January–February 1950), and *Superman: War of the Worlds* (October 1998) – and comic books, like *Secret Origins* (issue 5: 5 August 1986).[71]
  It remains uncertain whether or not coverage in the *Batman* comic was influenced by Cantril's study – the book, also published in April 1940, was mentioned frequently in the press prior to publication – but this example shows how the story was gaining substance upon the part of a wider audience from an early stage;
- the occasional broadcasting of repeats of the original programme or radio programmes based thereupon, particularly to mark anniversaries, as evidenced in 1988 by David Ossman's fiftieth anniversary production, starring Jason Robards, re-creating the 1938 drama for National Public Radio (now NPR). In 2013 the programme's seventy-fifth anniversary saw several remakes adapted to suit a radio station's target audience such as in Sydney, Australia (2SER) and Montana, USA (Montana Public Radio). Worthy of note is the LA TheaterWorks production starring Leonard Nimoy, *Star Trek's*

---

70. Jefferson Pooley and Michael Socolow, 'The myth of the War of the Worlds panic', Slate, 28 October 2013, http://www.slate.com/articles/arts/history/2013/10/orson_welles_war_of_the_worlds_panic_myth_the_infamous_radio_broadcast_did.single.html [accessed 12 February 2014].

71. See Chapter 10, pp. 188–90. John Gosling's three-part study of comics based on *The War of the Worlds* beginning, at http://www.war-ofthe-worlds.co.uk/comics_mars_1.htm [accessed 14 June 2014]; Gosling, *Waging the War of the Worlds*, pp. 169–74, 226–7.

Mr Spock, performed live in 1994 for broadcasting by KCRW, a radio station based at Santa Monica, California;

- the subject of television dramatic re-enactments – these included 'The Night America Trembled' (9 September 1957) and 'The Night That Panicked America' (31 October 1975) – and documentaries, such as 'Martian Mania: the true story of the *War of the Worlds*' (30 October 1998) and 'American Experience: War of the Worlds': PBS (29 October 2013);

- references in movie films, such as serving as the focus for one vignette in Woody Allen's *Radio Days* (1987), a film paying homage to radio's golden age. Orson Welles's programme featured also in *Spaced Invaders* (1990), a comedy in which a crew of Martians heard a repeat of the original broadcast and joined what they thought was an actual Martian invasion of earth;[72] and

- the central focus for academic studies published across the disciplinary range, including history, literature, media studies, politics, psychology and sociology.

Recently, perhaps, the most influential links have arisen from the way in which Orson Welles and the 1938 broadcast have been incorporated into such iconic programmes as 'Doctor Who: Invaders from Mars' (January 2002; BBC Radio Four, 24 September 2007), 'The X-Files' (5 January 1996) and 'The Simpsons' (5 November 2006). The *Doctor Who* reference highlights the manner in which the episode has proved the focus of numerous British radio and television programmes. Many were American-produced outputs – these include the original radio broadcast (27 October 1992) and documentaries, like *The Night That Panicked America* (23 December 1975) and *American Experience: War of the Worlds* (29 October 2013), as well as dramatizations like *Worldplay* (the 1994 LA Theater Works play: 27 February 2005). But some were original BBC productions, including *Orson Welles Sketchbook* (21 May 1955), *We Interrupt this Programme ...* (30 October 1988) and *Days that Shook the World* (3 November 2005).

These examples, albeit diverse in nature, acknowledge the extraordinary power radio exerted over listeners and their imaginations during the 1930s. Within this context, Orson Welles's 'The War of the Worlds' offered perhaps the most vivid example illustrating this point. Indeed, during the early 1960s Marshall McLuhan's use of the broadcast in *Understanding Media* (1964) to explore the conventions and resonating power of radio, cemented the broadcast's place in the history of mass communications: 'The famous Orson Welles broadcast about the invasion from Mars was a simple demonstration of the all-inclusive, completely involving scope of the auditory image of radio.'[73]

When responding to questions at his post-broadcast press conference, Orson Welles reminded those present that 'Radio is new and we are still learning about the effect it has on people.'[74] Moreover, when looking back from 1955, Orson

72. Gosling, *Waging the War of the Worlds*, pp. 177, 226; Flynn, *War of the Worlds*, p. 143.

73. McLuhan, *Understanding Media*, pp. 299–300.

74. 'The aftermath: Orson Welles "The War of the Worlds" Halloween press conference'.

Welles claimed that the 'Martian broadcast' was not as 'innocent' as represented by him at the time, given his alleged desire to educate Americans to the power of the 'new magic box' found in a large proportion of their homes:

> We were fed up with the way in which everything that came over this new magic box, the radio, was being swallowed ... was believed. So in a way our broadcast was an assault on the credibility of that machine; we wanted people to understand that they shouldn't take any opinion pre-digested, and they shouldn't swallow everything that came through the tap, whether it was radio or not.[75]

Radio audiences were large and still growing during the late 1930s, but relatively inexperienced regarding the mass media in general, insufficiently sceptical and frequently unclear about the boundaries between fact and fiction. Indeed, at the time some newspapers criticized radio listeners for their gullibility; thus, the *Chicago Tribune* went as far as to claim that many radio listeners were not 'very bright', even 'a trifle retarded mentally'.[76] Writing in the *New York Herald Tribune*, Dorothy Thompson argued that Orson Welles's broadcast exposed both the powers and dangers of radio as a new medium, including the susceptibility of listeners to 'popular and theatrical demagoguery' in troubled times.[77] In particular, the programme established the ability of radio drama to play on contemporary fears and insecurities.[78]

Was the resulting panic merely 'a media-driven myth'?

Today, the Orson Welles/Cantril line still occupies centre stage as regards perceptions of the 1938 broadcast. But there is an alternative revisionist view dismissing the whole episode as no more than – to quote W. Joseph Campbell – 'a tenacious media-driven myth'.[79] During recent decades, a growing number of commentators – they include Robert Bartholomew, W. Joseph Campbell, Edward Epstein, Jefferson Pooley and Michael Socolow – have conceded the programme's qualities

---

75. 'Orson Welles' Sketchbook'. Cantril claimed that 27.5 million families out of a total of 32 million possessed radios: Cantril, *Invasion from Mars*, p. xii.

76. Quoted, Campbell, *Getting it Wrong*, p. 42.

77. Thompson, 'On the Record'.

78. Cantril, *Invasion from Mars*, pp. 153–64, 195; N. and J. Mackenzie, *The Time Traveller*, pp. 411–12.

79. W. Joseph Campbell, 'Media Myth Alert', 29 October 2013, http://mediamythalert. wordpress.com/2013/10/29/pbs-squanders-opportunity-to-offer-content-that-educates-in-war-of-the-worlds-doc/ [accessed 15 February 2014]; Campbell, *Getting it Wrong*, p. 28; Parrinder, 'How far can we trust the narrator?', p. 15.

as radio drama and public entertainment. but downplayed reports concerning the broadcast's alleged role in causing mass panic and hysteria.[80]

For Edward Epstein, 'The program itself of course was a fiction. So was the "Mass Hysteria", which became part of American folklore about the power of the media.'[81] Confronting the sweeping claims made by the front page headlines of newspapers published on 31 October 1938, Campbell pointed to the anecdotal and poorly researched wire service summaries used to support press reports, particularly given the limited amount of time between the *CBS* broadcast and the moment when the morning newspapers went to press:

> The panic and mass hysteria so readily associated with the *War of the Worlds* program did not occur on anything approaching a nationwide dimension. The program did frighten some Americans, and some others reacted in less than rational ways. But most listeners, overwhelmingly, were neither frightened nor unnerved. They recognized the program for what it was – an imaginative and entertaining show on the night before Halloween.[82]

Pooley and Socolow echoed Campbell's thesis: 'The supposed panic was so tiny as to be practically immeasurable on the night of the broadcast. Despite repeated assertions to the contrary … almost nobody was fooled by Welles' broadcast'.[83]

Campbell pointed to the way in which one reader of the *Washington Post* challenged the image represented by the newspaper of widespread mayhem in the nation's capital. On 31 October 1938, the line taken by *The Washington Post* typified that taken by the American media as a whole when reporting that:

> Federal, State and municipal officials were hard put to it calming frightened thousands. At police headquarters here, in every precinct, in offices of the Park Police, morning newspapers and Station WSJV [the local radio station carrying the Mercury Theatre's play], switchboards blazed with insistent lights. Terrified, tearful voices asked, "What's it all about? Is it safe to stay here? Have they called

---

80. Robert E. Bartholomew, *Little Green Men, Meowing Nuns and Head-Hunting Panics: A Study of Mass Psychogenic Illness and Social Delusion* (Jefferson, NC: McFarland, 2001), pp. 217–19; Bartholomew and Radford, *The Martians Have Landed!*, pp. 16–22; Michael J. Socolow, 'The hyped panic over "War of the Worlds"', *Chronicle of Higher Education* 55 (9) (24 October 2008): B16–17; Campbell, *Getting it Wrong*, p. 28; Edward Jay Epstein, *Fictoid 7*, 'Mass Hysteria Over Martian Invasion', n.d. [2012], http://www.edwardjayepstein.com/nether_fictoid7.htm [accessed 15 February 2014]; Gosling, *Waging the War of the Worlds*, pp. 56–67; Pooley and Socolow, 'The myth of the war of the Worlds panic'.

81. Epstein, *Fictoid 7*.

82. Campbell, *Getting it Wrong*, pp. 26, 34–6.

83. Pooley and Socolow, 'The myth of the war of the Worlds panic'.

the Army, the Navy, the Marines?" ... For an hour hysterical pandemonium gripped the Nation's Capital and the Nation itself.[84]

For one reader, this seemed 'a totally false impression', a complete misrepresentation, of the actual situation.[85] During the broadcast, when walking down F Street, one of downtown Washington's main thoroughfares, he noticed 'nothing approximating mass hysteria': 'In many stores radios were going, yet I observed nothing whatsoever of the absurd supposed "terror of the populace". There was none.'

Sloppy and sensationalist news reporting, revisionists argue, resulted in a 'misleading historical narrative', based upon what was no more than a media-produced myth.[86] Moreover, the American press welcomed the opportunity to highlight the shortcomings of an up-and-coming media rival in the sphere of news, entertainment and advertising, albeit in a manner exposing inadvertently its own failings in respect of insufficient checking of wire reports and publishing false or improbable reports masquerading as fact based upon informed journalism. 'Terror by Radio', a critical editorial in the *New York Times*, reproached 'radio officials' for approving the interleaving of 'blood-curdling fiction' with news flashes 'offered in exactly the manner that real news would have been given'.[87] *Editor and Publisher*, the newspaper industry's trade journal, took advantage of the controversy to warn Americans about radio's shortcomings when reporting the news: 'The nation as a whole continues to face the danger of incomplete, misunderstood news over a medium which has yet to prove ... that it is competent to perform the news job.'[88]

Conclusion

In October 1988 Grover's Mill, New Jersey, marked the 50th anniversary of its brief moment of fame when it took centre stage in Orson Welles's radio drama based upon Wells's *The War of the Worlds*. A series of heritage events, including a 'panic run', culminated in the dedication of a memorial commemorating the original broadcast. Howard Koch, the programme's scriptwriter, was among those present in Van Nest Park to witness the unveiling ceremony. Depicting images

84. Marshall Andrews, 'Monsters of Mars on a Meteor Stampede Radiotic America', *The Washington Post*, 31 October 1938, quoted Jones, 'Washingtonians react to the *War of the Worlds*'.

85. A. McK. Griggs to editor, 3 November 1938, quoted Campbell, *Getting it Wrong*, p. 34; Pooley and Socolow, 'The myth of the war of the Worlds panic'.

86. Campbell, *Getting it Wrong*, p. 44. For a concise critique of Cantril's report, including its sources and methodology, see Pooley and Socolow, 'The myth of the War of the Worlds panic'.

87. 'Terror by Radio', *New York Times*, 1 November 1938.

88. Quoted, Pooley and Socolow, 'The myth of the War of the Worlds panic'.

of Orson Welles speaking into a microphone, a family listening in terror by their radio and a Martian tripod, the memorial carries a dedication following the line mapped out by Orson Welles and Cantril about the programme's impact:

> On the evening of October 30, 1938, Orson Welles and the Mercury Theatre presented a dramatization of H. G. Wells' *The War of the Worlds* as adapted by Howard Koch. This was to become a landmark in broadcast history, provoking continuous thought about media responsibility, social psychology and civil defense. For a brief time as many as one million people throughout the country believed that Martians had invaded the earth, beginning with Grover's Mill, New Jersey.[89]

Orson Welles's 1938 Martian broadcast made, and continues to make, a good story. Indeed, few radio programmes have inspired so much enduring interest, fascination, study and controversy. Apart from representing a significant chapter in media history, the radio drama remains a significant part of popular culture exerting wide-ranging impacts across the media and beyond. Moreover, as acknowledged in the dedication of the Grover's Mill memorial, the episode raised important questions about the media and society, particularly concerning the power of the media, the quality of news reporting, and the nature and response of audiences.

Whereas Wells's serialized and book versions of *The War of the Worlds* left much to readers' imaginations, Orson Welles's broadcast exploited radio's role as a theatre of the imagination by using smoke and mirrors to make fantastic fiction appear as terrifying fact to listeners living through anxious times. Building in part upon Wells's original reportage approach, the clever reworking of the narrative into an eye witness news reporting format gave new life and portability to his original creation: 'the effect of this, coming over CBS, a radio network on whose authenticity the public relied, was far more immediate and convincing than anything Wells himself had been able to achieve with a book'.[90]

Since 1938, Orson Welles's radio drama has played a major role in giving continuing visibility to Wells in general and *The War of the Worlds* in particular, while providing illuminating insights into the way in which his writings 'touched upon latent apocalyptic fears', as well as into popular psychology.[91] In turn, the continuing academic, media and popular focus upon the programme, including the radio adaptations based upon Orson Welles's template produced in other countries and discussed in the next chapter, has proved instrumental in prompting new generations across the world to access Wells's writings, by reading the book

89. Gosling, *Waging the War of the Worlds*, p. 167; Historical Marker Project: Martian Landing Site, n.d., http://www.historicalmarkerproject.com/markers/HM1764_martian-landing-site_West-Windsor-Township-NJ.html [accessed 12 May 2015].

90. N. and J. MacKenzie, *The Time Traveller*, p. 411; Self, 'Death on three legs'.

91. N. and J. MacKenzie, *The Time Traveller*, pp. 411–12; Cantril, *Invasion from Mars*, pp. ix–x.

upon which its script was based. Likewise, at the time publishers sought to take advantage of the controversy to market new editions of the book whose radio adaptation terrified the nation.

Even so, Orson Welles's Mercury Theatre drama has always remained centre stage, while retaining a perceived contemporary resonance, as highlighted by the way in which it continues to be referenced by the media and academic research. By often appearing to attract far more present-day attention than Wells's original text, Orson Welles's radio programme has seemed to have become the bigger story, possessing a life of its own. Indeed, the high visibility secured by the 1938 broadcast, in conjunction with the similarity of their surnames, has encouraged some people to treat Orson Welles as the person responsible for the original storyline, as suggested by a 1971 *New York Times*'s report headlined, 'Welles's "War of the Worlds" still stirs consternation', or the occasional use of 'H. G. Welles'.[92]

The traditional Orson Welles/Cantril narrative stressing mass panic and hysteria, has endured through the 1938 broadcast being frequently repeated, restaged on radio, or retold in print, on film, stage, television and online, particularly by those attracted by a highly engaging storyline, anxious to highlight examples of media power and influence, or celebrating the programme's anniversaries. As noted by Pooley and Socolow, 'the apocryphal apocalypse only grew in the retelling'.[93] Certainly, this line continues to exert a strong hold over the lay audience, if only through repetition in the media, the widespread availability of the 1938 broadcast and script and the frequency of academic studies thereof. Despite claiming to expose the mythologies surrounding the 1938 broadcast, revisionist accounts have experienced a tough time dislodging the hold of traditional narratives foregrounding popular fear and terror, especially as such perceptions have become deeply embedded in the national memory, media history and images of Orson Welles as – to reproduce a quote used on the billboard for a new play in which he was appearing in 1939 – 'the Man who scared the world'.[94] As he admitted in his typically modest manner', I'd suddenly become a sort of ... national event.'[95] In fact, it would be more accurate to say that Orson Welles had become a global celebrity, a central figure in *an international event*.

Account needs to be taken also of the usual difficulty encountered by revisionist histories in challenging popular mythologies and the fact that the priority for the media when targeting a popular audience, is to avoid appearing like a university seminar preoccupied with historical controversies and uncertainties, but rather to entertain through a clear and engaging storyline.[96] Typically, in October 2013,

---

92. 'Welles's "War of the Worlds" still stirs consternation', *New York Times*, 1 November 1971; 'The aftermath: Orson Welles "The War of the Worlds" Halloween press conference'.

93. Pooley and Socolow, 'The myth of the War of the Worlds panic'.

94. Quoted, Gosling, *Waging the War of the Worlds*, p. 94; Jeffrey Sconce, *Haunted Media: Electronic Presence from Telegraphy to Television* (Durham, NC: Duke University Press, 2000), p. 110.

95. 'Orson Welles' Sketchbook'.

96. Beck, *Presenting History*, pp. 30–9, 103–20. For example, a recent book by Alan

'American Experience: War of the Worlds', a Public Broadcasting Service (PBS) television documentary marking the broadcast's 75th anniversary, did little to undermine the narrative created by the American media in October 1938 and propagated subsequently by Orson Welles and Cantril, among others. Thus, it reminded viewers on both sides of the Atlantic about the major impacts exerted by the programme across the USA: 'Never before had a radio broadcast provoked such outrage, or such chaos. Upwards of a million people [were] convinced, if only briefly, that the United States was being laid waste by alien invaders, and a nation left to wonder how they possibly could have been so gullible.'[97] Images showing the next day's newspaper front-page headlines from across the country, portrayed the USA as a terrified and scared nation, reinforcing claims made in the commentary's introductory sentences. Following closely the framework defined by Cantril's 1940 study, the documentary then provided viewers with an account of the resulting mayhem, using actors to re-create the reactions of individual Americans.

Reportedly, Socolow, among others, had been contacted by the production team when preparing the programme, but the actual documentary did very little to apprise viewers of current scholarship.[98] Thus, a summary of the revisionist case was confined to a brief phrase – this read 'Ultimately the very extent of the panic would come to be seen as having been exaggerated by the press' – relegated to the end of a programme pushing throughout the impression of mass panic and hysteria.[99] No effort was made to indicate how recent academic research has increasingly questioned both the authenticity of the story and the quality of the supporting evidence.[100] For Campbell, *PBS* had squandered the opportunity to re-tell more accurately an infamous and repeatedly cited story.[101] Clearly the traditional narrative, albeit increasingly dismissed within academia as mythical, was deemed to provide a stronger and more engaging storyline for a television documentary than the more nuanced findings of revisionists stressing that the press was not reporting accurately what was happening, or rather not happening, across the USA on the evening of 30 October 1938.

Writing in 1998 at the time of the 60th anniversary of Orson Welles's dramatization, Bartholomew complained that 'for the better part of the past sixty years, many people may have been misled by the media to believe that the panic was

Gallop, though highly informative, ignores revisionist studies: Gallop, *The Martians are Coming!*

97. 'American Experience: War of the Worlds', *PBS*, 29 October 2013. The documentary was shown in both the UK and the USA on this date.

98. Pooley and Socolow, 'The myth of the War of the Worlds panic'.

99. The somewhat unbalanced nature of the programme was foregrounded by Richard Getler, whose critique written as *PBS*'s *Ombudsman* prompted a response from the show's producer: Richard Getler, 'War of Words', *PBS Ombudsman*, 31 October 2013, http://www.pbs.org/ombudsman/2013/10/war_of_the_words.html [accessed 13 February 2014].

100. Campbell, *Getting it Wrong*, pp. 26–44.

101. Campbell, 'Media Myth Alert'.

far more extensive and intense than it apparently was.'[102] Fifteen years on, the media was still doing the same thing. Today, there appears an unbridgeable divide between academic and lay perceptions regarding the Orson Welles's broadcast, but clearly the popular image thereof is deeply ingrained, indeed the myth has grown exponentially over the years and unfortunately revisionists seem engaged in a losing battle, if they think they are capable of changing it.

In 2013 a diverse range of newspaper and magazine articles, radio and television programmes and so on marking the 75th anniversary of Orson Welles's broadcast, reflected its perceived historical significance and iconic cultural status, even during a period when film, music and television, not radio, proved the principal formats through which present-day audiences access Wells's original storyline. Orson Welles's radio adaptation of Wells's novel, represented a defining event in the social history of *The War of the Worlds*. Over time, the radio programme has become a central part of society's cultural inventory, helping to illuminate the power of the media, most notably the challenge provided by new media formats. For Malmsheimer, it constitutes also an invaluable reference point for evaluating the impact of exaggerated and irrational scares: 'The broadcast is a well-known prototype which provides a projection of the consequences of responding to mass media in an insufficiently skeptical way. Moreover, it alludes to the problems which arise when individuals allow the collapse of ordinarily maintained boundaries between fiction and actuality.'[103]

102. Robert Bartholomew, 'The Martian Panic Sixty Years Later: What Have We Learned?', *Skeptical Inquirer* 22 (6) (1998), http://www.csicop.org/si/show/the_martian_panic_sixty_years_later_what_have_we_learned [accessed 15 February 2014].

103. Malmsheimer, 'Three Mile Island', p. 47; Campbell, *Getting it Wrong*, p. 43.

Chapter 13

'THOSE MEN FROM MARS' INVADE THE AMERICAS AND EUROPE AGAIN AND AGAIN AFTER 1938: THE POWER OF RADIO DRAMA

The enduring focus upon Orson Welles's 1938 radio drama proves in part a function of the fact that succeeding decades saw, or so it is alleged, similar panics elsewhere triggered by radio programmes dramatizing Wells's *The War of the Worlds* according to Orson Welles's template. In turn, these examples testify to the effectiveness of such a format for producing engaging radio drama as well as to the power exerted by radio over audiences in other parts of the world. As *Newsweek* commented in 1944, when reporting one such panic in Chile triggered by 'Those Men from Mars', 'Evidently radio's hold over the Latin American imagination is strong too'.[1]

Over time, the growing popularity of the cinema and the rise of television increasingly bypassed radio. Even so, during the 1940s and succeeding decades, drama programmes remained a staple part of the output of radio broadcasters and continued to attract audiences around the world. For some broadcasters, Orson Welles's 1938 recording proved a source of inspiration, most notably providing a programme template capable of the scriptural adaptations required to harmonize with the needs of audiences listening in different countries and time periods. As a result, radio dramas based upon 'The War of the Worlds' set in such countries as Brazil, Chile, Ecuador and Portugal, occasioned, it is reported, hysteria and panics similar to those occurring across the USA in October 1938. Moreover, the Martians returned repeatedly to the USA, especially to Buffalo and Providence, at least on people's radios. Generally speaking, such episodes, though acknowledging Wells as the author of the original book, tended to do far more for the global visibility of Orson Welles *vis à vis The War of the Worlds*.

The Martians land in Latin America

Reportedly, two South American radio programmes, based largely on Orson Welles's adaptation of Wells's book but set locally in the present-day, provoked

1. 'Those Men from Mars', *Newsweek*, 27 November 1944, p. 89.

even worse panics than that represented as occurring in the USA in 1938. Both programmes drew heavily also upon the techniques employed by Orson Welles to enhance their dramatic impact; thus, the use of the local topography was reinforced by their reliance upon faux news reporting. Notwithstanding warnings delivered both during and at the end of the programmes about their imaginative and fantastic nature, panics caused by radio dramas in which the Martians attacked Santiago in Chile and then Quito in Ecuador in 1944 and 1949 respectively, involved loss of life and prompted the inevitable post-mortems and controversies.[2] Similar difficulties were reported following a 1971 radio broadcast in Brazil featuring a Martian advance upon Rio de Janeiro.[3]

On 12 November 1944 Chile's *Radio Cooperativa Vitalicia* broadcast a programme in which the Martians were described as landing at Puente Alto, a town some fifteen miles from Santiago, before advancing upon the capital.[4] Reportedly, the fictional panic depicted on the radio was replicated on the streets of Chile's towns and villages. According to one newspaper, *La Opinión*, in Santiago people were 'petrified': 'The alarm was indescribable. People had flooded the streets.'[5] One resident of Valparaiso is alleged to have died from a heart attack.

Less than five years later, the Martians returned to South America. This time their target was Quito in Ecuador, a country featured in Wells's short story 'The Country of the Blind', published in *The Strand Magazine* in April 1904.[6] Replicating Orson Welles's *War of the Worlds* template, on 12 February 1949 a *Radio Quito* announcer interrupted a music programme to report 'urgent news', being the landing of the Martians at Cotocollao, the capture of the military airbase at Mariscal Sucre and their advance towards the capital Quito.[7] The resulting panic was considerable, given the lack of any prior warning about the fictional nature of the programme. No warning was delivered to listeners, until both the programme and the Martian invasion were already in progress. In Quito, the mood of the crowd turned from panic to anger when it became clear that the capital was not under actual threat. People began to attack and torch the building shared by the

2. Ibid., p. 89; '"Mars Raiders" caused Quito panic: Mob burns Radio Plant, kills 15', *New York Times*, 14 February 1949, p. 7; '"Invasion from Mars"', *The Times*, 14 February 1949, p. 4; '"Martian invasion" panics a city', *Daily Mail*, 14 February 1949, p. 1; Bartholomew, *The Martians Have Landed!*, pp. 23–6. These examples, though mentioned in press reports and regularly cited in the literature, still lack in-depth research testing the validity of reported events and reactions.

3. Gosling, *Waging the War of the Worlds*, pp. 143–8.

4. Ibid., pp. 99–102; Diego Zúñiga, 'Guerra de los Mundos: los marcianos también invadieron Sudamérica', *Pensar* 2 (4) (2005): 8–9.

5. Zúñiga, 'Guerra de los Mundos', p. 9.

6. For Michael Draper (aka Michael Sherborne), the events in Ecuador during 1949 showed the 'prophetic aptness' of Wells's story: Michael Draper, 'The Martians in Ecuador', *The Wellsian* 5 (1982): 36.

7. For extracts of the broadcast, see 'Quito panic after broadcast: 15 deaths in riots', *The Times*, 15 February 1949, p. 4.

radio station with *El Comercio*, Ecuador's leading newspaper and owner of *Radio Quito*. Press reports indicated at least six, but possibly as many as twenty deaths.[8]

Given the somewhat fragmentary nature of the evidence available upon events, the report sent by the British Legation in Quito to the Foreign Office in London is worth quoting, especially as the Foreign Office immediately linked the report with 'a similar fiasco' caused by 'a similar broadcast' in the USA:

> Incredible, though it may seem, Radio Quito chose to broadcast, without previous warning, the Orson Welles version of "The War of the Worlds" which caused some trouble in the United States a few years ago. Though there was some sort of preamble from which the astute might gather that what was to follow was part of the programme, the thing was so presented – in the form of emergency announcements between recordings of local music – that almost all listeners were deluded. Place-names were changed to those of places in the outskirts of Quito, and within a few minutes a large section of the population, especially in a suburb called Cotocallao (*sic*) (which was said to be immediately threatened by a death-dealing cloud) was in a state of acute panic.
>
> Several thousand people attempted to evade the Martian invasion by climbing the local mountain, Pichincha; presumably, as they had no way of hearing that the news was false, they stayed there all night. Others, however, rushed into town. When the truth filtered through, panic turned to rage, and a crowd rushed to attack the studio. Deliberately or otherwise, the building was set alight, and as the town's telephone operators had joined the mountain-climbers, the Fire Brigade arrived too late to be useful. Several lives were lost.[9]

The legation reported also that *El Comercio*, described as 'Quito's leading newspaper (and the only legible one)', had 'for some days previously been publishing obviously invented stories of flying saucers over Ecuador'. Claiming that 'we have hardly met any Ecuadorean who did not hear the programme', the British legation indicated that the Ecuadorian government was contemplating stricter controls over radio programming. Apparently the fire and the resulting destruction of the building housing both *El Comercio* and *Radio Quito*'s studios

8. Gosling, *Waging the War of the Worlds*, pp. 107–8; Zúñiga, 'Guerra de los Mundos', pp. 9–11; 'Mars Raiders caused Quito panic', p. 7; '20 Dead in the Quito Riot: 15 held for "Martian Invasion" radio show and panic', *New York Times*, 15 February 1949, p. 4; 'Quito panic after broadcast: 15 deaths in riots', *The Times*, 15 February 1949, p. 4.

9. British Legation, Quito, to the Foreign Office, 18 February 1949, Foreign Office Minute, 17 March 1949, FO371/74712/AS1502, British government records: Foreign Office (FO), The National Archives, Kew, London (TNA); Gosling, *Waging the War of the Worlds*, pp. 103–13; Draper, 'The Martians in Ecuador', pp. 35–6; 'Quito panic after broadcast: Two officials indicted', *The Times*, 15 February 1949, p. 4.

destroyed also any recording of the programme, which followed on at 2100 hours from *Radio Quito*'s scheduled re-broadcasting of a BBC News Bulletin.[10]

Nor was this the Martians' final assault launched against Latin America. On 22 November 1954, a radio transmission from Caratinga, Brazil, reporting a Martian landing and panic, attracted widespread media coverage.[11] Despite being soon revealed as a hoax, there is no evidence of a link with 'The War of the Worlds' apart from the episode being dismissed by the press – to quote Alexandre Busko Valim – as 'de mais uma brincadeira de mau gosto no estilo de um certo Sr. Orson Welles' ['one more bad joke in the style of a certain Mr. Orson Welles'].[12] Then on 30 October 1971 Brazil's *Rádio Difusora* reported Martian attacks upon São Luís and Rio de Janeiro.[13] Once again, Orson Welles's broadcast provided the template – for the radio station, this drama was represented as 'ficção científica baseada em Orson Welles' ['Science fiction based on Orson Welles'] – Halloween the trigger, hysteria and panic resulted.[14] As Valim argued, *Rádio Difusora* saw the broadcast as a sure way to secure national visibility in order to attract a larger audience and more advertisers.[15]

The Martians invade the Iberian Peninsula

Having hitherto targeted Britain and the Americas, in 1958 the Martians invaded continental Europe, or more specifically the Iberian Peninsula. On 25 June 1958, Portugal's *Rádio Renascença* broadcast the story using a translation of Howard Koch's script and a news reporting format, but with the names of places and characters changed to fit contemporary Portugal.[16] Thus, the Martians, having landed on a farm at Carcavelos, then targeted Lisbon. Significantly, the opening words, designed to reassure listeners, stressed that what followed was 'a radio adaptation of the famous play The War of the Worlds, by none other than the famous English novelist Herbert George Wells'. Despite this warning and the accompanying advice to remain calm, the broadcast prompted the usual media controversies, as evidenced by the next day's newspaper headlines and reports of panicking people. One distinctive feature of the programme was a brief sequence covering a news report *in English*, summarized in Portuguese, from London's

10. The re-broadcasting of BBC news bulletins in Latin America was a form of cultural propaganda funded through the Foreign Office's Information Department.

11. Gosling, *Waging the War of the Worlds*, pp. 114–19; Alexandre Busko Valim, "'Os Marcianos estão chegando!": as divertidas e imprudentes reinvenções de um ataque alienígena no cinema e no rádio', *Dialogos-Revista do Departamento de Historia e do Programa de Pós-Graduação em História* 9 (3) (2005): 198–200.

12. Valim, 'Os Marcianos', p. 199.

13. Gosling, *Waging the War of the Worlds*, pp. 143–8; Valim, 'Os Marcianos', pp. 200–3.

14. Valim, 'Os Marcianos', p. 202.

15. Ibid., p. 200.

16. Gosling, *Waging the War of the Worlds*, pp. 120–9; Valim, 'Os Marcianos', pp. 196–8.

BCC, presumably the deliberate use of a name similar to that of the BBC intended to give greater realism and authenticity to the programme.[17] Reporting the landing of strange cylindrical machines in both London and the rest of the country, the British news announcer mentioned over 5,000 deaths, scenes of panic and terror and the conquest of most of Essex and Kent.

By way of a postscript, on 30 October 1988 *Radio Braga* marked the fiftieth anniversary of Orson Welles's radio broadcast by recreating a Martian invasion of Braga, which seemingly caused some panic in northern Portugal.[18] Ten years later, in October 1998 the Martians launched yet another assault against Portugal, where Lisbon-based *Antena 3* celebrated Orson Welles's programme's sixtieth anniversary with a Martian landing at Palmela, near Lisbon.[19]

The Martians return to the USA: Buffalo and Providence

In October 2009 David Paterson, Governor of New York State, supported by the New York State Senate, declared Buffalo 'War of the Worlds Broadcast Capital of the World' by way of recognition that during recent decades Buffalo had suffered more than its fair share of Martian invasions.[20] Since 1968 the city of Buffalo proved the subject of several radio programmes on local radio stations dramatizing Martian attacks on the city. Unlike Orson Welles's programme which was broadcast nationwide by *CBS*, these adaptations had a much more limited reach as far as audiences were concerned and hence were focused upon a relatively small geographical area, in and around Buffalo. Nor had the people of Buffalo been totally unaffected by Orson Welles's 1938 radio broadcast, given the manner in which the Martians targeted New York State and one Martian cylinder was reported as landing near Buffalo.

Thirty years later – once again, Halloween was the prompt – the Martians returned to New York State in a 1968 WKBW programme produced and scripted by Jefferson Kaye.[21] Landing at Grand Island, northwest of the city, the Martians

17. Gosling, *Waging the War of the Worlds*, p. 124.

18. Peter Wise, 'Recreation of Orson Welles Broadcast Causes Panic in Portugal', 30 October 1988, http://www.apnewsarchive.com/1988/Recreation-of-Orson-Welles-Broadcast-Causes-Panic-in-Portugal/id-8d4d671ab4aa2a4591329a4bd0e3aac0 [accessed 2 April 2012]; Gosling, *Waging the War of the Worlds*, pp. 156–61; Valim, '"Os Marcianos"', pp. 196–8.

19. Gosling, *Waging the War of the Worlds*, pp. 162–3.

20. 'Buffalo named War of the Worlds capital', WIVB 4, Buffalo, NY, 16 October 2009. http://www.wivb.com/dpp/news/offbeat/Buffalo_named_War_of_the_Worlds_Capital_20091016 [accessed 18 March 2012]; Gosling, *Waging the War of the Worlds*, pp. 130–42.

21. The War of the Worlds (WKBW, Buffalo, 1968–71–75), n.d., http://www.war-ofthe-worlds.co.uk/war_worlds_wkbw_buffalo.htm [accessed 18 March 2012]; Bob Koshinski, 'WKBW's 1968 "War of the Worlds"', *Buffalo Broadcasters Association: Remembering*

advanced upon and took control of Buffalo. Despite advance warnings delivered over a three-week period, there were anecdotal reports of people believing that an invasion was really in progress, responses encouraged by Kaye's decision to use the radio station's own newsmen to report upon the Martian advance, as well as to be gradually killed off, like Carl Phillips in Koch's script, as the programme progressed. Updated versions were broadcast subsequently by WKBW in 1971 and 1975, with the 1971 version being repeated in 1988 to mark the fiftieth anniversary of Orson Welles's landmark broadcast. In turn, in 1998 the sixtieth anniversary of Orson Welles's broadcast and the 30th anniversary of Kaye's original programme, were marked by the Martians' return to Buffalo on local radio stations WGRF [97 Rock] and WEDG [The Edge] in a drama involving members of the original cast, including Kaye.

Introducing the 1971 broadcast, Kaye acknowledged Wells's 1898 novel and Orson Welles's 1938 radio programme as reference points, but stressed that the script, like that used for the 1968 programme, had been updated to take account of advances in the mass media – for example reporters were more mobile – in order to indicate how such an invasion would be covered by present-day newsrooms. Other updates covered such matters as press releases by NASA and the use of disc jockeys playing the hit records of the time. Rock 'n' roll replaced 1930s dance music. Kaye mentioned also the deliberate change of location from both Wells's novel and Orson Welles's broadcast, in order to make the programme 'more meaningful' to a radio audience in western New York State. Nor was Buffalo the only Martian target during this period, as evidenced on 30 October 1974 when WPRO, WKBW's sister radio station based in Providence, Rhode Island, chose Halloween to broadcast a programme based upon WKBW's 1971 script and centred on the island of Jamestown near Newport.[22]

'Wells, not Welles': BBC Radio's approach

In October 2013 *BBC Radio Four* marked the seventy-fifth anniversary of Orson Welles's programme by broadcasting the whole recording. However,

---

the Past, n.d., http://www.buffalobroadcasters.com/broadcast-history/WKBW's%C2%A0-
-War-of-the-Worlds/8 [accessed 18 March 2012]; 'Welles's "War of the Worlds" still stirs consternation', *New York Times*, 1 November 1971. Note the headline reference to Orson Welles, not H. G. Wells, thereby reinforcing his link with *The War of the Worlds* in popular culture. In 1998 WNED–TV broadcast a television programme about 'The Making of WKBW's *War of the Worlds*'.

22. Gosling, *Waging the War of the Worlds*, pp. 149–55; Holland Cooke, 'We blew up the Newport Bridge. Everyone in Fall River died', n.d., http://myri.tv/war.html [accessed 29 June 2012]; C. Eugene Emery Jr., 'The night WPRO's "War of the Worlds" shook up Rhode Island', *Providence Journal*, 30 October 2014 (first published 31 October 1993) http://www.providencejournal.com/article/20141030/Entertainment/310309989 [accessed 1 June 2015].

generally speaking BBC Radio has adopted a rather different approach to radio stations elsewhere when dramatizing *The War of the Worlds* for radio. As indicated above, most radio adaptations have played fast and loose with Wells's original text. Thus, they have not only updated the chronology, but also restaged the story in a local setting, defined either nationally or regionally, thereby loosening the story's link with Horsell, Woking, Surrey and London. By contrast, BBC radio adaptations (Table 13.1) have remained relatively faithful to Wells's original text and geography, but not always to his chronology. But there are exceptions, most notably a remake of the 1994 LA Theater Works production based upon Orson Welles's drama broadcast as 'War of the Worlds', a 'Play of the Week' on 26 February 2005. In January 2002 *Doctor Who: Invaders from Mars*, a BBC audio-drama set in the USA, made reference to the Orson Welles drama.[23]

In January 1950 the BBC commissioned Jon Manchip White to script six 30-minute radio programmes based upon *The War of the Worlds*.[24] Introducing the series in the *Radio Times*, White pointed to 'the immense impact' made by Wells's book on the late Victorian public, as well as to the way in which radio adaptations by Orson Welles and South American broadcasters had highlighted the story's realism.[25] For White, *The War of the Worlds* articulated 'Wells' lifelong impatience: his impatience to sweep away the dreary-looking world he saw about him in order to usher in the shining streamlined future that awaited his New Man'. As White informed prospective listeners, 'The serial you will hear will be Wells, not Welles. Wells at his most Wellsian, forceful, fantastic and fascinating'. Thus, he retained much of Wells's original dialogue alongside the geography and Victorian setting. Nor did he update the weaponry: 'Out of respect for the Martian Fighting-Machines – a bit obsolescent by the standards of jet-planes and anti-tank guns – the dramatized version of *The War of the Worlds* has not been brought up to date.' One key alteration concerned Wells's unnamed narrator, who White named as 'John Nicholson', an astronomer.

For White, the choice of music was vital, given its role to create the right atmosphere in support of the storyline; thus, he selected Holst's 'Mars, the bringer of war', from the Planet suite to open the serial. Members of the cast included Anthony Hawtrey (Nicholson), son of Charles Hawtrey, Peter Coke (Ogilvy, Nicholson's assistant), better known as BBC Radio's Paul Temple and Deryck Guyler (Sir James Stent, Astronomer Royal). Reportedly, White's scripts were adapted into French, Hindi and Urdu for broadcasting around the world.[26] Looking ahead to the series, the *Daily Mail* reminded readers about the panic and hysteria caused

23. Subsequently, it was broadcast on BBC7 (subsequently re-named BBC Radio Four Extra) in 2005 and 2006 and BBC Radio Four on 24 September 2007.

24. Andrew Pixley, 'Programme Notes', *The War of the Worlds* (London: BBC Audio, 2007).

25. Jon Manchip White, 'Wells at his Most Wellsian', *Radio Times*, 28 May–3 June 1950, p. 9.

26. Pixley, 'Programme Notes'.

Table 13.1 'The War of the Worlds' on BBC Radio

Date		Title	Details	No. of episodes
1950	30 May–4 July	*The War of the Worlds*	Book dramatized by Jon Manchip White	6
1967	9 June–14 July	*The War of the Worlds*	Jon Manchip White's 1950 scripts revised by John Powell	6
1973	15 January	BBC Schools	20 minute dramatization for BBC Schools Broadcasting	1
1987	13–22 April	*A Book at Bedtime*	Simon Ward reading John Scotney's abridged version	8
2005	26 February	BBC World Service	Re-broadcasting 1994 remake of Koch script starring · Leonard Nimoy	1

by Orson Welles's *War of the Worlds* 1938 broadcast and a similar programme in Ecuador when speculating whether 'British radio audiences are panic proof?' [27]

According to the BBC Audience Research Report panel members found the opening episode 'exciting' and gave it an above average appreciation index.[28] Following the final programme, the Audience Research Report recorded that while the serial 'had gripped listeners, arousing feelings of fascination and horror that "made them listen", the final episode, stressing the role of bacteria in stopping the Martians, was felt by many to have been something of an anti-climax, terminating the story too abruptly and tamely and leaving unexplored the tremendous possibilities of such an imaginative subject'.[29]

During the mid-1960s the BBC Drama Department decided to prepare a revised version of the 1950 serial for transmission in 1967.[30] Thus, White's scripts were revised by John Powell, the programme's producer, who retained the geographical locations, characters' names and episode titles from the 1950 version, but updated the time period to the present-day to include modern weaponry, including tanks, jet planes and helicopters and to transform the artilleryman into a helicopter pilot. Once again, the series had an impressive cast, including Paul Daneman (Nicholson), Martin Jarvis (Ogilvy), Harold Kasket (Stent) and Peter Sallis (the Parson). Writing in the *Radio Times* – his article was accompanied by Roger Payne's vivid illustration showing fighting machines attacking London – Powell warned listeners that 'This is not a comfortable work ... . *The War of the Worlds*, some seventy years after its first publication, remains a fearful tale from the pen of a writer who saw through a glass darkly'.[31] Significantly, during the week in which

27. 'Who ... why ... where ... in London', *Daily Mail*, 20 May 1950, p. 3.

28. BBC Audience Research Report, June 1950, p. 4, BBC Written Archives Centre, Caversham Park, Reading, UK (BBC).

29. BBC Audience Research Report, July 1950, p. 4 (BBC).

30. Pixley, 'Programme Notes'.

31. John Powell, 'The War of the Worlds', *Radio Times*, 9 June 1967.

the fifth episode was transmitted, the *Radio Times* included an article by Leonard Miall apprising readers about the panic caused by Orson Welles's broadcast.[32]

Reporting listeners' feedback, a BBC Audience Research Report concluded that the serial had worked well. Describing the serial as 'exciting', 'a magnificent thriller' and 'spine-chilling', most listeners felt it proved 'quite an experience'.[33] Nevertheless, many listeners, like those in 1950, opined that the ending, though 'plausible' and following Wells's text, proved 'rather flat', even 'a little tame', in the wake of an action-packed invasion. The production team was criticized for 'tampering with the classics' by modernizing the original.[34] Such an adaptation, many argued, detracted 'from the book's uniqueness and reduced it to the level of any contemporary science fiction tale'. The series received much praise also for its sound effects and accompanying music performed by the BBC Radiophonic Workshop, but some listeners claimed that Holst's *Planets*, as used for the 1950 series, would have been preferable.

Conclusion

Martian invasions of Brazil, Chile, Ecuador, Portugal and the USA, based upon *The War of the Worlds*, yielded good media copy at the time and continue to prove poplar topics for study. However, pending further in-depth research, media coverage of these events needs to be treated with care in order to guard against journalistic licence when reporting what happened, or rather did not happen. Also their actual popular impact needs to be evaluated in the light of the fact that by the 1960s, when the Martians turned towards Buffalo, radio was being rapidly overtaken by the advance of television and facing challenges to its role regarding the presentation of news.

Even so, the events recounted in this chapter, like those related in Chapter 12, can be taken as validating the words of Walter Lippmann: 'it is clear enough that under certain conditions men respond as powerfully to fictions as they do to realities, and that in many cases they help to create the very fictions to which they respond'.[35] Taking Wells's story and name in a fresh direction to new audiences across the world, radio versions, produced by Orson Welles and then based upon his formula, provided a strong foundation for the subsequent adaptation, including its chronological and geographical transplanting, of the story by the cinema and other branches of the media.[36] Notwithstanding BBC Radio's efforts to remain true to the geography, if not always the chronology, of Wells's original story, radio adaptations have invariably tended to do things very differently in the geographical and chronological senses.

32. Leonard Miall, 'The War of the Worlds', *Radio Times*, 29 June 1967.
33. BBC Audience Research Report, 16 August 1967, pp. 1–2 (BBC).
34. Quoted, Pixley, 'Programme Notes'.
35. Walter Lippmann, *Public Opinion* (New York: Harcourt, Brace, 1922), p. 14.
36. Valim, 'Os Marcianos', p. 203.

Chapter 14

THE WAR OF THE WORLDS REACHES CINEMA AND TELEVISION SCREENS AROUND THE WORLD: THE HOLLYWOOD FILMS OF 1953 AND 2005

The Time Machine was published in the same year as Louis and Auguste Lumière unveiled movie film and offered audiences an alternative way of moving through space and time, to that articulated in Wells's pioneering scientific romance. From this perspective, Wells's writing career can be viewed as running parallel to that of the cinema, particularly given the cinematic nature of his writing in the scientific romances and strong personal interest in the moving image. For Keith Williams, Wells's film-friendly and 'film-minded' writings, most notably his time travelling narratives and literary visualization skills, made a crucial contribution to 'the "cinematisation" of his own cultural epoch and beyond'.[1] In particular, Wells made 'time itself resemble a movie reel, speeded forwards and backwards, or stopped at will'. For Thomas Renzi, Wells's scientific romances pioneered what were to become key elements for filmmakers: highly visual scenarios combining the familiar with the fantastic; sharp variations in pace, including fast-forward, reverse and slow-motion action; alternative camera angles, as highlighted by the high angle shots from a balloonist observing the evacuation of London in *The War of the Worlds* (I.17: 172–3/104–5); and the imaginative use of special effects.[2] At the same time, Renzi conceded that Wells's science fiction writings lacked one element treated as an essential part of the filmmakers' template for a successful film, a love interest. Instead, Wells's scientific romances, Renzi observed, 'kept the romance in the thrill of the experience, not in the boy–girl relationship'.[3]

Reportedly, news about the advent of moving film pictures electrified Wells: 'Moving pictures! What a terrific thing!'[4] Naturally, Wells appreciated the basic

---

1. Keith Williams, *H. G. Wells, Modernity and the Movies* (Liverpool: Liverpool University Press, 2007), pp. 2, 5–7.

2. Renzi, *Wells*, pp. 5–9; Williams, *Wells, Modernity and the Movies*, p. 4.

3. Renzi, *Wells*, p. 188; Pal, 'Filming "War of the Worlds"', p. 102.

4. Quoted Thomson, 'Film Studies'. On Wells and film, see Sylvia Hardy, 'H. G. Wells and British cinema: *The War of the* Worlds', *Foundation: The International Review of Science Fiction* 28 (77) (1999): 46–58; Williams, *Wells, Modernity and the Movies*, pp. 1–23; Hughes, 'Radio and Film Adaptations', pp. 245–6.

differences between the literary and cinematic worlds, most notably the fact that, whereas filmmakers presented their own ready-made images to audiences, writers left readers to use their imaginations to fill gaps in the written narrative. However, unlike many of his literary counterparts, he took a close and informed interest in the cinema. Indeed, for Laura Marcus, 'Wells' engagement with film was as complete and as complex' as that of any writer of his time.[5] Recognizing the power and future potential of the moving image, he admired the ways in which filmmakers gave life and power to words.[6] For Charlie Chaplin, a longstanding friend, Wells's attitude towards film reflected 'an affected tolerance': "There is no such thing as a bad film," he said: "the fact that they move is wonderful!"'. [7] In addition, Wells's preparedness to advise on adapting *The War of the Worlds* for film, led one commentator to opine that this 'should mean more to the film than mere fidelity in retelling a story in a new medium'.[8] Naturally, this did not prevent him proving critical of the cinema's liberties with an author's text, given the inevitable tendency of films, like any other adaptation, to depart from the original storyline in one way or another. As Eric Fellner, the producer of *The Theory of Everything* (2015), observed, this results from not only variations between the original novel and the film script but also the process of film production, 'A film is a living animal … It changes from the moment you greenlight it'.[9] Or, as Kate Muir commented about *Suite Française* (2015), 'When Hollywood adapts great literature into movie, it is best not to expect too much, and merely feel thankful that anything has been salvaged.'[10]

Unsurprisingly, Wells soon became part of the fast-growing film world. In 1914 he made a Keystone Cops-type home movie with such literary luminaries as J. M. Barrie and G. K. Chesterton.[11] During the mid-1920s, Wells was a founding member of the Film Society in London, a group established to screen films unavailable through the commercial cinema, as well as to discuss film under the guidance of such guest lecturers as Sergei Eisenstein and Hans Richter. In November 1935 Wells visited Hollywood. Staying in Beverly Hills at the home of Charlie Chaplin, he relished the chance to link up with the film world, to be 'lionized' by the film community, to visit film studios and particularly to meet many 'pretty women'.[12]

For Wells, the cinema offered also yet another revenue stream through the

---

5. Laura Marcus, *Tenth Muse: Writings about Cinema in the Modernist Period* (Oxford: Oxford University Press, 2007), p. 45.

6. Wells to Evans, 3 February 1936, Smith, *Correspondence of H. G. Wells, IV*, p. 61.

7. Chaplin, *My Autobiography*, p. 270.

8. 'Mr H. G. Wells and the screen', *The Times*, 3 November 1932.

9. Quoted, Andrew Billen, 'After Stephen Hawking saw the film, he wanted to go to a club', *The Times*, 21 February 2015.

10. Kate Muir, 'Why can't Hollywood mind its French?', *The Times*, 13 March 2015, p. 7.

11. Sherborne, *H. G. Wells*, pp. 225.

12. Hugh Walpole, quoted N. and J. MacKenzie, *The Time Traveller*, p. 392; Wells, *H. G. Wells in Love*, pp. 207–8.

sale of film rights for his books – for example, in 1925 he sold the film rights for *The War of the Worlds* 'in perpetuity' to Paramount Studios and later received £10,000 for the film rights of *The Shape of Things to Come* – writing scripts and advising filmmakers. As Wells informed his literary agents, he welcomed any *bona fide* offers from Hollywood.[13] Although some of his other novels were adapted as plays for the theatre – they included The *Wheels of Chance*, dramatized as 'Hoopdriver's Holiday' (1903), *Kipps* (1912) and *The Wonderful Visit* (1921) – generally speaking Wells's scientific romances were viewed as – to quote Michael Sherborne – 'ill-suited to the stage', given their expansive nature and reliance upon special effects.[14] By contrast, 'the big screen proved more accommodating'. Following Gaumont's production of *The First Men in the Moon* (1919), during the early 1920s Stoll Productions filmed three of Wells's books, including *The Wheels of Chance* (1922).[15] Later, during the decade, Wells was credited as writing three silent 'shorts' – featuring Elsa Lanchester and Charles Laughton, they were directed by Ivor Montagu – even if his initial 'scribbled paragraphs' have been represented more as synopses or suggestions than shooting scripts.[16] Indeed, Frank Wells claimed that the script for *Bluebottles* (1928), written on a postcard, was merely 'Elsa blows a whistle'.[17]

During the 1930s, Wells's books were seen as offering filmmakers 'promising' material for the 'talkies', as evidenced by such films as the *Island of Lost Souls* (1932), Paramount's take on *The Island of Doctor Moreau*, Universal's *The Invisible Man* (1933) and London Film Productions' *Things to Come* (1936) based upon *The Shape of Things to Come* (1933).[18] Such films enjoyed varying degrees of commercial and critical success. However, like its source novel, *Island of Lost Souls*, a horror movie starring Charles Laughton, proved somewhat controversial. For James Robertson, *Island of Lost Souls*, which was repeatedly refused a certificate for screening in Britain by the 'British Board of Film Censors' until the late 1950s, occupies a 'notable' place in British censorship history.[19] Moreover,

13. Mrs G. P. Wells to Curtis Brown, 5 July 1935, WB72 (UIUC).

14. Sherborne, *H. G. Wells*, p. 245.

15. On filming *The Wheels of Chance*, see Gordon Parker, 'The Making of a Film', *Illustrated London News*, 6 August 1921, pp. 192–3.

16. Hardy, 'Wells and British cinema', p. 50.

17. Frank Wells to J. R. Hammond, 1 May 1961, 24 May 1961, HGW 1245/7/10–11 (BRO).

18. Sherborne, *H. G. Wells*, p. 304; Wells, *H. G. Wells in Love*, pp. 206–8, 211–13; N. and J. Mackenzie, *The Time Traveller*, pp. 390–2. For fuller coverage of films based on Wells's writings, see Renzi, *Wells*; Williams, *Wells, Modernity and the Movies*. The Invisible Man film was scripted by R. C. Sherriff, who wrote the play *Journey's End* (1928) and subsequently published a Wells-inspired post-apocalyptic novel called *The Hopkins Manuscript* (1939).

19. In Britain *Island of Lost Souls* was refused a certificate in 1933, 1951 and 1957: James C. Robertson, *The Hidden Cinema: British Film Censorship in Action 1913–1972* (London: Routledge, 2005), pp. 56–7.

during the weeks preceding his death, Wells was not only still working, but also engaged on a scenario for a new film called 'The Way the World is Going'.[20]

For Michael Sherborne, the adaptation of his scientific romances and other books for the cinema offers a good way 'to audit Well's public standing as a fiction writer' during the 1920s and after.[21] Wells welcomed films for ensuring that his books were 'still read as much as ever' and particularly, for introducing him repeatedly to new young audiences.[22] In addition, movies enabled filmmakers – they include George Pal, Steven Spielberg and Timothy Hines – to convert their admiration for Wells's books, most notably *The War of the Worlds*, into movies sharing his creativity with audiences around the world. Thus, Spielberg admitted his longstanding desire to make a film based on the book: 'I wanted to do *War of the Worlds* ever since I read the book in college before I actually became a filmmaker ... It was just that it's a great story. It's a great piece of nineteenth Century classic literature. It began an entire revolution in science-fiction and fantasy in my opinion – Jules Verne and H. G. Wells.' [23]

Filming The War of the Worlds

Wells's *The War of the Worlds* is distinguished by not only an engaging storyline but also what is frequently described as a highly visual, even cinematic, text adjudged as highly suitable for adaptation for film. Indeed, the story's visual potential means that there is always the risk that the filmmakers' focus upon special effects – these demand time and money – will compromise attempts to tell a good story. Significantly, the films released by Pal and Spielberg in 1953 and 2005 respectively, both won high praise for special effects – Pal's film even won an Oscar in this sphere – whereas Timothy Hines's 2005 release attracted strong criticism for its serious shortcomings in this area.

In 1925 Paramount purchased the film rights for *The War of the Worlds*. Notwithstanding repeated speculation during his lifetime that the story was to be turned into a movie, this did not happen until the early 1950s. Despite occasional reports of proposed film projects and the production of several draft scripts, such as by Roy J. Pomeroy in 1926, *The War of the Worlds* never reached the cinema screen during Wells's lifetime.[24] For Paramount, it proved 'a property that, due

20. 'H. G. Wells' last work: Atom', *Daily Sketch*, 14 August 1946. An anonymous undated note, stating that Wells was 'working very hard' on the project, gives brief details and stresses his copyright: Gregory Papers, note, n.d., SxMs14/1/7/2 (Sussex).

21. Sherborne, *H. G. Wells*, pp. 244–5.

22. Wells, *Experiment in Autobiography*, II, p. 561.

23. Faraci, 'Interview: Tom Cruise and Steven Spielberg'.

24. 'With the Producers and Players', *New York Times*, 27 June 1926; Gosling, *Waging the War of the Worlds*, p. 165; Flynn, *War of the Worlds*, pp. 56–7; Williams, *Wells, Modernity and Movies*, pp. 138–9.

to story and budget difficulties ... had a decades-long development history'.[25] Over time, producers linked to the project included Cecil B. DeMille, Sergei Eisenstein and Alfred Hitchcock. The early 1930s saw press speculation about a Gaumont-British film scripted by Ivor Montagu and Frank Wells and using Wells as an adviser.[26] Indeed, in March 1933 the *Daily Mail* reported that at Gaumont-British studios in Shepherd's Bush, 'a whole crew was engaged on "The War of the Worlds", which will be a year in production and will be produced on a gigantic scale'.[27] In reality, the project was doomed from the start, since the film rights were held by Paramount. Reportedly, Wells only remembered that he had already sold the film rights to Paramount after the script had been completed – this set the film in Britain but in a modernized setting.[28] Following his 1938 radio broadcast and RKO film contract (1939), *The War of the Worlds* was mentioned as one of Orson Welles's probable initial film projects in spite of the fact that RKO did not hold the book's film rights.[29]

George Pal's The War of the Worlds, *1953*

In the event, it was not until 1953, seven years after Wells's death, that a long anticipated film version of *The War of the Worlds,* starring Gene Barry and Ann Robinson, was released by Hollywood (Table 14.1; Figure 14.1).[30] Produced by George Pal, the film was directed by Byron Haskin. When seeking to follow up *Destination Moon* (1950) and *When Worlds Collide* (1951), Pal placed *The War of the Worlds* high up his list of priority projects. Apart from seeking to exploit the present-day 'big vogue for films of a science-fiction nature', he was motivated by the perceived challenge of filming such a story:

> Although written fifty-six years ago, in many respects it had withstood the advances of time remarkably well and remained today an exciting and visionary story of the future.

25. John M. Miller, *The War of the Worlds* (1953), *Turner Classic Movies*, n.d., http://www.tcm.com/this-month/article/188880%7C0/The-War-of-the-Worlds.html   [accessed 29 June 2012].

26. 'Mr H. G. Wells and the screen', *The Times*, 3 November 1932.

27. Seton Margrave, 'Behind the Scenes: at Britain's million a year talkie studios', *Daily Mail*, 13 March 1933, p. 4.

28. Williams, *Wells, Modernity and the Movies*, p. 237 n. 33. A draft script is held in the British Film Institute's Ivor Montagu holdings.

29. Callow, *Orson Welles, 1*, p. 464.

30. Hughes, 'Radio and Film Adaptations', pp. 246–8; Gilbert, 'Wars of the Worlds', pp. 331–6; Williams, *Wells, Modernity and the Movies*, pp. 146–53. Barry and Robinson appeared also in Steven Spielberg's 2005 film as grandparents, while the latter appeared in episodes of the TV serial (1988–9).

Table 14.1 The War of the Worlds at the cinema, on television and video

Year	Title	Director/Producer	Geography of Storyline	Production Company	Format
1953	The War of the Worlds	Byron Haskin/George Pal	USA	Paramount Pictures	Cinema
1983–5	'V': 2 mini-series (1983–4) plus 19-episode series (1984–5); (remade 2009–2011: 2 series with 22 episodes)	Kenneth Johnson, Richard T. Heffron/ Daniel Blatt, Robert Singer et al.	USA	Warner Brothers/NBC	TV
1983	Wojna swiatów – nastepne stulecie [War of the Worlds: the Next Century]	Piotr Szulkin	Poland	Zespol Filmowy 'Perspektywa', Poland	Cinema
1988–90	'War of the Worlds' 2 seasons: 43 episodes	Various, including Greg Strangis, Jonathan Hackett, William Fruet	USA	Hometown Films, Paramount Television	TV
2005	War of the Worlds	Steven Spielberg/Damian Collier, Kathleen Kennedy and Colin Wilson	USA	Paramount Pictures and DreamWorks Pictures	Cinema
2005	The War of the Worlds	Timothy Hines/Susan Goforth	Britain	Pendragon Pictures	DVD/Video
2005	H. G. Wells' War of the Worlds (aka Invasion)	David Michael Latt/David Rimawi	USA	The Asylum	DVD/Video
2008	War of the Worlds 2: The Next Wave	C. Thomas Howell/David Michael Latt, David Rimawi and Paul Bales	USA	The Asylum	DVD/Video
2012	War of the Worlds: The True Story	Timothy Hines/Susan Goforth and Donovan Le	Britain	Pendragon Pictures	Cinema
2012	War of the Worlds: Goliath	Joe Pearson/Kevin Eastman, David Abramowitz, Mike Bloemendal, Leon Tan	USA	Tripod Entertainment	Animation

Note: Format covers the principal initial format, as cinema films are released subsequently as DVDs and screened on television.

 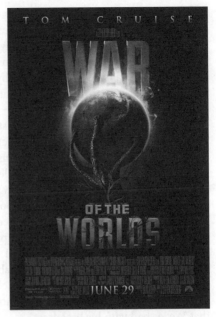

Figure 14.1 *War of the Worlds'* film posters, 1953 and 2005. Posters advertising the 1953 and 2005 Hollywood films of *The War of the Worlds*. Whereas the 1953 film poster gives prominence to Wells, his role as the author – this is noted to the left of 'June 29' – tends to be lost in the detail of the 2005 poster. By contrast, note the emphasis upon Tom Cruise and Steven Spielberg.

Source: Paramount Pictures, Los Angeles, California, USA

> It offered me my greatest challenge to date in figuring out how to film the Martian machines, their heat and disintegration rays and the destruction and chaos they might cause when they invade Earth.[31]

When preparing the project, Pal came across several unproduced scripts based on Wells's book in Paramount's story files.[32] Tossing aside archived scripts, he commissioned Barré Lyndon, a USA-based Londoner who had worked recently on DeMille's *The Greatest Show on Earth* (1952), to write the script. Meanwhile, soon after production began, Paramount discovered that its rights applied only to silent films; thus, it paid Frank Wells $7,000 to add the talkie rights.[33] Inevitably, like most films based upon books, Lyndon's script retained traces of the original novel, but in reality proved an extremely free adaptation thereof.

31. Pal, 'Filming "War of the Worlds"', pp. 100–1.

32. Miller, *The War of the Worlds*.

33. Flynn, *War of the Worlds*, p. 68. From this perspective, the abortive 1932–3 Gaumont–British project for a talkie film, as discussed above, was not barred by Wells's contract with Paramount.

Like Orson Welles, Haskin acknowledged that the impact of Wells's story upon readers was in part a function of the juxtaposition of fantasy and realism, most notably the threat posed to familiar ways of doing things and well known places by an unknown deadly force.[34] Thus, in the film – to quote James Gilbert – 'the suspension of reality is accomplished by intercutting between normal activities (a square dance in the small town) and the first attack by the enemy upon defenseless humans'.[35]

As the USA's National Film Registry recorded, Pal 'provocatively trans-planted' the storyline's location from Victorian England to mid-twentieth century Southern California, where the Martians landed at Linda Rosa, a fictional town, before moving on towards Los Angeles.[36] Entering the empty streets of Los Angeles, the Martian war machines blew up water towers and buildings, including City Hall. Responding to criticisms about removing the story from its original Victorian British context, Haskin claimed that the early 1950s Californian setting made the storyline meaningful for a present-day American cinema audience. He revealed also the influence exerted upon Hollywood filmmakers by Orson Welles's radio broadcast: 'It was identifiable to Americans, and that's who we were making the picture *for*. In making our choice we did as Orson Welles had done. We transposed it to a modern setting, hoping to generate some of the excitement that Welles had with his broadcast.'[37]

For 1950s American cinemagoers, the film's target audience, Wells's original Surrey locations represented an unknown world and, if used, were interpreted by the production team as impacting adversely upon box office returns. As Renzi acknowledged, 'the crises at Horsell, Woking, and Chobham might as well have occurred on Mars. By switching the action to America, he gave Americans a sense of the familiar and retained the dominant disturbing tone of Wells's story'.[38] When explaining why the film was not set in either a British location or the late Victorian period, Pal cited also financial and scheduling reasons arising from the large proportion of the budget, some seventy per cent, and time, roughly eight months, devoted to special effects.[39] But Britain was not completely blanked out, even if it was assigned merely a bit-part. Thus, midway through the film images of the Martian destruction of London, like that suffered also by other cities like New Delhi and Paris, were employed to give the impression of a worldwide confrontation and to indicate the apparent helplessness of all humankind, before the superior power of the Martians.

34. Haskin quoted, 1975, Renzi, *Wells*, p. 121.

35. Gilbert, 'Wars of the Worlds', p. 332.

36. '2011 National Film Registry More Than a Box of Chocolates', *News from the Library of Congress*, 28 December 2011, http://www.loc.gov/today/pr/2011/11-240.html [accessed 24 January 2014].

37. Quoted, 1975, Renzi, *Wells*, p. 121.

38. Ibid.

39. Pal, 'Filming "War of the Worlds"', pp. 103–7; Miller, *War of the Worlds*; Flynn, *War of the Worlds*, pp. 64–6. Pal's article detailed producing the special effects.

Nevertheless, Pal soon discovered that modernizing Wells's imaginative storyline to make the film 'entertaining, credible and believable to an audience geared to scientific awareness' posed its own problems:

> If for one moment you think the challenge of modernizing Wells' story was child's play, just take a scrap of paper and list the commonplace inventions and scientific discoveries which we utilize in our daily living that were utterly nonexistent when Wells wrote his story.
>
> There were no airplanes, atom bombs or tanks with which to fight the Martian machines at the time he wrote his tale. His readers followed his story on a flight of imagination. Our audience comes to the theatre today conversant with the terms: nuclear physics, atomic fission, gravitational fields and space platforms.
>
> Even the children play with space helmets and ray guns and are even more familiar with such expressions as "blast off" than their elders.[40]

Updating the time period, meant that Wells's tripods were transformed into streamlined flying machines shaped like manta rays with a long cobra neck. At the same time modern weaponry, even an atom bomb, was shown to be powerless against the superior Martian war-machines. However, in the end, as in the book, the Martian threat was foiled by micro-organisms. Taking up Wells's storyline, the closing narrative pointed out that the Martians lacked resistance to Earth's bacteria: 'thus, after science fails man in its supreme test, it is the littlest things that God in his wisdom had put upon the Earth that save mankind'.

Like Orson Welles and Spielberg, Pal used extracts from the book's opening paragraph. Sir Cedric Hardwicke, a leading British actor who had appeared in *Things to Come* (1936), delivered the opening narrative, his voice – to quote Pal – 'impersonating that of H. G. Wells in describing why the Martians were forced to migrate from their planet' and chose Earth as their target.[41] Inevitably, the film ushered in several character changes. The central character, based upon the book's narrator, was a nuclear physicist named Clayton Forrester, while the film industry's need for a romantic interest – for Pal, 'a boy-and-girl theme is necessary even in a science-fiction film of the scope of "War of the Worlds." Audiences want it' – led to the replacement of the narrator's wife by a new character, Sylvia van Buren, the niece of the curate.[42] Wells's anonymous curate, critiqued alongside religion in the novel, was named Pastor Matthew Collins and represented in the film very differently, as a heroic figure quoting scripture, walking bravely towards Martian fire, instant vaporization and death. For the National Film Registry, *The War of the Worlds*, highlighting Pal's frequent use of films, most notably apocalyptic-type movies, to portray his Catholic faith, replaced 'Wells's original commentary on the British class system with religious metaphor'.[43]

40. Pal, 'Filming "War of the Worlds"', p. 102.

41. Ibid., p. 110.

42. Ibid., p. 102.

43. '2011 National Film Registry'; Michael Bliss, *Invasions USA: The Essential Science*

Pal's fantasy alien invasion film was contextualized by not only the ongoing reality of the Cold War, most notably the 1950–3 Korean War and the Soviet Union's first hydrogen bomb test (August 1953), but also Hollywood's rediscovery of science fiction and the planet Mars. For many cinemagoers such films were merely escapist entertainment, but for filmmakers Mars and the Martian invasion became metaphoric vehicles to explore and exploit the contemporary threat posed by the Soviet Union, Cold War paranoia, the danger of World War Three and fears of a nuclear holocaust. From this perspective, science fiction – films released during the early 1950s included *Destination Moon* (1950), *The Day the Earth Stood Still* (1951), *When Worlds Collide* (1951) as well as *The War of the Worlds* (1953) – proved a popular film genre offering cinema audiences – to quote Gilbert – 'a vehicle for imagining the unthinkable'.[44] *The War of the Worlds*, released during a hot phase of the Cold War, capitalized – to quote the USA's National Film Registry – 'on the apocalyptic paranoia of the atomic age'.[45] Previewing the film for *Picture Post*, Robert Muller represented *The War of the Worlds* as epitomizing the contemporary vogue for sci-fi films as compared to Frankenstein-type horror films:

> Film producers … seem to have come to the conclusion that, after Belsen and Hiroshima, in an era of ever-improving hydrogen bombs, the only manufactured fear likely to satisfy and calm us is one which comes *from out of this world*. Hence the spate of films dealing with interplanetary conflicts … To take our mind off the war just behind us, and the war that we fear is just in front of us, we are getting bigger and better wars of growing incredulity, and, indeed after *The War of the Worlds*, mere human atomic war cannot appear as terrifying as before.[46]

Looking back, Spielberg recalled that 'One of the great things the Pal film did was to create, for its time, a tremendous sense of tension and dread … A contemporary dread. It really made me feel this event was actually happening.'[47]

Whether or not Wells would have recoiled with horror at what Hughes describes as a 'perversion of his work', remains a matter for debate, even if he must be viewed as likely to have seconded criticisms of the dialogue, van Buren's histrionics, the character changes, the switch of location and the change of time period.[48] Grossing $2 million, in 1953 the film was placed in the top fifty films at the box office in the USA, but John Flynn's claim that it 'became the biggest

Fiction Films of the 1950s (Lanham, MD: Rowman & Littlefield, 2014), pp. xvi, 91–2, 101–4.

44. Gilbert, 'Wars of the Worlds', p. 326.

45. '2011 National Film Registry'.

46. Robert Muller, 'War: Martians invade America!', *Picture Post* 58 (21 March 1953), p. 23.

47. Quoted Vicki Ecker, 'Lights! Camera! Martians!', *Fortean*, August 2005, http://www.forteantimes.com/features/articles/121/lights_camera_martians.html [accessed 14 January 2012].

48. Hughes, 'Radio and Film Adaptations', p. 247.

and most successful motion picture in Paramount's history' seems somewhat exaggerated.[49] In Britain, the film's X-certificate, reflecting concerns about such aspects as the incineration and vaporisation of bodies remaining merely as ash and themes regarding the possible end of humankind, restricted audiences to those aged over sixteen, thereby ruling out a substantial section of the potential audience.

Generally speaking *The War of the Worlds* proved a critical success. For *The New York Times*, the film was 'an imaginatively conceived, professionally turned adventure … suspenseful, fast and, on occasion, properly chilling making excellent use of special effects'.[50] Writing in *Variety*, 'Brog' echoed other reviewers in giving high praise for the special effects, while deploying Orson Welles's 1938 radio programme as a reference point for causing a 'good scare' by creating 'an atmosphere of soul-chilling apprehension so effectively [that] audiences will actually take alarm at the danger posed in the picture'.[51] Despite winning widespread praise for its action scenes and special effects, *The Times*'s reviewer, complaining about the 'drivelling dialogue' and the invariable failure of such adaptations to follow the original story, critiqued the film for 'ruthlessly' breaking with 'the mind and words of Wells'.[52]

Over time, the rise of the cinema and television increasingly bypassed radio drama, but it is worth noting not only Haskin's above-mentioned acknow-ledgement of Orson Welles's influence upon the project, but also the fact that the film inspired a radio spin-off. Thus, on 8 February 1955 *CBS*'s long running *Lux Radio Theater* series broadcast a sixty-minute radio adaptation starring Dana Andrews and Pat Crowley based upon the 1953 film. Moreover, today the film, which sold well when released as a video-cassette during the early 1980s, continues to take Pal's version of Wells's *The War of the Worlds* to audiences across the globe through television and DVDs. In turn, during the late 1980s, Paramount Pictures used the 1953 film, not Wells's book, as the reference point for *War of the Worlds*, a sequel shown as a weekly television series (October 1988–May 1990). This point was stressed by the lead character, Harrison Blackwood: 'In 1953 Earth experienced a War of the Worlds. Common bacteria destroyed the aliens but it didn't kill them. The aliens fell into a state of deep hibernation. Now the aliens have been resurrected more terrifying than before. In 1953 aliens started taking over the world. Today they're taking over our bodies.' [53]

49. Michael Gebert, *The Encyclopedia of Movie Awards* (New York: St. Martin's, 1996), p. 173; Flynn, *War of the Worlds*, p. 6.

50. 'The Screen in Review: New Martian Invasion is seen in War of the Worlds, which bows at Mayfair', *New York Times*, 14 August 1953.

51. 'Brog', Review from *Variety* dated April 6, 1953, Don Willis (ed.), *Variety's Complete Science Fiction Reviews* (New York: Garland Publishing, 1985), p. 95.

52. 'Film adaptation of H. G. Wells' story', *The Times*, 2 April 1953; John Baxter, *Science Fiction in the Cinema* (New York: A. S. Barnes, 1970), p. 149.

53. Quoted imdb (Internet Movie Database), 'War of the Worlds 1988–90', http://www.imdb.com/title/tt0094578/quotes [accessed 20 February 2014]. A similar statement was made in the series' promotional materials, as quoted by Flynn, *War of the Worlds*, p. 89.

The link with the 1953 movie was reinforced by representing Blackwood as the adopted son of Clayton Forrester, the film's hero, as well as by casting Ann Robinson as Sylvia Van Buren, the character she played in Pal's film. Whereas Wells's creative literary role was hidden from viewers, Orson Welles's radio broadcast came to the fore in episode five. Broadcast on 31 October 1988, fifty years on from Orson Welles's infamous radio drama, this programme centred upon the 50th anniversary celebrations held by the people of Grover's Mill, with aliens – the invaders were referred to as 'aliens', not Martians – arriving to find the spaceship that crashed there in 1938.

Pal's movie paved the way for numerous alien invasion films responsible for entertaining and frightening cinema audiences during subsequent decades.[54] In this vein, in 2011 his film was selected for inclusion in the Library of Congress's National Film Registry, whose brief is to preserve films deemed culturally, historically, or aesthetically significant. Rather like the pioneering contribution made by Wells's book to sci-fi literature, the 1953 film was seen as offering a template and a source of inspiration for alien invasion movies. Repeated showings on television around the world – it is still shown today – and releases on DVD/video have established the film as one of the most popular and influential science fiction movies.[55]

Steven Spielberg's War of the Worlds, *2005*

Following Pal's take on *The War of the Worlds*, over fifty years passed before Hollywood produced a new cinematic version of Wells's text, or rather what was represented by the film's publicity materials as 'a contemporary retelling of H. G. Wells's seminal classic'.[56] In fact, during the 1970s Paramount commissioned Anthony Burgess, the author of *The Clockwork Orange* (1962), to write a script for a remake of the story, but the project proved abortive. As a result, it was not until 2005 that Paramount, working with DreamWorks Pictures, released *War of the Worlds*, a star-studded big budget film produced by Steven Spielberg and starring Tom Cruise (Figure 14.1).

Spielberg claimed that for a long time he had believed that *The War of the Worlds* would make 'an amazing movie' partly through seeing George Pal's film on television and partly through reading Wells's book at college: 'I read the book for the first time, and I thought the book was extraordinary'.[57] Orson Welles's

---

54. Gebert, *Encyclopedia of Movie Awards*, p. 173; Flynn, *War of the Worlds*, pp. 52, 69, 74.

55. For example, Chapter 1 highlighted the film's role as a reference point, while the following section on Steven Spielberg establishes its influence upon other filmmakers. Pal's film was first shown on BBC television in March 1983.

56. Paramount Pictures and Dream Works, 'Production Notes: The War of the Worlds', n.d., http://www.waroftheworlds.com/productionnotes/index.html [accessed 3 June 2012].

57. Quoted, March 2005, Flynn, *War of the Worlds*, p. 115.

radio broadcast proved another important influence, as acknowledged in June 1994, when Spielberg paid $32,200 at an auction for what was represented as Orson Welles's own directorial copy of the script.[58] Moreover, he was familiar also with Jeff Wayne's musical version of the story through membership of the panel awarding Jeff Wayne's *War of the Worlds* music album a prize in 1979 as 'The Best Recording in Science Fiction and Fantasy'. Thus, in November 1979, he informed Jerry Wayne, Jeff Wayne's father, that he had been 'enormously entertained' by the music album and indicated his belief that 'it will make a unique and visionary film'.[59] However, a 'crammed' production schedule, Spielberg claimed, ruled him out of making such a film in the near future.

Subsequently, Spielberg steered clear of the project for fear that films like *Independence Day* (1996) had 'cherry-picked' the storyline to death.[60] For Spielberg, a new way was required to tell *The War of the Worlds* story as a film, especially as he wanted to represent aliens somewhat differently from those depicted in his earlier films, *Close Encounters of the Third Kind* (1977) and *E.T.* (1982): 'I grew up with the science-fiction films of the 1950s and 60s, in which flying saucers attack Earth and people have to resist the aliens with all their might. So I thought: before I retire I should direct a really mean invasion from outer space'.[61] Eventually Spielberg took up *The War of the Worlds'* project in 2002 when discussing future plans with Tom Cruise. In particular, they saw the storyline as possessing a strong resonance in a post-9/11 world scarred by the coordinated terrorist attacks launched on 11 September 2001, using aircraft targeted at the Twin Towers in New York and the Pentagon in Washington DC.

For Spielberg, the project came to be viewed through the prism of 9/11 paranoia about homeland security and contemporary anxieties about foreign terrorism: 'In the shadow of 9/11, there is relevance with how we are all so unsettled in our feelings about our collective futures. And that's why when I reconsidered War of the Worlds after 9/11, it began to make more sense to me.' [62] Spielberg indicated

58. 'Orson Welles War of the Worlds script inspired Steven Spielberg's movie', 4 November 2006, http://www.wellesnet.com/?p=110 [accessed 28 May 2015]; Ecker, 'Lights! Camera! Martians!'. In December 1988, the original radio script for *The War of the Worlds* was sold at auction in New York by Howard Koch for $143,000, a record for a radio script: 'Auctions', *New York Times*, 15 December 1988.

59. Steven Spielberg to Jerry Wayne, 23 November 1979, in Jeff Wayne, Damian Collier and Gaëtan Schurrer (eds), with Greg Brooks, *Jeff Wayne's Musical Version of The War of the Worlds: Collector's Edition* (London: Sony BMG, 2005), p. 18; Flynn, *War of the Worlds*, p. 83.

60. Quoted, March 2005, Flynn, *War of the Worlds*, p. 115; Ecker, 'Lights! Camera! Martians!'.

61. *Der Spiegel Online International*, 'Interview with Steven Spielberg and Tom Cruise', 27 April 2005, http://www.spiegel.de/international/spiegel/spiegel-interview-with-tom-cruise-and-steven-spielberg-actor-tom-cruise-opens-up-about-his-beliefs-in-the-church-of-scientology-a-353577.html [accessed 20 February 2014].

62. Quoted, Ecker, 'Lights! Camera! Martians!' For an illuminating contemporary view on 9/11 and Hollywood movies, see John Hoberman, 'All as it had been: Hollywood revises

agreement with the point made in Wells's original text (II. X: 300/190), as quoted to him by one reporter, to the effect that 'we cannot regard this planet as being fenced in and a secure abiding-place for Man; we can never anticipate the unseen good or evil that may come upon us suddenly out of space'.[63] Reaffirming the impact of 9/11 on the production team, David Koepp, the film's co-scriptwriter, admitted that 'we all come out of the same set of experiences'.[64]

Despite seeking to link up with a global theme – 'Earth goes to war' – Spielberg decided on a narrower personal focus as the most effective way of engaging with the target audience: 'The point of view is very personal. I think everybody in the world can relate to the point of view, because it's about a family trying to survive and stay together'.[65] For Spielberg, the film, though set exclusively within the USA, described 'a global catastrophe from a subjective point of view'.[66] The fate of one American family, the Ferriers, took centre stage, so that the audience experiences the war from an American family's perspective. Thus, the film covers the Ferriers's flight from their home, their struggle for survival and the transformation of Ray Ferrier, the character played by Tom Cruise, from a shambolic father into a responsible caring parent. Or, as Anthony Scott commented in the *New York Times*, 'Millions of deaths and incalculable property damage seem like pretty expensive family therapy'.[67]

When approached about writing the script, Koepp, whose writing credits included *Jurassic Park* (1993), *Mission: Impossible* (1996) and *Spider-Man* (2002), wondered 'what ground had been left uncovered that we could possibly stake out as our own?'.[68] After all, there were already numerous alien invasion and disaster movies as well as a previous Hollywood adaptation of Wells's book: 'But it became clear that, by sticking to the point of view of this one ordinary guy [the unnamed narrator], as Wells did, we could make a different, great movie'. For Koepp, the film's co-scriptwriter with Josh Friedman, this meant striking a balance between what the audience expected – 'you're writing in a genre, and that means your audience has certain expectations you can't ignore' – and the need for an element capable of surprising and challenging the audience. As always when scripting an adaptation, the first thing Koepp did was to look again at the novel: 'After I reread it, though, I was amazed to find that the best idea in the book was the one no one had ever used: this idea of showing a vast global event from a very limited perspective, only through the eyes of this unnamed narrator'. The resulting focus upon the human

history, joins the good fight', 4 December 2001, http://www.villagevoice.com/content/printVersion/167459/ [accessed 12 June 2012]; Williams, *Wells, Modernity and the Movies*, pp. 155–7.

63. *Der Spiegel*, 'Interview with Steven Spielberg'.

64. Friedman and Koepp, *War of the Worlds*, p. 143.

65. Quoted, Ecker, 'Lights! Camera! Martians!'.

66. *Der Spiegel*, 'Interview with Steven Spielberg'.

67. A. O. Scott, 'Another terror attack, but not by humans', *New York Times*, 29 June 2005.

68. Friedman and Koepp, *War of the Worlds*, pp. 141, 146; Mattin, 'Words on worlds'.

element through the trials and tribulations of the Ferrier family required the removal of the father's anonymity: 'I named him, because I'm not as brave as H. G.' and so decided to 'make a rule that we will not see anything unless Ray [played by Tom Cruise] sees it, and we'll not know anything unless Ray knows it'.

Inevitably, Spielberg's film, like its 1953 counterpart, was set in present-day USA, the base of the principal cinema audience, but followed Orson Welles, not Pal, by centring upon New Jersey and New York State in preference to California. Even so, this limited geographical perspective did not prevent the promotional material used to publicize the film's British release date adopting broader visions of a global war: 'On July 1, 2005, Earth goes to War!'. Nor, despite claiming 'great respect' for Wells's book, did Spielberg possess any desire to make a science fiction movie set in the Victorian period. Spielberg admitted that he felt more at home visualizing today's world: 'There are elements of Wells's novel in the movie. We have the tripods. We have the red weed growing all over. But I never thought of doing it as a period piece at the turn of the century. It just wasn't an interesting way to go. I just can't stand the styles of that time'.[69]

Set in the heavily populated urban industrialized American landscape centred upon Bayonne in New Jersey, but extending also to cover New York and Boston, the film employed stunning special effects taking advantage of computer-generated imagery (CGI) to depict the invaders and their powerful impacts inflicted upon ordinary people in their own homes. At the same time, the shadow of 9/11 fostered restraint; thus, Koepp admitted that the production team's guide-lines for the movie stipulated 'no destruction of famous landmarks, no shots of Manhattan getting the crap kicked out of it'.[70] By contrast, the 1897–8 American newspaper adaptations of the story, like Pal's film, had deliberately included the destruction of iconic buildings. Orson Welles's radio broadcast had been forced to avoid specifically naming targets.

Despite following Wells's version concerning the failure of the alien invasion, one major change concerned the identity of the invaders, who for once were not Martians.[71] Instead, alien tripods, crewed by pilots beamed down on bolts of lightning, erupt from beneath the earth to zap everyone and everything in sight, given Spielberg's view that this subterranean approach would possess a greater element of surprise. Having sprouted up from the ground like mushrooms, the alien tripods marauded across New Jersey and beyond leaving behind panicking people and a scorched landscape of vaporized bodies, incinerated buildings, wrecked cars and crashed planes. As John Gosling argued, the invader's change of identity was part of Spielberg's attempt to enhance the film's impact upon and appeal to cinema audiences: 'It was precisely the conundrum of how to work Martians into the story that caused Steven Spielberg to sever the connection to

69. Quoted, Flynn, *War of the Worlds*, pp. 119–20.

70. Quoted, Kevin Maher, 'When the killing had to stop', *The Times*, 30 June 2005.

71. Flynn's otherwise sound account of the film is marred by representing the Martians as the invaders, possibly because it seems to have been written before the film was actually released: Flynn, *War of the Worlds*, pp. 116–17.

Mars in his movie, reasoning that the public had seen too many pictures of a dead desert world to buy into the idea of a warlike civilisation waging war on the Earth.[72] Like the Martians, most of Wells's featured characters disappeared also. Despite retaining one character named Ogilvy, the script had no place for the artilleryman, the curate or the narrator's wife, even if Ogilvy, as played by Tim Robbins, might be viewed as embodying some of the traits possessed by Ogilvy, the artilleryman and the curate, as depicted in Wells's novel.

Dwarfing Pal's $2 million budget, Spielberg's *War of the Worlds* cost c. $132 million.[73] However, worldwide gross receipts of $591.7 million ensured that the film more than covered its production budget.[74] Taking fourth place in the table of box office receipts for 2005, *War of the Worlds* succeeded in attracting large numbers of cinema-goers across the USA and beyond. Notwithstanding Spielberg's prioritization of the American audience, the film's global appeal meant that sixty per cent of the receipts came from outside the USA. Nor were cinemas the only source of revenue and audiences. Reportedly, the film grossed some $113 million through the sale of 6.4 million DVDs, quite apart from accessing large audiences subsequently through television.[75]

Reviewers proved somewhat mixed in their reactions to the film, but most referred to Wells's original novel, including its geography and time period and/ or Orson Welles's radio broadcast as reference points.[76] The film's topicality, most notably preying upon contemporary anxieties in the wake of 9/11, proved a prime focus for discussion. For Nigel Morris, the film re-trod 'familiar Spielberg concerns', including disaster-movie spectacle, science fiction fantasy and family psychodrama: 'Its blockbuster treatment of America threatened by an unstoppable alien force is *Jaws* writ large'.[77] *The Times*'s James Christopher praised the film – 'it's a fabulously good watch' – particularly for the way in which 'fear wraps every scene'.[78] Nor was Christopher, who mistakenly mentioned Martians instead of aliens, unduly bothered by the switch of location:

> The Martians are back. Exactly 107 years after they invaded Woking … the aliens have finally scored a direct hit. Spielberg's version of H. G. Wells's novel, *War of the Worlds*, is quite simply the greatest B-movie ever made. Despite the

72. John Gosling, 'Best Sellers Illustrated – War of the Worlds', 2005, http://www. war-ofthe-worlds.co.uk/bestsellers_illustrated.htm [accessed 27 January 2014].

73. Pal, 'War of the Worlds', p. 101.

74. Box Office Mojo, http://boxofficemojo.com/movies/?id=waroftheworlds.htm [accessed 12 June 2012].

75. DVD Sales Chart (2005), Lees Movie Info, http://www.leesmovieinfo.net/Video-Sales.php?type=3 [accessed 27 January 2014].

76. Jenny McCartney, 'Alien tripods and their slippery ways', *Sunday Telegraph*, 3 July 2005; Christopher, 'Mars attacks – and it's a blast'.

77. Nigel Morris, *The Cinema of Steven Spielberg: Empire of Light* (London: Wallflower Press, 2007), p. 352.

78. Christopher, 'Mars attacks – and it's a blast'.

Hollywood change of address, Josh Friedman and David Koepp's screenplay is loyal to the original 1898 book, and the author's delicious sense of sadism. After slaughtering his bourgeois Woking neighbours as painfully as possible, Wells then selected South Kensington for – as he put it in a letter at the time – "feats of peculiar atrocity". Spielberg imposes the same horrors on contemporary New Jersey.

Writing in *The New York Times*, Scott claimed that *War of the Worlds* 'succeeds in reminding us that while Mr. Spielberg doesn't always make great movies, he seems almost constitutionally incapable of bad moviemaking. It's not much to think about, but it's certainly something to see.'[79] Describing the death-ray shooting alien tripods as 'wicked scary', Scott found the movie 'nerve-rackingly apocalyptic'. What really impressed him were the 'stunning' special effects, with several scenes and visual images – Scott mentioned the initial alien attack following the tripods' emergence from underground and the panicking crowd at a Hudson River ferry landing – showing 'how sublime, how aesthetically complete, a few moments of film can be'.

But others were less impressed. Writing in *The Guardian*, Peter Bradshaw, whose review highlighted also the way in which Orson Welles's programme continued to frame present-day thinking, described *War of the Worlds* as 'a fundamentally unambitious and often quite dull film': 'The whole film is a non-war of non-worlds: pseudo-aliens unequally matched with ersatz earthlings, and finally experiencing a reversal that apparently didn't affect them when they came to plant the underground tripods.'[80] Nor did its impact, Bradshaw claimed, rival that of the 1938 radio drama: 'Orson Welles's listeners thought they were experiencing the real thing. Viewers of this movie will think they are watching a demo for the tie-in video game'. Dismissing the film as 'a stinker', the *Daily Telegraph*'s Sukhdev Sandhu proved even more critical, citing the film's repeated failure 'to sustain the action for more than a few minutes' as well as his irritation with the film's key characters.[81] Nor was Sandhu convinced by Cruise's characterization as Ray Ferrier: 'Not for one minute do we believe he's the father of his children'.

In the event, such critical reviews failed to prevent the film proving a commercial success. Moreover, since its release and subsequent availability on DVD and release on television – it was first shown in BBC television in July 2008 – the film has probably taken Wells's *The War of the Worlds* to more people around the globe than any other adaptation. Apart from boosting Wells's name, leading to a spate of new editions of the book and lifting sales of a new Penguin Classics edition (2005), the film provided a sound foundation for Jeff Wayne to launch during the same year a stage show based upon his 1978 musical album, as discussed in the next chapter.

79. Scott, 'Another terror attack'.
80. Peter Bradshaw, 'War of the Worlds', *The Guardian*, 1 July 2005.
81. Sandhu, 'Close encounter of the wrong kind'.

Other film re-creations of The War of the Worlds

Although the two Hollywood movies released in 1953 and 2005 have gained the most attention in media and academia, as well as the largest audiences, during recent decades Wells's *The War of the Worlds* has attracted several other filmmakers (Table 14.1). Varying considerably in dramatic and visual quality, these films tended to have a low profile, frequently going straight to DVD and the television screen without either seeking or securing a cinema release. Inevitably, they varied also in the extent to which they acknowledged Wells's role as the original author, let alone kept faith with his storyline, geography and chronology.

The year 2005 was of course dominated by the Spielberg/Cruise movie, but that year also saw the release of two other films based upon Wells's *The War of the Worlds*. Neither of these low budget movies, directed by Timothy Hines through Pendragon Pictures and David Michael Latt through The Asylum, saw a cinema release.[82] Both went straight to DVD. Unsurprisingly, both films were eclipsed by Spielberg's Hollywood blockbuster, even if reportedly this did not stop Spielberg's team monitoring the progress of rival productions, readjusting film schedules to fast-track its film and using *Out of the Night* as an alias for its film's title during production.[83]

Having been introduced to Wells's *The War of the Worlds* as a child Timothy Hines (1960–) claimed that reading the book, like watching sci-fi films, fostered a deep fascination with science fiction in general and the Martian invasion genre in particular.[84] From an early age, he professed a strong desire to make his own film of the book, a view reinforced when he became aware of what had been done already on film and radio: 'I heard the [1938] radio broadcast, and was entirely taken and obsessed with this idea, this story of the Martians and their fighting machines. Later I saw the 50s version [Pal's film], and I can remember being disappointed that it didn't have walking machines, but still it was frightening.'

When planning to film *The War of the Worlds* during the early 2000s, Hines claimed that his aim was to provide the first authentic movie adaptation of Wells's novel in terms of text, time and geography, something rather different from the modern-day retelling of Spielberg's film under production at the same time: 'I wanted them [people] to see a different version of "War of the Worlds", the one based on the book and what Wells conceived'.[85] For Hines, his attempt to maintain 'the original integrity and original structure' of Wells's book – 'this is H. G. Wells' story' – and not to 'go off and do Tim Hines' story', proved far from easy. For

82. Flynn, *War of the Worlds*, pp. 135–6.

83. Ibid., pp. 108–16, 121; Snider, 'Interview: Timothy Hines'.

84. Snider, 'Interview: Timothy Hines'.

85. Quoted, *Flynn, War of the Worlds*, p. 109. Initial reports of Hines's film by the local press in Woking, took the line that his film would be set in the USA and 'wipe Woking away from the centre of action': Siobhan Ring, 'It's Monstrous!: Sci-fi's off to the USA', *Woking Informer*, 1 June 2001, p. 1. The article mentioned also Hines's hopes of securing Michael Caine as the film's narrator.

example, when seeking funding for the project, he discovered that a film set during the Victorian period was difficult to sell to potential backers.[86] Also 9/11 exerted important impacts. On the one hand, Hines saw 9/11 as imparting greater resonance to his project: '"War of the Worlds" is really a blueprint for survival in really complicated, difficult times. It's all about keeping your humanity together'.[87] On the other hand, 9/11 led to the loss of much of the initial $42 million funding already promised for the film; thus, Hines was forced to proceed with a less ambitious project, with a budget totalling a mere £25 million. Reportedly, Paramount spent this sum merely marketing Spielberg's rival version!

Representing a rare American-made *War of the Worlds*' excursion onto British soil, *The War of the Worlds* was released in 2005. In the event, Hines's efforts fell well short of his professed aims, as evidenced by the relatively negative stance adopted towards the film by most reviewers and commentators. For Williams, among others, 'stodgy playing, uninspired camerawork and lax editing do not match Hines' aesthetically original concept, making his version at best a brave but under-budgeted curiosity'.[88] For Gosling, watching this 179-minute long film proved something of an ordeal, 'a real endurance test'.[89] More importantly, whereas the films made by Pal and Spielberg won high praise for their special effects, a key element in any film of *The War of the Worlds*, this aspect proved a serious weakness, as lamented by Gosling:

> Turning to the special effects, one can only despair further. They are awful. Had this film been made by a couple of 15 year olds on their weekends with an old PC, I'd be calling it a masterpiece, a daring exciting production and a credit to their skills with a home computer, but this is meant to be a professional film and I'm sorry, but there is an expectation that the film will look like it has some production values.

Clearly the lack of a substantial budget proved a major constraint. Perhaps a more serious problem derived from Hines's apparent failure to appreciate the dangers of being too authentic, or the contrasting nature and demands of written and visual media. Hines's professed objective was to produce a true scene-by-scene recreation of Wells's novel set in Victorian England – for Gosling, the film, whose cast list includes the artilleryman, the curate and Ogilvy as well as lesser characters like Henderson, Gregg and Stent, followed 'the flow of the book in almost slavish detail' – and hence to prioritize authenticity over the template required of good movie films.

Nor despite its purported authenticity, did Hines himself treat the film as the definitive *The War of the Worlds* movie, as evidenced soon afterwards when

86. Snider, 'Interview: Timothy Hines'.

87. Quoted, *Flynn, War of the Worlds*, p. 111.

88. Williams, *Wells, Modernity and the Movies*, p. 157.

89. John Gosling, War of the Worlds, n.d., http://www.war-ofthe-worlds.co.uk/war_of_the_worlds_hines.htm [accessed 27 January 2014].

deciding upon a remake.[90] The result, Pendragon Pictures' *War of the Worlds: The True Story*, directed by Hines and produced by Donovan Le and Susan Goforth, was released in 2012. Representing the war fought between Earth and Mars in 1900 as part of world history – this was the conflict occupying centre stage in Wells's book – the movie was created as a faux documentary inspired by the reportage style adopted by Wells's book and Orson Welles's radio broadcast. Blurring the line between fiction and reality, *War of the Worlds: The True Story* treated Wells's fictional conflict as a historical fact, most notably by featuring interviews conducted in 1965 with eighty-six-year-old Bertie Wells, described as the only living survivor of Earth's first recorded interplanetary war:

> A 1965 film crew captured the memories of the last living survivor of the war between Earth and Mars that took place c. 1900. The filmed memoirs, discovered in a vault in 2006, were found with hours of previously unknown footage of the alien/Earth apocalypse, the actual Martian invaders and their war machines. This is the motion picture presentation of that eyewitness account.[91]

Other characters included Ogilvy, the astronomer who discovered the Martians' landing site on Horsell Common.

Premiered at Seattle in June 2012, Hines's film was shown nationwide as a 'special movie event' at selected cinemas across the USA on 30 October 2012, a date marking both Halloween and the anniversary of Orson Welles's broadcast. The film was made available also on DVD. Generally speaking, reviews of the remake were far more positive than those for Hines's 2005 effort. In particular, most reviewers acknowledged that previous weaknesses had now become strengths. For Gary Goldstein of the *Los Angeles Times*, *War of the Worlds: The True Story* proved a 'hugely inventive and ambitious' mock-documentary characterized by a 'clever mix of editing, special effects, visual artistry and offbeat storytelling … It's quite a production'.[92]

H. G. Wells' War of the Worlds, the third film version released in 2005, was yet another low budget film from an independent production company, The

90. Hines admitted that the 2005 film was 'rushed and unfinished', May 2012: Press Release, Pendragon Pictures, 19 May 2012, http://news.yahoo.com/war-worlds-true-story-15-journey-theaters-june-070415372.html [accessed 2 November 2012]; Jessica Martin, 'War of the Worlds: the true story', 13 July 2011, http://www.sfcrowsnest.com/articles/news/2011/War-of-the-Worlds-The-True-Story-16190.php [accessed 2 November 2012]. But the film still grossed $7 million.

91. Mattin, 'War of the Worlds'; Pendragon Pictures, *War of the Worlds: The True Story*, n.d., http://www.waroftheworldsthetruestory.com/ABOUT_THE_MOVIE.html [accessed 26 January 2014]; Steven Rose, Jr., '"War of the Worlds" comes close to historical reality in indie movie', *Sacramento Examiner*, 12 July 2012, http://www.examiner.com/review/war-of-the-worlds-comes-close-to-historical-reality-indie-movie [accessed 2 November 2012].

92. Gary Goldstein, 'Looking back at the Martian apocalypse', *Los Angeles Times*, 18 December 2012.

Asylum. Characterized by a strong emphasis upon horror and violence, the film went straight to DVD. Unlike Hines, David Michael Latt offered a modernized adaptation set in the USA, principally in and around Washington DC, but with a lead character, an astronomer called George Herbert, named by reversing Wells's Christian names. Subsequently, in 2008, The Asylum released *War of the Worlds: The Next Wave*, a sequel, which also went direct to DVD without making much impact upon either reviewers or audiences.

More recently, 2012 saw the release of *War of the Worlds: Goliath*, a 95-minute animated film, originating from Tripod Entertainment, produced in Kuala Lumpur, Malaysia and Seoul, South Korea. Despite offering a brief historical introduction dating back to the late 1890s, the film was basically a sequel, as outlined on the film's website:

> In 1899, the Earth was attacked by ruthless invaders from the planet Mars. The Martians' 80 ft tall, heat-ray spewing, Tripod battle machines laid waste to the planet, but the invaders ultimately fell prey to Earth's tiny bacteria.
>
> Fifteen years later, Man has rebuilt his shattered world, in large part by utilizing captured Martian technology. Equipped with giant, steam-powered Tripod battle machines, the international rapid reaction force, A.R.E.S., is Mankind's first line of defense against the return of the rapacious Martian invaders ...
>
> And return the Martians do. The rematch finds the multinational squad of the A.R.E.S. battle Tripod "Goliath" on the front-lines of a vicious interplanetary offensive when the Martian invaders launch their second invasion using even more advanced alien technology.[93]

Set in the USA, the film was centred upon New York, but extended as far as New Mexico.

Nor are these the only filmmakers to have been inspired by Wells's book and/ or audio-visual adaptations thereof. In 2004 Jeff Wayne concluded an agreement with Paramount Pictures for the production of a feature-length CGI-animated film using his music.[94] Despite the release of short preview sequences and a 2008 scheduled release date for cinema and television, the project was never completed. In the meantime, Jeff Wayne's music inspired other filmmakers, especially animators like Nathan Wilkes.[95] There was also a little known Polish

93. *War of the Worlds: Goliath*, The Movie, 2012, http://www.wotw-goliath.com/ [accessed 1 May 2015].

94. Jeff Wayne and Jemma Wayne, *Jeff Wayne's Musical Version of The War of the Worlds: The Story: The First 30 Years*, n.d., http://www.thewaroftheworlds.com/thestory/default. aspx [accessed 8 February 2014], p. 11.

95. Nathan Wilkes to the author, 15 June 2012. This was then in progress. No further update was provided in response to subsequent requests. Note also Richard Knotek, a Horsell resident: Rob Brown, 'Town's skyline is under fire', *Woking News and Mail*, 22 February 2007; Beth Woodger, 'High Rise thoughts on town's evolution', *Woking News and Mail*, 1 March 2007; Joe Finnerty, 'Town "needs" Martians', *Surrey Advertiser*, 29 June 2012.

film *Wojna Swiatów - Nastepne Stulecie* [*War of the Worlds: The Next Century*].
Released in 1983, Piotr Szulkin's film was dedicated significantly to both Wells and
Orson Welles. Its storyline opened during the closing days of 1999:

> A local reporter, Iron Idem, announces that the Martians have landed. Shortly
> after that his program loses its independence: he is given the script telling the
> crowds how to welcome the invaders. Then the chaos breaks out: the Martians
> and police mistreat the populace; things become violent. Idem's own wife is
> kidnapped and it seems somebody is trying to reduce his effectiveness as a
> reporter. Idem decides to fight back.[96]

Television adaptations

Although the Pal and Spielberg films have been shown on television screens across
the world and attracted large audiences, original television adaptations of *The War
of the Worlds* have proved rare in spite of the fact that any series proved ratings
successes. Also the resulting series, like 'V' (1983–5; remade 2009–11) and 'War
of the Worlds' (1988–90), tended to be sequels or alternative storylines rather than
professed adaptations of Wells's novel. Indeed, as discussed earlier in this chapter,
the 'War of the Worlds' series linked up with Orson Welles's radio broadcast and
Pal's film, not Wells's novel. Perhaps, worthy of mention here, also is the ambitious
BBC series 'The Tripods' (1984–5), based upon the book trilogy written by John
Christopher, imagining an alternative storyline in which the Martians arrived but
survived, rather than dying from earth's bacteria.[97]

One recent attempt by Hallmark Cards Entertainment Productions to produce
a television adaptation of *The War of the Worlds* proved abortive. Acting as
trustees of the Wells estate, Martin and Robin Wells, Wells's grandchildren and
the children of Frank Wells, concluded an agreement with Hallmark for the
production and distribution of a television mini-series based on *The War of
the Worlds*. However, Paramount, pointing to its agreement with Wells in the
mid-1920s and particularly its 1951 contract with Frank Wells, objected on the
grounds that its rights included exclusive ownership also of the television rights.
Wells's grandchildren and Hallmark argued that, though Paramount possessed
'extensive motion picture rights', the 1951 contract did not cover television rights.
In April 2002, the New York Manhattan Supreme Court Justice Ira Gammerman
ruled against the Wells's family and Hallmark, upon the grounds that 'there was
no distinction between a television mini-series and a motion picture': 'any motion
pictures that Paramount has the right to produce, it also has the right to televise'.[98]

---

96. Polish Cinema Database, n.d. quoted, http://www.imdb.com/title/tt0083335/
plotsummary [accessed 14 March 2014].

97. Flynn, *War of the Worlds*, pp. 169–73.

98. 'Hallmark Entertainment Productions, LLC v. Paramount Pictures Corp', *New
York Law Journal*, 25 April 2002, http://www.newyorklawjournal.com/id=1202504980801/

Conclusion

Although this chapter has concentrated upon cinematic adaptations of *The War of the Worlds*, Wells's seminal novel is widely acknowledged as an inspiration for many other films, especially those falling in the alien invasion genre.[99] Wells's *The War of the Worlds* has proved a focus for filmmakers for nearly a century following the sale of film rights during the mid-1920s, even if no film resulted until the early 1950s. By contrast, recent decades have seen a growing number of adaptations, with three films appearing in 2005 and two in 2012. Significantly Hines, Latt, Pal and Spielberg all pointed to the inspiration of Wells's original novel, as well as to the way in which their approach was influenced by Orson Welles's radio drama. Jeff Wayne, whose musical adaptation is discussed in the next chapter, has been cited also as impacting upon several recent filmmakers.

Film and television adaptations of *The War of the Worlds* have served to keep Wells's name in the public eye, to become cultural benchmarks in their own right and to take him to new audiences in a world imbued with a more visual, less literary, culture. Moreover, over time the quantum leap in digital technology offered new possibilities for science fiction filmmakers to render convincing fantasy scenarios, given the perceived significance of special effects for any film based on *The War of the Worlds*. The strings used to control the manta rays, visible to sharp-sighted cinema audiences watching Pal's film, are now a thing of the past.

For cinemagoers, the Pal and Spielberg films based upon *The War of the Worlds* films proved good escapist entertainment offering thrilling adventures and stunning action sequences. For Spielberg, like other filmmakers, movie adaptations of *The War of the Worlds* possess an enduring contemporary resonance and strong appeal in a troubled world, especially given the Martians' ability to serve as symbolic displacements of actual threats:

> Wells' novel has been made into a film several times, notably always in times of international crisis: World War II had just begun when Orson Welles terrified millions of Americans with his legendary radio play version, the headlines were dominated by reports on Hitler's invasion of Poland and Hungary. When the first screen version came into the movie theatres in 1953, the Americans were

HALLMARK-ENTERTAINMENT-PRODUCTIONS%2C-LLC-v.-PARAMOUNT-PICTURES-CORP#ixzz2vpnlnwVz [accessed 15 March 2014]; Dareh Gregorian, 'All's not Wells as Hallmark loses the "War"', *New York Post*, 20 April 2002, http://nypost.com/2002/04/20/alls-not-wells-as-hallmark-loses-the-war/ [15 March 2014]; Steve Green, 'Paramount wins "The War of the World" rights', 21 April 2002, https://groups.yahoo.com/neo/groups/ploktanewsnetwork/conversations/messages/165 [accessed 15 March 2014]. Reportedly Mammoth Screen is taking advantage of the expiry of copyright in 2017 to produce a television adaptation for ITV set in the story's original geogtaphy and period.

99. Flynn, *War of the Worlds*, pp. 127–46.

very afraid of a nuclear attack by the Soviet Union. And our version also comes at a time [i.e. 9/11] when Americans feel deeply vulnerable.[100]

Likewise, Piotr Szulkin's *Wojna Swiatów – Nastepne Stulecie* [*War of the Worlds: The Next Century*] (1983) was produced against the background of a period of turbulence in Polish and Soviet bloc politics, following the formation of the Solidarity Trade Union Movement (1980) and the subsequent declaration of martial law (1981) by the Polish government. In this manner, generally speaking, film adaptations of *The War of the Worlds* have reflected the collective fears, dreams and desires of people living in a rapidly changing world, most notably worries about homeland security and terrorism or uncertainties about the impact of scientific and technological advances upon weaponry and society.

During the 1950s, the appeal of alien invasion films, like Pal's *War of the Worlds* films, was conceptualized by André Bazin, the French film theorist, as the 'Nero Complex', a term describing the vicarious pleasure experienced by cinema audiences when viewing the mayhem and spectacular destruction of familiar cities and towns, major landmarks and so on.[101] Movies offered the vicarious 'fantasy of living through one's death and more, the death of cities, the destruction of humanity itself.'[102] Pointing to such blockbuster films as *Independence Day* (1996), an alien invasion movie in which the White House was annihilated and Manhattan obliterated, and Spielberg's *War of the Worlds* (2005), Kevin Maher observed that 'there's no catharsis greater than watching the neighbourhood get nuked'.[103]

In March 2012, Walt Disney Studios's release of *John Carter*, a film based on Edgar Rice Burroughs's novels, gave added popular cultural visibility to Mars during a period when NASA's Mars Curiosity rover was en route to the Red Planet. In the event, the film, like *Mars needs Moms* (2011), proved neither a critical nor commercial success. Glossing over the fact that perhaps these films themselves were not very good, Ben Fritz asserted that 'Movies featuring Mars as a setting or in the title have universally flopped at the box office over the past decade'.[104] Writing following the landing of NASA's rover on Mars, Fritz commented that:

The successful landing of the rover Curiosity on Mars on Sunday night captured

100. *Der Spiegel*, 'Interview with Steven Spielberg'. In fact, Orson Welles's broadcast, though following the 1938 Munich crisis, predated the outbreak of the 1939 war.

101. Eduardo Cintra Torres, 'Catastrophes in Sight and Sound', in Daniela Agostinho, Elisa Antz and Cátia Ferreira (eds), *Panic and Mourning: The Cultural Work of Trauma* (Berlin: Walter de Gruyter, 2012), p. 226; Maher, 'When the killing had to stop'; Hoberman, 'All as it had been'.

102. Susan Sontag, quoted Hoberman, 'All as it had been'.

103. Maher, 'When the killing had to stop'.

104. Ben Fritz, 'Mars Rover Curiosity is big hit – Mars movies are big flops', *Los Angeles Times*, 6 August 2012. Other Mars-themed 'flops' cited by Fritz included *Mars Attacks!* (1996); *The Red Planet* (2000); *Mission to Mars* (2000); and *Ghosts of Mars* (2001).

America's imagination in a way that few positive news events have in years. Hollywood, meanwhile, may have been left scratching its head over why it can't capture the same Martian magic ... The lesson? When it comes to Mars, it seems contemporary Americans are inspired more by reality, not science fiction.

In this vein, one can point also to the manner in which the Martians were replaced by anonymous aliens in Spielberg's film. Mars exploration, it appears, has limited the scope for sci-fi imagining of Martian scenarios, but enough question marks remain about the Red Planet to ensure that Mars will continue to attract sci-fi writers and filmmakers for some time to come. In part, the appeal of Wells's *The War of the Worlds* to filmmakers has proved a function of popular interest in Mars, but results largely from a wide range of other factors which combine to ensure that its appeal is enduring, not ephemeral. Indeed, in 2015 Ridley Scott's *The Martian*, a film well received both at the box office and by reviewers, made this point when taking Andy Weir's 2011 novel to the cinema.

Chapter 15

THE WAR OF THE WORLDS INSPIRES JEFF WAYNE'S ROCK OPERA AND REACHES THE MUSIC STAGE AROUND THE WORLD

For nearly four decades Jeff Wayne has taken, indeed introduced, Wells's *War of the Worlds* to yet another vast worldwide audience, listeners of music.[1] Initially, Jeff Wayne's music accessed this audience through vinyl records and cassette tapes and then CDs, but during the past decade he took *The War of the Worlds* as a music stage show to new audiences in large arenas in Britain, continental Europe and Australasia as well as through DVDs, radio broadcasts and screenings of the stage show at cinemas and on television. Taking root in the charts, the original album, whose sales exceed fifteen million, proved a commercial phenomenon. More significantly, given the deviant nature of most adaptations of *The War of the Worlds*, Jeff Wayne decided to remain true, or truer than most, to Wells's original template concerning time, place and storyline. In many respects, he offers the most definitive audio-visual retelling of Wells's *The War of the Worlds*.

Beginning and developing The War of the Worlds' *music project*

Born in New York in 1943, Jeffry 'Jeff' Wayne has worked chiefly in Britain for film, the record industry, stage and television as well as writing jingles for advertising agencies. He was first introduced to Wells's *The War of the Worlds* during the 1970s by his father, Jerry, an actor, lyricist and singer, who had starred as Sky Masterson in 'Guys and Dolls' on the London stage during the early 1950s: 'I had no knowledge of TWOTW [*The War of the Worlds*] and in my ignorance thought it was a modern piece, not an amazing Victorian tale'.[2] As Jeff Wayne admitted, 'Before he [my father] gave it to me, I had never heard of it. Nor was I familiar with Orson Welles's 1938 radio production, which had scared the wits out of some very naïve Yanks, or the 1953 Paramount film also set in America – which didn't scare anyone.'[3]

1. Jeff Wayne's Christian name is included to avoid confusion with his father.
2. Took, 'Interview'.
3. Jeff Wayne, 'H. G. Wells' The War of the Worlds: The Greatest Story'; Caroline Scott, 'Relative Values: How the West End Saved Our Family', *Sunday Times Magazine*, 25 November 2012, p. 6.

At the time Jeff Wayne and his parents were considering various books, principally science fiction titles, as the basis for a new music project to follow on from their collaboration in 'Two Cities', a musical based upon Charles Dickens's *Tale of Two Cities* and staged in London during the late 1960s. Jeff Wayne composed the music, his father the lyrics. Looking back to the time when evaluating possibilities with his wife – titles considered included Aldous Huxley's *Brave New World* (1932), Jules Verne's *20,000 Leagues under the Sea* (1870) and John Wyndham's *The Day of the Triffids* (1951) – Jerry Wayne recalled that finally they asked themselves, '"What's the greatest science fiction book ever written?" Doreen and I looked at each other and said, "*The War of the Worlds*"'.[4] They asked Jeff Wayne to read the book: 'After one read', he claimed, 'I was hooked'.[5]

In particular, Jeff Wayne was excited by the story's musical and visual potential: 'After just one reading I could already hear "sound". It was the one, which I felt could be adapted into a musical interpretation and not a spoken word recording with musical accompaniment'.[6] The storyline struck a chord: 'What inspired me about the book, other than its possibilities from a musician's perspective, was its underlying theme of man's struggle on Earth'.[7] The anti-imperial and war scare elements also resonated strongly. Further support for selecting *The War of the Worlds* emanated from the pop star David Essex, who had been working with Jeff Wayne on recordings and live shows: 'Jeff and I had done about five albums together. Then one day he said: "I'm thinking about doing this concept album, War of the Worlds." I told him it was a great idea, because it had been very controversial when Orson Welles did it as a radio play in America'.[8]

Having acquired the audio, electronic, graphic novel, radio and stage rights to the novel in 1975, Jeff Wayne began work on the lengthy process of retelling the story through a musical interpretation possessing its own sound, style, narrative and visual imagery: 'I envisaged my version of War of the Worlds as an opera: story, leitmotifs, musical phrases, sounds and compositions that relate to the whole'.[9] When they first met to discuss the project, Justin Hayward soon realized that Jeff Wayne was 'a man on a mission'.[10] For him, the project proved all-consuming. Working upon a draft script written by Doreen Wayne, his stepmother, and edited by his father, Jeff Wayne composed the music for his rock opera, described by one reviewer as musically 'an idiosyncratic mix of prog [progressive] rock

---

4. J. and J. Wayne, *Jeff Wayne's Musical Version: The Story*, pp. 7–8. See also 'Deconstructing Jeff Wayne's Musical Version of The War of the Worlds': The Making of DVD, disc 7, Jeff Wayne, Collier and Schurrer, *Jeff Wayne's Musical Versions: Collector's Edition*.

5. Wayne, 'H. G. Wells' The War of the Worlds'.

6. J. and J. Wayne, *Jeff Wayne's Musical Version: The Story*, p. 9;

7. Jeff Wayne, 'H. G. Wells' The War of the Worlds'; 'But Still They Come', *BBC Radio Four*, 22 December 2012; Took, 'Interview'.

8. Andrew Pulver, 'Jeff Wayne and David Essex: How We Made *The War of the Worlds*', *The Guardian*, 14 January 2014.

9. Pulver, 'Jeff Wayne'; J. and J. Wayne, *Jeff Wayne's Musical Version: The Story*, pp. 6, 11, 21.

10. Quoted, J. and J. Wayne, *Jeff Wayne's Musical Version: The Story*, p. 91.

and disco', in collaboration with Gary Osborne, a lyricist who had frequently worked with him on advertising jingles.[11] Recalling frequent journeys from his Hampstead home to discuss the music with Jeff Wayne, Osborne noted that they took him past not only one of Wells's residences in Camden Town, but also several landmarks mentioned in the book, like Regent's Park and Primrose Hill.[12]

Apart from preparing the music and finalizing the storylines, Jeff Wayne had to secure £240,000 to fund the production of a double album. *CBS Records* agreed to back the project, but only to the extent of £75,000, leaving Jeff Wayne to fund the rest himself.[13] Reportedly, the project's critical break-even figure was 150,000 album sales, a tall order for a so-called concept-album lacking an obvious target audience at a time when punk and disco music were all the rage.[14] Conversely science fiction films – 1977 releases, included George Lucas's *Star Wars*, Steven Spielberg's *Close Encounters of the Third Kind* and yet another movie adaptation of *The Island of Dr Moreau* – were doing well at the box office. Of course, one way to secure publicity and boost album sales was to recruit star names. When casting the recording, Richard Burton's agreement to act as the narrator, named as 'The Journalist' in Jeff Wayne's version, was a landmark event. Burton's high global profile in the film and theatre worlds, combined with the media focus upon his personal life and relationship with Elizabeth Taylor, proved a major marketing asset for the project. Indeed, the actor's busy work schedule meant that the recording of his contribution had to be conducted in Los Angeles.[15]

The recording benefited also from the participation of several star names from the world of popular music, including David Essex ('The Artilleryman'), Justin Hayward (the Sung Thoughts of 'The Journalist') of the Moody Blues, Phil Lynott ('Parson Nathaniel') of Thin Lizzy, Chris Thompson ('The Voice of Humanity') of Manfred Mann's Earth Band and Julie Covington (Beth, the parson's fiancée) who had appeared with David Essex in *Godspell*. Jerry Wayne performed 'The Voices of NASA Control'. Jeff Wayne's wife, Geraldine, helped out with sound effects. Reportedly, her kitchen saucepans played a key role in the chilling sequence on Horsell Common when the lid of the Martian cylinder was unscrewed and

11. Ian Gittins, 'The War of the Worlds – Review', *The Guardian*, 16 December 2012. Born in Hull, Doreen Wayne, Jeff Wayne's stepmother, was a novelist. Gary Osborne, was also well known, for his musical collaborations with Elton John.

12. J. and J. Wayne, *Jeff Wayne's Musical Version: The Story*, pp. 63–4.

13. Ibid., pp. 16–19; Nick McGrath, 'Jeff Wayne: "I spent my life savings on War of the Worlds"', *Daily Telegraph*, 22 December 2013.

14. Justin Hayward quoted, J. and J. Wayne, *Jeff Wayne's Musical Version: The Story*, p. 93. Speaking from experience, Justin Hayward confirmed that such albums always had problems finding their market and frequently never did.

15. J. and J. Wayne, *Jeff Wayne's Musical Version: The Story*, pp. 46–57; Pulver, 'Jeff Wayne'. Clips from the recording sessions with Burton – they indicated his initial mispronunciation of Billericay in Essex – were played in 'But Still They Come', BBC Radio Four, 22 December 2012. The text including Billericay was eventually edited out of the final album.

crashed to the ground in front of a crowd of local residents.[16] Several well-known musicians were involved, including Herbie Flowers on bass guitar, Chris Spedding on lead guitar and Jo Partridge on rhythm and acoustic guitars.

Speaking as 'The Journalist', Burton performed a pivotal role as the storyteller, 'the thread that ran through the whole thing': 'I wanted someone with a voice that would take the listener right inside this world. In my view, Richard Burton's voice was like a musical instrument'.[17] For Jeff Wayne, the emphasis upon working within Wells's original settings and time frame ruled out as narrator any person who was not British.[18] The brother's role in covering events in London was omitted to avoid confusion.[19] Re-invented as 'Parson Nathaniel', a totally different person from the somewhat passive character featured in Wells's text, 'The Curate' was given a wife, 'Beth', a new character. Introduced to give the story a female voice lacking in Wells's book, 'Beth' was used to add drama to the show through her relationship with Parson Nathaniel:

> [The] Parson is someone who you would think in times of an alien invasion, would be the person that people could go to for moral and spiritual comfort – but in fact Nathaniel is the first one to lose his sanity and thinks the Martians are the devils! ... He's the one that is the most insane and his wife Beth tries to "draw him back from his insanity" and to give him hope to live for and that there's good in life – and it's a major sequence in the show and it's a battle between those two.[20]

Ogilvy, the astronomer responsible for discovering the Martian landing place, was mentioned only during Burton's narrative.

Like Wells's novel, the production was divided into two acts (I: The Coming of the Martians; II: Earth under the Martians) replicating those in the original book. Likewise, a heavily edited version of the book's opening paragraph – 'No one would have believed, in the last years of the nineteenth century ...' (1.1: 1/7) and so on – was spoken by Burton as a 36-second narrative designed to set the mood for the show. This was followed musically by 'The Eve of the War', the only composition for which Jeff Wayne wrote both the words and music. Featuring Justin Hayward as 'The Sung Thoughts of the Journalist', the lyrics drew inspiration from Wells's text, in which Ogilvy asserted that 'the chances against anything man-like on Mars are a million to one' (1.1: 9/11) and the narrator asserted that everywhere things appeared safe and tranquil (I.1: 11/12).

16. J. and J. Wayne, *Jeff Wayne's Musical Version: The Story*, pp. 125–9.

17. Pulver, 'Jeff Wayne'.

18. Jeff Wayne, quoted Wayne, Collier and Schurrer, *Jeff Wayne's Musical Version*, p. 14; J. and J. Wayne, *Jeff Wayne's Musical Version: The Story*, p. 47.

19. J. and J. Wayne, *Jeff Wayne's Musical Version: The Story*, p. 25.

20. Suzanne Rothberg, 'Jeff Wayne's musical The War of the Worlds: Alive on stage', *Examiner.com*, 1 May 2010, http://www.examiner.com/article/jeff-wayne-s-musical-the-war-of-the-worlds-alive-on-stage [accessed 10 February 2014].

The album as a commercial and artistic success story

Completed in June 1977, the recording was handed over to *CBS* for approval, production and release.[21] Despite receiving a positive response from *CBS UK* for what was viewed as a 'truly original' and 'unique' work, the record company's American branch, Columbia Records, decided against releasing the recording in the USA where the head of 'A&R' ['Artists and Repertoire'], decided that such an unconventional work was unlikely to sell: 'It's an unusually good album, but we don't see a 95-minute continuous work happening anywhere in the world, especially in America!'.[22] Revealingly, Columbia Records, Wayne reported, viewed the story as *a classic American story* set in England, thereby indicating the manner in which exposure to Orson Welles's radio broadcast and Pal's film, encouraged Americans to claim ownership over the original book.[23]

Launched on 9 June 1978 at a multimedia presentation held at the London Planetarium, the album entered the British album charts the following week. Not only did sales rapidly overtake the critical 150,000 breakeven point, but within six weeks worldwide totals passed one million! [24] Sales exceeded all expectations, thereby soon forcing Columbia Records to reverse its decision regarding the album's release in the USA. By 2005, when the album had notched up thirteen million sales, 700,000 copies had been sold in the USA.[25] Peaking at number five in Britain's Top 200 Albums chart, the album never reached top spot, but remained in the chart for over thirty years. Released as singles, Justin Hayward's 'Forever Autumn' and Jeff Wayne's 'The Eve of the War' also charted in the UK. Charting in twenty-two countries, the album reached top position in eleven countries. In addition, the release of German, Spanish and Mexican Spanish versions meant that Richard Burton was joined by three other narrators: Curd Jürgens, Teófilo Martínez and Anthony Quinn.[26] The album's commercial success was reinforced by recognition of its artistic merit through two Ivor Novello awards (1979–80), as well as an award in 1979 for 'The Best Recording in Science Fiction and Fantasy', from a panel of judges including Alfred Hitchcock, George Lucas and Steven Spielberg.

Generally speaking, over time Wayne's rock opera weathered well both musically and conceptually. As one reviewer conceded, the album has had its

21. On recording the album (May 1976–June 1977), see Wayne, Collier and Schurrer, *Jeff Wayne's Musical Version: Collector's Edition*, pp. 66–71; J. and J. Wayne, *Jeff Wayne's Musical Version: The Story*, pp. 35–41, 67–83.

22. J. and J. Wayne, *Jeff Wayne's Musical Version: The Story*, pp. 133–7, pp. 142–3; Wayne, Collier and Schurrer, *Jeff Wayne's Musical Version: Collector's Edition*, p. 18.

23. 'But Still They Come'.

24. J. and J. Wayne, *Jeff Wayne's Musical Version: The Story*, p. 20.

25. Jeff Wayne, quoted, Wayne, Collier and Schurrer, *Jeff Wayne's Musical Version: Collector's Edition*, p. 19.

26. Dutch and Israeli versions were prepared for national radio broadcasts, but not for release as albums.

critics, but 'the playing, production and execution are all excellent'.[27] Moreover, the enduring nature of its sales, albeit boosted by the re-issue of the original vinyl double album as an audio-cassette, a CD, a remix album and so on, reflected the way in which this musical interpretation was instrumental in taking Wells's *The War of the Worlds* repeatedly to new young audiences. Reportedly, at one time the recording, most notably its extended, highly rhythmic, synthesizer-driven sections, became popular with DJs and audiences in discos and dance clubs in the USA. Nor when discussing new audiences should we forget that over time several computer games – these include a video game for the Sinclair Spectrum (1984), computer games for PCs and Sony PlayStation (1998–9) and mini-games introduced recently for the iPad and iPhone – have been developed around Jeff Wayne's *War of the Worlds*.[28]

Against this background, during the early 2000s, Jeff Wayne and his record company considered various ways of developing and updating the concept.[29] A key prompt was the forthcoming 25th anniversary of the original release of the album. One result was a re-mastered album in surround sound. Another outcome was a collector's edition of the album – this book was issued in 2005 – including the re-mastering of the original tracks into a surround sound version, remixes, outtakes, a documentary about making the original album and a book. Market research indicated that the new albums sold well not only to those who had previously purchased the 1978 album, but also to the fifteen to thirty age group.[30] However, Wayne's plans for a feature-length animated film of *The War of the Worlds* co-produced with Paramount Pictures, based upon his music, proved abortive.[31]

Moving on from the album to a stage show

Following an approach from 'Clear Channel' (now called 'Live Nation'), the concert promoters, Jeff Wayne agreed to stage a one-off concert rendition of the *War of the Worlds* at London's Royal Albert Hall on 7 September 2005, that is two months after the British release of Spielberg's film adaptation. The fact that tickets sold out in three hours, led him to recognize the case for something more permanent by taking the show on tour around Britain and beyond as a large scale spectacular multimedia extravaganza.[32]

27. Daniel Ross, 'Jeff Wayne: War of the Worlds', *The Quietus*, 18 June 2009, http://thequietus.com/articles/01901-jeff-wayne-s-war-of-the-worlds-special-edition-review [accessed 2 February 2014].

28. Flynn, *War of the Worlds*, pp. 81–2.

29. As recorded in Chapter 16, during 1996–7 there was an abortive attempt to arrange a concert of music from the album.

30. J. and J. Wayne, *Jeff Wayne's Musical Version: The Story*, pp. 182–3.

31. Ibid., p. 11.

32. Ibid., pp. 184–7.

The initial tour grew from one show to be staged in 2006, first to seven, then to ten and finally a fourteen-date tour including the 12,500 capacity Wembley Arena as well as the Royal Albert Hall. Five further tours followed (Table 15.1), principally within the UK, but also occasionally taking in Belgium, Ireland, Germany and the Netherlands as well as Australia and New Zealand. Since 2007 tours have included London's 20,000 capacity O2 arena. Most venues sold out, with extra shows being added to cover the high demand for tickets, from not only those familiar with the album but also from new audiences attracted by a spectacular musical stage show, based upon a book featured recently in Spielberg's Hollywood blockbuster. What was billed as the 'Final Arena Tour', the sixth tour, took place in 2014. Hitherto, no shows have been staged in the USA. Reportedly, discussions have taken place about touring the USA – New York's Radio City Music Hall was mentioned as a possible venue – but hitherto nothing has been finalized. As Jeff Wayne told one American interviewer:

> The problem is – (it's a nice problem) that once we mount the shows it's huge and a real live performance and technological ingredients but because of that you really need to have enough shows in any given territory to make it work financially. We know that there's interest from the [United] States in fact PBS ran our 2006 DVD which was our first tour last December; the feedback from that was pretty good – so we'll get to your side of the pond at some point. [33]

In the event, an American tour has yet to take place.

The size of venues – typically seating capacities ranged between 10,000 and 20,000 – placed a premium upon spectacle and the imaginative integration of sight and sound, even if the music remains the core: 'everything else has been built around that'.[34] Featuring the ten-piece Black Smoke Band and the forty-eight-piece ULLAdubULLA Strings conducted by Jeff Wayne, the stage show made extensive use of cutting-edge technology to re-enact a Martian invasion

Table 15.1 Jeff Wayne's music stage show, 2005–14

Year	Number of shows	Countries visited
2005	1	United Kingdom (UK)
2006	14	UK, Ireland
2007	8	Australia, New Zealand
2007	15	UK
2009	21	UK, Ireland, Germany, the Netherlands
2010	20	UK, Belgium, Ireland, the Netherlands. The planned tour to Germany was postponed
2012–13	22	UK, Ireland, Netherlands, Germany
2014	18	UK, the Netherlands

33. Rothberg, 'Jeff Wayne's musical'.
34. Ibid.

at arenas across Britain and overseas.[35] The storyline was streamlined to flow more easily, but revolved around the same characters as on the album: 'The Journalist', 'Parson Nathaniel', his wife 'Beth', 'The Artilleryman' and Carrie, the fiancée of 'The Journalist'. Even so, some rationalization occurred in the interests of making things easier for the audience and creating a more balanced musical line-up. Although Richard Burton had died in 1984, he featured still in the show as 'The Journalist', relating the story as a survivor of the invasion, but was now named George Herbert. Pictured initially in 2006 as a ten foot high talking head, from 2007 onwards Burton became an eleven foot high floating 3D hologram suspended over the stage.[36] Justin Hayward and Chris Thompson, who sang on the original 1978 recording, reprised their roles in the stage show. New cast members included Alexis James as 'The Artilleryman', Russell Watson as 'Parson Nathaniel' and Tara Blaise as 'Beth'. The role of 'Carrie', the fiancée of 'The Journalist', was performed by Anna-Marie Wayne, Jeff Wayne's daughter.

For most audiences, the star of the show was a thirty-five foot high Martian fighting machine (Figure 15.1). Providing visually powerful images, the giant machine descended towards the stage firing its heat-ray at the audience. As Wayne recorded, 'The machine's bug-like eyes scan the audience as they see themselves up on the big screen. It's really not as scary as it sounds, only the first three rows of the audience get incinerated – I kid of course!' [37] Nor should the contribution of CGI and video in counterpointing the live music be overlooked. Apart from replicating the Victorian era in which Wells had set the original novel, CGI and video projected onto a 100 foot wide screen backstage, contributed other audio-visual elements in support of the storyline, like showing people in flight, introduced 'Carrie' and provided special effects, most notably the black smoke and heat-rays.

The first stop on the initial tour, was Bournemouth's International Centre in April 2006. Reviewing the opening night of Jeff Wayne's *War of the Worlds* for the *Daily Telegraph*, David Cheal admitted being 'nonplussed' by the whole experience:

> This was easily one of the strangest shows I have ever seen. Featuring a dizzying array of special effects, a troupe of actor-singers, a cinema-sized video screen and a small army of musicians, and narrated by a virtual reincarnation of the late great Welsh actor Richard Burton, this weird multimedia version of Jeff Wayne's multi-million selling 1978 album The War of the Worlds was dazzling, puzzling, and utterly uncategorisable.[38]

---

35. The name 'ULLAdubULLA' is derived from the haunting 'Ulla' sound made by the Martians in Wells's novel (II.8: 275/164): Wayne, Collier and Schurrer, *Jeff Wayne's Musical Version: Collector's Edition*, p. 61.

36. J. and J. Wayne, *Jeff Wayne's Musical Version: The Story*, pp. 251–4.

37. Took, 'Interview'; J. and J. Wayne, *Jeff Wayne's Musical Version: The Story*, pp. 197–204.

38. David Cheal, 'The Martians have landed', *Daily Telegraph*, 15 April 2006.

Figure 15.1 Jeff Wayne's music stage show, 2014. The Martian Fighting Machine fires its deadly Heat Ray while Jeff Wayne conducts from his podium. On the right of the stage is the 36-piece ULLAdubULLA Strings. On the left of the stage is the 9-piece Black Smoke Band.

Source: Photographer Roy Smiljanic: http://www.thewaroftheworlds.com/.

Nor was he convinced by the show's storyline: 'as a narrative, it felt bitty and episodic. As drama, it didn't convince'. But Cheal was forced to admit that, 'As an experience, it was impressive'. Four years on, the stage show was still viewed by reviewers as very different: it was part live musical concert, part theatre, part audio-visual art and part multi-sensory experience. For *The Times*'s David Sinclair, it offered 'a curious mixture of orchestral rock music, singing, spoken narrative, theatre, film, pyrotechnics and lightshow'.[39]

By contrast, audiences proved far more receptive – even Cheal conceded that the packed audience was both enthusiastic and attentive – with sold-out venues and standing ovations greeting every performance. As two of the tour's promoters commented about the standing ovation after the opening show: 'The people have spoken'.[40] The first two tours played to c. 300,000 people on two continents.[41] What Jeff Wayne's multimedia extravaganza did was to give audiences a distinctive live show integrating images, music and words to bring Wells's 1898 novel 'noisily to life' in the twenty first century.[42] DVDs of the show filmed at Wembley Arena in April 2006 and a BBC radio broadcast in July 2009 took the stage show to the homes of a wider audience of listeners and viewers around the world. In Britain

39. David Sinclair, 'All fired up in Wayne's World', *The Times*, 14 December 2010.

40. Barry Clayman and Phil Bowdery quoted, J. and J. Wayne, *Jeff Wayne's Musical Version: The Story*, p. 236.

41. J. and J. Wayne, *Jeff Wayne's Musical Version: The Story*, p. 242.

42. Sinclair, 'All fired up'.

the DVD topped the Music DVD charts and spent over one year in the top forty charts. In the USA the DVD was shown on *PBS*.

Relaunching the stage show in 2012: 'The new generation'

Naturally over time, the stage show evolved such as in terms of retuning the presentation to top the previous tour, taking advantage of fast-advancing technology, introducing new musical content and making cast changes. Late 2012 saw the launch of Jeff Wayne's 'new interpretation', 'The New Generation' version of *War of the Worlds*, as a stage show and recording benefiting from revisiting the music, the script and the characters in the light of the ever-changing musical and technological landscape. In brief, the show continued to push the boundaries of music and performance.

Conducted by Jeff Wayne, the production featured the thirty-six-piece ULLAdubULLA Strings, the nine-piece Black Smoke Band and Liam Neeson in 3D holography in place of Richard Burton as George Herbert, 'The Journalist'. Jason Donovan, who had toured previously with the show as 'The Artilleryman', re-joined the cast as 'Parson Nathaniel'. New members of the cast included well-known names from popular music: Ricky Wilson ('The Artilleryman') of the Kaiser Chiefs, Marti Pellow ('The Sung Thoughts of the Journalist') of Wet Wet Wet, Kerry Ellis ('Beth'), and Will Stapleton ('The Voice of Humanity') of Jettblack. For the 2014 tour, Westlife's Brian McFadden replaced Marti Pellow and Carrie Hope Fletcher, who had appeared in *Les Miserables*, took the part of 'Beth'.

Significantly, Jeff Wayne used the final arena tour to allow Wells himself 'to have his say' through 'a technological recreation'.[43] As he promised, 'It's all written':

> The role is in three big pieces set at different times, one is when he's aged 33 which is a year after *War of the Worlds* came out, the next is 20 years later just after the First World War and then in 1945 just months before he died. He's looking back and forward and he gives a good insight into why he wrote it, which wasn't about a shoot-em-up-knock-em-down science fiction story, but it was actually making social commentary about the standing British Empire, about one's faith and challenging certain things. It's also about territorial invasion, which when you think about the world we live in today, not a lot has changed.

For David Sinclair, whose review of the previous show was cited above, the 'New Generation' show 'was hard to tell apart from those of previous generations'.[44]

---

43. Quoted, Val Siebert, 'The Quietus Interview: A life During Wartime: Jeff Wayne Interviewed', *The Quietus*, 20 December 2013, http://thequietus.com/articles/01901-jeff-wayne-s-war-of-the-worlds-special-edition-review [accessed 2 February 2014]; Jeff Wayne, 'The World of H. G. Wells', *Jeff Wayne's Musical Version of The War of the Worlds: Alive on Stage 2014* [Show Programme], 2014.

44. David Sinclair, 'Pop: The War of the Worlds', *The Times*, 11 December 2012.

Reviewing the film for *Screendaily*, Mark Adams admired the spectacle and the cast, but argued that it was 'essentially an event production, with as much attention paid to the animation and physical effects as to the singers'.[45] For *The Guardian's* Ian Gittins, Jeff Wayne's musical adaptation had 'not aged particularly well' either musically or as a show: 'this *War of the Worlds* is a flawed period piece'.[46] Once again, the mixed critical reactions contrast with those of audiences, which continue to be large, engaged and highly enthusiastic. One innovation was the cinema screening in April 2013 by More2Screen, a leader in event cinema, of a filmed version of the show staged at London's O2 in December 2012. Subsequently, the film became available as a DVD for home entertainment. Reviewing the film for *Screendaily*, Mark Adams feared that the show lost some of its impact through film: 'As with any filmed version of a live performance there is always a feeling that there is more fun to be had at the event itself than at any recording'.[47] *The Guardian's* Peter Bradshaw agreed, while adding that the music seemed 'bizarrely counterintuitive, given the story's horror'.[48]

Conclusion

The artistic and commercial success of his music recordings, combined with the sell-out audiences attracted by the stage shows and the substantial DVD sales thereof, places Jeff Wayne alongside Orson Welles, George Pal and Steven Spielberg on the list of people instrumental in their time taking Wells's *The War of the Worlds* to existing audiences and introducing the story to new audiences around the world.

In this vein, the music show staged since 2006, though attracting those who listened to the album, appealed also to a rather different audience. For over three decades, Jeff Wayne's *War of the Worlds* has taken Wells to a large worldwide audience, many of whom, like Wayne himself in the mid-1970s, will be new to the book. Undoubtedly, some listeners of the album and members of the show's audience, seeking something more than mere entertainment and musical escapism, will have been encouraged to read the book of the music and hence introduced to a literary world, which they might otherwise never have explored. For Marti Pellow, the show was in part 'about turning new people on to his [Jeff Wayne] vision, it delivers so much more to the original fans and will massively

45. Mark Adams, 'Jeff Wayne's Musical Version of The War of The Worlds – Alive On Stage! The New Generation', 5 April 2013, *Screendaily,* http://www.screendaily.com/reviews/the-latest/jeff-waynes-musical-version-of-the-war-of-the-worlds-alive-on-stage-the-new-generation/5053643.article [accessed 30 January 2014].

46. Gittins, 'The War of the Worlds'.

47. Adams, 'Jeff Wayne's Musical Version'.

48. Peter Bradshaw, 'The War of the Worlds – Alive on Stage! – Review', *The Guardian,* 4 April 2013.

inspire new ones'.[49] In this vein, Nathan Wilkes, a British film animator, was one young person inspired by the show to develop an animated film of *The War of the Worlds*: 'Our main influence has to be Jeff Wayne's Musical Version of War of the Worlds. This whole idea came about after watching it live on stage.' [50]

Jeff Wayne's multimedia musical version is distinguished by his effort to retain the story's fundamental integrity, given his decision 'to stick as close to H. G. Wells's original text as possible and to remain as faithful to it as the restrictions of a 96-minute musical work would permit'.[51] Indeed, when commencing the project during the mid-1970s, Jeff Wayne prioritized this point when requesting music rights to the book. Unsurprisingly, this feature, alongside the way in which his music has given Wells and *The War of the Worlds* visibility in today's world, represents a central part of what he views as his personal contribution to preserving and enhancing perceptions of Wells's legacy:

> At times my recordings have been used to introduce the story and get people aware of the story that was written in 1897. I know people, particularly in the United States, that only know the movies that have come out or the radio recording and think it's a tale of an alien invasion in contemporary America. It's nothing like that at all. If I have contributed at all I would be thrilled because I think it sets the record straight, so to speak.[52]

Despite his American roots, Jeff Wayne believed that the story 'lost its heart and soul' when placed in a modern North American setting; thus, what he called 'political' as well as musical reasons, led him to set the story in Britain.[53] Claiming to interpret the story musically exactly as the story was written, Jeff Wayne saw himself as helping to 'protect' what Wells created, as evidenced by the deliberate choice for the stage show of a Briton as narrator and the use of CGI and video to provide visual coverage of Victorian England. The show's focus upon Surrey and London was reflected in the inclusion of such songs as, 'Horsell Common and the Heat-Ray' and 'Dead London', as well as by mention of Horsell Common, Maybury Hill, Byfleet, Weybridge and London, but not Woking, in the linking narrative spoken by Burton and then Neeson as 'The Journalist'.[54]

49. 'Press Release: The Dazzling, Groundbreaking Arena Production Launches A New Generation!', n.d. [2012], http://www.thewaroftheworlds.com/live-events/2012-13-uk-eu/press.aspx [accessed 22 January 2013].

50. Nathan Wilkes to the author, 15 June 2012. See the use of Jeff Wayne's music by Richard Knotek for his 'YouTube' animated *War of the Worlds* video: Brown, 'Town's skyline is under fire'; Finnerty, 'Town "needs" Martians'.

51. J. and J. Wayne, *Jeff Wayne's Musical Version*, p. 24.

52. Siebert, 'The Quietus Interview'.

53. 'But Still They Come'.

54. Although Woking is not actually named, mention of both Maybury and Horsell Common places the initial setting in and around the town. Woking, like Horsell, Ottershaw and Pyrford, figured in the initial script narrated by Richard Burton, but subsequently was

Notwithstanding Jeff Wayne's claims about remaining true to Wells's story, some commentators have proved more critical. For example, Daniel Ross feared that those listening to the album or watching the music show, would treat *The War of the Worlds* as basically Jeff Wayne's work, his musical interpretation, rather than as a recording based upon a novel written by Wells: 'The main thing that goes unnoticed, however, is the shocking way in which Wayne has appropriated the Wells material, and almost billed it as his own. If one thinks of *The War of the Worlds* today, the Wells original must come into third place for most people, behind Wayne's and Spielberg's interpretations.' [55] Ross made no mention of Orson Welles's radio broadcast, but if he had this might have prompted him to relegate Wells's original to fourth place. What Ross objected to, was the alleged way in which Jeff Wayne's writing team had 'hacked the book to pieces', such as by cutting out philosophical, psychological, religious elements, toning down the horror and violence and re-imagining the original characters. For example, Jeff Wayne's script rewrote radically the curate's role in terms of re-titling him as a parson, naming him as Nathaniel and, as outlined above, transforming his character and marital status for dramatic effect.

Despite remaining true to a Victorian setting, the show, like the album, ended by striking a present-day resonance in the Epilogue through the closing NASA sequence performed by Jerry Wayne. Here American astronauts landed on the Red Planet, where communication problems led to the loss of contact with Earth. Listeners were left to draw their own conclusions. Echoing Ross's critique, David Sinclair pointed to the very different mood set by a popular music show offering a twenty-first-century take on Wells's pessimistic storyline: 'Although H. G. Wells's story has retained its appeal, it has become deracinated by the genteel familiarity of this production. While the Journalist speaks despairingly of the "rout of civilisation" and "the massacre of mankind", the music romps merrily along like *Tubular Bells* sets to a disco beat.'[56]

Clearly, any adaptation of Wells's *The War of the Worlds*, even one staying relatively close to the original geography and time period, will struggle to represent itself as *the definitive retelling* of a Martian invasion launched against Victorian Britain, given the perceived need to meet the specific requirements of an alternative audio-visual format, as well as the changing nature and expectations of present-day audiences. What Jeff Wayne can claim is his role in keeping Wells's name and *The War of the Worlds* in the public eye and taking both Wells and the story to existing and new audiences in today's multimedia world. Like other adaptations of Wells's original book, Jeff Wayne's music recording and stage show have become cultural landmarks in their own right. Reportedly, 2014 saw the final tour of the music show. Obviously, the music album and the show will live on through CDs, downloads on iTunes, DVDs and so on, but for Jeff Wayne the musician, it was now time 'to take *The War of The Worlds* in new

---

in effect left on the cutting room floor during the editing of the final recording: Wayne, Collier and Schurrer, *Jeff Wayne's Musical Version: Collector's Edition*, pp. 72–5.

55. Ross, 'Jeff Wayne'.

56. Sinclair, 'Pop: The War of the Worlds'.

directions'.[57] Thus, in November 2015 Jeff Wayne announced that after over eight years of touring arenas throughout the UK and internationally his musical version of Wells's *The War of the Worlds* would make its West End debut at London's Dominion Theatre in February 2016.[58]

57. Jeff Wayne, 'News', 18 November 2013, http://www.thewaroftheworlds.com/news/newsstory.aspx?id=212 [accessed 12 December 2013].

58. Jeff Wayne, 'News', 11 November 2015, http://www.thewaroftheworlds.com/news/newsstory.aspx?id=227 [accessed 10 December 2015].

PART IV

THE WAR OF THE WORLDS' LITERARY HERITAGE

Chapter 16

THE WAR OF THE WORLDS' LITERARY HERITAGE

The War of the Worlds' chapter headers – they include 'On Horsell Common', 'The Heat-Ray in the Chobham Road', 'What I saw of the Destruction of Weybridge and Shepperton' and 'What had happened in Surrey' – help explain why the county of Surrey, and particularly Horsell Common and the town of Woking, prove major heritage destinations for Wellsian enthusiasts and battlefield hunters, seeking to link up with the book's author and to explore the story's geographical setting.[1] Nor should the Wellsian heritage of London be overlooked, given such chapter headings as 'In London', 'The Exodus from London', 'The Man on Putney Hill' and 'Dead London'.

When reworking his *War of the Worlds* music album in 2002, Jeff Wayne decided to revisit places from the book responsible for inspiring his original project 'not just for myself as composer and producer, but also to help find the "spirit" of HG himself':

> My first port of call was Primrose Hill, where HG's Martians die at the end of his story … I would get caught up in my own world, usually sitting at the top of the hill overlooking London, imagining what it must have been like to live in the Victorian England of the book's setting, facing an invasion from a supremely intelligent force.[2]

Next, he travelled to Woking, where Wells planned, researched, wrote and set *The War of the Worlds*; where the story's narrator lived; and where the Martian invaders first landed:

> My next stop was Horsell Common in Woking, Surrey, where the first cylinder lands containing the initial batch of Martians and their amazing fighting machines. How clever these Martians were, I thought, with no sat-nav or traffic control bringing them in for a perfect landing. But land perfectly they did, right on Horsell Common's most open field with their cylinder pointing right-side-up.
>
> It was here I realised that these were incredibly smart dudes who had the ability to plan precisely not only where they wanted to land, but a place they

---

1. Shepperton, albeit placed in the historic county of Middlesex, is now part of Spelthorne in Surrey.
2. Wayne, 'H. G. Wells's *The War of the Worlds*'.

could safely leave their cylinder and set up camp to begin the process of taking over the Earth. And if anyone was to get in their way, well, they would have produced their heat rays and it would have been game over.

Place in literature

As recognized by Jeff Wayne's pilgrimages to Camden Town and Woking, place represents a central factor in understanding Wells and his writing. Place proves a variable in the creative life of writers, but for Wells the culturally specific meanings of one location or another, play a significant role in his attempt to engage with the real world through literature.

For Philip Hensher, 'psychologies are rooted in setting, and revealed through place and physical setting':

> Often, when I think of a novel I love, it is not the plot that comes to mind, or even, sometimes, the characters, but the setting. They can be real places – the blackened London that Maggie and Little Dorrit wander through, one long night – or the visionary skied blankness at the beginning of *Great Expectations* … I hardly ever walk towards the Royal Albert Hall, or through Peckham, or down Kings Road, without hearing Muriel Spark's dry tones. *The Girls of Slender Means*, *The Ballad of Peckham Rye* and *The Bachelors* don't render these places; they create them.[3]

As a result, Hensher reminds us, 'When the novelist's eye falls on a particular stretch of earth, it can transform it for ever.' Certainly Wells's words gave Horsell Common everlasting fame, the first place on earth visited by Martians, the location of the Martian encampment, the site of the initial military exchanges and the base for the Martian assault on London. Today, it remains a battlefield site where the invaders from another planet displayed the overwhelming power of their weaponry, as recorded by Jeff Wayne's 'Horsell Common and the Heat-Ray' in which an invisible heat-ray leapt from person to person: 'Every tree and bush became a mass of flames at the touch of this savage, unearthly Heat-Ray'.[4]

As recorded by Jeff Wayne, Horsell Common figures prominently on the literary heritage itinerary of Wellsian enthusiasts. In June 2013, Christopher Priest, author of *The Space Machine* and a vice president of the 'H. G. Wells Society', described just such a visit:

> We concluded our mini-tour of Wells memorabilia with a walk across the Common in search of the sandpit itself. It is not at all difficult to find… the walk … was an inspiring and reinvigorating experience. The sandpit itself is

3. Philip Hensher, 'The importance of place in fiction', *The Guardian*, 17 May 2013.
4. Jeff Wayne, 'Horsell Common and the Heat-Ray', Jeff Wayne, Collier and Schurrer, *Jeff Wayne's Musical Versions: Collector's Edition*, p. 27.

Figure 16.1 'Lynton', Maybury Road, Woking, 1966 and today. Photographs of 'Lynton', the house rented by Wells in Maybury Road, Woking, 1895-96. Recent modifications mean that the 1966 picture gives a better idea of the house's original appearance.

Source: The author; 'War of the Worlds was written in Maybury Road villa', *Woking Review*, Oct.1966, p. 5.

still much as it must have been in Wells's days, at least before the Martians came along and ploughed everything up.[5]

Over time, various attempts have been made to mark Horsell Common's central role in Wells's story. In 1978, the 'H. G. Wells Society', acting in collaboration with the 'Horsell Common Preservation Society' (H.C.P.S.), placed a seat, 'suitably inscribed' with a plaque, overlooking the sandpits. The aim was to celebrate Wells's 'association with the common' and his stay in Woking, 'one of the most fruitful periods of his life'.[6] Unfortunately, the seat was vandalized and the plaque disappeared. In part, this gap was filled in March 2007 when Horsell Common was awarded an 'alternative' blue plaque by BBC2's 'Culture Show'.[7] Whereas English

5. Christopher Priest, 'Journal: "Woking Work"', 6 June 2013, http://www.christopher-priest.co.uk/journal/1870/woking-work/ [accessed 1 April 2014]. But see below regarding the sandpits.

6. H. G. Wells Society, *Annual Report 1978/79*, n.d. [1979], p. 3, HGW/1727/50.4 (BRO); H. G. Wells Society, *Annual Report 1979/80*, n.d. [1980], HGW/1727/50.4, p. 2 (BRO); G. White, H.C.P.S., to W. Hammond, 29 September 1978, HGW/1727A/8 (BRO). In 1910 the H.C.P.S. took over responsibility for managing the common from Lord Onslow, the Lord of the Manor of Pyrford: *Horsell Common: A Brief History* (Woking: H.C.P.S., n.d.). In *The War of the Worlds*, the Lord of the Manor was named Lord Hilton (I.3: 23/19)

7. BBC2, 'The Culture Show', 31 March 2007; 'Horsell Common Blue Plaque', *The Common: Horsell Common Preservation Society Newsletter* 4 (1) (2007): 2; 'Alternative blue plaque marks common's cultural standing', *Get Surrey*, 15 March 2007, http://www.

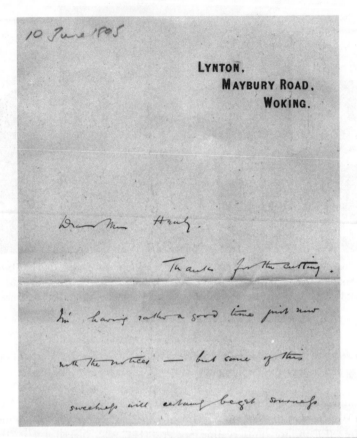

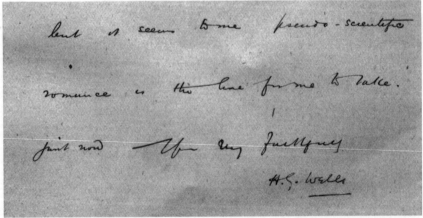

Figure 16.2 Wells's 'Lynton' Letterhead. Letter written by Wells to Elizabeth Healey, a friend from his student days, soon after the publication of *The Time Machine*. Pleased with initial reviews, Wells expresses his belief that scientific romances seemed the best course to take for the time being.

Source: Wells to Elizabeth Healey, 10 June 1895, 1894-98, 8 ALS, the Harry Ransom Center, The University of Texas at Austin.

Figure 16.3 'The Martian', Woking. Michael Condron's sculpture was erected in 1998 to mark the centenary of the publication of Wells's *The War of the Worlds.*

Source: The author.

Heritage's blue plaques commemorate famous individuals and their work, the alternative scheme championed by the 'Culture Show' marks significant events and places in British culture. Claiming that Wells's 'hugely influential 1898 novel' helped 'give birth to the science fiction genre', the plaque recorded that *The War of the Worlds* was set in Woking and that 'the first Martian landing happened here'.

Most tours of Wells memorabilia in Woking, like that conducted by Priest, also take in 'Lynton', the house in Maybury rented by Wells when writing *The War of the Worlds* (Figures 16.1–16.2). A commemorative blue plaque records that Wells lived there during 1895–6, even if building modifications mean that visitors need considerable imagination to picture the house as it looked at the time of his period of residence. Woking does not yet offer visitors a public statue of Wells – one is due to be unveiled in 2016 – but the town centre has 'The Martian' (Figure 16.3), a 'walking engine of glittering metal' (I.10: 71/46) located centrally less than a mile from 'Lynton'. Commissioned to mark the centenary of *The War of the Worlds*' publication, this public sculpture provides yet another dimension to the story's afterlife as

getsurrey.co.uk/ [accessed 17 April 2014]. Photos of Mark Kermode, the programme's co-presenter, holding the plaque were taken on the present-day sandpits. The plaque was not placed on public display.

a secular myth. As one journalist reminded readers of *The Boston Globe* at the time of the release of Spielberg's take on Wells's story, 'This is War of the Worlds Ground Zero', the most visible present-day sign of the town's starring role in the book.[8]

One visitor specifically attracted by Woking's 'Martian' was Simon Norton, a University of Cambridge mathematician, once hailed as a child mathematical prodigy and more recently the subject of a biography written by Alexander Masters. 'I'm going to see a Martian', Norton suddenly informed Masters, one day, 'He aaah, hnnn ... *it* lives in Woking'.[9] According to a tourist leaflet, Simon reported, 'it's seven metres high. It looks like a beetle trying to curtsey with its legs stuck in vacuum tubes. There's also a Woking Spaceship embedded in the pavement nearby, and Woking Bacteria, made out of splodges of coloured concrete brick.' Masters reluctantly agreed to accompany Norton to Woking. As happened with all their trips, they travelled by public transport, with Norton tracing their route on OS maps: 'Every fifteen or twenty minutes he'll ... look up, catch my attention and desperately point through the window at a "site of special historical interest" several seconds after it's disappeared from view'. Of course, for Norton, the trip's 'special historical interest' was located in Woking. Upon arrival at Woking station, Norton rushed off the train: 'Fretful with impatience, Simon bustled down Woking platform as fast as his holdall and gout would permit ... and ... made quickly for the centre of town':

> The Martian is at the end of a dreary pedestrian walkway, its legs buckled with despair at finding that it's travelled sixty million miles, the last hope of a dying civilisation, and ended up in Woking. In Woking, being punched by a lamp post and chased by fake Victorian bollards.
>
> Standing on a coloured microbe, Simon admired the sculpture, consulted a street map and ate a pack of Bombay mix he'd found wandering about his bag.
> 'Do you like this Martian?' I asked.
> 'It's all right,' he said.
> 'Do you like Woking?'
> 'It's all right'.

Britain's vibrant heritage industry

During recent decades. Britain's heritage industry has proved a major growth area in terms of employment, leisure, tourism and global visibility, with organizations like *English Heritage*, the *National Trust* and tourist bodies playing major promotional roles.[10] Castles, cathedrals and churches, historic houses and gardens, old towns, museums and battlefield sites, among other locations, attract ever-growing

---

8. Nick Walker, 'Gritty landing spot for alien invaders: H. G. Wells set his 1898 'War of the Worlds' in England, not the USA of today's movie', *The Boston Globe*, 26 June 2005.

9. Alexander Masters, *The Genius in My Basement: The Biography of a Happy Man* (London: Fourth Estate, 2011), pp. 73, 77, 93, 98.

10. Robert Hewison, *The Heritage Industry: Britain in a Climate of Decline* (London:

numbers of visitors from home and abroad. Britain's literary heritage, defined to embrace not only the places of birth, residence and death of writers, but also the locations featured in their work, has emerged as a central element in this industry. Literary events marking specific writer's anniversaries prove not only an increasingly common feature of the present-day cultural landscape but also – to quote Jasper Rees when writing about #DT100, the literary festival held in 2014 to commemorate Dylan Thomas – 'big business'.[11]

According to Chris Routledge, when writing about George Orwell, it seems also that 'Writers' houses are big business.'[12] Visitors from home and overseas flock to any houses within Britain still surviving and lived in at some time by, say, Jane Austen, Charles Dickens, Thomas Hardy, Beatrix Potter and William Wordsworth, as well as Wells, in order to view where they resided and wrote, perhaps also to identify factors influencing their thinking and writing as well as to explain why their work is so special: 'Maybe the answer is among the bric-a-brac and the antique furniture, if only you look hard enough. Except it isn't. Writers' houses promise to tell us something about the writers who lived in them, especially those open to visitors, but it is mostly an illusion. In any case by the time the curators and the tourists get there the writer is long gone.'

The writer may be 'long gone', but people still value the ability to experience the former home of a favourite writer, since even the commonest of places are enriched through their personal and intellectual associations with those who have lived there. Pointing to the manner in which he could not walk through many parts of London without recalling their past literary residents, the essayist and poet Leigh Hunt (1784–1859) admitted that, 'I can no more pass through Westminster, without thinking of [John] Milton' who was born there.[13] Hunt claimed also, that whenever possible he went out of his way to pass through Gerrard Street, where John Dryden (1631–1700), the dramatist and poet laureate, had lived to 'give myself the shadow of a pleasant thought'. Another famous resident of Gerrard Street was Dr. Johnson's biographer, James Boswell (1740–95), who admitted that 'there is something pleasingly interesting, to many, in tracing so great a man, through all his different habitations'.[14] More recently, in 2000 Surrey County Council published *Writers Inspired by Surrey* – Wells was one of the featured authors – to highlight the role of literature and place in heritage strategies:

Methuen, 1987), pp. 10–12, 131–46; Rodney Harrison, *Heritage: Critical Approaches* (Abingdon: Routledge, 2013), p. 7; Beck, *Presenting History*, pp. 11–12.

11. Jasper Rees, 'Land of my fathers? My fathers can keep it', *Sunday Times Magazine*, 6 April 2014.

12. Chris Routledge, 'George Orwell, Jura, and Nineteen Eighty-Four', 10 May 2009, http://chrisroutledge.co.uk/2009/05/10/george-orwell-jura-and-nineteen-eighty-four/ [accessed 15 September 2012].

13. Leigh Hunt, *Men, Women, and Books: A Selection of Sketches, Essays, and Critical Memoirs* (London: Smith, Elder, 1847), p. 141.

14. George Birkbeck Hill (ed.), *Boswell's Life of Johnson, I* (New York: Harper, 1889), p. 128.

The writers featured … represent the many associated with Surrey through the years. Some were born here, others lived or visited the county or have Surrey as their final resting place. The county inspired them, by providing local places and people to draw on in their writing or by offering a sympathetic working environment. All of these writers have gained from their association with Surrey, as indeed the world of literature has benefited.[15]

Time travelling back to Wells's original geography

Nor is Britain's literary heritage concerned only with authors. Today pilgrimages conducted to places mentioned in specific books, like those undertaken by Norton, Priest and Jeff Wayne to Woking, have become *de rigueur* for readers, especially regarding sites whose present-day appeal has been accentuated through recent film, music, radio and television adaptations, even those changing the story's chronology and geography. In this vein, locations mentioned in Wells's *The War of the Worlds*, like those figuring in Wells's life story, have become part of the heritage tourist trail for many people by way of complementing, reinforcing and enhancing their experience of reading the book, listening to the radio broadcast and music album, or watching the film, television programme or stage musical. In this sense, we all become time travellers reaching back into the Wellsian past, as represented by Wells himself, his biographers, academic studies, heritage locations and audio-visual adaptations.

Wells brought invasion and violent conflict to Victorian suburbia and London. Setting a fantasy scenario in actual places located in Surrey and London, *The War of the Worlds* blasted Horsell Common, Woking and Primrose Hill into the cultural consciousness of readers across Britain and the world. Moreover, previous chapters establish that Wells's original storyline, as published in the 1898 book as well as in a diverse and ever-extending range of multimedia adaptations, has not only remained popular and influential but also been treated by successive generations across the world as possessing present-day resonance. Wells's story might have been fictional, the product of a highly creative imagination, but for readers its impact and realism derived also from a strong sense of place, a belief that every location was known to, visited and scouted by him on foot or cycle, and then placed in the geography of the time period (Figure 16.4). Using OS maps, readers can identify where the Martians landed and conducted their initial military operations, follow their advance towards London and identify places – these include Horsell Common, Woking, Weybridge, Walton on Thames, Shepperton, Kingston upon Thames, Richmond upon Thames, Sheen, Putney and Camden Town – where key events occurred.[16]

Wells's detailed knowledge of the story's geography is revealed, while his incidental descriptions yield vivid glimpses of the region's urban and rural landscape over one century ago. Many specific places in Horsell, Maybury and

15. *Writers Inspired by Surrey* (Kingston upon Thames: Surrey County Council, 2000), p. 2.

16. Smith, *Wells*, p. 65.

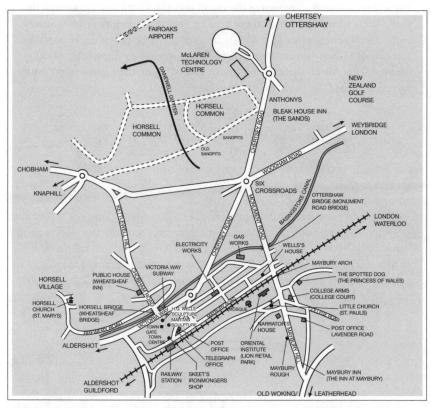

(I) Wells and *The War of the Worlds* in and around Woking. Present day locations/names of places are given in brackets

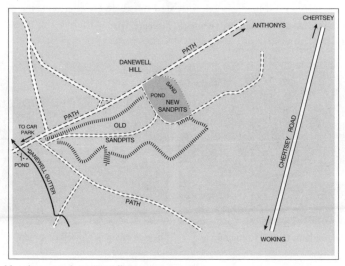

(II) The old and new sandpits, Horsell Common

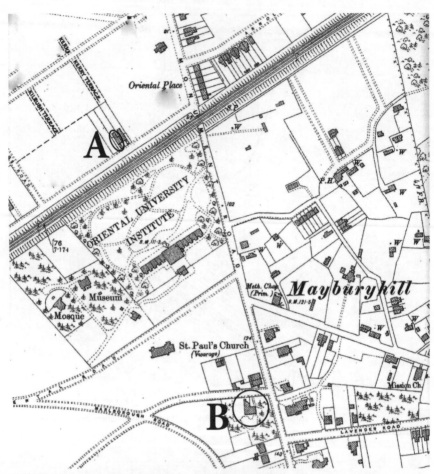

(III) Wells's house (A) and the narrator's house (B) Maybury, Woking

Source: Ordnance Survey map, 1894–96.

(IV) The old sandpits, Horsell Common   The new sandpits, Horsell Common

Source: The author.

Figure 16.4 Woking's Wellsian heritage

Woking are mentioned, including the railway station, the bridges crossing the Basingstoke Canal or carrying the railway, the Shah Jahan Mosque opened in 1889 and the Oriental Institute. Coverage of the Martians' destruction of 'the little church' (I: 9: 61/41) beside the Oriental Institute reveals the up-to-date nature of Wells's research, since the newly-constructed church had just been consecrated in November 1895.[17] The text's allusion to the noise from the gasworks (I.7: 46/32) acknowledged the works operating in Maybury since 1892. Mention of the fact that 'the electric lamps were all alight' (I.7: 46/32) recognized that Woking was one of the few provincial towns with electric streetlights, even if in practice the lights, supplied by a power station in Maybury, proved of variable reliability.[18]

The book's coverage of other parts of the county and the area beyond is equally strong topographically. A few miles away are Shepperton and Weybridge, two places destroyed by the Martians in a section of the text (I: 12: 96/60) benefiting from Wells's detailed description regarding the flow of the River Wey into the Thames at Weybridge, through several separate channels, the ferry crossing and the church at Shepperton visible from the Weybridge side of the river. Nor is the rural landscape neglected. Indeed, *The War of the Worlds* provides one of the more visual portrayals of Horsell Common during the late Victorian period. Likewise, the narrator's trip through country lanes to Leatherhead provides insightful contemporary images, such as when travelling down Maybury Hill towards Old Woking: 'In front was a quiet sunny landscape, a wheatfield ahead on either side of the road, and the Maybury Inn with its swinging sign ... The scent of hay was in the air through the lush meadows beyond Pyrford, and the hedges on either side were sweet and gay with multitudes of dog-roses' (I.9: 65/42–3; I.10: 67/44).

Life in Surrey was changing fast during the 1890s, but there remained still – to quote Crosby – 'a sense of timelessness about the landscape and the traditional farming practices'.[19] Most places figuring in the story remain, even if they have often changed in character and appearance over the years. During the mid-1890s, when living in and walking or cycling around Woking, Wells would have witnessed the boost in population and house building experienced by the town (Table 5.1) as well as the resulting encroachments upon the surrounding commons, farmland, nurseries, orchards and woods. Horsell Common remains a common – as Patrick Parrinder observed, 'Today the sandpits on Horsell Common near Woking are still instantly recognisable to a reader of *The War of the Worlds*' – but during the past century or so the rapid growth of trees, alongside the declining use of commonland for grazing animals, has qualified the openness characteristic of Wells's day when the narrator was able to view the common from his house on Maybury Hill.[20] In fact, the sandpits on Horsell Common used for extracting sand in Wells's day and referred to in his story, are now largely covered by trees. Nearby

17. Marion Field, A History of St. Paul's Church, Maybury (Woking: Marion Field, 2009), pp. 9–10.

18. Crosby, *History of Woking*, pp. 126–7.

19. Ibid., p. 112.

20. Parrinder, *Shadows of the Future*, p. 87.

are what are generally represented today as the sandpits mentioned in the book, but they were not dug until after the Second World War.

For the historian George Macaulay Trevelyan, walking a battlefield proved 'the greatest of outdoor intellectual pleasures'.[21] For visitors, such heritage sites offer knowledge, an emotional link with past events and a source of inspiration for imaginative rethinking of the past. As Trevelyan observed:

> The charm of an historic battlefield is its fortuitous character. Chance selected this field out of so many, that low wall, this gentle slope of grass, a windmill, a farm or straggling hedge, to turn the tide of war and decide the fate of nations and of creeds. Look on this scene, restored to its rustic sleep that was so rudely interrupted on that one day in all the ages.

Trevelyan's assertion was made about actual battlefields, but the popularity of battlefield tourism reinforces *The War of the Worlds'* appeal in terms of enabling Surrey and London to be treated as a virtual battlefield in the first interplanetary war, especially as fast-moving military developments can be followed with OS maps. However, in the case of *The War of the Worlds*, Wells, not 'chance', selected Horsell Common and the other battlefields featured therein. And, of course, any disturbance to Surrey's 'rustic' charms was fictional rather than actual.

Although Jeff Wayne's music album and stage shows continue to follow Wells's geography, most adaptations of *The War of the Worlds* have set the story thousands of miles away across the Atlantic, where they have created their own heritage sites, like Grover's Mill, the landing site for the Martians in Orson Welles's 1938 radio broadcast. Thus, when researching this episode, W. Joseph Campbell felt the need to visit Grover's Mill, 'the New Jersey hamlet that was ground zero for the Martian invasion' in Orson Welles's dramatization.[22] Subsequently, Spielberg's film added further sites to *The War of the Worlds'* heritage industry including the house at 11 Kennedy Boulevard, West First Street, Bayonne, lived in by Ray Ferrier, the character played by Tom Cruise, and Bayonne Bridge, which was destroyed by the invaders to cut off the town's link to Staten Island, New York.[23]

To some extent, these American-based sites, can be interpreted as qualifying the appeal of British heritage sites based upon the actual novel. However, adaptations, even those set across the Atlantic, have often created fresh media and popular interest within and outside Britain in the whole *The War of the Worlds* story, including the original topography. Writing for *The Guardian* in 2005 one journalist, inspired by Spielberg's film, decided to investigate the book's actual geography. Starting on Horsell Common, he moved onto nearby towns and villages: 'It's easy

21. George Macaulay Trevelyan, *Clio, A Muse and Other Essays Literary and Pedestrian* (London: Longmans, Green, 1914), pp. 27–8.

22. Campbell, *Getting it Wrong*, p. 7.

23. See, http://wikimapia.org/1117682/Tom-Cruise-s-house-in-the-movie-War-of-the-Worlds and http://www.movie-locations.com/movies/w/War_Of_The_Worlds_2005.html [accessed 25 February 2012].

now, walking across the common, past the sandpit to the crater-like dent that harbours a little lake, to imagine that first discovery just as Wells's narrator saw it. The dreadful events that follow take place in determinedly ordinary, comfortable, Surrey locations: Chertsey, Ottershaw, Chobham, Ripley, Ockham, Pyrford, Send.'[24] Likewise, Spielberg's film, most notably the way in which it reinforced the impression that 'celestial out-of-towners always seem to home in on the USA, at least on the big screen', prompted the *Boston Globe* to apprise readers of the story's British roots. Representing 'the massively popular Wells' as 'Woking's late-19th-century pop-culture icon', the *Boston Globe* linked Wells's role with that of the singer Paul Weller of 'The Jam' in putting the town on the world's popular cultural map.[25] Significantly, 'The Worldwide Guide to Movie Locations' website advised cinema-goers inspired by Spielberg's Martian-less film to visit Woking:

> If you want to see a gleaming silver, three-legged Martian war machine, as described by H. G. Wells, you need to visit the UK. Head down to the town centre of Woking, Surrey, where you'll find one striding across the pavement (sidewalk) at Crown Passage. In the original story, the Martian cylinders landed on Horsell Common, Woking, and the seven-metre-tall sculpture, by Michael Condron, celebrates the local author.[26]

Glossing over Woking's Wellsian heritage

Mention of the 'Martian' highlights the fact that for today's heritage tourists there exist additional attractions, given the manner in which during recent decades Woking, like other places touched by Wells's career and writing, has sought to exploit its Wellsian past through a range of commemorative projects. Notwithstanding Wells's fame as an author and a public figure, Woking took its time in acknowledging and publicizing its Wellsian heritage. Indeed, it was not until 1956 that Wells was listed in the town guide as a famous former resident. Even then, he was inserted seemingly as an afterthought out of alphabetical order between George Bernard Shaw and Dame Ethel Smyth, a composer, writer and suffragette.[27]

For much of the twentieth century, certainly during his lifetime, it appears that Wells was neither viewed nor represented by 'Woking' – this descriptor can be taken to cover the council, the press and residents thereof – as a significant known element in the town's past. In part, this might prove a function of the

24. David McKie, 'How Woking lost its war', *The Guardian*, 14 July 2005; 'Town centre invaded by television crew', *Woking Review*, 25 June 2005.

25. Walker, 'Gritty landing spot'.

26. 'The Worldwide Guide to Movie Locations: Exploring Film Locations Around the World: War of the Worlds Film Locations, http://www.movie-locations.com/movies/w/War_Of_The_Worlds_2005.html [accessed 25 February 2012].

27. 'War of the Worlds was written in Maybury Road villa', *Woking Review*, October 1966, p. 5.

fact that when resident in Maybury Road Wells, though featuring in the national and overseas media, did not appear to secure any public visibility in and around Woking itself, such as in terms of attracting local press coverage or undertaking public appearances in the town as a locally-based author writing successful and well-reviewed publications. Thus, when he moved away in 1896, Wells left no visible footprint in the town, especially as far as the local media were concerned. Despite having an occasional 'Art and Literature' section, during these years the *Woking News and Mail* mentioned writers like Jules Verne and George Gissing, but not Wells. No reviews were published of his books.[28] Nor, it appears, did *The War of the Worlds*' serialization in *Pearson's Magazine* in 1897, prompt any local press coverage recording Woking's prominent role in the conflict.

It was not until February 1898, a few weeks after *The War of the Worlds*' publication as a book that a public lecture delivered in Woking – as it was reported by both the *Woking News and Mail* and the *Surrey Advertiser* – highlighted links between the town and Wells's storyline.[29] The lecturer was Joseph McCabe (1867–1955), a former Roman Catholic priest who became a prolific freelance writer and speaker on free thought, religion and science.[30] McCabe's illustrated lecture, entitled 'Life in Other Worlds', was delivered before what was represented by the local press as a larger than usual audience for one of the regular free Sunday Afternoon Lectures hosted at Woking Public Hall. This proved one of McCabe's regular lecture topics and still figured in his repertoire a decade or so later.[31]

Reviewing the prospects of finding life on other planets McCabe moved on from Mercury and Venus to Mars before dealing with Jupiter, Saturn, Uranus and Neptune: 'Mars had atmosphere, water, clouds, snow and ice – apparently, in fact, all the necessary conditions of life. The probability was, therefore, that it was inhabited by living beings. *A novelist had recently described the invasion of earth by Martians who were supposed to have landed at Woking and begin their operations from there* [author's italics].[32] In this manner, McCabe employed Wells's fiction to complement, perhaps reinforce, his claims about life on the Red Planet.[33] He referred also, to the

28. For example, in December 1895 the Woking News' 'Art and Literature' section mentioned Gissing's latest novella, *A Paying Guest*, a story set in Surrey and highlighting the grotesque ambitions of suburban life: 'Art and Literature', *The Woking News*, 6 December 1895, p. 2.

29. Advertisements: Sunday Afternoon Lectures', *The Woking News and Mail*, 4 February 1898, p. 5; '"Life in Other Worlds": interesting speculations', *The Woking News and Mail*, 11 February 1898, p. 6; 'Sunday Afternoon Lectures at Woking', *Surrey Advertiser*, 9 February 1898, p. 5.

30. Nicolas Walter, 'McCabe, Joseph Martin (1867–1955)', *Oxford Dictionary of National Biography*, Oxford University Press, 2004, online edn, October 2009, http://www.oxforddnb.com/view/article/34674 [accessed 17 Feb 2013].

31. See for example, 'The Other Worlds. Mr McCabe's lecture', *The Press* (Canterbury, New Zealand), 29 May 1913.

32. 'Life in Other Worlds'.

33. McCabe and Wells eventually met and corresponded occasionally, but they do not

fact that telescopes had revealed on Mars a series of lines, which were possibly canals used for irrigation, while claiming that the Martians were probably far more intelligent than people on Earth.[34] Neither newspaper report indicated whether McCabe identified the name of the 'novelist' or the title of the book, let alone revealed that the story was largely written in Woking. Obviously, some people in Woking can be expected to have read *Pearson's Magazine*'s serialization of the story in 1897, a few might have even purchased the recently published book and such factors, in conjunction with the contemporary interest in Mars discussed in Chapter 3, might help to explain the above-average audience attracted by the lecture.

Exploiting the Wellsian heritage

In part, Wells's lack of visibility *vis à vis* Woking during the mid-late 1890s and the first half of the twentieth century reflected also the relative dearth of alternative audio-visual adaptations of the story readily available to British audiences until the early 1950s. Admittedly, Orson Welles's radio broadcast generated British media interest, but coverage rarely strayed from the press's initial preoccupation with alleged panic and hysteria throughout the USA. No real effort was made by the British media to question the shift of the storyline across the Atlantic. Wells's complaints about the rewriting of his original story were reported in general terms rather than through a specific focus upon the way in which Grover's Mill assumed the place formerly occupied by Woking and Horsell Common. Clearly, the release of Hollywood's *War of the Worlds* film in 1953, a time when British cinema audiences were booming, acted as one prompt for Wells's insertion in the 1956 town guide, just as national press coverage of the centenary of his birth in 1966 led the local press to focus upon the house he had lived in when writing *The War of the Worlds*.[35] Even then, one local newspaper complained that there was no plaque to indicate that Wells had ever lived in Maybury Road, let alone wrote *The War of the Worlds*, among other famous books, while based there. Reportedly, in 1966 the house's name was 'almost hidden under coats of red paint'.

During the early 1990s, the redevelopment of Woking's town centre through 'The Peacocks' shopping and entertainment complex reflected a desire to enhance the town's sense of identity as – to quote a 1992 Woking Borough Council press release – 'a place where people will want to be'.[36] In this vein, public art came to be viewed as a means of creating a sense of purpose and community, as well as a more attractive urban environment, particularly through exploiting the town's

seem to have been in contact with each other until after the First World War: Smith (ed.), *The Correspondence of H. G. Wells*, IV, pp. 432, 456–7, 487.

34. Subsequently McCabe, noting growing doubts about whether the lines on Mars were canals, reaffirmed that life, even 'very advanced life', seemed 'entirely probable to any student of science': Joseph McCabe, *The End of the World* (London: Routledge, 1921), pp. 129–37.

35. 'War of the Worlds was written in Maybury Road', p. 5.

36. Crosby, *History of Woking*, pp. 198–200.

past. Erected in 1992, the Town Gate offers a good example of the way in which public art has been employed to exhibit the town's rich and varied history. Located between Christ Church and Barclays' Bank, the gate, designed by Alan Dawson, includes images illuminating the role played by the canal and the railway in Woking's past. The Wellsian link is represented through a silhouette of a Martian fighting machine. Soon afterwards in 1994, Wells's residence in Woking was one aspect celebrated by a mural installed under the Victoria Arch railway bridge on the main road to Guildford as part of Woking Council's centenary celebrations. Unfortunately in 2009 the mural, which also depicted George Bernard Shaw, another one-time Woking resident (1901–3), was painted over when the bridge was spruced up for a major cycling event.

The years between 1996 and 1998, the period marking the centenary of Wells's residence in Woking and the publication of *The War of the Worlds*, witnessed the most conscious and sustained effort to celebrate Woking's Wellsian legacy. Initially, 'Woking's The War of the Worlds Celebrations' were justified on the mistaken grounds that 1996 marked 'the centenary of the first publication, in serialised form, of "The War of The Worlds", written in Woking by H. G. Wells and featuring the town and surrounding area as the setting for the fictional landing of Martian invaders.'[37] Subsequently, this rubric was corrected to take account of the fact that the story was not published until 1897–8; thus, the project's objective was now 'to celebrate Woking's association with the author H. G. Wells and the centenary of the writing of the first ever science-fiction novel, "The War of the Worlds".'

Perhaps the most significant outcome was Woking's 'Martian' (Figure 16.3) placed in Crown Square, on what is represented as the Martian invaders' route through the town. Commissioned in January 1997 by Woking Borough Council following a nationwide competitive bidding process, the sculpture, costing £30,000, was created by Michael Condron (1972–). Commissioning criteria specified the need for the sculpture, preferred to a statue of Wells himself, to 'create a positive welcome to the centre of Woking', 'have a space/science-fiction theme', 'be of a scale commensurate with the awesome nature of "War of the Worlds" narrative' and allow full public access.[38] 'Launched' on 8 April 1998 by Carol Vorderman, the TV presenter, the seven metres high chrome electro-polished stainless steel public sculpture proves a striking and innovative piece of public art, promoting the town's visibility and cultural image through the slogan, 'Woking: Where modern science fiction took off' and taking the town forward into the next millennium.[39]

37. David Vince, Arts Development Officer, Woking Borough Council, to Members of Steering Group, 13 November 1995; Woking Borough Council, 'A Public Art Commission Brief', n.d. [1996]. The Steering Group noted also that the dates of Wells's residence, as recorded on the plaque of 'Lynton' in Maybury Road, were incorrect. Reportedly, they were amended: Minutes, Woking's War of the Worlds Steering Group Committee, 3rd Meeting, 6 March 1996.

38. Woking Council, 'Public Art Commission Brief'.

39. '"The Martian" by Michael Condron' (Woking: Woking Borough Council, n.d. [1998]), p. 2; Paul Pickett, 'War of the Welds: Sculptor Creates a Martian in our Midst', *Woking Informer*, 13 March 1998; 'Martian lands in Woking – 100 years on', *Daily Telegraph*,

As Chris Smith, the Secretary of State for Culture, Media and Sport, noted when sending a message of support for the launch ceremony, the Martian, 'far from being an image of destruction', embodied a positive message regarding the town's hope and confidence for the future.[40] Traditional negative images, centring upon the Necropolis, death and all that, were effectively consigned to the past.[41]

Nearby is a cylindrical 'pod', resembling those in which the Martians arrived, shown ploughing into the ground. Patterns in the paving represent the shock waves resulting from the pod's landing. Several 'bacteria' slabs – these mark the bacteria responsible for eventually destroying the invaders – are set in the pavement. One 'broken' bacteria slab is placed under one of the tripod's legs, along which the bacteria are creeping upwards to destroy the seemingly invincible invader. Despite initial plans to support the Martian sculpture with an on-the-spot narrative nothing materialized, thereby leaving any onlookers, many of whom have seen Spielberg's film, but never read Wells's *The War of the Worlds*, to work out what it all means. In addition, tiled mosaics, depicting local scenes from the storyline, were placed nearby in the pedestrian subway under Victoria Way.[42]

An extensive series of *War of the Worlds*-themed commemorative events targeted all sections of the community. They included a Monster March Carnival, 'In the Footsteps of H. G. Wells (and his Martians)' heritage walks and lectures on Wells and Woking.[43] In September 1996, Carl Davis led the Philharmonia Orchestra in a War of the Worlds civic concert based upon a space-inspired programme of music from Holst's 'The Planets', as well as that used in such films as *2001 Space Odyssey* and *Star Trek*. Discussions were held with Jeff Wayne regarding the public performance of music from his *War of the Worlds* album/ CD in December 1996 – the narrator, it was suggested, should be someone of the stature of Anthony Hopkins – but these proved abortive.[44] Nor did it prove possible to use Jeff Wayne's recording in support of 'The War of the Worlds' fireworks display held in November 1996.[45]

7 April 1998; Steve Bennett, 'The Martian Chronicles: How Borough's Latest Landmark Took Shape', *Woking Informer*, 10 April 1998; Justine Stevenson, 'The Martian Landing', *Woking News and Mail*, 16 April 1998. Significantly, the above-mentioned *Daily Telegraph* article was set alongside the latest report about NASA's Mars Global Surveyor, which began mapping the planet's surface in 1996.

    40. Chris Smith, n.d. (1997–8), 'The Martian by Michael Condron'.

    41. See Chapter 7, pp. 131–5.

    42. The subway, now largely disused because of an improved surface crossing, leads to the Wheatsheaf Bridge, a rebuilt version of what is described as 'Horsell Bridge' in the story, Horsell and Chobham: 'Martian influence is appearing in Woking', *Woking Review*, 1 February 1997.

    43. 'Woking's "The War of the Worlds" Celebrations': Programme of Events, September 1996 to March 1997 (Woking: Woking Borough Council, 1996), SHC 4366/File 7 (SHC).

    44. Minutes, Woking's 'War of the Worlds Steering Group Committee', 6th Meeting, 26 July 1996; 7th. Meeting, 11 October 1996,

    45. Woking's 'War of the Worlds Steering Group Committee', 8th Meeting, 6 December 1996.

The resulting enhanced sense of Woking's Wellsian heritage means that Wells's name has been employed for a range of venues, most notably the *H. G. Wells Conference and Events Centre* located adjacent to the 'Martian'. The town's 'Wetherspoons' pub, 'The Herbert Wells', includes an Invisible Man sculpture and a time machine, while a few doors up Chertsey Road going towards the railway station the astronomer responsible for discovering the Martian cylinder, is commemorated by a pub re-launched in 2013 as 'The Ogilvy'.[46] When Wells lived in Woking, Chertsey Road was one of the town's principal shopping streets and probably it was along here that Ogilvy and Henderson walked to the railway station when telegraphing news about the cylinder's landing on Horsell Common (I.2: 17–18/16).

In this vein, Iain Wakeford has proved a prime mover in marking Wells's name locally through guide books, online material, articles in local newspapers and *The Wellsian* and heritage walks centred upon locations mentioned in Wells's *War of the Worlds*: 'Seeing local landmarks that were, for example, destroyed by the Martians' death-ray, really brings this story to life. The "War of the Worlds" is woven into this town's psyche just as much as any real-life developments. And Wells juxtaposing a doomsday scenario against quaint Middle England was typically masterful.'[47] Inspired by the belief that Wells based his story not only upon the local geography but also actual people he had encountered in the town, Wakeford has proved instrumental in drawing links between Wells's literary text and people and places referred to in *The War of the Worlds*, particularly those whose identity was disguised though a change of name or use. For example, Wakeford concluded that the pub called 'The Spotted Dog' (I.9: 63/42; I.10: 76/49), whose landlord hired the narrator a horse and dog-cart, is now 'The Princess of Wales'.[48] Alternatively, the unnamed 'enterprising sweetstuff dealer' (I.3: 22/19) was probably based upon Henry Flowerday, a fruit trader working from Woking's Chobham Road.[49]

Wells received the freedom of the City of London (1933) as well as of Brissago in Switzerland for his writing.[50] During his lifetime, he was never offered any honour by Woking, let alone its freedom, since as discussed above the town did not actively commemorate its Wellsian links during this period. But would he have accepted? In 1934, Wells exhibited no desire to add the freedom of Bromley, a part

46. 'Wetherspoons – Woking's newest pub – has a permanent guest', *Woking Review*, 3 June 1995.

47. Wakeford, quoted Walker, 'Gritty landing spot'.

48. Wakeford, 'Wells, Woking and *The War of the Worlds*', *Woking History Journal* 2 (1990): 11 [abridged version in *The Wellsian* 14 (1991): 18–29]; Iain Wakeford, 'Had victims of the Martians upset H. G. Wells?', *Woking Informer*, 25 June 2010, p. 4; Wakeford quoted, Louise Osborne, 'Our everlasting link with Wells's Martians', *Woking News and Mail*, 24 September 2009.

49. Wakeford, 'Wells, Woking and *The War of the Worlds*', *Woking History Journal*, p. 6.

50. Wells, *Experiment in Autobiography*, II, p. 666. Brissago figures in Chapter 4 of Wells's *The World Set Free* (1914).

of his life evoking highly negative images, to his existing honours.[51] By contrast, Wells, though destroying the town in *The War of the Worlds*, saw his residence in Woking much more positively, indeed it marked a transformational phase in his career as a professional writer. As a result, one would like to think that, if offered, Wells, the self-styled 'Man from Woking', would have been only too pleased to be honoured by Woking, the town in which he had achieved so much as a writer and a person. Today, Wells has now been installed as one of the major figures in Woking's past, a status recognized in print as well as by various present-day exhibits, sculptures and buildings in the town. As highlighted by the commemorative events held in 2016 to mark the 150th anniversary of his birth and the 70th anniversary of his death, Wells lives on in Woking, helping to create and reinforce a sense of pride and identity while drawing in people to engage with the town's Wellsian heritage.

Where Wells lived when writing The War of the Worlds

The buildings where Wells was born, lived, wrote and died represent central elements in our Wellsian literary heritage, especially because of his belief in a meaningful connection between the conditions under which people lived, their lifestyle and their state of mind. Every switch of residence proved symbolic as he moved on to the next phase in his life and career and to yet another home. For Wells, the 'quite dreadful conditions' of Atlas House, his Bromley birthplace, epitomized everything from which he sought to escape.[52] Staying nowhere for very long, Wells proved extremely mobile after leaving Bromley in 1880 (Tables 2.1–2.2), as recorded by Norman and Jeanne MacKenzie, 'The succession of homes that followed each has a similar symbolic significance for him. He projected the phases of his life into the places where he lived, and when he was done with one he was ready to be done with the other.'[53]

Wells's emphasis upon the symbolism of moving on was in part also a function of his strong sense of place and landscape, a point reflected by the readily identifiable topographical detail featured in *The War of the Worlds*. Visiting the properties where Wells lived and places where he walked, cycled and canoed while writing this story gives a sense of immediacy and reality that mere reading of the printed word cannot give. Moreover, the fact that the Martian invasion described in *The War of the Worlds* starts in Woking, where Wells was living when writing the story and effectively ended on Primrose Hill, near where he resided before moving to Woking, imparts added literary heritage resonance to his places of

---

51. Wells to F. H. Heyward, 15 October 1934, HGW/1245/1/39 (BRO); Tim Dickens, 'The truth about H. G. Wells "Morbid" Bromley', *Bromley Times*, 10 December 2010; Cahal Milmo, 'War of Words: How H. G. Wells Snubbed Bromley', *The Independent*, 29 December 2010. Milmo mistakenly lists Brussels for Brissago.

52. Wells, *Experiment in Autobiography*, I, p. 38.

53. N. and J. Mackenzie, *The Time Traveller*, p. 265; Sherborne, *H. G. Wells*, p. 134.

Table 16.1 Where Wells lived when writing *The War of the Worlds*

	Address during Wells's residence	Present-day address
1894–5	12 Mornington Road, London NW1.	12 Mornington Terrace, London NW1 7RR.
1895–6	'Lynton', Maybury Road, Woking, Surrey.	'Lynton', 141 Maybury Road, Woking, Surrey, GU21 5JR.
1896–8	'Heatherlea', The Avenue, Worcester Park, Surrey.	'Heatherlea', 41 The Avenue, Worcester Park, Surrey, KT4 7HD.

abode. Thus, *The War of the Worlds*, though largely written in Woking during 1895–6, can be linked with at least two more places of residence (Table 16.1).

Inevitably over time, places and houses change. Some of Wells's former houses, like that in Mornington Road, remain, albeit with a modified street name and a transformed urban environment. Some survive, but like 'Lynton' in Woking, look very different and some, like 'Heatherlea' in Worcester Park, have been demolished and replaced by a new building.[54] Nor will most present-day visitors to Monument Road, Woking, see 'a billowing tumult of white, firelit smoke' (I.7: 45/32) from steam trains crossing the bridge, given the advent of electric trains. Only a rare steam engine on a heritage journey can be seen today. All three houses are privately owned and hence, not open to the public.

a) 12 Mornington Road, London NW1, 1894–5

Although Wells did not start to write *The War of the Worlds* until after he had left Mornington Road, Camden Town continued to figure prominently in his thoughts and writing. Wellsian historiography offers competing versions regarding the original inspiration for *The War of the Worlds* – these were discussed in Chapter 7 – but one interview conducted with Wells in January 1898 pointed to a walk with his brother around Primrose Hill as the prime mover.[55] Camden Town features prominently in the closing sections of the story, with Primrose Hill proving the final resting place of the invaders (Figure 16.5). Having lived in and around Camden Town and Regent's Park for several years prior to his move to Woking (Table 2.2), Wells knew the area well. Wells visited relatives 'out Primrose Hill way' during the late 1880s and then between 1888 and 1891 lived in Fitzroy Road 'within pleasant walking distance' of Primrose Hill, Camden Town and Regent's Park.[56] In Spring 1889, he moved along Fitzroy Road from apartments above a 'hymn playing she-parson', to another house 'close to Primrose Hill & Regent's Park Rd instead of to Chalk Farm & the democratic Camden Town'.[57]

54. Frederick Sinclair, 'A Prophet came to Euston Road', *St Pancras Journal* 1 (8) (December 1947): 114–17; Rymill, *Worcester Park & Cuddington*, p. 28.

55. 'The Scientific Novel'.

56. Wells to Davies, 31 December 1887, Wells to Healey, 28 April 1888, Smith, *Correspondence of H. G. Wells, I*, pp. 77, 98. See also Wells to Healey, 28 Feb. 1888, p. 84.

57. Wells to Fred Wells, 28 May 1889, Smith, *Correspondence of H. G. Wells, I*, p. 121.

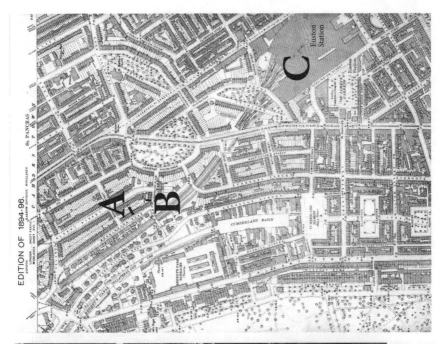

12 Mornington Road (Terrace)

Source: Photo by the author

Figure 16.5 Map: Camden Town's Wellsian heritage 1894–96

Source: Ordnance Survey map 1894–96.

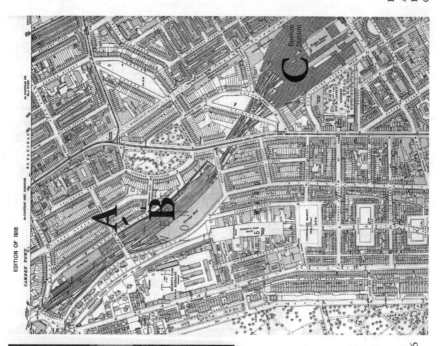

7 Mornington Place

Source: Photo by the author

Figure 16.5 Map: Camden Town's Wellsian heritage 1916

Source: Ordnance Survey map 1916

Key

A   12 Mornington Road
B   7 Mornington Place
C   Euston Station

Following his separation from Isabel, his first wife, in late December 1893, Wells lived with Jane in Camden Town until his move to Woking (Table 2.1). After a brief stay in Mornington Place, Wells and Jane moved just around the corner to rent a small two-room apartment in a five-storey lodging house at 12, Mornington Road. In May 1895 they went to Woking, but in October returned temporarily to Mornington Road by way of meeting the local residential requirements required for marriage at St Pancras Registry Office. Located on the east side of Mornington Road, their house, described by Booth's 1898 survey as one of the road's 'good lodging houses', faced semi-detached properties housing 'well-to-do' and 'middle class' residents.[58] Today, the house, though lacking a blue plaque commemorating Wells's stay, survives, but in a radically transformed urban environment, as reflected also in the change of road name to Mornington Terrace.

Soon after Wells's departure, the widening of the line into Euston Station used by the London & North Western Railway, plus the construction of a new carriage shed (opened 1905) next to Mornington Road, led to the requisitioning and demolition of the properties on the opposite side of the road to Wells's apartment.[59] As a result, today, Wells's former lodging house faces a wall bordering the railway tracks into Euston (Figure 16.5).[60] The railway widening also resulted in alterations to nearby bridges across the track, so that the bridge Wells would have used to cross the railway line was replaced by a new bridge continuing Mornington Street across the track to Park Village East.[61]

In the penultimate paragraph of *The War of the Worlds*, the narrator wrote about visiting London some years after the Martian war. Then the busy metropolis was a very different place from the 'dead city' he had encountered, following the

58. Booth's Survey Notebooks B357, p. 25, 28 October 1898, http://booth.lse.ac.uk/notebooks/b357/jpg/25.html [accessed 16 June 2013], Archives Division, British Library of Political and Economic Science, London School of Economics, London, UK (LSE). Charles Booth conducted a survey of life and labour in London (1886–1903). The original notebooks used to collect evidence contain interviews with Londoners from all walks of life and eye-witness descriptions of individual streets. The report was accompanied by a series of maps, with colour coding illustrating the various levels of prosperity and poverty.

59. Peter Darley to the author, 21 November 2013.

60. Peter Darley (ed.), *Camden Railway Heritage Trail: Primrose Hill to Camden Lock and Chalk Farm*, pp. 1–18 (London: Camden Railway Heritage Trust, 2009); K. A. Scholey, 'The Railways of Camden', *Camden History Society Occasional Paper* 4 (2002): 24. Details of the relevant legislation – this includes the London and North West Railway Acts of 1898, 1900 and 1907 and the Midland Railway Act of 1894 – provisions for compulsory purchase of land and property and contracts for rail widening between Euston and Camden Town can be read in British government records, Railways (RAIL), The National Archives, Kew, London (TNA): RAIL 410/910, RAIL 410/948, RAIL 410/952, RAIL 491/455 (TNA). Parliament became involved also due to delayed compensation payments to dispossessed householders: 'House of Commons', *The Times*, 27 March 1900, p. 10.

61. This area, including the bridges, is scheduled for further disruption as part of plans for HS2.

unsuccessful Martian invasion. As the narrator recorded, there remained two vivid reminders of the interplanetary invasion. At the Natural History Museum, a Martian was preserved in spirits (II. X: 298/178), while standing on Primrose Hill, 'as I did but a day before writing this last chapter', he saw people there 'walking to and fro among the flower-beds on the hill' and sightseers 'about the Martian machine that stands there still' (II. X: 303/180). Today, Primrose Hill remains an open space offering excellent views across the vast sprawling metropolis, as well as offering easy access to several of Wells's former residences. But there is no Martian machine to be seen.

However, during the mid-1970s the H. G. Wells Society, working with the Science Fiction Foundation, proposed erecting a large replica of a Martian fighting machine on Primrose Hill, by way of celebrating *The War of the Worlds* book and the role played therein by Primrose Hill. For George Hay, the society's Press Officer, 'A memorial like this is infinitely better than a host of blue plaques'.[62] In the event, the Department of the Environment's rejection of the proposal led to what proved an abortive search for another site, since local opposition led by the Heath and Old Hampstead Society ruled out Hampstead Heath, the preferred alternative. Thus, this particular Wellsian literary heritage project never went ahead, even if in time Woking's Martian more than filled the gap.

b) 'Lynton', Maybury Road, Woking, Surrey, 1895–6

Having signed a contract for the publication of *The War of the Worlds* soon after moving to Woking, Wells began writing the story in late summer 1895. By the time he departed for Worcester Park, Wells had completed the story scheduled for magazine serialization, the text providing the basis for the book. As recorded in Table 6.1, 'Lynton', the semi-detached villa rented by Wells in Woking for just over one year, proved a 'literary factory' and hence occupies an important place in the Wellsian literary heritage.

The house exists today, still named 'Lynton' (Figure 16.1) but now also numbered 141, Maybury Road. A blue plaque signifies its Wellsian link, but an extension constructed in a somewhat unsympathetic manner, detracts seriously from the house's appearance. Currently 'Fir Cottage', its semi-detached partner at 142 Maybury Road, provides a better idea of the exterior during Wells's period of residence, even if a photograph showing Wells and Jane outside the house

---

62. George Hay to Professor J. King, Queen Mary College, 11 September 1972, HGW/1727A/113 (BRO); Hay quoted, 'Heathman's Diary', *Hampstead and Highgate Express*, 3 October 1975, HGW/1727A/131 (BRO); H. G. Wells Society, *Annual Report 1975/76*, April 1976, pp. 2–3 (BRO); H. G. Wells Society, *Annual Report 1978/79*, n.d. [1979], p. 2 (BRO). Whereas Hay's letter proposed a 100 foot [30.48 meters) high replica based on Wells's own description, the 'Heathman's Diary' article mentioned a fifty foot [15.24 meters] Martian. 'Heathman's Diary' was accompanied by a photograph super-imposing a fighting machine on a picture of Parliament Hill. HGW/1727A/113 (BRO) includes draft sketches of a Martian fighting machine on Primrose Hill.

indicates that originally a covered glass walkway linked the front door to the road. The 1896 OS map reminds us that, despite the London Necropolis Company's land auctions – their variable success was discussed in Chapter 5 – and Woking's rapid rate of new building, residential housing still proved patchy across Maybury and particularly along Maybury Road.[63] As Wells wrote, beyond him 'in all directions stretched open and undeveloped heath land'.[64] 'Lynton' and 'Fir Cottage' were the only properties shown in the section of Maybury Road between King's Road and Monument Road. Most of the next stretch of Maybury Road extending from King's Road towards the railway station as far as North Road, was also empty and not placed on sale until 1898.[65] The section between New Road and Portugal Street was sold by auction in March 1896.[66]

The detached house next to 'Lynton, 140 Maybury Road, was built on land sold also to Raggett in September 1893, but the 1895–6 OS map records that no house had yet been built.[67] The semi-detached house next to 'Fir Cottage', now numbered 143 Maybury Road, was not built until 1905, even though this has not prevented this property being frequently mistakenly identified as the house in which Wells wrote *The War of the Worlds*.[68] For example, Christopher Priest, whose Woking visit has been mentioned already, recorded confusingly that:

> We went first to 143 Maybury Road, to which Wells had moved in June 1895. The house then was named 'Lynton', a small semi-detached villa opposite a railway line, but with a garden at the back … A commemorative blue plaque seems long overdue, because this is the house in which *The War of the Worlds* and *The Invisible Man* were written.[69]

Priest warned his blog's readers: 'Please note that the photograph of 143 Maybury Road shown on the Woking website about H. G. Wells is incorrect'. This house is also shown incorrectly on Wikipedia as the house rented by Wells.

'Lynton' and 'Fir Cottage' were built in 1893 on 'Maybury Common Estate', an extensive area of land comprising 201 plots in Maybury Road, Monument

63. OS Surrey Sheet XVII.5, 2nd edn 1896, rev. 1895.

64. Wells, *Experiment in Autobiography*, II, p. 543.

65. Alex Turner & Co., 'Sale Plan of Building Land in Maybury Road', eighteen plots, n.d. [1898–1903], SHC 2682/3 (SHC).

66. Paine & Brettell, 'Sale of Freehold Building Land in Maybury Road', twenty-four plots, 5 March 1896, SHC 4363/72 Folder 2 (SHC).

67. Land Registry title SY312926, '140 Maybury Road', edition date 16 April 2014.

68. Land Registry title SY381816, '143 Maybury Road', edition date 6 April 2014. Skeet, though not mentioned as a purchaser, is listed as the vendor in 1917 when he sold the house rented by Wells.

69. Christopher Priest, 'Journal: "Woking Work"'. Another example: Woking War of the Worlds.com, which originally showed a photo of Lynton, but represented it as 143 Maybury Road in the accompanying text. Now an unspecified house in Maybury Hill is claimed to be where Wells lived while resident in Woking.

Road, Walton Road, Queen's Road and Boundary Road auctioned by the London Necropolis and National Mausoleum Company in August 1888.[70] Plots facing the railway line in Maybury Road, like that on which 'Lynton' was built, were deemed to be the most attractive location, as indicated by the larger size of plots – they possessed a frontage of sixty feet with a depth of 200 feet – and a contractual restriction placed upon the minimum value of properties constructed thereupon.[71] Thus, their conditions of sale stipulated that no semi-detached or detached house should be built upon the plots having a value of less than £350 or £400 respectively. Significantly, the sales particulars stressed the plots' proximity to the railway station – they were represented as merely a short walk away – and Woking's regular and fast rail links with London. Apart from offering the opportunity for people to purchase a freehold residence within easy reach of London, the sales particulars pointed also to the rapid growth of Woking and hence, the prospects of a speculative investment rising in value and providing a good rental return.

'Lynton' and 'Fir Cottage' were built by George Raggett, a local builder who had purchased the plot from William Agar in January 1893.[72] According to the 1913 Land Valuation Survey, each house was 'a well-built modern semi-detached brick slated villa containing: – 3 bedrooms, dressing room, bathroom, dining room, drawing room, kitchen, scullery, larder, WC'.[73] The valuer's report noted also the 'minute greenhouse' mentioned by Wells in his autobiography.[74] Upon completion in 1893, the two semi-detached villas were sold for £400 each to William Robert Skeet, a local ironmonger who came to play a significant part in the town's history. Like many of his contemporaries, Skeet saw property as an attractive form of investment. Indeed, prior to purchasing 'Lynton' and 'Fir Cottage', he was already renting out other properties, including two houses in Horsell Moor.[75] Subsequently, Skeet purchased the houses constructed on either side of 'Lynton' and 'Fir Cottage'.

Born in Aldershot on 4 April 1867, Skeet followed his father's trade by becoming an ironmonger. Setting up shop in Woking, he rented a house and shop opposite the northern entrance to the railway station at 1 High Street.[76] During 1903 the

70. Wm. R. Nicholas, 'Sale of Freehold Building land known as the "Maybury Common Estate"', 24 August 1888, SHC 6852/8/2/4, p. 4 (SHC); Land Registry Title, no. SY400247, edition date 17 December 2010. The Necropolis Company auctioned another section of this estate covering Oriental Road, Pembroke Road, Marlborough Road and Onslow Crescent at the same time: SHC 6852/8/2/3 (SHC).

71. Crosby, *History of Woking*, pp. 84–5.

72. Land Registry Title, no. SY400247, '"Lynton" 141 Maybury Road, edition date 17 December 2010'. Documents in the SHC indicate that Agar owned land and a substantial number of properties for rent in Woking.

73. Reports ref. no. 606–7, December 1913, Valuer's Field Book, Parish of Woking, TNA, IR58/34499.

74. Wells, Experiment in Autobiography, II, p. 542.

75. Supplemental Valuation List, Woking, 1891, SHC 6198/13/17, p. 3 (SHC). Each house had an estimated annual rental of £10.

76. Valuation List, Woking, 20 August 1891, SHC 6198/13/4, no. 1647 (SHC); Valuation

site was taken over by the London, County and Westminster Bank – today the NatWest Bank occupies the site – with Skeet opening a larger shop, including stabling, nearby in Chobham Road.[77] Working with D. H. Jeffes, the resulting firm 'Skeet and Jeffes' became a prominent part of Woking's shopping landscape, while Skeet himself performed an active role in the local community, such as by serving as a Justice of the Peace, a member of the 'Education Committee' and president of 'Woking Tradesmen's Alliance' (1899).[78]

During the first decade or so of his ownership of 'Lynton' and 'Fir Cottage', Skeet rented out both properties, with Wells proving an early, possibly his first tenant, at Lynton for an annual rental of c. £28.[79] Interestingly, given Wells's views on religion, the occupier at the time of the 1901 census was George Roy Badenoch, a Church of Scotland Minister. However, by the time of the 1911 Census Skeet and his family had moved into 'Lynton', whose recent numbering as 141, Maybury Road, reflected the way in which vacant plots of land along one side of the road had now been built upon. The railway track left no space for building on the opposite side of Maybury Road. According to the 1911 census return eight people – Skeet, his wife, five children and one servant – occupied the house, a point offering perspective to Wells's complaints about the lack of dedicated writing space and his need for a larger house. Skeet sold both 'Lynton' and 'Fir Cottage', as well as the house next door at 140 Maybury Road, in November 1917 and during the 1920s lived nearby at 'Tilloy', in Oriental Road.[80]

Maybury, was also the location of the house occupied by the narrator of *The War of the Worlds*. No exact address, let alone a road name, is given in the text, but the text suggests a probable location on Maybury Hill, given the narrator's route along Monument Road and ability to look across from his house to Horsell Common. Another clue is given while the narrator was loading the cart before leaving for Leatherhead. A soldier was running up Maybury Hill calling upon people to leave home. After a brief exchange of words with the narrator, the soldier 'ran on to the gate of the house on the crest' (I.9: 64/42), thereby placing the narrator's house on the slope of Maybury Hill Road, below Maybury Rough, the house on the crest.

List, Woking, 26 August 1895, SHC 6198/13/5a, no. 715 (SHC). The owner of Skeet's High Street shop was listed as William Wells, who owned a shop and rented out several properties in Woking, but appears not to be related to H. G. Wells.

77. Reports ref. no. 1212 and 1215, January 1914, Valuer's Field Book, Parish of Woking, IR58/34505 (TNA); Woking Council Building Control Plan Register 1906–12, SHC 6198/5/3, p. 12, 31 January 1907 (SHC). For a time, the business was known as 'Skeet, Fooks & Jeffes'. Today, the site is occupied by O'Neill's pub.

78. Skeet and Jeffes closed in 1996.

79. Supplemental Valuation List, Woking, 20 June 1893, no page [p. 13], SHC 6198/13/19 (SHC); Valuation List, Woking, 26 August 1895, SHC 6198/13/5a, no. 285 (SHC). The 1895 list recorded Wells as the occupier and Skeet as the owner. The present-day monetary equivalent of Wells's 1895 annual rent of £28 is £3,288.

80. Land Registry Title, no. SY400247, edition date 17 December 2010. The 1913 Land Valuation Survey valued each house at £450.

Frequently, Maybury Knolle [Knowle], an unusual looking house in The Ridge resided in by George Bernard Shaw from 1901–3, has been identified as the probable narrator's house. Admittedly, it would have possessed a view across to Horsell Common, but was not built until after Wells left Woking. For Iain Wakeford, 'Pooks Hill', a large detached house located on the corner of Maybury Hill and Pembroke Road but now sub-divided into eight flats, seems the most likely possibility.[81] When Wells was living in Woking this house, built in 1888 for William Drury, was called 'Kilcarberry', and rented for £70 per annum by Arthur W. Smyth.[82] Described by the Land Valuation Survey as a 'well built detached brick tiled residence' with a study, dining room, drawing room and six bedrooms, Kilcarberry was valued at £1,550.[83] Nearby, on Maybury Hill is 'Heatherbrae', which was not mentioned in *The War of the Worlds* but was occupied between 1901 and 1903 by Henley, the magazine editor responsible for both serializing *The Time Machine* and putting Wells in touch with Heinemann, *The War of the Worlds*' publisher.

c) *'Heatherlea', The Avenue, Worcester Park, Surrey, 1896–8*

From Woking, Wells moved some fifteen miles across Surrey to Worcester Park, where he rented 'Heatherlea' in The Avenue.[84] While Wells lived here, *The War of the Worlds* appeared as a serial in both Britain and the USA and then he prepared *The War of the Worlds* for publication as a book.

Claimed by developers to offer a blend of town and country relatively near the metropolis, during the 1890s, Worcester Park emerged as a residential suburb, offering reasonable access by train to London as well as being close to such places as Epsom, Hampton Court and Kingston upon Thames. As detailed in Chapter 9, Wells's residence at 'Heatherlea' illuminated his fast-changing circumstances and escalating demands as a writer. The move up the property ladder from a semi-detached villa with a small garden, to a detached house with a large garden reflected his growing status and wealth, even if he preferred still to rent rather than to purchase a property. Even so, the annual rent was more than double that charged for 'Lynton'. The house met also his desire for more space to work as a writer, enjoy his leisure, entertain relatives, friends and literary acquaintances and provide accommodation for Jane's elderly mother.

81. Iain Wakeford, H. G. Wells, *Woking and the Real War of the Worlds: Maybury Hill* (Old Woking: Iain Wakeford, 2005), pp. 9, 11; Iain Wakeford, 'Site of narrator's house is not where some people think it is', *Surrey Advertiser*, 16 August 2013; Iain Wakeford, 'Wells, Woking and *The War of the Worlds*', *Woking History Journal* 2 (Spring 1990): 12.

82. Valuation List, Woking, 26 August 1895, SHC 6198/13/5a, no. 201 (SHC). Kelly's 1895 directory lists him as Arthur William Smith. The plot was sold to Drury, a Bournemouth resident, by William Agar on 30 October 1888: Land Registry Title no. SY464283, edition date 1 November 2001.

83. Report ref. no. 2207, March 1914, Valuer's Field Book, Parish of Woking, IR58/34515 (TNA).

84. Report ref. no. 41, Valuer's Field Book, Parish of Cuddington, IR58/80995 (TNA); Land Registry Title no. SY321516, edition date 16 April 2014. The Avenue was often named 'The Great Avenue', such as by the Land Valuation Survey and OS maps.

At the same time, 'Heatherlea', built on land purchased in 1875 from the Landed Estates Company, provides a good example of the downside of literary heritage, most notably the lack of legal protection offered to properties linked to the lives of leading writers. During the mid-1950s, the house was demolished to make way for a new property bearing the same name and road number. As a result, visitors to The Avenue, though able to check out the house's location and to appreciate the transformation of Worcester Park as a suburb since Wells's day, will have to use photographs of 'Heatherlea' to fill the gap, most of which show the house in a dilapidated start prior to demolition.[85]

Wells and Bromley

In February 1898, the recent publication of *The War of the Worlds* led *The Bromley Record* to apprise the people of Bromley about the way in which Wells, who had been born in the town, had become one of Britain's most successful writers.[86] Then, in 1929 E. L. S. Horsburgh's history of Bromley described Wells as the town's 'most distinguished' son, the person 'who has attained the greatest fame'.[87]

Today, relatively little is left of the town and buildings which Wells knew as a boy.[88] Although Bromley did not figure in his scientific romances written during the 1890s, Wells's writings, most notably *The War in the Air* (1908) and *The New Machiavelli* (1911), frequently recorded the fast-disappearing world of his childhood years due to the spread of London, the boom in building and the resulting encroachments upon the surrounding countryside.[89] Thus, anyone travelling to Bromley to visit 'Atlas House' at 47, High Street, the house where Wells was born, will find only a blue plaque, not the actual house which was demolished during the 1930s. More confusingly, the street's renumbering means that anyone visiting the actual location should look for number 172, not 47, High Street, where a large Primark store sports a blue plaque marking Wells's place of birth. In fact, this plaque is one of the few remaining visible indicators of Wells's links with the town, even if Bromley's Central Library, a short walk away from Primark, houses an invaluable archive of Wells's correspondence and publications, including sketches of Atlas House.[90] Naturally, Bromley still celebrates its Wellsian heritage. For example, on 15 September 1966, Wells's son, Frank, opened an exhibition at Bromley Town Hall, marking the centenary of Wells's birth.[91] From the mid-1980s onwards a Wells-themed mural adorned the Market Square, but during 2004–5 was replaced by a Charles Darwin mural.

85. See postcards in SHC 6348/Box 4; SHC PC49/12, PC49/16 (SHC); Rymill, 'History: pens and paintbrushes in Worcester Park', p. 7.

86. 'Record Portraits', pp. 20–1.

87. Horsburgh, *Bromley, Kent*, pp. 283, 369.

88. A. H. Watkins (ed.), *Catalogue of the H. G. Wells Collection in the Bromley Public Libraries* (Bromley: London Borough of Bromley, 1974), p. viii.

89. See Chapter 2.

90. William Baxter, 'Sketches of 47 High Street before alterations in 1931', n.d. [1930s], HGW/1276(i), p. 1 (BRO).

91. Watkins, *Catalogue of the H. G. Wells Collection*, pp. 175–6.

Significantly, Wells himself proved somewhat unenthusiastic about maintaining contact with his 'native place'.[92] Refusing repeatedly to speak there, he showed little interest in undertaking public engagements in Bromley. Despite agreeing to subscribe to the forthcoming history, Wells proved a reluctant contributor of material to the book.[93] The history, albeit published in 1929 in Horsburgh's name, was in fact the product of a local committee upon which William Baxter, a contemporary of Wells's elder brother Frank and a fellow pupil at Morley's Academy, took it upon himself to collect material about 'Bromley's most noted citizen'.[94] As a result, from c. 1904 onwards, Baxter conducted a lengthy correspondence with Wells, focused upon both the history of Bromley and his personal life and career. Unsurprisingly, Wells frequently complained about the repeated, often repetitive, enquiries made by Baxter about his Bromley years: 'your questions are rather a lot for a busy man'.[95] Responding somewhat cynically to one of Baxter's numerous missives, Wells asserted 'I'm sorry but I do not remember being born'.[96] Increasingly, he left his wife and then, following Jane's death, his daughter-in-law, Marjorie Wells, to respond.[97]

Writing in the published history Horsburgh claimed that:

> Ineffectual efforts have been made to induce Mr. H. G. Wells, perhaps the most distinguished of all Bromley's sons (for he was born at 47 High Street), to contribute some of his reminiscences of Bromley to this volume, but all that has been obtained from him is the assurance that his old schoolmaster, Thomas Morley, does not figure in any of his novels.[98]

92. Wells to Dear Sir [possibly Borough Librarian], 19 September 1906, HGW/1245/1/5 (BRO); Wells to Baxter, 28 February 1907, HGW/1245/1/7 (BRO); Wells to Baxter, 15 April 1925, HGW/1245/1/24 (BRO).

93. Wells to Baxter, n.d. [1923?], HGW 1245/1/20 (BRO); Wells to Baxter, 15 April 1925, HGW 1245/1/24 (BRO); Catherine Wells to Baxter, n.d., HGW 1245/3/3 (SHC).

94. Baxter to Catherine Wells, 4 July 1924, HGW/1245/5/1 (BRO). The history project began during the mid–late 1900s, but made slow progress until the formation of a new committee in 1921.

95. Wells to Baxter, n.d. [1919?], HGW/1245/1/16 (BRO).

96. Wells to Baxter, n.d. [6 October 1927], HGW/1245/1/29 (BRO).

97. M. Wells to Baxter, 11 January 1928, HGW/1245/6/7 (BRO). Baxter also corresponded with Frank Wells: HGW/1245/6/1–6 (BRO).

98. Horsburgh, Bromley, pp. 283, 287, 369. In 1898 an article, published in *The Bromley Record* shortly after the publication of *The War of the Worlds* as a book, highlighted Wells's links with Bromley and would have struck a chord with former members of Morley's Academy, the school attended by Wells. The article quoted at length from a 1895 short story, 'On schooling and the phases of Mr. Sandsome', published subsequently in *Certain Personal Matters* (1898): 'It is not, of course, a portrait of Mr. Morley, but to any former "Morley's Bull Dog" the flavour of reminiscence will be evident enough', 'Record portraits', pp. 20–1. Claiming the credit for the first-ever public notice of H. G. Wells – in October 1866 the journal published notice of his birth – *The Bromley Record* acknowledged using material from Arthur H. Lawrence's interview published in *The Young Man* (1897), as 'The Romance of the Scientist', a source cited in this book.

As a result, Wells, though mentioned in the section about the history of education in Bromley as a 'famous novelist' and former pupil of Morley's academy in the High Street, did not figure very prominently in the actual text. However, the history did mention 'Atlas House' in the section on 'The Market-Place', record the cricketing exploits of Wells's father and include a brief paragraph outlining Wells's life story until 1880: 'The subsequent career of Mr. Wells and his remarkable achievement and success are a source of much pride to Bromley. These triumphs have not, however, had any direct association with the town, and do not require more than this brief notice.' [99]

Admittedly, Wells begrudged the repeated enquiries made by Baxter – certainly they tried his patience – and limited use was made of his responses in the published history, but notwithstanding Horsburgh's above-mentioned comment, he did provide Baxter with a considerable amount of information about both the town and his own life. In 1914, Baxter drew upon his research when speaking about Wells to the 'Bromley Reading Circle' and then writing the material up for the *Bromley Chronicle*.[100] Shortly after Horsburgh's history of Bromley was published, Wells's autobiography offered a more personal, frequently, negative perspective on his boyhood years in Bromley, particularly as viewed in the broader context of the many starts and escapes made throughout his life and career, following his departure from the town and especially 'Atlas House' in 1880.[101] In this vein, as mentioned above, in 1934 Wells refused the town's offer of the freedom of Bromley: 'Bromley has not been particularly gracious to me nor I to Bromley'.[102]

Conclusion

Our ability to establish and make links with past writers varies. In Wells's case, relatively little is left heritage-wise in Bromley or Worcester Park, whereas Camden Town and Woking offer much more in terms of a Wellsian literary heritage, particularly as regards *The War of the Worlds*. Nor should Midhurst, a location important for Wells's move, from the drapery counter into science and as a setting for such stories as *The Invisible Man*, and Sandgate, where the 'early Wells' gave way to the 'Later Wells', be overlooked, even if neither place is linked closely to *The War of the Worlds*.[103] During recent decades, Wells's birthplace of Bromley has

99. Horsburgh, *Bromley*, p. 401.

100. 'Mr. H. G. Wells and Bromley: The Distinguished Author's Birthplace', *Bromley Chronicle*, 4 June 1914.

101. Wells, *Experiment in Autobiography*, 1, p. 109; N. and J. Mackenzie, *The Time Traveller*, p. 265; Sherborne, *H. G. Wells*, p. 134.

102. Wells to Heyward, 15 October 1934, HGW/1245/1/39 (BRO); Dickens, 'The truth about H. G. Wells "Morbid" Bromley'; Milmo, 'War of Words'. Growing up in Bromley during the 1960s and early 1970s, Hanif Kureishi used his autobiographical *The Buddha of Suburbia* (1990) to highlight a desire to escape from the suburbs to London.

103. Mary O'Neill, Kim Leslie and Martin Hayes, *H. G. Wells in West Sussex* (Chichester: West Sussex County Council, 1996); *H. G. Wells and Midhurst* (The Midhurst Society,

offered Wellsian heritage tourists little more than a plaque on a Primark store. In effect, as happened to the mural, Wells has been brushed out of sight by Bromley, excepting the invaluable research role still played by Bromley Central Library and the occasional heritage event. Camden Town claims substantial Wellsian associations, through residence and textual references, but in London's crowded literary landscape, Wells tends to be merely one writer among many.

By contrast, Woking has begun to harness its Wellsian literary heritage more consciously, most notably through public art; honouring Wells's name; exhibitions, like the Lightbox's 'Alien Invasion Exhibition' (2013–14); and commemorative events. Indeed, 'the Martian' and the new sculpture of Wells unveiled in 2016 provide a substantial artistic dimension to *The War of the Worlds*' afterlife. Significantly, in 2010 Jonathan Lord, elected recently as Woking's MP, used his maiden speech to remind Parliament that Woking was 'proud of our Victorian, literary and cultural heritage', most notably the fact that Wells was a 'famous citizen of Woking':

> On one of my first home surgery visits, I visited a modest, semi-detached villa in the heart of Woking, only to be told that it was the very house where H. G. Wells had penned "The War of the Worlds", which envisaged Martians landing on beautiful Horsell common and laying waste to the whole of Woking and, indeed, vast swathes of southern England. We now celebrate H. G. Wells's imagination with a large, modern, Martian tripod sculpture in the centre of our town.[104]

Lord moved on from talking about Wells, the science fiction writer, to the innovative technology of McLaren, the Woking-based Formula One team and luxury sports car manufacturer. Subsequently, 'Vision for Woking', a report produced in 2012 by Matthews Associates for Woking Council as the basis for its five-year development plan, highlighted the Wellsian heritage as a 'unique' but hitherto under-exploited element in developing the town's image and tourist potential.[105] Thus, the Wellsian literary heritage continues to figure in local mindsets, even if as the 2012 'Vision for Woking' report pointed out, that far more could be done by way of exploiting the link to enhance the town's national and international profile.

Over the years, Woking has been much maligned as both a cemetery town and – to quote Patrick Parrinder – 'the town famous only because the Martians supposedly destroyed it'.[106] In this vein, the town's destruction has often been viewed as evidence of Wells's dislike of Woking, an interpretation overlooking the fact that his fiction destroyed also much of the rest of Surrey as well as London,

Midhurst: 2004); Paul Allen, 'A day of significance at Sandgate', *H. G. Wells Society Newsletter* 28 (2014): 12–15. In 2014, Midhurst co-hosted the 'Film Hub South East's project Sci-Fi: Days of Fear and Wonder'.

104. Jonathan Lord, 27 October 2010, *Hansard Parliamentary Debates (Commons)*, Vol. 517, col. 379.

105. Matthews Associates, *Woking Borough Council, Economic Development Strategy and Action Plan, 2012–2017* (April 2012): 30–1, 49; John Ellul, 'McLaren and H. G. Wells could boost town's economy', *Surrey Advertiser*, 2 December 2011, p. 1.

106. Parrinder, 'How far can we trust the narrator?', p. 15; Aldiss, 'Introduction', p. xvii.

places much loved by Wells. Even so, the way in which most adaptations of *The War of the Worlds* have revised Wells's geography has qualified the extent to which Woking and Surrey are identified globally with the story.[107] Obviously, both would be even more famous if Spielberg had followed Wells's text more closely in his 2005 film, thereby encouraging people from around the world to place them more firmly on the heritage tourist trail.

Set on America's East Coast, Spielberg's movie followed Orson Welles's 1938 radio broadcast and George Pal's 1953 Hollywood film in cheating Woking of another fifteen minutes of fame and the global visibility accruing from yet another popular and successful multimedia adaptation of Wells's original story. Pointing out how the dreadful events described in Wells's original story took place in 'determinedly ordinary, comfortable, Surrey locations', the release of Spielberg's film led David McKie to record that Woking lost its war:

> All of that in the Spielberg version is replaced by a bleak industrial 21st-century urban American landscape. Had Spielberg honoured Wells's intentions, thousands might have been flocking to north-west Surrey, giving the often maligned and traduced town of Woking a place on the tourist trail alongside Stratford, Edinburgh and Bath.
>
> The terrifying scenes when Tom Cruise and his son and daughter fight their way on to a ferry across the Hudson, only to find not safety but even more terrible menace, could so easily have been filmed not on the Hudson but on the Thames at Chertsey, or more faithfully still on the waterway that flows so conveniently close to Horsell – the Basingstoke canal ...
>
> Yet as the story unfolded – as it transpired that the role which might have been played by Horsell bridge, and the church of All Saints at Ockham, and the picturesque ruins of Newark Priory, had here been usurped by soulless motorways, domineering flyovers, brutal and ominous factories.[108]

When discussing whether it was possible to 'cash in' on Spielberg's film to promote Woking as a tourist destination for fans of Wells's *The War of the Worlds*, local councillors acknowledged that it was difficult to exploit the film because the story was set in the USA, not Surrey.[109] As one councillor observed, 'Anyone who saw that film would not have any idea the story was originally based in Woking'. However, as pointed out earlier, McKie-type media articles, though carrying a negative message for Woking and Surrey as far as the Spielberg film

---

107. Woking rarely figured in his subsequent writing. Thus, one character merely left the train at Woking station in *Love and Mr Lewisham*: H. G. Wells, *Love and Mr Lewisham* (London: Penguin, 2005), p. 117. Canoeing on the canal at Woking, walking along a lane towards the town, buying electricity from a company there and referring to a former school friend working in Woking as a monumental artist in Woking, figured in *Tono-Bungay*: H. G. Wells, *Tono-Bungay* (London: Penguin, 2005), pp. 31, 316, 347, 373.

108. McKie, 'How Woking lost its war'.

109. 'Time to cash in on War of the Worlds film, says councillor', *Woking News and Mail*, 21 July 2005.

was concerned, had a positive impact in terms of indirectly offering global media visibility by reminding people indirectly about Wells as the author and his book's original geography. Moreover, soon afterwards, Jeff Wayne's music stage show began to help redress the balance, given its emphasis upon Wells's original geography and ability to attract large audiences within and outside Britain.

Looking back on the formation of the society in 1960, a 1964 report commissioned by the 'H. G. Wells Society' concluded that for many people, the only homage paid to a favourite writer was to read his/her books, to discuss their writings and critical commentaries thereupon with fellow enthusiasts, or to join with others to form literary societies dedicated to specific authors.[110] For many people, visiting the places where their favourite writer lived and wrote, or locations mentioned in their work remains an enjoyable and engaging way of linking up with favourite writers, especially with those like Wells often first encountered during their schooldays. Quoting from a survey of the society's membership, the report recorded that roughly 60 per cent of respondents first made contact with Wells's publications when a boy and at school.[111] Very few respondents claimed to have come to Wells through either film (seven per cent), or radio (2 per cent) versions of his writings. Unsurprisingly, members, though agreeing 'that Wells was a very great man', gave different reasons for their interest in and admiration of him: 'Some revere Wells the novelist, the creator of Messrs Kipps, Polly, and Lewisham. Some claim him as the father of respectable science fiction; others hail Wells in his roles as world historian, sociologist, humanist, educationalist, prophet of world government; one at least worships him, among other things, as the founder of a world faith.'[112]

For over fifty years, the 'H. G. Wells Society' has played its part in maintaining, enhancing and publicizing Wells's literary heritage through *The Wellsian* journal, conferences, website and other activities commemorating his life and writings. Like the early members of the 'H. G. Wells Society', we all have our own vision of Wells, composed of images which are no doubt adapted, modified, even jettisoned, over time. Moreover, since the 1960s, Wells has become less studied and read as a writer – even so within academia, he figures prominently still in science fiction modules – but is now accessed principally through alternative multimedia formats, most notably comics, computer software/apps, film, graphic novels, music, radio and television.

110. Hammond, 'The Wellsians', n.d. [1964?], pp. 1–2, HGW/1727A (BRO). The report is anonymous, but the text (p. 2) suggests that the author's surname is Hammond. John Hammond, the author of several publications on Wells and one-time President of the Wells Society, denies authorship. Neither he nor Patrick Parrinder recalls who wrote it: John Hammond to the author, 9 July 2013; Patrick Parrinder to the author, 23 December 2013.

111. 'The Wellsians', n.d. [1964?], p. 7, HGW/1727A (BRO). The survey provided no information about the gender of respondents, some of whom commented that they first read Wells 'as a boy'. However, Fay Weldon, among others, has admitted first encountering Wells as a girl: Weldon, 'Great Lives'.

112. 'The Wellsians', n.d. [1964?], p. 3, HGW 1727A (BRO).

PART V

Conclusion

Chapter 17

WELLS AND *THE WAR OF THE WORLDS*

Looking back to the 1880s and 1890s when he was an emerging author, Arthur Conan Doyle recalled 'there was a general jeremiad in the London press about the extinction of English literature, and the assumed fact that there were no rising authors to take the place of those who were gone'.[1]

> The real fact is that there was a most amazing crop, all coming up simultaneously, presenting perhaps no Dickens or Thackeray, but none the less so numerous and many sided and with so high an average of achievement that I think they would match for varied excellence any similar harvest in our literary history ... Many of these I met in the full flush of their youth and their powers.

Among the rising authors met by Conan Doyle and named by him as 'winning their spurs' was Wells, alongside such writers as J. M. Barrie, Rudyard Kipling and George Bernard Shaw. The rapid growth in the reading public and a rising demand for newspapers, journals, magazines and books made the late Victorian period – to quote Wells – 'an extraordinarily favourable time for new writers', most notably those displaying 'literary freshness' in terms of offering readers engaging, distinctive and original stories.[2] Publishers were searching constantly for new writing talent, so that, as Wells admitted, 'Quite a lot of us from nowhere were "getting on"', even those, like him, from humble origins.

Wells as an original new writer

A few months before the publication of *The War of the Worlds* as a book, the *Illustrated London News*' reviewer opined that *The Invisible Man* had further enhanced Wells's reputation as 'a very ingenious story-teller', capable of making 'credible, and even scientific', the seemingly impossible idea of an invisible man, as well as forcing readers to think seriously about issues raised by the story: 'Mr Wells has a remarkable faculty of invention, and a still more remarkable gift of

---

1. Conan Doyle, *Memories and Adventures*, pp. 111–12.
2. Wells, *Experiment in Autobiography*, II, pp. 506–7.

persuasion ... Mr Wells's peculiarity is that he not only claims your attention when you are actually reading him, but exercises the same fascination over your subsequent reflections.'[3] Moreover, his ability to give the storyline 'the atmosphere of reality, of cold, hard facts' gave him 'a signal advantage over his contemporaries'. This skill, the reviewer predicted, would 'carry him very far'.

Certainly, Wells's next book, *The War of the Worlds*, more than lived up to such expectations. Indeed, in January 1898 William L. Alden, whose regular 'London Letter' apprised readers of *The New York Times* about the ever-changing British literary scene, echoed comments made by the *Illustrated London News*' reviewer:

> Mr H. G. Wells's new books, "The Invisible Man" and "The War of the Worlds", are, of course, doing well. Mr Wells is one of the cleverest men of the day, and he already has his own public. "The War of the Worlds" is to my mind by far the best work that he has done. The subject must have struck ninety-nine men in a hundred just as it did me – a subject with which it would be impossible to do anything that would rise above the level of Jules Verne. But Mr Wells made an infinitely better book than Verne ever made. He made the coming of the Martians and their raid on London not only terribly impressive, but actually probable. Nothing short of true genius could have accomplished this feat. My only fear is that someday the Martians will put Mr Wells's suggestion into practice. Last month I was in Florence, and every time an earthquake or a cart passed along the street, the thought that the first of the Martians cylinders had arrived forced itself on me.[4]

Fuelled by Wells's vivid imagination and scientific knowledge, *The War of the Worlds* possessed a highly visual, even cinematic quality, enabling Alden, like other readers, to see things, no matter how fantastic, as actually happening in their own minds. The highly positive reception accorded to this book marked a further stage in the literary world's recognition of Wells as a successful and popular new writer, much admired for his 'literary mastery' and creative skills.[5] In this vein, his next scientific romance, *When the Sleeper Wakes* (1899), was represented in the *New York Times* as typically Wellsian, an innovative blend of fantasy and realism for readers: 'Picture after picture rises before them, grotesque and arabesque, tinged with bizarre imagery, painted with colors such as never were on sea or sky or land, and yet everything somehow so matter of fact, so astoundingly real, that the impossible and outrageous seem sober, commonplace, and quite natural.'

Wells's name sold books and soon he built up a substantial readership – as Alden acknowledged, 'his own public' – on both sides of the Atlantic for his pioneering scientific romances. Pinker, his literary agent, reaffirmed this point

3. 'Writer of the Day: XXVIII', *Illustrated London News* CXI (3050) (2 October 1897), p. 456.

4. William L. Alden, 'London Letter', *The New York Times*, 15 January 1898. Reportedly, Mark Twain described Alden (1837–1908), the author of *Shooting Stars as observed from 'The Sixth Column' of the New York Times* (1878), as 'the funniest man on earth'.

5. 'Review: *When the Sleeper Wakes*', *The New York Times*, 19 August 1899.

in 1897, when informing Wells about subscriptions for *The Plattner Story*: 'Six hundred subscribed – not bad for volume of S. S.' [short stories].[6] In turn, the popularity of the scientific romances, offered a strong springboard for the launch of the 'Later Wells', with *Love and Mr Lewisham* (1900) selling 4,100 copies at home and abroad prior to publication.[7]

Viewing Wells from the literary world

During the mid–late 1890s Wells, though frequently depicted still as a new young writer, was viewed increasingly by the literary world as someone who had arrived and was now 'sure of himself' as a writer, an impression reinforced by the success of his books and serials on both sides of the Atlantic and the Channel.[8] *The War of the Worlds*, the first scientific romance serialized in the USA, indeed serialized there three times during 1897–8, figured prominently in such perceptions. As the influential New York-based literary agent, Paul Revere Reynolds (1864–1944), told Pinker, 'when you mention H. G. Wells to a man with reference to serial publications, he immediately thinks of *The War of the Worlds* when he reads the story'.[9] Moreover, when published as a book, *The War of the Worlds* sold well in not only Britain, but also the USA. Indeed, by mid-1898 it was listed as one of the six best-selling books in such diverse places as Cleveland, Ohio, and Los Angeles.[10]

Prior to its publication, reviewers writing for *The Bookman* (USA) claimed that Wells had yet to reach a large American audience. Admittedly, he had published short stories in such newspapers as the *New York Times* in 1896 and secured good reviews and reasonable sales for *The Time Machine*, *The Wonderful Visit* and *The Wheels of Chance*, but for *The Bookman* (USA) Wells had yet to become a really popular writer in the USA.[11] For *The Bookman* (USA), *Cosmopolitan*'s successful serialization of *The War of the Worlds* in the USA, suggested that the resulting book would be read 'eagerly and generally': 'it would seem as if his hour has now

6. Pinker to Wells, 28 April 1897, Loing, *Wells à l'oeuvre*, p. 434.

7. Wells to his mother, 7 June 1900, Wells, *Experiment in Autobiography*, I, p. 410.

8. 'Review: *When the Sleeper Wakes*'.

9. P. Reynolds to Pinker, 4 October 1904, Pinker, Vol. 3 (Ransom); St John, *Heinemann*, p. 67. For this reason, Reynolds, who had been appointed Heinemann's representative in New York in 1893, told Pinker that he would be unable to place *Kipps* (1905), a social novel, as a serial in the USA.

10. 'English Letter: London, February 21 to March 19', 1898', *Bookman* (USA) VII (3) (May 1898): 267; 'Book Mart', *The Bookman* (USA) VII (4) (June 1898): 365; 'Book Mart', *The Bookman* (USA) VII (5) (July 1898): 445.

11. See Mathilde Weil, 'A modern Don Quixote', *The Bookman* (USA) IV (4) (December 1896): 362–3; 'Chronicle and Comment', *The Bookman* (USA) IV (5) (January 1897): 414; 'Chronicle and Comment', *The Bookman* (USA) VI (1) (September 1897): 12; Claudius Clear, 'The Fantastic Fiction; or, "The Invisible Man"', *The Bookman* (USA) VI (3) (November 1897): 250.

come'.[12] Wells's name was spreading rapidly also across the Channel to continental Europe, as readers there accessed his scientific romances in both English and increasingly in translation (Table 7.2). For example, writing from Rome, Gissing informed Wells about seeing a notice about his 'Martian book' on the front page of *Il Messaggero*.[13]

Notwithstanding what seemed at times a difficult, seemingly unsurmountable task to succeed as a professional writer, within a decade of conducting his 'first literary experiments' in the *Science Schools Journal*, Wells's position had been transformed.[14] Growing wealth accruing from sales of books and serial rights was complemented by praise and recognition from the media and the literary world. Newspapers and magazines on both sides of the Atlantic published profiles about Wells and sought interviews to discuss his writing. For many literary commentators, Wells stood out from the pack of new young writers, as a fast rising talent widely praised for the originality of his writing. The highly positive reception accorded *The War of the Worlds*, as discussed in Chapter 7, showed that Wells attracted widespread praise from reviewers, like Strachey in the *Spectator*, for his 'literary workmanship', 'very remarkable gift of narration' and distinctive choice of topics.[15] For Strachey, the key point was that Wells proved 'singularly original'. Nor was he alone in this view. Welcoming *The War of the Worlds* as 'a very strong and a very powerful book' setting 'our minds agog', Shorter asserted that 'among the younger writers of the day, Mr Wells is the most distinctly original, and the least indebted to predecessors'.[16] Writing shortly after the publication of *The War of the Worlds*, Stead, the editor of the *Review of Reviews*, portrayed Wells as 'a young and rising novelist, who has given more proof of original genius than any of his contemporaries'.[17] It is striking how often the word 'original' appeared as a descriptor for Wells's writing.

Even so, the need for up-and-coming writers to be seen as 'new' but not 'strange', meant that Wells was frequently represented 'to be "a second" – somebody or other'.[18] As Wells complained, 'In the course of two or three years I was welcomed as a second Dickens, a second Bulwer Lytton and a second Jules Verne'. Naturally, he resented descriptors about being 'the English Jules Verne' or – to quote Oscar Wilde – 'a scientific Jules Verne' – even more once he had made his name.[19] For Wells, Verne's practical scientific approach dealing with

12. 'Chronicle and Comment', *The Bookman* (USA) VI (3) (November 1897): 178; Clear, 'The Fantastic Fiction', pp. 250–1.

13. Gissing to Wells, 20 December 1897, Mattheisen, Young and Coustillas, *The Collected Letters of George Gissing*, 7, pp. 19–20.

14. M. Wells to Baxter, 11 January 1928, HGW/1245/6/7 (BRO).

15. Strachey, 'Books: *The War of the Worlds*', pp. 168–9.

16. Shorter, 'Mr Wells "War of the Worlds"', pp. 246–7.

17. Stead, 'The Book of the Month', p. 389.

18. Wells, *Experiment in Autobiography*, II, p. 508.

19. H. G. Wells, *The Scientific Romances of H. G. Wells* (London: Victor Gollancz, 1933), p. vii. See also Wells to the Editor, *Outlook*, 23 March 1905, Smith, *Correspondence of*

probable happenings in such works as *A Journey to the Centre of the Earth* (1864) and *Twenty Thousand Leagues Under the Sea* (1870) contrasted vividly with his scientific romances exploring mere possibilities, even impossibilities: 'there is no literary resemblance whatever between the anticipatory inventions of the great Frenchman and these fantasies'.[20]

Praised by Batchelor as 'a magnificently sustained superimposition of fantasy and closely observed reality', *The War of the Worlds* highlighted Wells's skill – what he represented as a 'magic trick' – in combining fantastic scenarios with everyday realities, thereby blurring, even breaking down, the boundaries between fact and fiction.[21] Wells believed that he could hook readers only by setting strict limits to the fantasy element and then domesticating events by keeping everything else 'human and real'. Offering readers a new angle, Wells saw himself as a creative writer capable of engaging an ever-growing reading public with something very different: 'I was doing my best to write as other writers wrote, and it was long before I realized that my exceptional origins and training gave me an almost unavoidable freshness of approach and that I was being original in spite of my sedulous efforts to justify my discursive secondariness'.[22] Of course, when writing about the future, there was always the risk of being overtaken by events. When looking back to what he had written in the past, Wells was always happy to claim credit for the accuracy of his predictions, but did concede occasionally, that 'The reader will find it amusing now to compare the guesses and notions of the author with the achieved realities of today'.[23]

Clearly Wells's approach appealed to William Heinemann, the first publisher of his scientific romances. Writing about trends in fiction in June 1900, Heinemann stressed his openness to all kinds of fiction regardless of literary fashion:

> The only sure guide to success is the consideration of freshness and novelty, either in subject or in treatment, or in *genre* ... Too often the very elementary axiom seems to be forgotten that the reader is in search of a novel experience or sensation with each new book, and that it is useless to try and interest him in the same sort of story, or character, or surroundings, over and over again.[24]

Certainly, Wells ticked all of Heinemann's boxes, even if he proved a difficult, frequently exasperating, author to deal with. Nor did Heinemann, albeit retaining

H. G. Wells, II, p. 66; Wilde quoted, Borges, *Other Inquisitions*, p. 86; 'Mr H. G. Wells', *The Graphic*, 7 January 1899.

20. Wells, *The Scientific Romances*, p. vii.

21. Batchelor, *H. G. Wells*, p. 24; Wells, *Seven Famous Novels*, p. viii.

22. Wells, *Experiment in Autobiography*, II, p. 509.

23. Wells, *War in the Air* (1921), p. 5. For one attempt to check Wells's speculations against future events, see Gangale and Dudley-Rowley, 'The War of the Worlds: An After Action Report', pp. 36–56.

24. William Heinemann, 'Fashion in fiction?', *Literature*, 23 June 1900, quoted St John, *Heinemann*, pp. 40–1.

the lucrative rights to three scientific romances, manage to hold onto Wells for very long. Inevitably, other publishers as well as magazine and newspaper editors, literary agents, publishers and influential literary critics, like Edward Garnett and Edmund Gosse, were making contact by way of reflecting the literary world's view that he had made it as a writer.[25] Prestigious literary groupings celebrated Wells's achievements. For example, in December 1896 *The New Vagabonds Club of London* hosted a dinner in honour of Wells, whose 'picshua' of the event depicted such literary figures as Jerome K. Jerome, Sidney Low, the editor of the *St James's Gazette* and Kenneth Grahame, the author of *The Wind in the Willows* (1908), in attendance and bowing in homage to him.[26] In this vein, Wells was winning praise from and networking with an ever wider range of fellow writers, like Grant Allen, J. M. Barrie, Arnold Bennett, Joseph Conrad, Stephen Crane, George Gissing, Ford Madox Ford (aka Ford Madox Hueffer), Henry James and George Bernard Shaw.[27]

An early literary contact was Grant Allen (1848–99), then a well-known novelist responsible for such 'Hilltop novels' as *The Woman Who Did* (1895) and *The British Barbarians* (1895), but now largely forgotten.[28] He was also the uncle of Grant Richards, who worked with Stead on the *Review of Reviews*. In 1895, Wells travelled by train from Woking to Haslemere and then walked on to Hindhead, where Allen's house, 'The Croft', stood on the edge of the Devil's Punchbowl, 'a lonely place in a great black, purple and golden wilderness of heath' and near where Conan Doyle was building a new house.[29] Representing Allen as an 'aggressive' Darwinist, Wells acknowledged being influenced by both 'Pallinghurst Barrow' (1892) and *The British Barbarians* (1895).[30] The reference to Allen in *The Time Machine* reflects Wells's view that they were fellow time travellers: 'I flatter myself that I have a certain affinity with you. I believe that this field of scientific romance with a philosophical element which I am trying to cultivate, belongs properly to you.'[31] For Peter Morton, Allen's biographer, their 1895 meeting, which

25. Wells to Gosse, 2 October 1897, n.d. [1898], Wells to Garnett, 26 June 1900, Smith, *Correspondence of H. G. Wells, I*, pp. 290–1, 299, 358–9, 412–13 n.1. In *Boon* (1915) Wells represented Gosse as the 'official British Man of Letters': H. G. Wells, *Boon: The Mind of the Race, the Wild Asses of the Devil, and the Last Trump* (London: T. Fisher Unwin, 1915), pp. 76–7. When first published, Reginald Bliss was given as the author. Both Garnett and Gosse worked with Heinemann, the publisher of three of Wells's scientific romances: St John, *Heinemann*, pp. 14–16. For Gosse's praise of Wells's writing, see Edmund Gosse, 'The Abuse of the Supernatural in Fiction', *The Bookman* (USA) VI (4) (December 1897): 298–9.

26. Wells, *Experiment in Autobiography*, II, pp. 557, 559–60.

27. See for example, Gissing to Hick, 20 April 1898, in Mattheisen, Young and Coustillas, *The Collected Letters of George Gissing, 7*, p. 85.

28. Trotter, *The Hilltop Writers*, pp. 84–7.

29. Wells, *Experiment in Autobiography*, II, p. 552.

30. Ibid., p. 546; Ruddick, *The Time Machine*, p. 105 n.2.

31. Wells to Allen, n.d. [1895], Smith, *Correspondence of H. G. Wells, I*, pp. 245–6; H. G. Wells, *The Time Machine* (London: Penguin, 2005), p. 44; Ruddick, *The Time Machine*,

was joined by Le Gallienne, possessed considerable literary significance. Wells, 'a new and aggressive beginner' in the world of books, was welcomed by Allen, an already well-established figure in the publishing world:

> Wells was only twenty-nine, and his career was just starting … Allen could hardly have failed to recognize that a brilliant new star was in the ascendant, working the same patch that he himself had worked as best he could, but with incomparably more energy and inventiveness. Over the last few years of Allen's life, the young Wells marched from triumph to triumph, demonstrating his ability to "domesticate" (as he called it) a scientific hypothesis in a fashion which Allen, even at his best, could never emulate.[32]

'Fairly launched at last' as a writer

When interviewing Wells in 1897 Arthur Lawrence asked him for advice to pass on to young writers: "'Young writers?' Mr Wells exclaims … 'What am I but a young writer?'".[33] Wells's rapid emergence on the literary scene, rendered it easy to overlook the fact that a mere two or three years earlier he was virtually unknown and when interviewed by Lawrence, was still only thirty-years-old. Already, aspiring writers were treating Wells as a role model.[34]

Indeed, in February 1898, soon after the publication of *The War of the Worlds*, Percy Redfern, who appears like Wells to have been a shop assistant, solicited his advice about becoming a professional writer.[35] Apart from acknowledging implicitly the 'exceptional' nature of his own literary talent, Wells used his response to stress the need for ability, hard work and courage. He took the opportunity also

p. 105; David Y. Hughes, 'A queer notion of Grant Allen's', *Science Fiction Studies* 25 (2) (1998): 271–84.

32. Peter Morton, *"The Busiest Man in England": Grant Allen and the Writing Trade, 1875–1900* (Basingstoke: Palgrave Macmillan, 2005), pp. 110–11; Wells, *Experiment in Autobiography*, II, p. 552. Allen (1848–99), who died in 1899, was cremated at Woking. A memorial address was delivered by Frederic Harrison, the historian and jurist, who wrote *Annals of an Old Manor House: Sutton Place, Guildford* (1893), the property leased by his family (1874–99).

33. Lawrence, 'The Romance of the Scientist', p. 257.

34. For example, see Orwell to Symons, 10 May 1948, in Peter Davison (ed.), *George Orwell: A Life in Letters* (London: Harvill Secker, 2010), p. 406.

35. Wells to *Redfern*, n.d. [February 1898], Smith, *Correspondence of H. G. Wells, I*, pp. 305–7, 357 n.1; Wells to Redfern, 9 October 1907, Smith, *Correspondence of H. G. Wells, II*, p. 162; John Huntington, 'My Martians; Wells's success', *Foundation: The International Review of Science Fiction* 28 (77) (1999), pp. 26–7. Redfern, who served as Secretary of the Manchester Tolstoy Society, published a biography on *Tolstoy* (1907) and *The New History of the C.W.S.* (1938). On Redfern, see Charlotte Alston, 'Tolstoy's Guiding Light', *History Today* 60 (10) (2010): 35–6.

to reflect upon his early life and struggles to become an established writer: 'I know that to be an assistant in a shop is not a pleasing way of life, very irksome in a hundred ways, very hopeless for a man without command or hope of capital, & socially not very useful, or at least not obviously very useful.'

> And I know that itch to write & how attractive the freedom & repute of writing must seem to you. But the transition means a perilous journey – make no mistake about that. It is not like changing your trade. A draper may be a second rate hand or a third rate hand, and still find a place in the world for him. But for the man from below, there is no place in the world of journalism & literature unless he is an exceptional man.

The runaway success of his scientific romances renders it easy to overlook the fact that only a few years earlier Wells, having tried teaching, educational journalism and theatre reviewing, had been, like Redfern, yet another young man seeking success as a professional writer.[36]

'Living from hand-to-mouth', Wells had struggled at times to make ends meet, while attempting also to deal with a range of personal issues appertaining to his problematic health, his relationships with Isabel and Jane and the care of his elderly parents.[37] When he moved to Woking in May 1895, Wells was still making his way and name as a professional writer following a decade or so characterized by 'a series of false starts' and failed career moves.[38] By the time he left Woking just over one year later, Wells's career as a full-time writer was – to quote from his autobiography – 'Fairly Launched At Last': 'We were "getting on".'[39] In this vein, in September 1897, *The Sketch Magazine* headlined Wells as 'A Young Novelist Who Has "Arrived"'.[40] One month later the *Illustrated London News* made him its 'Writer of the Day'.[41] Introducing its serialization of *When the Sleeper Wakes* in January 1899, *The Graphic* pointed out that 'of the younger schools of writers few indeed have sprung into a success as sudden and as well-deserved as Mr H. G. Wells': 'It is but a few years since one knew no more of his writing or personality than that an anonymous contributor to the *Pall Mall Gazette* was enlivening that paper with a series of delightful little sketches which stood out on its pages no less for their insistent humour than for their shrewd observation.'[42]

However, Wells did not remain in the by-roads of journalism for long. Benefiting from the support and mentoring of Henley, among others, he soon established a reputation as a highly original writer capable of presenting his

36. Lawrence, 'The Romance of a Scientist', p. 256.

37. Wells to unknown American correspondent, 25 November 1897, Loing, *Wells à l'oeuvre*, p. 436.

38. Batchelor, *H. G. Wells*, p. 2.

39. Wells, *Experiment in Autobiography*, II, pp. 505, 636.

40. 'A Young Novelist Who Has "Arrived"', p. 317.

41. 'Writer of the Day: XXVIII', p. 456.

42. 'Mr H. G. Wells', *The Graphic*, 7 January 1899.

imaginings, his prophetic glimpses into an uncertain future, in a most enthralling and engaging form. Reviewing the wide range of Wells's writings to date, *The Graphic* opined 'that, given health and opportunity, there might be no limit to the possibilities of the new writer, for Mr Wells is a young man, and to the young all things are possible':

> Mr Wells stands out as a most original and daring writer, with a brain so active in its imaginings that at times one fancies he must see the whole future of the world written on the scroll of his fancy, right ahead to the day when the earth's fires shall have grown cold, and it shall revolve like some barren moon unenlivened on its dreary way by the vagaries of the teeming life upon its surface... that is why one looks to Mr Wells with such high augury for the future.

Wells's 'annus mirabilis' *in Woking*

Wells's rapid emergence was also a function of his stay in Woking. This period proved what Christopher Rolfe represented as a real '*annus mirabilis*' [wonderful year], a brief but decisive stage transforming his personal life and literary career.[43] What Wells wrote and published in Woking, was to prove instrumental in making his name and fortune not only in Britain but also across both the Atlantic and the Channel. As John Hammond pointed out, the Woking period was also a liberating episode, most notably enabling him to concentrate upon writing as a full-time career, giving him greater self-confidence as a writer and freeing him from both the drapery counter and the financial insecurities of jobbing journalism:

> After 1896 he was launched on an amazing career as a novelist, short story writer, prophet, historian, educationist and visionary. But he never forgot the Woking years. Here he found happiness; he found a landscape which stimulated his imagination; and he found the self-confidence to settle down to sustained writing – and in the process produced *The War of the Worlds*, one of the finest scientific romances in the English language.[44]

In retrospect, Wells's arrival at Woking occurred at a propitious time, given the recent serialization of *The Time Machine* and its forthcoming appearance, as a book on both sides of the Atlantic. Highly supportive comments about its serialization, gave Wells confidence that *The Time Machine* would do well as a book. *Select Conversations with an Uncle* also appeared in May 1895. However, these publications should not obscure the fact that at the time Wells was still relatively unknown in the literary world, as emphasized in August 1895 by *The Bookman's* article, representing him as a 'new writer'.[45] Subsequently, *The Time Machine's*

43. Rolfe, 'From Camden Town', p. 4.
44. Hammond, 'Wells and Woking', p. 7.
45. 'New writers', *The Bookman*, pp. 134–5.

success raised questions regarding Wells's ability to build upon his initial scientific romance, and hence fulfil his promise as a creative imaginative writer making distinctive use of science in literature. Or, would he prove yet another one-book wonder, especially following the negative reception accorded to *The Island of Dr Moreau*? By way of response, throughout his stay in Woking, Wells worked extremely hard as a writer 'banging away', 'with the idea of keeping myself before the public' and establishing that *The Time Machine* was not a one-off.[46]

Looking back to 'the Woking period' in his autobiography, Wells pointed to not only his literary achievements, but also a wide range of positives regarding his personal life. Perhaps the most important was the marked improvement in his health, as well as that of Jane, resulting from their escape from London's polluted atmosphere and their active pursuit of a range of recreational activities. The resulting upswing in Wells's health and general wellbeing, meant that his next serious relapse did not occur until nearly two years after he left Woking. Wells's stay in Woking ushered in a period of 'stability and respectability' in his personal life, after the traumas consequent upon the breakdown of his marriage and recent divorce from Isabel.[47] Wells and Jane, who made their relationship respectable in the eyes of Victorian society through marriage in October 1895, enjoyed life and leisure together, undertaking such suburban pleasures as boating, cycling, gardening and walking, broadening their circle of friends and acquaintances, as well as by working together in support of Wells's writing.[48] Likewise, their 'sordid exultation about royalties and cheques', enabled them increasingly to push aside longstanding worries about money.[49] Wells confessed to his need as a writer to feel 'an ample solvency', given the fluctuating nature of his earnings and the extent of his financial commitments: 'Until the summer of 1896 I never was £100 ahead of the gulf ... Since then – thanks chiefly to Pearson's high cheques & liberal advertisement of me – I have come upon better conditions'.[50] For Wells and Jane, it seemed all very exciting: 'we were very young still, we had had a hard and risky time and it was exciting to succeed'.[51]

In brief, the fact that Wells, still a relatively inexperienced writer, continued to write as much, if not more than ever, without a serious breakdown in his fragile health, testified to the manner in which Woking provided him with a conducive environment in which to work and relax as well as to launch his burgeoning career as a professional writer. Certainly, Woking fulfilled Wells's hopes that it would be a good place to work.[52] It proved an extremely productive period, perhaps the

46. Wells to unknown American correspondent, 25 November 1897, Loing, *Wells à l'oeuvre*, p. 436.

47. Wells, *Experiment in Autobiography*, II, p. 639.

48. Ibid., p. 546.

49. Ibid., p. 553.

50. Wells to Dent, 19 November 1897, Smith, *Correspondence of H. G. Wells, I*, pp. 294–5. Pearson serialized *The War of the Worlds* and published *The Invisible Man*.

51. Wells, *Experiment in Autobiography*, II, p. 553.

52. Wells to Tommy [Simmons], Spring 1895, WS31 (UIUC).

most productive period, of his whole writing career. Looking back in 1898, Wells recorded that during the past few years he had been a creative writer working 'at a ghastly pace' and 'writing away for dear life'.[53] The 'great spurt' in his writing during the mid–late 1890s meant that Wells became – to quote David Smith – 'a veritable writing machine' and "Lynton," a literary factory'.[54] Following *The Time Machine*'s success, editors, publishers and readers demanded more and more from Wells. Their demands, combined with Wells's focus upon financial security and ability to write at speed, ensured that books as well as short stories, book reviews and non-fiction articles kept on coming as part of a kind of literary surge. Far from seeing a scaling down of his journalistic and literary activities, as anticipated by Wells in November 1895, the mid-1890s were marked by a rapid advance on all writing fronts.[55]

Writing in November 1897 to Dent, the publisher, Wells saw Summer 1896, when he was still resident in Woking, as a key reference point for his writing: 'All my published work up to now & all appearing in 1898, except revisions of The Invisible Man, six short stories … & the revision of The War of the Worlds was finished before August 1896.'[56] Thus, the dining table of 'Lynton' proved the source of a lengthy list of publications. Today, Woking's association with Wells is represented and commemorated largely in terms of *The War of the Worlds*. Obviously, the significance of this linkage should not be underestimated, but Table 6.1 establishes the need to look far more widely when discussing Woking's Wellsian heritage, particularly given the manner in which Wells's projects often extended over a lengthy time period covering inspiration, planning, research, writing, rewriting and publication. While living at Woking, Wells, whose arrival there coincided with the publication of *The Time Machine* as a book, planned, researched, set and wrote *The War of the Worlds* for serialization, completed *The Island of Dr Moreau*, wrote *The Wonderful Visit* and *The Wheels of Chance* and much of *The Invisible Man* and began writing *When the Sleeper Wakes* and *Love and Mr Lewisham*.

As recorded in Chapter 6, Henley was not alone in urging Wells to slow down, because of fears about adverse impacts upon not only his fragile state of health but also the quality of his writing. In the event, Wells proved reluctant to check his pace, but subsequently, when looking back to his early books did admit that they were produced at speed by 'a beginner' too anxious for publication, yet loath to devote sufficient time to rewriting and improving the text.[57] Rather than writing two or more per year, he would have liked the opportunity to spend two years on one book and then be free to burn the manuscript, if he disliked the final result:

53. Wells, *Experiment in Autobiography*, I, pp. 398–9; Wells to Healey, n.d. [4 January 1898], Wells, HG Letters Healey, Miss 1894–8 8 *ALS* (Ransom).

54. Smith, *Wells*, pp. 48, 58; 'The Literary Regimen', G. and M. Rinkel, *Picshuas of H. G. Wells*, p. 184.

55. Wells to Grant Richards, 6 November 1895, W–R13–1 (UIUC).

56. Wells to Dent, 19 November 1897, Smith, *Correspondence of H. G. Wells*, I, pp. 294–5.

57. Wells to Quilter, n.d. [1898], Smith, *Correspondence of H. G. Wells*, I, p. 333; Wells, *Experiment in Autobiography*, I, p. 20.

'No novelist can do his best work until he feels free to do that'.[58] Acknowledging the 'slap dash' nature of some of his early writing and that he was becoming 'more anxious about the quality' of his work, Wells frequently took the opportunity to improve and rewrite his published work, as well as to boost the didactic element.[59] For example, he revised and extended *The War of the Worlds* between serialization and publication of the book, but even then opined that the resulting book was 'a clotted mass of fine things spoilt'.[60] Unsurprisingly, during the next decade or so he continued to make minor changes to the text. Within the space of one decade, he decided to revise radically the text and modify the title of *When the Sleeper Wakes* to *The Sleeper Awakes*. Wells came to represent *The Wonderful Visit* as 'a juvenile work', while speculating about the possibility of making *The Wheels of Chance* 'practically a new book': 'the young woman is a dummy of wood'.[61] At the same time, such comments should be viewed in context, given the tendency of most writers to accept that their previous publications could be improved in some way or another, as epitomized by Martin Amis's claim that he was 'appalled' by his initial writing: 'When I look back at my early stuff, I'm horrified by how crude it is'.[62]

Whereas Wells's stay in Woking proved highly productive, his residency in Worcester Park, though successful in terms of his pursuit of an active social life and literary recognition, was characterized by what he depicted as a 'long silence', a marked change of pace downwards.[63] Apart from completing both *The Invisible Man* and *The War of the Worlds* for publication as books, Wells 'worked to and fro' on *Love and Mr Lewisham* and *When the Sleeper Wakes*, but without finishing them.[64] Next, Sandgate, like Woking, proved another place to 'get good work out of myself every day'. Here Wells finished *When the Sleeper Wakes* for serialization in *The Graphic* and publication as a book, completed *Love and Mr Lewisham* and worked on 'a comic novel' [*Kipps*]: 'There are more ideas in a day here than in a week of Worcester Park'.[65] Fortunately, in the meantime his previous publications kept on selling, bringing in regular royalty cheques.

58. Quoted, 'The Output of Authors', p. 460; Wells to the Editor, *Pearson's Magazine*, n.d. [March 1897], Smith, *Correspondence of H. G. Wells, I*, p. 284.

59. Wells to Gosse, 2 October 1897, Smith, *Correspondence of H. G. Wells, I*, p. 290; 'A young novelist who has "arrived"', p. 317.

60. Wells to Quilter, n.d. [1898], Smith, *Correspondence of H. G. Wells, I*, p. 333.

61. Ibid, p. 333; Wells to St John Ervine, n.d. [1920?], Smith, *Correspondence of H. G. Wells, III*, p. 40.

62. Bryan Appleyard, 'Interview: Martin Amis talks to Bryan Appleyard', *Sunday Times, Culture Section*, 17 August 2014, p. 6.

63. Wells to his father, 18 December 1898, Wells, *Experiment in Autobiography*, I, pp. 408–9.

64. Wells to Dent, 19 November 1897, Smith, *Correspondence of H. G. Wells, I*, pp. 294–5.

65. Wells to his father, 18 December 1898, Wells, *Experiment in Autobiography*, I, pp. 408–9.

'Mr Science Fiction'

Synthesizing ongoing debates about Wells's contribution to literature, Patrick Parrinder observed that:

> Where Wells's contemporaries saw him as adding what [John] Tyndall had called the 'scientific imagination' to nineteenth-century romance, the twentieth century regarded him as the greatest of the forerunners of modern science fiction. His tales of future evolution, alien intelligence, interplanetary warfare, and technological dystopia anticipated most of the genre's thematic repertory. He stands midway between the older traditions of the learned satire, the utopia, and the marvellous voyage, and the twentieth-century growth of mass-entertainment technological fantasy.[66]

In this vein, Ford Madox Ford saw Wells as instrumental in claiming a place, indeed a respected place, for science fiction in the literary world.[67] For many commentators, the key literary legacy of *The War of the Worlds* arises from its role in supporting Wells's claim to be one of the founders, even *the founder*, of science fiction and particularly the originator of the time travel and alien invasion sub-genres. For Robert Silverberg, *The War of the Worlds* proved a landmark work:

> Not only is *The War of the Worlds* by H. G. Wells the first of all alien-invasion stories – a pathbreaking novel of stark originality by the finest mind that ever applied itself to the writing of science fiction – but it's possible to discern the hand of Wells behind almost every one of the major themes of modern science fiction. His achievement was dazzling and dizzying. He opened all the doors for us, a century ago, and we have been following in his myriad paths ever since.[68]

Indeed, widespread recognition of his pioneering role is reflected by frequent descriptors of Wells as – to quote Silverberg – 'the true father of today's science fiction, for it was he who set the canons of subject and technique that most contemporary writers follow': 'Wells ... systematically conceived and explored each of the major themes of modern science fiction: the conflict between worlds, the social consequences of great inventions, the voyage in time, the possibility of

---

66. Patrick Parrinder, 'Wells, Herbert George'. John Tyndall (1820–93), who worked at the Royal Institution (1853–87), was an early popularizer of science.

67. Ford, *Mightier than the Sword*, pp. 147–9.

68. Robert Silverberg, 'Introduction', in Glenn Yeffeth (ed.) *The War of the Worlds: Fresh Perspectives on the H. G. Wells Classic* (Dallas, TX: BenBella, 2005), p. 1. In 2004 the Science Fiction Writers of America designated Silverberg a Grand Master.

the world's destruction, the future of warfare, and much else'.[69] For Jack Williamson also, Wells, 'was more than anybody else the creator of modern science fiction'.[70]

Represented subsequently, as 'science fiction' in terms of the fictional projection and imaginative use of scientific knowledge, Wells's scientific romances proved instrumental in securing literary and public recognition for this new literary genre. Or, as Michael Harrington remarked, 'Wells is easily the greatest literary and intellectual figure to have written science fiction, though he did not know that he was doing anything of the kind'.[71] Harnessing his creative and vivid literary imagination, the scientific romances highlighted Wells's ability to draw upon his scientific education to explore new vistas, identify the challenges posed for humankind by science and technology in a fast-changing world, and provide a framework of ideas, topics and techniques defining the nature of science fiction as a literary genre as it took shape after 1926 on the pages of Hugo Gernsback's *Amazing Stories*. Unsurprisingly, Wells's writings featured prominently in *Amazing Stories'* early years, with *The War of the Worlds* published therein during August and September 1927.

Madox Ford, a one-time neighbour, praised Wells for originating 'a perfectly new brand' of literature combined with science: 'It did not take us long to recognize that here was genius. Authentic, real Genius. And delightful at that'.[72] For the late Victorian literary world, science was viewed as somewhat remote, even vulgar and certainly not something which men of letters should worry about, let alone treat as a suitable topic for literature. As Madox Ford recorded, 'In those days no one bothered his head about Science. It seemed to be an agreeable parlour game like stamp collecting ... One did very well without it in those days'. Then along came Wells, an imaginer using scientific ideas as a literary tool for explorations in fantasy. Emerging with 'extraordinary speed', seemingly from nowhere, he treated science as a treasure trove of fantastic ideas capable of being pressed into the untrodden field of literature: 'And we welcomed Science – Mr Wells's brand of Science – with acclamations. Fairy tales are a prime necessity of the world, and he and Science were going to provide us with a perfectly new brand. And he did.' Moreover, Wells's stories, each proving 'an entertaining and magnificently machined gem of fiction', possessed widespread appeal:

> All Great London lay prostrate at his feet. Mr Wells struck the Empire with all the impact of Mr Kipling. He struck everybody. He delighted the bourgeois

69. Silverberg, 'Introduction', *Mirror of Infinity*, p. viii; Robert Gunn, 'The Man who invented tomorrow', n.d. [2000], http://www.sfcenter.ku.edu/tomorrow.htm [accessed 12 September 2014]; Lester del Rey, *The World of Science Fiction, 1926–1976: The History of a Sub-Culture* (New York: Garland, 1980), p. 19; Michael Harrington, 'Second Sight: Dream of a sci-fi prophet', *Sunday Telegraph*, 27 August 1995, p. 27. Note Brian Aldiss, BBC Radio Four, 'Stranger than Truth', 2 July 1970.

70. Jack Williamson, 'Foreword: H. G. Wells: The Star', in Robert Silverberg (ed.), *The Mirror of Infinity: A Critics' Anthology of Science Fiction* (New York: Harper & Row, 1970), p. 3.

71. Harrington, 'Second Sight'.

72. Ford, *Mightier than the Sword*, pp. 147–9.

profane with his imagination, and we intelligentsia snorted with pleasure at the idea of a Genius whom we could read without intellectual effort. And with immense admiration for his "technique". One could ask no more ... So we devoured Mr Wells.

Praising *The Invisible Man* and *The War of the Worlds*, Joseph Conrad was another prominent author welcoming Wells as 'a very original writer, *romancier du fantastique*, with a very individualistic judgement in all things and an astonishing imagination'.[73] Moreover, Wells evoked the same response from the general reading public by making his fantasies accessible, engaging and real for readers, thereby creating and building an audience with a taste for science fiction.[74] For many commentators, Wells's page-turning stories did more to make science fiction literature acceptable, readable, entertaining and saleable than any previous writer.[75] Unsurprisingly, Wells became a major source of inspiration for many scientific fiction writers, particularly as he proved the author of one of the first science fiction stories most ever read. As one reviewer of *The War of the Worlds* noted in 1898, 'Already Mr Wells has his imitators'.[76] Numerous science fiction scenarios derive from the stories sketched out by Wells's pen, with *The War of the Worlds* proving – to quote David Lodge – 'the mother of all aliens-invade-earth novels'.[77] In addition, as studied in Part 3, he provided stories which were soon regarded as highly adaptable for representation in alternative literary and audio-visual formats.

Popularizing science

Writing *Nature*'s obituary of Wells, who he often described as both his oldest and his dearest friend, Sir Richard Gregory, the journal's long-time editor (1919–39) and currently President of the British Association for the Advancement of Science, described the scientific romances as an imposing series of works making him 'the greatest international scientific educator of his times'.[78] For Gregory, 'Wells knew, better than any other man of letters, what such natural events and processes had been and [that] they were due to forces acting continually and uniformly. It was this scientific knowledge, combined with brilliant powers of expression, that made him unique in his own particular field'.[79] Science revolu-

73. Conrad quoted, Dryden, 'Wells and Joseph Conrad', p. 4.

74. Andy Sawyer, 'Science Fiction: the sense of wonder', in Christine Berberich (ed.), *The Bloomsbury Introduction to Popular Fiction* (London: Bloomsbury, 2015), p. 96.

75. Del Rey, *World of Science Fiction*, pp. 19–20; Adam Roberts, *Science Fiction: The New Critical Idiom* (London: Routledge, 2000), pp. 48–9.

76. 'Review', *The Academy*, 29 January 1898, quoted Danahay, *The War of Worlds*, p. 229.

77. David Lodge, 'Top 10 H. G. Wells books', *The Guardian*, 4 May 2011.

78. Gregory, 'H. G. Wells: a survey', p. 406; Richard Gregory to Gip (Wells), n.d. (1946), Gregory Papers, SxMs14/1/7/2 (Sussex).

79. Gregory, 'H. G. Wells: A survey', p. 401.

tionized Wells's life and impacted heavily upon his writing, even if as a scientist he wore his learning lightly.[80] Writing more recently in *Nature*, Roy Porter, a historian of science active in taking science outside academia, dubbed Wells, the writer, as 'Mr Science'.[81] According to Steve Jones, a former Reith Lecturer actively involved also in promoting the public understanding of science, 'what is extraordinary is the excellence of H. G. Wells's science and the almost uncanny way in which he anticipated its advances over the next century'.[82]

For Steven McLean, debates about Wells as a founding father of science fiction, have diverted attention away from the way in which his early fiction provided – to quote Wells – 'a mouthpiece for science, philosophy and art' and hence, reflected the way in which fiction was 'widening its territory'.[83] Drawing upon ongoing discourses touching upon a range of scientific disciplines, Wells's scientific romances took science almost by stealth to a non-specialist readership.[84] Thus, they performed an educational role in terms of popularizing scientific concepts and dramatizing science's potential impacts upon society in a vivid and engaging narrative. For example, whereas *The Invisible Man* highlighted the barriers existing between science and society, most notably the reluctance of scientists to address a public audience, *The War of the Worlds* engaged with several branches of science, including astronomy and evolutionary theory. Both *The Island of Dr Moreau* and *The Invisible Man* revealed Wells's fears about the downside of science, the dangers of how scientists might misuse science, without being subject to the appropriate controls.

Writing at a time when science was beginning to play an increasingly important role in politics, the economy and society, Wells led the way in bridging the gap between science and culture by harnessing the power of his scientific knowledge to literature, in order 'not only to describe his own world, but also to offer a glimpse into worlds that might be'.[85] His initial writing about travelling through time, provided the foundation for further scientific romances based upon what Norman and Jeanne Mackenzie described as his 'trick-of-the-pen formula', designed to force his readers to suspend their disbelief at the fantastic stories unfolding on the page before their very eyes: 'He heard of some new concept or invention. He next set the novel theory in a conventional background. Then, having made the incredible acceptable by his attention to detail, his imagination was free to make what fantasies he pleased out of the resulting conflict.'[86] Building upon his early journalism, taking science to the man in the street and his articles in *Nature* about popularizing science and science in schools, Wells's scientific romances rooted fantasy in the

80. Batchelor, *Wells*, p. 30.

81. Roy Porter, 'Mr Science, Warts and All', *Nature*, 361, 4 February 1993, p. 413.

82. Jones, 'View from the Lab'.

83. *Weekly Sun Literary Supplement*, 1 December 1895, quoted Smith, 'A chat with the author', p. 6; Mclean, *Early Fiction of H. G. Wells*, p. 2.

84. Mclean, *Early Fiction of H. G. Wells*, pp. 3, 89–90, 189–92.

85. Smith, *H. G. Wells*, p. xii.

86. N. and J. MacKenzie, *The Time Traveller*, p. 65.

real world.[87] Reviewing *The War of the Worlds*, Gregory, then assistant editor of *Nature*, pointed to the role of such fiction 'in furthering scientific interests; they attract attention to work that is being done in the realm of natural knowledge, and so create sympathy with the aims and observations of men of science.'[88]

As a story benefiting from Wells's creative imagination and literary reputation as a populist, *The War of the Worlds* was written to be read, to entertain, to engage readers and to sell to purchasers of *Pearson's Magazine*, *Cosmopolitan* and the books published by Heinemann and Harper. From this perspective, didactic elements were downplayed. Subsequently, the 'Later Wells' was more prone to claim that his early scientific romances had an intended meaning. Yet, in December 1895, when writing for the *Saturday Review*, he critiqued any attempt to make literature a tool for pamphleteering purposes: 'the philosopher who masquerades as a novelist ... discredits both himself and his message, and the result is neither philosophy nor fiction.'[89] Even so, the scientific romances, albeit depicted primarily as mere 'stories', are frequently interpreted as offering far more in terms of pushing messages centred upon *fin de siècle* themes and Wells's uncertainty about the future, due to 'a profound scepticism about man's knowledge of final reality' and worries about the use and misuse of science.[90]

Indeed, Hammond claimed that:

It is frequently overlooked that these are not simply "stories". Each was written with a didactic intent, and some of them ... are really parables: satires written in the form of allegory. To Wells, the novel was a vehicle for the discussion of ideas, and although this became much more evident in his later works, the serious intent was there from the very beginning.[91]

Echoing Hammond's line, David Smith described the scientific romances as '"good reads", shot full of science that made them believable, but also with a message; and a message which increased in intensity as time went on', especially that the intervention of science could be as evil as it could be good.[92] For Norman and Jeanne MacKenzie, the diverse range of the scientific romances cannot disguise the fact that, 'They are all variations on a single theme – the nature of the evolutionary process and Man's precarious place in the scheme of things. At the heart of each

87. H. G. Wells, 'Popularising Science', *Nature* 50, 26 July 1894, pp. 300–1; H. G. Wells, 'Science, in School and after School', *Nature*, 50, 27 September 1894, pp. 525–6.

88. Richard Gregory, 'Science in fiction', *Nature*, 57, 10 February 1898, p. 340.

89. H. G. Wells, 'Mr Grant Allen's new novel', *The Saturday Review* 80 (14 December 1895), pp. 785–6.

90. Smith, *Wells*, pp. 85–6; H. G. Wells, 'Preface to Volume I', *The Works of H. G. Wells*, Atlantic Edition, Vol. I (London: T. Fisher Unwin, 1924), pp. xxi–xxiii.

91. J. R. Hammond, 'Nottingham Countryside: H. G. Wells and the Midlands', *Nottingham Topic*, April 1976, p. 10, HGW 1727A/53 (BRO).

92. Smith, *Wells*, p. 85.

story Wells states the same negative idea ... man is only temporarily dominant on a planet which itself is doomed.' [93]

A biography of The War of the Worlds *as a book*

In many respects, this study provides a biography of *The War of the Worlds* as a book, and particularly its afterlife, given the manner in which the storyline was taken to audiences in an ever wider range of literary and audio-visual adaptations. From this biographical perspective, Part 1 provides an introductory survey setting the scene and contextualizing the book. Part 2 offers a critical study of the project in terms of inspiration; negotiations with literary agents, editors and publishers; the signing of contracts for publication as a book and a serial; research, writing and rewriting; publication first as a serial and then as a book; reception, sales, reviews, readership and impact; translations; parodies, sequels and so on. Then, Part 3 highlights the way in which over time, Wells's *The War of the Worlds* has been adapted for a wide range of alternative formats, including comics, computer games, films, graphic novels, music, newspapers, radio and television. Finally, Part Four illuminates *The War of the Worlds'* ongoing legacy as a central element in the Wellsian literary heritage.

By definition, most science fiction writing has a short shelf life. Overtaken rapidly by scientific and technological advances, many science fiction stories soon become redundant. By contrast, Wells's scientific romances, though published more than one century ago, continue to live on in today's world, even if *The War of the Worlds* has fared and still fares, much better than most. Combining literary and imaginative qualities appealing to audiences during both the late 1890s and today's multimedia world, *The War of the Worlds'* enduring present-day resonance and appeal, has proved a function of Wells's skills as a magician, an illusionist, capable of encouraging audiences willingly to suspend their disbelief by mixing doses of fantasy with substantial portions of real life. *The War of the Worlds* remains in print. Indeed, it has never been out of print. Today the book continues to attract large numbers of readers, while the timeless nature of the storyline ensures that it remains capable still during the twenty-first century of inspiring numerous adaptations. Indeed, *The War of the Worlds* has enjoyed a much more active afterlife than most books, so that for many people the story has come to mean, say a film, a music show or a radio programme, not a book.

Despite being frequently portrayed as 'a rattling good yarn', this does not mean that *The War of the Worlds* lacks a purposive role. Indeed, the story's enduring appeal to audiences across the world derives in part from its ability to reflect and advance present-day issues points for debate. As Will Self commented about Wells's writings, 'Writing about the future is best understood as a function of

---

93. N. and J. MacKenzie, *The Time Traveller*, pp. 127–9; Batchelor, *Wells*, p. 30.

contemporary anxiety'.[94] Thus, as discussed in Chapter 3, Wells's fantasy storyline about an interplanetary invasion rooted in the real world plays on readers' fears and anxieties about the future in the light of the changing global power balance, growing threats to national security and the advance of science. In brief, Wells used the Martians to speculate, predict, warn and exhort society to reappraise existing modes of thought, or else face the consequences.

Discussing the history of imaginative writing about Mars, Crossley contextualized Wells's *The War of the Worlds*:

> The way people imagine other worlds is an index of how they think about themselves, their immediate world, their institutions and conventions, their rituals and habits. Mars, in other words, is a site for both critical exposure and imaginative construction. As [Kim Stanley] Robinson observes at the opening of *Red Mars*, the literary history of Mars is a history of our own minds because "we are all the consciousness that Mars has ever had." The Mars that has for so long attracted human attention is the product both of evolving scientific understandings of the planet and of the stories that have been told about it... human beings have created Mars in their own image even as scientists have labored to discover and authenticate the truths about the planet. The *Mars* of the literary imagination is the complex product of an interplay between fact and fancy, between evidence and desire, between knowing with the head and knowing with the heart.[95]

Within this context, the various adaptations of *The War of the Worlds* discussed in Part 3, help to audit Wells's standing in contemporary popular culture during the 1890s and after.[96] They serve not only to reaffirm the book's role as an influential source about attitudes towards Mars, but also to represent further chapters in a long-running story, with every new version reflecting what David Mattin represented as present-day 'communal angst', treating Wells's Martians as symbolic displacements of perceived contemporary threats:

> *War of the Worlds* seems to occupy a place all of its own in the modern Western psyche. Wells' novel, published in 1898, played on British anxiety over German militarisation. In 1938, the world tense on the eve of war, Orson Welles revived the tale in a faux documentary radio broadcast so credible that it famously had Americans fleeing their homes in panic.[97]

As Koepp, the co-scriptwriter of Spielberg's '9/11' take on the story, remarked, 'The genius of the story is that everyone can fit their own personal fears around it,

94. Self, 'Death on three legs'.

95. Crossley, *Imagining Mars*, p. xiv; Kim Stanley Robinson, *Red Mars* (New York: Bantam, 1993), p. 2.

96. Sherborne, *H. G. Wells*, pp. 244–5.

97. Mattin, 'Words on Worlds: Spielberg's Writer'.

that someone out there – the fascists, the communists, the Americans – is coming to get them.'

Conclusion

Wells, died at his Regent's Park home on 13 August 1946 aged seventy-nine. A few days later, he was cremated at Golders Green Crematorium, where J. B. Priestley delivered a short address bidding farewell to 'the great prophet of our time … the chief prophet … long foreshadowing … the shape of things to come'.[98] Subsequently, Wells's sons scattered his ashes over the sea off the coast of Dorset.[99] Then, on 30 October, over 600 people attended his Memorial Service at the Royal Institution, an event broadcast on BBC Radio's Third Programme. Lord Beveridge read a tribute from Clement Attlee, the prime minister, describing Wells as the great awakener of the men and women of his generation.[100] Paradoxically, Wells, though honoured by a service held at the Royal Institution, never secured a much cherished Fellowship of the Royal Society.[101] Nor was he knighted. In his autobiography, Wells speculated that 'I might have been knighted; I might have known the glories of the O. M': 'But Ann Veronica (bless her!) and my outspoken republicanism saved me from all that.'[102]

The time traveller's journey was over, but his writings, most notably the scientific romances, lived on.[103] Of course, Wells's literary reputation came to rest on far more than *The War of the Worlds* and the other scientific romances, but the 'Later Wells', though occasionally returning to science fiction type writings, falls beyond the bounds of this study. Despite normally represented as a twentieth-century author, Wells's literary career really took off during the closing years of the nineteenth century, with the mid–late 1890s seeing what most commentators view as his best, most popular, most enduring and most influential writing. However, the massive success of his scientific romances was not enough for Wells, who sought recognition subsequently, as both a serious novelist and a public intellectual, pointing his readers and listeners towards new ways of thinking. However, much of his post-1900 literary output, except such books as *First Men in the Moon* (1901), *Kipps* (1905) and *The History of Mr Polly* (1910), has minimal present-day visibility and appeal.

Like any major writer, over time Wells's literary standing and popularity have waxed and waned, as has the extent to which his writings have been studied

98. Hammond, *H. G. Wells*, p. 84; Priestley, 'Right or wrong'.

99. Anthony West, *H. G. Wells*, pp. 153–4.

100. 'Public Homage to H. G. Wells', *The Times*, 31 October 1946, p. 6. On preparing the tribute meeting, see Gregory Papers, file SxMs14/1/7/2 (Sussex).

101. Smith, *Wells*, pp. 461–4, 483; Sherborne, *H. G. Wells*, pp. 342–3; N. and J. MacKenzie, *The Time Traveller*, pp. 436–7. In 1943, Wells was awarded a University of London D. Sc. The Royal Institution and The Royal Society are separate bodies.

102. Wells, *Experiment in Autobiography*, II, pp. 639, 651, *et seq*. Nor did his confrontation of contemporary moral codes, through his love life, help his honours' prospects.

103. N. and J. MacKenzie, *The Time Traveller*, p. 447.

within academia. But throughout this period, his scientific romances, especially *The War of the Worlds*, continued not only to attract readers but also to take Wells to new audiences, because of their enduring contemporary resonance and capability for adaptation by alternative multimedia formats. Moreover, his personal life, most notably his love life, defiance of conventional ways of thinking about personal relationships and the manner in which he constantly reinvented himself, has emerged as a prime topic of interest for biographers and readers, particularly following the eventual publication in 1984 of *H. G. Wells in Love*, the final volume of his autobiography. Wells's frank account of his marriages and love affairs, added a new dimension to his life story, while inspiring such publications as Andrea Lynn's *Shadow Lovers: The Last Affairs of H. G. Wells* (2001) or David Lodge's factional *A Man of Parts* (2010).

Moreover, recent decades have witnessed a growing preoccupation with the Wellsian literary heritage, that is the towns and villages where Wells was born, lived, worked, was inspired by, used in his writing and died. In 2016, the 150th anniversary of his birth and the 70th anniversary of his death, accentuated the focus upon this aspect. Several places, most notably, Bromley, Midhurst, Sandgate, Sutton, Woking and Worcester Park, figure alongside London, especially Camden Town, in the Wellsian literary heritage, since much of his life, particularly until c. 1900, was one of repeated 'breakouts', from family poverty, from limited schooling, from drapery indenture, from institutionalized religion and from marriage, to yet another place.[104]

In 1900, *Love and Mr Lewisham* reflected a new Wells, an author motivated by a growing desire to write something perceived by him as more prestigious than scientific romances and henceforth, to be known as a writer of mainstream novels rather than fantastic fiction: 'I finished the *War of the Worlds* in the summer of 1896. Then, said I, let me do something worthy to prove I'm no charlatan'.[105] Like any author, Wells's writing proved somewhat uneven in terms of literary quality, but it is generally agreed – to quote Patrick Parrinder – 'that his best writing came relatively early and, apparently, with such ease that he himself set little store by it'.[106] Paradoxically, it was *The War of the Worlds*-type books, the work of the 'early Wells', not the 'new Mr Wells' or the 'Later Wells', that made and preserved his reputation and gave him a secure place not only in literature, but also in popular culture, through an ever extending range of adaptations reaching new audiences across the globe. As Strachey wrote in 1898, when reviewing *The War of the Worlds*, 'As a writer of scientific romances, he [Mr Wells] has never been surpassed'.[107] As regards science fiction, many would argue that such sentiments remain equally true today at a time when the book still remains in print and has

104. Hughes and Geduld, *Critical Edition*, p. 11.

105. Wells to Healey, n.d. [4 January 1898], Wells, H. G. Letters Healey, Miss 8 *ALS* 1894–8 (Ransom); J. E. H. W., 'The new Mr Wells', p. 155.

106. Patrick Parrinder, 'The War of Wells's Lives', *Science Fiction Studies* 38 (2) (2011): 329.

107. Strachey, 'Books: *The War of the Worlds*', p. 168.

a buoyant afterlife, such as evidenced by the staging of Jeff Wayne's music show in London's West End (2016), Stephen Baxter's forthcoming sequel about the Martians' return (2017), and the first British television adaptation (2017). Indeed, in January 2016, when noting the forthcoming 150th anniversary of Wells's birth, A.A. Gill, the *Sunday Times*' critic and reviewer famed for his acerbic commentaries, gave readers a highly positive assessment of Wells as an author, even if 'late Victorian' might be preferred to 'Edwardian' as a descriptor:

> No other Edwardian writer can have had a greater influence on contemporary popular culture than Herbert George. Along with Jules Verne, he invented science fiction, the abiding format of today's films, games and fiction - not just one strand, but a whole library of fantasy genres, from alien invasion to time travel, dystopian futures, hallucinations and medical nightmares. Wells also wrote history, journalism and the rules for war games ... He has always been a significant influence on television – there would be no Doctor Who without Wells.[108]

In today's multimedia world *The War of the Worlds* has not only survived and accommodated itself to fast-changing circumstances but also flourished as a book inspiring an ever expanding range of adaptations. In turn, the latter have proved a major source for new readers. For example, when published in 2005 as a Penguin Classic over 250,000 copies of *The War of the Worlds* were sold to readers seeking an engaging and iconic science fiction story, studying the story as a set text or wishing to read the book linked to Orson Welles's famous radio broadcast, Jeff Wayne's new stage music show or Spielberg's recently released film. Indeed, a special film tie-in version of the Penguin Classic secured substantial sales. Clearly *The War of the Worlds* plays a major role in explaining Wells's central place in popular culture today, and – to quote Damien Timmer when announcing the forthcoming British television version of the story – further adaptations promise merely 'to reaffirm H.G. Wells' position as one of this country's most important writers.'[109]

108. A. A. Gill, 'Brainstorming inventor fails a character test', *Sunday Times Magazine*, 31 Jan. 2016, p. 16.

109. Quoted, Jake Kanter, 'War of The Worlds set for UK television adaptation', 15 Dec. 2015 http://www.broadcastnow.co.uk/news/war-of-the-worlds-set-for-uk-television-adaptation/5098070.article" http://www.broadcastnow.co.uk/news/war-of-the-worlds-set-for-uk-television-adaptation/5098070.article# [accessed 18 Jan. 2016].

BIBLIOGRAPHY

Citations record the edition of a book used for referencing the text, not necessarily its initial date of publication, which is recorded in square brackets. Some website addresses are no longer accessible.

Primary sources (unpublished)

Official documents

General Register Office:
Birth, marriage and death certificates of H. G. Wells

Land Registry:
Property titles

The National Archives, Kew, London (TNA):
British government records: Foreign Office (FO); Railways (RAIL); Land Valuation
Survey, 1910–1915: Plans (IR121–125) and Field Books (IR58); British Census
Records 1891, 1901, 1911

Surrey History Centre, Woking, Surrey (SHC):
Woking Borough Council Records; Anchor Hotel, Ripley, Cyclists Books; Land Sales
Particulars; Photos and Postcards

Private papers

Archives & Local History, Manchester Central Library, Manchester (Manchester):
Percy Redfern Collection

**Archives Division, British Library of Political and Economic Science, London School
of Economics, London, UK (LSE):**
Booth's Survey Notebooks

BBC Written Archives Centre, Caversham Park, Reading, UK (BBC):
BBC Audience Research Reports

**Beinecke Rare Book and Manuscript Library, Yale University, New Haven,
Connecticut, USA (Yale):**
H. G. Wells Correspondence

**Bromley Local Studies and Archives, Bromley Central Library, Bromley, Kent, UK
(BRO):**
H. G. Wells and H. G. Wells Society Collection

Harry Ransom Humanities Research Center, University of Texas at Austin, Texas, USA (Ransom):
H. G. Wells Correspondence

Random House Group Archive & Library, Rushden, Northants, UK (Rushden):
William Heinemann Archive, Author File H. G. Wells

Rare Book & Manuscript Library, University of Illinois at Urbana-Champaign, Urbana-Champaign, Illinois, USA (UIUC):
H. G. Wells Correspondence; Sarah Wells's Diaries

University of Sussex Special Collections, The Keep, Falmer, Brighton (Sussex):
Mass Observation Archive, The Mass Observation Project: the Universe and Outer Space 2005 (MO); Sir Richard Gregory Papers.

Primary sources (published)

Official documents

Hansard Parliamentary Debates, Official Reports: House of Commons.
Woking Borough Council, 'A Public Art Commission Brief', 1996

Magazines, newspapers and comics

Articles from magazines and newspapers are listed individually in the footnotes. Note that the British Library's Newspaper Library at Colindale, as referenced in the footnotes, has now closed.

Correspondence and diaries

Davison, P. (ed.), *The Complete Works of George Orwell, XII: A Patriot After All, 1940–1941*, London: Secker and Warburg, 1998.
Davison, P. (ed.), *George Orwell: A Life in Letters*, London: Harvill Secker, 2010.
Jean-Aubry, G. (ed.), *Joseph Conrad: Life and Letters,* New York: Doubleday, Page, 1927.
Lellenberg, J., Stashower, D. and Foley, C. (eds), *Arthur Conan Doyle: A Life in Letters*, New York: Penguin Press, 2007.
Loing, B. *H. G. Wells à l'oeuvre: les débuts d'un écrivain (1894–1900)*, Paris: Didier Erudition, 1984.
Mattheisen, P. F., Young, A. C. and Coustillas, P. (eds), *The Collected Letters of George Gissing, 6: 1895–1897; 7: 1897–1899; 8: 1900–1902*, Athens, OH: Ohio University Press, 1995–96.
Smith, D. C. (ed.), *The Correspondence of H. G. Wells, 1–4*, London: Pickering & Chatto, 1998.

Publications by H. G. Wells

Autobiographies

'H. G. Wells', in A. Einstein *et alia*, *Living Philosophies*, New York: Simon & Schuster, 1931, pp. 78–92.

Experiment in Autobiography: Discoveries and Conclusions of a Very Ordinary Brain (since 1866), I–II, London: Victor Gollancz and the Cresset Press, 1934.

Wells, G. P. (ed.), *H. G. Wells in Love: Postscript to an Experiment in Autobiography*, London: Faber and Faber, 1984.

Books, including collections of short stories and articles

Textbook of Biology, 1–2, London: W. B. Clive, University Correspondence College Press, (with Gregory, R. A.) *Honours Physiography*, London: Joseph Hughes, 1893.

The Time Machine: An Invention, London: William Heinemann, 1895.

The Time Machine: An Invention, New York: Random House, 1931.

The Time Machine: An Invention, (ed.) N. Ruddick, Peterborough, ON: Broadview, 2001.

The Time Machine: An Invention, (ed.) P. Parrinder, London: Penguin, 2005.

Select Conversations with an Uncle (now extinct) and Two Other Reminiscences, London: John Lane, 1895.

The Stolen Bacillus and Other Incidents, London: Methuen, 1895.

The Wheels of Chance & The Time Machine, London: J. M. Dent, 1935. [1896/95].

The Wonderful Visit, London: Dent/New York: Macmillan, 1895.

The Island of Dr Moreau, (ed.) P. Parrinder, London: Penguin, 2005 [1896].

The Invisible Man, (ed.) P. Parrinder, London: Penguin, 2005 [1897].

The Plattner Story and Others, London: Methuen, 1897.

Thirty Strange Stories, New York: Arnold, 1897.

Certain Personal Matters, A Collection of Material, Mainly Autobiographical, London: Lawrence & Bullen, 1898.

The War of the Worlds, London: William Heinemann, 1898.

The War of the Worlds, (ed.) P. Parrinder, London: Penguin, 2005.

The War of the Worlds, (ed.) M. A. Danahay, Peterborough, ON: Broadview, 2003.

The Sleeper Awakes, (ed.) P. Parrinder, London: Penguin, 2005 [1899].

Love and Mr Lewisham, (ed.) S. J. James, London: Penguin, 2005 [1900].

The First Men in the Moon, London: Newnes, 1901.

Anticipations, London: Chapman & Hall, 1901.

Kipps, (ed.) S. J. James, London: Penguin, 2005 [1905].

The Future in America: A Search After Realities, London: George Bell, 1906.

First and Last Things: A Confession of Faith and Rule of Life, London: Archibald Constable, 1908.

The War in the Air, and particularly how Mr Bert Smallways fared while it lasted, London: Collins, 1921 [1908].

The War in the Air, and particularly how Mr Bert Smallways fared while it lasted, (ed.) P. Parrinder, London: Penguin, 2005.

Ann Veronica, (ed.) S. Schutt, London: Penguin, 2005 [1909].

Tono-Bungay, (ed.) P. Parrinder, London: Penguin, 2005 [1909].

The History of Mr Polly, (ed.) S. J. James, London: Penguin, 2005 [1910].

The New Machiavelli, (ed.) S. J. James, London: Penguin, 2005 [1911].

The Country of the Blind and Other Stories, London: Nelson, 1911.
The Discovery of the Future, New York: B. W. Huebsch, 1913.
The World Set Free, London: Macmillan, 1914.
Boon: The Mind of the Race, the Wild Asses of the Devil, and the Last Trump, London:
    T. Fisher Unwin, 1915.
Mr Britling Sees It Through, London: Cassell, 1916.
The Works of H. G. Wells, Atlantic Edition, I, III, London: T. Fisher Unwin, 1924.
The Scientific Romances of H. G. Wells, London: Victor Gollancz, 1933.
Seven Famous Novels, New York: Knopf, 1934.
Star-Begotten, London: Chatto & Windus, 1937.

*Other publications (Wells's early publications were often published anonymously
and then published under his name, in a collected edition)*

"'Specimen Day": From a Holiday Itinerary', *Science Schools Journal* 33 (1891): 17–20.
'Man of the Year Million: A Scientific Forecast', *Pall Mall Gazette*, 6 November 1893, p. 3.
'Out Banstead Way by An Amateur Nature Lover', *Pall Mall Gazette*, 25 November 1893,
    p. 11. Re-published in H. G. Wells, *Certain Personal Matters*, London: Lawrence &
    Bullen, 1898, pp. 254–61.
'On a Tricycle: Cycling and the Higher Criticism', *Pall Mall Gazette*, 18 May 1894.
    Re-published in H. G. Wells, *Select Conversations with an Uncle*, London: John Lane,
    1895.
'The Stolen Bacillus', *Pall Mall Budget*, 21 June 1894. Re-published in H. G. Wells, *The
    Stolen Bacillus and Other Incidents*, London: Methuen, 1895.
'Popularising Science', *Nature* 50 (26 July 1894): 300–1.
'The Extinction of Man: Some Speculative Suggestions', *Pall Mall Gazette*, 25 September
    1894, p. 3. Re-published with minor amendments and additions in H. G. Wells,
    Certain Personal Matters, London: Lawrence & Bullen, 1898, pp. 172–9.
'Science, in School and after School', *Nature* 50 (27 September 1894): 525–6.
'Review: *The Woman Who Did*', *Saturday Review* 79 (9 March 1895): 319–20.
'Argonauts of the Air', *Phil May's Annual* 5 (December 1895): 45–64.
'Mr Grant Allen's New Novel', *The Saturday Review* 80 (14 December 1895): 785–6.
'Intelligence on Mars', *The Saturday Review* 81 (4 April 1896): 345–6.
'The Rajah's Treasure', *The New York Times*, 6–8 July 1896.
'In the Abyss', *The New York Times*, 7–10 August 1896.
'The Sad Story of a Dramatic Critic', in H. G. Wells, *The Plattner Story and Others*,
    London: Methuen, 1897, pp. 262–73.
'The Output of Authors', (with W. L. Alden et al.), *Pearson's Magazine* 3 (16) (April 1897):
    456–61.
'A Perfect Gentleman on Wheels', *Woman at Home*, April 1897, pp. 673–81. Re-published
    in the *New York Daily Tribune*, 16 May 1897 and in Jerome K. Jerome et al. (ed.), *The
    Humours of Cycling: Stories and Pictures*, London: James Bowden, 1897, pp. 5–14.
'The Novels of Mr George Gissing', *Contemporary Review*, 72, August 1897, pp. 192–210.
'The War of the Worlds', *Pearson's Magazine* 3 (16)–4 (24) (April–December 1897).
'The War of the Worlds', *The Cosmopolitan* 22 (6)–24 (2) (April–December 1897).
'The Crystal Egg', *The New Review*, May 1897.
'The Star', *The Graphic*, December 1897.

'Fighters from Mars, or The War of the Worlds', *New York Evening Journal*, 15 December 1897–7, January 1898.

'Fighters from Mars: The War of the Worlds in and near Boston', *Boston Post/Boston Sunday Post*, 9 January–3 February 1898.

'On Schooling and the Phases of Mr Sandsome', in H. G. Wells, *Certain Personal Matters*, London: Lawrence & Bullen, 1898, pp. 49–55.

'The Things that Live on Mars', *Cosmopolitan* 44 (4) (March 1908): 335–42.

'War of the Worlds: Introduction: An Experiment in Illustration', *Strand Magazine*, lix, February 1920, pp. 154–63. Includes Wells's condensing of *The War of the Worlds*.

'The War of the Worlds, Parts 1–2', *Amazing Stories* 2 (5) (August 1927): 422–50; 2 (6): (September 1927): 568–97.

'Fiction about the Future', December 1938, in P. Parrinder and R. M. Philmus (eds), *H. G. Wells' Literary Criticism*, Brighton: Harvester, 1980, pp. 246–51.

Secondary sources

A. D. 'An interview with Mr J. B. Pinker', *The Bookman* 14 (79) (April 1898): 9–10.

Adams, M., 'Jeff Wayne's Musical Version of The War of The Worlds – Alive On Stage! The New Generation', *Screendaily*, 5 April 2013, http://www.screendaily.com/reviews/the-latest/jeff-waynes-musical-version-of-the-war-of-the-worlds-alive-on-stage-the-new-generation/5053643.article [accessed 30 January 2014].

Alden, W. L., 'London Letter', *New York Times*, 15 January 1898.

Alden, W. L., 'London Literary Letter', *New York Times*, 12 March 1898.

Alden, W. L., 'London Literary Letter', *New York Times*, 19 March 1898.

Alden, W. L., 'London Literary Letter', *New York Times*, 23 April 1898.

Aldiss, B., *Billion Year Spree: The True History of Science Fiction*, New York: Doubleday, 1973.

Aldiss, B., '*In the Days of the Comet*: An Introduction', *The Wellsian* 8 (1985): 1–6.

Aldiss, B., 'The referee of *The War of the Worlds*', *Foundation: The International Review of Science Fiction* 28 (77) (1999): 7–14.

Aldiss, B., 'Introduction', in H. G. Wells, *The War of the Worlds*, London: Penguin, 2005, pp. xiii–xxix.

Allen, G., 'The Episode of the Diamond Links', *Strand Magazine*, 12 July 1896, pp. 97–106.

Allen, P. M., 'A Day of Significance at Sandgate', *H. G. Wells Society Newsletter* 28 (2014): 12–15.

Alston, C., 'Tolstoy's Guiding Light', *History Today* 60 (10) (2010): 30–6.

An Ambler, 'The Gentle Art of Cycling', *Macmillan's Magazine*, January 1898, p. 206.

Anderson, K. J. (ed.), *War of the Worlds: Global Dispatches*, New York: Bantam, 1996.

Andrew, C., *Secret Service*, London: Heinemann, 1985.

Appleyard, B., 'The Plot to Hide H. G. Wells's Genius', *The Sunday Times*, 26 June 2005.

Appleyard, B., 'Interview: Martin Amis Talks to Bryan Appleyard', *Sunday Times, Culture Section*, 17 August 2014, pp. 4–6.

Aron, J., 'While Reaching Mars', *New Scientist* 21/28 (December 2013): 25.

Aron, J., 'What's flying over Mars… Could it be auroras? Volcanoes? Even aliens?' *New Scientist*, 21 February 2015, pp. 10–11.

Ash, B., *Who's Who in H. G. Wells*, London: Elm Tree Books, Hamish Hamilton, 1979.

Attlee, C., *As it Happened*, London: William Heinemann, 1954.

Ayer, N. W., *N. W. Ayer & Sons American Newspaper Annual containing a Catalogue of American Newspapers 1898, Part 1*, Philadelphia, PA: N. W. Ayer, 1898.

Ayer, N. W., *N. W. Ayer & Sons American Newspaper Annual containing a Catalogue of American Newspapers 1899, Part 1*, Philadelphia, PA: N. W. Ayer, 1899.

Banerjee, J., *Literary Surrey*, Headley Down: John Owen Smith, 2005.

Bartholomew, R. E., 'The Martian Panic Sixty Years Later: What Have We Learned?', *Skeptical Inquirer* 22 (6) (1998), http://www.csicop.org/si/show/the_martian_panic_sixty_years_later_what_have_we_learned [accessed 15 February 2014].

Bartholomew, R. E., *Little Green Men, Meowing Nuns and Head-Hunting Panics: A Study of Mass Psychogenic Illness and Social Delusion*, Jefferson, NC: McFarland, 2001.

Bartholomew, R. E. and Radford, B., *The Martians Have Landed!: A History of Media-Driven Panics and Hoaxes*, Jefferson, NC: McFarland, 2011.

Bassett, T. J., 'The Production of Three-Volume Novels, 1863–1897', *Papers of the Bibliographical Society of America* 102 (1) (2008): 61–75.

Batchelor, J., *H. G. Wells*, Cambridge: Cambridge University Press, 1985.

Baxter, J., *Science Fiction in the Cinema*, New York: A. S. Barnes, 1970.

Baxter, S., 'H. G. Wells's *The War of the Worlds* as a controlling metaphor for the twentieth century', *The Wellsian* 32 (2009): 3–16.

Baylen, J. O., 'W. T. Stead and The Early Career of H. G. Wells, 1895–1911', *Huntington Library Quarterly* 38 (1) (1974): 53–79.

Beck, P. J., *Presenting History: Past and Present*, Basingstoke: Palgrave Macmillan, 2012.

Bennett, S., 'The Martian Chronicles: How Borough's Latest Landmark Took Shape', *Woking Informer*, 10 April 1998.

Bergonzi, B., *The Early H. G. Wells: A Study of the Scientific Romances*, Manchester: Manchester University Press, 1961.

Bergonzi, B., 'A global thinker', *The Times Higher Education Supplement*, 3 October 1986.

Billen, A., 'After Stephen Hawking saw the film, he wanted to go to a club', *The Times*, 21 February 2015.

Bliss, M., *Invasions USA: The Essential Science Fiction Films of the 1950s*, Lanham, MD: Rowman & Littlefield, 2014.

Bone, C., *The Authors Circle*, Godalming: Tremlett's Books, 1998.

Borges, J. L., *Other Inquisitions, 1937–1952*, Austin, TX: University of Texas Press, 1964.

Bowerman, L., 'Early Cycling on the Surrey Roads with particular reference to the "Ripley Road"', *Surrey History* III (4) (1987): 157–60.

Bradshaw, P., 'War of the Worlds', *The Guardian*, 1 July 2005.

Bradshaw, P., 'The War of the Worlds – Alive on Stage! – Review', *The Guardian*, 4 April 2013.

Braunstein, R., 'SSRC. The Immanent Frame: *"I would love to read the biography of a book..."*', 13 April 2011, http://blogs.ssrc.org/tif/2011/04/13/i-would-love-to-read-the-biography-of-a-book/ [accessed 22 September 2014].

Brimblecombe, P., *The Big Smoke: A History of Air Pollution in London Since Medieval Times*, London: Routledge, 2011.

Broderick, J. F., *The Literary Galaxy of Star Trek: An Analysis of References and Themes in the Television Series and Films*, Jefferson, NC: McFarland 2006.

'Brog', 'Review from *Variety* dated April 6, 1953', in D. Willis (ed.), *Variety's Complete Science Fiction Reviews*, New York: Garland, 1985, p. 95.

Brome, V., *H. G. Wells: A Biography*, London: Longmans Green, 1951.

Brown, E., 'Ulla, Ulla', in Mike Ashley (ed.), *The Mammoth Book of Science Fiction*, New York: Carroll & Graf, 2002, pp. 1–26.

Brown, R., 'Town's Skyline is Under Fire', *Woking News and Mail*, 22 February 2007.

Brown, R. J., *Manipulating the Ether: Power of Broadcast Radio in Thirties America*, Jefferson, NC: McFarland, 2004.

Calder, J., 'The Story of Clegg's Aunt', *New Statesman*, 19 November 2007, http://www. newstatesman.com/politics/2007/11/moura-budberg-british-gorky [accessed 30 August 2012].

Callow, S., *Orson Welles, 1: The Road to Xanadu*, London: Vintage, 1996.

Callow, S., *Orson Welles, 2: Hello Americans*, London: Penguin, 2007.

Campbell, W. J., *The Year That Defined American Journalism: 1897 and the Clash of Paradigms*, New York: Routledge, 2006.

Campbell, W. J., *Getting it Wrong: Ten of the Greatest Misreported Stories in American Journalism*, Berkeley, CA: University of California Press, 2010.

Campbell, W. J., 'Media Myth Alert', 29 October 2013, http://mediamythalert.wordpress. com/2013/10/29/pbs-squanders-opportunity-to-offer-content-that-educates-in-war-of-the-worlds-doc/ [accessed 15 February 2014].

Cantril, H., *The Invasion from Mars: A Study in the Psychology of Panic*, New York: Harper Torchbooks, 1966 [1940].

Casey, S. and Wright, J., 'Introduction', in S. Casey and J. Wright (eds), *Mental Maps in the Era of Two World Wars*, Basingstoke: Palgrave Macmillan, 2008, pp. xii–xix.

Chang, K., 'On Mars Rover, Tools to Plumb a Methane Mystery', *New York Times*, 22 November 2011.

Chaplin, C., *My Autobiography*, London: Penguin, 2003 [1964].

Chaudhry, Y. M., *Yeats, The Irish Revival and the Politics of Print*, Cork: Cork University Press, 2001.

Cheal, D., 'The Martians have landed', *Daily Telegraph*, 15 April 2006.

Chesney, G., 'The Battle of Dorking: Reminiscences of a Volunteer', *Blackwood's Edinburgh Magazine* 109 (May 1871): 539–72. Originally published anonymously.

Christopher, J., 'Mars attacks – and it's a blast', *The Times*, 30 June 2005.

Cian, D., *Megawar*, New York: ibooks, 2005.

C. K. S., 'A Literary Letter', *Illustrated London News*, CXII (3064), 8 January 1898, p. 50.

Clark, S., 'Across the Universe: Curiosity Rover: Why Nasa isn't Looking for Life on Mars', *The Guardian Science Blog*, 5 August 2012 http://www.guardian.co.uk/science/across-the-universe [accessed 5 August 2012].

Clarke, I. F., *Voices Prophesying War: Future Wars 1763–1984*, Oxford: Oxford University Press, 1966.

Clarke, J. M., *London's Necropolis: A Guide to Brookwood Cemetery*, Stroud: Sutton, 2004.

Clarke, J. M., *The Brookwood Necropolis Railway*, 4th edn, Monmouthshire: Oakwood Press, 2006.

Clear, C., 'The Fantastic Fiction; or, "The Invisible Man"', *The Bookman* (USA), VI (3) (November 1897): 250–1.

Conan Doyle, A., 'The Adventure of the Naval Treaty', *The Strand Magazine* 6 (34–5) (October–November 1893): 392–468.

Conan Doyle, A., *Memories and Adventures*, Boston, MA: Little Brown, 1924.

Connell, J., *W. E. Henley*, London: Constable, 1949.

Cooke, H., 'We blew up the Newport Bridge. Everyone in Fall River died.' http://myri.tv/war.html [accessed 29 June 2012].

Crick, B., *George Orwell: A Life*, London: Secker & Warburg, 1980.

Crick, B., 'Introduction', in George Orwell, *George Orwell: Essays*, London: Penguin, 2000, p. ix.

Crosby, A., *A History of Woking*, Chichester: Phillimore, 2003.

Crossley, R., *H. G. Wells*, Mercer Island, Wash: Starmont House, 1986.

Crossley, R., *Imagining Mars: A Literary History*, Middletown, CT: Wesleyan University Press, 2011.

Darley, P. (ed.), *Camden Railway Heritage Trail: Primrose Hill to Camden Lock and Chalk Farm*, London: Camden Railway Heritage Trust, 2009.

Davidson, B., 'The *War of the Worlds* Considered as a Modern Myth', *The Wellsian* 28 (2005): 39–50.

Davison, P. (ed.), *Orwell's England*, Penguin, London: 2001.

Dawson, F., *A Sensational Trance*, London: Downey, 1895.

Del Ray, L., *The World of Science Fiction, 1926–1976: The History of a Sub-culture*, New York: Garland, 1980.

Der Spiegel Online International, 'Interview with Steven Spielberg and Tom Cruise, 27 April 2005, http://www.spiegel.de/international/spiegel/spiegel-interview-with-tom-cruise-and-steven-spielberg-actor-tom-cruise-opens-up-about-his-beliefs-in-the-church-of-scientology-a-353577.html [accessed 20 February 2014].

Dickens, Charles, *Bleak House*, London: Vintage, 2008 [1852–3].

Dickens, Charles, *Our Mutual Friend*, London: Vintage, 2011 [1864–5].

Dickens, T., 'The truth about H. G. Wells "Morbid" Bromley', *Bromley Times*, 10 December 2010.

Dickson, L., *H. G. Wells: His Turbulent Life and Times*, London: Readers Union, Macmillan, 1971.

Dodsworth, B., *The Foundation of Historic Irvington*, Irvington-on-the-Hudson, NY: The Foundation for Economic Education, 1995.

Douglas, S. J., *Listening In: Radio and the American Imagination*, Minneapolis, MN: University of Minnesota Press, 2004.

Douglas-Fairhurst, R., 'Scratching An Endless Itch', *Daily Telegraph*, 8 May 2010.

Doyle, M., 'The burning question is, why the Cremators?', Woking *Football Club Programme*, 9 December 2006.

Doyle, M., 'How the Cremator name came to be', *Woking News and Mail*, 12 December 2013, p. 38.

Draper, M., 'The Martians in Ecuador', *The Wellsian* 5 (1982): 35–6.

Dryden, L., 'H. G. Wells and Joseph Conrad: A Literary Friendship', *The Wellsian* 28 (2005): 2–13.

Ecker, V., 'Lights! Camera! Martians!', *Fortean*, August 2005, http://www.forteantimes.com/features/articles/121/lights_camera_martians.html [accessed 14 January 2012].

Edginton, I. and D'Israeli, *Scarlet Traces*, Milwaukie, OR: Dark Horse Comics, 2003.

Edginton, I. and D'Israeli, *Scarlet Traces: The Great Game*, Milwaukie, OR: Dark Horse Books, 2007.

Eggert, P., *Biography of a Book: Henry Lawson's While the Billy Boils*, University Park, PA: Penn State University Press, 2013.

Ellul, J., 'McLaren and H. G. Wells Could Boost Town's Economy', *Surrey Advertiser*, 2 December 2011, p.1.

Emery Jr., C. E., 'The night WPRO's "War of the Worlds" shook up Rhode Island', *Providence Journal*, 30 October 2014, http://www.providencejournal.com/article/20141030/Entertainment/310309989 [accessed 1 June 2015] [31 October 1993].

Englund, S. A., 'Reading the Author in *Little Women*: A Biography of a Book', *ATQ* 12 (3) (1998): 199–220.

Epstein, E. J., *Fictoid 7: 'Mass Hysteria Over Martian Invasion'*, n.d. (2012), http://www.edwardjayepstein.com/nether_fictoid7.htm [accessed 15 February 2014].

Faraci, D., 'Interview: Tom Cruise and Steven Spielberg (War of the Worlds)', 29 June 2005, http://www.chud.com/3533/interview-tom-cruise-and-steven-spielberg-war-of-the-worlds/ [accessed 20 February 2014].

Ferguson, N., 'H. G. Wells warned us of how it would feel to fight a "War of the World"', *Daily Telegraph*, 24 July 2005.

Ferguson, N., *The War of the World: Twentieth Century Conflict and the Descent of the West*, New York: Penguin, 2006. The British edition's sub-title is *History's Age of Hatred*.

Ferguson, N., 'The War of the World: Twentieth-Century Conflict and the Descent of the West', *Carnegie Council Public Affairs Program*, 26 September 2006, http://www.carnegiecouncil.org/studio/multimedia/20060926/index.html [accessed 22 February 2012].

Field, M., *A History of St Paul's Church, Maybury*, Woking: Marion Field, 2009.

Finnerty, J., 'Town "needs" Martians', *Surrey Advertiser*, 29 June 2012.

Flanders, J., *The Victorian City: Everyday Life in Dickens' London*, London: Atlantic, 2012.

Flynn, J. L., *War of the Worlds from Wells to Spielberg*, Owings Mills, MD: Galactic, 2005.

Ford, F. M., *Mightier than the Sword: Memories and Criticisms*, London: George Allen & Unwin, 1938.

Fowler, C., 'Forgotten Authors no. 34: John Collier', *The Independent on Sunday*, 24 May 2009.

Frederic, H., 'Henley's art as editor', *New York Times*, 5 April 1896.

Freeman, N., *Conceiving the City: London, Literature and Art, 1870–1914*, Oxford: Oxford University Press, 2007.

Friedman, J. and Koepp, D., *War of the Worlds: The Shooting Script*, New York: Newmarket Press, 2005.

Fritz, B., 'Mars Rover Curiosity is big hit – Mars movies are big flops', *Los Angeles Times*, 6 August 2012.

Gallop, A., *The Martians are Coming!: The True Story of Orson Welles' 1938 Panic Broadcast*, Stroud: Amberley, 2011.

Gangale, T. and Dudley-Rowley, M., 'When was the War of the Worlds?', *The Wellsian* 29 (2006): 2–20.

Gangale, T. and Dudley-Rowley, M., '*The War of the Worlds*: An After Action Report', *The Wellsian* 30 (2007): 36–56.

Gangale, T. and Dudley-Rowley, M., 'Strategy and Tactics in the War of the Worlds', *The Wellsian* 31 (2008): 4–33.

Gannon, C. E., '"One swift, conclusive smashing and an end": Wells, War and the Collapse of Civilisation', *Foundation: The International Review of Science Fiction* 28 (77) (1999): 35–46.

Gannon, C. E., *Rumors of War and Infernal Machines: Technomilitary Agenda-Setting in American and British Speculative Fiction*, Lanham, MD: Rowman & Littlefield, 2005.

Gebert, M., *The Encyclopedia of Movie Awards*, New York: Martin's, 1996.

Getler, R., 'War of Words', *PBS Ombudsman*, 31 October 2013, http://www.pbs.org/ombudsman/2013/10/war_of_the_words.html [accessed 13 February 2014].

Gilbert, J. B., 'Wars of the Worlds', *Journal of Popular Culture* 10 (2) (1976): 326–36.

Gill, A. A., 'I don't think we can save this one, Doctor', *The Sunday Times*, 24 August 2014.

Gill, A.A. 'Brainstorming inventor fails a character test', *Sunday Times Magazine*, 31 Jan. 2016, pp. 16–17.

Gittins, I., 'The War of the Worlds – Review', *The Guardian*, 16 December 2012.

Gold, T., 'Hilary Mantel', *The Sunday Times Magazine*, 8 December 2013, p. 37.

Goldstein, G., 'Looking back at the Martian apocalypse', *Los Angeles Times*, 18 December 2012.

Gosling, J., 'Best Sellers Illustrated – War of the Worlds (Best Sellers Illustrated, 2005)', http://www.war-ofthe-worlds.co.uk/bestsellers_illustrated.htm [accessed 27 January 2014].

Gosling, J., *War of the Worlds*, http://www.war-ofthe-worlds.co.uk/war_of_the_worlds_hines.htm [accessed 27 January 2014].

Gosling, J., 'Comics: 1–3', http://www.war-ofthe-worlds.co.uk/comics_mars.htm [accessed 12 March 2015].

Gosling, J., *Waging the War of the Worlds: A History of the 1938 Broadcast and Resulting Panic*, Jefferson, NC: McFarland, 2009.

Gosling, S., 'H. G. Wells' letter goes on display', BBC News, 1 February 2011, http://news.bbc.co.uk/local/kent/hi/people_and_places/history/newsid_9373000/9373313.stm [accessed 28 January 2012].

Gosse, E., 'The Abuse of the Supernatural in Fiction', *The Bookman* (USA) VI (4) (December 1897): 297–300.

Graves, C. L. and Verrall Lucas, E., *The War of the Wenuses*, Bristol: Arrowsmith, 1898.

Green, S., 'Paramount Wins "The War of the World" Rights', 21 April 2002 https://groups.yahoo.com/neo/groups/ploktanewsnetwork/conversations/messages/165 [accessed 15 March 2014].

Gregorian, D., 'All's not Wells as Hallmark loses the "War"', *New York Post*, 20 April 2002, http://nypost.com/2002/04/20/alls-not-wells-as-hallmark-loses-the-war/ [accessed 15 March 2014].

Gregory, R. A., 'Book Review: A Journey to the Planet Mars', *Nature* 40 (25 July 1889): 291.

Gregory, R., 'Science in fiction', *Nature* 57 (10 February 1898): 339–40.

Gregory, R. A., 'Mars As A World', *The Living Age* 225 (2209) (April–June 1900): 21–8.

Gregory, Sir R., 'H. G. Wells: A Survey and Tribute', *Nature* 158 (21 September 1946): 399–406.

Griest, G. L., *Mudie's Circulating Library and the Victorian Novel*, Bloomington, IN: Indiana University Press, 1970.

Gunn, R., 'The Man Who Invented Tomorrow', from *The Science of Science Fiction Writing* (2000), http://www.sfcenter.ku.edu/tomorrow.htm [accessed 12 September 2013].

Gurney, David. 'War, Woking and H. G. Wells', *Surrey County Magazine* 27 (12) (December 1996): 18.

Hammond, J., *An H. G. Wells Companion: A Guide to the Novels, Romances and Short Stories*, London: Macmillan, 1979.

Hammond, J., 'Wells and Woking', *Foundation: The International Review of Science Fiction* 28 (77) (1999): 3–7.

Hammond, J., *A Preface to H. G. Wells*, Harlow: Longman/Pearson Education, 2001.

Hammond, J. R., 'Nottingham Countryside: H. G. Wells and the Midlands', *Nottingham Topic*, April 1976, p. 10.

Hammond, J. R. (ed.), *H. G. Wells: Interviews and Recollections*, London: Macmillan, 1980.

Hand, R. J., *Terror on the Air!: Horror Radio in America, 1931–1952*, Jefferson, NC: McFarland, 2006.

Hardy, S., 'H. G. Wells and British Cinema: *The War of the* Worlds', *Foundation: The International Review of Science Fiction* 28 (77) (1999): 46–58.

Harrington, M., 'Second Sight: Dream of a Sci-fi Prophet', *Sunday Telegraph*, 27 August 1995, p. 27.

Harrison, R., *Heritage: Critical Approaches*, Abingdon: Routledge, 2013.

Hashimoto, Y., 'Victorian Biological Terror: A Study of "The Stolen Bacillus"', *The Undying Fire: The Journal of the H. G. Wells Society, The Americas* 2 (2003): 3–27.

Haynes, R. D., 'Book Review', *The Wellsian* 31 (2008): 70.

Henley, W. E., *Song of Speed*, London: David Nutt, 1903.

Hensher, P., 'The importance of Place in Fiction', *Guardian*, 17 May 2013.

Hewison, R., *The Heritage Industry: Britain in a Climate of Decline*, London: Methuen, 1987.

Heyer, P., 'America Under Attack 1: A Reassessment of Orson Welles' 1938 *War of the Worlds* Broadcast', *Canadian Journal of Communication* 28 (2003): 149–65.

Heyer, P., *The Medium and the Magician: Orson Welles, the Radio Years, 1934–1952*, Lanham, MD: Rowman & Littlefield, 2005.

Hill, A., 'The Secret Loves of H. G. Wells Unmasked', *Observer*, 7 January 2001.

Hill, G. B. (ed.), *Boswell's Life of Johnson, 1*, New York: Harper, 1889.

Hillegas, M. R., 'Victorian "Extraterrestrials"', in J. H. Buckley (ed.), *The Worlds of Victorian Fiction*, Cambridge, MA: Harvard University Press, 1975, pp. 391–414.

Hoberman, J., 'All as it had been: Hollywood revises history, joins the good fight', 4 December 2001, http://www.villagevoice.com/content/printVersion/167459/ [accessed 12 June 2012].

Horsburgh, E. L. S., *Bromley, Kent: From the Earliest Times to the Present Century*, London: Hodder and Stoughton, 1929.

Houseman, J., 'The Men from Mars', *Harper's Magazine* (December 1948), pp. 74–82.

Houseman, J., *Run Through: A Memoir*, New York: Simon & Schuster, 1972.

Houseman, J., 'The War of the Worlds', *The Times*, 27 January 1973, p. 8.

Houseman, J., *Unfinished Business: A Memoir*, London: Columbus, 1986.

Howsam, L., *Old Books and New Histories: An Orientation to Studies in Book and Print Culture*, Toronto: University of Toronto Press, 2006.

Hudson, D., *Munby, Man of Two Worlds: The Life and Diaries of Arthur J. Munby 1828–1910*, London: Sphere, 1974.

Hughes, D. Y., *An Edition and a Survey of H. G. Wells' The War of the Worlds*, Ph.D. diss., Urbana, IL: University of Illinois, 1962.

Hughes, D. Y., 'Radio and Film Adaptations', 'The War of the Worlds in the Yellow Press', in D. Y. Hughes and H. M. Geduld, *A Critical Edition of The War of the Worlds: H. G. Wells's Scientific Romances*, Bloomington, IN: Indiana University Press, 1993, pp. 237–48, 281–9.

Hughes, D. Y., 'A Queer Notion of Grant Allen's', *Science Fiction Studies* 25 (2) (1998): 271–84.

Hughes, D. Y. and Geduld, H. M., *A Critical Edition of The War of the Worlds: H. G. Wells's Scientific Romances*, Bloomington, IN: Indiana University Press, 1993.

Hunt, L., *Men, Women, and Books: A Selection of Sketches, Essays, and Critical Memoirs*, London: Smith, Elder, 1847.

Huntington, J., 'My Martians: Wells's Success', *Foundation: The International Review of Science Fiction* 28 (77) (1999): 25–34.

Huxley, T. H., 'The Romanes Lecture', *Oxford Magazine*, May 1893, http://aleph0.clarku. edu/huxley/comm/OxfMag/Romanes93.html [accessed 4 February 2012].

James, H., *Portraits of Places*, Boston, MA: James R. Osgood, 1883.

James, S. J., '*Fin-de-cycle*: Romance and the Real in *The Wheels of Chance*', in S. McLean (ed.), *H. G. Wells: Interdisciplinary Essays*, Newcastle: Cambridge Scholars, 2008, pp. 34–48.

James, S. J., *Maps of Utopia: H. G. Wells, Modernity and the End of Culture*, Oxford: Oxford University Press, 2012.

James, S. J., 'When I see a quotation on the internet: Wells, the bicycle and the human race', *H. G. Wells Society Newsletter* 27 (2014): 2–3.

James, S. J., 'Digital Wells', H. G. Wells Society AGM, 28 June 2014.

J. E. H. W., 'The New Mr Wells', *The Bookman* 18 (107) (August 1900): 155.

Jones, J., 'London Burning: History Just Went Sci-fi', 8 August 2011, http://www.guardian. co.uk/artanddesign/jonathanjonesblog/2011/aug/08/london-riots-sci-fi-dystopian [accessed 5 September 2011].

Jones, M., 'Washingtonians react to the *War of the Worlds*', *Boundary Stones: WETA's Local History Blog*, 29 October 2013, http://blogs.weta.org/boundarystones/2013/10/29/ washingtonians-react-war-worlds [accessed 14 February 2014].

Jones, S., 'View from the Lab: A Century's Worth of Wisdom Since the Martians First Landed', *Daily Telegraph*, 18 February 1998.

Judd, D., 'Diamonds are forever?: Kipling's Imperialism', *History Today* 47 (6) (June 1997): 37–43.

Kanter, J., 'War of The Worlds set for UK television adaptation', 15 Dec. 2015, http://www.broadcastnow.co.uk/news/war-of-the-worlds-set-for-uk-television-adaptation/5098070.article [accessed 18 Jan. 2016].

Karol, P. and Catling, D., *NASA: Mars Chronology: Renaissance to the Space Age*, 29 October 2003, http://www.nasa.gov/audience/forstudents/9-12/features/F_Mars_ Chronology.html [16 October 2014].

Kemp, P., *H. G. Wells and the Culminating Ape: Biological Imperatives and Imaginative Obsessions*, Basingstoke: Macmillan, 1996.

Kennerly, B., 'Mystery of Mars still attracts space lovers', *Florida Today*, 1 August 2012, http://www.usatoday.com/tech/science/space/story/2012-08-01/mars-mystery-attracts/56650542/1 [accessed 5 August 2012].

Kipling, R., 'Recessional', *The Times*, 17 July 1897, p. 13.

Koch, H., *The Panic Broadcast: Portrait of an Event*, Boston, MA: Little Brown, 1970.

Koshinski, B., 'WKBW's 1968 "War of the Worlds"', *Buffalo Broadcasters Association: Remembering the Past*, n.d., http://www.buffalobroadcasters.com/broadcast-history/ WKBW's%C2%A0--War-of-the-Worlds/8 [accessed 18 March 2012].

Kuchta, T., *Semi-Detached Empire: Suburbia and the Colonization of Britain, 1880 to the Present*, Charlottesville, VA: University of Virginia Press, 2010.

Lanchester, J., 'Making War on Woking: H. G. Wells Memorial', *Daily Telegraph*, 30 January 1999, p. A 5.

Langford, D., 'The History of Mr Wells', *Fortean Times*, 199 (2005), http://www.ansible. co.uk/writing/ft-wells.html [accessed 14 January 2012].

Laver, A., 'Herbert George Wells, Godalming and Tono-Bungay', *The H. G. Wells Newsletter* 5 (16) (Spring 2008): 13–20.

Lawrence, A. H., 'The Romance of the Scientist: An Interview with Mr H. G. Wells', *The Young Man* 128 (August 1897): 253–7. Re-published in J. R. Hammond (ed.), *H. G. Wells: Interviews and Recollections*, London; Macmillan, 1980, pp. 2–6.

Le Gallienne, R., *The Romantic '90s*, London: Robin Clark, 1993 [1925].

Le Gallienne, R., *Travels in England*, London: John Lane, 1900.

Le Queux, W., The *Great War in England in 1897*, 11th edn, London: Tower, 1895 [1894].

Le Queux, W., *The Invasion of 1910: With a Full Account of the Siege of London*, London: Eveleigh Nash, 1906.

Lee, S., 'A New Theatre of Operations', *Sunday Times*, 19 March 2006, p. 27.

Leslie, S., 'What have the Brits done for sci-fi?', *The Times*, 21 April 2005.

Lippmann, W., *Public Opinion*, New York: Harcourt, Brace, 1922.

Livingston, M., 'The Tripods of Vulcan and Mars: Homer, Darwin, and the Fighting Machines of H. G. Wells's *The War of the Worlds*', *The Wellsian* 32 (2009): 54–60.

Locke, G., 'Wells in Three Volumes?: A Sketch of British Publishing in the 19th Century', *Science-Fiction Studies* 3 (3) (1976): 282–6.

Lodge, D., *The Novelist at the Crossroads and other Essays on Fiction and Criticism*, London: Ark, 1986.

Lodge, D., 'Top 10 H. G. Wells books', *The Guardian*, 4 May 2011.

Lodge, D., *A Man of Parts: A Novel*, London: Harvill Secker, 2011.

Lodge, D., *Lives in Writing*, London: Harvill Secker, 2014.

Luckhurst, R., *Science Fiction*, Cambridge: Polity, 2005.

Lynn, A., *Shadow Lovers: The Last Affairs of H. G. Wells*, Boulder, CO: Westview Press, 2001.

MacKenzie, N. and J., *The Time Traveller: The Life of H. G. Wells*, London: Weidenfeld & Nicolson, 1973.

Maher, K., 'When the killing had to stop', *The Times*, 30 June 2005.

Malmsheimer, L. M., 'Three Mile Island: Fact, Frame, and Fiction', *American Quarterly* 38 (1) (1986): 35–52.

Marcus, L., *Tenth Muse: Writings about Cinema in the Modernist Period*, Oxford: Oxford University Press, 2007.

Margrave, S., 'Behind the Scenes: at Britain's Million a Year Talkie Studios', *Daily Mail*, 13 March 1933, p. 4.

Markley, R., *Dying Planet: Mars in Science and the Imagination*, Durham, NC: Duke University Press, 2005.

Martin, J., 'War of the Worlds: The True Story', 13 July 2011, http://www.sfcrowsnest.com/articles/news/2011/War-of-the-Worlds-The-True-Story-16190.php [accessed 2 November 2012].

Masters, A., *The Genius in my Basement: The Biography of a Happy Man*, London: Fourth Estate, 2011.

Matthews Associates, *Woking Borough Council, Economic Development Strategy and Action Plan, 2012–2017*, April 2012.

Mattin, D., 'Words on Worlds: Spielberg's Writer', *The Times*, 20 July 2005.

McCabe, J., *The End of the World*, London: Routledge, 1921.

McCarthy, P. A., 'Heart of Darkness and the Early Novels of H. G. Wells: Evolution, Anarchy, Entropy', in H. Bloom (ed.), *H. G. Wells*, New York: Chelsea House, 2005, pp. 193–216.

McCartney, J., 'Alien Tripods and their Slippery Ways', *Sunday Telegraph*, 3 July 2005.

McDonald, D. and Dronfield, J., *A Very Dangerous Woman: The Lives, Loves and Lies of Russia's Most Seductive Spy*, London: Oneworld, 2015.

McGrath, N., 'Jeff Wayne: "I spent my life savings on War of the Worlds"', *Daily Telegraph*, 22 December 2013.

McKie, D., 'How Woking Lost Its War', *Guardian*, 14 July 2005.

McLean, S. (ed.), *H. G. Wells: Interdisciplinary Essays*, Newcastle upon Tyne: Cambridge Scholars, 2008.

McLean, S., *The Early Fiction of H. G. Wells: Fantasies of Science*, Basingstoke: Palgrave Macmillan, 2009.

McLuhan, M., *Understanding Media: The Extensions of Man*, London: Ark, 1987 [1964].

Mee, A., 'Brookwood', *The Kings' England: Surrey: London's Southern Neighbour*, London: Hodder and Stoughton, 1938.

Mehew, E., 'Henley, William Ernest (1849–1903)', *Oxford Dictionary of National Biography*, Oxford University Press, May 2006, http://www.oxforddnb.com/view/article/33817 [accessed 27 March 2012].

Mesta, G., *The Martian War: A Thrilling Eyewitness Account of the Recent Invasion as Reported by Mr H. G. Wells*, New York: Pocket Books, 2005.

Miall, L., 'The War of the Worlds', *Radio Times*, 29 June 1967.

Miller, J. J., 'Badly Wrong in the War of the World Views', *Wall Street Journal*, 21 June 2005.

Miller, J. M., *The War of the Worlds* (1953), *Turner Classic Movies*, n.d., http://www.tcm.com/this-month/article/188880%7C0/The-War-of-the-Worlds.html [accessed 29 June 2012].

Miller, T., *Picturesque Sketches of London: Past and Present*, London: Office of the National Illustrated Library, 1852.

Milmo, C., 'War of Words: How H. G. Wells Snubbed Bromley', *The Independent*, 29 December 2010.

Mollmann, S., 'The War of the Worlds in the Boston Post and the Rise of American imperialism: "Let Mars Fire"', *English Literature in Transition, 1880–1920* 53 (4) (2010): 387–412.

Mollmann, S., 'Fighters from Mars, or The War of the Worlds in and near Boston', 21 April 2009, http://steve-mollmann.livejournal.com/124003.html [accessed 6 February 2012].

Moorcock, M., 'Before Armageddon', in M. Moorcock and A. Kausch (eds), *Michael Moorcock: London Peculiar and other Nonfiction*, Oakland, CA: PM Press, 2012, pp. 189–201.

Moore, A. and O'Neill, K., *League of Extraordinary Gentlemen*, II, La Jolla, CA: America's Best Comics, CA: 2003.

Moretti, F., 'Geography of "invasion literature" (1871–1906)', *Atlas of the European Novel, 1800–1900*, London: Verso, 1999.

Morris, N., *The Cinema of Steven Spielberg: Empire of Light*, London: Wallflower Press, 2007.

Morton, P., *"The Busiest Man in England": Grant Allen and the Writing Trade, 1875–1900*, Basingstoke: Palgrave Macmillan, 2005.

Mott, F. L., *A History of American Magazines, 1885–1905*, Cambridge, MA: Harvard University Press, 1957.

Muir, K., 'Why can't Hollywood mind its French?', *The Times*, 13 March 2015, p. 7.

Muller, R., 'War: Martians Invade America!', *Picture Post* 58, 21 March 1953, pp. 21–3.

NASA, *Mars Science Laboratory Launch: Press Kit*, November 2011.

Nevins, J., *A Blazing World: The Unofficial Companion to the Second League of Extraordinary Gentlemen*, Austin, TX: MonkeyBrain Books, 2004.

Niles, D., *War of the Worlds: New Millennium*, New York: Tor, 2005.

Nordau, M., *Degeneration*, London: William Heinemann, 1895.

O'Neill, M., Leslie, K. and Hayes, M., *H. G. Wells in West Sussex*, Chichester: West Sussex County Council, 1996.

Orwell, G., 'The Male Byronic', *Tribune*, 21 June 1940, pp. 20–1.

Orwell, G., 'Wells, Hitler and the World State', *Horizon* (August 1941), in P. Davison (ed.),

The Complete Works of George Orwell, XII: A Patriot After All, 1940–1941, London: Secker and Warburg, 1998, pp. 536–40.

Orwell, G., 'The True Pattern of H. G. Wells', *Manchester Evening News*, 14 August 1946.

Orwell, G., 'Such, Such Were the Joys', c. 1946–7 [first published 1952], in P. Davison (ed.), *Orwell's England*, London: Penguin, 2001.

Osborne, L., 'Our everlasting link with Wells' Martians', *Woking News and Mail*, 24 September 2009.

Pal, G., 'Filming "War of the Worlds"', *Astounding Science Fiction* LII (2) (October 1953): pp. 100–11.

Panek, L. L., *The Special Branch: The British Spy Novel, 1890–1980*, Bowling Green, OH: Bowling Green University Popular Press, 1981.

Paramount Pictures and Dream Works, 'Production Notes: The War of the Worlds', n.d., http://www.waroftheworlds.com/productionnotes/index.html [accessed 3 June 2012].

Parker, E., *Highways and Byways in Surrey*, London: Macmillan, 1908.

Parker, G., 'The Making of a Film', *Illustrated London News*, 6 August 1921, pp. 190–5.

Parrinder, P., *Science Fiction: Its History and Criticism*, London: Methuen, 1980.

Parrinder, P., 'The Roman Spring of George Gissing and H. G. Wells', *The Gissing Newsletter* XXI (3) (July 1985): 1–12.

Parrinder, P., *Shadows of the Future: H. G. Wells, Science Fiction, and Prophecy*, Liverpool: Liverpool University Press, 1995.

Parrinder, P., 'How far can we trust the narrator of *The War of the* Worlds?', *Foundation: The International Review of Science Fiction* 28 (77) (1999): 15–24.

Parrinder, P., 'Biographical Note', 'Note on the text', in H. G. Wells, *The War of the Worlds*, London: Penguin, 2005, pp. vii–xii, pp. xxxii–vi.

Parrinder, P., 'Introduction', (with Barnaby, P.), 'Timeline: European Reception of H. G. Wells', in P. Parrinder and J. S. Partington (eds), *The Reception of H. G. Wells in Europe*, London: Thoemmes Continuum, 2005, pp. 1–7, pp. xxiii–xl.

Parrinder, P., 'Wells, Herbert George', *Oxford Dictionary of National Biography*, http://www.oxforddnb.com/view/article/36831 [accessed 27 March 2012].

Parrinder, P., 'The War of Wells's Lives', *Science Fiction Studies* 38 (2) (2011): 327–33.

Parrinder, P. (ed.), *H. G. Wells: Critical Heritage*, London: Routledge, 1972.

Parrinder, P., *Utopian Literature and Science: From the Scientific Revolution to Brave New World and Beyond*, Basingstoke: Palgrave Macmillan, 2015.

Parrinder, P. and Philmus R. M. (eds), *H. G. Wells' Literary Criticism*, Brighton: Harvester, 1980.

Partington, J. S., 'The Pen as Sword: George Orwell, H. G. Wells and Journalistic Parricide', *Journal of Contemporary History* 39 (1) (2004): 45–56.

Partington, J. S., 'Review of John Gosling's *Waging the War of the Worlds*', *Kritikon Litterarum*, 37 (2010): 268–73.

Pendragon Pictures, Press Release, 1 May 2012, http://news.yahoo.com/war-worlds-true-story-15-journey-theaters-june-070415372.html [accessed 2 November 2012].

Pendragon Pictures, *War of the Worlds: The True Story*, n.d., http://www.waroftheworlds thetruestory.com/ABOUT_THE_MOVIE.html [accessed 26 January 2014].

Picaroon, 'Portrait of Mr H. G. Wells', *The Chap-Book* (Chicago) 5 (1) (May 1896): 366–74.

Pickett, P., 'War of the Welds: Sculptor Creates a Martian in our Midst', *Woking Informer*, 13 March 1998.

Pittock, M. G. H., 'Le Gallienne, Richard Thomas (1866–1947)', *Oxford Dictionary of National Biography*, Oxford University Press, 2004; online edn, May 2008, http://www.oxforddnb.com/view/article/34477 [accessed 17 August 2012].

Pixley, A., 'Programme Notes', *The War of the Worlds*, London: BBC Audio, 2007.

Planetary Society, 'Visions of Mars', 2007, http://www.planetary.org/explore/projects/vom/ [16 October 2014].

Planetary Society, Press Release, 'Phoenix Takes Image of First Library on Mars', 27 May 2008, http://www.planetary.org/press-room/releases/2008/0527_Phoenix_Takes_Image_of_First_Library_on.html [accessed 16 October 2014].

Pooley, J. and Socolow, M., 'The Myth of the War of the Worlds Panic', *Slate*, 28 October 2013, http://www.slate.com/articles/arts/history/2013/10/orson_welles_war_of_the_worlds_panic_myth_the_infamous_radio_broadcast_did.single.html [accessed 12 February 2014].

Porter, R., 'Mr Science, Warts and All', *Nature*, 361, 4 February 1993, p. 413.

Powell, J., 'The War of the Worlds', *Radio Times*, 9 June 1967.

Priest, C., *The Space Machine*, London: VGSF, 1988 [1976].

Priest, C., 'Journal "Woking Work"', 6 June 2013, http://www.christopher-priest.co.uk/journal/1870/woking-work/ [accessed 1 April 2014].

Priestley, J. B., 'Right or wrong. H. G. Wells was a major prophet of this age: he saw the shape of things to come', *Daily Mail*, 14 August 1946.

Procter, B. H., William *Randolph Hearst: The Early Years, 1863–1910*, New York: Oxford University Press, 1998.

Pulver, A., 'Jeff Wayne and David Essex: How We Made *The War of the Worlds*', *Guardian*, 14 January 2014.

Ramsden, C., *A View from Primrose Hill: The Memoirs of Caroline Ramsden*, London: Hutchinson Benham, 1984.

Ray, G. N., 'H. G. Wells's Contributions to the Saturday Review', *The Library* XVI (1) (1961): 29–36.

Ray, M., 'Conrad, Wells and *The Secret Agent*: Paying Old Debts and Settling Old Scores', *The Modern Language Review* 81 (3) (1986): 560–73.

Rees, J., '"Land of my fathers? My fathers can keep it"', *The Sunday Times Magazine*, 6 April 2014.

Reginald, R., *Invasion! Earth vs. the Aliens* (formerly *War of Two Worlds*), Rockville, MD: Wildside Press, 2007.

Reginald, R., *The Martians Strike Back*, Rockville, MD: Wildside Press, 2011.

Renzi, T. C., *H. G. Wells: Six Scientific Romances Adapted for Film*, Metuchen, NJ: Scarecrow Press, 1992.

Richards, G., *Memories of a Misspent Youth*, New York: Harper, 1933.

Ring, S., 'It's Monstrous!: Sci-fi's off to the USA', *Woking Informer*, 1 June 2001, p. 1.

Rinkel, G. K. and Rinkel, M. E., *The Picshuas of H. G. Wells: A Burlesque Diary*, Urbana and Chicago, IL: University of Illinois Press, 2006.

Robb, B. J., *A Brief Guide to Star Trek*, London: Constable & Robinson, 2012.

Roberts, A., *Science Fiction: The New Critical Idiom*, London: Routledge, 2000.

Robertson, J. C., *The Hidden Cinema: British Film Censorship in Action 1913–1972*, London: Routledge, 2005 [1989].

Robinson, D., *Chaplin: His Life and Art*, London: Collins, 1985.

Robinson, K. S., *Red Mars*, New York: Bantam, 1993.

Roiphe, K., *Uncommon Arrangements: Seven Marriages*, New York: Dial, 2007.

Rolfe, C., 'From Camden Town to Primrose Hill', *Camden History Review* 10 (1982): 2–4.

Rose, Jr., S., '"War of the Worlds" comes close to historical reality in indie movie', *Sacramento Examiner*, 12 July 2012, http://www.examiner.com/review/war-of-the-worlds-comes-close-to-historical-reality-indie-movie [accessed 2 November 2012].

Ross, D., 'Jeff Wayne: War of the Worlds', *The Quietus*, 18 June 2009, http://thequietus.
com/articles/01901-jeff-wayne-s-war-of-the-worlds-special-edition-review [accessed
2 February 2014].

Rothberg, S., 'Jeff Wayne's Musical The War of the Worlds: Alive on Stage', *Examiner.com*,
1 May 2010, http://www.examiner.com/article/jeff-wayne-s-musical-the-war-of-the-
worlds-alive-on-stage [accessed 10 February 2014].

Routledge, C., 'George Orwell, Jura, and Nineteen Eighty-Four', 10 May 2009, http://
chrisroutledge.co.uk/2009/05/10/george-orwell-jura-and-nineteen-eighty-four/
[accessed 15 September 2012].

Rubinstein, D., 'Cycling in the 1890s', *Victorian Studies* 21 (1) (1977): 47–71.

Ruddick, N., 'Introduction', 'Note on the text', in N. Ruddick (ed.), H. G. Wells, *The Time
Machine: An Invention H. G. Wells*, Peterborough, ON: Broadview, 2001, pp. 11–45,
52–3.

Rymill, D., *Worcester Park & Cuddington: A Walk Through the Centuries*, Worcester Park:
The Buckwheat Press, 2000.

Rymill, D., 'History: Pens and Paintbrushes in Worcester Park', *Worcester Park Life* 29
(October 2010): 7–8.

Sandbrook, D., 'Classic Sci-fi', *The Times*, 15 November 2014.

Sandhu, S., 'Close Encounter of the Wrong Kind', *Daily Telegraph*, 1 July 2005.

Sawyer, A., 'Science Fiction: The Sense of Wonder', in C. Berberich (ed.), *The
Bloomsbury Introduction to Popular Fiction*, London: Bloomsbury, 2015, pp. 87–97.

Scheick, W. J. and Cox, J. R. (eds), *H. G. Wells: A Reference Guide*, Boston, MA: Hall,
1988.

Schneirov, M., *Dream of a New Social Order: Popular Magazines in America 1893–1914*,
New York: Columbia University Press, 1994.

Scholey, K. A., 'The Railways of Camden', *Camden History Society Occasional Paper* 4 (2002).

Sconce, J., *Haunted Media: Electronic Presence from Telegraphy to Television*, Durham,
NC: Duke University Press, 2000.

Scott, A. O., 'Another terror attack, but not by humans', *New York Times*, 29 June 2005.

Scott, C., 'Relative Values: How the West End Saved Our Family', *The Sunday Times
Magazine*, 25 November 2012, p. 6.

Secord, J. A., *Victorian Sensation: The Extraordinary Publication, Reception, and Secret
Authorship of 'Vestiges of the Natural History of Creation'*, Chicago: University of
Chicago Press, 2000.

Self, W., 'Death on Three Legs', *The Times*, 23 January 2010.

Serviss, G., *Edison's Conquest of Mars*, Burlington, ON: Apogee, 2005 [1898; 1947]

Shaw, W. N., 'The London Fog Inquiry', *Nature*, 64, 31 October 1901, pp. 649–50.

Sherborne, M., 'Book Review', *The Wellsian* 30 (2007): 58.

Sherborne, M., *H. G. Wells: Another Kind of Life*, London: Peter Owen, 2010.

Shorter, C., 'Review: The Invisible Man', *The Bookman* 13 (1) (October 1897): 19.

Shorter, C., 'Mr Wells's "War of the Worlds"', *The Bookman* (USA) VII (3) (May
1898): 246–7. Also in *The Bookman* 14 (78) (March 1898), pp. 182–3.

Siebert, V., 'The Quietus Interview: A life During Wartime: Jeff Wayne Interviewed', *The
Quietus*, 20 December 2013, http://thequietus.com/articles/01901–jeff-wayne-s-war-
of-the-worlds-special-edition-review [accessed 2 February 2014].

Silverberg, R., 'Introduction', in R. Silverberg (ed.), *The Mirror of Infinity: A Critics'
Anthology of Science Fiction*, New York: Harper & Row, 1970, pp. vii–xi.

Silverberg, R., 'Introduction', in G. Yeffeth (ed.) *The War of the Worlds: Fresh Perspectives
on the H. G. Wells Classic*, Dallas, TX: BenBella, 2005, pp. 1–13.

Sinclair, D., 'All fired up in Wayne's World', *The Times*, 14 December 2010.

Sinclair, D., 'Pop: The War of the Worlds', *The Times*, 11 December 2012.

Sinclair, F., 'A Prophet came to Euston Road', *St Pancras Journal* 1 (8) (December 1947): 114–17.

Sinclair, I., 'Woking at War', *Guardian*, 26 June 2004.

Smith, D. C., *H. G. Wells: Desperately Mortal. A Biography*, New Haven, CT: Yale University Press, 1986.

Smith, D. C., 'A chat with the author of *The Time Machine*, Mr H. G. Wells', *The Wellsian* 20 (1997): 3–9.

Smith, G. H., *The Second War of the Worlds*, New York: Daw, 1976.

Snider, J. C., 'Interview: Timothy Hines, Pendragon Pictures', *Sci-fi Dimensions*, November 2004, http://www.scifidimensions.com/Nov04/timothyhines.htm [accessed 20 February 2014].

Socolow, M. J., 'The hyped panic over "War of the Worlds"', *Chronicle of Higher Education* 55 (9) (24 October 2008): B16–17.

Squire, Sir J., 'An "unconquerable soul": "W. E. Henley" by John Connell', *Illustrated London News* 245 (5762) (24 September 1949): 452.

St John, J., *William Heinemann: A Century of Publishing, 1890–1990*, London: Heinemann, 1990.

Stead, W. T., 'The Book of the Month: The latest Apocalypse of the End of the World', *The Review of Reviews* XVII ((4) (April 1898): 389–96.

Stearn, R. T., 'Wells and War; H. G. Wells's Writings on Military Subjects, Before the Great War', *The Wellsian* 6 (1983): 1–15.

Stearn, R. T., 'General Sir George Chesney', *Journal of the Society for Army Historical Research* 75 (1997): 106–18.

Stedman-Jones, G., 'Friedrich Engels', *Oxford Dictionary of National Biography*, September 2012, http://www.oxforddnb.com/view/article/39022 [accessed 27 March 2012].

Stevenson, J., 'The Martian Landing', *Woking News and Mail*, 16 April 1998.

Strachey, J. St L., 'Books: The *War of the Worlds*', *The Spectator* 3631 (29 January 1898), pp. 168–9. This review was published unsigned.

Sussman, H. L., *Victorians and the Machine: The Literary Response to Technology*, Cambridge, MA: Harvard University Press, 1968.

Symons, A., *London: A Book of Aspects*, Minneapolis, MN: Private Printing, 1909.

Taylor, D. C., 'A. J. Munby in Surrey', *Surrey History*, II (5) (1983): 217–21.

Thompson, D., 'On the Record', *New York Herald Tribune*, 2 November 1938.

Thomson, D., *In Camden Town*, London: Hutchinson, 1983.

Thomson, D., 'Film Studies: Science vs Imagination: The Cinematic Vision of H. G. Wells', *The Independent*, 8 May 2005.

The Times, 'Editorial: The Bicycle as a Social Force', *The Times*, 15 August 1898, p. 7.

The Times, 'Editorial: H. G. Wells', *The Times*, 14 August 1946, p. 5.

Took, M., 'Interview: Jeff Wayne', n.d. [2010], http://www.whatsonwales.co.uk/interviews/i/18910/ [accessed 12 January 2012].

Torres, E. C., 'Catastrophes in Sight and Sound', in D. Agostinho, E. Antz and C. Ferreira (eds), *Panic and Mourning: The Cultural Work of Trauma*, Berlin: Walter de Gruyter, 2012, pp. 211–32.

Trevelyan, G. M., *Clio, A Muse and Other Essays Literary and Pedestrian*, London: Longmans, Green, 1914.

Trotter, W. R., *The Hilltop Writers: A Victorian Colony Among the Surrey Hills*, Headley Down: John Owen Smith, 2003.

Valim, A. B., "'Os Marcianos estão chegando!": as divertidas e imprudentes reinvenções de um ataque alienígena no cinema e no rádio', *Dialogos-Revista do Departamento de Historia e do Programa de Pós-Graduação em História* (Universidade Estadual de Maringá, Brazil) 9 (3) (2005): 185–208.

Vreeland, F., 'Charlie Chaplin, Philosopher, Has Serious Side', *New York Herald*, 11 September 1921.

Wakeford, I., 'Wells, Woking and *The War of the Worlds*', *Woking History Journal* 2 (Spring 1990): 4–15 [abridged as Wakeford, I., 'Wells, Woking and *The War of the Worlds*', *The Wellsian* 14 (1991): 18–29].

Wakeford, I., *Heritage Notes: Maybury Hill*, Old Woking: Iain Wakeford, 2000.

Wakeford, I., *H. G. Wells, Woking and the Real War of the Worlds: Maybury Hill*, Old Woking: Iain Wakeford, 2005.

Wakeford, I., 'Had victims of the Martians upset H. G. Wells?', *Woking Informer*, 25 June 2010, p. 4.

Wakeford, I., 'Site of narrator's house is not where some people think it is', *Surrey Advertiser*, 16 August 2013.

Waldrop, H., 'Night of the Cooters', *Omni* 9 (7) (April 1987): 84–91.

Walker, N., 'Gritty landing spot for alien invaders: H. G. Wells set his 1898 'War of the Worlds' in England, not the USA of today's movie', *Boston Globe*, 26 June 2005.

Walter, N., 'McCabe, Joseph Martin (1867–1955)', *Oxford Dictionary of National Biography*, Oxford University Press, 2004; online edn, October 2009, http://www.oxforddnb.com/view/article/34674 [accessed 17 February 2013].

Watkins, A. H. (ed.), *Catalogue of the H. G. Wells Collection in the Bromley Public Libraries*, Bromley: London Borough of Bromley, 1974.

Wayne, J., *Jeff Wayne's Musical Version of The War of the Worlds: The Story: The First 30 Years*, n.d., http://www.thewaroftheworlds.com/thestory/default.aspx [accessed 8 February 2014].

Wayne, J., 'H. G. Wells' The War of the Worlds: The Greatest Story Ever Told', *Independent*, 13 June 2005.

Wayne, J., 'Deconstructing Jeff Wayne's Musical Version of The War of the Worlds': The Making of DVD, disc 7, in J. Wayne, D. Collier and G. Schurrer (eds), with G. Brooks, *Jeff Wayne's Musical Version of The War of the Worlds: Collector's Edition*, London: Sony BMG, 2005.

Wayne, J., 'News', 18 November 2013, http://www.thewaroftheworlds.com/news/newsstory.aspx?id=212 [accessed 12 December 2013].

Wayne, J., 'News', 11 November 2015, http://www.thewaroftheworlds.com/news/newsstory.aspx?id=227 [accessed 10 December 2015].

Wayne, J., 'The World of H. G. Wells', *Jeff Wayne's Musical Version of The War of the Worlds: Alive on Stage 2014* [Show Programme], 2014.

Wayne, J., Collier, D. and Schurrer, G. (eds), with G. Brooks, *Jeff Wayne's Musical Version of The War of the Worlds: Collector's Edition*, London: Sony BMG, 2005.

Weil, M., 'A modern Don Quixote', *The Bookman* (USA) IV (4) (December 1896): 362–3.

Welles, O., 'Can a Martian help it if he's colored green?', in O. Welles (ed.), *Invasion from Mars: Interplanetary Stories, Selected by Orson Welles*, New York: Dell, 1949, pp. 5–7.

Wells, G. H., *The Works of H. G. Wells: a bibliography*, London: George Routledge, 1926.

West, A., 'Letters', *Scientific American* (CCLII) (October 1960): 16.

West, A., *H. G. Wells, Aspects of a Life*, London: Hutchinson, 1984.

West, G., *H. G. Wells: A Sketch for a Portrait*, London: Howe, 1930.

West III, J. L. W., *American Authors and the Literary Marketplace Since 1900*, Philadelphia, PN: University of Pennsylvania Press, 1988.

Whatmore, E., 'Now War of the Worlds pub beats the developers', *Woking Informer* 18 (April 2008).

White, J. M., 'Wells at his Most Wellsian', *Radio Times*, 28 May–3 June 1950, p. 9.

White, P., *Thomas Huxley: Making the "Man of Science"*, Cambridge: Cambridge University Press, 2003.

Whittington–Egan, R. and Smerdon, G., *The Quest of the Golden Boy: The Life and Letters of Richard Le Gallienne*, London: Unicorn, 1960.

W. H. S. A., 'Rambles in Surrey', *Illustrated London News*, XCV, no. 2622, 20 July 1889, p. 92.

Williams, K., *H. G. Wells, Modernity and the Movies*, Liverpool: Liverpool University Press, 2007.

Williams, K., 'Alien Gaze: Postcolonial Vision in *The War of the Worlds*', in S. McLean (ed.), *H. G. Wells: Interdisciplinary Essays*, Newcastle-upon-Tyne: Cambridge Scholars, 2008, pp. 49–73.

Williams, K. B., 'H. G. Wells: The War of the Worlds', *The Literary Encyclopedia*, 8 June 2009, http://www.litencyc.com/php/sworks.php?rec=true&UID=8092 [accessed 9 August 2013].

Williamson, J., 'Foreword: H. G. Wells: The Star', in R. Silverberg (ed.), *The Mirror of Infinity: A Critics' Anthology of Science Fiction*, New York: Harper & Row, 1970, pp. 3–7.

Wilson, A., 'Science Jottings', *Illustrated London News*, C (2758), 27 February 1892, p. 272.

Wilson, A., 'Science Jottings', *Illustrated London News*, CXXX (3536), 26 January 1907, p.146.

Wise, P., 'Recreation of Orson Welles Broadcast Causes Panic in Portugal', 30 October 1988, http://www.apnewsarchive.com/1988/Recreation-of-Orson-Welles-Broadcast-Causes-Panic-in-Portugal/id-8d4d671ab4aa2a4591329a4bd0e3aac0 [accessed 2 April 2012].

Woodger, B., 'High Rise Thoughts on Town's Evolution', *Woking News and Mail*, 1 March 2007.

Wright, J., 'H. G. Wells and Surrey', *Surrey County Journal* 1 (3) (January–March 1947), pp. 61–2.

Wynn, H., 'H. G. Wells and Woking', *Surrey Today*, September 1965, p. 34.

Yeats, W. B., *Autobiographies*, London: Macmillan, 1955.

Zúñiga, D., 'Guerra de los Mundos: los marcianos también invadieron Sudamérica', *Pensar* 2 (4) (2005): 8–11.

Anonymous publications ordered by date

'Woking Cemetery', *Illustrated London News* XXI (579–80), 18 September 1852, p. 214.

'The London Necropolis and National Mausoleum', *Illustrated London News* XXI (598), 18 December 1852, p. 548.

'The Great Cemetery at Woking', *Illustrated London News* XXVIII (795–6), 25 April 1856, pp. 462, 464;

'A Visit to Woking Cemetery', *Illustrated London News* XXXIII (928), 24 July 1858, p. 77.

'A Rondel in the Fog', *Punch*, 4 December 1886, p. 273.

'The Winter Art Exhibitions', *Punch*, 4 December 1886, p. 274.

'Home News', *Illustrated London News* XCVIII (2701) (24 January 1891), p. 98.

'Our London Correspondent', *The Woking News*, 26 October 1894, p. 2.

'Deserted and Betrayed Wife', *Sheffield Evening Telegraph*, 11 January 1895, p. 4.

'The New Review', *Review of Reviews* XI (March 1895), p. 263.

'Heinemann's advertisement, *The Standard*, 29 April 1895, p. 9.

'The May Magazines', *The Yorkshire Herald*, 6 May 1895, p. 6.

'Heinemann's advertisement, *The Times*, 28 May 1895, p. 12.

'Books of the Day', *Freeman's Journal and Daily Commercial Advertiser* (Dublin), 7 June 1895, p. 2.

'The World several millions of years hence: a vision of the fate of man', *Review of Reviews* (New York) XI (June 1895): 701–2.

'The Time Machine', *Nature*, 52, 18 July 1895, p. 268.

'Art and Literature', *The Woking News and North-West Surrey Gazette*, 2 August 1895, p. 2.

'Literary Gossip', *The Belfast News-Letter*, 5 August 1895, p. 8.

'Heinemann's advertisement, *The Times*, 5 August 1895, p. 6.

'Engels' funeral – yesterday', *Reynolds's Newspaper*, 11 August 1895.

'Obituary: The Late Friedrich Engels', *The Times*, 12 August 1895, p. 10.

'Personal', *Illustrated London News*, CVII (2939), 17 August 1895, p. 198.

'Fiction', *Saturday Review of Politics, Literature, Science and Art*, 17 August 1895, p. 216.

'New books', *The Pall Mall Gazette*, 26 August 1895.

'New Writers: Mr H. G. Wells', *The Bookman* 8 (47) (August 1895), pp. 134–5.

'Reviews: A. D. 802,701', *The Pall Mall Gazette*, 10 September 1895, p. 4.

'Novels and Stories', *The Glasgow Herald*, 3 October 1895, p. 7.

'The New Books. Notes from Our London Correspondent', *Review of Reviews* (New York) XII (October 1895), pp. 496–8.

'The Woking News: Our Public Roads', *The Woking News*, 22 November 1895, pp. 4–5.

'The Cycling Craze', *Hampshire Telegraph and Sussex Chronicle* (Portsmouth), 23 November 1895, p. 12.

'Art and Literature', *The Woking News*, 6 December 1895, p. 2.

'The Woking News', *The Woking News*, 6 December 1895, p. 4.

'Books of the Day', *Morning Post*, 19 December 1895, p. 7.

'Train timetables', *The Woking News*, 27 December 1895, p. 8.

'Novels', *Daily News*, 8 January 1896, p. 6.

'The Cycling Craze', *Hampshire Telegraph and Sussex Chronicle* (Portsmouth), 15 February 1896, p. 12.

'The Cycling Craze', *The Sheffield and Rotherham Independent* (Sheffield), 25 March 1896, p. 6.

'Recent Novels', *The Times*, 17 June 1896.

'Chronicle and Comment', *The Bookman* (USA) III (4) (June 1896), p. 293.

'English Letter, London, April 20 to May 23, 1896', *The Bookman* (USA) III (5) (July 1896): 471.

'Review: The Island of Dr Moreau', *The New York Times*, 16 August 1896.

'New Views About Mars', *Edinburgh Review* 184 (October 1896), pp. 368–85.

'The Wheels of Chance', *The Bookman* 11 (64) (January 1897), p. 124.

'Chronicle and Comment', *The Bookman* (USA) IV (5) (January 1897), p. 414.

'The Cycling Craze', *Western Mail* (Cardiff), 27 February 1897, p. 7.

'The Output of Authors', *Pearson's Magazine*, 3 (16) (April 1897): 456–61.

'Surrey as a Health resort', *The Woking Mail*, 29 May 1897, p. 6.

'Local Affairs: The Improvement Association', *The Woking Mail*, 10 July 1897, p. 4.

'Local Affairs: Woking's Growth', *The Woking Mail*, 4 September 1897, pp. 4–5.

'Woking's Changing Aspect: Some Significant Signs of Progress and Prosperity', *The Woking Mail*, 4 September 1897, pp. 4–5.

'A young novelist who has "arrived": a chat with Mr H. G. Wells', *The Sketch Magazine*, 15 September 1897, p. 317.

'Chronicle and Comment', *The Bookman* (USA) VI (1) (September 1897), p. 12.

'Writer of the Day: XXVIII', *Illustrated London News*, Vol. CXI (3050), 2 October 1897, p. 456.

'Woking Improvement Association', *The Woking Mail*, 9 October 1897, p. 5.

'Surrey in 1897: Looking Backward', *Surrey Advertiser*, 1 January 1898, p. 2.

'More News from Mars: A "Scientific Shocker"', *Daily News*, 21 January 1898.

'Heinemann's advertisement', *The Times*, 25 January 1898, p. 12.

'The Scientific Novel. A talk with Mr H. G. Wells', *Daily News*, 26 January 1898.

'News Notes', *The Bookman* 13 (76) (January 1898), pp. 113–16.

'Advertisements: Sunday Afternoon Lectures', *The Woking News and Mail*, 4 February 1898, p. 5.

'"Life in Other Worlds": interesting speculations', *The Woking News and Mail*, 11 February 1898, p. 6.

'Sunday Afternoon Lectures at Woking', *Surrey Advertiser*, 9 February 1898, p. 5.

'Record Portraits: No. XXV, H. G. Wells', *The Bromley Record and Monthly Advertiser* 475 (February 1898), pp. 20–2.

'Heinemann' advertisement', *The Times*, 19 April 1898, p. 12.

'English Letter: London, February 21 to March 19, 1898', *Bookman* (USA) VII (3) (May 1898): 267.

'Book Mart', *The Bookman* (USA) VII (4) (June 1898), p. 365.

'Book Mart', *The Bookman* (USA) VII (5) (July 1898), p. 445.

'News Notes', *The Bookman* 14 (84) (September 1898), p. 149.

'Mr H. G. Wells', *The Graphic*, 7 January 1899.

'Observations', *The Courier* (Lincoln, Nebraska), 11 March 1899, p. 2.

'Review: *When the Sleeper Wakes*', *The New York Times*, 19 August 1899.

'House of Commons', *The Times*, 27 March 1900, p. 10.

'London Fog Inquiry, 1901–02', *Nature*, 67, 9 April 1903, pp. 548–9.

'A Stupendous Swindler: Whittaker Wright's Exposure', *The Argus* (Melbourne), 1 March 1904, p. 7.

'The Other Worlds. Mr McCabe's Lecture', *The Press* (Canterbury, New Zealand), 29 May 1913.

'Mr H. G. Wells and Bromley: The Distinguished Author's Birthplace', *Bromley Chronicle*, 4 June 1914.

'We Are Safe From Such Jesting', *New York Times*, 19 January 1926.

'With the Producers and Players', *New York Times*, 27 June 1926.

'Entertainment' Advertisements, *The Times*, 9, 16, 23 September 1931.

'Mr H. G. Wells and the Screen', *The Times*, 3 November 1932.

'Radio Listeners in Panic, Taking War Drama as Fact', *New York Times*, 31 October 1938, p. 1.

'Fake Radio "War" Stirs Terror Though U. S.', *New York Daily News*, 31 October 1938, p. 1.

'The Aftermath: Orson Welles "The War of the Worlds" Halloween Press Conference', 31 October 1938', *Radio Guide Magazine*, 1938, http://www.wellesnet.com/?p=296 [accessed 25 May 2015].

'Radio Station's "Attack by Mars" panics thousands', *Universal Newsreel*, 31 October 1938.

'Terror by Radio', *New York Times*, 1 November 1938.

'Panic Caused by Broadcast: A Wells Fantasy in America', *The Times*, 1 November 1938.

'Mr Wells "deeply concerned"', *Manchester Guardian*, 1 November 1938.

'Letters: Alvin Bogart of Cranford, NJ', *New York Times*, 2 November 1938, p. 22.

'Press and Public Divided in Reaction to Mars Program', *Broadcasting*, 15 (10), 15 November 1938, pp. 14–15, 28.

'Editorial: Well, Wells, Welles', *Broadcasting* 15 (10) (15 November 1938), p. 40.

'New York Stage: Playgoers Without New Plays', *The Times*, 29 November 1938.

'Those Men from Mars', *Newsweek*, 27 November 1944, p. 89.

'H. G. Wells' Last Work: Atom', *Daily Sketch*, 14 August 1946.

'Public Homage to H. G. Wells', *The Times*, 31 October 1946, p. 6.

'"Mars Raiders" cause Quito panic: Mob burns Radio Plant, kills 15', *New York Times*, 14 February 1949, p. 7.

'"Invasion from Mars"', *The Times*, 14 February 1949, p. 4.

'"Martian invasion" panics a city', *Daily Mail*, 14 February 1949, p. 1.

'20 Dead in the Quito Riot: 15 held for "Martian Invasion" radio show and panic', *New York Times*, 15 February 1949, p. 4.

'Quito panic after broadcast: 15 deaths in riots', 'Quito panic after broadcast: two officials indicted' *The Times*, 15 February 1949, p. 4.

'Who… why… where… in London', *Daily Mail*, 20 May 1950, p. 3.

'Film Adaptation of H. G. Wells' story', *The Times*, 2 April 1953.

'The Screen in Review: New Martian Invasion is seen in War of the Worlds, which bows at Mayfair', *New York Times*, 14 August 1953.

'The War of the Worlds', *Classics Illustrated*, no. 124 (1955).

'War of the Worlds was written in Maybury Road villa', *Woking Review*, October 1966, p. 5.

Superman from the Thirties to the Seventies, New York: Bonanza Books, 1971.

'Welles's "War of the Worlds" Still Stirs Consternation', *New York Times*, 1 November 1971.

'Writers' Houses by Paul Hogarth: 10; H. G. Wells's House', *Illustrated London News* 268 (6987), 25 October 1980, p. 87.

'Auctions', *New York Times*, 15 December 1988.

'Wetherspoons – Woking's newest pub – has a permanent guest', *Woking Review*, 3 June 1995.

'Martian influence is appearing in Woking', *Woking Review*, 1 February 1997.

'Martian Lands in Woking – 100 Years On', *Daily Telegraph*, 7 April 1998.

Writers Inspired by Surrey, Kingston upon Thames: Surrey County Council, 2000.

'Hallmark Entertainment Productions, LLC v. Paramount Pictures Corp.', *New York Law Journal*, 25 April 2002, http://www.newyorklawjournal.com/id=1202504980801/ HALLMARK-ENTERTAINMENT-PRODUCTIONS%2C-LLC-v.-PARAMOUNT-PICTURES-CORP#ixzz2vpnlnwVz [accessed 15 March 2014].

H. G. Wells and Midhurst, Midhurst: The Midhurst Society, 2004.

'Town centre invaded by television crew', *Woking Review*, 25 June 2005.

'Time to cash in on War of the Worlds film, says councillor', *Woking News and Mail*, 21, http://www.getsurrey.co.uk/reporter/July 2005 [accessed 22 February 2012].

The Batman Chronicles, 1, New York: DC Comics, 2005.

'Orson Welles War of the Worlds script inspired Steven Spielberg's movie', 4 November 2006, http://www.wellesnet.com/?p=110 [accessed 28 May 2015].

'Horsell Common Blue Plaque', *The Common: Horsell Common Preservation Society Newsletter* 4 (1) (2007): 2.

'Alternative blue plaque marks common's cultural standing', *Get Surrey*, March 2007http://
www.getsurrey.co.uk/ [accessed 17 April 2014].

'Buffalo named War of the Worlds capital', WIVB 4, Buffalo, NY, 16 October 2009,
http://www.wivb.com/dpp/news/offbeat/Buffalo_named_War_of_the_Worlds_
Capital_20091016 [accessed 18 March 2012].

'The War of the Worlds (WKBW, Buffalo, 1968–71–75)', n.d., http://www.war-ofthe-
worlds.co.uk/war_worlds_wkbw_buffalo.htm [accessed 18 March 2012].

'The War of the Worlds Game', 2011, http://www.paramount.com/games/the-war-of-the-
worlds/details [accessed 4 June 2012].

'2011 National Film Registry More Than a Box of Chocolates', *News from the Library
of Congress*, 28 December 2011, http://www.loc.gov/today/pr/2011/11-240.html
[accessed 24 January 2014].

Horsell Common: A Brief History, Woking: H.C.P.S., n.d.

'Wells' Law', *Encyclopedia of Science Fiction*, n.d., http://www.sf-encyclopedia.com/entry/
wellss_law [accessed 2 May 2014].

'Press Release: The Dazzling, Groundbreaking Arena Production Launches A New
Generation!', n.d. [2012], http://www.thewaroftheworlds.com/live-events/2012-13-
uk-eu/press.aspx [accessed 22 January 2013].

'Mars of the Mind', *The Indian Express*, 5 November 2013, http://www.indianexpress.com/
news/mars-of-the-mind/1190930/ [accessed 10 November 2013].

'Mars in Popular Culture', *Times of India*, 6 November 2013, http://articles.timesofindia.
indiatimes.com/2013-11-06/india/43730963_1_mars-attacks-from-venus-from-mars
[accessed 10 November 2013].

'Mars, The Muse: How Red Planet Has Inspired Earth', *Hindustan Times*
6 November 2013, http://www.hindustantimes.com/StoryPage/Print/1147655.aspx
[accessed 10 November 2013].

History of Maybury', Lynch Sales & Lettings, n.d., http://www.housesinwoking.com/
GenericPage.aspx?type=AreaProfile&key=history_maybury [accessed 11 May 2015].

Radio and television sources

KTSA Radio, San Antonio, 'H. G. Wells meets Orson Welles', 28 October 1940, *The
Mercury Theatre on the Air*, http://www.mercurytheatre.info/ [accessed 19 February
2012].

BBC TV., 'Orson Welles' Sketchbook: Episode 5', 21 May 1955, http://www.wellesnet.com/
sketchbook5.htm [accessed 12 February 2014].

BBC Radio Four, B. Aldiss, 'Stranger than Truth', 2 July 1970.

BBC Radio Four, B. Bergonzi, 'Best Seller, 6: The War of the Worlds by H. G. Wells', 19
April 1978.

BBC Radio Four, Jonathan Ross, Roy Hattersley and Patrick Moore, 'H. G. Wells and Me',
20 March 2005.

BBC Radio Four, R. Snoddy, 'The Riot that Never Was', 16 June 2005.

BBC2. TV., 'The Culture Show', 31 March 2007.

BBC Radio Four, J. Gardiner, 'The History of the Future: 8: H. G. Wells', 19 September
2012.

BBC Radio Four, J. Wayne, 'But still they come', 22 December 2012.

PBS, 'American Experience: War of the Worlds', 29 October 2013.

BBC Radio Four, F. Weldon, 'Great Lives: H. G. Wells', 8 May 2014. [12 October 2001].

BBC2. TV. D. Sandbrook, 'Tomorrow's Worlds: The Unearthly History of Science Fiction',
22 November 2014.

INDEX